J2EE
AND BEYOND

ART TAYLOR

PRENTICE HALL
PROFESSIONAL TECHNICAL REFERENCE
UPPER SADDLE RIVER, NJ 07458
WWW.PHPTR.COM

ISBN 0-13-141745-2

Library of Congress Cataloging-in-Publication Data

Taylor, Art
  J2EE and beyond/Art Taylor
    p. cm.
  ISBN 0-13-141745-2
    1. Java (computer program language) 2. Business—Data processing. I. Title.

QA76.73J38 T385 2003
005.13'3—dc21

2002042491

Editorial/production supervision: *Kerry Reardon*
Cover design director: *Jerry Votta*
Cover designer: *Anthony Gemmellaro*
Art director: *Gail Cocker-Bogusz*
Manufacturing manager: *Alexis Heydt-Long*
Manufacturing buyer: *Maura Zaldivar*
Senior managing editor: *John Neidhart*
Editorial assistant: *Brandt Kenna*
Marketing manager: *Kate Hargett*
Full-service production manager: *Anne R. Garcia*

 © 2003 Pearson Education, Inc.
Publishing as Prentice Hall Professional Technical Reference
Upper Saddle River, New Jersey 07458

Prentice Hall books are widely used by corporations
and government agencies for training, marketing, and resale.

For information regarding corporate and government bulk
discounts please contact:
Corporate and Government Sales (800) 382-3419 or corpsales@pearsontechgroup.com

Printed in the United States of America
10 9 8 7 6 5 4 3 2 1

ISBN 0-13-141745-2

Pearson Education LTD.
Pearson Education Australia PTY, Limited
Pearson Education Singapore, Pte. Ltd.
Pearson Education North Asia Ltd.
Pearson Education Canada, Ltd.
Pearson Educación de Mexico, S.A. de C.V.
Pearson Education–Japan
Pearson Education Malaysia, Pte. Ltd.

CONTENTS

             AND AUTHORIZATION API (JAAS)   221

    Introduction   221

    Package History and Design   222

    The JAAS Package   223

    Authentication with JAAS   224

    Code Example   226

    Application Execution   246

    Summary   251

CHAPTER 10   THE JAVA SECURE SOCKETS EXTENSION: JSSE   253

    Introduction   253

    The JSSE API   254

    The SSL Protocol   255

    JSSE Installation   256

    The JSSE Package   259

    JSSE Code Sample   260

    The SSLServer Class   264

    The SSLServer Class Constructor   266

    The SSLClient Class   268

    The SSLClient Class Constructor   270

    The Client Superclass   271

    Summary   275

CHAPTER 11   USING CRYPTOGRAPHY WITH JAVA   277

    Introduction   277

    Package Design   278

CHAPTER 31   USING SWING APPLICATIONS WITH RMI   779

PART III   J2EE APPLIED

CHAPTER 32   JAVA DESIGN PATTERNS   799

CHAPTER 33   J2EE APPLIED: CREATING A FRAMEWORK-BASED SHOPPING CART APPLICATION   813

CHAPTER 34   J2EE APPLIED: THE MOVIE STORE APPLICATION   833

PREFACE

Within a few short years, the World Wide Web and its associated Internet or Net development has permeated our culture so that we now consider it commonplace. From Web browsers running on the ubiquitous PC in the United States to the Internet cafe in Bangalore India, the Web is everywhere. And despite the fickle currents of national economies and the fates of dubious technical startups, the most common and the most promising application development platform continues to be the Web.

Web technologies abound, and for a developer or manager who must make a key decision regarding the best Web development platform, the decision is in no way simple or straightforward. But as many have found in the past few years, there is one choice that provides a rich set of technologies, flexible development and deployment options, and a robust, mature, and secure infrastructure. That choice is the Java language offering for the enterprise, commonly known as the Java 2 Enterprise Edition, or J2EE.

J2EE is a superset of Java, both a language and a set of technologies that extends over 3,000 APIs at this writing. As such, J2EE cuts a wide swath through the Java APIs so that a comprehensive discussion of J2EE could require volumes. But by being concise and focusing on the commonly used technologies, this book provides the succinct coverage of J2EE APIs that developers require.

J2EE is a development environment for creating distributed applications. These are applications which are composed of components running on one or more servers. In developing J2EE applications, we make logical distinctions on the types of components we create. We distinguish between these components as separate tiers of development. In the first section of this book we will discuss these logical tiers in some detail, but in order to understand the design of this book just know that they are as follows.

Resource tier	Stores the persistent data for the application.
Integration tier	Interacts with the resource tier and business tier.
Business tier	Encapsulates business logic of the application.
Presentation tier	Prepares the application presentation for the client tier.
Client tier	Interacts with the user, the client of the application.

Not every application uses every tier. To add to the confusion, many architectural discussions refer to only three of these tiers, a client tier, a middle tier and a resource (data) tier. But to truly understand J2EE and be able to use it correctly, a developer should understand all of these tiers of development and how J2EE packages can be used on each of them. That is the approach used in this book.

The J2EE development paradigm differs from that of client/server architectures where a client application communicates directly with a database resource (the resource tier) and offers a variety of technologies. A J2EE developer therefore needs to understand both the technology of J2EE and the proper architectural strategies for designing multi-tiered, distributed J2EE applications.

This book provides the information the prospective J2EE developer or architect needs to know. Sections deal with the architecture and design of solutions with J2EE, J2EE technology, and J2EE applications. The goal is to provide significant technical coverage in each section and to use a consistent set of code examples throughout. This book goes beyond Java Server Pages (JSPs), Enterprise JavaBeans (EJBs), and servlets that many J2EE books are limited to and covers key J2EE APIs and packages, such as

- Java Web Services, SOAP (JAXM)
- Java XML (JAXP)
- Relational database connectivity (JDBC)
- Remote Method Invocation (RMI)
- Java networking
- Logging
- Java Naming and Directory Interface (JNDI)
- Java email (JavaMail)
- Servlets
- Java Server Pages (JSP)
- Enterprise JavaBeans (EJB)
- Java messaging (JMS)
- SSL support (JSSE)
- Cryptography (JCE)

- Java security
- Security Authentication and authorization (JAAS)
- GUI development (Swing)

This broad coverage explains the book's bulk and also provides value for the reader. While it would be easy to write a complete book about any of these APIs, the goal of this book was to provide a large and significant portion of what the developer needs to know to actually use these APIs and packages. The purpose of each core technology is explained and demonstrated through both minimal examples (just what is needed to use the technology) and more complex examples, many of which are demonstrated as part of a complete application.

Creating a solid object-oriented design is an important part of creating a good J2EE-based application. Since the J2EE technology and object-oriented development in general may be unfamiliar to many readers, this book devotes several chapters to the discussion of good architectural design with J2EE. These chapters include a discussion of object-oriented modeling and design and the application of these principles to J2EE development.

Application of Java design patterns is an important part of good J2EE development. This book provides a discussion of Java design patterns and then applies them when appropriate throughout the examples in the text.

BOOK SECTIONS

This book is divided into three parts, starting with architecture and design and proceeding through a detailed discussion of a large swath of important J2EE APIs. These sections are as follows.

- Part 1: J2EE Architecture and Design
- Part 2: Core J2EE Technology
- Part 3: J2EE Sample Applications

Part 1, J2EE Architecture and Design, covers J2EE architecture and design, offering practical steps for creating a solid J2EE architecture based on user requirements. It includes several chapters on object-oriented analysis and design applied to J2EE and a set of case studies that provide an example of how to architect a J2EE system.

Part 2, Core J2EE Technology, provides extensive coverage of the J2EE packages identified above. Basic introductory code examples are used to introduce the package and then more complex code examples, many of which are used by examples in later sections, are used to more detailed information on how to use the package.

Part 3, J2EE Sample Applications, builds on the work of the previous sections to demonstrate the use of J2EE packages to develop two applications: a shopping cart application and a discussion group application. The shopping cart application uses the Struts framework, servlets, JSPs and EJBs. Code examples from the previous chapters are used in the creation of this application.

The development of a discussion group application using JSPs, tag libraries, and Java Bean components is also shown. Users are allowed to enter and modify their own messages and add messages to a message thread.

COVERING J2EE APIS

In determining the order in which to cover the numerous J2EE APIs, we will use the option that provides the most meaningful coverage for someone who is relatively unfamiliar with J2EE technologies and packages. Using the multiple tiers of development as our guide mentioned previously, we start with the APIs most commonly used on the integration tier of development and proceed from there back to the client tier. Since most J2EE applications must manage some form of data and must be able to persist this data (the application state) as needed, we begin our discussion with the J2EE package used for interacting with relational databases, JDBC. Since managing security has become a concern of many organizations (and rightly so), we then move our discussion to Java security and the related security APIs (JAAS, JSSE, JCE).

Naming services provide a convenient facility for accessing resources in J2EE applications and are discussed in the chapter on the JNDI package. A good logging API was something lacking in early J2EE releases and has now become part of the J2EE collection. Both the core Java logging package is discussed as well as the Apache log4j package.

Much has been written in the technical press about XML and SOAP. These technologies and protocol standards represent some very valuable facilities for managing data interchange, moving data between components and applications. We will spend several chapters discussing XML and will use XML related APIs in examples throughout the text.

Our discussion then moves on to various APIs and J2EE packages which are useful on the business tier—Java networking, Remote Method Invocation (RMI), Web services and XML messaging with Java (JAXM), Java messaging with JMS and using email with Java using the JavaMail package. EJBs are then discussed across a number of chapters in the text.

Once we understand what can be done on the business tier, we spend several chapters discussing the presentation tier (Web tier) components J2EE provides. This involves coverage of JSPs and servlets. As you would expect, these applications build on the material presented in the previous chapters.

Finally, the client tier is discussed—how to use Java APIs and J2EE to create client tier, GUI applications. Like the presentation tier code shown, the client tier code builds on the previous chapters, demonstrating application code that accesses databases using JDBC, and uses RMI to communicate with remote objects that encapsulate data access functionality.

CODE EXAMPLES

Working code examples are presented throughout this book. These code examples provide a sample of how specific technology can be used. They range from simple, minimal implementations of a J2EE package to more complex components that are part of a complete sample application. As a reader learning J2EE, you may want to use these code samples to supplement your learning experience. These examples are available at the Web site for this book: http://www.phptr.com/taylor/j2ee. On that same page you can find an email link to contact me, the author.

WHO SHOULD READ THIS BOOK

This book is intended for the Java developer who is somewhat familiar with the Java language and wants to learn about developing applications using the various J2EE packages. Knowledge of Java object-oriented concepts (classes, objects, interfaces) and how to write Java programs is required. Knowledge of servlets, JSPs, EJBs, XML, Java XML Messaging (SOAP), Java security, and the various other packages and technologies of J2EE are not required—that's what this book is for.

ACKNOWLEDGMENTS

If you look over the table of contents for this book, it looks like a lot—and it is. Many people have helped me complete this sizable effort.

Thanks to Karen McLean and John Neidhart at Prentice Hall for their undying and patient support of this project. Thanks also to Kerry Reardon for production editing and to Carol Lallier for a detailed copy editing effort.

Pravin Mundkur and Dave Goyette provided timely technical review of this extensive technical tome. Thanks to them for finding time to do this in their busy schedules.

As always, the "home support staff" was patient and understanding. These projects take a great deal of time that has a tendency to pull me away from what really matters. But they are understanding and patient. So, to Carolyn, Hannah, and Eric, "the best there is," much love and thanks.

CHAPTER 1

J2EE and Beyond

INTRODUCTION

To paraphrase the old adage, to understand where you are going, it is always good to know exactly where you are. It is no different with J2EE. To truly understand J2EE and how it can help you do your job, it is important to know exactly what it is and how it came to be. Once you have done that, then understanding the architecture and technology of J2EE makes much more sense.

Building from that knowledge, we can then examine the architecture of J2EE—how applications should be architected using this technology. This chapter covers these basic architectural concepts, building on the technical discussion of J2EE and progressing to an architectural view. Successive chapters build on this discussion to determine which design patterns are best for J2EE and which tools work best for certain applications and not so well for others.

WHEN IT ALL BEGAN

J2EE leaped onto the scene in 1999. Considering the historical context of this product release you find that the cost of creating, deploying, and maintaining PC-based client/server software was becoming increasingly expensive. Partly in response to this, interest in the Internet and Web applications had been gathering steam for several years.

Java had been released only 4 years earlier and continued to demonstrate value in cross-platform development. The technology, the APIs beyond Java, continued to grow at a dizzying pace; therein lay part of the problem. The development of APIs was not always coordinated, and Java users would often need to struggle to cobble together a set of APIs that would perform the task required.

With its excellent crossplatform support, Java was already becoming the language of choice for middleware development, but there were issues in the development of middleware. Most notably, there was no consistent standard for development of services among vendors. Additionally, each vendor provided a different set of services for the applications. Clearly, there was an opportunity to impose some order on the industry.

By 1998, the Java programming language and its constituent set of APIs was burgeoning. Java had moved far beyond its original goal of being used as an embedded language. But the proliferation of APIs and standards was becoming difficult to work with. Developers found it increasingly difficult to find what they needed, and version release schedules between dependent APIs were not always synchronized.

The Java development team at Sun Microsystems saw several opportunities in this environment. First, the conglomeration of APIs and standards that was Java could be organized in such a way that it would be easier for developers to build applications, specifically Web applications, with Java. Second, Java could make more inroads in middleware development with a clear and consistent middleware standard. And third, the various Java technologies that were currently being used to develop Web applications could be combined with the middleware APIs to create a convenient package for developers to use to create applications. The result of this repackaging and branding exercise was the J2EE released in December 1999.

As part of this effort, the Java Development Kit (JDK) was split into three parts: Java 2 Standard Edition (J2SE), Java 2 Enterprise Edition (J2EE), and the Java 2 Micro Edition (J2ME). This split provided a convenient repackaging of the myriad APIs that was Java. What is confusing in relation to J2EE is that the J2SE is part of the J2EE release. In order to run the J2EE, the J2SE must be installed. To avoid this confusion, you should think of the J2SE as the core Java installation component. J2EE is built on the J2SE.

J2EE includes a number of APIs; the most important and the ones most frequently associated with J2EE are EJBs (Enterprise JavaBeans), JSPs, and servlets. The EJB specification preceded the J2EE specification and was no doubt partly intended to improve the portability of these components.

MULTITIERED DEVELOPMENT WITH J2EE

The development of J2EE applications requires a *multitiered* approach to application development. Unlike the fat-client approach in which a single application included presentation logic, business logic, and data access (resources) logic, the distributed application takes this functionality and places it in various *components* across multiple logical tiers. The components represent pieces or portions of the application.

The division of the application into components is based on the responsibilities of the component. The logical association of component to tier is based on the same responsibilities. The use of multiple tiers requires a different development approach, one that takes into account the capabilities of the components, the resources available on that tier, and the skill of the developers who will create the components—for instance, in creating a component that would control the user interface.

A simplified version of a multitiered architecture involves three logical tiers: client tier, business tier, and resource tier. The client tier manages the client interface and communicates with the business tier to obtain the information needed to present to the user. The business tier reacts to client calls and retrieves data from the resource tier as needed.

A common problem with this multitiered approach is to allow functionality that should be executed on the business tier to creep into the client tier. The client tier may be deployed across numerous platforms, so business logic that has been allowed to creep into the client application now resides on numerous platforms and must be updated on each platform.

The J2EE architecture expands on the three-tiered architecture to provide for additional delineations of responsibility and to acknowledge the specific requirements of the Web application. The multiple tiers commonly identified with J2EE development are listed in Table 1–1 and are explained in more detail in the following sections.

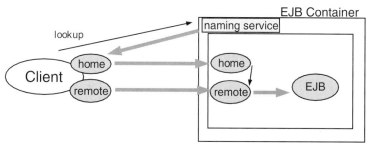

Figure 1–1   *Components on multiple architectural tiers.*

Table 1–1   *J2EE Development Tiers*

Tier	Description
Client	The portion of the application which is responsible for interacting with the end -user.
Presentation	Responsible for creating the presentation used by the client to interact with the user.
Business	Responsible for executing the business logic of the application. Applies the business logic to the information received from the integration tier.
Integration	Performs the data access operations for the application.
Resource	Contains the persistent data of the application. This is usually a database.

Client Tier

The client tier logically enough represents the client application. The purpose of this tier is to render the presentation prepared by the presentation tier and to react to the input from the user. The client tier must also communicate with the presentation tier and relay the user's input to that tier.

The client tier can be a Web browser, an applet and Swing applet, or a WebStart client. Using a thin-client architecture, the component should have a minimal footprint. The goal is to avoid the problems of fat-client architectures where deploying to the client tier was difficult and expensive.

In order to keep this client a thin client, the responsibilities of this tier must be minimized. By minimizing and focusing the responsibilities of this tier, the amount of information that must be sent to the tier will be minimized. If we determine that this tier should only render the display and respond to the user's input, then decisions on what to display and how to display it should be left to another tier.

Presentation Tier

The presentation tier is responsible for the preparation of the output to the client tier. Since in a Web application we are usually preparing these pages dynamically, this tier must be able to store and retain information between calls, either in memory or in a data store.

If we are using a Web browser as our client, then the protocol between the client tier and the presentation tier is Hypertext Transport Protocol (HTTP). The most logical server for the presentation tier is a server that can perform HTTP, such as Apache.

Additionally, we would like the server to be able to manage dynamic content using a robust language such as Java. The Tomcat server, the reference implementation of the Java servlet engine, provides this capability using servlets and JSP pages.

The components used most often on this tier are either Java servlets, JSP pages, JavaBeans, and tag libraries. But the component could also be an applet running in a Web browser. The question we need to answer at the design stage is which type of component should be used. If we want to create components on this tier that require minimal support from Java developers, then JSP should be used to provide the bulk of the presentation logic. JavaBeans and tag libraries could be used to isolate more complex logic, leaving a JSP page that would be familiar and maintainable by most Web page developers.

By maintaining this separation of roles, staff with more specialized skill sets can maintain the presentation tier components. If these components are primarily Hypertext Markup Language (HTML), then developers familiar with HTML can be used to maintain these pages. Java provides a number of technologies that make this approach even more attractive: tag libraries and Java Bean integration into the JSP page. Using these technologies, presentation tier logic can be isolated in the JSP page and any additional logic can be moved to backend-components like Java Beans and Tag libraries. The resulting JSP page, composed primarily of HTML elements, can be maintained by an HTML developer.

The end result of this separation of roles is a flow of control for the application, which extends from the client browser to the servlet or JSP page and from the servlet or JSP page to the business tier. The business tier will execute any business logic and access the resource tier as needed.

Business Tier

The business tier isolates, encapsulates and codifies the business logic (the business rules) of the organization in the application. These are rules such as how to select sales regions for sales reports, including the usual list of exceptions that always seem to exist for many business rules.

Logic that could have resided in the presentation tier in Web components such as JSP pages or servlets is effectively pushed off and managed in this tier. Here in the business tier, under their auspices of an application server, the component is easy to look up and use, thus enhancing reusability.

The components on this tier can be created using a variety of Java technologies: Java Beans, tag libraries, and EJBs, or remote components delivered using RMI.

Integration Tier

The purpose of the integration tier is to apply the logic needed to extract data from the resource tier. This logic may involve performing necessary data conversions or applying business logic filters on the data. The data store can be any data source required by the application, such as a relational database, a legacy mainframe system, or a flat file.

Resource Tier

The resource tier is represented by the data store which could be a relational database, an object-relational database, an object database, or any technology which provides data storage (persistence services) for the application.

The resource tier is responsible for providing persistence services for the application. This usually involves storing and maintaining the consistency of application data. Communication with the resource tier is accomplished with a standard API such as JDBC for relational databases.

CORE J2EE PACKAGES

J2EE is effectively a superset of J2SE, meaning that it encompasses or contains all of J2SE. In addition to the various standard packages of J2SE, several optional packages are added to the J2EE distribution. The APIs or packages that are commonly used are identified in Table 1–2 and explained in the sections below.

A J2EE application may use additional APIs or tools to create a distributed application. It is not uncommon and is in fact useful to use the frameworks and tools of the open source community, notably the Apache Software Foundation, to augment J2EE and shorten the time-to-market cycle for application development. (Chapter 33 34 and 35 demonstrate a J2EE application which uses the Struts framework, an Apache open-source project.)

JDBC

The Java Database Connectivity (JDBC) API is an important part of J2EE applications. Every application needs data, and today that data is usually kept in a relational database. JDBC provides an open, vendor-independent API for accessing relational databases. The common goal of most applications is to make them database-neutral; JDBC contains a number of features that can aid in this effort. Later additions to the API provide for accessing JDBC resources for a specific database through naming services (using `DataSource` implementations) and batch updates. The JDBC package is covered in chapters 5, 6 and 7.

Table 1–1　　*Core J2EE Packages*

API	Description
JDBC	Provides connectivity to relational databases.
JNDI	Provides Java access to naming services (LDAP, Windows Registry).
XML Processing (JAXP)	Provides for manipulation of XML documents.
Web Services (JAXM)	Provides the ability to send and recieive XML messages using protocols such as SOAP.
JSSE	Allows secure SSL communications both as a server and a client.
JCE	Allows common encryption techniques to be used with Java applications.
RMI	Allows Java objects to be invoked remotely using the Remote Method InvocationRMI protocol.
servlets	Provides a Web tier component using the HTTP protocol.
JMS	The Java Messaging Service. Provides access to message queues and topics both as a client and a server.
JSPs	Provides a scripting language for insertion into HTML documents.
Java-IDL	Allows Java applications to interact with CORBA servers.
EJBs	Allows the use of business tier components operating within an abstract container that provides a number of services.
JavaMail	Allows access to email servers using common protocols such as POP3 and IMAP.

JNDI

The Java Naming and Directory Interface (JNDI) package provides consistent access to a variety of naming services. These naming services provide for storage and access of various objects. They are effectively lightweight databases with very specific uses. For instance, Domain Naming Service (DNS) servers provide naming resolution services to resolve network domain names to IP addresses. Lightweight Directory Access Protocol (LDAP) servers allow a variety of objects to be stored in hierarchical fashion. LDAP servers are used to store information such as the location of various system resources, or to authenticate information such as the user names and passwords for system users. With the introduction of JNDI, these LDAP servers are now more commonly being pressed into use to store arbitrary Java objects. JNDI also supports Windows platform naming services such as the Windows Registry.

The advantage of using JNDI is that system-wide configuration information, such as the name and location of a database server, can be stored in a central location and broadcast to interested applications. Should the location of the resource change, it would need to be changed in only a single location. The various applications using the resource would then receive the new location information the next time they connected to the naming service. Unlike the alternative method of either hardcoding the configuration information into the source code files or using Java properties files, this method is simple and automatic. The JNDI package is covered in detail in Chapter 12.

JAXP

The Extensible Markup Language (XML) has become the de facto standard for information interchange. XML allows data to be stored in a simple text file using tags that are easy to read and understand. Parsers and transformers allow XML documents to be easily read and transformed into other formats. This allows the development of service components that create XML documents for a number of different clients. The client application can access the XML document and transform it to the format required.

The JAXP package contains a number of classes that provide parsers and transformation services for Java applications. Chapters 14, 15 and 16 discuss XML and the JAXP package.

JAXM

Web services combine the data interchange capabilities of XML and the openness of the HTTP protocol to create a service delivered over the Web. While it has been suggested that this facility could be used to create complete applications, it is more likely to be used to facilitate information interchange between applications, an important and often time-consuming task for developers.

The Java for XML Messaging (JAXM) package contains classes and interfaces that provide access to Web Services. This package allows SOAP clients and servers to be developed. Using this package, an enterprise, for example, could expose a service to provide information on stock availability or allow products to be ordered. The JAXM package is covered in Chapter 22 and 23.

RMI

The RMI package allows an object to be created which exposes specific methods to remote clients. This package also provides for client access to these remote methods. RMI is relatively simple and easy to use and is the lower level protocol used by a number of J2EE application servers to provide access to their EJB components.

RMI also allows a client to provide access to its methods as a call back service to the server. Chapter 17 discusses the Java networking API and Chapter 18 and 19 discuss the RMI package.

Java servlets and JSPs

The servlet was the original Java Web component. The servlet is a Java class implementation that is invoked and run within a container. The container (operating in a Web server) provides various services for the servlet, such as lifecycle management and security.

JSPs provide for Web page scripting, allowing Java code fragments to be embedded in an HTML page. The JSP is converted into a servlet and runs within the servlet container. Both servlets and JSPs are covered in Chapter 27.

JavaMail

Email is used by Java applications for a variety of purposes: for example, to send a warning message to an administrator or user or to transmit data to another application. The JavaMail package provides access to these services using a flexible API. Common protocols, such as POP3 and IMAP, are supported. The JavaMail API is covered in Chapter 21.

JMS

The JMS package provides access to asynchronous messaging services. Many applications do not require an instant synchronous response to a request. These applications can pass a request to another application, leaving it to yet some other application to determine the success or failure of the operation and to manage it accordingly.

This messaging service can be used to exchange data within a transactional context (using the Java Transaction API, JTA), supporting distributed transactions across multiple data sources. Message queues are not new, but before JMS, there was no consistent standardized API for message queues in the Java language. JMS queues can support concurrent consumption of messages.

With the release of EJB 2.0, JMS has now been integrated into EJBs with the addition of message-driven beans (MDBs). With MDBs, an EJB can be exposed as a message queue, thus simplifying the creation of message queues and allowing them to be controlled within the same context as EJBs. The JMS package provides access through a service provider interface to common messaging servers. This package is covered Chapter 21.

EJBs

The EJB is the middleware component of J2EE. Like the servlet, this component runs in a container, which provides a variety of services. The services for the EJB are provided by the application server and are often significant. Application servers are usually, but not always, used for applications that expect a high usage load and/or must be highly available with very little downtime. But even if an application does not have these requirements, EJBs provide a development paradigm that isolates business logic into easily accessible components, which can be accessed by Web tier components, such as JSPs or servlets, or even directly by client tier components such as a Swing GUI. EJBs are covered in Chapter 24, 25 and 26.

Java-IDL

Java-IDL provides the ability for Java applications to interact with Common Object Request Broker Architecture (CORBA) components written in any language. Applications using Java-IDL can invoke operations on remote services using the OMG IDL (Object Management Group's Interface Definition Language).

J2EE COMPONENTS

The J2EE environment is based on the concept of a *software component*—an abstract object that operates within some type of environment. The specific component that J2EE technology is built on is the *distributed software component*, a component that can be invoked remotely and can accept and receive parameters and return values.

This ability to build applications with components provides a great deal of flexibility in constructing and deploying an application and is one of the primary reasons for the interest in J2EE technology. A distributed component can be deployed on a single server and made available to multiple applications that have access to the server. The component can thus be deployed in a centralized fashion, allowing information technology (IT) management control over the operating environment of the critical business services provided by the application components.

The J2EE specification provides for different types of components that can be used to create an application. While for many the focus of a J2EE application is on the middle tiers (the presentation tier, the business tier, and the integration tier), there are J2EE components that can be used on the client tier. Most of these components are Java objects that operate within a logical *container*, an environment that provides a number of services for the component. The following sections identify these components.

Client Tier Components

The client tier represents the portion of the application that interacts with the user. For Web applications, this would be whatever component is running within the Web browser, potentially a simple HTML page, an HTML page with JavaScript, an HTML page running a Java applet, or a Java WebStart component.

The HTML Page

The HTML page is the most common form of interacting with the end user in a Web application. From its fairly simple, modest birth at CERN in the late 1980s, HTML and the accompanying HTTP have provided the framework for a burgeoning Web economy.

HTML is adequate for simple presentation of material but is limited in the GUI controls it can use. The basic GUI controls are available—the listbox, the radio button, the checkbox—but more sophisticated controls such as sliders and number wheels are beyond its abilities. HTML also does not allow immediate reaction to the user's actions; should a user enter a Q in a field that is designated *Sex'* and expects an entry of M or F, the most common approach is to allow this information to be posted back to the server, where it will be examined, and if there is an error, an error page is returned to the browser. Editing complex input pages with HTML can be a tedious experience for the user.

There are some alternatives to basic HTML. The Dynamic HTML (DHTML) standard expands upon HTML, and JavaScript provides a scripting language that most browsers support (though with a subtle variation of maddening differences). But the support for these languages varies among browser types and versions so that using them entails some risk.

The applet Component

The applet was the first Java *component*. The applet runs within a *container* provided by the browser. The container is an abstraction that provides a number of services for the applet, such as lifecycle management (starting and stopping the applet) and security (limiting the applet from accessing local resources by default).

At one time applets were considered to be the choice tool for expanding the capabilities of the Web browsers, but limitations of the GUI and the bandwidth required to download large applets led to limited usage of these components. Today many of the limitations of the GUI have been addressed (with Swing JApplet), and bandwidth is continuing to improve. Though not as commonly used as JSPs or servlets, the Java applet still represents a viable technology for applications that require a more robust interface than that of an HTML page with JavaScript.

A Java applet is effectively a class that is downloaded each time it is used. If this class uses other classes, as is common, those classes are also downloaded. As the size and complexity of the applet grows, the size of the download may also grow. A moderately complex applet could easily be 200 to 400 kilobytes in size, requiring a 2- or 3-minute download on a connection using a 56-K modem. For users used to 20-second start times for PC-based applications, running an applet of this size could appear painfully slow.

The Java applet was also designed to be secure. Since it can be downloaded over an open network, it is relatively easy for a malicious user to introduce applets that could circulate among client machines and damage them. By default, applets had restrictive security; they could not access local machine resources such as the hard disk or the printer, and they could access network resources only on the machine from which they were downloaded. While these restrictions on applets did provide solid security, they also severely limited the general usefulness of the applet (which could not send output to the printer or save a file to disk).

The initial version of the Java applet used the Java Abstract Windowing Toolkit (AWT) for the creation of the GUI, a set of widgets that was limited and paled in comparison to what was in the Microsoft Foundation Classes. The Java applet has now become the Java Swing applet, or JApplet, which provides access to a more mature set of GUI widgets. These applets, however, require the Java 2 Web server plug-in to be installed in the browser.

The Java WebStart Component

The Java WebStart component is similar to that of the applet. But unlike Java applets, the developer of the WebStart application can choose to have the application downloaded once and then stored on disk. Java WebStart can make deploying an application a much simpler process.

The Java WebStart application requires a plug-in be installed in the Web browser and can optionally install updates to all classes in the application or only to certain classes. This allows robust, client/server applications to be created and installed on a central site and then updated to client machines on an intelligent basis, updating only those classes that need to be changed. A Java WebStart application can also be run offline, without access to the server from which it was downloaded.

Java WebStart applications run in a dedicated Java runtime environment and use a default security model that is restrictive. Security involves the use of signed JAR (Java ARchive) files using digital signatures that can help insure that the code being executed by the client is the code received from the host server and not a *trojan horse* intruder with malicious intent. WebStart applications may or may not use this restrictive security model, and WebStart application applets may also be digitally signed, in which case they are considered "trusted" and are able to run in a less restrictive environment.

The GUI Client

The client application could also be a standalone application that uses a graphical user interface (GUI) to interact directly with the end user. Though this type of application is used less and less these days because of deployment and support issues, the GUI interface is still superior in terms of functionality of controls and performance to what can be delivered using a Web browser working with HTML and JavaScript.

Sun has aggressively improved the Swing API over the past few years and today a number of notable GUI applications including Integrated Development Environments (IDE) and OOAD modeling tools have been developed as cross-platform applications using Swing. For applications that require a more robust user interface, developing the application in Java Swing may be the preferred alternative. We demonstrate the use of the Swing GUI in Chapter 30 and 31.

PRESENTATION TIER COMPONENTS

J2EE presentation tier components can be developed using Java servlets and Java Sever Pages (JSP). These components both operate within a conceptual container as do Java applets. These containers provide various services for the component that allow it to run in a secure, efficient environment.

These components are often referred to as a Web tier components since they are primarily designed to interact with Web browsers using the HTTP protocol. Java servlets were the first Web component. A servlet is a Java object which is a subclass of certain servlet API classes. The servlet accepts an HTTP request and provides an HTTP response within the body of certain methods called by the servlet container. If the response is being returned as an HTML document, then the Java code within the body of the method being called by the container.

The JSP specification followed the initial servlet specification. JSP pages are created by interspersing JSP scriplets amongst HTML. The JSP is then converted into a Java servlet and executed within a servlet container. Thus JSP can easily be implemented on top of an existing servlet container.

BUSINESS TIER COMPONENTS

The J2EE specification describes an end-to-end environment for the development of enterprise applications—from client GUI libraries, to Web browsers, to Web servers running JSPs and servlets, to the business tier, to the resource tier.

Business tier components run on the middle tier and thus have historically been referred to as *middleware*. These components run within an *application server,* which provides the *container* for the components. As with applets, this container provides various services for the component: lifecycle management, pooling, security, and automatic failover.

Prior to the EJB specification, developers creating middleware components needed to write code to specifically manage the infrastructure and provide services for the component. The EJB specification provides for the services in a consistent manner, thus providing the developer with a certain degree of portability in being able to move a component or set of components from one application server to another. In order to understand the creation and development of a J2EE application, it is important to understand the middleware technology provided with J2EE. For this reason, the next section discusses EJBs in more detail.

EJBs

EJBs lie at the core of the J2EE architecture. They represent the middleware component specification for Java. The pure object-oriented nature and platform-independence, and security and network I/O features of Java made it a natural for the development of distributed components.

Following the release of the first EJB specification, the specification was quickly embraced and implemented by a number of application server vendors, and at last count, there were over 30 J2EE application servers available with varying costs and compliance levels (not all 30 are J2EE-certified by Sun Microsystems). Among these vendors, many try to distinguish themselves by offering specialized services. Not all vendors implement the complete J2EE specification, and many may implement a version of J2EE but not the current version.

As stated previously, EJBs operate within a logical container that provides a number of services; it is these services, in combination with the advantages of an object-oriented development, that make J2EE such an attractive development environment.

The following sections introduce some of the basic concepts of EJBs. But this nontrivial topic will not be dealt with in detail at this point; chapters 24 – 26 discuss EJBs in detail.

Client Interaction with EJBs

The EJB is a remote object used by clients. The exact nature of the client can vary. The client can be another EJB, a Web component such as a servlet or JSP, a stand-alone Java application, or an application or component written in another language. These clients are referred to as *rich clients*.

An EJB client accesses the services provided by the EJB in a two-step process. First, the object is looked up using a naming service, which returns a reference to the *home interface* for the EJB. Next, the home interface is used to create a *remote reference* for the EJB. This remote reference is then used to access the services (the methods) of the EJB (see Figure 1-2: EJB Access).

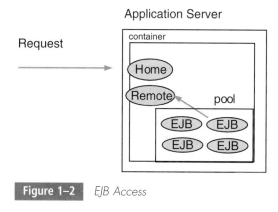

Figure 1–2 *EJB Access*

The remote reference is effectively used as any other object would be used. Parameters may be passed to the remote object, and values may be returned from the object. Method parameters are passed by value, not by reference, as they are done with objects in the local Java Virtual Machine (JVM). Parameters passed must be serializable.

Communication with the EJB is *by proxy*. The client never holds a reference directly to the EJB, but instead holds an indirect reference to a remote interface (the remote object in the server). The remote interface communicates with its counterpart in the application server, which in turn communicates with the EJB. This allows the container of the application server to intervene and manage communication with the EJB. It is this indirection that allows the container to implement the various services identified below.

The EJB Container

With EJBs, the container is implemented by what is commonly called an *application server*. Application server vendors and open source development groups may add additional services above and beyond the EJB specification and have some discretion on how services are implemented, but in order to be compliant, they must provide a core set of services, as follows:

- security
- transactions
- naming
- scalability
- lifecycle management

J2EE emphasizes the use of declarative programming for many of these services. Rather than use complicated, error-prone method calls to implement a particular service, a declarative scheme under the control of the container is used to manage the service. The developer makes entries in a configuration file (known as the *deployment descriptor*), which describes specifically how the service should be implemented. These services and some background information on how they may be implemented are discussed in the following sections.

Security. EJB application servers must implement a specific role-based security model and must provide a role reference facility that allows a role reference name to be established for the role. Role permissions are then associated with methods and can be assigned to all methods within a component.

EJB security does not deal with authentication—the expectation is that this is managed in the presentation tier or the client tier. EJB security is concerned with the user's role and whether or not the user (in his or her role) has permission to perform the action he or she is attempting to perform (executing a method or accessing a resource).

Transactions. The EJB specification provides for transactions related to components and for transaction managers that transparently manage transactions with a single data source or with multiple data sources combined. Transactions can be managed either by the container using container-managed transactions or programmatically through specific method calls using bean-managed transactions.

Components may run within a transaction and may propagate transactions down the call chain. This means that a method may have one transaction mode and call another method. That method being called may elect to use or not use the transaction of the method that called it, depending on the configuration of the component. This provides an easy mechanism to manage transactions based on component boundaries.

Naming. The naming services provided by the EJB application server allow the component to use a JNDI naming service to access J2EE resources. A JNDI naming service allows an arbitrary name to be associated with a resource. The resource is represented by a Java object reference that provides access to the services of the resource.

The J2EE resources accessed through the naming service could be an EJB component, a JDBC data source, or an environment entry that provides configuration information for the component. The naming service allows entries to be retrieved as object references that may be cast or *narrowed* to their specific Java type.

Scalability. The EJB server should provide scalability features, which should be enjoyed by the components transparently. The EJB specification does not provide details on what these scalability features should be or how they should be implemented (though it does specify that pooling of EJB components may be done and provides callback methods to allow some control over the process). Virtually all EJB application servers provide some type of scalability feature, though the type and sophistication varies.

Lifecycle Management. The EJB server should provide lifecycle management services for the component. This means that the application server should find the bean when it is requested and should be able to return a home object reference for the bean. When the home object attempts to create or locate the bean, the application server should create or access the remote object reference and return it to the client that requested the component.

Lifecycle management also includes the passivation of EJBs. If an EJB component has not been accessed for some time, the application server can elect to passivate the bean. When the EJB component is later requested, the application server must be able to find the bean and restore its state.

EJBs can be instantiated before use and kept in a pool. Then, when an EJB is requested by a client, it is simply retrieved from the pool and made available to the client, thus avoiding the overhead of object instantiation (for the EJB) at runtime. See Figure 1–3.

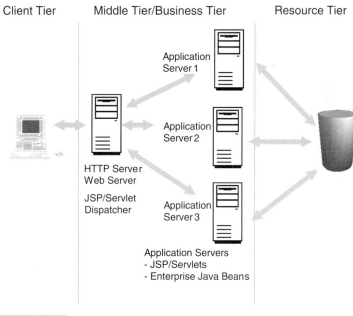

Client Tier   Middle Tier/Business Tier   Resource Tier

Application Server 1

Application Server 2

HTTP Server
Web Server

JSP/Servlet
Dispatcher   Application Server 3

Application Servers
- JSP/Servlets
- Enterprise Java Beans

Figure 1–3   *EJB component pooling.*

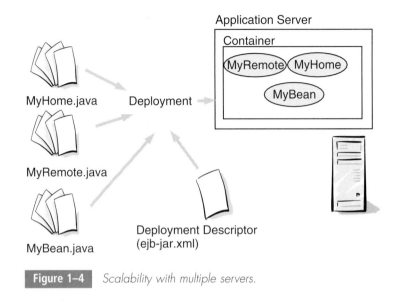

Figure 1–4   *Scalability with multiple servers.*

Scalability and Failover

The scalability of an application represents the application's ability to handle an increase in usage without a significant drop in performance. For a Web site, usage is generally represented by the number of concurrent users or the number of page hits for the site for some increment of time (day, hour, minute, second).

Scalability is not addressed directly in the J2EE specification, but is addressed indirectly in the design of the components and how they interact with the container. Scalability is usually provided using a feature known as *load balancing,* where a dispatcher component can dispatch service requests over one or more servers. This load balancing depends on another feature known as application server clustering, where multiple application servers are attached to a cluster or group of servers. These servers usually work together to provide both scalability and failover capabilities for the distributed application.

Load balancing can be done using various algorithms, from a simple round-robin algorithm where requests are distributed evenly among all available servers, to a weighted average form of load balancing where requests are distributed among servers based on some statistical weight (see Figure 1–4).

Application servers may also provide some form of failover capabilities. The failover capabilities of a server represent the server's ability to survive a failure of some sort caused by either the server hardware or the operating system. Specifically, failover generally applies to the ability of session activity to survive the failure of one of the servers in the cluster. This failover may be transparent, meaning that if the server on which the session is running fails, the other servers in the cluster will manage its workload transparently to the client application.

Flavors of EJBs

EJBs come in three flavors as of the EJB 2.0 specification: session beans, entity beans, and message-driven beans. These variations are for a purpose. Each bean has specific functionality that makes it amenable for providing certain services, as detailed in the following sections.

Session Beans

Session beans represent a session between a client and an EJB, a client conversational state. Using the service model, a client will request a service from the bean through some conversation and the bean will respond with a result. This communication between the client process and the bean may or may not require the EJB to retain state information between invocations. If a session bean retains state between invocations, then it is considered a *stateful session bean*. If a session bean does not retain state between invocations, then it is considered a *stateless session bean*.

Any stateless session bean, since it does not retain state between invocations, should not use instance members or class members, because they will not be guaranteed to have sensible values—values specific to a client session—between invocations. In this vein, stateless session beans should receive a request, perform all work necessary to complete the request, and then return results for the request all within the space of the invocation (the method call).

Entity Beans

Entity beans represent a unique element in a persistent data store. They represent persistent data, and in relational database terms, they are said to represent a row in a database table (or potentially, a unique record composed of a join across multiple tables).

Since they represent a unique relation in a persistent data store, an entity bean is represented by a primary key, a unique representation for the entity bean. A primary key can be represented by one or more columns in the underlying table.

An entity bean does not need to be mapped into a relational database. An entity bean could be mapped into a legacy database system or even into a set of files, though the most common implementation is that of object-relational mapping, using the entity bean to represent some portion of a relational database.

Entity beans must remain synchronized with the persistent data store. This is accomplished using a set of callback methods called by the container for certain lifecycle events. These methods must be implemented by the entity bean. Specifically, the `ejbLoad` method is used to load the bean from the database, and the `ejbStore` method is used to synchronize the bean with the database.

An entity bean developer can write the code for the `ejbLoad` and `ejbStore` methods (and a few others), or the application server vendor can provide a tool that will write the code for these methods. If the developer provides the code for the entity beans database synchronization, then the bean is using bean-managed persistence (BMP). If the developer allows the application server tool to create the code for the Entity Bean persistence, then the entity bean is using container-managed persistence (CMP).

As part of the EJB 2.0 specification, additional features have been added to entity beans to improve performance, address some of the limitations of the previous specification, and enhance the implementation of CMP. A query language (EJB-QL) has also been added, which allows internal selects and the navigation of related beans, values, and dependent objects.

Message-Driven Beans

MDBs have been added as part of the EJB 2.0 specification. These beans represent a useful integration of the JMS and the EJB. Am MDB allows asynchronous invocation of an EJB component. The MDB is stateless and is invoked by the container upon the arrival of a message.

Declarative Authorization and Security with EJBs

As indicated previously, the EJB container provides a number services for the distributed component including security and transactions. Part of the design for the EJBs stresses the use of declarative syntax versus traditional programming for certain properties. Using declarative syntax, entries in an XML file, an individual can define the security and transaction properties of an enterprise Java bean. This allows for easier integration of existing components from a variety of sources.

The alternative is to programmatically define the security of an application. This is a common approach with other applications, where the specific security of an application is defined in a series of Java language statements. Though common, this approach is prone to error. Using EJB declarative security provides a cleaner approach.

Deploying the EJB

Once the interfaces and classes for the EJB have been declared, they must be *deployed* into the application server. This deployment process reads a *deployment descriptor*, an XML-encoded document that describes various properties of the EJB (see Figure 1–5). These properties include but are not limited to transactional

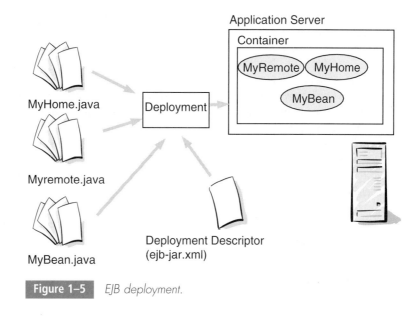

Application Server

Container

MyRemote   MyHome

MyBean

MyHome.java

Deployment

Myremote.java

Deployment Descriptor
(ejb-jar.xml)

MyBean.java

Figure 1–5   *EJB deployment.*

behavior, whether a session bean is stateful or stateless, and whether an entity bean is using CMP or BMP.

The application vendor is expected to provide a tool that will perform the deployment process. The process includes reading the deployment descriptor, finding the classes and interfaces required, possibly generating implementation code for the interfaces, and making entries into the name server.

SUMMARY

This chapter provided an introduction to J2EE and using distributed components to create an application. We examined the various packages that are commonly associated with J2EE and examined the Web tier and business tier components in additional detail.

We saw that distributed components are logically organized into tiers, groups of components that generally have some physical or logical relation to one another. These logical tiers are an important part of the architectural process. They are used to set guidelines for the design of the components that comprise an application. In the architectural process, associating a component with a specific logical tier identifies the responsibilities of the component. These responsibilities in turn drive the detailed design of the component and will be used to identify the behaviors and members that will be assigned to the component.

We also examined the J2EE components that operate on these logical tiers. We provided a high level overview of the packages used to create these components, providing some details on how these packages originated and how they are developed using J2EE. Later sections will provide more detail and include examples of usage.

Now that we understand just what J2EE is, let's start at the beginning of the development process and discuss how a J2EE application should be designed. As with any complex technology, it is important to impart structure on the design process, otherwise what may result from the development effort would be an unworkable collection of components instead of a coherent, flexible application. The following chapters in this section will discuss the basic principles of the J2EE architecture and application design process.

CHAPTER 2

J2EE Architecture and Design

INTRODUCTION

J2EE is an enterprise-wide set of technologies. As explained in the previous chapter, it involves the creation of applications from one or more sets of components, which operate on different logical tiers. Relative to the creation of monolithic and client/server applications, or applications developed with structured languages instead of object-oriented languages, development with these tools involves a different architecture and design.

This chapter introduces the basic concepts of designing a J2EE system and determining the architecture—the structure—for the application. Since this is essentially an object-oriented technology, we will also take this opportunity to review some basic object-oriented concepts and apply them to J2EE technology.

An architectural discussion can be potentially open-ended and vague. Architecture can mean different things to different people. To avoid ambiguity and confusion, we will clearly define what we consider architecture as applied to J2EE applications.

Architecture Defined

The dictionary definition of architecture is the study of design; the orderly arrangement of parts or structure. Interestingly enough, one dictionary defines architecture as the "art or science of building ...," lending credence to the argument that architecture is more of an art than a science.

More specifically, when the term architecture is applied to the computer science field as a *system architecture,* the definition applies to the overall design of a system, including the hardware and software required. When applied to software as a *software architecture,* the term applies to the grouping of components into mutually dependent parts that create a logical whole. The emphasis is on structure and not the specifics, the details, of the system. The selection of the components and the determination of the dependencies of the components is a large part of what comprises the architectural process.

Since we need to apply this concept of architecture to J2EE, we will define *J2EE architecture* as the study of how to design of J2EE applications. This design includes the types of components to be used (servlet, JSP, EJB, JMS), and the hardware that will be used to run the components.

Architecture and J2EE

Developing an architecture for J2EE involves object-oriented analysis, but instead of looking only at classes and groups of classes, we look at components—the J2EE components we discussed in the previous chapter

The architectural process, since it is somewhat of an art, does not require a strict procedure be used each time a J2EE architecture must be created; a variety of approaches can be used depending on the size of the project and the project constraints. But the outcome must be the same: an architecture that provides a cohesive, clear solution.

Architecture requires compromises and tradeoffs be made. As we will see in the sections below, various constraints are applied to the system design process. These constraints must be balanced with the goals of the system and the nonfunctional requirements (the critical success factors) for the system.

Goals of the Architectural Process

There are some general principles that are usually applied during the architectural process. These principles help guide the analysis and decision making that must be performed during the process:

- Create an architecture that has clarity.
- Create an architecture that is extensible.
- Create an architecture that is maintainable.

By creating an architecture that has clarity, you create a system that can be understood, a system that is not overly complex. This is not always an easy task to achieve, since many systems are by the nature of their requirements complex. But object-oriented design allows us to encapsulate that complexity into the components we create so that the resulting architecture is clear and understandable and does not require detailed knowledge of the complex inner workings of its constituent components.

One design process that can help to simplify the system architecture is the creation of *subsystems*. A subsystem completely encapsulates its functionality and exposes only a small, simple interface. The functionality it encapsulates could comprise some complex set of processes, but the client objects are shielded from this complexity through the simple interface it exposes. The result is a design, a system architecture, that is clearer and easier to understand (see Figure 2–1 and Figure 2–2).

Cohesion and Coupling

The final product of the architectural process should create an architecture that is clear and understandable and can be maintained and extended with minimal difficulty. To get to this point, it is important that during the architectural process, we create a design that manages the interaction of our components. The components we design must interact, but this interaction must be controlled. As we group our components, we create groups that have a high degree of *cohesion*, a term that indicates the members of the group have a high degree of dependence on each other. High

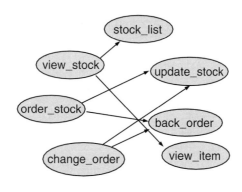

Figure 2–1   *Before subsystem.*

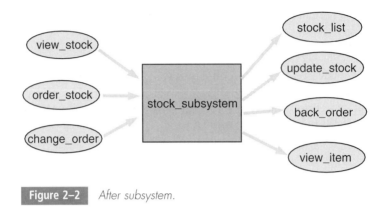

Figure 2–2   *After subsystem.*

cohesion indicates that the groupings make sense, that the members do belong together.

The groups created (represented as packages in our UML diagrams) will then interact. This interaction is referred to as *coupling*. The coupling between groups, the interdependence of groups, must be managed and minimized as much as possible. A high degree of coupling between groups creates a system where a change to one group could have a rippling effect of requiring a change to many other groups, an expensive and time-consuming proposition. What is desired instead is loose coupling between components.

Loose Coupling, High Cohesion

The general rule of thumb we can take from this advice is *loose coupling, high cohesion*—a simple enough set of terms, but not so easy to implement in the design process where systems can be very complex and system interaction reflects that complexity. But J2EE provides a varied set of tools that can help to manage the complexity of the process. Understanding what these tools are and the technology that makes them work is part of the responsibility of the J2EE architect. For example, interaction between systems often adds complexity to system design. Legacy systems often have rigid, inflexible interfaces that must be used. Tools such as XML with XSLT can be used to package the data that travels between the new system and the legacy system, and can generalize and simplify the transformation process, creating an interface that is easy to change (by changing the XSLT) and manage.

Additionally, exposing a service to client systems or components could also be a difficult process. Without the correct tools, this could involve defining a communication protocol and defining data transmission packets. But once again, XML can save the day using the Simple Object Access Protocol (SOAP). SOAP allows an interface to be created and a schema for the data interchange to be defined. Data is transmitted in XML, a format understood by a wide number of tools. The end result of defining a SOAP service for the interface would be a simple, relatively easy to implement interface for the system.

Knowing that these technologies exist and how they can simplify the design process is an important part of the role of the J2EE architect. Technical proficiency is every bit as important as design proficiency for the J2EE architect.

THE ARCHITECTURAL PROCESS

The following sections describe an architectural process for developing J2EE architectures. As these sections indicate, this process is part object-oriented analysis (applied to distributed components), part technology selection, and part project management, as illustrated in Figure 2–3.

The architectural process is about decisions, about managing tradeoffs. For every project, there is a series of decisions that need to be made during the design process. These decisions are critical; they have a tremendous impact on the success or failure of the project. As an architect, you must approach this decision-making process in a logical manner, using principles and goals to guide your decisions. There are two key elements that can help guide the creation of an effective J2EE architecture:

* architectural goals
* nonfunctional requirements (critical success factors)

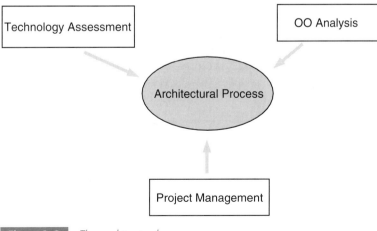

Figure 2–3   *The architectural process.*

The architectural goals represent guiding principles that apply mainly to the design of J2EE components. These goals defy strict measurement and as such are somewhat nebulous. But they are nevertheless vitally important to the creation of a successful J2EE architecture:

- clarity
- performance
- reliability
- extensibility
- reusability

Any system will have a set of functional requirements that should clearly define what functions the system must perform correctly in order to be considered successful. For any system, there are a set of equally important nonfunctional requirements that must also be met in order for the system to be considered successful. These nonfunctional requirements, when distinguished from functional requirements, are sometimes referred to as critical success factors, reflecting their importance. The nonfunctional requirements generally associated with a J2EE project are as follows:

- security
- manageability
- reliability
- scalability
- capacity
- extensibility
- flexibility
- performance
- project constraints

It is unfortunately not uncommon for systems to be developed that meet all of their functional requirements, yet fail to meet their nonfunctional requirements and are thus deemed a failure. An accounting system that meets all functional requirements for its user interface and account updates, but does not meet the nonfunctional requirements of scalability up to a user load of 100 simultaneous users would not be considered a successful system.

This identification of goals and nonfunctional requirements is by design a simplification of the process. Creating a good architecture requires careful consideration of a variety of elements and requires the architect to draw on a large pool of knowledge from the areas of computer technology and systems analysis. Specifically, using a top-down approach, we define this architectural process as follows.

1. Perform initial requirements gathering.
2. Create abstract definition of system.
3. Identify nonfunctional requirements.
4. Identify high-level components.
5. Refactor component design and group components by tier.
6. Identify software technology required.
7. Identify hardware required.
8. Create deployment diagrams, component diagrams, and other documentation to describe the system architecture.

These steps are not cast in stone. The specifics of a project may dictate exactly how many of these steps are used and how often they are repeated to hone and refactor the design. These steps are explained in more detail in the following sections.

Perform Initial Requirements Gathering

Before we can define our system, we need to understand the functional requirements for the system, even if they are at a very high level. This requires that at least some use case analysis be performed with designated stakeholders to determine what the major functions of the system will be. This will be used to drive the next step in this process, providing an abstract, high-level definition of the system.

NOTE

Use Case Analysis

Use case analysis is a form of gathering requirements from the users of a system, the stakeholders, based on their view of the system. A *use case* identifies a user, someone outside of the system who gains value from the system. Each particular use case identifies a distinct way the user gets value from the system.

As of this time, use case analysis is probably the most widely accepted technique for requirements gathering. Part of the reason for this success is that it allows the user to describe the system from their perspective instead of from the perspective of the systems analyst.

Create Abstract Definition of System

The very start of the project provides an opportunity to clarify and ensure that the application being designed has been clearly defined in a manner that is understandable by the users. Creating a high-level, abstract, description can help to clarify the system for those on the project team.

An abstract definition of the system should be created among the team members. This abstract definition should indicate the purpose of the system and provide some guidance for the definition of the nonfunctional requirements of the system. This definition will most likely be built using a set of high-level use cases identifying the basic requirements for the system. To develop a good understanding of the interactions required of the system, these use cases should take a careful look at relationships with other use cases and with other systems.

It is important to take a breather at this point in the development effort and ensure that the requirements provided up to this point are clear and that the end users have been involved in the process from the beginning. Requirements must not be contradictory, and if they are, they must be refactored working with the end users who helped to create the documents.

Requirements must also be stable and fixed, and not subject to the whims of higher level management. Appropriate domain experts should be identified for the project, and their time should be allocated to the design of the project. In the end, it is the use cases which by definition detail the value of the system. The user input in this process is therefor critical.

Identify Nonfunctional Requirements

The nonfunctional requirements of the system identify what the system must achieve in order for it to be considered successful. They are distinguishable from the *goals* of a system in that they are considered *measurable* requirements, whereas the goals of a system are not measurable. Each of the nonfunctional requirements here has an identifiable metric associated with it (though testing or tracking that metric is another matter entirely).

What these requirements or factors indicate is that even if the system meets all of its *functional requirements,* the functions identified by the end users or the proponents of the system, and performs its operations flawlessly, if it fails to achieve its nonfunctional requirements, then the system itself has failed. When you examine these factors., it is easy to see why that is the case. For the purposes of this text, the nonfunctional requirements of a J2EE system are as follows:

- security
- manageability
- reliability
- availability
- scalability
- capacity
- extensibility
- flexibility
- performance

- project constraints
- testability

Security

The security of a system is a measurement of the potential for a security breach of the system. Based on the fact that almost any system can experience a security intrusion if enough time is available, this is usually measured in some increment of time.

Security is a broad term that applies to both authentication and authorization; *authentication* is the ability to identify who a principal is (for example, obtaining and verifying a password), and authorization is granting an authenticated principal permission to perform certain operations.

Security intrusions can involve modifying information for maliciousness or gain, viewing sensitive information, or destroying information. The security policy for a system should be able to protect against these various intrusions. A metric applied commonly to this nonfunctional requirement is how many hours a malicious intruder would require to compromise the system.

Manageability

The manageability of a system measures how much effort is required to manage the current configuration. Generally speaking, as the number of machines and the extent of the network increases, or the more complex the technology used, the more difficult it is to manage the system. This is usually measured in the number of person hours required to manage the system.

Reliability

Reliability is a measurement of how well the system can maintain the integrity and consistency of an application. Reliability is usually attained using transactions. Transaction management can be used to insure that the data source is maintained in a consistent state even though multiple users may be accessing the database or the applications accessing the database may have failed.

Note that with the definitions used here, reliability is different from availability, so that even though a highly available system may be referred to as being reliable, that is not the definition being used for our purposes. We use the term reliable in reference to transactional integrity, and we use the term availability in reference to the uptime, the time a system is available to be used, on the system.

Availability

Availability is an indicator of how often a resource will be available and when the resource might be unavailable. The usual metric for this requirement is the mean time between failure (MTBF) for a system or technology. It may also be measured in an expression of the time period in which the system should be available, such as 99.99 percent uptime (the infamous "four nines").

Scalability

Scalability is considered to be the ability to support a specified level of performance as the load on the system increases. As with the performance and capacity nonfunctional requirements, the definition of scalability is very subjective and specific to the application being developed.

Scalability metrics are a statement of desired performance level as load increases, such as the ability to load a page in 15 seconds with a user load of 500 concurrent users. These metrics would be expressed as a response curve based on additional load and the additional application of system resources (CPU/memory, additional application servers) to manage the load. *Vertical scalability* is considered the addition of hardware resource (CPU/memory) on an individual server. *Horizontal scalability* is considered the addition of servers to manage the load.

Capacity

Capacity is the measure of the number of jobs or use cases that can be performed for a given unit of time. Capacity is a nonfunctional requirement that represents a measure of performance at a specified load. It is a specific measure of the workload the system can manage. The greater the capacity, the more work the system can perform.

Capacity is directly related to scalability. As system load increases, capacity should begin to decrease in a nonlinear fashion; this is the measure for scalability.

In order to develop a suitable metric for capacity, a clear definition of the jobs to be performed by the system is required. With batch-oriented systems, the definition of this is clear, since the system is designed to perform fixed job sets. With Web applications and other end-user systems, the concept of a job is less clear. The standard metric of page hits is also somewhat nebulous, since different pages exact different tolls on the system. The capability to cache pages can also affect these measures. Obviously, a page that has been cached will be returned more quickly than a page that has not been cached.

The best approach is to select a cross-section of pages that represent a common user path into the system and a cross-section of pages that will be cached and pages that will not be cached by the system (the selection of caching strategies is obviously an important part of performance tuning).

To further clarify, a system could have a requirement to manage 500 simultaneous users—that represents a statement of capacity. The system requirements could further define the user's request at that load will take no more than 1.5 seconds to process and return an acknowledgment—that is a measure of performance.

Extensibility

Extensibility is not a measure of system performance, but a measure of how easy it is to extend a system. As such, it is difficult to measure or quantify, and only in very specific cases is this a clear nonfunctional requirement (as opposed to a design goal). An example of a very specific non-functional requirement for extensibility is that a system should allow modifications to accommodate additional sites at a cost of 2 person-months of effort and $250, 000 in hardware.

Flexibility

Flexibility identified here as a non-functional requirement is considered by many to be a general design goal that should be the byproduct of good object-oriented design. Flexibility is the ability of a system to support architectural or hardware changes. A system that is designed with a minimum of collusion will be flexible and not brittle, and will provide the ability to support the changes required during the system's life cycle.

Flexibility is difficult to measure. There have been attempts at measuring flexibility, such as determining the number of intersection points between objects to measure coupling between components, but these measurements are not standard.

Performance

Performance is the ability of the system to execute the work required in the given timeframe required. Performance with multitiered component-based systems can involve a broad set of measures that apply to the various components being used.

The performance, scalability, and availability requirements of a system can have a significant impact on the system architecture. A system that does not need to be available 24 hours a day, 7 days a week (24/7) and available 99.99 percent of the time at peak performance levels will require a different architecture than a system that does not require high availability and constant peak performance levels.

For an end-user system, various performance goals would be the time to load a page, the time required to execute a page, and the time required to create a report. But these end-user actions can involve the invocation and execution of a number of components, all of which have an effect on the performance as seen by the end user. A Web page may be presented by a JSP page, may use a servlet to load part of the page, and may invoke a JavaBean that invokes an EJB that executes a query from the database; poor performance from any one of these components could lead to poor performance for the application as a whole.

While it is important to measure performance from the end user's perspective, the performance of individual components must also be carefully examined during the development cycle. In this way, potential performance bottlenecks can be identified before they impact end-user performance.

Testability

In order to manage the quality of a system, it is important to be able to test for flaws. If functional and nonfunctional requirements are nebulous (as they sometimes can be), then testing becomes more difficult, and the quality of the system may suffer. For this reason, testability is identified as a nonfunctional requirement. In order for the system to be successful, it is important to consider testability in the design process as requirements are being identified. If an end user has provided requirements that are not clear and testable, then the requirement should be refined.

Project Constraints

The project constraints are real-world constraints on a project. The elements of this non-functional requirement are listed in Table 2–1.

Table 2–1	Project Constraints
Environmental	Hardware, hardware environment, and software constraints on the system architecture
Personnel Resource	Staffing constraints
Budgetary	Monetary constraints that limit other resources available for the system
Time	Time constraints on the start and completion of a project

The *environmental constraints* on a system are those factors in the system environment that can limit the design or operation of the system. These are hardware and hardware environment issues that can affect the system architecture as well as the software environment constraints of the system.

A hardware constraint imposed on a system architecture could limit the system to be developed and run on existing hardware only. Such a limitation would mean that the system would very likely have to share resources with other systems that are operating.

Hardware environmental constraints involve issues such as the space available in the computer room for additional hardware and the power supply or air conditioning limitations where the computer is located.

There can also be software environment constraints on the system architecture. The information technology department may insist that all software operate on the Windows NT operating system and may further restrict the version of the operating system to be used. Software restrictions may also extend to the client software to be used, limiting that to the Windows environment using the Internet Explorer browser.

Personnel resource constraints could constrain a project by limiting project staffing only to members of the department, staff members who may not have any experience with J2EE technology. Personnel resources may also involve limiting the total number of staff members who will be allowed to work on a project.

The *budgetary constraints* on a system architecture can often be the most limiting. The purchase of additional hardware to create a truly robust, highly available system may be restrained by budgetary limitations. This could also have a significant impact on the staffing resources available. Staffing—paying for good technical staff—is often the most significant cost of a project. (As of this writing, good J2EE developers with experience and credentials can cost upwards of $3,000 to $5,000 per week.)

The *time constraints* for the system impact the design and staffing requirements. To a certain extent, additional development staff can perform more work for a given period of time. This works up to the point of diminishing returns ("Nine women don't make a baby in one month"—Fred Brooks). Just where the point of diminishing returns is depends on the project. If the time constraints for a project are rigid and inflexible and are coupled with restrictive budget and staffing constraints, then the design of the system may need to be revisited to reduce the amount of functionality for the initial release of the system.

Identify High-Level Components and Their Interactions

In order to correctly determine the appropriate architecture of the system, a good deal of information about the required system operation must be understood. End users may be inclined to simply say, "I need a reporting system to print sales reports and allow some orders to be modified. So how long will that take?" But the devil is in the details, and a certain amount of details must be known to determine the architecture.

The true complexity of the system can be gleaned from good object-oriented analysis. While some object-oriented analysis is an important part of the architectural process, the true, detailed object-oriented analysis that determines object class definitions is not specifically in the architectural role (though in many organizations it is not unusual for the J2EE architect or the system architect to play a role in the lower level design process.)

The high-level components for the system are identified through various object-oriented analysis techniques. Use-case analysis, class responsibility cards (CRCs), and other analysis techniques should be used to determine the various high-level entities that comprise the system. The interaction of the these entities can then be determined using sequence diagrams and other techniques. What ultimately feeds the architectural process is the high-level entities, control objects, boundary objects, and business objects for the system.

Refactor Component Design and Group Components by Tier

A good design effort refactors the design several times before attempting to implement the design. Each iteration in the design process leads to a more detailed and potentially lower level design for the system. The architect does not need the final, low-level design of the system. The architect just needs to understand the composition and interaction of the high-level objects for the system.

Once the architect has provided the high-level design of the system, it should be examined, reviewed, discussed, and then refactored. The architect should prepare several alternative approaches for the system architecture and identify the costs and benefits of each approach.

Creating and using additional documents may also be useful during this step. For instance, with Web applications, the creation of a *wire diagram* may be useful. This diagram provides a detailed process-flow diagram that shows the execution path (the pages executed) for a Web application. Viewing the page flow of an application is essential to determining the processing that must be done to support the process flow. Some also find the use of CRCs helpful in determining component interactions.

Identify Software Technology Required

The next two steps in the architectural process involve a technology evaluation. This involves evaluating hardware and software alternatives, including any potential off-the-shelf or open-source solutions if corporate policy allows. The only requirement for the evaluation of these technologies, in the scope of this discussion, is that they be compatible with J2EE—this leaves a wide array of potential technologies available.

A technology evaluation should include as part of the process a matrix that identifies the technology, the benefits of the technology, and the potential issues with the technology. The technology must also be evaluated based on its impact on the nonfunctional requirements of the system. For example, a technology such as Remote Method Invocation (RMI) may be appropriate for a small to moderate user load, but for a system with a nonfunctional scalability requirement that it must handle thousands of requests an hour, RMI may quickly be ruled out in favor of a more scalable technology. So, at a minimum, the various criteria that should be identified as part of the technology evaluation for software are as follows:

- Technology name
- Estimated acquisition cost
- Benefits of technology
- Potential issues with the technology

- Impact on nonfunctional requirements
- Impact on project goals

As an architect, it is important for you to carefully document each step in the decision-making process. When you consider the ultimate expenditure involved in even a small J2EE effort, it is worthwhile to be able to explain why specific decisions were made. Creating a comparative matrix such as the sample in Table 2–2 is an important part of this process.

Table 2–2   *Sample Technology Comparison*

Name	Cost	Benefits	Issues	NFR Impact	Goals Impact
JSP	None (Tomcat)	HTML page scripting. Non-technical users can develop pages. (With limited development staff, we could use the help of several system administrators.)	Pages must be pre-compiled else performance issue on first hit. Potential for mixing presentation with business logic.	Positive;. good performance, scalable, modular.	Good; modular.
SOAP (JAXM)	None (JWS)	Flexible, interoperable with MS world (part of our NFR).	Data typing not fully implemented in JAXM, messaging not as robust as message queues with JMS.	Positive; scalable.	Positive; modular.
RMI	None (JDK)	Lightweight, easy to use.	Not as scalable as other solutions (EJBs). Protocol can be slow.		

As this sample shows (and it is by no means complete), the various technologies must be evaluated against the needs, the nonfunctional requirements of the project. This requires that you consider the capabilities of the technology that are relevant for the project. This is done at several points in Table 2–2 where JSPs are considered based on the ability of nontechnical staff to help build pages (and the project has limited staffing—not an unusual constraint), and the use of SOAP is considered beneficial because the nonfunctional requirements require interoperability with Microsoft systems. As is clear from this example, this process may require you to review use cases and possibly request end-user clarification to determine what is the correct technology for a component. Several iterations of reviewing this matrix will most likely be required. As the evaluation nears completion, it may be useful to apply statistical weights or grades to the various technologies to provide a convenient means of ranking them—for example, grading a technology's overall appropriateness for a project on a scale of 1 to 10.

As part of this process, you—the wise architect and technology expert—will most likely be asked to evaluate the alternative implementations of a technology. Though this may not be required in some cases (many IT shops have already standardized on a J2EE application server), it is a distinct possibility. Such an evaluation should consider the J2EE compliance of the application server (not all are J2EE-compliant) and the prebuilt modules they may provide. There are currently over 25 J2EE application servers available, many of which are specialized and provide modules (groups of J2EE components) that perform common e-commerce operations, such as personalization (tracking user preferences), logins, catalogs, and shopping carts. Using what has been developed and tested could help reduce the person-hours required to complete a project.

The benefits of considering existing software technology at this stage cannot be overstated. Applying the notion of "borrow where you can" can save your project a tremendous number of development person-hours. This applies not only to the products of independent software vendors (ISVs) but also to the products of open-source development efforts.

J2EE technology goes beyond the Web tier and business tier components commonly associated with J2EE. J2EE includes RMI and messaging services that could meet the technological requirements for a component. The capabilities of Web Services (SOAP) may meet the interoperability requirements for a component. The use of XML technologies such as XSLT could allow a single J2EE component to interface with a variety of user front ends (HTML browsers, hand-helds/palm-tops, Swing GUI).

Additionally, there are open-source efforts like Jakarta-Apache Struts (as demonstrated in the application in Chapter 33, 34 and 35, which provide frameworks for Web development. These technologies can greatly reduce the effort necessary to create a Web application.

Identify Hardware Required

Since J2EE software operates in a networked environment, the servers in which the components run are usually spread across more than one machine on a network. Such a configuration has a positive impact on performance by spreading the task of executing a request across more than one server. Using more than one server also has a positive impact on availability, since if one machine is not available, another machine can execute requests for it (the degree to which this is done is dependent upon the server support and the configuration of the application).

J2EE servers, specifically application servers, can run in clustered environments. These clustered environments furnish the services that provide high availability and superior performance. The more robust J2EE servers can recognize a failure of a machine in the cluster and migrate the session for a component and its state to another server, which will then service the requests for that component. This can be done transparently to the user. (Though many J2EE application servers provide this *transparent failover* capability, not all do, and it is not a requirement for J2EE compatibility.)

The factors that must be considered for hardware configurations are varied and highly dependent upon the project constraints, specifically the environmental and budgetary constraints. A limited budget will obviously impact the choice of hardware platforms. Additionally, limitations on the computer room configuration and environment can also impact hardware decisions.

Create Deployment Diagrams, Component Diagrams, and Other Documentation to Describe the System Architecture

The final step in this development process is to create various pieces of documentation that describe the system architecture. Diagrams, which are an important part of the architectural process, have even more importance at this point. These communication tools are especially useful in helping you communicate the results of the architectural design process—how the system should be developed and deployed. Since these deployment decisions can represent a significant portion of the project expense, it is important to clearly detail what they are and how they should be implemented. These diagrams will be described in more detail in Chapter 3, but to illustrate our point, it is useful to take a quick look at a sample here. Figure 2–4 is an example of a component diagram.

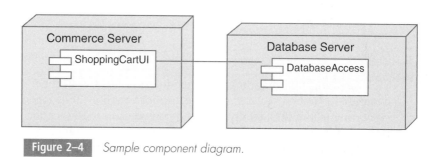

Figure 2–4   *Sample component diagram.*

This diagram details the interaction between physical implementations of a design, and so is useful to describe exactly what the results of the architectural process have been. This is also extremely useful in describing alternative implementations of the architecture.

The deployment diagram takes this visualization further, detailing the deployment of components across the various hardware platforms which will make up the system as shown in Figure 2–5.

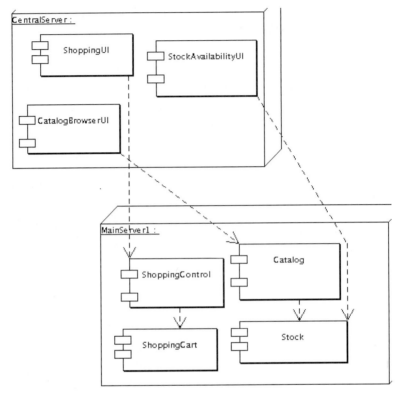

Figure 2–5   *Sample deployment diagram.*

Creating this diagram involves determining the number and types of J2EE components to be used to create the application. For J2EE, this means you need to perform a technology evaluation and comparison to determine whether the component will be a Web component (servlet, JSP), an EJB component, a message queue, an RMI component, a Web Service (SOAP), a JavaBean, or a Java helper class.

As part of this final step, several alternative approaches should be identified along with the pros and cons of each approach. This helps clarify the architectural reasoning for management and other members of the team and may present additional alternatives that involve novel approaches based on existing approaches.

It is possible that more than one iteration would be involved in the creation of the deployment diagram. Refactoring the final architectural design and making choices among the alternatives is a useful approach to determining this final architecture.

The information contained in this final deliverable details the architecture of the system through several pieces of documentation. The work items delivered are as follows:

- Unified Modeling Language (UML) deployment diagrams
- UML component diagrams
- Hardware configuration diagrams
- Use-case documentation
- Supporting documentation

The UML deployment diagrams detail the components that will be deployed and indicate where they will be deployed. The use-case documentation is effectively the supporting documentation for the deliverables. It details the use cases through UML diagrams and paper documents detailing the use-case events.

The hardware configuration diagrams detail the hardware, preferably the make and model of the machines and information about the network configuration for the hardware, including the location of one or more security firewalls if they are included.

Summary

Architecture can be a nebulous concept. It is therefore important that we clearly define what we mean by architecture and how the process of developing a valid J2EE architecture will unfold. This chapter introduced the basic concepts for J2EE architecture and discussed the architectural process. The steps involved in the architectural process and the work that must be performed during those steps was also discussed.

In the following chapters we continue this discussion of OOAD and examine the tools we use to perform this task. As part of this effort we will examine the de facto standard for modeling languages: the Unified Modeling Language (UML).

CHAPTER 3

Analysis, Design, and Development Techniques with J2EE

INTRODUCTION

As a J2EE architect, you are required to organize various J2EE components into groups and determine how those components will interact. To a large extent, this is object-oriented analysis and design (OOAD) with an eye towards the technology that will be used to implement the components. All of this analysis is conducted within the context of various project goals and nonfunctional requirements as we identified in the previous chapters.

As an architect, you must control the coupling between components and packages, and whenever possible, capitalize on the use of component associations. This requires you to work with the project team and communicate architectural ideas clearly. This entails the use of visual modeling using object-oriented (OO) diagramming to express the modeling ideas developed during requirements analysis and the subsequent development of the architecture. The most common OO modeling language in use today is the Unified Modeling Language (UML), which provides a visual medium for the expression of object and component design, object relationships, and control flow. This chapter describes UML as it is used in practice and lays the foundation for the use of these diagrams throughout this text.

Following the discussion of UML, we examine the analytical process and apply appropriate OOAD concepts to the J2EE architectural process. As always, analysis and design is about managing complexity and producing as concise and robust a design as possible. This chapter will provide various for you on how to control and manage the complexity of a J2EE architecture.

THE ARCHITECTURAL PROCESS

As we saw in Chapter 2, the architectural process is complex, requiring a mix of object-oriented analysis, requirements gathering, project management, and technology evaluation. As an architect, you are truly a jack of all trades. The process we detailed in Chapter 2 is as follows.

1. Perform initial requirements gathering.
2. Create abstract definition of system.
3. Identify nonfunctional requirements.
4. Identify high-level components.
5. Refactor component design and group components by tier.
6. Identify software technology required.
7. Identify hardware required.
8. Create deployment diagrams, component diagrams, and other documentation to describe the system architecture.

In the end, we would like the architecture and its supporting documentation to articulate the structure of the system and identify the components that comprise it and their interactions. Subsystems should be used to reduce coupling and clarify interactions.

Scattered throughout several of these steps, primarily steps 1, 3, 4, and 7, is the need to adequately document the analysis and design process with diagrams. A variety of diagrams may be used to show the components, their interaction, the security requirements, and the flow of information through the system. Fortunately, there is a core set of diagrams that represents something of a standard in OOAD. Before we can have a detailed discussion of J2EE architectural process, we must identify a core set of diagrams, our facility for communicating, and discuss how they should be used.

PROJECT COMMUNICATION AND THE UNIFIED MODELING LANGUAGE

One of the most important aspects of any architectural development effort is the communication between members of the development team. Careful examination and review of architectural alternatives is critical, and this can be done well only if all team members, both technical and in some cases nontechnical, can understand the design.

The analysis diagram is a visual presentation of a technical concept. As such, analysis diagrams have been around for some time; some have been formally standardized and others are merely arrows and circles used in a logical manner. The UML is an attempt to standardize diagramming for OOAD, which has become the de facto standard for OO analysis.

The UML is based on work done by Grady Booch, James Rumbaugh, and Ivar Jacobson. There are nine diagrams supported by UML, as listed in Table 3–1.

Of these nine diagrams, seven are commonly used:

1. use case diagram
2. class diagram
3. sequence diagram

Table 3–1   *Nine UML Diagrams*

Diagram	Description
Use Case Diagram	Describes the operation of the system from the user's point of view.
Component Diagram	Defines how pobjects are grouped into packages.
Sequence diagram	Object interaction for a set of actions. Indicates order and flow of processing.
Deployment diagram	Details object deployment across hardware platforms.
State diagram	Provides a diagram of the object lifecycle.
Collaboration diagram	Creates a diagram describing object collaboration.
Activity diagram	Details the process flow of an event.
Object diagram	Describes instantiations of classes. (Not used often.)
Class diagram	Describes the design for a class, including class members, instance members, and methods.

4. activity diagram
5. state diagram
6. component diagram
7. deployment diagram

These diagrams represent the core set you will use to describe the development of the J2EE architecture you create. Additional diagrams may also be used (for example, the process flow diagram to show the flow of data, and an entity-relationship diagram to show the relationship of data entities), but these UML diagrams listed here represent the core, which the following sections will explain.

Use Case Diagram

Use case analysis is used to gather the functional requirements for a system. Consequently, the use case diagram helps to describe this process in a way that is easily understandable to the end user. The use case diagram uses a gender-neutral stick figure to represent the user. The stick figure is referred to as the actor, an individual outside of the system who must interact with the system. The actor initiates an event, and ovals are used to represent the event the actor is initiating. A rectangle can be used to represent an external system, and lines are used to represent relationships between the actors and events. In the example in Figure 3–1, a user initiates events for a login, for reading a message or for creating a new message.

Each use case diagrammed should describe a discrete benefit for the actor. A well-focused use case should be expressed in 30 words or less, and the action taking place should happen within a single session for the actor. Excessive complexity in a use case is probably an indication that the use case should be subdivided into separate use cases. Describing complex use cases and managing these complexities is discussed in further detail in the following sections.

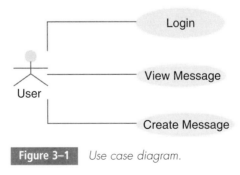

Figure 3–1   *Use case diagram.*

Class Diagram

The class diagram may be the most commonly used of UML diagrams. This diagram describes the composition of an object class, specifically the attributes and behaviors that comprise the class. Boxes are used to represent the class, with the top section reserved for the members of the class and the bottom section reserved for the methods (behaviors) of the class. Multiple classes can be described in the same diagram with lines between the classes used to represent the relationship of the classes, as shown in Figure 3–2.

An arrow going from one class to another represents inheritance: The class to which the arrow points is the superclass, and the class where the arrow originated is the subclass.

A common representation, representing a technique that is an important part of Java object-oriented programming, is the UML stereotype. The UML stereotype indicates that the object will implement specific behavior, but the object diagrammed is not the implementation itself. In Java, the properties of the UML stereotype are provided using the Java interface. An example of this is the

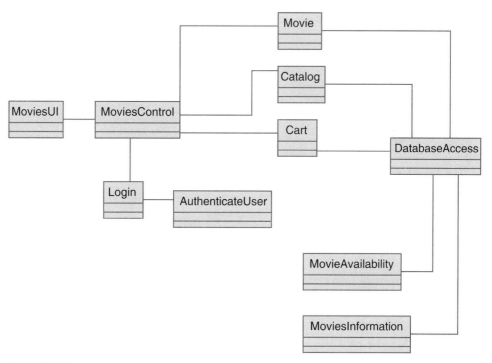

Figure 3–2   *UML class diagram.*

Runnable interface, which allows a program to start an independent thread of execution. The Runnable interface does not provide a thread implementation itself; it is up to the class that implements the interface to provide the implementation. This is shown in the UML class diagram with the << characters above the name, as shown in Figure 3–3.

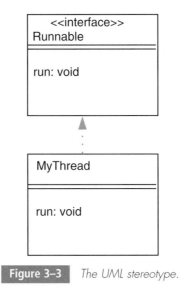

Figure 3–3   *The UML stereotype.*

From a development perspective, the use of interfaces provides a great deal of flexibility. They provide a very clear description of the implementation behavior expected of an object—a clear contract. An object implementing multiple interfaces can participate in multiple relationships for the interface, exhibiting a behavior similar to that of multiple inheritance (something not provided in Java).

The class diagram provides for the grouping of classes into packages, as shown in Figure 3–4. This is an important part of the design process, since the organization of these classes and how they interact can have a significant impact on a system. This is where optimizing cohesion and minimizing coupling are managed. By creating consistent diagrams throughout the development process, excessive coupling can be discerned earlier in the development process rather than later when it is difficult to correct. This topic will be revisited later in this chapter.

Sequence Diagram

Once again, it is critical that we understand how our objects interact, how they will work with each other. The UML sequence diagram is an excellent tool for visualizing these types of relationships. Sequence diagrams represent control flow across

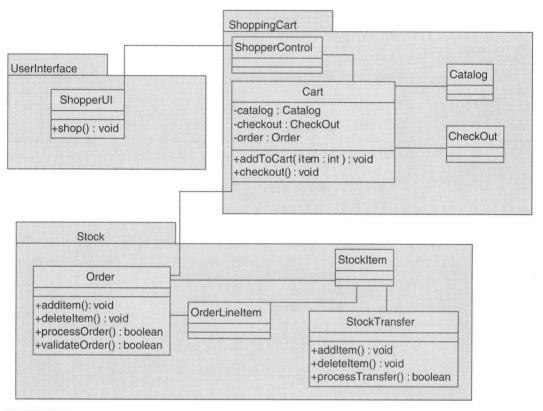

Figure 3–4 *Class diagram with package groupings.*

a series of objects or components and provide a useful visual medium for determining object relationships in the design phase. While the common terminology for the elements in this diagram are objects, with J2EE architectural analysis and design, these objects are more commonly J2EE components: JSPs, servlets, or EJBs.

Using sequence diagrams, it is easy to determine the amount of collaboration between two or more objects. This can help determine how to group objects and whether or not a given object is becoming too complex.

In the example in Figure 3–5, a sequence diagram is used to detail a user login process.

As a user logs into the system, the login process in turn executes an authentication process, which then passes control to a flow control process that will decide what the user's next action will be based on his or her authentication.

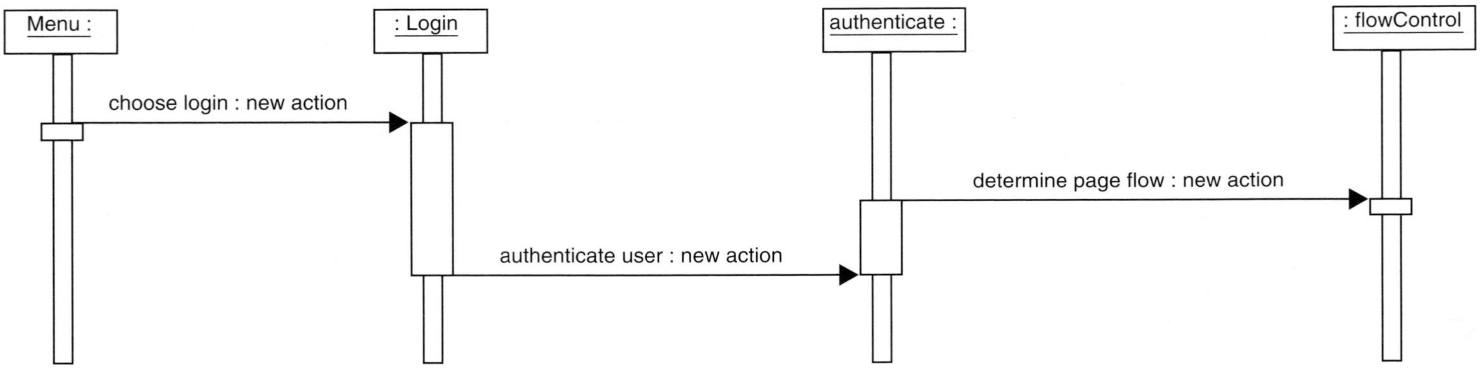

Figure 3-5 UML sequence diagram.

Activity Diagram

Use case activities can be further analyzed using activity diagrams. Though these diagrams are frighteningly similar to the much maligned programming flow chart (sometimes called "flaw charts"), they are built on distinctly different rules and work at a higher level of detail than the flow chart. As one of the set of diagrams you will use to describe the design of your J2EE system, this is a useful tool for visualizing the processing of an event.

UML activity diagrams break down the activities into a series of events that help provide insights on the processing behind the event. These diagrams, coupled with more detailed textual documents, can help you facilitate discussions with stakeholders. The example shown here Figure 3–6) documents part of a user login.

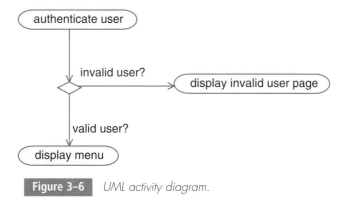

Figure 3–6 *UML activity diagram.*

As this diagram details, if the user login is valid, then a menu is displayed. If, however, the login is invalid, then a page describing the invalid login is displayed.

State Diagram

Some objects move through various states of activity, often in response to some set of events. The lifecycle of an EJB or servlet is an example of this. For these objects you may find it useful to use a UML state diagram that details the states of that object.

A state diagram shows the various states' existence for an object, thus providing a representation of the lifecycle of an object or component, as shown in Figure 3–7.

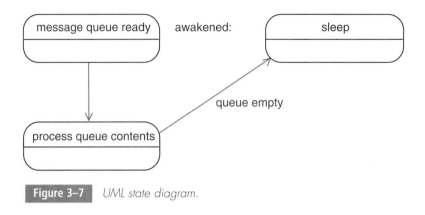

Figure 3–7   *UML state diagram.*

This diagram details the lifecycle of an object that processes messages from a message queue. The message queue processor is in a ready state until it is awakened. When it is awakened, the contents of the queue are processed until there are no more contents to process. The queue processor is then put back to sleep until it is needed again.

Component Diagram

As it has no doubt become clear, J2EE involves creating distributed applications, applications where components will run on one or, more than likely, multiple servers on a network. Once you have identified the top-level objects or components of the system becomes clear, you then need to determine how the objects will be distributed across servers. Two UML diagrams help to visualize this process: the component diagram and the deployment diagram.

The UML component diagram represents the relationships of the physical implementation of components and so is sometimes referred to as an implementation diagram, as demonstrated in Figure 3–8.

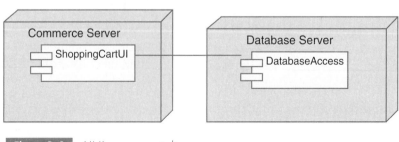

Figure 3–8   *UML component diagram.*

In this example, a shopping-cart user interface component is shown interacting with a database access component. As the diagram makes clear, both reside on separate network nodes (servers). As part of a more complex architecture, this diagram could help discern excessive coupling or potential bottlenecks between components residing on separate servers where interaction will require network communication and possibly create a performance bottleneck.

Deployment Diagram

Similar to the component diagram, the deployment diagram illustrates the physical deployment of system components. Three-dimensional boxes are drawn to illustrate servers, and components are drawn as boxes with connectors (vaguely similar to an electrical plug), as shown in Figure 3–9.

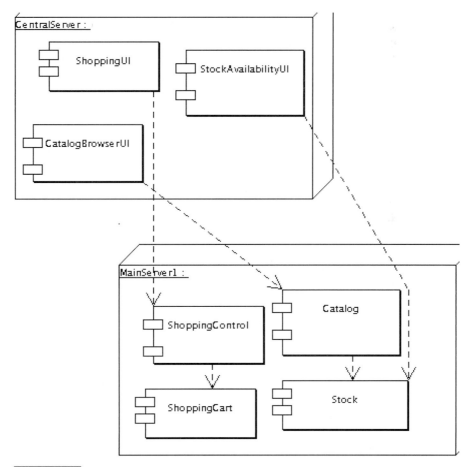

Figure 3–9 *UML deployment diagram.*

This diagram shows the potential deployment of a shopping cart system across several servers. The lines between components represent associations. As with the component diagram, this visualization of distributed components can help identify potential bottlenecks and excessive coupling between components and modules (groups of components) in the system.

THE ANALYTICAL PROCESS, J2EE STYLE

There are a number of different analytical methodologies that could be applied to the development of a J2EE system and virtually infinite hybrids that could be developed to suit the needs or constraints of a particular project. But one of the more popular methodologies, and one that most projects will borrow from to some degree, is the Rational Unified Process (RUP). The following section provides a brief overview of this process and explains how it can be applied to the J2EE architectural process.

The RUP Phases

The RUP analytical process divides the software development lifecycle into several phases of development:

- inception
- elaboration
- construction
- transition

These steps are executed in order in a cyclical fashion. Each pass through these steps should result in a usable software product, but not necessarily a product that meets the full requirements of the system. Software development with RUP is like building a house, then adding a garage, then adding a pool, until at last you have the house you originally set out to build.

This iterative process is considered an evolutionary approach to software development. Each iteration results in improvements and a product that is one step closer to the goal of a complete system. Each phase in the process may also involve multiple iterations before they are complete.

The *inception* phase represents the starting block—the absolute birth of the project. It involves the articulation of the vision for the system and the establishment of a formal project to build the system. This should be something more than the good idea scribbled on the back of a dinner napkin. A clear vision should be expressed, a business case expressed, and the scope of the project defined. These work items will be the foundation for the next phase.

In the *elaboration* phase, the problem domain will be detailed and the scope of the project will be defined to greater detail. Both the functional and nonfunctional requirements for the system should be defined at this point. The nonfunctional requirements can be recast as critical success factors, which describe the degree of risk involved in the development of the system.

The end result of this phase is the baseline architecture of the J2EE system and a schedule for the production of the system. Described as a baseline architecture in RUP documentation, any changes made in the construction phase should be minor.

The *construction* phase begins by working out the details of the baseline architecture and producing a final architecture. As with other phases of the development, it is expected that the construction phase may involve multiple iterations.

During the *transition* process, the system is turned over to the end user. The end user may require training and may find bugs that need fixing. Several iterations may be required before the user signs off on the formal acceptance criteria for the system.

RUP Best Practices

RUP involves several guiding principals or best practices that tie in well with J2EE:

- Develop software iteratively.
- Manage requirements.
- Use component-based architectures (and technologies).
- Visually model software.
- Control the software change process.

Develop Software Iteratively

As differentiated from other software methodologies that preceded it, RUP does not require strict, sequential execution of steps, a waterfall approach. Such a process was seen as slow and ineffective. Instead, steps are executed as cycles with the completion of each step representing a generation. A generation includes a software release and its supporting documentation. The release may not be the completed concept, but it represents a useful product nonetheless. Through its life, a software product is expected to evolve and thus continue the cycle, creating successive releases.

Manage Requirements

As on any project of sufficient size, the requirements of the project must be managed. Though this is really more of a project management issue than an architectural issue, the technical architect is generally in a position to advise the project manager of "scope creep." Additional requirements that may appear trivial to management could have a serious, costly impact on a project's architecture, and the J2EE architect must manage these requirements by clearly articulating the cost and impact of such changes.

Use Component-Based Architectures (and Technologies)

Though not particular to OO development, RUP has been used with success in the construction of component-based architectures. The complexity of component-based technology and OO technologies in general requires additional upfront analysis in order to create extensible, robust systems. Thus, component-based technologies benefit from the structured yet flexible RUP approach.

Visually Model Software

The role of the architect as a communicator involves communicating complex processes to less technical project team members. Communicating the complex components and component interactions of a J2EE system require that you use visual modeling techniques. The UML visual modeling language discussed in the preceding sections help facilitate this communication process.

Control the Software Change Process

Similar to the issue of changing requirements, the software change process can impede and slow the development of a system. As an architect, you must first understand and be able to predict (with reasonable accuracy) the impact of software changes on the system. You must then communicate this cost and impact to management.

J2EE Architectural Analysis

For purposes of our J2EE architecture, we do not need to complete the design process (in fact, we would not expect it to be complete), but we do need to have some idea of high-level requirements and components. This is what is referred to in RUP as the *baseline architecture*, an architecture that is further refined and is not completed until the construction phase. As we have identified throughout these first few chapters, we have a number of forces acting on the architectural design process as shown in Figure 3-10: J2EE Architectural process.

The analytical steps we would need to complete our initial architecture are as follows:

1. Gather initial requirements using use cases.
2. Refine and clarify use cases.

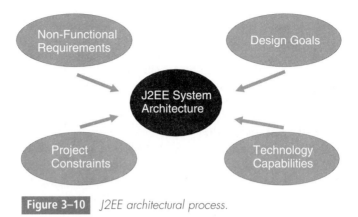

Figure 3–10   *J2EE architectural process.*

3. Identify top-level domain objects.
4. Perform technology evaluations.
5. Associate business domain objects with technologies.
6. Create component diagrams and deployment diagrams.

As these steps indicate, initial requirements are gathered using use cases. Use cases are developed, clarified, and refined, and they ultimately lead to the identification of top-level domain objects. These business domain objects are essentially what will become the components—the servlets, JSPs, and EJBs—of the J2EE system being developed.

At this point we need to determine what technology to use for these components. We would then perform technology evaluations to determine appropriate candidate technologies for implementing these business objects. The end result is a set of services and business objects (or components) and associated J2EE technologies.

Finally, we take the services and associated components that we have identified and group them into packages. At this point we also need to indicate the hardware and software requirements of our system. The UML component and deployment diagrams help to visualize the potential deployments for J2EE components.

We would expect these steps to be completed in order. But as with RUP, we would also expect these steps to be repeated iteratively. Once again, architecture involves choices among alternatives, and as the development effort continues, choices will need to be made. Through the duration of the project, functional and nonfunctional requirements may change to reflect new priorities or altered project constraints; the architecture must respond to these changes. Each iteration of refining and improving the architecture will involve responding to this inevitable change and making the choices that need to be made.

Use Case Analysis

Use case analysis is the most common technique used to identify the requirements of the system, information that is then used to define processes and later to design classes that will ultimately fulfill the use case. The importance of these requirements cannot be overemphasized. They are the foundation on which the system is built. If they are incomplete or, worse yet, incorrect, then the system development effort will obviously suffer.

You should begin use case analysis by identifying the participants, the users or stakeholders of the system. These are individuals who may have a variety of responsibilities within the organization, from manager to clerk. The common thread among these individuals is the interest in the direction and success of the system.

These stakeholders should be individuals who have a "buy-in" to the success of the system and are willing to stay with the project for the duration. It is unfortunately a recurring problem that many chosen stakeholders start with an interest in a system but then begin to lose interest as the project wears on. Choosing stakeholders whose job is directly affected by the success or failure of the system can help alleviate this problem.

If these stakeholders are outside of the system being developed and interact with the system, then they represent actors for the purposes of use case analysis. You should select more than one stakeholder with varied backgrounds, gathering the opinions not only of management (who are often only the consumers of system information), but of the administrative and professional users of the system who must input and manage the information in the system.

During the use case sessions, the session facilitator will work on creating the use case diagrams, most likely UML diagrams, to help visualize the requirements of the system. This process involves determining how the users extract value from the system. The value they extract is not only information retrieved from the system in the form of reports or queries, but the processing that the system will perform for them, processing that would otherwise need to be done manually or through one or more disparate legacy systems.

Managing Use Case Complexity

A use case should represent a discrete benefit for the actor. A well-defined use case should be expressed succinctly, and the action taking place should happen within a single session for the actor. If that is not the case and a use case involves excessive complexity, then it may require refactoring the use case into one or more separate use cases. Fortunately, UML provides diagrammatic syntax to help manage this complexity.

Use cases can *include* other use cases, or a use case may *extend* another use case; these techniques allow use cases to be designed in such a way that complexity of individual use cases is reduced and the overall model retains simplicity. An include operation indicates that the use case absorbs the behavior of another use case. Alternatively, an extend operation indicates that the use case depends on the behavior of the base use case and may optionally add the execution of its events to it.

Figure 3–11 contains an example of a use case include. In this example, the actor initiates the "navigate system" use case. This use case event includes the events of viewing existing messages and create or deleting a message. Using this technique, the complexity of a use case can be managed using the "divide and conquer" approach, where complex events are broken into smaller, more manageable use case events, which are included into other use case events.

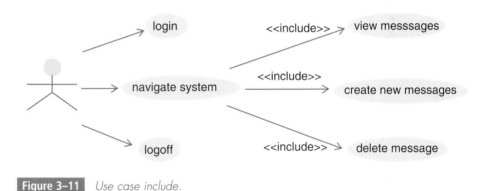

Figure 3–11   *Use case include.*

Abstraction is an important object-oriented technique that is often used to simplify complex behaviors. The benefits of abstraction can also have an impact on use case analysis. A complex use case can be made abstract and then other use cases can call on its abstract behavior, as shown in Figure 3–12.

Actors can also be generalized in use cases. If different actors have similar interactions with the system, then consolidating those interactions into a single actor could be a useful abstraction. Use case generalization can be used to model this behavior, as shown in Figure 3–13.

Evaluating Object Relationships

As objects are being identified during the analytical process, relationships between the objects will also be identified. As you identify objects during the OOAD process, you must also identify relationships between objects. These relationships

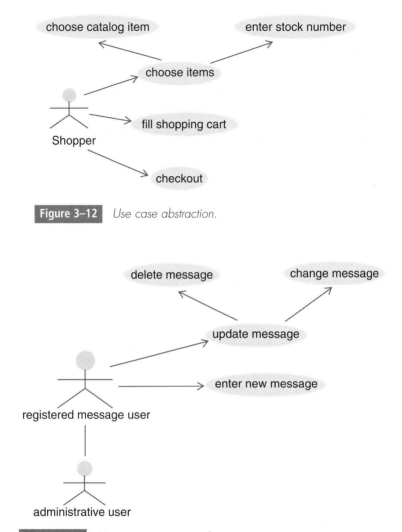

Figure 3–12   *Use case abstraction.*

Figure 3–13   *Use case actor generalization.*

or associations between objects are important and represent one of the key analysis areas where we can exert control over coupling and facilitate cohesion (discussed in more detail later in this chapter).

When an object creates a reference to another object, even though it may carry the reference for only a short time, an object *association* exists between the two objects. Careful selection of object relationships can lead to more robust, flexible applications. The selection of these relationships have additional meaning when working with J2EE, since the relationships between some objects must be realized through network connections. Passing objects to and from J2EE business tier components (EJBs) is by value, not by reference, as is done in a local JVM. This creates a performance penalty, albeit a very manageable penalty, that must be factored into decisions on how to use these components.

Though Java is a true object-oriented language that thoroughly supports inheritance, careful thought should be given to the use of this feature, since in many cases an alternative is to use a more flexible object relationship. The commonly identified object relationships are as follows:

- dependency
- association
- aggregation
- composition

The distinction between these relationships is based on the duration and the nature of the relationship. This list identifies the relationships from weakest to strongest as explained below.

Dependency

An object dependency exists when there is a short-term relationship between the objects. For instance, the relationship between a shopping cart and a checkout object would be short term, since once the checkout operation is complete, the checkout object would no longer be needed. The same relationship would exist for a stock transfer object that needed to use a stock item object to get the information on the stock item being transferred. The stock transfer object would have a *dependency* relationship with the stock item object; the stock transfer object would read the transfer information and could then discard the stock item object and continue processing. Dependency is shown in UML with a dashed line with an arrow between the client class and the class use, as shown in Figure 3–14.

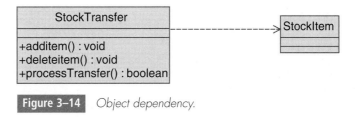

Figure 3–14 *Object dependency.*

Association

An object association represents a more long-term association than the dependency relationship. The controlling object will obtain a reference to the association object and then use the reference to call methods on the object. The relationship between a car and a driver is representative of this relationship. The car will have a driver who will be associated with the car for a period of time.

Another example is a business object that performs an end-of-day processing routine by reading the contents of a message queue. The object that provides access to the message queue would have an association with the business object, since the relationship would persist for some time until the message queue was exhausted, at which time it could be discarded (see Figure 3–15).

Figure 3–15 *Object association.*

Aggregation and Composition

The *aggregation* and *composition* relationships involve a tighter binding between the related objects. The related objects have a long-term relationship and have some level of mutual dependency, which may be exclusive, that defines their existence.

With an aggregation relationship, the contained object is part of the greater whole. There is a mutual dependency between the two objects, but the contained object can participate in other aggregate relationships and may exist independently of the whole. For example, a `FileReader` object that has been created using a `File` object represents a mutual dependency where the two objects combine to create a useful mechanism for reading characters from a file. The UML symbols for expressing this relationship as shown in Figure 3–16 involve a line connecting the two classes with a diamond at the object that represents the greater whole.

With the composition relationship, the client object is *owned* by the greater whole. The contained object cannot participate in more than one compositional relationship. An example of this is a customer object and its related address object; the address object cannot exist without a customer object. This relationship is shown with a darkened diamond at the object, which represents the greater whole, as shown in Figure 3–17.

Figure 3–16 *Object aggregation.*

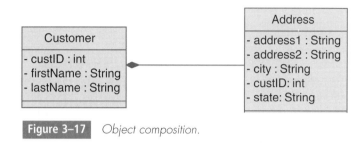

Figure 3–17 *Object composition.*

To summarize this nebulous and esoteric topic, a variety of associations may exist, the differences lying in the duration of the association. Table 3–2 summarizes the relationships discussed in the previous sections.

Table 3–2 *Object Relationships*

Association	Description
Dependency	Short term, transitive relationship. Associated object is quickly discarded by the object which initiated the relationship. Associated object can exist on its own.
Association	More long-term relationship than dependency. The controlling object will use the associated object to make method calls. Associated object can exist on its own.
Aggregation	Long-term relationship and mutual dependency. Part of a greater whole. May participate in multiple aggregate relationships.
Composition	Long-term relationship and mutual dependency. Part of a greater whole. Can participate in only one compositional relationship. May not be able to exist on its own.

Navigability of Object Relationships

Another topic related to the concept of object associations is the navigability of objects relationships—that is, the direction in which object relationships operate. In many cases, the contained object can be used by the container object but not vice versa. For instance, in the composition relationship described earlier between a customer and an address object, the customer object would use the address object to reference the address information, but the address object would have no reason to reference the customer object. This one-way navigability is represented in UML with an arrow towards the direction of the navigability, as shown in Figure 3–18.

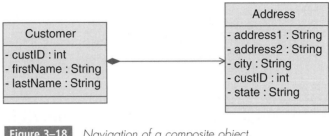

Figure 3–18   *Navigation of a composite object.*

Interestingly enough, the UML standard is not specific about the meaning of a line with no arrows. A line with no arrow, as shown in Figure 3-15 could indicate bidirectional navigability or possibly even unknown or undecided navigability. The project team should decide on the meaning of this symbol at the start of the project and then maintain consistency throughout the effort.

Multiplicity of Object Relationships

An object association may involve only one of each object, the controlling object and the associated object, or it may involve multiple instances of either. Multiplicity is used to indicate the number of objects that may exist in a relationship. An object may contain one and only one instance of another object, or it may contain several instances of another object.

Following the example of the customer and address object relationship shown earlier, a customer object could have more than one related address object to manage the inclusion of a home address and a business address for the customer. The diagram should indicate the number of instances of an associated object that may exist. This is represented by a set of numbers near the referenced object, which indicates its multiplicity, as shown in Figure 3–19.

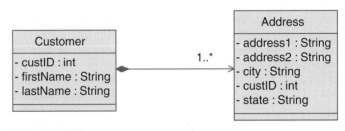

Figure 3–19   *A composite object with multiplicity.*

NOTE There is no default multiplicity defined in UML; an absence of multiplicity notation indicates that multiplicity is undetermined.

Object Association Versus Object Inheritance

You should use object association to extend the capabilities of a class whenever possible. There are alternatives, some that are worth consideration and others that represent poor programming. One alternative is to simply let the object design grow more complex. This has the downside of reducing the manageability, flexibility, and extensibility of the code contrary to the key goals for our J2EE development effort.

Another alternative, and one worth consideration, is the use of the class inheritance. Class inheritance allows one class to be extended with the capabilities of another and is a perfectly acceptable OO design. But there are two issues with this approach.

One issue is that class inheritance adds overhead to the object creation process. For each class in the inheritance hierarchy, the JVM must find the appropriate members and call the appropriate constructor. Relative to a more simple class design, this adds overhead.

The other issue is that Java limits us to a single inheritance model, and thus for complex classes that may be required to exhibit several different behaviors of distinct classes, inheritance is not a good alternative. For instance, if we are modeling a business customer as an object and the customer may also be a preferred retail customer who is also a B2B customer, using inheritance to model this object requires at least three levels of inheritance hierarchy (since Java does not support multiple inheritance). But modeling this object using object association would simply involve adding the distinct business objects (the preferred retail customer object, the B2B customer object) to be members of the business customer object.

There are cases where class inheritance is appropriate. When an important business domain object must be created and it clearly fits the inheritance model (for instance, the classic manager extends employee hierarchy, or a preferred customer extends customer), then inheritance is a good choice. But for a large number of cases, object association is the preferable technique.

Cohesion and Coupling

A mentioned in Chapter 2, it is important to group objects in such a way that members of the group are logically related. If the relationships between members of the group are sound, then we have strong *cohesion* in the group. But if the relationships are weak or artificial, we have weak cohesion.

The concept of cohesion is applied to different levels of the analytical process. It is applied to an object design (a class) and its members, it is applied to objects in a group (a package), and for large systems it can be applied to packages in a module.

The term *coupling* applies to the level of dependence between different groups. If there is a high degree of interdependence between groups, the groups are described as having tight coupling. As with cohesion, coupling can be applied to a number of different levels, to members of a class, to objects in a package, and to components in a module.

Shopping Cart Example

Consider the following example for an e-commerce site shopping cart. Though this is a well-worn example, it is illustrative of some of the design issues that must be tackled in creating a J2EE application. The first UML diagram, shown in Figure 3–20, shows the a subset of the various classes that will be used to create the application.

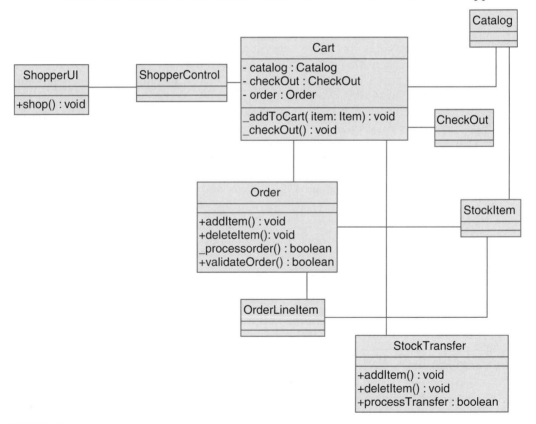

Figure 3–20   *Shopping cart class diagram.*

The shopping cart class (Cart) uses a catalog that lists the available stock items for purchase and uses an order object to process the order. For purposes of this example, the specific types of relationship (association, dependency, aggregation, composition) are not identified; they will be clarified in a later design step.

The question that arises is, how do we group these objects into packages? If we create a `Cart` package, which makes sense given the cohesion of the objects in that group, we must still manage the relationships with the stock classes, which we will group into the `Stock` package. The relationships between the `Catalog` and `StockItem` and `Cart` and `Order` represent coupling between the packages. While this may not seem like much to be concerned about, order processing and selection of stock items for sale often involve the application of a great deal of business logic; this is business logic that, if placed in our `ShoppingCart` package, would represent a high degree of coupling between the `ShoppingCart` package and the `Stock` package. We therefore decide to group classes based on their usage, which is ultimately reflected in cohesion between the members of the package, as shown in Figure 3–21.

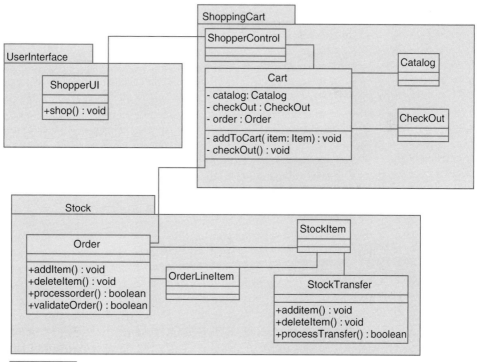

Figure 3–21   *Shopping cart classes with package groupings.*

Since the business logic cannot be eliminated, and some degree of coupling between the two packages is required, the solution is to create a subsystem to manage the processing. This subsystem would reside in the `Stock` package and would encapsulate the business logic of the access to its package members. This is shown in Figure 3–22with the inclusion of the `StockAccess` class. This object manages access to all stock objects and applies any business logic that is necessary. It exposes a small, concise interface to the other packages that contain members that must access `Stock` objects. This approach reduces the exposure, the *friction*, between this package and the other packages, and should there be a change to the `Stock` package, it is much less likely to affect the other packages.

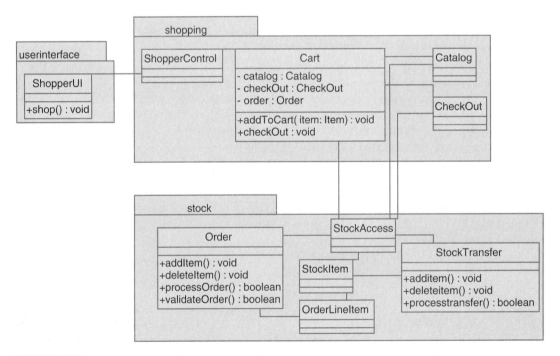

Figure 3–22   *Shopping cart class diagram with subsystem.*

OBJECT TYPES

As part of the analytical process, we must discern the types of objects or components that will be used in the application. There are a number of common object types that have been identified based on their usage, and as it happens, these object types relate directly to J2EE components. These object types are as follows.

- entity
- boundary
- control
- lifecycle

Not all object definitions will fit clearly into one of these categories. In fact, it makes very good sense to create helper objects or convenience objects to facilitate development. But the top-level domain objects, which we referred to earlier, should each fall into one of these categories. The following sections explain these object types in more detail.

Entity Objects

An entity object is an object that encapsulates business knowledge within the system. These objects are responsible for ensuring that the business logic of the organization is applied correctly in the system. Entity objects really represent a category of objects that perform a range of functions, including applying business logic and managing data retrieval operations. Java design patterns provide additional guidance on how to design these components.

The entity object within a J2EE system is generally represented by an EJB running within the application server. In some cases, a JavaBean component may be used to encapsulate this functionality.

Boundary Objects

A boundary object represents an interface of some type, either a system interface or a user interface. This is a component that is responsible for interacting with the user and relaying user input back to the entity objects (the business tier components) through control objects.

In J2EE architectures, these objects are represented by presentation tier components, servlets, or JSP pages. They could also be represented by client tier components such as applets or Java WebStart components.

Control Objects

Control objects are responsible for workflow, managing the progression of work and application navigation through the system. These objects marshal the resources of the entity and boundary objects of the system. They do not execute business logic per se, as that is the responsibility of the entity objects.

In J2EE architecture, these objects are most commonly represented using EJBs, specifically the EJB session bean. But workflow may also be managed to some extent on the presentation tier using servlets, where these Web tier control objects would interact with JavaBeans and Java helper classes to execute workflow logic.

Lifecycle Objects

Lifecycle objects encapsulate the logic of finding, instantiating, and later destroying the object resources used by the control objects. These objects effectively isolate this logic and enhance maintainability by locating this activity in a small set of objects. Lifecycle objects can also be used to ensure that proper housekeeping is being done and that resources are being freed when they are no longer needed. In J2EE, these objects are most likely to be Java helper objects used by the control objects to marshal the resources needed to perform their work.

The sequence diagram in Figure 3–23 provides an example of these objects to a portion of a system. The shoppingUI object represents a boundary object. This object interacts with the user and initiates the shopping process. The shoppingUI calls the shoppingAccess object to create the various objects needed to begin the shopping process. Once the initiateShopping call to the shoppingAccess object has completed, the shoppingUI will then interact with the shoppingControl object; the shoppingAccess object, as a lifecycle object, is responsible for simply finding, creating, and deleting objects.

The shoppingAccess object will return a reference to the shoppingControl object, a control object. This object controls the access to the various objects needed to use the shopping cart. In this example, most of that work is performed through the Cart object, an entity object that provides access to the shopping cart. The Cart object in turn manages access internally to the Order, Catalog and CheckOut objects.

Java design patterns expand on many of these concepts and provide additional guidance on how to design objects for Java applications. These design patterns have been applied directly to the J2EE architecture and are presented in detail in Chapter 32. At this point it is suffice to say that the principals we have outlined here are not invalidated by Java design patterns, but are instead supported and expanded.

SUMMARY

Creating a solid architecture that is appropriate for the application is a vital step in the development of a J2EE system. In this chapter we covered the process of performing J2EE architectural analysis and design, and examined the various work artifacts created during this process. Since J2EE applications involve the construction and communication of distributed objects, object-oriented analysis can be applied directly to the architectural process, which we covered extensively in this

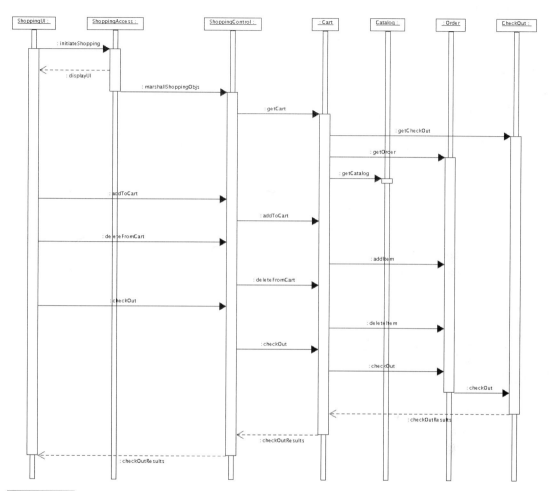

Figure 3–23   *Shopping cart sequence diagram.*

chapter. The types of objects to create and optimal object associations were also covered.

As we saw in this chapter, UML is an excellent communication tool for object designs. UML documents should be used at each step in the design process to document the current state of the architecture and to communicate the design clearly to other members of the development team, both technical and non-technical members of the team.

In the next chapter, we will use two case studies to demonstrate this architectural design process. Later in the text, applications will be developed which implement portions of this design.

CHAPTER 4

J2EE Case Studies

INTRODUCTION

Now that we've covered the architecture of J2EE and have some understanding of the technology behind it, we can begin to examine how to implement a system using this technology. The case study is a time-tested method of teaching through examples, so that approach will be used in this chapter. The following sections detail examples of systems that will be used later in the book to provide a more detailed examination of J2EE technology.

The previous chapters outlined a number of architectural analysis and design principles. These principles will be applied in this case study discussion up to a point. Since we have not discussed or shown the J2EE technology in detail, we will not complete the steps of the analysis and design process that involve the selection of J2EE technology.

THE DISCUSSION GROUP SYSTEM

The first case study examines the creation of a discussion group system that provides access to message lists. Assume that a client wants to create an online discussion group that can manage threaded message discussions in which one user enters a message on a topic and other users can respond to the message. The initial message and all responses to the message can be viewed as a *message thread*. This type of application is often referred to as a *threaded message list* or knowledge base in which knowledge provided by multiple users is exchanged.

Initially, the client would like the system to be used as a problem-tracking system for the IT department, to track problems and resolutions to problems for its internal systems. A problem could be posted, and various resolutions to the problem would be posted to the initial message as part of the message thread. The client would like to track information about the postings, such as who posted the message or response and the date it was posted. Though the system will initially be used as a problem tracking system, the client would like the system to be flexible enough to be used as a general-purpose discussion group system for a variety of topics.

The client wants users to be able to review messages anonymously, without having to log into the system. But it should require that users log into the system in order to post a message. User should be able to modify or delete only their own messages. The client would also like the ability to moderate the discussions, potentially deleting messages that are considered inappropriate.

The client expects this system to be a Web-based system but does not expect it to be run over the Internet. Therefore, there are no requirements for the use of more stringent security measures, such as Secure Sockets Layer (SSL) encryption. The expectation is that the system will be run on an internal network with a moderate number of users. The system does not need to be available 24/7, but preferably would not go down for days at a time.

While the client is aware that an email-based system can provide similar functionality, it prefers that this system be stored in a relational database allowing messages to be referenced and searched more easily and, through the database, would provide a direct backup and restore facility for the corresponding message data. Since the client is not certain which database vendor it will use to store this information, it would like this system to be able to store messages in any database, so the application must be vendor-neutral.

Architectural Analysis and System Design

In Chapter 2 we outlined a number of steps for creating an architecture for a J2EE application. The steps we identified are as follows:

1. Perform initial requirements gathering.
2. Create abstract definition of system.
3. Identify nonfunctional requirements.
4. Identify high-level components.
5. Refactor component design and group components by tier.
6. Identify software technology required.
7. Identify hardware required.
8. Create deployment diagrams, component diagrams, and other documentation to describe the system architecture.

As mentioned, we will not cover all of these steps in this chapter. In this chapter, we will cover steps 1 through 3.

Perform Initial Requirements Gathering

Using the information provided above in the description of the message system, we can develop some initial use cases to help us understand the system better. The use cases in Figure 4–1 show a message system user (actor) and associated use cases. Use cases are identified for posting a new message thread, posting to an existing message thread, updating an existing message, and deleting an existing message. Though not mentioned in the initial description, we have also added use cases for a menu to allow the user to navigate the system and a login process, since users will need to be registered and logged into the system to add new messages or to update their existing messages. We also have use cases to enter the user registration information and to update existing registration information.

These use cases can be simplified through generalization. Assume that additional analysis with the end user has revealed that the operation of posting a new message to start a message thread or posting a message to an existing message thread will use the same page. This information allows us to generalize the process of posting a new message.

Additional analysis has determined that the same page can be used for registration information, just making a minor adjustment for entering new information or updating existing information. The users have indicated that the system user should not be able to delete his or her registration information; that will be an administrative function to be added later.

We have also determined that the process of updating or deleting a message involves the use of the same pages and the same validations (the user owns the message); the only difference is the database update that is performed.

Though not identified in the initial requirements, analysis has also determined that there is a need for an administrative user to perform the moderator function. This user will be allowed to review and update all messages, including messages entered by other users, and to delete any message on the system. This

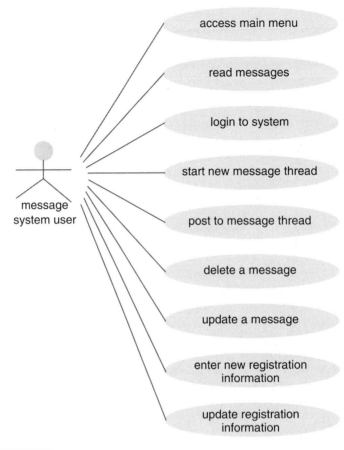

Figure 4–1   *Message system use cases.*

additional analysis has led to the creation of a more generalized use case model, as shown in Figure 4–2.

This use case model demonstrates that generalization applied to use cases and actors. The actor has been generalized to include the system administrator. While the use case model does not have syntax to show the details of the use case, certain use cases could only be performed either by the user who entered the message or by the administrative user. (The text documentation or UML [Unified Modeling Language] action diagrams for the use case would provide this information.) The use case model also generalizes use cases for posting a new message, updating (a database update or delete) an existing message, and entering registration information.

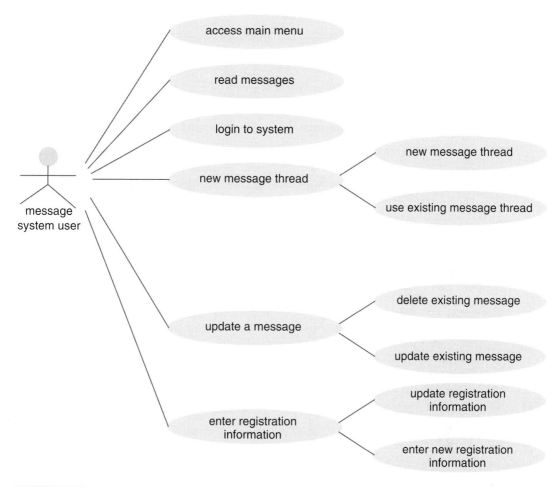

Figure 4–2   *Generalized use case model for message system.*

Create High-Level Definition of System

Based on the information gathered in the first step, we can define this system in terms of its functional requirements as follows.

> To provide a general-purpose discussion group system allowing entry of message threads. Messages will be stored in a relational database and accessible using a Web browser interface. The system will support a message moderator role and will enforce security with which a person will be able to update only his or her own messages. The system need not be available 24X7.

Identify Nonfunctional Requirements

The nonfunctional requirements for this system are addressed indirectly in the description. The application does not need high availability and is not expected to have a high user load. We can assume that all other project goals, such as clarity, extensibility, and maintainability, are relevant here.

Identify High-Level Components

The class diagram for the message system identifies the top-level components (objects) for the system (see Figure 4–3). In this diagram, we have identified a user object to represent the system user and a message object to represent the message.

In order to make the system flexible, we have created a somewhat complex database structure. It is therefore useful to encapsulate the complexity of the database update operation into an object; we have done that with the `MessageUpdate` class. A `DatabaseAccess` class is used to encapsulate the specifics of database access, making it easier to code database access that is vendor-neutral (which is one of our functional requirements).

The sequence diagram in Figure 4–3 demonstrates how we expect these objects will interact. The `LoginControl` object manages the login process, and the `MessageControl` object manages the workflow through the message system. The `MessageUpdate` object interacts with the `DatabaseAccess` object to perform the database update.

In terms of object types, we can see that the `LoginControl` and the `MessageControl` objects are *control* objects (and are aptly named). The `MessageUI` is a *boundary* object, which interfaces with the end user. The `Message`, `User`, and `Registration` objects represent *entity* objects.

THE MOVIE SHOPPING SYSTEM

Our second case study is for a retail store that sells videos. The store has a number of retail stores that sell movie videos and DVDs to consumers at a deep discount. They would like to begin selling their movies on the Web.

Use cases for the message group system indicate that the users of the system would like to be able to browse a catalog of movies available over the Web. Use cases alsoinclude listing the customer's shopping cart.

The movie store e-commerce system would allow a default customer to enter the Web site and browse its contents. This default customer could even use the shopping cart. But the actual purchase of movies would require the customer to register on the site. Registered users would have a different view of the site,

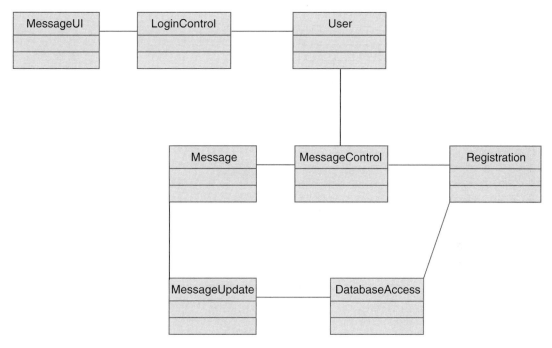

Figure 4–3 *Message system class diagram.*

including informational messages customized to their interests. (No pop-up browser windows would be used, since the client considers this type of Internet advertising annoying and the scourge of e-commerce.)

Though the bulk of Movies R Us is a business-to-consumer (B2C) site, it does sell some stock to other retailers, providing a business-to-business (B2B) service. Movies R Us would like to expose a stock information and availability request service via the Internet that would allow other interested businesses to perform a search for a specific movie title, and if the title is found, return information on the title, including the price and availability.

Movies R Us has a pretty loyal following and consider it likely that with its deep discounts on videos and unique titles, the company will be able to attract attention on the Internet. It therefore considers it essential that the site be able to scale up to a large number of page hits per day. It would also like the flexibility to use different client front ends for the services offered by the Movies R Us site.

Architectural Analysis and System Design

The steps we have identified for the architectural process are as follows:

1. Perform initial requirements gathering.
2. Create abstract definition of system.
3. Identify nonfunctional requirements.
4. Identify high-level components
5. Refactor component design and group components by tier and show subsystems.
6. Evaluate and identify technologies and hardware. Associate technologies with components.
7. Create deployment diagrams, component diagrams, and other documentation to describe the system architecture

We cover the first four steps in the following sections.

Perform Initial Requirements Gathering

The use case analysis for this system yielded the set of use cases shown in Figure 4–4. These use cases include a generalization for the shopping cart use case and an external system actor that accesses the stock information use case. (According to our information, the user-actor, the consumer, will not access those services; they are for other businesses—B2B.)

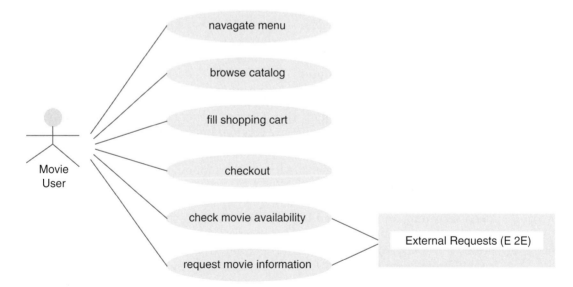

Figure 4–4   *Movies shopping system use cases.*

Even with our limited knowledge of the checkout operation, it would be safe to assume that this is potentially a complex operation involving several steps. It is therefore reasonable to expect that further refactoring of the checkout use case will lead to splitting this use case into multiple use cases.

The sequence diagram for this case (see Figure 4–5) reveals additional details that will map neatly into object definitions for this case study. The user interface is abstracted into a single object in this example. We know that the user interface will undoubtedly require a number of pages.

The `MoviesUI` object interfaces with the login object to perform the login operation. The login object in turn uses the `UserAuthenticate` object to validate the user.

Once the user has been validated, the sequence diagram demonstrates the process flow for a browse-catalog operation. This highlights how the `MoviesControl` object creates several objects to use and then controls the access to these objects. The `MoviesUI` (which we can assume is a presentation tier component) does not need to know the details of the operation. It only needs to request a catalog page from the `MoviesControl` object.

The `MoviesControl` object creates and manipulates several entity objects for the `Catalog`, `Movies`, and `Cart` objects. The `MoviesUI` also does not need to know the details of adding an item to the `ShoppingCart`. Those details are managed with a call to the `MoviesControl` object, requesting that it add an item to the shopping cart.

Create High-Level Definition of System

Based on the description of the system and our use case analysis, we can create the following high-level definition of the system.

> The movies e-commerce system will provide the ability for a user to browse available movies and add them to a shopping cart. The user will need to register on the site and log in to make a purchase. The system will provide B2B functionality through public services that allow the queries on movies that are available and information about the movies.

Identify Nonfunctional Requirements

Based on the description of the system and the nonfunctional requirements, the system must be able to support high availability and be able to scale up to a heavy user load. The exact user load is not known at this point, but the system architecture must support that ability for the system to scale. The system will initially be developed to support a Web client front end, but the architecture must also be able to support other front-end systems that may be added in the future.

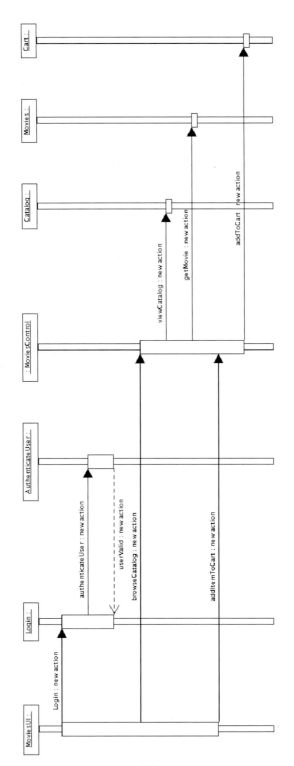

Figure 4–5 Movies shopping system sequence diagram.

82

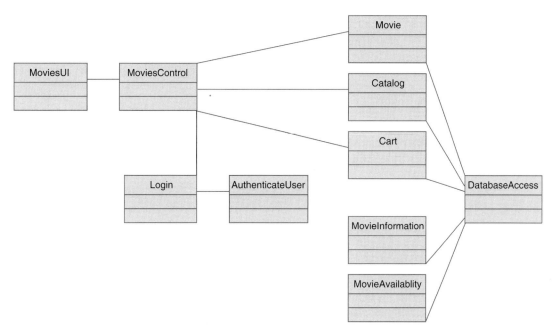

Figure 4–6   *High-level class design for the movies system.*

Identify High-Level Components

The class diagram for the movies system is shown in Figure 4–6. This contains the classes we identified in our sequence diagram plus the stock information classes (`MovieInformation` and `MovieAvailability`) for B2B e-commerce, as identified in the use case diagram. The user interface is abstracted into a single class in this design (`MoviesUI`). in the final design this will be expanded into a number of components to reflect the user interface details discovered during use case analysis. A class has also been designed (`DatabaseAccess`) to manage the specifics of database access and further abstract those operations.

In terms of object types, we can see that our analysis identified *boundary* objects in the `MoviesUI` class, *control* objects with the `MoviesControl` class, and *entity* objects with the `Movie`, `Catalog`, and `Cart` objects. Later design iterations could include *life cycle* objects to be used by the control and boundary objects to perform lookups and instantiation of other objects required.

SUMMARY

This chapter provided an introduction to the case studies that will be used throughout this book. These case studies provide examples of problems that real-world applications must tackle. After covering the various constituent technologies of J2EE (and there are more than a few), we will revisit these case studies and use them to create two examples of J2EE applications.

CHAPTER 5

The JDBC API: JDBC Basics

INTRODUCTION

As we mentioned in the introduction, J2EE provides a number of different APIs that can be used across multiple operational tiers. To provide a consistent and clear coverage of these APIs, we will start at the integration tier (which accesses data from the resource tier) and discuss the APIs that apply to that tier. This means that the JDBC API or package will be where we start our discussion. That will be the focus of the first few chapters of this section of the book.

To write a database application, certain events need to take place: You must load a database driver, you must create a connection to the database, you must execute a query, and if the query has results, you must receive the results and process them. It is precisely this sequence of events that has driven the design of the Java Database Connectivity (JDBC) package.

Relational databases are the predominant database in use today. JDBC was designed to work with relational databases, but technically it is not limited to working with relational data. This chapter covers the JDBC package, including the details of the API, how to load a JDBC driver, and how to use JDBC in J2EE applications.

Later chapters will provide more detail on the various features provided by the API, such as the ability to gather information about the data being retrieved (the metadata) and how to use scrollable cursors.

CONNECTING TO THE RELATIONAL DATABASE

Modern relational databases are complex applications that support access by multiple users. These users are considered connections by the database application. When an application connects to a relational database, it must create some internal representation to manage the database connection. This is usually referred to as a *connection handle* or just a connection for short.

Once the connection is established, the application must be able to use the connection by moving data back and forth across the connection, executing transactions and performing other relevant operations. This requires what is known as a *database driver*.

JDBC is not specific to any one database vendor, instead it is vendor-neutral. This means that in order to use JDBC, the JDBC implementation code must search through multiple drivers before an appropriate database driver is found and loaded by the application. Once the driver has been loaded, the application can use the connection. When the application is finished with the connection, it should close the connection to release the resources it was using in the database.

There are two distinct methods for loading and using JDBC drivers: using the Java class loader to load the driver class directly with the `DriverManager` or using a `DataSource` to load the JDBC driver using a naming service. The `DataSource` method is by far the most common approach and the easiest to use, but we will demonstrate both approaches in this chapter.

THE JDBC PACKAGE

The purpose of the JDBC package is to provide vendor-neutral access to relational databases. The implementation differences of the various databases used are *abstracted* from the user through the use of the JDBC API. Though the specification does not indicate that the API is to be used solely for relational databases (in fact, it can be used to access any tabular data, including a spreadsheet or flat file), historically it has been used primarily for relational database access.

The developers of the JDBC API specification have tried to keep the API as simple as possible so that it can be a foundation upon which other APIs are built. For instance, the `Connector` API can be implemented on top of an existing JDBC API using appropriate resource adapters.

JDBC is composed of a number of interfaces. These interfaces are implemented by driver developers. The API is implemented by either a vendor or a third party to create a JDBC *driver*. There are four different types of JDBC drivers that have been implemented, as indicated in Table 5–1.

Table 5–1 *JDBC Driver Types*

Driver	Description
Type 1	Implements JDBC by mapping JDBC calls to other Call-Level Interface (CLI) calls. Communicates with a binary library written in another language, using some form of inter-process communication to use the library. Requires software on the client machine. For example, the JDBC-ODBC bridge driver.
Type 2	Driver is partially composed of Java code and partially native code using another CLI. Requires some client-side binary code. Native code runs in the Java Virtual Machine (JVM).
Type 3	Pure Java driver; uses middleware to convert JDBC calls to vendor-specific calls and protocol required to access the database.
Type 4	Pure Java driver that implements the native protocol. Does not require middleware or any client-side binary. Can be downloaded to a client if necessary.

The Type 4 JDBC driver is considered the best driver to use for two reasons. One reason is that since the driver has been written completely in Java, it is extremely portable. Another reason is that the driver is not required to map JDBC calls to corresponding native CLI calls. This avoids the overhead of mapping logic required by the Type 1 or Type 2 driver, or the overhead of communicating with middleware required by the Type 3 driver. Such improvements in efficiency should allow the driver to execute faster than the other types of JDBC drivers.

Package Organization

The JDBC package is divided into two packages: `java.sql` and `javax.sql`. The `java.sql` is the core package initially created circa 1997 for the JDBC 1.0 release. The JDBC 2.0 release included a set of extensions to the JDBC package that were separated into the `javax.sql` package. With JDBC 3.0, the standard extensions were added to the main package distribution (though they kept the same package name) to comprise the complete JDBC package. The contents of standard package (`java.sql`) are summarized in Table 5–2.

These interfaces defined in these packages are implemented by database vendors and independent software vendors to create the JDBC database driver.

Table 5–2 *The java.sql Package Classes/Interfaces*

Class/Interface	Description
java.sql.Array	Represents the Array data type.
java.sql.BatchUpdateException	Java exception for batch updates.
java.sql.Blob	Represents the BLOB data types. .
java.sql.CallableStatement	Used to create and execute stored procedures.
Clob	Respresents the CLOB data type.
Connection	Used to create a connection to the database.
DataTruncation	An exception thrown for data truncation errors.
DatabaseMetaData	Used to gather information about the underlying data source.
Date	Represents the Date data type.
Driver	The database driver for a specific database.
DriverManager	Automatically loads the drivers used by a JDBC instance. Provides access to the drivers loaded using a number of static methods.
DriverPropertyInfo	Provides information on the properties of a driver.
ParameterMetaData	Provides information on parameters as part of the JDBC 3.0 specification.
PreparedStatement	Used to create and execute prepared statements, statements that have been registered and stored within the database before the statement is executed.
Ref	Represents the Ref (reference) type. .
ResultSet	Used to iterate through a set of tuples retrieved from the database.
ResultSetMetaData	Used to gather information about a ResultSet.
Savepoint	Used to create a transactional savepoint as part of the JDBC 3.0 specification.
SQLData	Used for the custom mapping of SQL types. Not expected to be called by the programmer;. intended for use internally by vendor tools.
SQLException	Standard Java exception for JDBC.
SQLInput	An SQL input stream.
SQLOutput	An SQL output stream.
SQLPermission	A reference to an SQL structured type.
SQLWarning	Contains information about the SQL warning generated by the last statement executed.
Statement	Used to create and execute an SQL statement.
Struct	Used to represent the Struct data type.
Time	Used to represent the Time data type.
Timestamp	Used to represent the TimeStamp data type.
Types	Defines constants used to define generic SQL types.

The most common implementations of these interfaces are used for creating a connection to the database and retrieving data.

```
DriverManager
Connection
Statement
PreparedStatement
ResultSet
```

The following sections provide a brief introduction into how these classes are used in a JDBC application.

The DriverManager Class

The `DriverManager` class is responsible for managing access to the drivers that have been loaded by the JDBC application and returning connections to the underlying database. Since more than one driver can be loaded at any particular time, the `DriverManager` must select among the drivers to determine which driver will be used. It makes this determination based on a call to its `getConnection` method. The `getConnection` method is passed a string, which provides the URL of the database to be used for the connection. Based on the contents of this database URL, the `DriverManager` selects a driver to manage the connection and then returns a `Connection` object to be used by the application (see Figure 5–1).

(As we will see later in this chapter, the `DriverManager` class is not used directly when using a `DataSource` to connect to the database. Instead, the `DataSource` configuration properties contain the information on how the database connection is made and the connection is made through the `getConnection` method of that class.)

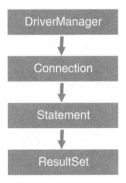

Figure 5–1   *The JDBC DriverManager.*

The Connection Class

The Connection class represents the connection to the database and is returned by the DriverManager as a return value from the getConnection method. The database connection returned is the database specified in the URL passed to the getConnection method. The DataSource class also returns a Connection object to the database specified in the configuration for the DataSource.

The Connection class also provides a number of methods to determine the properties and state of the connection to the database. Transactions are managed through this class, which contains a method for committing data to the database and for altering the autocommit behavior of the connection. (By default, JDBC drivers will commit the results of each single SQL statement to the database, which means that you must make an explicit call on the Connection object to begin using transactions which span multiple SQL statements.)

Since there is significant overhead to creating connections to a database (this is due to resources that must be allocated in the database server and is not an issue with the JDBC driver or the Java language), it is useful to create a pool of connections with physical database connections on application startup and then use connections from this pool. The javax.sql.PooledConnection class is an optional though widely implemented interface that provides this capability. Pooled connections are virtually transparent to the developer; they require no special coding on the part of the developer. Connection pools are commonly implemented through extensions of the DataSource interface discussed later in this chapter.

The Statement Class

The Statement class is used to execute SQL statements against a database. The statements can be SQL Data Manipulation Language (DML) statements such as the select statement or some type of update statement such as the insert, update, delete statement. A Data Definition Language (DDL) statement (create table, create index). The result of the execution of a select statement is stored in a ResultSet object. The result of the execution of an update statement returns an integer value indicating the number of rows updated by the statement.

The PreparedStatement Class

The PreparedStatement class is similar to the statement class in that it allows a SQL statement to be executed against the database. But unlike the Statement class, the PreparedStatement class presents the query to the database before it is executed. The database then processes the query (which includes parsing the statement and determining the most efficient method of executing the statement) and stores a reference to the processed or *prepared* statement. When a call against the PreparedStatement object is made to execute the statement, the prepared statement in the database is used to perform the operation. For statements that must be executed multiple times, using the `PreparedStatement` can potentially provide improved performance.

The ResultSet Class

The `ResultSet` class is used to iterate through a set of rows (or tuples) returned from the execution of a SQL `select` statement. This class provides methods to iterate serially through the set, or if the JDBC driver and database support it, to iterate backwards and forwards through the `ResultSet`. In order to use a scroll cursor capability, the underlying data base must support this capability. A method is available to determine the type of the `ResultSet` object, which indicates whether or not the cursor is scrollable.

THE JAVAX.SQL PACKAGE

The `javax.sql` package was originally introduced as part of the JDBC 2.0 Standard Extensions, an optional package that was not part of the JDBC core package. In JDBC 3.0, it is considered part of the core JDBC API, though drivers are not required to support all of the features to be compliant. The `java.sql` package includes the methods listed in Table 5–3.

The `javax.sql` package does not replace the JDBC API but instead supplements the API. For the `javax.sql` package to be used, an existing JDBC implementation must be in place.

The DataSource Class

The `DataSource` class, the implementation of `javax.sql.DataSource`, provides an abstraction for a connection to a database. The `DataSource` encapsulates the details of the database connection, thus removing from the application the responsibility of managing these details.

The `DataSource` object is usually retrieved using the Java Naming and Directory Interface (JNDI). This allows the configuration and location of the database to be controlled at a central location and referenced by a name. Any application which requests the `DataSource` using its designated name can access the database resource provided by the `DataSource` (see Figure 5–2).

The `DataSource` interface has also been extended to provide additional features. For instance, connection pooling and distributed transaction support are both implemented through vendor extensions to the `DataSource` interface.

Table 5–3   *The javax.sql Classes/Interfaces*

Class/Interface	Description
javax.sql.ConnectionEvent	Used to create event listeners for database connections.
javax.sql.ConnectionEventListener	Used to create event listeners for database connections.
javax.sql.ConnectionPoolDataSource	Used to create a connection to a data source which supports connection pooling.
DataSource	A data source which represents and underlying data store and manages connections to the data store.
PooledConnection	A connection that interfaces with an underlying pool of database connections.
RowSet	Extends the ResultSet class and adds support for JavaBeans; a RowSet can be used as a JavaBean.
RowSetEvent	Used to manage events on a RowSet.
RowSetInternal	Manages RowSetObjects.
RowSetListener	Provides an event listener for a RowSet.
RowSetMetaData	Used to gather information on a RowSet.
RowSetReader	Provides a reader for RowSet.
RowSetWriter	Provides a writer for a RowSet.
XAConnection	A connection that supports distributed transactions.
XADataSource	A connection to an XADataSource used to provide distributed transactions.

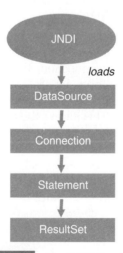

Figure 5–2   *The JDBC DataSource.*

Connection Pooling

Connection pooling provides for the efficient management of connections to the database being supported. The process of connecting to a database is time consuming and needs to be avoided for any application that must create and then drop a large number of connections.

Connection pooling is implemented through a `DataSource` object, so a client application would need to obtain an appropriate data source object to use connection pooling.

Use of connection pooling is transparent to the application code; the object pooling and management required to implement this feature are managed in the JDBC driver. An application coded for a non-pooled connection should not require code changes to begin using a pooled connection.

Distributed Transactions

Distributed transaction support allows database transactions to span multiple databases from different vendors on multiple servers. This requires the support of a *transaction manager*, which communicates with the various participants in the transaction. An implementation of the `XADataSource` interface provides this functionality (see Figure 5–3).

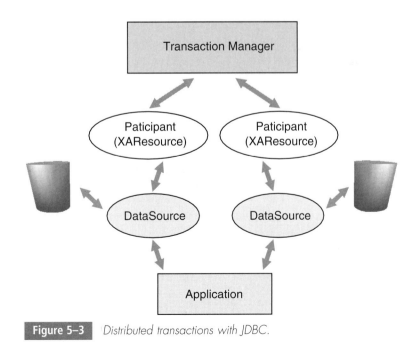

Figure 5–3   *Distributed transactions with JDBC.*

JavaBean Wrapper Support (Rowsets)

The RowSet class effectively wraps the ResultSet class with JavaBean event functionality. This class makes it easier for the developers of visual programming environments to create JDBC objects for integration into those environments.

USING JDBC

The best place to start in understanding an API is with a minimal implementation example. The following code demonstrates just such an implementation using only four JDBC classes as listed in Table 5–4.

Table 5–4   *Core JDBC Classes*

Interface/Class	Purpose
DriverManager	Loads the JDBC driver and manages the database connection. Controls access to the database driver.
Connection	Connects to the database and allows the creation of Statement objects.
Statement	Allows the execution of SQL statements and returns results, either integer values for the number of rows updated or ResultSet objects representing the rows returned by the execution of a SQL select statement.
ResultSet	Allows access to individual rows in the set of rows returned by a SQL select statement query.

The basic process for a simple data retrieval operation with JDBC is as follows.

- A JDBC driver is loaded;
- A database Connection object is created using the DriverManager (using the database driver loaded in the first step);
- A Statement object is created using the Connection object;
- A SQL statement is executed using the Statement object, and a ResultSet is returned.
- The ResultSet is used to step through (or iterate through) the rows returned and examine the data.

The following code sample demonstrates this sequence of calls.

JDBCExample1.java

```
1.import java.sql .*;
2.
3.public class JDBCExample1 {
4.
5.public static void main( String args[] ) {
6.
7.String connectionURL =
8. "jdbc:postgresql://localhost:5432/movies;user=puser;password=puser";
9.
10.try {
11.
12.      // load the Driver class
13.      Class.forName("org.postgresql.Driver");
14.
15.      // create the connection using the static getConnection method
16.      Connection con = DriverManager.getConnection( connectionURL );
17.
18.      // create a Statement class to execute the SQL statement
19.      Statement stmt = con.createStatement();
20.
21.      // execute the SQL statement and get the results in a ResultSet
22.      ResultSet rs   =
23.      stmt.executeQuery(
24.              "select movie_name, release_date from movies" );
25.
26.      // iterate through the ResultSet, displaying two values
27.      // for each row using the getString method
28.      //
29.      while ( rs.next() )
30.              System.out.println( "*****************" + "\n" +
31.                              "movie_name: " + "\t" +
32.                                      rs.getString("movie_name") + "\n" +
33.                              "release_date: " + "\t" +
34.                                      rs.getString("release_date")  );
35.
36.}
37.catch (SQLException e) {
38.      e.printStackTrace();
39.}
40.catch (Exception e) {
41.      e.printStackTrace();
42.}
43.finally {
44.      // should always close the connection when done
45.      //
46.      con.close();
47.}
48.
```

```
49.}
50.
51.}
```

This is a simple, straightforward sample of JDBC code. In an effort to be succinct and keep the sample easy, the JDBC calls to load the driver, create the connection, and create the statement are all located in one block of code (the Java `main` programming block, no less). In production code, this code, which is responsible for locating and loading the driver, should be placed elsewhere. It is generally considered good practice to encapsulate the process of locating and loading the database driver in a separate method or using various helper classes.

This code sample also shows the original (JDBC 1.0) method of loading the database driver: using the `class.forName` call to load the `Driver` class and then passing a connection URL to the static `DriverManager getConnection` method to obtain a connection to the database. The preferred method for connecting using JDBC is to use a `DataSource` object. This involves locating and retrieving a `DataSource` object and then using the object to create a connection to the database.

Though the `DataSource` method is the better approach to performing these tasks, the actual difference in the code for the two approaches is not significant. And demonstrating the older method in this example helps highlight the benefits of using a `DataSource` implementation as shown later in this chapter.

Since only the core JDBC classes are used in this example, an import statement on line 1 only imports `java.sql`. On lines 7 and 8, a string is created and initialized to store the connection URL for the database. The connection URL contains the details of the database connection in a format that tends to vary for each database vendor. To find the correct format for a connection URL, it is necessary to consult the vendor's documentation. The URL specified in this example is as follows.

```
jdbc:postgresql://localhost:5432/movies;user=puser;password=puser
```

The basic structure of the connection URL is that of the character constant `jdbc` followed by colon character (`:`) and a subprotocol, then followed by a colon character (`:`) and a subname, as follows.

```
jdbc:<subprotocol>:<subname>
```

The subprotocol identifies a database connectivity mechanism that the driver may support. In this example, the subprotocol of `postgresql` is specified, indicating the protocol of the underlying database will be used by the JDBC driver.

The URL then contains the subname for the connection. The subname is dependent on the subprotocol. If a network address is to be used as part of the subname, then the naming convention should follow that of standard URL server names, as follows.

```
//hostname:port/
```

Using this scheme, the URL for the PostgreSQL database would be as shown below (and in the code example).

```
//localhost:5432/movies;user=puser;password=puser
```

The server name and port is then followed by the name of the database to connect to and the user name and password for the connection. This information is optional, and the format is specific to the database vendor.

Following the example, on line 13 the database driver is loaded using the `Class.forName` call to dynamically load the class when the program is executed. In this example, the string "`org.postgresql.Driver`" is used to indicate the fully qualified class name of the `Driver` class. The content of this string is also vendor-specific.

Once the driver has been loaded, a connection is obtained using the static `getConnection` method of the `DriverManager`. As shown on line 16 in the code sample, the call to the `getConnection` method takes the connection URL string shown above. Using the information in the connection URL, the `DriverManager` determines which database driver to use (since multiple drivers may be loaded) and then makes the internal calls to connect to the database. It returns a `Connection` object representing a connection to the database as specified in the connection URL.

The `Connection` object is used to create `Statement` objects to use to execute SQL statements against the database. This is done on line 19 in the example shown above.

The `Statement` object uses different methods to execute a query, depending on whether the query is an `update` statement (`executeUpdate`) or a `select` statement (`executeQuery`). In this example, the `executeQuery` method is called on line 23. This method will execute a SQL `select` statement and return its results in a `ResultSet` object.

On line 29, a Java `while` loop is used to iterate through the results returned. The `ResultSet` class has a `next` method. The first call to this method will position the underlying cursor before the first row returned in the `ResultSet`. The `next` method returns a boolean value indicating whether or not there is a current row. (So a `select` query that returned no rows would return `false` on the first call to the `next` method.) As long as the `next` method returns `true`, then there is a row that can be examined and the `while` loop will continue.

The `ResultSet` class includes a set of `getXXXX` methods that can be used to examine the results in the current row. There is a `getXXXX` method for the various data types that can be returned from a database query. Most current relational database implementations are flexible about allowing nonstring data types to be converted to strings. In this example, both columns are retrieved using the `getString` method, but the `release_date` column retrieved on line 34 is not a string but is a SQL `Date` data type. The call to the `getString` method will do the conversion for us.

The majority of the JDBC methods which interact with the database throw an `SQLException`. This requires that they be called in a `try/catch` block, allowing the execption to be caught and managed in the local program block where it occurred. (Alternatively, it could be thrown to another level on the call stack, though that is not shown here.) On line 46 in the `try/catch`, the `Connection` is closed within the `finally` block of the `try/catch` block. Since Java guarantees that the `finally` block will always be executed (even in the event an exception has been thrown), we can be assured that the call to the `close` method will always occur.

USING THE CONNECTION CLASS

Before we can do anything significant with JDBC, we must get connected to the database. As we will find in this chapter, we will not connect directly to the database; we will connect with one or more layers of software, which will control our connection to the database.

As mentioned earlier, there are two distinct approaches for connecting to a database using JDBC: using a `DriverManager` directly or using a `DataSource` connection. This chapter presents both approaches.

Loading the Database Driver

There is unfortunately no standard protocol for direct communication with relational databases. Each relational database vendor has created a proprietary low-level protocol for communicating with its database engine.

In the intensely competitive world of database software, there is a continuous effort to make database operations fast, efficient, and accurate. Part of the effort to create fast and accurate communication has involved tweaking the communication protocol and the APIs that use that protocol. For this reason, database vendors regard their low-level communication protocols as trade secrets. This competition led to the creation of different database APIs for each vendor's product.

In order for the standardized API to work, a driver must be created to map the standard JDBC calls to the vendor's proprietary API. And since each database vendor has a different API, a different driver is needed for each vendor.

Prior to the JDBC 2.0 API, the only method available for loading a JDBC driver was to use a *driver manager* by calling static members of the `DriverManager` class. Using this approach, the JDBC driver would be loaded when the class was loaded, using the `Class.forName` call, as shown below.

```
...
Class.forName( "org.postgresql.driver");
...
```

This call leads to the class identified by the fully qualified class name provided as a parameter to the `forName` call to be loaded. When coded as shown, with a string constant for the class name, it tends to tie the source code to the particular driver and reduces the portability of the code. Following this call, a call must be made to connect to the database. That call must address the specifics of the connection, as shown in the following code snippet.

```
...
Connection con = DriverManager.getConnection(
   "jdbc:postgresql://localhost:5432/movies;user=puser;password=puser");
...
```

This connection URL reveals a number of details about the database connection (including in this example the user name and password for the connection). Placing this in the application further reduces the portability of the code.

One solution to this problem of binding the source code to the database vendor is to take the connection details out of the application and place them in a properties file. The application will then read the properties file at startup. A Java properties file can contain lines for the connection URL and the driver manager class, as follows.

Properties File with JDBC DB Connection Information

```
connectionURL: jdbc:postgresql://localhost:5432/movies;user=puser;password=puser
driverManager: org.postgresql.driver
```

The properties file is then read when the application is started. The calls to load the driver manager (`Class.forName`) and connect to the database (`DriverManager.getConnection`) will use the properties from the properties file, as shown in the following code snippet.

```
1.import java.sql.*;
2.import java.util.*;
3.import java.io.*;
4....
5.try {
6.
7.      Properties prop = new Properties();
8.      prop.load( new FileInputStream( "basic.properties" ) );
9.
10.     // load the Driver class
```

```
11.     Class.forName(
12.             prop.getProperty( "driverManagerClass" ) );
13.
14.     // create the connection using the static getConnection method
15.     Connection con = DriverManager.getConnection(
16.                     prop.getProperty( "connectionURL") );
17....
```

In this example, the appropriate package names are imported on lines 1 through 3 to allow the use of the `Properties` class (part of the `java.util` package), the `FileInputStream` class (the `java.io` package), and the JDBC API (the `java.sql` package). On line 7 a `Properties` object is created and loaded on line 8 with a call to the `load` method. The `load` method requires an `InputStream` object argument, which is returned by the `FileInputStream` constructor (which subclasses `InputStream`).

Once the `Properties` class `load` method has been called, the properties can be accessed using the `get` method. The end result of these efforts is that on lines 12 and 16 the details for loading the database driver and the connection to the database are not written into the application. The details are retrieved from a properties file (`basic.properties`). Should these details change because a database has been moved or a server name has been changed, then the change would need to be made only in the properties file. The application code could remain untouched.

This does provide a solution to the problem of binding database specifics to application code. But this solution generally requires a file to be present on the machine where the application is run. This means that if the application is moved from one machine to another, the file must follow and must be placed in the correct directory. Should the application be deployed across several machines, each machine would require a copy of the file. Should some of the database details change and the application is deployed across several machines, the file would need to be changed on each machine.

But a more robust and flexible solution is available through the JDBC 2.0 standard extension (and part of JDBC 3.0). As stated earlier, that is the use of `DataSource` implementations accessed through JNDI. Using JNDI, a `DataSource` is looked up through a service that returns an appropriate `DataSource` object reference. Using the `DataSource` object reference, a connection can be established with the database that corresponds to the `DataSource`. To understand the benefits of this approach, it is important to understand the functionality provided by JNDI (explained in detail Chapter 12). The following section provides an example.

JNDI AND DATASOURCES

The JNDI API is integral to the use of DataSources. JNDI and DataSource objects have the potential to make the life of the Java developer and the application deployer easier. The following code snippet provides an example of using JNDI to obtain a JDBC connection.

```java
import java.sql.*;
import javax.sql.*;
import javax.naming.*;
import java.util.*;
public class JNDIExample {
public static void main( String args[] ) {
Connection con=null;

try {
    PreparedExample pe = new PreparedExample();
    //
    // get our InitialContext from an LDAP naming service
    //
    Hashtable env = new Hashtable();
    env.put( Context.INITIAL_CONTEXT_FACTORY,
            "com.sun.jndi.ldap.LdapCtxFactory" );
    env.put( Context.PROVIDER_URL, "ldap://localhost:389");
    env.put( Context.SECURITY_AUTHENTICATION, "simple");
    env.put( Context.SECURITY_CREDENTIALS, "secret");
    env.put( Context.SECURITY_PRINCIPAL,
            "cn=movies,dc=movies,dc=com");
    //
    // get the initial context
    //
    InitialContext ctx = new InitialContext( env );
    //
    // get the DataSource from the JNDI name server
    //
    DataSource ds = (DataSource) ctx.lookup("cn=movies");

    //
    // get the initial context
    //
    InitialContext init = new InitialContext( env );
    Context ctx = (Context) init.lookup(
    "o=jdbc, o=general-application-objects, dc=movies, dc=com" );
    //
    // get the DataSource from the JNDI name server
    //
    DataSource ds = (DataSource) ctx.lookup("cn=movies");
    //
```

```
// get the connection from the DataSource
//
con = ds.getConnection( );
```

In this application, a `Hashtable` is used to hold the various environment entries required by JNDI to connect to the naming service. These entries are used to create the JNDI `InitialContext` that will be used to find the `DataSource`. Two key/value entries are added into the `Hashtable`: the initial context factory, used for creating the initial or topmost context for the directory server, and the provider URL for making the connection to the directory server provider. For local resources, which this example demonstrates, these two entries are required to create the `InitialContext`. Some Java containers, such as application servers, place these properties in the `InitialContext` environment for the developer, and they do not need to be set explicitly in the code. Additionally, if the directory server is on a remote machine, then a security manager must be provided and configured.

The constructor for the `InitialContext` is then called and passed the `Hashtable`. This returns an `IntialContext` entry (an access point for the naming context), which is then used to return a subdirectory in the directory tree where the JDBC `DataSource` objects are located.

We then use the `lookup` method to return a specific DataSource which must be cast up to the correct object type. In our case, we cast the reference as an implementation of the `DataSource` interface.

Once we have a `DataSource` object, we can call the `getConnection` method to make a connection to the underlying database. Since the `DataSource` object encapsulates the connection details, we do not need to specify the database connection specifics in our `getConnection` call.

Creating a Connection Using a DataSource

We have seen that the `DataSource` represents a layer of software above the database driver and uses the database driver to add features to the database communication process.

In the previous section, we demonstrated the use of the `DataSource` accessed through JNDI. The following code sample adds completes this picture, accessing the `DataSource`, creating a `Connection` and then using a `ResultSet` to iterate through the results.

```
import javax.sql.*;
import javax.naming.*;
public class BasicExample {
public static void main( String args[] ) {
Connection con=null;
try {
    //
    // the initialization properties for the
```

```
    // InitialContext constructor will be read from
    // the jndi.properties file in the CLASSPATH

    //
    // Create the initial naming context
    //
    InitialContext ctx = new InitialContext( );
    //
    // get the DataSource from the JNDI name server.
    // ('movies' name has been defined in poolman.xml and
    // bound to the naming service by Poolman).
    //
    DataSource ds = (DataSource) ctx.lookup("movies");
    //
    // get a connection from the DataSource
    //
    con = ds.getConnection( );
    //
    // create a Statement class to execute the SQL statement
    //
    Statement stmt = con.createStatement();
    //
    // execute the SQL statement and get the
    // results in a ResultSet
    //
    ResultSet rs   = stmt.executeQuery(
             "select movie_name, release_date from movies" );
    //
    // iterate through the ResultSet, displaying two values
    // for each row using the getString method
    //
    while ( rs.next() ) {
          System.out.println( "*******************" + "\n" +
                              "movie_name: " + "\t" +
                              rs.getString("movie_name") + "\n" +
                              "release_date: " + "\t" +
                              rs.getString("release_date")  );
    }

}
catch (SQLException e) {

    // display SQL specific exception information
    System.out.println("*************************" );
    System.out.println("SQLException in main: " +
                          e.getMessage() );
    System.out.println("** SQLState: " + e.getSQLState());
    System.out.println("** SQL Error Code: " + e.getErrorCode());
    System.out.println("*************************" );
    e.printStackTrace();
}
catch (NamingException e) {
```

```
        System.out.println( "NamingException in main: " +
                                e.getMessage() );
}
catch (Exception e) {
    System.out.println("Exception in main: " + e.getMessage() );
    e.printStackTrace();
}
finally {
    try {
        // close the connection
      if ( con != null )
            con.close();
    }
    catch (SQLException e) {
            e.printStackTrace();
  }
 }
}
}
```

This example demonstrates the use of a DataSource with JNDI to manage a connection. In order to use JNDI, a JNDI Service Provider Interface (SPI) is required. This means that a server must be running to provide the lookups and return the appropriate objects requested. For this example the reference implementation of the JNDI SPI for the rmiregistry (http://java.sun.com/products/jndi/) was used. This required that an appropriate set of JAR files be placed in the CLASS-PATH for the application. The JNDI InitialContext class needs information on what SPI is being used (what ContextFactory needs to be accessed and other pertinent information). This information can be provided in one of several ways, but for this example a jndi.properties file in the current CLASSPATH is used. The jndi.properties file has the following entries.

```
java.naming.factory.initial: com.sun.jndi.rmi.registry.RegistryContextFactory
java.naming.provider.url: rmi://localhost:1099
```

Since the initialization properties for the InitialContext is read from the properties file, there is no need to load a Hashtable with this information, as shown in the previous example, and the InitialContext constructor can be called with no arguments.

The InitialContext returns a Context object, which provides the utilitarian lookup call. As shown in this example, this call can take a string parameter with the name of the object to look up, and then returns a Java Object reference. Since in this example we know the type of the object reference being returned, we can cast it to the DataSource type. So, with no more knowledge than a string for the name of the DataSource, the application is able to obtain an object for the DataSource.

Once the data source has been obtained, it can be used to return a Connection object that represents a connection to the database. This Connection object can be used just as if the DriverManager class had returned it. As shown in this example, a Statement is created from the Connection object and is then used to execute a query which returns a ResultSet object (explained in more detail in the next chapter). The ResultSet is then iterated through to the end of the set using the Java while loop. The code within this while loop will print out a set of columns for each row returned.

In order to create a DataSource, details about the connections to the underlying database must be identified and placed in a configuration file or registry. For this example, the open source PoolMan driver was used to add the DataSource functionality onto the existing PostgreSQL database. This driver uses the poolman.xml file to define data sources. The following fragment shows the definition of the movies DataSource.

```
1....
2.    <datasource>
3.
4.       <dbname>movies</dbname>
5.       <jndiName>movies</jndiName>
6.       <driver>org.postgresql.Driver</driver>
7.<url>jdbc:postgresql://localhost:5432/movies;user=puser;password=puser        </url>
8.
9.       <username>puser</username>
10.      <password>puser</password>
11.
12.      <connectionTimeout>300</connectionTimeout>
13.      <minimumSize>0</minimumSize>
14.      <maximumSize>10</maximumSize>
15.      <debugging>true</debugging>
16.      <logFile>/lin2/tmp/testdb.log</logFile>
17.
18.   </datasource>
19....
```

As can be seen from this example, a JNDI data source name is provided on line 5 of the configuration file. This name will be bound in the JNDI name server to the DataSource described in this file.

On line 6, the driver for the DataSource is declared. This driver is the class name for the driver to be used to manage the database connection. On line 7, the database connection URL is provided as a value for the <url> tag. As expected, this URL provides the details on how to make the database connection. Lines 9 and 10 provide the user name and password to be used for authentication when the connection is made.

Lines 12 through 15 provide various configuration parameters for the `DataSource` connection. These entries are proprietary, and though the entries shown here are specific to the PoolMan driver (no longer available as of this writing), other `DataSource` implementations provide similar configuration parameters.

A `connectionTimeout` entry on line 12 indicates how long a `DataSource` connection object will be kept alive before being destroyed and returned to the pool. The `minimumSize` parameter on line 13 indicates the minimum number of objects that will be kept in the pool, and the `maximumSize` parameter on line 14 indicates the maximum size the object pool will be allowed to grow. The `debugging` entry on line 15 indicates the debugging level for the `DataSource`, and the `logfile` entry on line 18 indicates which log file to use for the `DataSource`.

Another example of JDBC configuration is the following entry which appears in a Tomcat server configuration file (server.xml).

```
...
<Resource name="jdbc/movies" auth="container"
          type="javax.sql.DataSource"/>
    <ResourceParams name="jdbc/movies">
        <parameter>
            <name>user</name>
            <value>art</value>
        </parameter>
        <parameter>
            <name>password</name>
            <value>YES</value>
        </parameter>
        <parameter>
            <name>driverClassName</name>
            <value>org.gjt.mm.mysql.Driver</value>
        </parameter>
        <parameter>
          <name>driverName</name>
          <value>jdbc:mysql://localhost/movies</value>
        </parameter>
    </ResourceParams>
</Resource>
...
```

In this file, a resource is identified with the name "`jdbc/movies`". This will be the name used to lookup the JDBC `DataSource` using JNDI. Note that this name is only visible from within the Tomcat server container.

Successive entries in the file identify the user name and password to be used to access the database, and the Java class name of the database driver to use and the URL used to access the database.

Additional Capabilities Provided by the DataSource

The JDBC 2.0 Standard Extension API introduced the `DataSource` interface and provided two additional interfaces that could optionally be used to create a `DataSource` with more specific capabilities. These additional interfaces are the `ConnectionPoolDataSource` and `XADataSource` interfaces.

The `ConnectionPoolDataSource` and the `XADataSource` interfaces are expected to be implemented by a data source in addition to the `DataSource` interface. For this reason, the JNDI lookup for a `ConnectionPoolDataSource` would be the same as for a standard `DataSource` interface, as shown in the following code snippet.

```
. . .
InitialContext ctx = new InitialContext();
// lookup the data source to be used for connection pooling
DataSource ds = (DataSource) ctx.lookup("MoviesDBConnPool");
. . .
```

The `ConnectionPoolDataSource`, as the name implies, provides a data source with an underlying connection pool. The `XADataSource` adds transaction management capabilities to the data source, allowing a transaction to span multiple databases, potentially databases from different vendors.

Connection pooling has become the standard for middleware database drivers. The process of creating a connection, always an expensive, time-consuming operation, is multiplied in these environments where a large number of users are accessing the database in short, unconnected operations. Repeatedly creating connections in these environments is simply too expensive.

The transaction profile for Web applications, probably the most common application in use today, is that of a large number of users performing short, discrete database operations. These applications usually perform work centered around creating a Web page, which will be sent back to the user's browser. Transactions are generally short-lived and user sessions are often limited in time.

A connection pool operates by performing the work of creating connections ahead of time. In the case of a JDBC connection pool, a pool of `Connection` objects is created at the time the application server (or some other server) starts. These objects are then managed by a *pool manager* that disperses connections as they are requested by clients and returns them to the pool when it determines the client is finished with the `Connection` object. A great deal of housekeeping is involved in managing these connections.

When the connection pool server starts, it creates a predefined number of `Connection` objects. A client application would then perform a JNDI lookup to retrieve a reference to a `DataSource` object that implements the `ConnectionPoolDataSource` interface. The client application would not need to make any special provisions to use the pooled data source; the code would be no different from code written for a nonpooled `DataSource`.

When the client application requests a connection from the `ConnectionPoolDataSource`, the data source implementation would retrieve a physical connection from the preexisting pool, perform some housekeeping, and return the connection to the client application. The `ConnectionPoolDataSource` would return a `Connection` object that implemented the `PooledConnection` interface.

The `PooledConnection` interface dictates the use of *event listeners*. These event listeners allow the connection pool manager to capture important connection events, such as attempts by the client application to close the connection. When the driver traps a close-connection event, it intercedes and performs a pseudo-close operation that merely takes the `Connection` object, returns it to the pool of available connections, and performs any housekeeping that is necessary.

The operation of the connection pool should be completely transparent to the client application. The triggering of connection events, the manipulation of the object pool, and the creation and destruction of physical connections are all managed by the pool manager. The activities of the connection pool are, however, configurable by the application developer or the application deployer.

Summary

Almost every J2EE application requires data, and that data most commonly comes from a relational database. The API of choice for working with a relational database is JDBC. This chapter covered the basics of the JDBC package, how the API is designed, and how it is used. But at this point we've barely scratched the surface of JDBC. The next few chapters provide additional details about and examples of using JDBC.

CHAPTER 6

JDBC: Connecting to the Database and Using the Data

INTRODUCTION

The `java.sql.Connection` object is a required part of any database interaction with JDBC. The `Connection` object represents the physical connection to the database, usually using an underlying network connection, and is responsible for maintaining and managing the connection.

Though the `Connection` represents a physical connection, the process of obtaining a connection may not represent the creation of a physical connection to the database, since connection pooling may simply use an existing connection instead of creating a new connection.

A `Connection` object can provide information about the tables in the database, the supported SQL grammar, the stored procedures available, and the general capabilities of the database connection by using the `DatabaseMetaData` object returned by the `getMetaData` method.

Transactions and Autocommit Mode with JDBC

A JDBC connection is in autocommit mode by default. With autocommit set, each SQL update statement (insert, update, delete) executed is automatically committed to the database separately on successful execution of the statement. In order to group a set of database updates together, the autocommit mode must be set off (using the setAutoCommit method of the Connection interface). Once the autocommit behavior has been turned off, every SQL statement is part of a transaction and must be explicitly committed using the Connection commit method to become a permanent part of the database. Failure to commit with autocommit turned off will generally cause an implicit rollback by the database when the connection is closed and any updates will be lost.

Table 6–1 provides a description of the methods in the Connection class. All methods throw a SQLException.

Table 6–1   *java.sql.Connection Class Methods*

Method	Description
void clearWarnings()	Clears the various warnings that may have accumulated for this Connection object.
void close()	Closes the database connection. Terminates the relationship of this object to the underlying data store. (With pooled connections, retains the connection and returns it to the pool of available connections.)
void commit()	Places all updates in a permanent state in the underlying data store. A transactional *commit* operation. Releases any locks currently held by the connection.
Statement createStatement()	Creates a Statement object for the execution of SQL statements.
Statement createStatement(int resultSetType, int resultSetConcurrency)	Creates a Statement object for the execution of SQL statements. Parameters are provided to indicate that the ResultSet generated by the statement should be of the ResultSet type specified and should provide the concurrency specified.
boolean getAutoCommit()	Returns a boolean value for the auto-commit state of the Connection. If true, auto-commit is on. If false is returned, auto-commit is not on.
String getCatalog()	Returns a string with the catalog name for the current catalog of the connection.

Table 6–1 *java.sql.Connection Class Methods (cont.)*

Method	Description
DatabaseMetaData getMetaData()	Returns a DatabaseMetaData object for the underlying database for the current connection.
int getTransactionIsolation()	Returns an integer value representing the transaction isolation mode for the current database connection. Integer value returned relates to the integer constants in the Connection class.
Map getTypeMap()	Returns a java.util.Map object to be used for the custom type mapping of User- Defined Types (UDTs) in the current database.
SQLWarning getWarnings()	Returns a SQLWarning object containing the warnings for the current connection.
boolean isClosed()	Returns a boolean value indicating true if the database connection has been closed with a call to the close method, and false if the database connection is open. (If the connection has been invalidated for some other reason, the client may need to catch an exception and react accordingly.)
boolean isReadOnly()	Returns a boolean true if the database is a read-only database, and a boolean false ifs the database can be updated.
String nativeSQL(	Converts a SQL statement into the native SQL of the underlying database. Returns a string containing the converted SQL statement.
String sql) CallableStatement prepareCall(String sql)	Creates and returns a CallableStatement object (an object to be used for calling database stored procedures) using the SQL statement passed as a parameter to be used with the current database connection. (An object to be used for calling database stored procedures.)
CallableStatement prepareCall(String sql, int resultSetType, int resultSetConcurrency)	Creates and returns a CallableStatement object for use with the current connection. (An object to be used for calling database stored procedures.) Indicates that the ResultSet returned will be of the defined type and will use the specified concurrency. Usually throws an SQLa SQLException if the ResultSet type is not supported by the database or the driver.
PreparedStatement prepareStatement(String sql)	Creates a *prepared* SQL statement, a parsed, precompiled, reusable statement for use with the current database connection. Returns a PreparedStatement object.

Table 6–1   *java.sql.Connection Class Methods*

Method	Description

`PreparedStatement prepareStatement(`
`String sql,`
`int resultSetType,`
`int resultSetConcurrency)`
	Creates and returns a `PreparedStatement` object for use with the current database connection. The `ResultSet` returned will have the specified `ResultSet` type and will use the specified `ResultSet` concurrency mode.

`void rollback()`	Will roll -back or undo the changes (updates) made in the current transaction. (The auto-commit mode must be turned off.) Will release any database locks held by the connection.
`void setAutoCommit(boolean` `autoCommit)`	Will set the auto-commit mode based on the boolean parameter passed to the method. If the boolean value is true, the auto-commit mode is set on, meaning each SQL statement represents a transaction. If the parameter is false, then auto-commit is turned off and it is possible to create multi-statement database trans-actions.
`void setCatalog(String catalog)`	Sets the database catalog to the string catalog name passed into the method.
`void setReadOnly(boolean readOnly)`	Sets the current database connection to read-only mode as a hint for database optimizations.
`void setTransactionIsolation(int` `level)`	Sets the transaction isolation mode to the specified value.
`void setTypeMap(Map map)`	Sets the type map for the database connection based on the `Map` object passed as a parameter. The Map object provides mapping between the UDTs and cor-responding Java classes.

Given the importance and the prevalence of the `Connection` class in JDBC, it is worthwhile to review the various methods that are available in this class. The following sections cover these methods.

The close Method

The `close` method closes the connection to the database. This effectively termi-nates the relationship between the client application and the database, and releas-es all resources held in the database. Resources released include any transactions that were open and any locks held implicitly or explicitly by the connection. This means that any transaction that was open and uncommitted is rolled back by calling the `Connection` close method. This rollback is performed quietly, without any exception being thrown. The following code snippet demonstrates this.

```
1....
2.//
3.      // get the initial context
4.      //
5.      InitialContext ctx = new InitialContext(  );
6.
7.      //
8.      // get the DataSource from the JNDI name server
9.      //
10.      DataSource ds = (DataSource) ctx.lookup("movies");
11.
12.      //
13.      // get the connection from the DataSource
14.      //
15.      con = ds.getConnection( );
16.
17.      //
18.      // create a Statement class to execute the SQL statement
19.      //
20.      Statement stmt = con.createStatement();
21.
22.      //
23.      // turn auto-commit  off
24.      //
25.      con.setAutoCommit( false );
26.
27.      //
28.      // we are now in a transaction ... perform a series of updates
29.      //
30.      updateResult = stmt.executeUpdate(
31."insert into users (user_id, first_name, last_name, address1," +
32." city, state_province, postal_code, country)  " +
33." values ( 0, 'Fred', 'Smith', '2020 Nowhere Lane', 'Newark', 'NJ', '09090',
'US');" );
34.
35.      updateResult = stmt.executeUpdate(
36."insert into users (user_id, first_name, last_name, address1," +
37." city, state_province, postal_code, country)  " +
38." values ( 0, 'Sally', 'Smith', '2020 Nowhere Lane', 'Newark', 'NJ', '09090',
'US');" );
39.
40.      updateResult = stmt.executeUpdate(
41."insert into users (user_id, first_name, last_name, address1," +
42." city, state_province, postal_code, country)  " +
43." values ( 0, 'Harry', 'Henderson', '3030 Milbourne', 'Tuckamarin', 'NJ',
'08090', 'US');" );
44.
```

```
45.
46.     // oops ... forgot to commit !
47.     // con.close() call will cause all of the updates above
48.     // to be lost !
49.     //
50.      con.close();
51....
```

In this example, a `DataSource` is obtained using a JNDI lookup, and a `Statement` object is obtained via the `Connection`. A series of database updates is performed on lines 30 through 43, but because there is no commit call (`con.commit()`), all of the updates are lost when the `Connection close` method call is executed on line 50. A call to the `Connection commit` method on the previous line would have saved the work.

The getAutoCommit and setAutoCommit Methods

The autocommit state of the database driver indicates how the driver will manage transaction logging with the database. The default value for autocommit is on (a setting of true), which means that every SQL statement executed is a separate transaction and is committed to the database separately.

The `getAutoCommit` method returns a boolean value that indicates the current autocommit state of the database. A boolean value of true indicates that autocommit is turned on (the default), and a boolean value of false indicates that autocommit is turned off. In order to create a transaction (i.e., group a set of SQL statements together), the autocommit behavior must be turned off, as shown in this code snippet.

```
1....
2.// get the initial context
3.     //
4.     InitialContext ctx = new InitialContext(  );
5.
6.     //
7.     // get the DataSource from the JNDI name server
8.     //
9.     DataSource ds = (DataSource) ctx.lookup("movies");
10.
11.     //
12.     // get the connection from the DataSource
13.     //
14.     con = ds.getConnection( );
15.
16.     //
17.     // create a Statement class to execute the SQL statement
18.     //
19.     Statement stmt = con.createStatement();
20.
```

```
21.      //
22.      // turn auto-commit
23.      //
24.      con.setAutoCommit( false );
25.
26.
27.      //
28.      // we are now in a transaction ... perform a series of updates
29.      //
30.
31.      updateResult = stmt.executeUpdate(
32."insert into users (user_id, first_name, last_name, address1," +
33." city, state_province, postal_code, country)   " +
34." values ( nextval('user_id'), 'Fred', 'Smith', '2020 Nowhere Lane', 'Newark',
'NJ', '09090', 'US');" );
35.
36.      updateResult = stmt.executeUpdate(
37."insert into users (user_id, first_name, last_name, address1," +
38." city, state_province, postal_code, country)   " +
39." values ( nextval('user_id'), 'Sally', 'Smith', '2020 Nowhere Lane', 'Newark',
'NJ', '09090', 'US');" );
40.
41.      updateResult = stmt.executeUpdate(
42."insert into users (user_id, first_name, last_name, address1," +
43." city, state_province, postal_code, country)   " +
44." values ( nextval('user_id'), 'Harry', 'Henderson', '3030 Milbourne',
'Tuckamarin', 'NJ', '08090', 'US');" );
45.
46.
47.      // user_id = 2 is renting a movie
48.      updateResult = stmt.executeUpdate(
49.         "insert into user_rentals (user_id, rental_date, movie_id) " +
50.         " values ( 2, current_date, 1 ); " );
51.      // user_id = 3 is renting a movie
52.      updateResult = stmt.executeUpdate(
53.         "insert into user_rentals (user_id, rental_date, movie_id) " +
54.         " values ( 2, current_date, 3 ); " );
55.
56.
57.      //
58.      // need to perform a commit to save the work
59.      //
60.      con.commit();
61.
62.      // 'finally' block will close the connection
63....
```

This example obtains a `DataSource` from JNDI, and then obtains a `Connection`. Using the connection, a `Statement` object is created. Before the actual database update statements are executed, a call is made to the `setAutoCommit` method on line 24 to turn autocommit off. This is done by passing the `setAutoCommit` method a boolean value of false. Following the `setAutoCommit` call, a series of database update statements are executed on lines 31 through 52. Since autocommit mode is not on, these statements will not be committed to the database until the `Connection commit` method is executed at line 60. (Note that there is no explicit `begin` or `beginWork` method with JDBC; with autocommit off, all work against the database is effectively in a transaction.)

The commit and rollback Methods

The `commit` and `rollback` methods provide for direct programmatic control over transaction logging in the client application. The `commit` method commits all database update activity in the current transaction to the database. The `rollback` method rolls back or ensures that all update activity in the current transaction will not be committed to the database. If the autocommit state is on (the default), then each statement executed is automatically committed to the database, leaving nothing for the `commit` or `rollback` method to work with. The autocommit state of the database driver must be set off (false) in order to for these methods to work correctly. The following code snippet demonstrates the use of these methods.

```
1....
2.//
3.      // get the initial context
4.      //
5.      InitialContext ctx = new InitialContext(  );
6.
7.      //
8.      // get the DataSource from the JNDI name server
9.      //
10.      DataSource ds = (DataSource) ctx.lookup("movies");
11.
12.      //
13.      // get the connection from the DataSource
14.      //
15.      con = ds.getConnection( );
16.
17.      //
18.      // create a Statement class to execute the SQL statement
19.      //
20.      Statement stmt = con.createStatement();
21.
22.      //
23.      // turn auto-commit  off
24.      //
25.      con.setAutoCommit( false );
26.
27.      //
28.      // we are now in a transaction ... perform a series of updates
```

```
29.      //
30.      updateResult = stmt.executeUpdate(
31.      "insert into users (user_id, first_name, last_name, address1," +
32.      " city, state_province, postal_code, country)  " +
33.      " values ( nextval('user_id'), 'Fred', 'Smith', '2020 Nowhere Lane',
'Newark', 'NJ', '09090', 'US');" );
34.
35.      updateResult = stmt.executeUpdate(
36.      "insert into users (user_id, first_name, last_name, address1," +
37.      " city, state_province, postal_code, country)  " +
38.       " values ( nextval('user_id'), 'Sally', 'Smith', '2020 Nowhere Lane',
'Newark', 'NJ', '09090', 'US');" );
39.
40.      updateResult = stmt.executeUpdate(
41.      "insert into users (user_id, first_name, last_name, address1," +
42.      " city, state_province, postal_code, country)  " +
43.       " values ( nextval('user_id'), 'Harry', 'Henderson', '3030 Milbourne',
'Tuckamarin', 'NJ', '08090', 'US');" );
44.
45.      // user_id = 2 is renting a movie
46.      updateResult = stmt.executeUpdate(
47.      "insert into user_rentals (user_id, rental_date, movie_id) " +
48.                      " values ( 2, current_date, 1 ); " );
49.      // user_id = 3 is renting a movie
50.      updateResult = stmt.executeUpdate(
51.      "insert into user_rentals (user_id, rental_date, movie_id) " +
52.                      " values ( 2, current_date, 3 ); " );
53.
54.      // need to perform a commit to save the work
55.      // this expression tests true about half the time
56.      //
57.      if ( ( (int)(Math.random() * 10) % 2) > 0 ) {
58.          con.commit();
59.          System.out.println("Transactions have been committed.");
60.      }
61.      else {
62.          con.rollback();
63.          System.out.println("Transactions have been rolled back.");
64.      }
65.
66.      //
67.      // 'finally' block will close the connection
68.      //
69.
70.
71....
```

This example gets a `DataSource` from the `InitialContext` and then creates the `Connection` from the `DataSource`. The database driver autocommit is turned off at line 25, and a series of database updates are performed on lines 30 through 52. At line 57, a random value (the expression will randomly generate a 0 or 1) is generated to make a decision whether to commit or roll back the transaction. The `Connection commit` method is called at line 58 to commit the transaction, or the `Connection rollback` method is called at line 62 to roll back the transaction.

The clearWarnings and getWarnings Methods

When a connection is made to a relational database, a series of warnings may be generated by the database. These warnings potentially, but not necessarily, provide information about the level of ANSI SQL support, how null values are handled, and other pertinent information. (Whether or not warnings are used at all is dependent on the database being used; developers should review the documentation for the driver to determine what information is relayed in warnings.)

Other JDBC objects return `SQLWarnings` for the database operations they represent (`Statement`, `ResultSet`). These warnings are returned by the underlying database and are represented as *chains* of warnings, with each `SQLWarning` object retrieved potentially containing a reference to an additional `SQLWarning` object.

The `getWarnings` method returns a `SQLWarning` object (`java.sql.SQLWarning`), which is an exception (a subclass of `java.sql.SQLException`). The `SQLWarning` class contains a `getNextWarning` method, which returns a `SQLWarning` object if another warning exists in the chain or a null reference if no more warnings exist. The following code snippet provides an example of using the `getWarnings` and `clearWarnings` methods.

```
...
DataSource ds;
...
Connection con  = ds.getConnection();
//
// check for warnings from the database connection
//


SQLWarning sqlw = con.getWarnings();
//
// warning may be null reference
//
if (sqlw != null) {

    //
    // iterate through the chain of warnings
    //
```

```
    while ( sqlw != null )
        System.out.println("Warning: " + sqlw );
          sqlw = sqlw.getNextWarning();
    }
else
    System.out.println("There are no warnings.");
//
// clear all warnings on the connection
//
con.clearWarnings();
...
```

In this example, a connection is made to a database using a `DataSource`, and a `Connection` object is returned. The `Connection` object will potentially have a series of warnings (`SQLWarning` objects) attached to it as a result of the database connection operation. Since the `getWarnings` method may have returned a null object reference, a conditional statement is first used to test for this condition. If the `SQLWarning` object is not null, then a `while` loop is used to extract the entire chain of objects.

For an application that must connect to various databases with varying levels of support that may not be known when the application is developed, the `SQLWarning` may provide useful information. As shown in the previous code snippet, warnings are not thrown like exceptions; the programmer must make the `getWarnings` call on the `Connection` object to obtain the first warning (if any), and then iterate through the warnings to examine all warnings.

Though warnings may warrant examination if the database uses them, in practice, the `DatabaseMetaData` class provides more finely grained and useful information on database support than the `SQLWarning` object.

The createStatement Method

The `createStatement` method is used to create SQL statements for execution. Both database `select` and `update` statements are created using this method. The `createStatement` method has been overloaded to take two sets of arguments, as shown below.

```
Statement  createStatement()
Statement  createStatement(int resultSetType,
                           int resultSetConcurrency)
```

One version takes no arguments and returns a `Statement` object. The other version takes arguments for the type of result set to be returned and the type of result set concurrency to use. The `ResultSet` class contains the constants that can be used for these calls. The possible values are shown in Table 6–2.

Table 6–2 *ResultSet Constants*

Constant	Type	Description
CONCUR_READ_ONLY	Concurrency	Indicates that read-only concurrency will be used. The ResultSet object will not be updated.
CONCUR_UPDATABLE	Concurrency	Indicates that the ResultSet created may be updated.

There are two concurrency types that impact how the ResultSet (cursor) created by the Statement object will manage updates. The type of concurrency selected must be supported by the underlying database and driver.

Using the CONCUR_READ_ONLY parameter value creates a regular cursor—a ResultSet without update capabilities. Using the CONCUR_UPDATABLE parameter creates a ResultSet with update capabilities. The second argument to the createStatement method takes an integer value corresponding to the scrolling and concurrency type, which would take one of the values shown in Table 6–3. (The JDBC 3.0 API overloads this method and adds a cursor holdability parameter indicating whether or not a cursor will be held open after a commit.) This method usually throws an exception if a ResultSet type requested is not supported by the database or the driver.

Table 6–3 *Scrollable ResultSet Constants*

Constant	Type	Description
TYPE_FORWARD_ONLY	Scroll	Indicates that the ResultSet will only be processed in a forward direction; it is not a scroll cursor.
TYPE_SCROLL_INSENSITIVE	Scrolling	Indicates that the cursor is scrollable but is not sensitive to changes made in the database while the cursor is being moved.
TYPE_SCROLL_SENSITIVE	Scrolling	Indicates that the cursor is scrollable and is sensitive to changes made in the database while the cursor is being used.

The ResultSet created by the Statement object is implemented with a database cursor. A database cursor can be either a *serial cursor,* meaning that it will be traversed in one direction only from the beginning of the cursor to the end of the cursor. The other type of cursor is the *scroll cursor.* This type of cursor allows the entire result set to be traversed in an arbitrary fashion. Cursor evaluation can start at the first row, jump to the fifth row, and then move to the second row. The database may also offer flexibility with concurrency (simultaneous database updates to the rows being evaluated by the cursor). The cursor may optionally be sensitive to changes in the rows being evaluated and refresh the rows from the database if needed.

The type parameters passed to the `createStatement` method indicate the type of cursor to be created for the `ResultSet` that will be produced by the execution of the SQL statement. The `TYPE_FORWARD_ONLY` creates a normal cursor that does not provide scroll capability. The `TYPE_SCROLL_INSENSITIVE` scroll cursor is not sensitive to changes in the database; changes in the database are effectively ignored by the cursor. The `TYPE_SCROLL_SENSITIVE` scroll cursor is sensitive to changes in the database, potentially re-reading database rows if they have changed.

The following code snippet reads rows from the movies database using a `ResultSet` to iterate through the results. This demonstrates the use of the `createStatement` method.

```
1. ...
2.
3.      // get the DataSource from the JNDI name server
4.      DataSource ds = (DataSource) ctx.lookup("movies");
5.
6.      // get the connection from the DataSource
7.      con = ds.getConnection( );
8.
9.      // create a Statement class to execute the SQL statement
10.      Statement stmt = con.createStatement();
11.
12.      // execute the SQL statement and get the results in a ResultSet
13.      ResultSet rs    = stmt.executeQuery(
14.          "select movie_name, release_date from movies" );
15.
16.      // iterate serially through the ResultSet, displaying two values
17.      // for each row using the getString method
18.      //
19.      while ( rs.next() ) {
20.          System.out.println( "******************" + "\n" +
21.                          "movie_name: " + "\t" +
22.                            rs.getString("movie_name") + "\n" +
23.                          "release_date: " + "\t" +
24.                            rs.getString("release_date")  );
25. ...
```

The `Connection` object obtained on line 7 is used to create a `Statement` object using the `createStatement` method on line 10. This form of the method takes no arguments and creates a `Statement` object that will return a `ResultSet` using the default cursor type, a serial cursor. The `ResultSet` is created on line 13 and then used to step through the results serially, using a `while` loop on line 19.

Alternatively, a *scroll cursor* can be used to move through a `ResultSet` in an arbitrary manner. This requires the `createStatement` method to identify the cursor to be created as a scroll cursor. The following code snippet demonstrates this approach.

```
1. ...
2.      //
3.      // load the DataSource
4.      //
5.      DataSource  ds   = PoolMan.findDataSource("movies");
6.
7.      //
8.      // create the connection using the static getConnection method
9.      //
10.      Connection con = ds.getConnection( );
11.
12.      //
13.      // create a Statement object to execute the SQL statement
14.      // define the cursor type to get a scroll cursor
15.      //
16.      Statement stmt = con.createStatement(
17.                       ResultSet.TYPE_SCROLL_INSENSITIVE,
18.                       ResultSet.CONCUR_UPDATABLE );
19.
20.      // execute the SQL statement and get the results in a ResultSet
21.      ResultSet rs   = stmt.executeQuery(
22.         "select movie_name, movie_id, release_date from movies" );
23. ...
```

In this example, a `DataSource` is obtained from the `InitialContext`, and a connection is created from the `DataSource` on line 10. On line 16 a `createStatement` method is executed using the optional arguments to define concurrency and cursor type. In this example, a scroll-insensitive cursor is declared, meaning the cursor will be a scroll cursor but will not be sensitive to changes made in the database while the cursor is being used by the client application. The `createStatement` method also accepts a parameter for the concurrency and in this case defines concurrency to be *updatable,* meaning that updates may be performed using the `ResultSet`.

The getMetaData Method

The `getMetaData` method returns a `DatabaseMetaData` object. Every relational database has metadata—data about data. Metadata can provide a wealth of information about a database and is useful to developers who write applications that must work with many different databases. Metadata information is not only useful when working with databases from different vendors, but can also help when working with different versions of the same database.

While much of the information delivered by the DatabaseMetaData class is available through database system catalogs or database functions, JDBC provides a consistent API to access this information regardless of the database vendor. The ability to access and use this information is one of the more significant benefits of JDBC. The following code snippet demonstrates the use of the getMetaData method.

```
1....
2.      //
3.      // load the DataSource
4.      //
5.      DataSource  ds   = (DataSource) ctx.lookup("movies");
6.      //
7.      // create the connection using the static getConnection method
8.      //
9.      Connection con = ds.getConnection( );
10.        // create a meta-data object for the connection
11.       //
12.      DatabaseMetaData dmd = con.getMetaData();
13.         // get a list of System functions
14.         //
15.
16.      String sysFuncts = dmd.getSystemFunctions();
17.      System.out.println("System functions: " + sysFuncts );
18.         //
19.         // get a list of tables in the database
20.         //
21.      ResultSet tables = dmd.getTables("","","",null);
22.      while ( tables.next() )
23.            System.out.println( "tables: " +
24.            tables.getString("TABLE_NAME")  );
25....
```

In the code snippet above, a DataSource is retrieved using a JNDI lookup, and a Connection is obtained from the DataSource. The getMetadata method is then called on the Connection object to retrieve a DatabaseMetaData object on line 12. One of the more common operations to perform on a DatabaseMetaData object is to list the tables available in the database. This is done on line 21 using the getTables method of the DatabaseMetaData class. This method returns a ResultSet, which is then used to iterate over the results, listing the tables in the database using the while loop on line 22.

The getTransactionIsolation and setTransactionIsolation Methods

The getTransactionIsolation method returns the isolation mode of the current database connection in the form of an integer. The integer value must then be evaluated against the integer constants in the Connection class to determine what the current isolation mode is.

The isolation mode can optionally be changed using the setTransactionIsolation method and passing a valid integer value for the isolation mode to which the connection should be changed. If the database does not support the isolation mode requested, then a SQLException will be thrown. The following code snippet demonstrates the use of this method.

```
...
 // get the initial context
    InitialContext ctx = new InitialContext( );
    // get the DataSource from the JNDI name server
    DataSource ds = (DataSource) ctx.lookup("movies");
    // get the connection from the DataSource
    con = ds.getConnection( );
    // examine the isolation mode
    //
    System.out.println("Transaction isolation mode is: " +
            formatIsolationMode( con.getTransactionIsolation()) );
    //
    // let's set the isolation mode to allow dirty reads since
    // we are just creating a simple report
    //
    con.setTransactionIsolation(
            Connection.TRANSACTION_READ_UNCOMMITTED );
...
static String formatIsolationMode( int isolationMode ) {
//
// Translate integer value for Transaction Isolation Mode
// into an appropriate string and return string value
//
switch (isolationMode) {
    case Connection.TRANSACTION_NONE:
            return "No Transaction Isolation Mode" ;
    case Connection.TRANSACTION_READ_COMMITTED:
            return "Read Committed Isolation Mode" ;
    case Connection.TRANSACTION_READ_UNCOMMITTED:
            return "Read Uncommitted  Isolation Mode" ;
    case Connection.TRANSACTION_REPEATABLE_READ:
            return "Repeatable Read Isolation Mode" ;
    case Connection.TRANSACTION_SERIALIZABLE:
            return "Serializable Isolation Mode" ;
}
// if at this point, then this is an invalid value
```

```
// so return a null reference
//
return null;
}
...
```

This code snippet examines the isolation mode and displays the output. A formatting routine is used to convert the integer value constant to a meaningful string. The isolation mode is then explicitly set to the read-uncommitted isolation mode (a *dirty read'*). This is an isolation mode that requires fewer locks be held in the database engine. Using a less restrictive isolation mode such as this should improve performance for database operations that do not require locking.

The prepareStatement Method

The `prepareStatement` method is used to optionally prepare a SQL statement for processing. Most relational databases support the capability to preprocess a SQL statement before it is actually used. This allows the database to optimize the SQL statement and determine how to process the statement before it is used. While this may sound like a trivial process, determining the best way to process a complex SQL statement with 10 table joins and 20 lines of `where` clause filters is not trivial. Being able to preprocess a SQL statement that will be executed multiple times can lead to a significant performance improvement. The following code snippet demonstrates the use of these methods.

```
...
// get the DataSource from the JNDI name server
    DataSource ds = (DataSource) ctx.lookup("movies");

    // get the connection from the DataSource
    con = ds.getConnection( );

    // create a Statement class to execute the SQL statement
    PreparedStatement pstmt = con.prepareStatement(
  " select distinct first_name, last_name, state_province, " +
  " movie_name, rental_date "                             +
  " from users, movies, user_rentals "                    +
  " where (users.user_id    = user_rentals.user_id and " +
  "        movies.movie_id  = user_rentals.movie_id) and " +
  "        user_rentals.user_id = ? " );

    // set the PreparedStatement parameters
    pstmt.setInt(1, 2); // set to user_id = 2

    // execute the SQL statement and get the results in a ResultSet
    ResultSet rs   = pstmt.executeQuery();

    // iterate through the ResultSet, displaying two values
```

```
// for each row using the getString method
//
while ( rs.next() ) {
        System.out.println( "Name: " + "\t" +
                    rs.getString("first_name").trim() + "\t" +
                    " " + "\t" + rs.getString("last_name").trim() +
                    "\t" + " Movie: " + "\t" +
                    rs.getString("movie_name") + "\t" +
                    "" Rental Date: " + "\t" +
                    rs.getString("rental_date") );
```
. . .

In this example, the `prepareStatement` method of the `Connection` class is called and returns a `PreparedStatement` object. The call to the `prepareStatement` method is passed a query string, which joins several tables to list the movie rental transactions in the database for a specific user ID. The `PreparedStatement` uses the `"?"` as a placeholder to indicate where a parameter value will be substituted when the statement is executed. As the code shows, the values of parameters are set with `setXXXX` calls before the statement is executed with the `executeQuery` method of the `PreparedStatement` class.

RETRIEVING AND MANIPULATING DATA: THE STATEMENT CLASS AND JDBC EXCEPTIONS

The `Statement` class allows a SQL statement to be presented to the database for execution. As part of that process, the `Statement` class allows suggestions to be sent to the database on how to process the query and how to return the results.

Extensions to the `Statement` class allow batches of updates to be sent to the database and processed together. The SQL syntax can vary slightly across different databases. The JDBC API provides for *escape processing* to allow a standard JDBC syntax to be used for various statements (such as stored procedure calls). The JDBC driver is then responsible for providing the correct syntax for these statements before presenting them to the database server.

Processing Data

As we have seen, a JDBC application must load the appropriate driver and connect to a database. In practice, this involves very few method calls. The bulk of the work in a database application takes place in the processing of the database data. That involves using primarily three JDBC classes: the `Statement` class, the `PreparedStatement` class, and the `ResultSet` class.

The designers of the JDBC API made a distinction between the execution of a SQL statement and the processing of results from a statement. For this reason, there are distinct classes designed for executing SQL statements (`Statement`, `PreparedStatement`) and examining the results (`ResultSet`).

The `Statement` class encapsulates the calls used to create and execute SQL statements. Where the `Statement` class expects to receive and execute a SQL statement once, the `PreparedStatement` class allows a SQL statement to be processed before it is used and then executed multiple times with potentially different parameters. A `Statement` object can execute both SQL and Data Manipulation Language (DML) statements, including `select`, `insert`, `update`, and `delete`. The `Statement` class can also be used to execute Data Definition Language (DDL) statements, including `create table`, `alter table`, `create schema`, and `drop table`.

Both the `Statement` and the `PreparedStatement` class provide methods that can return results. The results returned by these methods are encapsulated in the `ResultSet` class. The `ResultSet` allows database results to be extracted either serially, in the arbitrary order in which they are received from the database, or using a *scroll cursor* capability where the dataset returned can be reviewed in random order if the database server and the JDBC driver support it. A `ResultSet` may also provide the ability to update the database using the `ResultSet` object.

A Program Example

A good place to start is with a complete working example that shows all of the parts necessary to complete the puzzle. The following code example demonstrates the retrieval and processing of data from a data source. It is similar to examples shown in the previous chapter, with a few new twists.

```
1.import java.sql.*;
2.import javax.sql.*;
3.import javax.naming.*;
4.
5.public class StatementExampleX {
6.
7.public static void main( String args[] ) {
8.
9.ResultSet rs     = null;
10.Connection con  = null;
11.
12.try {
13.
14.    //
15.    // Either connect to an existing poolman instance
16.    // or start poolman here. This will register JNDI name
17.    // with the JNDI service provider and initialize pools
18.    //
19.
20.    //
21.    // JNDI startup parameters are stored in
```

```
22.        // the "jndi.properties" file in the classpath.
23.        //
24.          InitialContext ctx = new InitialContext( );
25.
26.        // get the DataSource from the JNDI name server
27.         DataSource ds = (DataSource) ctx.lookup("moviesmysql");
28.
29.        // get the connection from the DataSource
30.        con =  ds.getConnection( );
31.
32.        // create a Statement class to execute the SQL statement
33.        // create two statements from the same connection
34.        Statement stmt = con.createStatement();
35.
36.        //
37.        // execute a query. can be an update or a select will still
38.        // use the same code to process the query
39.        //
40.        String[] queries = {"select * from users",
41.                             "select * from movies",
42.      "update users set country = 'USA'", // perform update
43.      "select * from users"};             // view update results
44.
45.for ( int n = 0; n < queries.length; n++ ) {
46.
47.      //
48.      // execute the query
49.      //
50.      System.out.println("\n** Executing query: " + n + " : " +
51.                          queries[n] );
52.      boolean isResultSet = stmt.execute( queries[n] );
53.
54.      //
55.      // if we were successful, get a ResultSet
56.      //
57.      if ( isResultSet ) {
58.          rs = stmt.getResultSet();
59.      }
60.
61.      //
62.      // print the results whether this an update or a select
63.      //
64.      if ( isResultSet ) {  // it's a ResultSet
65.          System.out.println( "\nSelect Performed - Results: " );
66.
67.          while ( rs.next() ) {
68.             //
69.             //
70.             //
71.             System.out.println("** Table: " +
72.                         rs.getMetaData().getTableName(1) );
73.
```

```
74.
75.                       //
76.               // loop through all columns in the ResultSet
77.                 //
78.           for ( int i = 1;
79.                       i < rs.getMetaData().getColumnCount();
80.                       i++ ) {
81.                  System.out.println( "\tColumn: "    +
82.                            rs.getMetaData().getColumnName(i) +
83.                  " - value :\t" +
84.                            rs.getObject(i) ); // value
85.                  }
86.          }
87.
88.        }
89.     else {              // it's an update
90.        System.out.println("\n Update Performed - Rows updated: " +
91.                            stmt.getUpdateCount() );
92.        }
93.
94.rs =  null; // reset this for the next loop
95.
96.} // end for loop
97.
98.}
99.catch (SQLException e) {
100.
101.     // display SQL specific exception information
102.     System.out.println("*************************" );
103.     System.out.println("SQLException in main: " + e.getMessage() );
104.     System.out.println("** SQLState: " + e.getSQLState());
105.     System.out.println("** SQL Error Code: " + e.getErrorCode());
106.     System.out.println("*************************" );
107.     e.printStackTrace();
108.}
109.catch (Exception e) {
110.     System.out.println("Exception in main: " + e.getMessage() );
111.     e.printStackTrace();
112.}
113.finally {
114.
115.    try {
116.
117.    if ( con != null )
118.            con.close();
119.    }
120.    catch (SQLException e) {
121.            e.printStackTrace();
122.    }
123.}
124.
125.
```

```
126.
127.}
128.
129.}
130.}
```

This program connects to a data source, executes several SQL statements, and examines the results of the statement execution. Though for convenience and simplicity, the SQL statements are hardcoded into the program, they are treated in a generic way by the code. This means that once the program code begins processing the query, it assumes that it doesn't know what type of database query it is. The program does not know whether or not the query is a select query or an update query.

The program code begins by identifying the package names for import on lines 1 through 4. Several variables that will be used in the program are declared on lines 9 through 11. An initial JNDI context is obtained on line 24 and used to look up a `DataSource` reference for the `moviesmysql` data source on line 27. The `DataSource` object is then used to obtain a `Connection` object on line 30.

The `Connection` object is used to obtain a single `Statement` object on line 33. This statement object is used to process all of the queries to be executed by the program. A String array is used to store the queries that will be processed in this example. This array is declared and populated on lines 41 through 43.

A `for` loop starting at line 45 is used to process the array of queries. All processing within the `for` loop makes no assumption about the nature of the query being processed. The queries are effectively treated as *dynamic queries* within this loop.

The loop iterates for the length of the queries array (`< queries.length`). as indicated on line 45. For reach iteration of the loop, it will execute the query and examine the results. The `Statement` class `execute` method is used to execute the query on line 52. It takes a string argument representing the query to be executed. The query can be either a database update or a `select` statement. The `execute` method returns a boolean value, which is stored in the `isResultSet` boolean variable. If the value is true, then the first statement executed by the execute method returned a `ResultSet`. If it returns false, then the first SQL statement executed was an update.

The `if` conditional statement on line 57 tests the result `isResult` boolean variable, and if it is set true, will continue processing the query results. If the method returns true, then the `ResultSet` is retrieved using a call to the `Statement` class `getResultSet` method on line 58.

The next section of the code processes the `ResultSet`, if in fact there is a `ResultSet`; otherwise, it processes the update count for the update operation that was performed. If there is a `ResultSet`, then the `while` loop is executed on lines 67 through 86 to process the results in the `ResultSet`.

This processing of the ResultSet makes few assumptions about the contents of the ResultSet. It is intended to demonstrate some of the features available for managing dynamic queries. Within the processing on line 72 loop, a ResultSetMetaData object is obtained for the ResultSet. This object can be used to gather information about the contents of the ResultSet. In this example, the ResultSetMetaData object is used to determine the name of the table for the column being output and the name of the column. Later in the program, on line 81, the ResultSetMetaData object is used to determine the number of columns in the ResultSet, allowing the loop on line 81 to iterate through all of the columns in the current ResultSet row.

If the else condition on line 89 is executed, then the ResultSet reference was null and the query is assumed (and the program logic would ensure it) to have been an update query. The update count is obtained on line 91 with a call to the Statement class getUpdateCount method.

On line 94, the ResultSet reference rs is set to null. This is required, since this variable is used as an indicator in the program and would be set incorrectly on successive update loops.

Lines 94 through 122 are used to catch the various exceptions that may be thrown in the main program block. As a result of executing this program, the following output would be produced.

```
** Executing query: 0 : select * from users
Select Performed - Results:
** Table: users
        Column: user_id - value :      101
        Column: first_name - value :  Cal
        Column: last_name - value :   Coder
        Column: address1 - value :     12 Joe DiMaggio Rd.
        Column: address2 - value :     null
        Column: city - value :West Amwell
        Column: state_province - value :      NY
        Column: postal_code - value : 12134
        Column: country - value :      UK
** Table: users
        Column: user_id - value :      201
        Column: first_name - value :  Carrie
        Column: last_name - value :   Coder
        Column: address1 - value :     25 Norma Jean La.
        Column: address2 - value :     null
        Column: city - value :East Amwell
        Column: state_province - value :      NY
        Column: postal_code - value : 21393
        Column: country - value :      UK
** Executing query: 1 : select * from movies
Select Performed - Results:
** Table: movies
        Column: movie_id - value :     3
        Column: movie_name - value :  Stamping Out the Evil Null Reference
```

```
     Column: release_date - value :        2001-01-01
     Column: movie_desc - value :  ** not provided **
     Column: special_promotion - value :  1
     Column: update_date - value : 2002-01-14
     Column: category - value :     Comedy
** Table: movies
     Column: movie_id - value :     4
     Column: movie_name - value :  The Last Compile
     Column: release_date - value :        2000-01-11
     Column: movie_desc - value :  ** not provided **
     Column: special_promotion - value :  2
     Column: update_date - value : 2002-01-14
     Column: category - value :     Comedy
** Table: movies
     Column: movie_id - value :     602
     Column: movie_name - value :  The Final Test
     Column: release_date - value :        1997-01-22
     Column: movie_desc - value :  ** not provided **
     Column: special_promotion - value :  1
     Column: update_date - value : 2001-01-10
     Column: category - value :     Thriller
** Table: movies
     Column: movie_id - value :     601
     Column: movie_name - value :  One Last Try Before the Lights Go Down
     Column: release_date - value :        1998-01-11
     Column: movie_desc - value :  ** not provided **
     Column: special_promotion - value :  2
     Column: update_date - value : 2002-01-14
     Column: category - value :     Comedy
** Table: movies
     Column: movie_id - value :     902
     Column: movie_name - value :  Another Dog Day
     Column: release_date - value :        2002-05-22
     Column: movie_desc - value :  ** not provided **
     Column: special_promotion - value :  1
     Column: update_date - value : 2001-10-20
     Column: category - value :     Documentary
** Executing query: 2 : update users set country = 'USA'
 Update Performed - Rows updated: 2
** Executing query: 3 : select * from users
Select Performed - Results:
** Table: users
     Column: user_id - value :     101
     Column: first_name - value :  Cal
     Column: last_name - value :   Coder
     Column: address1 - value :    12 Joe DiMaggio Rd.
     Column: address2 - value :    null
     Column: city - value :West Amwell
     Column: state_province - value :      NY
     Column: postal_code - value : 12134
     Column: country - value :     USA
** Table: users
```

```
Column: user_id - value :      201
Column: first_name - value :   Carrie
Column: last_name - value :    Coder
Column: address1 - value :     25 Norma Jean La.
Column: address2 - value :     null
Column: city - value :East Amwell
Column: state_province - value :     NY
Column: postal_code - value : 21393
Column: country - value :      USA
```

This example provided an introduction to using JDBC to retrieve rows and review them. But it did not use all of the methods available in the `Statement` class—that would have made for a very long and tedious example. To be thorough, the following sections cover the `Statement` class in more detail, using code snippets to demonstrate many of the methods within the class.

The Statement Class

In any JDBC application, a `Connection` object is obtained either from the `DriverManager` or from the `DataSource`. This object is an instance of the `Connection` class, which encapsulates the functionality of the data source connection and acts as a *factory* (effectively implementing a Factory design pattern) for the creation of `Statement` and `PreparedStatement` objects.

A SQL `select` statement that is expected to return results is executed using the `executeQuery` method of the `Statement` class. This method returns a `ResultSet` object, which contains the results of the query. A SQL `update` statement is executed using the `executeUpdate` method, which returns an integer representing the number of rows affected by the update.

The `Statement` class is best used when a query is going to be executed only once and return results. If a query is going to be executed repeatedly, then the `PreparedStatement` class provides better performance. (The `PreparedStatement` class is described in the following section of this chapter.)

Efficient SQL Execution

If a statement is to be executed multiple times, it is better for performance reasons to use the `PreparedStatement` class to execute the SQL statement. A prepared statement is sent to the database engine to be parsed and optimized before being used. Therefore, each time the statement is executed, the overhead of parsing and optimization is eliminated.

Executing the Query

The `Statement` class provides a number of methods for executing queries. Which method is used depends on the nature of the application. The methods available are called using the following signatures.

- `boolean execute(String sql)`
- `ResultSet executeQuery(String sql)`
- `int executeUpdate(String sql)`
- `int[] executeBatch()`
- `void addBatch(String sql)`
- `void clearBatch()`

The `execute` method in the `Statement` class takes a string argument that contains the SQL statement to execute. The SQL statement can be any type of SQL statement—an `insert` or `update` statement, a `select` query, or a `create table` statement, or a stored procedure that returns multiple results. The `execute` method returns a boolean value indicating true if the statement executed was a `ResultSet` or false if it was an `update` statement. If the SQL statement executed using the `execute` method returns multiple `ResultSet` objects, then the `getMoreResults` method can be called to determine if there are more results to retrieve, and the `getResultSet` method can be called to retrieve the next `ResultSet`. The previous example demonstrated the use of this method but did not call `getMoreResults`, since only one `ResultSet` was returned by the executed statement. Generally speaking, the `execute` method is a convenient method to use if the specific type of SQL statement being executed is not known.

The `executeQuery` method is used to execute queries against the database. The intention of the name is to imply that only queries or `select` operations are to be executed with this method. Unfortunately, the term *database query* is often applied to database update operations as well as to database select operations. This method, however, should be used to execute only database `select` queries that are expected to return a `ResultSet`. It is allowed that the `ResultSet` returned may be empty (and that is not an error).

The `executeQuery` method accepts a string that contains a valid SQL query. If escape processing is turned on for the database, then the string may have valid JDBC escape sequences in the SQL statement. Only one SQL statement should be passed in the string.

The `executeQuery` method returns a `ResultSet`. As with most Java methods, this return value could be ignored, but this is not common practice with JDBC. (The `execute` method provides more coherent syntax for select operations where results will be ignored.) The following code snippet provides an example of the `executeQuery` method.

```
. . .
    // get the DataSource from the JNDI name server
    DataSource ds = (DataSource) ctx.lookup("movies");

    // get the connection from the DataSource
    con = ds.getConnection( );

    // create a Statement class to execute the SQL statement
    Statement stmt = con.createStatement();

    // execute the SQL statement and get the results in a ResultSet
    ResultSet rs   = stmt.executeQuery
                    ("select movie_name, release_date from movies" );
. . .
```

In this code snippet, a `Connection` object is obtained from the `DataSource` and is used to create a `Statement` object. The `executeQuery` method is used to execute a SQL `select` statement to retrieve specific columns for all rows in the `movies` table.

The `executeUpdate` method is used to execute queries that perform database update operations. This method returns an integer count for the number of records updated by the update operation. While it appears to be common practice to ignore the return value from this method, this is not recommended. The following code snippet provides an example of the `executeUpdate` method.

```
. . .
DataSource ds = (DataSource) ctx.lookup("movies");
    //
    // get the connection from the DataSource
    //
    con = ds.getConnection( );
    //
    // create a Statement class to execute the SQL statement
    //
    Statement stmt = con.createStatement();
    //
    // turn auto-commit
    //
    con.setAutoCommit( false );
    //
    // we are now in a transaction ... perform a series of updates
    //
    int updateResult = stmt.executeUpdate(
  "insert into users (user_id, first_name, last_name, address1," +
  " city, state_province, postal_code, country)   " +
  " values ( 0, 'Fred', 'Smith', '2020 Nowhere Lane', " +
  " 'Newark', 'NJ', '09090', 'US');" );
. . .
```

In this example, a `DataSource` is obtained for the `movies` data source and then used to create a `Statement` object. Then, as is common with database update operations, a transaction boundary must be established to span multiple database update operations. Since the autocommit facility of JDBC is turned on by default, it must be set off before a multistatement transaction can be created. The `executeUpdate` method is then called, and the results of the update operation—how many rows were updated by the `update` statement—are returned as an integer value and stored in the `updateResult` variable. At some later point in the code (not shown), the transaction will be either committed or rolled back based on the success or failure of the individual SQL statements being executed.

Working with Batches

As of JDBC 2.1, the JDBC API supports batch operations for updates if the underlying driver and database support it. Batch update operations allow multiple updates to be directed at the database at one time, thus providing the potential of improved update performance. Batches are supported using the following methods.

- `int[] executeBatch()`
- `void addBatch(String sql)`
- `void clearBatch()`

The `addBatch` method takes a string argument that contains the SQL update operation to be added to the batch. This method is called repeatedly with each separate SQL statement to be added to the batch. Alternatively, the `clearBatch` method could be called to clear the batch of any existing entries; this method should be called in any code that may be reusing a `Statement` object for batch operations.

Once all SQL entries have been added to a batch statement, the batch can be executed using the `executeBatch` method. The `executeBatch` method returns an integer array containing corresponding integer values for each update operation performed in the batch. The integer entries correspond in sequence to the update operations, so the first update operation results would be stored in the result array element zero, the second in the result array element one, and so on. The following code snippet provides an example of the batch update operations in JDBC.

```
...
//
// get the DataSource from the JNDI name server
//
DataSource ds = (DataSource)
        ctx.lookup("movies-mysql");
//
// get the connection from the DataSource
```

```
      //
      con = ds.getConnection( );
      //
      // create a Statement class to
      // execute the SQL statement
      //
      Statement stmt = con.createStatement();
      //
      // add a batch of SQL statements
      //
      stmt.addBatch(
"insert into users (user_id, first_name, last_name) " +
" values ( 101, 'Sam', 'Snape')" );

      stmt.addBatch(
"insert into users (user_id, first_name, last_name) " +
" values ( 102, 'Sal', 'Snake')" );

      stmt.addBatch(
"insert into movies (movie_id, movie_name) " +
                          " values ( 201, 'The Evil Null Reference')" );
      stmt.addBatch("update movies   " +
                          " set movie_desc = '** not provided **' " );
      // execute the batch and get the results
      //
      int results[] = stmt.executeBatch();
      //
      // print the results. integer values represents rows updated
      //
      for (int n=0;n<results.length;n++)
          System.out.println("Result from query " + n +
                             " = " + results[n] );
...
```

In this code snippet, the DataSource is obtained for the movies-mysql data source. The DataSource object obtained is used to create a Statement object, and the addBatch method of the Statement class is then called repeatedly to add SQL update statements to the Statement object. Once all appropriate update statements have been added to the batch, the executeBatch method is called, and the results are stored in an integer array. This integer array is then examined in a for loop to determine the results of the batch update operation.

Examining Query Results

Once a SQL statement has been executed, the program needs to examine the results. If the SQL statement was a select query, then a ResultSet is returned, and the results of the query are examined using ResultSet class methods (covered later in this chapter). If the query was an update query, then results of the statement execution can be examined with the `Statement` class methods listed below.

- `int getUpdateCount()`
- `boolean getMoreResults()`
- `ResultSet getResultSet()`

The `getUpdateCount` method returns the number of records updated by the last executed `update` statement. If the last statement executed was a `select` query, then this method should return a –1.

The `getMoreResults` method returns a boolean value indicating whether or not there are more `ResultSet` objects available from the last executed query. This method closes any currently open `ResultSet` objects returned by the `Statement` object and requires a call to the `getResultSet` method to obtain the next `ResultSet`.

```
. . .
//
// get the DataSource from the JNDI name server
//
DataSource ds = (DataSource) ctx.lookup("movies-mysql");
//
// get the connection from the DataSource
//
con = ds.getConnection( );
//
// create a Statement class to execute the SQL statement
//
Statement stmt = con.createStatement();
//
// execute a query that returns multiple ResultSet objects
//
isResultSet = stmt.execute( query );
if ( isResultSet )  {

    //
    // loop through all returned results
    //
    while( stmt.getMoreResults() ) {
        //
    // if true, then we have a result set
    //
        rs = stmt.getResultSet();
        //
        // process the ResultSet
        //
        processResults( rs ) ;
    }
```

```
    }
    else {                // it's an update
        System.out.println("\n Update Performed - Rows updated: " +
                            stmt.getUpdateCount() );
    }
...
```

In this code snippet, the `DataSource` is used to obtain a `Connection` object, which is then used to create a `Statement` object. A query that will return multiple `ResultSet` objects is executed using the `Statement execute` method.

The return value from the `execute` method is a boolean value that indicates whether or not the execute method has returned results. If the method returns a true value, then a `ResultSet` has been returned. In this code snippet, the return value from the execute method (`isResultSet`) is used in an `if` statement; if the value is true, then a `while` loop is executed using the `getMoreResults` method. As long as the `getMoreResults` method returns true, then there is a `ResultSet` that can be retrieved using the `getResultSet` method.

If, however, the return value from the `execute` method is false, then the `execute` method executed an update, and the `getUpdateCount` method is called to return the number of rows that have been updated.

Controlling and Tuning Results Processing

When a `select` query is executed, results are provided in the form of a `ResultSet` object as returned by the `Statement` object. The behavior of this `ResultSet` object is partly controlled by the `Statement` object. (This is largely because the database system should be informed of how the results will be processed when the statement is executed.) A number of methods are available that may optionally be used by the driver to control the processing of database queries. These methods are as follows.

- `int getFetchSize()`
- `int getMaxFieldSize()`
- `int getMaxRows()`
- `void setFetchSize(int rows)`
- `void setMaxRows(int max)`
- `void setMaxFieldSize(int max)`

These methods allow examination and manipulation of the size of the *fetch* buffer. The process of retrieving rows from the database is often referred to as a fetch operation. The integer value returned by the `getFetchSize` method is the number of rows that will be retrieved in increments during the processing of a `ResultSet`. The default value for the fetch size is dependent on the database vendor. The `setFetchSize` method can be used to set the size of the fetch buffer for the database driver by passing an integer value for the size of the fetch buffer in rows.

Performance can be improved by tuning the fetch buffer size to an appropriate size for the operation being performed. For example, if the application component being developed will probably only work with 50 rows from a `select` query, then setting the fetch buffer size to 50 would improve performance. If in this example you consider the alternative of setting the fetch buffer size to 200, then the component would be required to wait for 150 rows to be placed in the fetch buffer (instead of the 50 that the client is ready to use), rows that may never be used by the application. Additionally, in this hypothetical example, the 200 rows would require allocation of additional memory that is not really needed by the application.

The fetch buffer size is an internal buffer size that provides a hint or some advice to the database driver. The database driver and the database are not required to use this information. If the fetch buffer size is set to zero, then the hint for the fetch buffer size is explicitly ignored by the database driver and an internal default value is used; this is the default value for this parameter.

The `getMaxRows` method can be used to determine the maximum number of rows that a driver can return for `select` query processing. This method returns an integer indicating the current setting for the maximum number of rows to be returned by a `ResultSet`. A return value of zero indicates that there is no fixed limit to the number of rows returned (a common default setting). The default value returned is vendor-specific. Per the JDBC specification, if this limit is exceeded, then additional rows are silently dropped; that is, no exception is thrown. Setting and using this limit should therefore be done with caution.

The `getMaxFieldSize` method returns an integer representing the maximum number of bytes that certain fields should have. The `setMaxFieldSize` method takes an integer argument representing the number of bytes that certain fields can contain before being returned by the driver. These methods apply only to the JDBC data types of `BINARY`, `VARBINARY`, `LONGVARBINARY`, `CHAR`, and `VARCHAR`. These fields are quietly truncated if the size is exceeded; this means that no exception will be thrown. The following code snippet provides an example of these methods.

. . .

```
// get the DataSource from the JNDI name server
DataSource ds = (DataSource) ctx.lookup("movies-mysql");
// get the connection from the DataSource
con = ds.getConnection( );
// create a Statement class to execute the SQL statement
Statement stmt = con.createStatement();
//
// get some information about the fetch limits
//
System.out.println( "Fetch size: " + stmt.getFetchSize() );
System.out.println( "Field size: " + stmt.getMaxFieldSize() );
```

```
System.out.println( "Max rows: " + stmt.getMaxRows() );
//
// tune these parameters
//
stmt.setMaxRows( 500 );
stmt.setFetchSize( 100 );
...
```

In this code snippet, the `Connection` object returns a `Statement` object, which is used to obtain the current settings (the default settings) for the fetch buffer size, the maximum field size, and the maximum number of rows to be retrieved using a `ResultSet`. Running this portion of the application against a MySql database returns the following output.

```
Fetch size: 0
Field size: 1048576
Max rows: 0
```

This indicates the that fetch buffer size for the data source is set to zero, indicating the fetch buffer size hint has not been set to any particular value (this is the default), the field size for the data types affected by `setMaxFieldSize` is 1,048,576 bytes, and there is no limit on the number of rows returned by a `ResultSet`. The settings for the fetch buffer size and the maximum number of rows are then changed to suit the application.

Controlling Query Processing

Several aspects of query processing are dictated by the `Statement` object. The amount of time the driver will wait for a query to execute and the type of concurrency to be used by the database can be controlled using `Statement` object methods. The direction in which a `ResultSet` will be processed can also be passed to the database as a hint for execution of the query. The methods used to control this behavior are as follows.

- int getQueryTimeout()
- int getResultSetConcurrency()
- int getResultSetType()
- int getFetchDirection()
- void setFetchDirection(int direction)
- void setQueryTimeout(int seconds)

The `getResultSetConcurrency` method returns the concurrency type (as specified by integer constants in the `ResultSet` class) defined for `ResultSet` objects created by the `Statement`. The `getResultSetType` returns an integer, which indicates the type of `ResultSet` created by this `Statement` as defined by the integer constants in the `ResultSet` class. There are no corresponding set methods for these methods in the `Statement` class because the `ResultSet` behavior is set when the `Statement` object is created. The `ResultSet` behavior for `ResultSet` objects created by a `Statement` object is dictated when the `Statement` object is created using an overloaded version of the `Connection` `createStatement` method, as follows.

```
Statement createStatement(int resultSetType,
                          int resultSetConcurrency)
```

The `ResultSet` type and `ResultSet` concurrency values passed into this method are integer constants from the `ResultSet` class. Possible values for concurrency are `ResultSet.CONCUR_READ_ONLY` and `ResultSet.CONCUR_UPDATABLE`. Possible values for type are `ResultSet.TYPE_FORWARD_ONLY`, `ResultSet.TYPE_SCROLL_INSENSITIVE`, and `ResultSet.TYPE_SCROLL_SENSITIVE`.

The time the driver will wait for a query to execute can be set using the `setQueryTimeout` method. This method is passed an integer indicating the number of seconds to wait for a query to execute. If the value specified is exceeded, then an exception is thrown. The `getQueryTimeout` method returns an integer indicating the current setting of this parameter. The default value is vendor-specific. A value of zero indicates an unlimited timeout and is a common vendor setting. (Note that even with an unlimited setting for a query timeout parameter, network socket timeout values could potentially cancel a long-running query.) Many database vendors also allow query timeout parameters to be set, which can be used to timeout a query initiated by a client irrespective of the client timeout setting.

The `setFetchDirection` method takes an integer argument representing a hint to the database driver on the direction in which query processing will proceed. The `getFetchDirection` method returns an integer argument representing the fetch direction. The integer value is one of the integer constants in the `ResultSet`, as follows.

- `ResultSet.FETCH_FORWARD`
- `ResultSet.FETCH_REVERSE`
- `ResultSet.FETCH_UNKNOWN`

The default value is `ResultSet.FETCH_FORWARD`. Corresponding methods for getting and setting the fetch direction also exist in the `ResultSet` class. Since many databases provide optimizations based on how a `select` query will be processed, it may be best to set these parameters in the `Statement` object before the query is executed.

Miscellaneous and Utility Methods

A number of miscellaneous methods are available to control processing and retrieve useful information about the `Statement`. These methods are as follows.

- void setCursorName(String name)
- void setEscapeProcessing(boolean enable)
- Connection getConnection()
- void clearWarnings()
- SQLWarning getWarnings()
- void cancel()
- void close()

The `setCursorName` method can be passed a string argument for the cursor name to set the cursor name for all cursors to be created by the `Statement` object. This name can then be used in positioned `update` and `delete` statements. This method will only work on databases and JDBC drivers that support positioned update as indicated by the `DatabaseMetaData supportsPositionedUpdate` method; otherwise, this method will quietly fail.

As of JDBC 2.0, drivers may optionally support updates through `ResultSets`. This provides a vendor-neutral facility for positioned updates. While it is assumed that JDBC drivers will map this capability to the vendor-specific syntax, this is not required.

Controlling JDBC Escape Processing

The `setEscapeProcessing` method can be used to turn escape processing in the driver on or off. By default, escape processing is turned on in the JDBC driver. JDBC escape processing allows the JDBC driver to intervene in the processing of SQL queries. Since some SQL features are not implemented by all databases, and some features are implemented differently, the escape processing feature of the JDBC driver allows a standard JDBC "escape syntax" to be used to access these features and leaves it to the JDBC driver to implement the database-specific syntax. This enhances the portability across databases of the JDBC application. JDBC escape processing uses special characters in the SQL string to inform the driver that it must preprocess that portion of the query.

The escape processing feature is implemented for scalar functions, date and time literals, outer joins, stored procedures, and `where` clause matching. For instance, escape processing can be used to provide a standard syntax for date literals and timestamp literals, as the following code snippet shows.

```
ResultSet rs = stmt.executeQuery(
                "select *  from movies " +
```

```
"where movie_date = {d '2001-01-12'} and  "
" return_timestamp = {d '2002-01-28' 12:00:00' ");
```

Virtually every database vendor provides a unique syntax for processing outer joins. JDBC provides a standard escape processing syntax using the following format.

```
{oj <table_name> [LEFT|RIGHT|FULL] OUTER JOIN
          <table_name> | <outer_join>
          on <search_condition> }
```

Using this syntax, a left outer join could be used to join the `user_rentals` and `movies` table, thus returning all movies whether or not they have been rented. The following code snippet demonstrates this join using JDBC escape syntax.

```
...
Statement stmt;
DatabaseMetaData dmd;
...
  System.out.println( "supportsFullOuterJoins: " +
                      dmd.supportsLimitedOuterJoins() );
  ResultSet rs = stmt.executeQuery(
          "select user_id, movies.movie_id, movie_name, rental_date " +
      " from {oj movies LEFT OUTER JOIN user_rentals " +
      " on movies.movie_id=user_rentals.movie_id} " );
...
```

Stored procedures can also be called using escape syntax, as the following code demonstrates.

```
...
  //
  // execute the processMovieTransfers stored procedure
  //
  CallableStatement stmt2 = conn.prepareCall(
              "{?= call  processMovieTransfers(?)}");
    stmt.registerOutParameter(0, Types.VARCHAR);
    stmt.setObject(2, new Integer(43));
    if (stmt.execute()) {
      ResultSet rs = stmt.getResultSet();
...
```

The getConnection Method

The `getConnection` is a convenience method that retrieves the database connection that was used to create this `Statement` object. Having this method available provides access to the methods of the `Connection` object, methods which allow transactions to be managed and metadata information about the database to be retrieved (through a `DatabaseMetaData` object).

Processing Statement Warnings

The `clearWarnings` method clears all warnings off the `Statement` object. The `getWarnings` method retrieves the warnings for the `Statement` object. Warnings are received in a chain, one warning chained to the next in the chain, so that all warnings must be iterated through to determine the full extent of the warnings retrieved. The following code snippet demonstrates.

```
...
//
// check for warnings on the Statement
//
SQLWarning sqlw = statement.getWarnings();

//
// warning may be null reference
//
if (sqlw != null) {

    //
    // iterate through the chain of warnings
    //
    while ( sqlw != null ) {
        System.out.println("Warning: " + sqlw );
        sqlw = sqlw.getNextWarning();
    }
else
    System.out.println("There are no warnings.");
...
```

This code retrieves a `SQLWarning` object reference for the `Statement`. The code then checks to determine whether or not the warning object is null (which is common). If the `SQLWarning` object is not null, then the warnings are iterated through using a `while` loop. Each warning message is displayed using the `toString` method of the `SQLWarning` interface implementation.

The cancel Method and the close Method

The `cancel` method allows a database query to be canceled through the `Statement` that executed the query. Since the various execute methods (`executeQuery`, `execute`, and others) block while an `execute` method is processing, some other processing thread must be used to cancel the currently executing processing thread (the thread that executed the query with the `Statement` object).

The `close` method closes the database connection associated with the `Statement` object. If the `Statement` object had a `ResultSet` object, it is also closed. (Closing a `Connection` object also closes any associated objects and is the most common approach for releasing database resources.)

Exceptions and Errors and Warnings

The JDBC API provides a number of exceptions and warnings that capture error information useful to database programmers.

The SQLException Class

A `SQLException` is thrown by a large number of the JDBC methods. This exception inherits from `java.lang.Exception` and provides the usual exception reason or message through the inherited `getMessage` method. But this exception also provides information specific to databases, such as the SQLCode of the error and the SQLState—standardized database error reporting facilities.

The `SQLException` class contains a string, which is the reason given by the database server or JDBC driver for the exception; the SQL state, which is a standardized string containing information about the state of SQL processing for the exception; and an integer error code containing an error code specific to the database vendor or provider. Table 6–4 contains the constructors for this exception class.

The `SQLException` contains a small number of methods to provide access to its internal data about the exception that was thrown. Table 6–5 provides a list of these methods.

Table 6–4   *Constructors for the SQLException Class*

Constructor	Description
`SQLException()`	Creates a new `SQLException` with null values for the reason, SQLState, and vendor error code.
`SQLException( String reason)`	Creates a new `SQLException` with the reason provided as a parameter. Substitutes a null value for the SQLState and vendor error code.
`SQLException(String reason, String SQLState)`	Creates a new `SQLException` with the reason provided as a parameter and the SQLState provided as a parameter. Substitutes a zero for the vendor error code.
`SQLException(String reason, String SQLState, int vendorCode)`	Creates a new `SQLException` with the reason provided, the SQLState provided, and the vendor error code provided as a parameter.

Table 6–5	Methods for the SQLException Class

Method	Description
`int getErrorCode()`	Returns the vendor error code for the exception that was thrown to create the exception.
`SQLException getNextException()`	Retrieves the next exception in the chain, if there is another exception.
`String setNextException(SQLException e)`	Sets the next exception in the chain of exceptions attached to the current object.

The SQLWarning Class

The `SQLWarning` is similar in use and functionality to the `SQLException` class except that warnings are by definition some event or occurrence that the application can possibly overcome. A `SQLWarning` is not thrown by the application, as is an exception, so declaring a `catch` block for `SQLWarning` will have no effect (and would generate a compile-time error). Instead, the `SQLWarning` is returned by the `getWarnings` methods of the `Connection` and `Statement` classes. Table 6–6 lists the constructors for the `SQLWarning` class.

The `SQLWarning` class is a subclass of `SQLException` and so inherits the methods of that class, making those methods available to call if needed. Table 6–7 lists the methods in this class.

Table 6–6	Constructors for the SQLWarning Class

Constructor	Description
`SQLWarning()`	Creates a new `SQLWarning` with null values for the reason, SQLState, and vendor error code.
`SQLWarning( String reason)`	Creates a new `SQLWarning` with the reason provided as a parameter. Substitutes a null value for the SQLState and vendor error code.
`SQLWarning(String reason, String SQLState)`	Creates a new `SQLWarning` with the reason provided as a parameter and the SQLState provided as a parameter. Substitutes a zero for the vendor error code.
`SQLWarning(String reason, String SQLState, int vendorCode)`	Creates a new `SQLWarning` with the reason provided, the SQLState provided, and the vendor error code provided as a parameter.

Method	Description
`SQLException getNextWarning()`	Retrieves the next warning in the chain if there is another exception.
`String setNextWarning(SQLWarning w)`	Sets the next warning in the chain of warnings attached to the current object.

The DataTruncation Class

The `DataTruncation` class is a subclass of `SQLException` and provides a warning or exception that specifically reports on errors of data truncation. On SQL `select` operations, a `DataTruncation` warning would be placed on the `Statement` and could be retrieved using the `getWarnings` method. On write operations or database updates, a `DataTruncation` exception would be thrown. The following constructor is available for this class (see Table 6–8).

Table 6–8   *DataTruncation Class Constructor*

Constructor	Description
`DataTruncation( int index, boolean parameter, boolean read, int dataSize, int transferSize)`	Creates a `DataTruncation` object using the specified parameters

The `DataTruncation` class is a subclass of `SQLWarning` and the `SQLException` class and so has access to the inherited methods of that class. The class contains a number of methods to reveal information about truncation that took place, as shown in Table 6–9.

The BatchUpdateException Class

The `BatchUpdateException` is a class that is thrown by the batch update methods in the `Statement` class. This class is a subclass of `SQLException` and simply augments the behaviors of that class to include a method that returns the update counts for the batch just executed. Table 6–10 contains the constructors for this method.

Table 6–9   *DataTruncation Class Methods*

Method	Description
int getDataSize()	Returns an integer indicating the size of the number of bytes that should have been written.
int getIndex()	Returns an index to the column or parameter that was truncated.
Boolean getParameter()	Returns a boolean indicating whether or not the value truncated.
Boolean getRead()	Returns a boolean true if the truncation occurred on a database read operation.
int GetTransferSize()	Returns an integer representing the number of bytes actually transferred.

Table 6–10   *Constructors for the BatchUpdateException Class*

Constructor	Description
BatchUpdateException()	Creates a new BatchUpdateException with null values for the reason, zero for the update counts, and the SQL state.
BatchUpdateException(int[] UpdateCounts)	Creates a new BatchUpdateException with null values for the reason, and the update counts.
BatchUpdateException(String reason, int[] updateCounts)	Creates a new BatchUpdateException with the designated parameters.
BatchUpdateException(String reason, String SQLState, int updateCounts)	Creates a new BatchUpdateException with the designated parameters.

The BatchUpdateException class inherits the methods of its superclass, the SQLException class, which is itself a subclass of the Exception class. This leaves a number of methods available to BatchUpdateException instances. The BatchUpdateException class adds a single method, as shown in Table 6–11.

The getUpdateCounts method returns an integer array. The integer array contains the update counts, the number of records updated for each of the update statements in the batch that generated the exception.

Table 6–11	*Method for the BatchUpdateException Class*

Method	Description
`Int[] getUpdateCounts()`	Returns an integer array of the update count for the updates executed by the batch before the exception was thrown.

SUMMARY

The process of accessing a database with JDBC involves first accessing an appropriate database driver and then obtaining a connection to the database. In this chapter we explored the process of connecting to the database by examining the JDBC interface that describes the connection to the database—the `Connection` interface.

Once a connection has been made, we must present a SQL statement to the database to either extract data (using a `select` query) or update data (using an `update` query). This requires an appropriate object. In this chapter we examined the `Statement` interface, which encapsulates the methods required to execute SQL statements against the relational database. The `PreparedStatement` interface extends the `Statement` interface and provides similar functionality; that interface is examined in Chapter 7.

JDBC: Preparing SQL Statements and Examining Results

INTRODUCTION

The previous chapters introduced us to the all-important JDBC package and saw how to connect to the database and execute SQL statements. In this chapter, we will look at a common technique for optimizing SQL statement execution using prepared statements and we will examine how we examine the results of our queries using result sets.

As we will see, the `PreparedStatement` interface provides methods to optimize the query process using the capability of many databases to prepare a database query before it is executed. This preparation process usually involves parsing the query, identifying the query path (how the data in the tables will be accessed), and saving the information so that the query can be executed by simply finding the prepared information for the query and applying the query to the database.

Using this class, a *prepared* SQL statement is created with placeholders for any parameters in the SQL statement. Parameters can be values in the `where` clause for a `select` or `update` statement, the `values` clause of an `insert` statement, or the `set` clause of an `update` statement. The SQL statement and any parameters are then presented to the database to be *preprocessed*. When the database receives the query, it parses, optimizes, and then retains the query for processing again. Repeated calls to the prepared statement are more efficient, since they do not require the database server to parse and optimize the query. This chapter examines the `PreparedStatement` class in detail.

This chapter also examines the `ResultSet`, the JDBC interface that describes the object that represents the rows returned from the database by the execution of a `select` query. The best place to start with the `ResultSet` class is with an example that shows serial progression through a `ResultSet`, moving from the first row to the last row. An example of random access or scroll cursor `ResultSet`s will also be shown together with a description of the methods used with this type of `ResultSet`. Finally, a demonstration of an *updateable* `ResultSet` will be provided along with the methods used with the `ResultSet`.

THE PREPAREDSTATEMENT

The `PreparedStatement` provides a certain degree of convenience for the Java database developer. Once a SQL statement has been prepared, its object representation becomes the `PreparedStatement` object. The parameters of the query can be changed not by restating the query, but by making method calls on the `PreparedStatement` object.

If the full range of queries to be presented to an application are known when the application is being developed, and the range of queries is limited and manageable, then it may make very good sense to use the `PreparedStatement` class to develop the application.

If all of the queries an application may need to run are known beforehand and the number of queries is limited, then it probably makes sense to use the `PreparedStatement` class over the `Statement` class. This chapter presents an example of just such a JDBC application.

Like the `Statement` class, the `PreparedStatement` class encapsulates the processing of a SQL statement. But unlike the `Statement` class, the `PreparedStatement` class allows a statement to be presented to the database for *preprocessing*, creating *prepared* statement.

A large portion of the `PreparedStatement` class is devoted to setting the values for the prepared statement. The methods to perform these operations make up the bulk of the API.

There are several advantages to using the `PreparedStatement` class over the `Statement` class. As stated previously, the most notable advantage is the improved performance gained by preparing the query before using it. In today's large, complex, intelligent databases there is a certain degree of effort involved in processing a query. Decisions must be made about access paths, memory must be set aside in the database server for the fetch buffer, control blocks must be created to control query processing and manage any threads that may be used, and various other activities must be performed. While this may seem trivial for small queries, for larger, more complex queries (which are not uncommon), this processing could require over a second. For a query that must be executed repeatedly by thousands of users, this would represent a significant drag on performance.

Another advantage of using PreparedStatement objects is that they help modularize the database processing. Each prepared statement object can represent a specific database query and be managed accordingly. The alternative, as shown in previous code snippets and examples, to continually create query strings by appending or inserting query text, can quickly become tedious and cumbersome. For these reasons, the more common approach to query processing with JDBC when the query is known at development time is to use the PreparedStatement class. The following code snippet demonstrates the use of this class.

```
...
//
// initial context information is in jndi.properties file
// get the initial context
//
InitialContext ctx = new InitialContext( );

// get the DataSource from the JNDI name server
DataSource ds = (DataSource) ctx.lookup("movies-mysql");

//
// get the connection from the DataSource
//
con = ds.getConnection( );

//
// create a Statement class to execute the SQL statement
//
PreparedStatement pstmt = con.prepareStatement(
    " select distinct first_name, last_name, state_province, " +
    " movie_name, rental_date "                          +
    " from users, movies, user_rentals "                 +
    " where (users.user_id    = user_rentals.user_id and " +
    "         movies.movie_id  = user_rentals.movie_id) and " +
    "         user_rentals.user_id = ? " );

//
// set the PreparedStatement parameters
//
pstmt.setInt(1, 2); // set to user_id = 2

//
// execute the SQL statement and get the results in a ResultSet
//
ResultSet rs   = pstmt.executeQuery();
```

```
//
// iterate through the ResultSet, displaying two values
// for each row using the getString method
//
while ( rs.next() ) {
        System.out.println( "Name: " + "\t" +
            rs.getString("first_name").trim() + "\t" +
                " " + "\t" +
            rs.getString("last_name").trim() + "\t" +
                " Movie: " +        "\t" +
            rs.getString("movie_name") +
                "\t" +
                " Rental Date: " + "\t" +
            rs.getString("rental_date") );
}
...
```

In this example, a `DataSource` object for the `movies-mysql` data source is obtained from the JNDI name server and used to create a `Connection` object. The `Connection` object is then used to create the `PreparedStatement`. This is done using the `prepareStatement` method, which takes a string argument for the SQL statement to prepare.

The SQL query string passed to this method performs a join between the `users`, `movies`, and `user_rentals` tables. The `where` clause of this query performs a filter operation using the `user_id`; the query will select only movies rented by the `user_id` specified in the `where` clause. The value for the `user_id` is not supplied in the string passed to the `prepareStatement` method. Instead, a ? *placeholder* is placed in the `where` clause where the value should go.

The values for the placeholders in the prepared statement are supplied using various `setXXXX` methods with a separate `setXXXX` method for each JDBC data type. The `setXXXX` methods take two parameters: an integer representing the ordinal position of the parameter moving in a left to right direction in the query statement and *starting at one* (not zero, as Java indexes and almost everything else in Java does). In this example, the first placeholder element to appear in the query string (and the only one) is an integer at position one. The `PreparedStatement` `setInt` call is used to set this integer parameter value to 2. This will have the query execute with a filter clause to retrieve only the movies rented by the user with the user ID of 2 (`user_id = 2`).

One, Not Zero

Arrays, string indexing, and collections all have something in common in Java: they use 0-based ordinal positions. That is, they begin counting positions starting at position 0, so that a substring of the string 0123 from position 0 through position 3 inclusive—in Java syntax, `"0123".substring(0,3)`—would be 012.

But JDBC is a different beast. The positions in a select string list of columns start at 1, not 0. For example,

```
select first_name, last_name, age
from customers
```

In this query, any reference to the first_name would be as column 1, and last_name would be column 2, and so on. Similarly, if we are setting parameters in the where clause, positional parameters are also referenced starting from position 1, as shown below.

```
select first_name, last_name, age, status_code
from customers
where age > ? and
      status_code in (?, ?, ?)
```

In this example, the first parameter to be referenced, the parameter being compared to the age column, is parameter 1, and the next parameter is the first item in the status_code list, which is parameter 2.

This same 1-based strategy persists throughout the JDBC API. For the database developer, it can be a source of frustration, but as shown throughout the code examples in this book, by making minor adjustments in loop control logic, it is easily managed.

(The origin of this seeming inconsistency may be that relational databases and SQL syntax have often referred to these parameters in the same fashion. Thus, to more easily reconcile the JDBC API with existing relational database Call Level Interfaces (CLIs), the JDBC API uses the same approach.)

The PreparedStatement query is then executed using the executeQuery method. As with the Statement class, this method returns a ResultSet representing the rows returned by the query execution.

The processing of the ResultSet is the same as with the Statement class. The values of the ResultSet are examined using a while loop, which will continue to loop as long as the ResultSet next method returns true.

Per the JDBC specification, the PreparedStatement interface extends the Statement interface, so any class that implements the PreparedStatement interface will also provide implementations for all of the Statement interface methods.

The most important and obvious aspect of using the PreparedStatement class is the setting of parameters. The developers of the JDBC driver specification have elected to create separate set methods for each data type. All of these methods take an initial (first) method argument that is an integer indicating the ordinal position of the parameter (or placeholder) in the SQL statement. This parameter position is from left to right as the parameters appear in the statement, starting with the number 1 and progressing up to however many parameters exist in the statement. The second method argument is the value to substitute for the parameter. In several cases, additional arguments are used with the set method signature to clarify the data value (for example, a Calendar object with the setDate method).

Since this class is a subclass of the Statement class (the PreparedStatement interface extends the Statement interface), the various get methods of the Statement class are available. Several methods are provided to manage the parameter substitution mechanism for prepared statements. The following sections explain these methods and provide some code examples as appropriate.

Setting Parameters

As mentioned previously and as will be shown in the following example, the PreparedStatement class allows substitution parameters to be identified in the SQL statement to be executed. These parameters can then be set using various set methods. This approach allows SQL statement parameters to be changed easily using a simple method call. It also avoids the problems associated with placing large and unwieldy parameter values in SQL statement strings. For very large character strings, such as large blocks of text or large binary strings (a CLOB or BLOB column, for example), creating SQL statements as a string becomes difficult if not impossible.

The clearParameters method is used to clear all existing parameter values from the Statement object. Statement objects are generally used to execute a query numerous times with different parameters each time the query is executed. Setting a parameter automatically clears a previous value and substitutes the new value for the parameter. But in cases where not all parameters may be set by the application, the clearParameters method is convenient, since it ensures that all parameters are set to default values.

A PreparedStatement Example

The following code example demonstrates the use of the PreparedStatement class to repeatedly execute queries. The application creates a report, a common usage for the PreparedStatement. The program design was to create a PreparedStatement which reflects the data to be retrieved for each query in the report. These queries are prepared at the start of the program. Then, when the reports are run, the PreparedStatement objects are executed using the parameters provided for the report.

Each report is generated by executing a separate method that accepts parameters for the report and returns a ResultSet. The report is generated by a generic method that accepts a ResultSet and a label for the report. The complete code for this example follows.

PreparedExample.java

```
1.import java.sql.*;
2.import javax.sql.*;
3.import javax.naming.*;
4.import java.util.*;
5.import java.text.*;
6.import java.io.*;
7.import com.codestudio.sql.PoolMan;
8.
9.
10.public class PreparedExample {
11.
12.PreparedStatement rentalsbyDate;
13.PreparedStatement rentalsbyUserID;
14.PreparedStatement rentalsbyCustName;
15.
16.public static void main( String args[] ) {
17.
18.ResultSet rs;
19.
20.Connection con=null;
21.try {
22.
23.      PreparedExample2 pe = new PreparedExample2();
24.
25.      // get the initial context
26.      InitialContext ctx = new InitialContext(  );
27.
28.      // get the DataSource from the JNDI name server
29.      DataSource ds = (DataSource) ctx.lookup("movies");
30.
31.      // get the connection from the DataSource
32.      con = ds.getConnection( );
33.
34.      // prepare statements
35.      pe.doPrepares( con );
36.
37.      // execute a report
38.      // get all records for customer id = 2
39.      rs = pe.getRentalsbyCustName( "Smith" );
40.
41.      // print results
42.      if ( rs != null )
43.          pe.printResults( "Rentals by Customer Name: Smith", rs );
44.
45.      // execute another report
46.      // greater all records greater than or equal to this date
47.      rs = pe.getRentalsbyDate( "2001-01-01" );
48.
49.      // print results
50.      if ( rs != null )
```

```
51.           pe.printResults( "Rentals by Date: > 1/1/2001", rs );
52.
53.      // execute another report
54.      // get all records for customer id = 2
55.      rs = pe.getRentalsbyUserID( 2 );
56.
57.      // print results
58.      if ( rs != null )
59.           pe.printResults( "Rentals by Customer ID: 2", rs );
60.
61.}
62.catch (SQLException e) {
63.
64.      // display SQL specific exception information
65.      System.out.println("*************************" );
66.      System.out.println("SQLException in main: " + e.getMessage() );
67.      System.out.println("** SQLState: " + e.getSQLState());
68.      System.out.println("** SQL Error Code: " + e.getErrorCode());
69.      System.out.println("*************************" );
70.      e.printStackTrace();
71.}
72.catch (Exception e) {
73.      System.out.println("Exception in main: " + e.getMessage() );
74.      e.printStackTrace();
75.}
76.finally {
77.
78.      try {
79.           // close the connection if it exists
80.      if ( con != null )
81.             con.close();
82.      }
83.    catch (SQLException e) {
84.           e.printStackTrace();
85.      }
86.}
87.
88.} // end main
89.
90.void doPrepares( Connection con) {
91.
92.// use instance members to store PreparedStatements
93.try {
94.    rentalsbyDate = con.prepareStatement(
95.       " select distinct first_name, last_name, state_province, " +
96.       " movie_name, rental_date "                      +
97.       " from users, movies, user_rentals "             +
98.       " where (users.user_id    = user_rentals.user_id and " +
99.       "         movies.movie_id  = user_rentals.movie_id) and " +
100.      "         user_rentals.rental_date >= ? " );
101.
102.
```

```
103.    rentalsbyUserID = con.prepareStatement(
104.         " select first_name, last_name, state_province, " +
105.         " movie_name, rental_date "                         +
106.      " from users, movies, user_rentals "                +
107.      " where (users.user_id    = user_rentals.user_id and " +
108.      "          movies.movie_id  = user_rentals.movie_id ) and " +
109.      "          user_rentals.user_id = ? " );
110.
111.    rentalsbyCustName = con.prepareStatement(
112.         " select distinct first_name, last_name, state_province, " +
113.         " movie_name, rental_date "                              +
114.      " from users, movies, user_rentals "                +
115.      " where ( users.user_id    = user_rentals.user_id and " +
116.      "          movies.movie_id = user_rentals.movie_id ) and " +
117.      "          users.last_name like ? " );
118.
119.}
120.catch (SQLException e) {
121.
122.     // display SQL specific exception information
123.     System.out.println("**************************" );
124.     System.out.println("SQLException in doPrepares(): " +
125.                           e.getMessage() );
126.     System.out.println("** SQLState: " + e.getSQLState());
127.     System.out.println("** SQL Error Code: " + e.getErrorCode());
128.     System.out.println("**************************" );
129.     e.printStackTrace();
130.}
131.
132.}
133.// *************************************************************
134.ResultSet getRentalsbyUserID ( int custID ) {
135.
136.ResultSet rs = null;
137.
138.try {
139.
140.// set the customer ID parameter as an integer
141.rentalsbyUserID.setInt(1, custID);
142.
143.// execute the query using the PreparedStatement object
144.rs = rentalsbyUserID.executeQuery();
145.
146.}
147.catch (SQLException e) {
148.
149.     // display SQL specific exception information
150.     System.out.println("**************************" );
151.     System.out.println("SQLException in getRentalsbyUserID(): " +
152.                           e.getMessage() );
153.     System.out.println("** SQLState: " + e.getSQLState());
154.     System.out.println("** SQL Error Code: " + e.getErrorCode());
```

```
155.     System.out.println("*************************" );
156.     e.printStackTrace();
157.
158.}
159.finally {
160.  // return the ResultSet object reference
161.  return rs;
162.}
163.}
164.
165.// ****************************************************************
166.ResultSet getRentalsbyDate( String rentalDate ) {
167.
168.ResultSet rs = null;
169.
170.try {
171.
172.// convert rentalDate string to java.sql.Date and pass
173.rentalsbyDate.setDate(1,  java.sql.Date.valueOf( rentalDate ) );
174.
175.// execute the query using the PreparedStatement object
176.rs = rentalsbyDate.executeQuery();
177.
178.}
179.
180.catch (SQLException e) {
181.
182.     // display SQL specific exception information
183.     System.out.println("*************************" );
184.     System.out.println("SQLException in getRentalsbyDate(): " +
185.                         e.getMessage() );
186.     System.out.println("** SQLState: " + e.getSQLState());
187.     System.out.println("** SQL Error Code: " + e.getErrorCode());
188.     System.out.println("*************************" );
189.     e.printStackTrace();
190.
191.}
192.finally {
193.// return the ResultSet object reference
194.  return rs;
195.}
196.
197.}
198.// ****************************************************************
199.ResultSet getRentalsbyCustName( String custName ) {
200.
201.ResultSet rs = null;
202.
203.try {
204.// set the custName parameter
205.rentalsbyCustName.setString( 1, custName );
206.
```

```
207.// execute the query using the PreparedStatement object
208.rs = rentalsbyCustName.executeQuery();
209.
210.}
211.catch (SQLException e) {
212.
213.     // display SQL specific exception information
214.     System.out.println("***************************" );
215.     System.out.println("SQLException in getRentalsbyCustName(): " +
216.                        e.getMessage() );
217.     System.out.println("** SQLState: " + e.getSQLState());
218.     System.out.println("** SQL Error Code: " + e.getErrorCode());
219.     System.out.println("***************************" );
220.     e.printStackTrace();
221.}
222.finally {
223.   return rs;
224.}
225.
226.}
227.
228.// ****************************************************************
229.void printResults( String header, ResultSet rs) {
230.
231.try {
232.
233.// output a report header
234.System.out.println("*********************************************");
235.System.out.println("\n******** " + header.trim() + " ********" );
236.System.out.println("*********************************************");
237.System.out.println(
238.         "First \tLast \t State \t Movie \t\t\t\tRental Date ");
239.System.out.println(
240.         "----- \t---- \t ----- \t ----- \t\t\t\t----------- ");
241.
242.// output results
243.while ( rs.next() ) {
244.   System.out.println( rs.getString( "first_name") + "\t" +
245.                       rs.getString( "last_name" ) + "\t" +
246.                       rs.getString( "state_province" ) + "\t" +
247.                       formatString( rs.getString( "movie_name" ),
248.                                22) +
249.                            "\t\t" +
250.                       rs.getString( "rental_date" )  ) ;
251.}
252.System.out.println("*********************************************");
253.
254.
255.
256.}
257.
258.catch (SQLException e) {
```

```
259.
260.        // display SQL specific exception information
261.        System.out.println("*************************" );
262.        System.out.println("SQLException in printResults(): " +
263.                                e.getMessage() );
264.        System.out.println("** SQLState: " + e.getSQLState());
265.        System.out.println("** SQL Error Code: " + e.getErrorCode());
266.        System.out.println("*************************" );
267.        e.printStackTrace();
268.
269.}
270.finally {
271.}
272.
273.}
274.// ********************************************************
275.
276.String formatString( String s, int size ) {
277.
278.// declare local work buffers
279.String blanks = "                        ";
280.String retString = null;
281.
282.// pad or trim the string to be exactly 'size' in length
283.
284.if ( s.length() < size )      // need to pad string
285.    retString = s + blanks.substring( 0, size - s.length()) ;
286.else                          // need to trim (substring) string
287.    retString = s.substring( 0, size );
288.
289.return retString;
290.
291.}
292.void clearAllParams() {
293.
294.try {
295.//
296.// call clearParameters on each PreparedStatement object
297.// this will clear all existing parameter settings
298.//
299.rentalsbyDate.clearParameters();
300.rentalsbyUserID.clearParameters();
301.rentalsbyCustName.clearParameters();
302.}
303.catch (SQLException e) {
304.        // display SQL specific exception information
305.        System.out.println("*************************" );
306.        System.out.println("SQLException in clearAllParams(): " +
307.                                e.getMessage() );
308.        System.out.println("** SQLState: " + e.getSQLState());
309.        System.out.println("** SQL Error Code: " + e.getErrorCode());
310.        System.out.println("*************************" );
```

```
311.        e.printStackTrace();
312.
313.}
314.
315.}
```

PreparedExample.java: main Program Block

This code example performs a number of imports on lines 1 through 7, and then declares the `PreparedStatement` instance members on lines 12 through 14; these are declared as instance members to avoid the overhead of passing them as parameters throughout the program.

Since the work performed in this code example is not static and requires an object instance, an instance of the `PreparedExample2` class is created on line 32. Next, the usual JDBC startup operations are performed. The JNDI initial context is obtained on line 26 and used to obtain a `DataSource` object reference on line 29. A `Connection` object is then obtained from the `DataSource` object on line 32.

The remainder of the `main` program block is then devoted to calling the methods that will perform the work for the application. The methods will create the `PreparedStatement` objects, execute the prepared statements and return the results, and then output the results.

Before the prepared statements can be used, they must be declared, and the parameter values must be set. A single method is used to prepare all of the statements. This has the advantage of placing the SQL query strings for the statements in a single location in the code. Since there is a distinct possibility that these statements could change over time, this consistency makes code maintenance easier. The prepared statements are created with a call to the `doPrepares` method on line 35.

The application is now ready to generate a report. To generate a report, a method must be called to execute the appropriate prepared statement and return the results. The method must also be passed the parameters to use to run the report. In this code example, the execution of the prepared statements is contained in several `getXXXX` methods, the first of which is called on line 39. This method, named `getRentalsbyCustName`, is called with a string, which is the customer name. The method uses the string argument to the method, the customer name, and assigns it to a parameter (placeholder) in the prepared statement, and then executes the prepared statement. The method returns the results of the execution of the query in the form of a `ResultSet`.

Once the `getRentalsbyCustName` method is called, the `ResultSet` returned is passed to the `printResults` method. The job of the `printResultsMethod` is to take the `ResultSet` returned by any of the `getXXXX` methods (which all return the same column values in a `ResultSet`) and a string argument that represents the header for the report. These argument values are used to output a simple character-based report. According to the logic in the `main` program block, the `printResults` method is called only if the `ResultSet` object reference returned by the `getXXXX` methods is not null. A null `ResultSet` returned by a `getXXXX` method would indicate an error condition.

Next, in the `main` program block, the `getRentalsbyDate` method is called. This method is passed a date in the format of a string (not a `java.sql.Date` object) and returns a `ResultSet`. As was done previously in the application, the `printResults` method is called to output the results.

Finally, the `getRentalsbyUserID` method is called. This method is passed an integer value for the user ID and returns a `ResultSet`, which is then output using the `printResults` method.

Now that we see the control logic of the `main` program block, we can move on to examine the various methods that perform the work for this application. These are covered in the following sections.

The doPrepares Method

The `doPrepares` method on lines 90 through 132 is used to create the `PreparedStatement` objects used in the application. This method is passed the `Connection` object created in the `main` program block; this is needed to execute the `createPreparedStatement` method called on lines 94, 103, and 111. The `createPreparedStatement` method calls that are executed in this method are passed strings, which contain the SQL statement and appropriate placeholders for the prepared statement. The `createPreparedStatement` method returns a `PreparedStatement` object reference, which is stored in the instance members declared on lines 12 through 14 in the application. The `rentalsbyName` `PreparedStatement` reference is created on line 94, the `rentalsbyUserID` reference is created on line 103, and the `rentalsbyCustName` reference is created on line 111. These instance members will be used by the `getXXXX` methods to execute the prepared statements and return results.

The getRentalsbyUserID Method

The body for the `getRentalsbyUserID` method is started on line 134 and completed on line 162. This method searches the database for movie rentals for a given user ID, using the `rentalsbyUserID` `PreparedStatement`, and will return the results.

Before the `rentalsbyUserID` prepared statement can be executed, the parameter or placeholder for the user ID value must be set to the integer value for the user ID that was passed into the method as an argument. This is done with a call to the `PreparedStatement` `setInt` method on line 141. The prepared statement is executed on line 144 using the `PreparedStatement` `executeQuery` method on line 144. This overloaded version of the `executeQuery` method takes no arguments (since the query string is actually part of the `PreparedStatement` object, arguments do not need to be passed as they do with a `Statement` `executeQuery` method). The method returns a `ResultSet` reference. A `try/catch` block is used to catch exceptions locally so that specific error messages can be returned, a strategy that makes the debugging process easier.

The `ResultSet` reference is returned in the `finally` block which allows for the possibility of an exception being thrown by the `executeQuery` method. Since the `ResultSet` reference is set to null on line 136, if the `executeQuery` method throws an exception, it will not return a `ResultSet` reference, and a null value reference will be returned on line 161 in the `finally` block. This is okay, since the code in the `main` program block quietly treats a null `ResultSet` reference as an error and does not attempt to manipulate it.

> Failures of specific queries directed at specific database tables are not uncommon in database programming, since database administrators may sometimes change tables without informing developers. Being able to trap and identify queries against which tables are failing within an application helps to isolate the problem. Catching the `SQLException` in the local program block where the exception was thrown makes it easier to identify the query that failed. If the `SQLException` is merely thrown to the calling method (declaring the method block with throws `SQLException`), the process of identifying where the exception was thrown and why becomes more difficult.

The getRentalsbyDate Method

The `getRentalsbyDate` method begins on line 166 and runs through line 195. This method uses the `rentalsbyDate PreparedStatement` to search the database for movie rentals greater than or equal to a given date. The rental date is passed to the method as an argument, but the argument is not the same data type as the database column with which it will be used. The corresponding column for the rental date in the `user_rentals` table is the `rental_date` column, which is a `Date` data type (in the PostgreSQL database). The `Date` data type maps to the `java.sql.Date`. Though most databases will freely convert data types from string representations, the conversions are in many cases vendor-specific. Since we would like to limit our dependence on vendor-specific features and behavior as much as possible, we will try to provide specific code to convert to the appropriate data types wherever possible.

The conversion of the `date` string takes place in the call to `PreparedStatement setDate` on line 173. The version of the `setDate` method called on this line takes an integer argument for the parameter (placeholder) index in the SQL statement and a second argument for the value of the parameter. The second argument for this version of the `setDate` method is a `java.sql.Date` data type. (The `java.util.*` package also contains a `Date` class, and since that package namespace is included in this program, we must clarify the `Date` class name with the fully qualified class name: `java.sql.Date`.)

The static `valueOf` method in the `java.sql.Date` class takes a string in the correct format and returns a `java.sql.Date` object having the date value passed into the method. This object is then passed to the `setDate` method on line 173.

The `PreparedStatement executeQuery` method is then called on line 176 for the `rentalsbyDate PreparedStatement` object. This call returns a `ResultSet` object reference, which is returned on line 194.

The getRentalsbyCustName Method

The `getRentalsbyCustName` method body begins on line 199 and extends to line 226. This method scans the database for rentals made by a customer of the specified name supplied as a method argument. It searches the database using the `rentalsbyCustName PreparedStatement` object.

The customer name is set with a call to the `PreparedStatement setString` method on line 208, which is used to set the value of the customer name parameter in the `rentalsbyCustName PreparedStatement` object.

The `executeQuery` method of the `rentalsbyCustName` object is called on line 208. This method executes the `rentalsbyCustName` query declared in the `prepareStatements` method and returns its results as a `ResultSet` reference. The `ResultSet` reference is returned on line 223.

The printResults Method

The `printResults` method declared on line 229 is used to print the contents of the `ResultSet` object reference passed as the second argument, using the first argument string as a header for the report. The `while` loop on line 243 prints the contents of the `ResultSet`. The columns in the `ResultSet` are printed as unformatted strings with the exception of the `movie_name` column on line 247, which is passed to the internal `formatString` method (explained below) for formatting. Also note that the `rental_date` column is retrieved on line 250 as a string when the data type for the column (as identified earlier) is `Date`. This is allowed because the database and the JDBC driver (as required by the specification) will freely convert to string data types in most cases. In this case, the default format for the `java.sql.Date` data type is in the JDBC date escape format, as follows.

```
yyyy-mm-dd
```

where `yyyy` is the year in 4-digit format, `mm` is the 2-digit month, and `dd` is the 2-digit day.

Since the `java.util.Date` class is the superclass of `java.sql.Date`, all of the robust formatting facilities available to format `java.util.Date` objects are available for `javs.sql.Date`. Using this knowledge, the `rental_date` column could have been formatted as follows.

```
//

// create a date formatter which uses the LONG format by
default

//

DateFormat df = DateFormat.getDateInstance( DateFormat.LONG );

...


//

// format the rental_date field using the LONG date format

//

System.out.println( "Rental Date: " +

                 df.format( rs.getDate( "rental_date" ) )
);

...
```

This would produce dates formatted using the `long` date format: January 1, 2000. Substituted in this application, this would produce the following results:

```
    ...

******** Rentals by Customer Name: Smith ********

*********************************************

First  Last   State      Movie
Rental Date

___    __     ___    ___        _____

Fred   Smith  NJ     Gone with the Java   January 1, 2000
Fred   Smith  NJ     Gone with the Java   February 1, 2001
Fred   Smith  NJ     Here in the Code     January 1, 2000
...
```

The formatString Method

The `formatString` method is declared on line 276. The purpose of this method is just to improve the output of the report by forcing the string passed into the method to be a consistent, specified length. The method either pads or trims the string to get the specified length and returns the formatted result as a Java string.

The clearAllParams Method

The `clearAllParams` method is declared on line 292 and is used to ensure that all existing parameters on the `PreparedStatement` have been cleared. The `PreparedStatement clearParameters` method clears all existing parameter settings for a `PreparedStatement` object. This type of method is useful in an application where the `PreparedStatement` object is being used repeatedly.

    The various `setXXXX` methods used to set parameter values implicitly reset the parameter before inserting the new value. In an application where each parameter is set every time the `PreparedStatement` object is used, it is not necessary to use this method (and doing so merely adds overhead to the application). But in large, complex applications where it may not be possible to ensure that parameter values have not been touched by other objects, using this method could provide a useful insurance policy for statement execution. (Given the design of this example, it is technically not necessary to call this method; it is shown here to provide an example of its use.)

PreparedExample.java: Program Output

The `PreparedExample.java` application prints a few simple reports using a set of `PreparedStatement` objects. The output of this sample application follows.

```
* * * * * * * * * * * * * * * * * * * * * * * * * * * * * * * * * * * * * * * * * * * * * * * * * * * * *

* * * * * * * *  Rentals by Customer Name: Smith  * * * * * * * *
* * * * * * * * * * * * * * * * * * * * * * * * * * * * * * * * * * * * * * * * * * * * * * * * * * * * *
First   Last     State   Movie               Rental Date
---     ---      ---     ---
Fred    Smith    NJ      Gone with the Java  2000-01-01
Fred    Smith    NJ      Gone with the Java  2001-02-01
Fred    Smith    NJ      Here in the Code    2000-01-01
Fred    Smith    NJ      Major Tom           2000-01-01
Fred    Smith    NJ      Major Tom           2001-02-01
Sally   Smith    NJ      Gone with the Java  2001-01-01
Sally   Smith    NJ      Gone with the Java  2002-01-01
Sally   Smith    NJ      Here in the Code    2001-01-01
Sally   Smith    NJ      Major Tom           2001-01-01
* * * * * * * * * * * * * * * * * * * * * * * * * * * * * * * * * * * * * * * * * * * * * * * * * * * * *

* * * * * * * * * * * * * * * * * * * * * * * * * * * * * * * * * * * * * * * * * * * * * * * * * * * * *
```

```
******** Rentals by Date: > 1/1/2001 ********
*****************************************************************
First   Last    State   Movie               Rental Date
---     ---     ---     ---                 ------
Fred    Smith   NJ      Gone with the Java  2001-02-01
Fred    Smith   NJ      Major Tom           2001-02-01
Sally   Smith   NJ      Gone with the Java  2001-01-01
Sally   Smith   NJ      Gone with the Java  2002-01-01
Sally   Smith   NJ      Here in the Code    2001-01-01
Sally   Smith   NJ      Major Tom           2001-01-01
*****************************************************************
*****************************************************************

******** Rentals by Customer ID: 2 ********
*****************************************************************
First   Last    State   Movie               Rental Date
---     ---     ---     ---                 ------
Fred    Smith   NJ      Gone with the Java  2000-01-01
Fred    Smith   NJ      Gone with the Java  2001-02-01
Fred    Smith   NJ      Here in the Code    2000-01-01
Fred    Smith   NJ      Major Tom           2000-01-01
Fred    Smith   NJ      Major Tom           2001-02-01
*****************************************************************
```

Executing Queries with the PreparedStatement Class

The `PreparedStatement` class provides several overloaded methods to perform statement execution. These methods overload the corresponding methods in the `Statement` class to account for the parameter-driven nature of `PreparedStatements`. These methods are as follows.

- boolean execute()
- ResultSet executeQuery()
- int executeUpdate()

The `PreparedStatement execute` method, called with no arguments, takes the existing parameters and executes the query regardless of the type of SQL query.

As shown in the code example in the previous chapter using the `Statement` class and shown again in the code snippet below, the execution of this method returns a boolean value, which indicates whether a SQL `select` or `update` query was executed. If the value is true, then the execute method executed a `select` query and there are one or more `ResultSet` objects available. The `getMoreResults` method returns true if there are more than one `ResultSet` objects, and the `getResultSet` method is used to return the `ResultSet`.

```
...
PreparedStatement pe;
...

// execute either a 'select' or 'update'
boolean isResultSet = pe.execute();
if ( isResultSet) {                    // if true, it was a 'select'
    while ( rs.getMoreResults() ) {
            ResultSet rs = pe.getResultSet();
            processResults( rs );
    }
}
else {                                 // false, it was an 'update'
    int updateCount = pe.getUpdateCount();
}
...
```

Like the `execute` method, the `PreparedStatement executeUpdate` method is called with no arguments. The method takes existing parameter value substitutions and executes the prepared `update` query, returning an integer representing the number of rows updated by the execution of the statement.

The `PreparedStatement executeQuery` method takes no arguments, takes the existing parameter value substitutions, executes the prepared SQL `select` statement, and returns a `ResultSet` representing the results of the statement execution.

Working with Batches and PreparedStatements.

The `PreparedStatement` class can also work with batch updates if the driver supports it. Batch updates are used as they are with the `Statement` class, the difference being the manner in which the individual updates are added to the batch. The following code example demonstrates this.

```
1.import java.sql.*;
2.import javax.sql.*;
3.import javax.naming.*;
4.
5.
6.public class BatchExample {
7.
8.public static void main( String args[] ) {
9.
10.ResultSet rs    = null;
11.Connection con  = null;
12.try {
13.
14.
15.
16.
```

```
17.       InitialContext ctx = new InitialContext();
18.       DataSource ds = ctx.lookup( "movies" );
19.        con = ds.getConnection();
20.
21.       // add a batch of SQL statements
22.       //
23.       PreparedStatement ps = con.prepareStatement(
24.          "insert into users (user_id, first_name, last_name) " +
25.          " values ( ?, ?, ?)" );
26.       ps.setInt( 1, 101);                // user_id
27.       ps.setString( 2, "Cal" );          // first_name
28.       ps.setString( 3, "Coder" );        // last_name
29.
30.       // add the first batch update
31.       ps.addBatch();
32.
33.       ps.setInt( 1, 201);                        // user_id
34.       ps.setString( 2, "Carrie" );               // first_name
35.       ps.setString( 3, "Coder" );                // last_name
36.
37.       // add the second batch update
38.       ps.addBatch();
39.
40.       ps.setInt( 1, 401);                        // user_id
41.       ps.setString( 2, "Sal" );                  // first_name
42.       ps.setString( 3, "Snake" );                // last_name
43.
44.       // add the third batch update
45.       ps.addBatch();
46.
47.       //
48.       // use the inherited Statement class addBatch
49.       // these queries can't contain parameter placeholders
50.       //
51.       ps.addBatch("insert into movies (movie_id, movie_name) " +
52.                              " values ( 501, 'Trying Again')" );
53.       ps.addBatch("update movies   " +
54.                   " set movie_desc = '** not provided **' " );
55.
56.       //
57.       // execute the batch and examine the results
58.       //
59.       int results[] = ps.executeBatch();
60.
61.       //
62.       // print the results. integer values represents rows updated
63.       //
64.       for (int n=0;n<results.length;n++)
65.          System.out.println("Result from query " + (n+1) + " = " +
66.                              results[n] );
67.
68.}
```

```
69.catch (SQLException e) {
70.
71.     // display SQL specific exception information
72.     System.out.println("***************************" );
73.     System.out.println("SQLException in main: " + e.getMessage() );
74.     System.out.println("** SQLState: " + e.getSQLState());
75.     System.out.println("** SQL Error Code: " + e.getErrorCode());
76.     System.out.println("***************************" );
77.     e.printStackTrace();
78.}
79.catch (Exception e) {
80.     System.out.println("Exception in main: " + e.getMessage() );
81.     e.printStackTrace();
82.}
83.finally {
84.
85.     try {
86.
87.     if ( con != null )
88.             con.close();
89.     }
90.     catch (SQLException e) {
91.             e.printStackTrace();
92.     }
93.}
94.
95.}
96.
97.}
```

In this example, the JDBC driver is loaded using a `Class.forName` call, and the `Connection` object is obtained using a `DriverManager getConnection` call on line 17. The `PreparedStatement` is created on lines 23 through 25. This statement will be used to insert users into the users table. Placeholders are provided for the `user_id`, `first_name`, and `last_name` columns in the SQL `insert` statement.

On lines 26 through 27 several calls are made to `setXXXX` methods to set the values for the `user_id`, `first_name`, and `last_name` placeholders. On line 31, the `PreparedStatement addBatch` method is called with no arguments. This version of the method uses the current values of the parameters to create the SQL `insert` statement to be used in the batch update operation.

On lines 33 through 36 the `setXXXX` methods are called again with a different set of values for a different user. The `PreparedStatement addBatch` method is called once again on line 38, this time adding an `insert` statement with the values specified on lines 33 through 36. The operation is repeated a third time, with the values set on lines 40 through 42 and added with a call to the `addBatch` method on line 45.

On line 51 a demonstration of the use of the inherited `Statement` methods is provided with a call to the `addBatch` method using a string argument. The string argument contains a SQL `update` statement, which performs an insert into the `movies` table. The SQL `update` statements added using `addBatch` cannot contain any placeholders (?); only standard SQL statements can be added. On line 53 an additional query is added using the `addBatch` method with a string parameter, this time adding an `update` statement to the batch instead of an `insert` statement.

Finally, on line 59 the `executeBatch` method is called. This method returns an integer array with the update counts for each of the SQL `update` statements contained in the `PreparedStatement` batch. On lines 64 through 66 a `for` loop is used to iterate through the results integer array and output the result count for each update performed. This program provides output as follows.

```
Result from query 1 = 1
Result from query 2 = 1
Result from query 3 = 1
Result from query 4 = 1
Result from query 5 = 5
```

THE RESULTSET CLASS

The `ResultSet` class encapsulates the rows or tuples resulting from the execution of a SQL select query. Originally, in the early releases of the JDBC API, the `ResultSet` class allowed only for the serial progression through a set of results, from the first to the last. Random movement through the results was not allowed. Additionally, data in the `ResultSet` could only be read; updates through the `ResultSet` were not allowed.

With the JDBC 2.0 optional extensions, additional capabilities were added to the `ResultSet` specification, which allow results to be reviewed in a random order. This is referred to as a *scrollable* `ResultSet` or *scrollable cursor*. Later JDBC releases also added the capability to perform updates through `ResultSets`.

Though these additional features are provided in the current API, it is up to the JDBC driver provider to provide them—they are not required for compliance. Fortunately, partly because of the demand, a large number of JDBC drivers provide these features.

Using a ResultSet for Serial Access

The default behavior for a `ResultSet` object and the behavior required for JDBC compliance is serial access, accessing the rows or tuples returned from the first row to the last in a serial fashion. Using this type of access, once a row has been read, it cannot be read again. For many applications, such as producing reports or informational pages for a Web site, this is a perfectly acceptable form of access. The following code sample uses this type of access.

ResultSetExample1.java

```
1.import java.sql.*;
2.import javax.sql.*;
3.import javax.naming.*;
4.import com.codestudio.sql.PoolMan;
5.
6.public class ResultSetExample1 {
7.
8.
9.public static void main( String args[] ) {
10.
11.Connection con=null;
12.try {
13.      //
14.      // JNDI startup parameters are stored in
15.      // the "jndi.properties" file in the classpath.
16.      //
17.      InitialContext ctx = new InitialContext( );
18.
19.      // get the DataSource from the JNDI name server
20.      DataSource ds = (DataSource) ctx.lookup("movies-mysql");
21.
22.      // get the connection from the DataSource
23.      con = ds.getConnection( );
24.
25.      // create a Statement class to execute the SQL statement
26.      Statement stmt = con.createStatement();
27.
28.      // execute the SQL statement and get the results in a ResultSet
29.      ResultSet rs   = stmt.executeQuery(
30.         "select movie_name, release_date from movies" );
31.
32.      // display the ResultSet type
33.      System.out.println(
34.            "\nResultSet type: " +
35.            getCursorTypeString( rs.getType()) +
36.            "\n" );
37.
38.      // iterate through the ResultSet, displaying two values
39.      // for each row using the getString method
40.      //
41.      while ( rs.next() ) {
42.            System.out.println(
43.               "******************" + "\n" +
44.          "movie_name: " + "\t" +
45.             rs.getString("movie_name") + "\n" +
```

```
46.                      "release_date: " + "\t" +
47.                         rs.getString("release_date")  );
48.      }
49.
50.}
51.catch (SQLException e) {
52.
53.     // display SQL specific exception information
54.     System.out.println("**************************" );
55.     System.out.println("SQLException in main: " + e.getMessage() );
56.     System.out.println("** SQLState: " + e.getSQLState());
57.     System.out.println("** SQL Error Code: " + e.getErrorCode());
58.     System.out.println("**************************" );
59.     e.printStackTrace();
60.}
61.catch (Exception e) {
62.     System.out.println("Exception in main: " + e.getMessage() );
63.     e.printStackTrace();
64.}
65.finally {
66.
67.     try {
68.          // close the connection
69.     if ( con != null )
70.             con.close();
71.     }
72.     catch (SQLException e) {
73.             e.printStackTrace();
74.     }
75.}
76.
77.
78.} // end main
79.
80.static String getCursorTypeString( int type ) {
81.
82.if ( type == ResultSet.TYPE_FORWARD_ONLY )
83.     return "Forward Only ResultSet.";
84.
85.if ( type == ResultSet.TYPE_SCROLL_INSENSITIVE )
86.     return "Scroll Insensitive ResultSet.";
87.
88.if ( type == ResultSet.TYPE_SCROLL_SENSITIVE )
89.     return "Scroll Sensitive ResultSet.";
90.
91.return "Unknown";
92.
93.}
94.
95.}
```

In this example, rows are retrieved from the `movies` table in the movies database to produce a listing of the movies available. In code that is no doubt familiar at this point, the application obtains an initial JNDI context on line 17, obtains a `DataSource` reference on line 20 for the `movies-mysql` data source, and then creates a `Statement` object on line 26.

On line 27 a SQL `select` statement query is executed using the `Statement` `executeQuery` method. This statement merely selects the `movie_name` and `release_date` columns from the `movies` table.

On line 33 the `getType` method of the `ResultSet` class is called to retrieve the type of `ResultSet` we have obtained by executing the query. The `getType` method returns an integer, which is matched with the integer constants from the `ResultSet` interface in the `getCursorTypeString` method, which is declared on line 80. The `getCursorTypeString` method converts the value of the integer argument into an appropriate string for display.

The loop that is started on line 44 demonstrates a typical loop used to output the contents of a normal serial `ResultSet`. The `ResultSet` `next` method is called as the controlling argument to the `while` loop. The first call to the `ResultSet` `next` method after the `ResultSet` has been created will position the cursor or pointer for the `ResultSet` before the first record in the result set and return true if there are records to be retrieved. If the query has failed to return records, then the call to the `ResultSet` `next` method will return false. As this program loop is designed, a failure to return any records will cause it to quietly fail.

Selecting Zero Rows

Since it is not uncommon for a query that worked fine during programmer testing to fail to return rows in production, it is a good practice to create code that will manage this situation correctly. Note that a `select` query that fails to return rows will not necessarily throw an exception; the programmer must test for this condition. When we examine the `ResultSetMetaData` class, we will find other methods for determining the contents of a `ResultSet`. Still, testing for rows using the `ResultSet` `next` method is a common and simple approach for determining whether or not there are rows to process.

A `catch` block on line 51 catches the `SQLException` that may be thrown by the various JDBC calls being made. This catch block displays information on the SQL state and SQL error code. These methods can provide additional information on a SQL error when they occur (though not all JDBC drivers will provide this information).

The `finally` block on line 65 closes the `Connection` object if it is non-null. Closing the connection in this block insures that the connection will be closed even in the event an exception is thrown (since the `finally` block is always executed).

On line 80, the `getCursorTypeString` method is declared. This method takes the integer argument and maps it to the appropriate `ResultSet` integer constant. It returns a meaningful string for the type of cursor that the `ResultSet` implements. The output of this program is as follows.

```
ResultSet type: Forward Only ResultSet.

* * * * * * * * * * * * * * * * * *
movie_name:     The Evil Null Reference
release_date:   2001-01-01
* * * * * * * * * * * * * * * * * *
movie_name:     The Last Reference
release_date:   2001-01-01
* * * * * * * * * * * * * * * * * *
movie_name:     Just One More Compile
release_date:   2001-01-01
* * * * * * * * * * * * * * * * * *
movie_name:     One More Lonely Harley
release_date:   2001-01-01
* * * * * * * * * * * * * * * * * *
movie_name:     One Last Try Before the Lights Go Down
release_date:   2002-01-11
```

The ResultSet getXXXX methods

There are a number of `getXXXX` methods in the `ResultSet` class, one set for each JDBC data type defined in *java.sql.Types*. Each `getXXXX` method references a column in the select list. The column can be referenced in two ways. One common process for addressing the column is through the identification of the offset or ordinal position of the column in the select list, starting at the far left with the number 1 and moving to the right through the number of columns in the select list.

The other process for addressing the column in the select list is to provide a string name for the column in the list (for example, `movie_name`). For each data type, there are two versions of the `getXXXX` method, one for each type of access.

The process of using the `getXXXX` methods is as shown in the various examples in this and other chapters. The rear portion of the method name represents the type such that the method signatures are as follows.

```
get<type_name>( integer <column_index>);
get<type_name>(String <column_name>);
```

The return type from these methods is the return type that is being retrieved, whether it is a Java primitive data type or an object reference of the specified type. There are a few cases of variation from this standard format where a third argument is added to indicate precision or length of the data type being retrieved from the `ResultSet`.

Moving in the ResultSet: Scrollable ResultSets

One of the more notable omissions in the early releases of the JDBC API was the inability to position the `ResultSet` pointer or cursor within the result set. The `ResultSet` could only be read in a serial fashion, from the first record to last record. Once a row was read and the `ResultSet` pointer was moved to the next row in the set, the previous row could not be read again. But relational databases generally provided more robust access facilities through their proprietary APIs (referred to as CLIs).

Fairly early in the history of relational databases, relational database vendors provided proprietary APIs to access database data. These APIs have for some time supported *cursors*, the ability to execute a SQL `select` statement and review the results in some native language, such as C or C++, or using a database stored procedure language. These vendor APIs have generally supported *scroll cursors*, cursors that allow `select` results to be reviewed serially and randomly. Using a scroll cursor, a completely random access order can be used. For example, the first, second, and third row of a result set could be read, then the second row could be read again, then the third and then the fifth row could be read.

Using Scroll Cursors

The `ResultSet` class contains a number of methods that provide for this random access or scroll cursor capability. These methods allow positioning within the results serially, by absolute record number from the start of the result set, or by a relative record number from the current position in the result set. The major database vendors all provide this capability in their JDBC driver, as do many of the open source databases. But technically, a scroll cursor or random access `ResultSet` capability is not required in the JDBC driver for JDBC compliance. The following code example demonstrates the use of scroll cursors using JDBC.

ScrollExample2.java

```
1.import java.sql.*;
2.import javax.sql.*;
3.
4.
5.public class ScrollExample2 {
6.
7.public static void main( String args[] ) {
```

```
8.
9.try {
10.     // get the initial context
11.     InitialContext ctx = new InitialContext(  );
12.
13.     // get the DataSource from the JNDI name server
14.     DataSource ds = (DataSource) ctx.lookup("movies-mysql");
15.
16.     // create the connection using the static getConnection method
17.     Connection con = ds.getConnection( );
18.
19.     // create a Statement class to execute the SQL statement
20.     Statement stmt = con.createStatement(
21.                         ResultSet.TYPE_SCROLL_INSENSITIVE,
22.                         ResultSet.CONCUR_UPDATABLE );
23.
24.     // execute the SQL statement and get the results in a ResultSet
25.     ResultSet rs   = stmt.executeQuery(
26.           "select movie_name, movie_id, release_date from movies" );
27.
28.     // show the cursor type
29.     System.out.println("Cursor Type: " +
30.                 getCursorTypeString( rs.getType() ) );
31.
32.     // iterate through the ResultSet, displaying two values
33.     // for each row using the getString method
34.      System.out.println("Cursor has the following rows.");
35.      while ( rs.next() )
36.             System.out.println( "*******************" + "\n" +
37.                         "movie_id: " + "\t" +
38.                     rs.getString("movie_id") + "\n" +
39.                     "movie_name: " + "\t" +
40.                     rs.getString("movie_name") + "\n" +
41.                     "release_date: " + "\t" +
42.                     rs.getString("release_date")  );
43.
44.    // jump to the first record
45.    if ( rs.first() {
46.       System.out.println("\n\nThis is the first record.");
47.       System.out.println( "******************" + "\n" +
48.                   "movie_id: " + "\t" +
49.               rs.getString("movie_id") + "\n" +
50.                   "movie_name: " + "\t" +
51.               rs.getString("movie_name") + "\n" +
52.                   "release_date: " + "\t" +
53.               rs.getString("release_date")  );
54.     }
55.    // jump to the last record
56.     if ( rs.last() ) {
57.        System.out.println("\n\nThis is the last record.");
58.        System.out.println( "******************" + "\n" +
59.                         "movie_id: " + "\t" +
```

```
60.                              rs.getString("movie_id") + "\n" +
61.                                  "movie_name: " + "\t" +
62.                              rs.getString("movie_name") + "\n" +
63.                                  "release_date: " + "\t" +
64.                              rs.getString("release_date")  );
65.       }
66.     // jump to the third record - absolute
67.     if ( rs.absolute(3) ) {
68.        System.out.println("\n\nThis is the third record.");
69.        System.out.println( "*******************" + "\n" +
70.                               "movie_id: " + "\t" +
71.                         rs.getString("movie_id") + "\n" +
72.                               "movie_name: " + "\t" +
73.                         rs.getString("movie_name") + "\n" +
74.                               "release_date: " + "\t" +
75.                         rs.getString("release_date")  );
76.     }
77.
78.     // jump to the last record - 2
79.     if ( rs.absolute(-2) ) {
80.        System.out.println("\n\nThis is the second to last record.");
81.        System.out.println( "*******************" + "\n" +
82.                               "movie_id: " + "\t" +
83.                     rs.getString("movie_id") + "\n" +
84.                               "movie_name: " + "\t" +
85.                     rs.getString("movie_name") + "\n" +
86.                               "release_date: " + "\t" +
87.                     rs.getString("release_date")  );
88.      }
89.     // jump to the last record
90.     if ( rs.relative(1) ) {
91.        System.out.println("\n\nThis is the last record - again.");
92.        System.out.println( "*******************" + "\n" +
93.                               "movie_id: " + "\t" +
94.                         rs.getString("movie_id") + "\n" +
95.                                "movie_name: " + "\t" +
96.                   rs.getString("movie_name") + "\n" +
97.                               "release_date: " + "\t" +
98.                   rs.getString("release_date")  );
99.      }
100.    // close the connection
101.    con.close();
102.
103.}
104.catch (SQLException e) {
105.
106.    // display SQL specific exception information
107.    System.out.println("*************************" );
108.    System.out.println("SQLException in main: " + e.getMessage() );
109.    System.out.println("** SQLState: " + e.getSQLState());
110.    System.out.println("** SQL Error Code: " + e.getErrorCode());
111.    System.out.println("*************************" );
```

```
112.      e.printStackTrace();
113.}
114.catch (Exception e) {
115.      System.out.println("Exception in main: " + e.getMessage() );
116.      e.printStackTrace();
117.}
118.finally {
119.
120.      try {
121.
122.    if ( con != null )
123.              con.close();
124.      }
125.      catch (SQLException e) {
126.              e.printStackTrace();
127.      }
128.}
129.}
130.
131.static String getCursorTypeString( int ctype ) {
132.
133.if ( ctype == ResultSet.TYPE_FORWARD_ONLY )
134.      return "Forward Scrolling Only";
135.
136.if ( ctype == ResultSet.TYPE_SCROLL_INSENSITIVE )
137.      return "Scrolling Insensitive";
138.
139.if ( ctype == ResultSet.TYPE_SCROLL_SENSITIVE )
140.      return "Scrolling Sensitive";
141.
142.return "Unknown";
143.
144.}
145.}
```

None of this code looks much different from that shown in the previous examples. It is the `Connection` class `createStatement` method on line 20 that looks different. This overloaded version of the `createStatement` method contains arguments for the cursor type (`ResultSet.TYPE_SCROLL_INSENSITIVE`) and the concurrency type (`ResultSet.CONCUR_UPDATABLE`). This indicates to the JDBC driver that we will be using scroll cursor functionality and we will allow concurrent updates to the data we will be reading in our `ResultSet`; thus we are *sharing* the data with other database users.

Though the specification does not require it, requesting a `ResultSet` type that is not supported usually throws an exception. If a `ResultSet` type is `TYPE_FORWARD_ONLY`, then any attempt to try to position the `ResultSet` pointer (absolute, relative, first, last) will throw an exception. (Note that the `createStatement` method in the `Connection` class that requests the `ResultSet` type may not throw an exception.)

On line 25 we call the executeQuery method, passing in a SQL statement that selects a number of columns from the movie table. The executeQuery method returns a ResultSet, which is used throughout the remainder of the program.

On line 30 a call is made to the getCursorTypeString method (declared as part of this class—not part of the JDBC API) to display the type of cursor implemented by the ResultSet. The getCursorTypeString method is passed an integer, which relates to one of the integer constants in the ResultSet class. The getCursorString maps the integer parameter to a string, which indicates the cursor type. This string is returned by the method.

The remainder of the program iterates through the ResultSet, moving in various directions to demonstrate the use of the scroll cursor functionality. A while loop on line 35 demonstrates that simple serial iteration is available by making successive calls to the ResultSet next method to move the ResultSet pointer to the next record in the results. This while loop iterates through all of the results, from the first record to the last record in the ResultSet.

Once the while loop has completed, the ResultSet first method is called on line 45 to move iteration back to the first record in the ResultSet. On lines 47 through 53 the value of the columns in the first record are displayed.

On line 56 the ResultSet last method is called to move the ResultSet pointer to the last record in the ResultSet. On lines 58 through 63 the values of the columns in the last record are displayed.

The next positioning call is made on line 67 where a call is made to the absolute method. This method takes an integer argument that indicates the absolute position within the result set for the move. In this example, the integer 3 is passed into the method, indicating that the third record in the ResultSet should be retrieved.

The ResultSet absolute method is called again on line 79 where a negative 2 (–2) is passed as an argument to the method. A negative number passed to the absolute method indicates that the positioning is relative to the last record, so an argument of –2 will move the cursor to the second to last record.

The negative numbers passed into the absolute method can be confusing. The call on line 79 of absolute(-2) has moved us to the record before the last record in the ResultSet. A call of absolute(-1) it would have moved the ResultSet pointer to the last record. This makes sense when you consider we are working from a base of 1, not 0, so that 1 is the first record, 2 is the second record, and so on. Using this logic, –1 should be the last record, –2 the record before last, and so on.

Since the ResultSet pointer is on the second to the last record, moving one position from where we are currently would place us on the last record. This is exactly what is done on line 90 with a call to the ResultSet relative method. The method call on line 90 passes a value of 1 into the method (relative(1)), thus placing the ResultSet pointer on the last record. The value of the records columns are displayed on lines 92 through 98.

A number of `catch` blocks are used on lines 115 through 128 to catch the various exceptions that may be thrown by the JDBC calls. In the `finally` block started on line 129, the connection is closed (if it has been created). As usual, it is good practice to close the connection and release resources in the `finally` block, which we know will be executed even in the event an exception is thrown by one of the many JDBC method calls being made.

On line 131 the body of the `getCursorTypeString` method is declared. This method simply maps the integer value passed into the method to one of the `ResultSet` constant values. It returns the name of the cursor type being used. The output from the execution of this program is as follows.

```
Cursor Type: Scrolling Insensitive
Cursor has the following rows.
* * * * * * * * * * * * * * * * * *
movie_id:      1
movie_name:    Stamping Out the Evil Null Reference
release_date:  2001-01-01
* * * * * * * * * * * * * * * * * *
movie_id:      2
movie_name:    The Last Compile
release_date:  2000-01-11
* * * * * * * * * * * * * * * * * *
movie_id:      3
movie_name:    The Final Test
release_date:  1997-01-22
* * * * * * * * * * * * * * * * * *
movie_id:      4
movie_name:    One Last Try Before the Lights Go Down
release_date:  1998-01-11
* * * * * * * * * * * * * * * * * *
movie_id:      5
movie_name:    Another Dog Day
release_date:  2002-05-22
* * * * * * * * * * * * * * * * * *
movie_id:      6
movie_name:    Trying Again
release_date:  2001-01-28


This is the first record.
* * * * * * * * * * * * * * * * * *
movie_id:      1
movie_name:    Stamping Out the Evil Null Reference
release_date:  2001-01-01


This is the last record.
* * * * * * * * * * * * * * * * * *
movie_id:      6
movie_name:    Trying Again
```

```
release_date:   2001-01-28


This is the third record.
******************
movie_id:       3
movie_name:     The Final Test
release_date:   1997-01-22


This is the second to last record.
******************
movie_id:       5
movie_name:     Another Dog Day
release_date:   2002-05-22


This is the last record - again.
******************
movie_id:       6
movie_name:     Trying Again
release_date:   2001-01-28
```

This example demonstrated the use of the versatile scroll cursor `ResultSet`. While this example demonstrated a number of the methods available, to thoroughly understand what a scroll cursor `ResultSet` can do, you should be aware of all the methods in the `ResultSet` class that pertain to this capability. The following section details these methods.

Methods for the Scroll Cursor ResultSet

As mentioned previously, the underlying database and the JDBC driver must support scrollable `ResultSets` for these methods to be usable. (If they have not been implemented, the driver will usually throw an exception indicating the method has not been implemented.) The `DatabaseMetaData` method `supportsResultSetType` can be called to determine whether or not the underlying database supports the scrollable `ResultSet`. An example of this call follows.

```
...
//
// get the DatabaseMetaData object from the Connection
//
DatabaseMetaData dmd = con.getMetaData();


//
// test for scrolling
//
if ( dmd.supportsResultSetType(ResultSet.TYPE_SCROLL_INSENSITIVE) ) {
    // it's ok to create and use scroll cursor ResultSet
...
```

Table 7–1 lists the methods available for scrollable `ResultSets`.

All of these methods will throw a `SQLException` if the cursor is not a scrollable cursor, a cursor created as one of `ResultSet.TYPE_SCROLL_SENSITIVE` or `ResultSet.TYPE_SCROLL_INSENSITIVE`.

These methods will not throw an exception if an invalid request is made to move to a nonexistent row (for example, making an `rs.absolute(20)` call when only 10 rows are in the `ResultSet`). What they will do on an invalid call is return a boolean value false. Applications should test for a value of true before proceeding to work with the `ResultSet` row (this was the technique shown in the previous example).

The `previous` method moves the cursor or pointer to the record before the current record. This method returns a boolean value if there is a record at the requested position, or it returns false if there is no previous record.

Table 7–1   *Scroll Cursor ResultSet Methods*

Method	Description
`boolean previous()`	Moves the `ResultSet` pointer from the current row to the previous row.
`boolean isBeforeFirst()`	Returns true if the `ResultSet` pointer is currently before the first row in the ResultSet.
`boolean isFirst()`	Returns true if the `ResultSet` pointer is currently at the first row of the `ResultSet`.
`boolean isLast()`	Returns true if the `ResultSet` pointer is currently at the last row of the `ResultSet`.
`boolean last()`	Moves the `ResultSet` pointer to the last row in the `ResultSet`.
`void afterLast()`	Moves the `ResultSet` pointer to after the last row.
`void beforeFirst()`	Moves the `ResultSet` pointer to before the first row;. the cursor to the front of this `ResultSet` object, just before the first row.
`boolean isAfterLast()`	Returns true if the `ResultSet` pointer is currently after the last row in the `ResultSet`.
`boolean first()`	Moves the `ResultSet` pointer to the first row in the ResultSet.
`Boolean relative(int rows)`	Moves the `ResultSet` pointer to the row specified by the integer argument. This movement is relative to the current `ResultSet` pointer position. A positive number argument moves forward. A negative number argument moves back.
`boolean absolute(int row)`	Moves the `ResultSet` pointer to the first row in the `ResultSet`.

The `isBeforeFirst` method returns a boolean true if the cursor is before the first record in the `ResultSet`. The `beforeFirst` method moves the cursor to before the first record in the `ResultSet`; this is where the cursor (`ResultSet` pointer) should be before the first call to the `ResultSet next` method.

The `isAfterLast` method returns `true` if the cursor or pointer is after the last record in the `ResultSet`. The `afterLast` method moves the cursor to after the last record in the `ResultSet`.

The `first` method moves the cursor or pointer to the first record in the `ResultSet`. The `isFirst` method returns true if the cursor is on the first record of the `ResultSet`. Alternatively, the `last` method moves the cursor to the last record in the `ResultSet` and the `isLast` method returns true if the cursor is at the last record in the `ResultSet`. (A call to the `last` method followed by a call to the `getRows` method returns the number of rows in the `ResultSet`.)

The `relative` method takes an integer argument that represents the number of positions the cursor will move in the `ResultSet` *relative* to the current position in the `ResultSet`. A positive value integer argument indicates the cursor should move forward in the `ResultSet`, and a negative number indicates the cursor should move back in the `ResultSet`. This method will throw an exception if there is no current row in the `ResultSet` (the cursor is before the first row or after the last row). This method can be called with a zero integer argument (`relative(0)`), but the cursor will not be moved (which is exactly what was requested by the call).

The `absolute` method takes an integer argument that represents the number of positions to move relative to the *absolute* start or end of the `ResultSet`. A positive value provided as an argument indicates the position being requested is relative to the beginning of the `ResultSet`. A negative value provided as an argument requests a position relative to the end of the `ResultSet`. Calling the method with an argument of zero (`absolute(0)`) will throw an exception. Calling the method with positional value beyond the beginning of the `ResultSet` will position the cursor before the first record. Calling the method with a positional value beyond the end of the `ResultSet` will position the cursor after the last record.

Using Updateable ResultSets

As of JDBC 2.0 it is possible to update the database using a `ResultSet`. This provides a convenient mechanism for browsing and updating a database using the same object. Though most major relational database vendors and open source relational database organizations provide a JDBC driver that supports this feature, it is not required for JDBC compliance.

Using `ResultSet` updates may place some requirements on the type of query used to create the `ResultSet`. The JDBC driver must be able to locate the row in the database table that corresponds to the row being updated. This requires either a unique row ID for the current row or knowledge of the primary key for the current row. The driver must be able to effectively create an `update` statement to update the columns of the current record to the appropriate database row. The following code example demonstrates `ResultSet` updates.

ResultSetExample2.java

```
1.import java.sql.*;
2.import java.util.*;
3.import javax.sql.*;
4.import javax.naming.*;
5.//import com.codestudio.sql.PoolMan;
6.
7.public class ResultSetExample2 {
8.
9.
10.// demonstrate updatable resultsets
11.
12.
13.public static void main( String args[] ) {
14.
15.// set ourDate to the current date
16.java.sql.Date ourDate =  new java.sql.Date(
17.                   Calendar.getInstance().getTime().getTime() );
18.
19.Connection con = null;
20.ResultSet  rs  = null;
21.try {
22.
23.      // load the database driver
24.      Class.forName("org.gjt.mm.mysql.Driver");
25.      // create the connection
26.      con= DriverManager.getConnection(
27.         "jdbc:mysql://localhost/movies?user=art&password=YES");
28.
29.      // create a Statement class to execute the SQL statement
30.      Statement stmt = con.createStatement();
31.
32.      // ** with this driver: must use a table with
33.      // ** a primary key defined; must select the pk and
34.      // ** must only use one table; must select the columns
35.      // ** we are going to update
36.      //
37.      // execute the SQL statement and get the results in a ResultSet
38.      rs   = stmt.executeQuery("select movie_id, update_date, " +
39.                           " movie_name, release_date, " +
40.                           " category, special_promotion" +
41.                           " from movies" +
42.                   " where category='Comedy'" +
43.                   " order by movie_id" );
44.
45.      // display the ResultSet type
```

```
46.        System.out.println(
47.              "\nResultSet type: " +
48.              getCursorTypeString( rs.getType()) +  "\n" );
49.
50.        // iterate through the ResultSet, displaying two values
51.        // for each row using the getString method
52.        while ( rs.next() ) {
53.              System.out.println( "*******************" + "\n" +
54.                        "movie_name: "    + "\t" +
55.                        rs.getString("movie_name") + "\n" +
56.                        "special_promotion: "  + "\t" +
57.                        rs.getString("special_promotion") + "\n" +
58.                         "update_date: "  + "\t" +
59.                        rs.getDate("update_date") +  "\n" +
60.                        "release_date: " + "\t" +
61.                        rs.getString("release_date")  );
62.
63.             // change the update date to today
64.           rs.updateDate( "update_date", ourDate );
65.
66.        // change the special_promotion to 5
67.        rs.updateInt( "special_promotion", 5 );
68.
69.        // update the database row
70.        rs.updateRow();
71.     }
72.
73.     // perform an insert
74.     //
75.     // first, set the values
76.     rs.moveToInsertRow();
77.     rs.updateInt( "movie_id", 601 );
78.     rs.updateDate( "update_date", ourDate );
79.     rs.updateString( "movie_name",
80.              "One Last Try" );
81.     rs.updateDate( "release_date", ourDate );
82.     rs.updateString( "category", "Comedy" );
83.     rs.updateInt( "special_promotion", 0 );
84.
85.     // perform the insert
86.     rs.insertRow();
87.
88.     // let's examine the results
89.     rs   = stmt.executeQuery("select movie_id, movie_name, "  +
90.              " update_date, release_date, special_promotion " +
91.              " from movies" +
92.              " where category = 'Comedy'" );
93.
94.     System.out.println( "\n ** After updates: \n" );
95.
```

```
96.      while ( rs.next() ) {
97.              System.out.println( "*******************" + "\n" +
98.                "movie_name: "    +         "\t" +
99.                rs.getString("movie_name") + "\n" +
100.               "special_promotion: "   + "\t" +
101.               rs.getString("special_promotion") + "\n" +
102.              "update_date: "   +          "\t" +
103.               rs.getDate("update_date") +  "\n" +
104.                "release_date: " +          "\t" +
105.               rs.getString("release_date")  );
106.      }
107.
108.}
109.catch (SQLException e) {
110.
111.     // display SQL specific exception information
112.     System.out.println("*************************" );
113.     System.out.println("SQLException in main: " + e.getMessage() );
114.     System.out.println("** SQLState: " + e.getSQLState());
115.     System.out.println("** SQL Error Code: " + e.getErrorCode());
116.     System.out.println("*************************" );
117.     e.printStackTrace();
118.}
119.catch (Exception e) {
120.     System.out.println("Exception in main: " + e.getMessage() );
121.     e.printStackTrace();
122.}
123.finally {
124.
125.   try {
126.        // close the connection
127.    if ( con != null )
128.             con.close();
129.       }
130.      catch (SQLException e) {
131.           e.printStackTrace();
132.       }
133.   }
134.
135.} // end main
136.
137.static String getCursorTypeString( int type ) {
138.
139.if ( type == ResultSet.TYPE_FORWARD_ONLY )
140.     return "Forward Only ResultSet.";
141.
142.if ( type == ResultSet.TYPE_SCROLL_INSENSITIVE )
143.     return "Scroll Insensitive ResultSet.";
144.
145.if ( type == ResultSet.TYPE_SCROLL_SENSITIVE )
```

```
146.     return "Scroll Sensitive ResultSet.";
147.
148.return "Unknown";
149.
150.}
151.
152.}
```

This example begins by performing a number of imports on lines 1 through 4. On line 16 a local variable is declared as a `java.sql.Date` type variable and set to an initial value of the current date.

A `Connection` and `ResultSet` object are declared on lines 19 and 20. The JDBC driver is loaded on line 24, and a `Connection` is obtained from the database driver at line 26 using a URL database connection string. On line 30 a `Statement` object is created from the connection using the `createStatement` method with no arguments. (The default database concurrency for this database supports updates. A call to the `getConcurrency` method at this point would return a value of `ResultSet.CONCUR_UPDATABLE`.)

The `Statement executeQuery` method is called on line 38 with a SQL `select` query. On line 45 the `getCursorTypeString` method is called and is passed the value returned by the `ResultSet getType` call. The `getCursorTypeString` simply maps the `ResultSet` integer value to a string representing the name of the concurrency type.

Next, on line 52, to demonstrate the versatility of the `ResultSet`, a while loop is started to iterate through the results of the query. This block of code should look familiar, since it has been used several times already in this book. The `ResultSet next` method is used to move from record to record in the `ResultSet`, from the beginning to end of the result set.

But within this `while` loop, a number of updates are performed on the database, using the `ResultSet`. The `update_date` field for the current record is changed on line 64 and is set to the value of the `ourDate` variable (which has been assigned the value of today's date on line 16). The value for the `special_pro-motion` field is set to the value of 5. The `ResultSet  updateRow` method is called on line 70 to update the current row to the underlying data store. These updates are performed for each record examined by the `ResultSet` within the loop, which is terminated on line 71.

The next portion of this program performs a SQL insert operation. Before an insert can be done, the cursor must be positioned over the insert row. This is done with a call to the `moveToInsertRow` method on line 76. (If this were not done, then the values of the current row would simply be overwritten by the updates to the insert row.) A series of `updateXXXX` methods are then called on lines 77 through 83. These methods are called for database updates just as they are called for database insert operations. On line 86, the `insertRow` method is called to insert the row into the underlying database.

On line 89 a query is executed to review the results of the update operation. This `ResultSet` is used to control the loop that is executed on line 96. The columns within the `ResultSet` are displayed using the `println` method call on line 97.

The remainder of this program contains code that was explained in the previous program example and is shown again for completeness. The `finally` block for the main program on line 123 contains the method call to close the connection, and the `getCursorTypeString` method on line 137 is used to map the cursor type integer constant to a corresponding string value. The output of this program is as follows.

Output of ResultSetExample2.java

```
ResultSet type: Scroll Insensitive ResultSet.

* * * * * * * * * * * * * * * * * *
movie_name:     The Evil Null Reference
special_promotion:     0
update_date:    2001-01-22
release_date:   2001-01-01
* * * * * * * * * * * * * * * * * *
movie_name:     Just One More Compile
special_promotion:     1
update_date:    2001-10-22
release_date:   2001-01-01
* * * * * * * * * * * * * * * * * *
movie_name:     Another Funny Story
special_promotion:     1
update_date:    2001-10-22
release_date:   2001-01-01

  ** After updates:

* * * * * * * * * * * * * * * * * *
movie_name:     The Evil Null Reference
special_promotion:     5
update_date:    2002-01-11
release_date:   2001-01-01
* * * * * * * * * * * * * * * * * *
movie_name:     Just One More Compile
special_promotion:     5
update_date:    2002-01-11
release_date:   2001-01-01
* * * * * * * * * * * * * * * * * *
movie_name:     One Last Try Before the Lights Go Down
special_promotion:     0
update_date:    2002-01-11
release_date:   2002-01-11
* * * * * * * * * * * * * * * * * *
```

```
movie_name:        Another Funny Story
special_promotion:       5
update_date:    2002-01-11
release_date:   2001-01-01
```

The updateXXXX Methods of the ResultSet Class

The `ResultSet` class contains a number of methods used to provide updateable `ResultSets`. As with the `getXXXX` methods used to retrieve `ResultSet` data, the `ResultSet` class has been designed to contain a group of `updateXXXX` methods with a method for each data type used in JDBC. The naming convention used for these methods is as follows.

```
update<type_name>( integer <column_index>,
                   <data_type_value>);
update<type_name>( String <column_name>,
                   <data_type_value>);
```

Given this naming convention, the method name for updating a `String` column would be as follows.

```
void updateString(int columnIndex, String value);
```

In addition to the methods for updating the column values in the `ResultSet`, methods are provided to perform the database update operations. The `updateRow` method updates the database with the values of the updated columns that have been previously updated with the appropriate `updateXXXX` methods.

The `updateRow` method does not return a status value. The `rowUpdated` method must be called to determine the status of the update operation. This method returns true if the update succeeded *and* the JDBC driver can detect updates. But since not all database drivers can detect updates, it is possible that this method will return false even if the update succeeded.

The `insertRow` method sends the updated values of the inserts on the `ResultSet` to the database. As shown in the previous code example, inserting using a `ResultSet` for SQL insert updates requires moving to the *insert row* using the `moveToInsertRow` method and then using the appropriate `updateXXXX` methods to update the column values in the insert row. Then, once the updates have been performed, the `insertRow` method is called to apply the updates (in this case, a database insert) to the database.

As with the `updateRow` method, the `insertRow` method does not return a status value. The `rowInserted` method must be called to determine the status of the insert operation. This method return a boolean true if the insert succeeded and the driver can detect database updates. It will return false if the insert failed *or* if the driver simply cannot determine the status of the update.

The `deleteRow` method is used to delete the current row. Naturally, as with any delete operation, this should be used with caution. The code should include various checks using `getXXXX` methods to determine that the correct row is being deleted.

As with the `updateRow` and `insertRow` methods, the `deleteRow` method does not return a value. The `rowDeleted` method must be called to determine the status of the operation. This method return a boolean true if the JDBC driver can detect deletes and the delete succeeded. The method will return a false value if the delete operation failed or if the JDBC driver cannot determine the status of the operation.

Obviously, a return value of false from `rowDeleted` or `rowUpdated` creates red flags for using an updateable `ResultSet`. If the JDBC driver admits it cannot determine whether or not an update or delete has succeeded, it is probably best not to make use of the updateable `ResultSet` with that driver.

DATA TYPE MAPPING

As you might expect, the data types of the Java language do not have the same names as the data types of the various relational databases. In fact, relational databases do not have consistent naming among all of the data types they use. Though most relational databases implement some or all of the ANSI SQL 92 data types, most have added additional data types. Part of the reason for this was an effort to distinguish database products and provide additional functionality that users desired, functionality such as a more robust set of data types to serve users' needs.

The data type picture becomes more interesting when the ANSI SQL 99 data types are added to the mix. The ANSI SQL 99 specification includes distinct data types, the ability of the database users to create types as they see fit. This powerful capability adds significant extensibility to a database, which is no longer limited to the set of data types that have been with us virtually since the dawn of the computer (integers, strings, decimals). But adding this extensibility in the database server requires that drivers using the server also support the same extensibility. The JDBC 3.0 specification does provide support for distinct data types and provides a flexible mechanism for driver developers to extend data types as needed.

Since relational databases do not use Java data types, the database data type must be mapped to a Java data type. The mapping operations are fairly logical and are listed in Table 7–2 and discussed in more detail in the following sections.

Table 7–2   *java.sql Package Classes/Interfaces*

SQL Type	Java Type
CHAR	String
VARCHAR	String
LONGVARCHAR	String
NUMERIC	java.math.BigDecimal
DECIMAL	java.math.BigDecimal
BIT	boolean
TINYINT	byte
SMALLINT	short
INTEGER	int
BIGINT	long
REAL	float
FLOAT	double
DOUBLE	double
BINARY	byte[]
VARBINARY	byte[]
LONGVARBINARY	byte[]
DATE	java.sql.Date
TIME	java.sql.Time
TIMESTAMP	java.sql.Timestamp

SQL CHAR Data Type

The SQL CHAR data types all map into the Java String data type. Java has no fixed-length character string arrays; character string arrays in Java should be treated as String data types that can assume a variable length. There is therefore no need to distinguish between variable-length and fixed-length character strings with Java. The SQL data types of CHAR, VARCHAR, and LONGVARCHAR all can be stored in a Java String data type.

SQL DECIMAL and NUMERIC

The SQL DECIMAL and NUMERIC data types are used to represent fixed-point numbers. These two data types are represented using a java.math.BigDecimal data type. This data type is a subtype of the java.lang.Number type. This type provides math operations for Numeric data types to be added, subtracted, multiplied, and divided with Numeric types and other data types.

SQL BINARY, VARBINARY, and LONGVARBINARY

These three data types all can be expressed as byte arrays in Java. Because the LONGVARBINARY data type can be very large, JDBC allows the programmer to set the return value of a LONGVARBINARY to be a Java input stream.

BIT Data Type

The SQL BIT type can be mapped to the Java boolean type. A call to the ResultSet getObject method will return java.lang.Boolean reference for a BIT column.

TINYINT, SMALLINT, INTEGER, and BIGINT

The SQL TINYINT, SMALLINT, INTEGER, and BIGINT types can be mapped to the Java byte, short, int, and long data types respectively. A call to the ResultSet getObject method will return a subclass of java.lang.Number for an integer column. The TINYINT, SMALLINT, and INTEGER will map to java.lang.Integer. The BIGINT will map to java.lang.Long.

REAL, FLOAT, and DOUBLE

The SQL floating-point data types of REAL, FLOAT, and DOUBLE can be mapped as follows. The REAL data type can be stored in a Java float data type, and the REAL and DOUBLE can be stored in a Java double.

DATE, TIME, and TIMESTAMP

SQL provides three date- and time-related data types: DATE, TIME, and TIMESTAMP. The java.util.Date class provides date and time information, but this class does not directly support any of the three SQL date and time data types. To accommodate these SQL data types, three subclasses were declared from java.util.Date; they are java.sql.Date, java.sql.Time, and java.sql.TimeStamp. The java.util.Date class can be used to store SQL date data. The java.util.Time class can be used to store SQL time information. And the java.sql.Timestamp can be used to store SQL timestamp data.

Summary

This chapter continued coverage of the JDBC package and examined what we can do after we have connected to the database. Using the `PreparedStatement` class, we can present our queries to the database before we use them, allowing the database to optimize the query and increasing the speed with which the query will execute when we do use it in our application.

After we have executed our query, we often return data from the database. The JDBC `ResultSet` interface describes the object we will use to examine the rows returned from the database. JDBC `ResultSet` objects have been expanded over the years to allow scrollable cursors, the ability to move randomly through a returned data set, and to conveniently update the database using the same `ResultSet` object.

In the next chapter we will shift our focus to the topic of security. This discussion will begin by examining the Java security architecture and how Java manages system security. We will then focus on the various security APIs that J2EE provides.

Java Security

INTRODUCTION

The Java environment was designed with security in mind. As a language destined for network operation, Java's developers at Sun Microsystems were well aware of the dangers of potential hackers manipulating code being moved over a network. The Java language has built-in security features that can provide tight control over the process of class loading and the interaction of the application to its operating environments (e.g., the disk, the network ports).

As this chapter details, Java security is designed around two types of security: application security and system security. Java provides security features and packages to manage both types of security.

JAVA SECURITY AND PROTECTION DOMAINS

Java security is concerned with two protection domains or areas of the program environment where we will apply security: the *application protection domain* and the *system protection domain*.

The exact configuration of the application protection domain depends on the needs of the particular application. The Java language does not provide a general solution that applies to all application security, but instead provides the the Java Authentication and Authorization (JAAS) package to allow custom security solutions to be developed. We will examine the JAAS package in Chapter 9.

Java system security is concerned with program operations at the system level. This includes accessing disk resources and network connections. Java provides a number of security facilities that control how the application accesses system resources. It is these facilities that will be the subject of this chapter.

THE JAVA SECURITY ENVIRONMENT

Java was originally designed as a language for embedded systems, code that runs in environments where there may or may not be an operating system. This is part of the reason for Java's platform independence. Because of this, Java does not depend on any particular operating system for system security features. Java maintains security through its own set of facilities.

As we just mentioned in the previous section, system level security involves controlling access to such resources as the disk, any system peripherals and the network. Java controls access to these resources through a security manager (`java.lang.SecurityManager`) and an access controller (`java.security.AccessController`) which operate in the Java runtime environment. Access to these system resources is performed through Java base classes (J2SE core classes). When these classes perform an action which attempts to access these resources, the Java runtime environment calls the security manager or access controller to determine whether or not the action is permissible. We will examine the activities performed by these classes later in the chapter.

Figure 8-1 provides a class diagram of the classes used to implement the Java security environment. As we can see, this security environment includes not only access to system resources, but the class loading process. Class loading also represents a security vulnerability for Java applications. As you undoubtedly know at this point, a Java application is comprised of a set of classes. When a Java program starts, it loads these classes using its class loading facilities. Java was designed to be a network programming language and thus certain Java applications can be loaded over a network.

Because of this approach to loading the code for a program, the network represented a potential security vulnerability for the Java application. An individual, the quintessential malicious hacker, could monitor the network and could potentially manipulate network traffic to substitute his or her own version of the class file being loaded over the network. Assuming this individual had bad intentions, the class being substituted could provide a much different set of instructions that

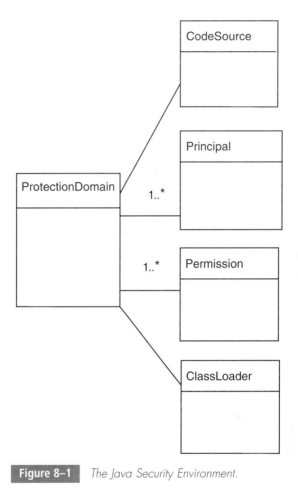

Figure 8–1   *The Java Security Environment.*

what the programmer of the application had intended. This is referred to in security parlance as a 'spoofing attack'.

To protect against this type of attack, the Java class loader was designed to distinguish between classes loaded locally from the local domain and classes loaded over the network. Classes loaded over the network run in a more restricted environment and do not have full system security permissions, which means that they are not allowed to use local system resources. Mechanisms are provided to digitally sign the code loaded over the network and allow it to be trusted by the local JVM; if this is done, then the local JVM may decide to permit access to local resources. We will discuss using digital signatures later in this chapter.

JAVA SECURITY CLASSES

To explain the implementation of Java security we must first understand several key terms. Java system security, in a nutshell, is concerned with *protection domains* as implemented by the `java.security.ProtectionDomain` class. A protection domain associates a code source (`java.security.CodeSource`) with a principal (`java.security.Principal`) and also associates a code source with a set of permissible actions (`java.security.Permission`) (see Figure 8–1).

A code source (`CodeSource`) represents the location where the code was loaded, what is commonly known as a codebase (`java.net.URL`). This could be a local file system or a network location. Associated with the code source are principals represented by the security certificates. These certificates provide a public key, which can be used to validate that a code source has been signed by the private key of the certificate holder.

A principal (`Principal`) represents an authenticated user. The principal is not necessarily a physical user and could also be represented by another system or some other entity. And finally, a permission is used to represent access to a system resource and the associated actions that can be performed on that resource.

To secure Java application code, the developer does not need to provide specific implementations of these classes.

As we will see in the next section, the Java runtime environment uses a security policy file to make specific security declarations. The entries in this file make associations between entries in the policy file which declare the security intentions of the application and the security classes which encapsulate their security declaration. We will see more about the security policy file in the next section.

The Security Policy

A security policy is effectively a set of code sources, associated principals, and associated permissions for a protection domain and is represented by the `java.security.Policy` subclass, as outlined in the previous section. The methods to be implemented in the `Policy` abstract class are listed in Table 8–1.

These methods highlight the associations used by the `Policy` class. Any `Policy` class implementation would logically need to contain members that stored a collection of `Permission` objects referenced by a `CodeSource` object or `ProtectionDomain`.

Note that the `Policy` class is not directly concerned with the `Principal` allowed to use the `PermissionCollection`; instead, that relationship is specified in the `ProtectionDomain`.

The `CodeSource` objects contain a reference to certificates (`java.security.cert.Certificate`), which can be used to validate the signature of a given code source.

| Table 8–1 | *Policy Class Methods* |

Method	Description
`PermissionCollection getPermissions(CodeSource codesource)`	Retrieves a `PermissionCollection` for a given code source.
`PermissionCollection getPermissions(ProtectionDomain domain)`	Retrieves a `PermissionCollection` for a given protection domain.
`static void getPolicy()`	Retrieves a reference to this `Policy` object.
`boolean implies(ProtectionDomain domain, Permission permission)`	Returns a boolean true if the protection domain passed contains the specified permission.
`static void refresh()`	Reloads the settings for this `Policy` object.
`SetPolicy(Policy policy)`	Sets the this `Policy` object to the value of the `Policy` object passed.

The default policy implementation is set with the `policy.provider` parameter in the `java.security` configuration file. A custom implementation could be substituted here, but note that this is something that should be done with care so as not to leave gaping security holes in your application. As we will see shortly, Java provides a robust and finely grained configuration mechanism by default, which should meet the needs of a majority of applications.

The AccessController

Before any system resource can be accessed, the `AccessController` in effect evaluates the request made by the code. The `AccessController` determines whether or not the current security policy allows the action requested. This is determined by the `AccessController` class calling the `checkPermission` method. If none of the callers in the call chain have the correct permissions, then an `AccessControlException` is thrown.

The `AccessController` uses the current policy provider (as set by the `policy.provider` parameter in the security properties file) to determine the current policies. By default, the Java implementation loads a `PolicyFile` implementation of `Policy`, which will read system security policies from a policy configuration file.

The `AccessController` is accessed indirectly at runtime through the installed security manager. The `java.lang.SecurityManager` class contains a `checkPermission` method, which in turn calls the `AccessController` `checkPermission` method. The `AccessController` `checkPermission` method checks the permission against the current `Policy` implementation to determine if the action being attempted is allowed.

The `AccessController` object can also be used to mark a block of code as privileged, to determine whether or not access to a privileged system resource is allowed, and to create a current context to be used to provide access validation services for other blocks of code.

Configuring the Security Policy

Configuring the security policy is done primarily by making entries in the Java security policy file used by the application. By default, this file is located in `JAVA_HOME/jre/lib/security` directory in the `java.policy` file. The Java application can be instructed to read the security policy from another file by changing the setting of the system property `java.security.policy` to the URL of the file to use. The file must of course be in the correct format for a Java security policy file.

Note that by default standalone Java applications (Java code that is not running in a container such as a Web server or J2EE application server) do not load a `SecurityManager`. They must be explicitly instructed to do so. This can be done either programmatically through explicit calls to the `System setSecurityManager` method, or on the command line by setting the `java.security.manager` property.

Each program ultimately has a runtime security context, a security domain. Since Java applications may have multiple threads of execution the Java runtime environment ensures that these threads inherit the security context of their parent.

The Syntax of the Security Policy File

The security policy file allows permissions to be granted to provide access to system resources. This file is composed of various entries concerning the system security of the Java runtime environment.

If a policy file contains a code base that references an alias, or if it contains a reference to a principal, then a keystore file must be available. (The keystore is a file used to store public and private keys, usually in the form of a certificate; it is discussed in more detail in a later section.) A single keystore entry is optionally entered in the security policy file as follows.

```
keystore "keystore_url", "keystore_type";
```

The first entry is the string `keystore`, the second entry is the URL for the keystore, and the third entry is the type of keystore (for example, "`JKS`"). The URL may be an absolute URL or a relative URL. If it is relative, then it is relative to the security properties file being read. The type describes the format of the entries in the keystore with the default being JKS, the proprietary Sun format.

After the keystore entry, one or more grant entries may appear in the file. The syntax for these entries is as follows.

```
grant [SignedBy "signer"] [, CodeBase "<code_base_URL"]
    [, Principal [class_name] "principal_name"]
... {
    permission class_name [ "<target>" ]
                [, "action"] [, SignedBy "signer_names"];
    permission ...
};
```

The only required clauses for the grant entry are the permission class name and the permission. Elimination of one of the clauses indicates the entry applies to all of the instances of the element that could be referenced in the clause. For example, the following entry applies to all code bases, all principals, and any signers.

```
grant {
    permission java.net.SocketPermission "localhost:1024-", "listen";
    permission java.util.PropertyPermission "java.version", "read";
    permission java.util.PropertyPermission "java.vendor", "read";
};
```

Since the code base, principal, and signer entries are eliminated, this entry would grant the specified permissions globally. Note that multiple permissions may be assigned in the same grant block.

The SignedBy clause is used to indicate the name or names used to sign the code. The CodeBaseURL supports wildcard syntax, which differs slightly from common file system wildcard syntax. A trailing / matches all class files in the referenced directory, and a trailing /* matches all files, both class files and JAR files, in the directory referenced and recursively through all subdirectories. If omitted, then the grant entry applies to any code base. For example, the grant entry

```
grant CodeBase "file://my_apps/Java/*" { ...
```

would provide all code loaded from the URL specified in the CodeBase entry, regardless of their names, with the permissions specified in the grant entry.

The SignedBy element may contain a comma-separated list of signers (the command indicating an and boolean assignment, not an or). The signer name is an alias that must be associated with a certificate in the keystore. As with the code base entry, if the signer element is omitted, then the grant entry applies to any signer.

The permission entry references the implementation of the Permission class. The Permission class may also optionally be signed, and a SignedBy element in the grant statement can be associated with the Permission class.

The permissions assigned using the `grant` statement are subclasses of the `java.security.Permission` class. Some of the more commonly used system resource permissions, which are subclasses of the `Permission` class, are listed in Table 8–2.

Table 8–2 *Permission Subclasses*

Permission	Description
FilePermission	This permission identifies which files and/or directories may be accessed using file I/O and the types of access that are allowed.
SocketPermission	This permission identifies which sockets may be accessed and what type of access may be used on those sockets.
RuntimePermission	The base permission class for runtime operations; provides the capability to restrict operations such as exiting the virtual machine (VM) and loading specific libraries.
AllPermission	This class provides all permissions allowed on all actions. Recommended for testing, *not* for runtime production use.

The `AllPermission` class is a convenience mechanism that relaxes all security for the code base to which it is granted. An example of the use of `AllPermission` is as follows:

```
grant codeBase "file:/lin/local/jdk/j2sdkee1.3.1/lib/j2ee.jar" {
    permission java.security.AllPermission;
};
```

In this example, all permissions are granted to the `j2ee.jar` code base, the core classes for the J2EE package. Since this particular JAR is considered trusted code, this does not undermine system security.

Hackers usually access a system through a network connection. Most firewalls make a significant effort to reduce the exposure of a server to the network by shutting down unused ports and limiting the protocols and packets that are allowed into the network. Java applications can also be configured to limit their exposure to the network. With the `SecurityManager` installed, all code bases are prohibited from making network connections unless explicitly granted permission to do so. The `SocketPermission` class is used to allow a network socket connection to be made, as the following entry demonstrates.

```
// any service can access these ports
grant codebase "file:./service/-" {
```

```
    permission java.net.SocketPermission "localhost:3306",
                                          "connect,accept";
    permission java.net.SocketPermission "localhost:389",
                          "connect,accept";
};
```

Many hacker programs have managed to infiltrate a system and execute applications on those systems in order to wreak their havoc. With a `SecurityManager` installed, Java completely restricts the execution of programs on the local machine. Should an application need to execute a program, a `FilePermission` can be granted to the file to allow execution, as follows.

```
grant codebase "/batch/-" {
    permission java.io.FilePermission "/local/batch/runjobs.sh", "execute";
};
```

Granting these permissions would allow the code base with the defined URL (`/batch`) the permission to execute the file specified (`/local/batch/run-jobs.sh`).

To make the programming of a policy file somewhat easier, environment variable values are accessible in the `security.policy` file, as shown below.

```
grant codeBase "file:${java.home}/lib/ext/*" {
        permission java.security.AllPermission;
};
```

In this example, the code base is specified relative to a Java home, which is provided via environment variable expansion.

The AllPermission Class

One of the more dangerous permissions that can be granted is the `AllPermission`. This permission effectively turns security off for the specified code base. When used as shown below, it turns system security off for all code bases and allows unfettered access to all code.

```
grant {
        permission java.security.AllPermission;
}
```

In this security policy grant example, no code base is identified and so the permission is applied to all code loaded by the application. No parameters are passed to the permission class. As written, this `grant` statement allows free, unfettered access to system resources. While this may be convenient for application development (and is still not recommended), this is definitely not recommended for production.

The Java Security Configuration File

Java uses a security configuration file to assign various properties that affect the execution of security policies and the use of security facilities such as encryption and secure sockets layer (SSL). This file is located in `JAVA_HOME/jre/lib/security` and is named `java.security`.

The entries in this file have direct control over how security will be implemented. Java cryptography providers can be identified in this file, and since more than one provider may implement the same algorithm, a priority can be assigned to the provider (perhaps on the basis of the most efficient or strongest and most secure). A few minor entries and changes in this file can greatly strengthen the security for a system. The following sections detail the entries in this file.

Security Provider Entries

The providers identified in this section must provide a concrete subclass of the abstract `Provider` class. More than one provider may be identified using the following syntax.

```
security.provider.<n>=<className>
```

In this example, the `<n>` represents a priority number where the number 1 is used for the default provider (the one used when no specific provider is identified). A common set of providers, the set shipped with the JDK 1.4 release, is as follows.

```
security.provider.1=sun.security.provider.Sun
security.provider.2=com.sun.net.ssl.internal.ssl.Provider
security.provider.3=com.sun.rsajca.Provider
security.provider.4=com.sun.crypto.provider.SunJCE
security.provider.5=sun.security.jgss.SunProvider
```

Login Configuration

The JAAS package provides a facility for authentication and authorization using pluggable modules. The login configuration file setting can be used to specify the configuration of the login modules, specifying which login module will be used for which application.

The System Policy

The system policy controls the loading of the default security policy for an application. This can be changed at runtime with a call to the `Policy setPolicy` method (if permissions allow it to be changed). This entry specifies an implementation of the `java.security.Policy` abstract class and is set as follows.

```
policy.provider=sun.security.provider.PolicyFile
```

The previous entry specified the class that will implement the security policy. The default implementation of the `Policy` class reads the system security policy from a file. The file URL can be set with entries in the security configuration file, or it can be set (or appended) by setting the system property `java.security.policy`. The following are the two default entries provided in the default security configuration file.

```
policy.url.1=file:${java.home}/lib/security/java.policy
policy.url.2=file:${user.home}/.java.policy
```

There is a feature that allows environment properties to be expanded in the policy file. While this is a somewhat convenient feature, it also presents a security loophole that could be exploited by would-be hackers. This feature can be turned off using the following configuration file entry.

```
policy.expandProperties=true
```

As mentioned previously, security policy files can be passed into a program on the command line (by setting the `java.security.policy` system property). Once again, this is convenient but does present a potential security flaw. This feature can be turned off using the following entry.

```
policy.allowSystemProperty=true
```

JAR Signing and Keystores

The JDK 1.1 version used a slightly different version of JAR signing. This setting allows the `IdentityScope` to be ignored, and if the identity is found, the code base is granted all permissions.

```
policy.ignoreIdentityScope=false
```

Java supports different formats for the keystore (certificate database) file. The default keystore type is set with the following entry.

```
keystore.type=jks
```

The system scope, the database of identities, is identified with the following entry.

```
system.scope=sun.security.provider.IdentityDatabase
```

Controlling Package Access

Several important system packages contain methods and members that could be misused if placed in the hands of hackers. The `ClassLoader loadClass` method first determines whether or not a class is accessible by calling the `SecurityManager checkPackageAccess` method. The `package.access` parameter shown below contains the list of network names or partial names that will be examined by the class loader before loading the class. The common practice is to place entries here that are used internally but should not be used by other code.

```
package.access=sun.
```

A similar security breach could involve the insertion of rogue classes in trusted Java packages. This behavior can be controlled using the package definition entry shown below.

```
package.definition=sun.
```

By default, there are no package names provided for this property. A secure application would want to identify trusted packages (for example, `sun.`, `java.lang.`) and place the package names in this list.

Overriding Security Properties

One potential security intrusion would be to override critical security properties when loading a class. This can be prohibited using the following entry.

```
security.overridePropertiesFile=true
```

Default Key Manager Algorithm

The default key manager algorithm can be specified with the following entry.

```
ssl.KeyManagerFactory.algorithm=SunX509
ssl.TrustManagerFactory.algorithm=SunX509
```

JSSE Parameters

The Java Secure Sockets Extension (JSSE) package creates secure sockets which provide secure communications over public networks like the internet. A default socket factory and server socket factory can be identified using these properties.

The entries below are commented out, allowing the Java implementation to use the SSL implementation which is packaged with the standard version of Java.

```
#ssl.SocketFactory.provider=
#ssl.ServerSocketFactory.provider=
```

Network-Specific Settings

The Java language provides several methods that perform a domain name lookup. The following property allows the number of seconds to cache an entry to be defined. A negative value indicates the domain name should be cached forever. A positive number is the number of seconds to cache an address, and a 0 indicates the address should not be cached.

You should be careful when changing any of these parameters. A DNS spoofing attack would take advantage of cached values so that aggressive name caching could lead to a DNS spoofing attack. The following entry sets the cache to exist forever.

```
networkaddress.cache.ttl=-1
```

The following property affects the length of time in seconds that failed lookups will be kept in the cache. It sets the time to live (TTL) failed lookup timeout to 10 seconds.

```
networkaddress.cache.negative.ttl=10
```

PROVIDING SECURITY THROUGH ENCRYPTION

Java programs and components involve the manipulation of information in some form. In many cases, this information should be kept secure. Prior to rapid growth of the Internet, a common solution to keeping information secure was to create a secure point-to-point network, one in which it would be difficult or impossible for some untrusted third party to access the network.

Today, however, the use of the Internet for transfer of information is a very practical and cost-effective solution. What must be managed is the security and integrity of the information being transferred over the public network. This is accomplished by effectively hiding the information in plain sight through the application of cryptography.

Cryptography is the science of encryption of information. In essence, encryption allows information to be transmitted over open channels, in open view of those who want unauthorized access to the information. Encryption scrambles the information being transmitted in such a way that descrambling that information is so difficult and would take such a large amount of time and CPU power that it is practically impossible for the unauthorized user to gain access to the information.

Cryptography is by no means new. In fact, much of the advanced math that is the foundation of modern cryptography had its roots in the effort to code military messages during World War II. The processing power of modern computers now make it possible to perform these intensive computations relatively quickly and thus allow advanced encryption to be used for the mundane purpose of information interchange.

These encryption techniques take a given set of bytes, which could be a string of text data, an integer number, or the byte codes of a Java program. This data is manipulated or encrypted in such a way that the result is completely indecipherable to anyone who does not understand the encryption technique. To make this encryption process more effective, the manipulation of the data that produces the encrypted format uses a *key* to perform the encryption process. Exactly how that key is used defines the type of encryption used.

Symmetric encryption involves the process of providing both the sender or producer of the encrypted data and the receiver of the encrypted data with the same key, which is known as a *secret key*. The sender and receiver must agree on the key and the cryptographic algorithm before the process starts. The sender encrypts the data with the secret key, and the recipient uses the secret key to decrypt the data.

The secret key used by these parties must be kept secret. If a third party were to gain access to the secret key, he or she could use it to decrypt the messages being transferred and would thus be able to compromise the security of the communications.

Secret key encryption can be efficient and effective but is also problematic for two of the reasons cited already. Both parties must have knowledge of the encryption algorithm to use, and both must have possession of the secret key. Dissemination of the secret key may not be a problem for a small group of 20 or 30 users, but for an e-commerce site with 20,000 users, disseminating a key before encryption is used would be difficult.

Private key encryption manages to solve some of the problems of symmetric encryption using a technique known as asymmetric encryption. With this type of encryption the recipient of a message sends a public key to the sender of the message. Using an agreed-upon encryption algorithm, the sender of the message encrypts the message and sends it. Even if a hacker managed to obtain the public key for the encryption and knew the algorithm, he or she would not be able to decrypt the message. (The caveat is that using present-day computing power and spending 30 years of computer time to crack the encryption is not practical.)

Public key encryption solves the problem of key dissemination. The sender of the message does not need to provide secure transfer of private keys. The recipient, however, must have a private key that corresponds to the public key he or she uses and must keep the private key secure.

Asymmetric encryption solves the key dissemination issue of symmetric encryption, but it does so at a cost. Asymmetric encryption requires much more CPU power than secret key encryption, so the encryption of large amounts of data using this technique is not currently feasible.

Given the issues with both of these techniques, you may think that some process that takes the best of both approaches would be a viable solution. In fact, that is a very big part of what SSL provides, as we will see in Chapter 10, "The Java Secure Sockets Extension: JSSE."

Message Digest

With the knowledge that encryption will always exact its toll on CPU resources, we need to carefully consider when to encrypt and what needs to be encrypted. In many cases, security procedures do not require that all information be concealed. Much business data (for example, the number of staff retiring in the Denver, Colorado, office) is not of any practical use to a hacker or even to an individual with knowledge of the company's business. But what needs to be prevented is the manipulation of this information. Simple manipulation of data provides an outlet for the destructive security hack—an unsophisticated yet problematic security breach.

A message digest can provide this level of security without the overhead of complete message encryption. A message digest is computed by scanning the bytes of a message and using a one-way hash algorithm, computing a string that is representative of the contents of the message. The result is a digital signature computed using an algorithm that makes it extremely difficult to convert from the digital signature string back into the message text. This signature is in turn encrypted using a technique that can be decrypted by the recipient of the message.

The recipient of the message decrypts the digital signature and then recomputes the one-way hash of the message. If the signatures match, the recipient can be assured that the message has not been tampered with. The MD5 (message digest 5) and SHA-1 are common message digest algorithms.

THE JAVA KEYSTORE

The keystore file is a database containing a collection of public/private key pairs in the form of a certificate. The certificate type is usually an X.509 certificate, though other formats are supported. A key entry in the keystore holds the cryptographic keys in an encrypted format, encrypted using the password for the keystore. The key entry is usually a *secret key* or *private key* or a *public key/private key* pair.

A recipient of a message containing a digital signature would require a certificate containing the public key of the digital signature. The digital signature has been encrypted using a private key but can be decrypted using a public key. The public key for the decryption can be distributed in the form of a certificate. The recipient can then use the public key to decrypt the digital signature.

The recipient will most likely want to verify that the certificate he or she is using is in fact the certificate from the intended sender. The recipient can verify the signature with a trusted Certificate Authority (CA), a third party that can validate the certificate as authentic when the certificate is received.

A verifiable certificate is created by having the originator of the certificate send the certificate to the CA. The CA signs the certificate and sends it back to the originator. The originator can then send the certificate to a client who requests a secure message. The client can receive the certificate and request the CA to validate the certificate. If the CA validates the certificate, the client can be sure that he or she is communicating with the correct party and the security certificate can be trusted.

Certificates can be self-signed, which may be acceptable on a local network, but will probably not be adequate (and may not be accepted) for Internet communications.

What is actually stored in the keystore file is a certificate chain. The certificate chain is a group of certificates that all relate to the same security entity.

Security Certificates

Security certificates are a facility used in public key encryption that provide a means of distributing public keys efficiently and securely. Certificates are usually digitally signed using a one-way hashing algorithm. This ensures that the signature can be decrypted only by the corresponding public key for the private key that was used to sign the certificate.

Signed certificates are distributed with the public key that corresponds to a private key of the signer of the certificate. The distributor of the certificate can using hash algorithms to ensure that the contents of a particular file has not been tampered with. The distributor of the file executes a hash algorithm on the contents and generate a checksum. The checksum is encrypted using the private key of the sender. The recipient receives the file and uses the public key to decrypt the hash. The recipient can then recompute the hash on the file received, and if it does not match the hash he or she has decrypted, the recipient knows the file has been tampered with.

To avoid the overhead of distributing certificates to all possible recipients of a encrypted document, Certificate Authorities (CA) can be used. A CA represents a trusted third party who will verify a certificate. This allows the distributor of a public key to pass the certificate to potential recipients who need to receive encrypted messages. The recipients can then validate the certificate with the CA to ensure they have not received a certificate from some other (potentially malicious) party.

One of the more common certificate formats is X.509, but other formats are also used and supported by the Java security packages.

USING THE KEYTOOL UTILITY

The JDK provides a command-line utility named `keytool` for manipulation of the keystore key database. This tool is run from the command line and accepts a number of parameters that allow it to be used to create new certificates, to import certificates, to delete certificates, or to generate certificate-signing requests (CSRs) for Certificate Authorities.

The following sections detail some of the more common actions that can be executed with this command and the parameters used to execute the actions. If all required parameters have not been passed in the command, then the `keytool` command will prompt for additional parameters. For the commands shown below, the `keytool` command will prompt the user for one or more passwords.

Generating a Key

Keys can be generated by running `keytool` from the command line using the `-genkey` parameter. Executing this command will generate the key and automatically wrap the key in a self-signed certificate. The `-keystore` parameter is usually used with the command to identify the name of the keystore database for the certificate. If the keystore does not exist, it will be created. A `-alias` parameter can be used to associate a name with the certificate. The following provides an example of generating a new certificate key.

```
keytool -genkey -alias myKey -keystore myCerts
```

Execution of this command will prompt for a password for the keystore and will then prompt the user with a series of questions about the certificate, such as the name to be associated with the certificate, the organizational unit, and a password. When completed, the certificate will reside in the keystore specified and will be referenced using the alias name specified. If the keystore `myCerts` does not exist, it will be created.

Listing a Key Certificate

The `keytool` command allows the certificates in a keystore to be listed. This is executed on the command line using a `-list` parameter. If a specific certificate is not specified, then all certificates in the keystore will be listed. If a `-alias` parameter is passed with the alias of a certificate, then the certificate specified will be displayed. If no alias is specified, then all certificates in the keystore will be displayed. The `-v` parameter will provide verbose output. The following command lists the contents of the `myKey` certificate.

```
keytool -list -v -alias myKey -keystore teststore -keypass password
```

The output of this command is as follows.

```
Alias name: artskey
Creation date: Thu May 09 20:07:27 EDT 2002
Entry type: keyEntry
Certificate chain length: 1
Certificate[1]:
Owner: CN=Art Taylor, OU=Books Inc., O=Books Inc., L=Unknown, ST=Unknown, C=US
Issuer: CN=Art Taylor, OU=Books Inc., O=Books Inc., L=Unknown, ST=Unknown, C=US
Serial number: 3cdb0f31
Valid from: Thu May 09 20:07:13 EDT 2002 until: Wed Aug 07 20:07:13 EDT 2002
Certificate fingerprints:
        MD5:  C2:C6:84:03:26:79:2F:A8:D1:F0:24:E5:4F:0D:04:F5
        SHA1: 6E:EE:8E:A7:96:24:1E:59:66:64:4E:A1:6C:1E:48:DC:67:C2:2E:76
```

Exporting a Certificate

A certificate containing a public key could be distributed to client applications to decrypt documents encrypted with the corresponding private key. This would require that the certificate be manually exported using the `-export` parameter in combination with the `-alias` parameter. The `-file` parameter could be used to export the certificate to a specific file, as the following command demonstrates.

```
keytool -export -alias myKey -file artskey.cer -keystore myKeystore
```

This command exports the `myKey` certificate to the file named `artskey.cer`. The keystore database used would be the `myKeystore` database. If the `-file` parameter is not specified, then the certificate would be exported to the console (standard out).

Generating a CSR

Passing a certificate to a CA for signing allows the certificate to be authenticated by clients (many of which will not accept a self-certified certificate). A certificate can be exported from the keystore using the `keytool -certreq` parameter. Using this command requires the `-alias` parameter to be used to identify a specific certificate and a file to be used for exporting the CSR. The following is an example of using this command.

```
keytool - certreq -alias c2 -keystore myKeystore -file c2.csr
```

This command generates a CSR in a file named `c1.csr` for the certificate alias of `c2`. This CSR is then sent to a CA for signing. The reply from the CA is imported into the keystore (and added to the certificate chain for the certificate in the process).

Importing a Certificate

Executing the `keytool` command with the `-import` parameter will import certificates directly into the keystore. This would be used to import a certificate that has been exported from another keystore or to import a certificate reply from a CA. A `-file` parameter is required to indicate the file to import. An example of using this parameter is shown below.

```
keytool -import -file artskey.cer -alias artskey -keystore newstore
```

This command imports the certificate specified by the `-file` parameter using the alias specified by the `-alias` parameter. The keystore to be used is the one specified by the `-keystore` parameter. The end result is that the certificate contained in the file `artskey.cer` will be imported into the `newstore` keystore database.

Creating a Self-Certifying Certificate

A self-certifying certificate is often used for testing purposes or within a corporate firewall. This command is executed using the `-selfcert` parameter with the `-alias` parameter to specify the certificate to self-certify. The following command demonstrates the use of these parameters with an additional parameter to specify a keystore to use.

```
keytool -selfcert -alias artskey -keystore teststore
```

Using the jarsigner Tool

One of the notable advantages of Java is that some or all of the application can be downloaded over the Internet. Java classes loaded via a class loader can be retrieved over a network connection. This advantage comes with risks. A hacker, an impersonator, could intercept a class-loading event and insert a malicious version of a class. Without some mechanism for verifying the contents of a code loaded over the network, the application could be compromised.

A `jarsigner` utility is available for attaching a digital signature to a JAR file. This digital signature is verified against a signature in a keystore to authenticate the

JAR file. Certain key permissions can then be verified using the `SignedBy` clause in the security policy file. To digitally sign a JAR file, the following command is used.

```
jarsigner -keystore acctKeyStore accounting.jar apkey
```

This command associates the alias `artskey` with the contents of the JAR file. To verify the signature of a JAR file, the following command is used.

```
jarsigner -verify -keystore acctKeyStore accounting.jar apkey
```

Using this command, if any of the components of the JAR file have not been signed, the output of the `-verify` command will indicate this.

A signed JAR file can then be distributed and authenticated by client programs holding the public key certificate for the certificate used to sign the JAR. For instance, a certificate `secureJar` could be created as follows.

```
keytool -genkey -alias secureJar
```

The key could be made self-certifying as follows.

```
keytool -selfcert -alias secureJar
```

The jar file could then be signed as follows.

```
jarsigner test.jar secureJar
```

The certificate then needs to be exported (to export the public key) as follows.

```
keytool -export -alias secureJar -file secureJar.cert
```

This exported certificate then must be made available to the client program by importing the certificate into the keystore for the runtime environment for the program. This is done as follows.

```
keytool -import -alias secureJar -file secureJar.cert
```

The policy file indicates that any code loaded needs to be signed using the `secureJar` certificate. The following grant entry provides that security.

```
...
grant SignedBy "secureJar"  {
    permission java.io.FilePermission "<<ALL FILES>>", "execute";
};
...
```

Any Java application running with a security manager would need to be signed using the `secureJar` certificate. The following code snippet shows execution of the UNIX `logger` command, which will write an entry to the UNIX system log (`syslog`). Since a file is being accessed (`logger`), the Java program requires execute permission for that file.

```
...
try {
    Runtime.getRuntime().exec(
            "logger Error on Queue L120 Access." );
}
catch (java.io.IOException e ) {
    System.out.println("exception in main: " + e );
    e.printStackTrace();
...
```

Sealed JAR Files

A sealed JAR file is a file that indicates that the contents of a specific package must be retrieved from this JAR file and not from some other source. This furthers security by providing assurances that malicious code cannot be inserted into the package. In fact, using sealed JAR files in combination with signed JAR files, it is extremely difficult to insert malicious code into a package. (I do not say impossible, since cracking the encryption techniques for the digital signatures or gaining password access to the keystores and manipulating the certificates would allow the JAR files to be compromised.)

Placing the `Sealed` directive in the manifest file for the archive indicates that either the entire archive is sealed or the previously named package is sealed. The syntax for this entry is as follows.

```
...
Name: /com/taylor/accounting/
Sealed: true
```

Appearing in a manifest, the entry above indicates that the contents of the `com.taylor.accounting` package are sealed. Any code attempting to run as part of this package would need to be loaded by the class loader from this JAR file.

If the `Sealed` directive is placed on the first line of a manifest entry, the entire contents of the archive are considered. The directive to seal an entire archive could be made in exclusion of other packages in the archive, as shown below.

```
Sealed: true
Name: com/taylor/misc
Sealed: false
...
```

These entries indicate that the entire archive is sealed to the exclusion of the `com.taylor.misc` package. These entries would appear in the manifest and would be included in the JAR file with the following syntax.

```
jar -cvmf acctgManifest extensions
```

The policytool Program

In a rare departure from command-line tools, Sun provides the Policy Tool program for the manipulation of policy files. Though it is often easier to code the policy file by hand (the parser is pretty clear about errors), the GUI tool does provide some useful prompts for those unfamiliar with the syntax of policy files. Figure 8–2 provides an example of the `policytool` interface.

Figure 8–2   *Java Policy Tool.*

SUMMARY

Java provides a great number of security features, but they are not used by default. As developers, we must understand these features and know how to use them and implement in any application requiring security.

This chapter explained the various Java language security features available: policy files, class loaders, access controllers, JAR file signing, and certificate keystore manipulation. If used appropriately, these features can provide a high level of security for your Java applications.

We saw that encryption can help secure information being passed over a network. This is a vitally important feature since many Java applications make use of the internet, a public network accessed by millions any one of which could read unencrypted information traveling over the network. We provide additional coverage of these topics in Chapter 10 which covers the JSSE package which provides access to the SSL protocol to secure a network channel, and Chapter 11 which covers the JCE package which provides access to various cryptography facilities.

The next chapter explores the Java authentication and authorization package, which augments the basic Java security features with additional security features, including login modules (authentication) and permission checking (authorization).

The Java Authentication and Authorization API (JAAS)

INTRODUCTION

Though Java has always had strong system-level security, it lacked an API for authentication of users (verifying that a user is who he or she claims to be) and authorization of users (verifying that a user is allowed to perform a specific operation). The Java Authentication and Authorization Service (JAAS) provides a security API for the Java language that, as the name implies, provides classes and interfaces that can be used to provide authorization and authentication services.

As applications change over time, the security components of the application must also change. An application could start as a character-based application with no user interface, and then later be developed with a GUI component for user interaction. JAAS was designed with a pluggable architecture. Certain modules can be changed and swapped, while application code remains unchanged. In this chapter we examine both the authentication and authorization components of the JAAS package.

PACKAGE HISTORY AND DESIGN

The JAAS package was introduced as an optional package in Java 1.2 and 1.3 versions; it is now part of the core set of APIs for the Java 1.4 version. JAAS is tightly integrated with the Java security classes, interacting with the active `SecurityManager` and `AccessController` class instances when needed.

Before JAAS was available, Java security only allowed code to be executed based on where the code had originated. With JAAS, applications can now examine who is running the application and make security decisions based on that information.

JAAS is designed to be modular and pluggable, meaning that certain portions can be swapped with other similar modules as needed. These pluggable components could be developed as part of your project or could be third-party components. As technology changes and authentication or authorization techniques improve, improved modules could be added to your application.

JAAS does not replace the Java security framework, but instead adds to that framework to provide a set of features that was lacking in previous releases. The functionality added is authentication and authorization, which we define as follows.

> **Authentication** is the ability to determine with reliability the entity is running the application code.
>
> **Authorization** is the ability to determine that the entity attempting to perform an action has the permission to do so.

As are other portions of the Java security framework, JAAS is built on the concept of principals and subjects. An entity is the focus of our security efforts. Conceptually, an entity could be an individual, a group of individuals, a corporation, or a login ID with which we decide to associate security rights.

A principal is an entity that has been granted specific security rights. This is the identity we choose to use for security purposes. The principal is expanded with the concept of a *subject*. A subject can have multiple principals associated with it, reflecting the real world where a user may have permission to use multiple systems or multiple functions within a system. A user may have one identity (principal) used to access an accounting system and one identity to access a human resources system. We expect that a robust application development environment would be able to manage these requirements using a single login operation, what is known as a *single-sign-on*.

A subject represents the focus of our security processing and must be authenticated by our login process. A subject may also have a set of associated security credentials. These credentials may be private, intended to be kept secret, or public, intended to be viewed by the world at large. The JAAS subject can support both types of credentials.

Table 9-1	*Common JAAS Classes*

Class/Interface	Purpose
LoginModule	Responsible for validating the user (either with a CallbackHandler or through some other means) and assigning principals to the subject.
CallbackHandler	Responsible for interacting with the user to validate the user's identity.
Subject	The focus of the login process; associated with one or more principals.
Principal	An entity that has been granted access rights.

THE JAAS PACKAGE

The JAAS package is composed of a number of classes and interfaces. While it is beyond the scope of this chapter to cover all of the classes, it is worthwhile to cover some of the more commonly used classes, listed in Table 9–1.

Together these classes provide the authentication and authorization services of JAAS.

The Subject Class

The Subject class represents the object of our security. An instance of the Subject class would contain one or more principals that represent the authenticated identity of our subject. The Subject class is the result of the JAAS authentication process. If a JAAS login process is successful, then it will result in a subject and associated principals for the login. The Subject class also provides authorization services through several methods which allow the privileged execution of an action; we will examine this facility later in this chapter.

The Principal Class

The Principal class represents an authenticated entity. Though the principal is often a person—a system user—a principal could also be a business entity, a group of users sharing a common login, or an external system that must be used for data interchange. If a Subject instance has a set of associated principals, then it we assert that the subject has been authenticated.

The LoginModule Class

The `LoginModule` is an interface implemented by authentication providers to provide authentication services. The implementation of this interface must provide the methods for initialization, the login process, and committing or aborting the login process.

The `LoginContext` represents the controller for the login process. It has access to the `LoginModule` and `Subject` to use to perform the authentication process. The context either is provided a `Subject` to use or creates its own `Subject`.

The CallbackHandler Class

The `CallbackHandler` interface is implemented to handle the login process. The implementation of this interface interacts with the `LoginModule` to authenticate the entity attempting the login.

Using Credentials

A security credential is a general concept representing relevant security properties. There is a great deal of variation in the nature and structure of security credentials, so the JAAS does not attempt to define a specific credential. Instead, any object may represent a credential in JAAS. The package provides collections for storage of credentials in the `Subject` class.

The credential may optionally implement two interfaces to provide some functionality for the credential. The `javax.security.auth.Refreshable` interface provides a set of methods for refreshing the credential, which can be used by callers to request that the credential be refreshed. Similarly the `javax.security.auth.Destroyable` exposes methods that allow callers to request that the credential be destroyed.

AUTHENTICATION WITH JAAS

As we develop any secure application, we must make certain that the user who is running the program is in fact the user we expected. This requires a login process. Almost every user interface requires a login process. If ever there was a process with code reuse potential, it is the login process. This point was not lost on JAAS designers.

JAAS authentication revolves around the `LoginModule` (`javax.security.auth.spi.LoginModule`). The `LoginModule` is a pluggable interface that provides the login services and completes the connection of the authentication process with the `Subject`. The implementation of the `LoginModule` is loaded by a `LoginContext`, which controls the login process. The `LoginContext` can optionally work with a `CallBackHandler` (`javax.security.auth.call-back.CallbackHandler`) to manage the interaction required to perform the authentication. The overloaded constructor for the `LoginContext` provides parameters for the `CallbackHandler`, `Subject`, and the name of the JAAS configuration to use (see Figure 9–1).

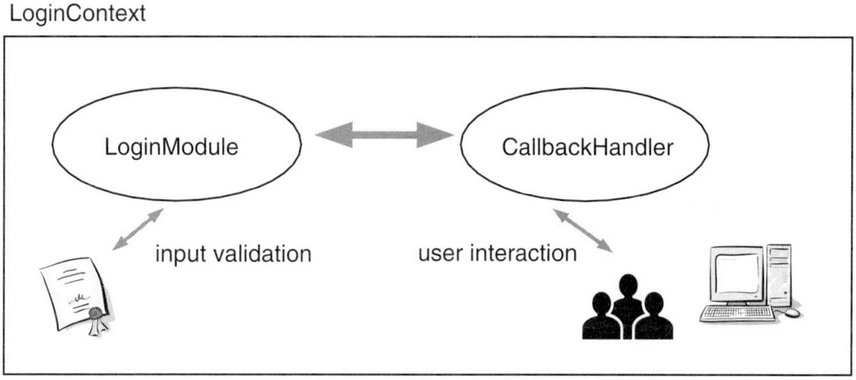

LoginContext

Figure 9–1   *CallbackHandler–LoginModule interaction.*

The login process is initiated using the `login` method of the `LoginContext`. The implementation of this method is expected to make calls on the `LoginModule` to perform the login process and optionally commit or roll back, depending on the results of the login. The `CallbackHandler` can be used to handle the events triggered by the login process. The following sections provide an example to demonstrate this nontrivial process.

JAAS Configuration

JAAS is designed to be highly configurable. A configuration file can be used to define one or more `LoginModule` implementations for a specific login configuration. This approach simplifies to the adaptation of an application to different environments where different login modules may be used, and allows multiple login modules and requirement parameters to be defined. The ability to define multiple login modules for a single configuration also helps with the implementation of a *single sign-on* security implementation, where a user can log in once and be automatically logged into multiple security accounts.

A `LoginModule` configuration in the JAAS configuration file can be assigned a value of `required`, `sufficient`, `requisite`, or `optional`. The specific values for these parameters and their meaning and impact on the login process are defined by the LoginModule implementation. A sample login configuration file is shown below.

```
SimpleLogin {
  com.ourgroup.logins.SimpleLogin required;
}

SecureAppLogin {
com.ourgroup.logins.MainLoginModule required;
com.sun.security.auth.module.NTLoginModule sufficient;
com.sun.security.auth.module.UnixLoginModule optional;
com.foo.Kereberos optional debug=true;
}
```

This configuration file contains two login configurations. If we were using this configuration file, then when the LoginContext is instantiated, it would reference one of these configurations. The first configuration is named SimpleLogin and identifies a single login module, which is required. It can be assumed that this login is being used by an application that does not have complex security requirements with different principals required to perform actions.

The second configuration file entry is named SecureAppLogin and contains a number of entries for various LoginModule implementations. The first entry identifies a MainLoginModule as a required login module. The NTLoginModule and the UnixLoginModule are also identified as login modules whose login information may be used as part of the login process. Using these modules can save development effort by allowing information collected by OS logins to be used as part of the authentication process.

CODE EXAMPLE

Using JAAS involves the interaction of a number of classes and configuration files. The classes involved in using JAAS are not just the classes in the JAAS package, but include the Java SecurityManager and the AccessController, classes that are part of the Java security framework. In addition to these classes, entries in the security policy file, the Java security configuration file, and the JAAS configuration file may also be required.

The following example demonstrates the use of JAAS for both authentication and authorization. First, the user is authenticated using one of several LoginContext initializations. Following a successful login, authorization is tested by executing several privileged actions using the Subject class.

The first order of business in this example is to create a `LoginContext` instance. We then use the `LoginContext` instance to perform our authentication using the `LoginContext login` method.

To instantiate the `LoginContext`, we use one of the overloaded constructors for the class. In this particular example, we want to test several methods of processing the authentication, so we allow a command-line parameter to be passed into the program. This command-line parameter is then used to create an instance of the `LoginContext` using one of four different sets of parameters.

The first parameter to the `LoginContext` constructor is a string that relates to a login configuration entry in the JAAS configuration file. The second optional entry is a reference to a handler for the login processing callbacks (the events triggered by the login process). This parameter is optional, so the constructor can be called with a single parameter, the configuration name, in which case a default callback handler as defined by the `auth.login.defaultCallbackHandler` security property will be used. If that property is not set, then the JAAS package assumes that the `LoginModule` (as specified in the JAAS configuration file) will manage the callbacks as needed.

The login configurations identified by the first string passed into these constructors references implementations of the `LoginModule` interface. As indicated earlier, one or more `LoginModule` implementations can be specified. Though not shown explicitly in this example, multiple login modules in the configuration file will be executed depending on the parameters associated with the login configuration. We will examine the rest of the `DemoJAAS` class before we review the alternative `LoginModule` implementations used.

Once the `LoginContext` has been created (and the associated `LoginModule` or `LoginModule` implementations have been identified and loaded), the `LoginContext login` method is called to perform the login process. The execution of this method leads to interaction between the `LoginModule` or `LoginModule` implementations identified and the optional `CallbackHandler` that has been identified.

It is common practice that if a user has entered an incorrect password, he or she should be given another chance to enter the password. To provide this functionality, in this example, the login process is executed in a loop. If the user enters an invalid login, then we allow him or her to retry. Programmatically, we limit the user to three tries within the loop, and if the user fails to enter a valid login, the program will fall through and fail somewhat gracefully. If the login process was successful, then a collection of the principals loaded by the login process is displayed.

The DemoJAAS Class

```
import javax.security.auth.login.*;
import javax.security.auth.*;
import javax.security.auth.callback.*;
```

```java
import java.security.Principal;
import java.security.AccessController;
import java.security.PrivilegedAction;
import java.io.*;
import java.util.Set;
import java.util.Iterator;

import com.sun.security.auth.callback.*;

// com.sun.security.auth.module.JndiLoginModule

public class DemoJAAS {

public static void main(String args[] ) {

//
// get the login context
//
LoginContext lc = null;

DemoJAAS demoJAAS = new DemoJAAS();

//
// create the login context based on command line
// input
//
int choice = 1;
if ( args.length > 0 ) {
    choice = Integer.parseInt( args[0].trim() );
}


try {
  switch (choice) {
    case 1:  lc = new LoginContext("TestJAAS",
                    demoJAAS.new MyCallbackHandler() );
            break;
    case 2:  lc = new LoginContext("DemoJAAS" );
            break;
    case 3:  lc = new LoginContext("TextJAAS",
                    new TextCallbackHandler() );
            break;
    case 4:  lc = new LoginContext("JDBCJAAS",
                    new TextCallbackHandler() );
            break;
  }
}
catch (LoginException e) {
    System.err.println(
      "Could not create login context: " + e );
    e.printStackTrace();
}
```

```
//
//   now try the login
//
int tries=1;
boolean success=false;
for (;tries <= 3;tries++ ) {

    try {
      lc.login();
      break;   // we succeeded, so end the loop
    }
    catch(LoginException e ) {
        System.err.println(
        "LoginException: authentication failed: " + e );
        e.printStackTrace();
    }
}

if (  tries <= 3   )   {
    Set principals = lc.getSubject().getPrincipals( );
    Iterator i = principals.iterator();

    //
    // output results
    //
    System.out.println("Login successful.");
    System.out.println("Principals loaded: ");

    while ( i.hasNext() ) {
       success=true;
       String name = ((Principal) i.next()).getName();
        System.out.println("\tPrincipal: " + name );
    }

}

else {

    System.out.println("Login failed.");
}
```

Executing Privileged Code: Using JAAS Authorization

Once we have completed the authentication of the user, we then move on to the task of executing privileged code as shown in the next code sample. The authenticated user is now reflected in a Subject composed of one or more principals. Only principals that have been designated to execute the privileged code should be allowed to do so.

JAAS does not provide for privileged execution directly. JAAS builds on the existing Java security framework and therefore uses the `java.security.PrivilegedAction` interface to identify and wrap the privileged code. This interface identifies a single `run` method. It is within the body of this `run` method that we place our privileged code.

JAAS provides several methods within the `Subject` class to allow privileged code to execute. We use the `Subject.doAsPrivileged` method. This method has been overloaded to accept a number of different parameters. In this example, the static `Subject doAsPrivileged` method is called with parameters to pass the `Subject` instance (as returned by the `LoginContext`). The second parameter to this method must be an object that implements the `PrivilegedAction` interface. By passing the `Subject` instance reference from our `LoginContext`, we are assured that the `doAsPrivileged` method will recognize the `Subject` we have populated. The successful completion of this method indicates that the `Subject` (and its associated principals) have been assigned the permission the `UserPropertiesAction`.

An alternative method of executing the privileged code is also shown in this example. We use the same `Subject` instance as the previous example, but in this case we create an anonymous object as a user action. This provides an inline code location where the `SecurityManager checkPermission` method can be used to check whether or not a permission has been granted to our principal.

The `checkPermission` method uses the current system context to identify whether or not the user has permission to perform the action. Since the first parameter we have passed to the constructor is the `Subject` from our login process, we an be assured that the `doAsPrivileged` method will use the current `Subject` object.

The body of the `Action` method is used to execute a series of `checkPermission` methods on permission entries which have been made in the security policy file. If the call to `checkPermission` fails, a `SecurityException` is thrown and program execution jumps to the catch block for the exception. If however the permission has been granted, program execution continues with the next line following the `checkPermission` method call. This allows us to programmatically check a particular block of code.

The interesting aspect of using the `SecurityManager checkPermission` method is that the `Subject` we have populated is only visible to the `checkPermission` method within the body of the `PrivilegedAction` object we have created. The `Subject` is placed in the `AccessControlContext` for the `SecurityManager` at that point on the call stack.

```
...
//
// try doAsPrivileged()
//
try {
```

```
   System.out.println("\nExecuting Subject doAsPrivileged ... " );
   String s = (String) Subject.doAsPrivileged( lc.getSubject(),
           new UserPropertiesAction(), null );
   System.out.println(
      "Privileged action completed. Value Returned: " + s + "\n");
}
catch (SecurityException e) {
   System.out.println("Exception in doPrivileged. " );
   System.out.println("exception: " + e );
   e.printStackTrace();
}



//
// try checkPermission
//

   if ( System.getSecurityManager() == null ) {
       System.out.println( "SecurityManager not installed.");
   }
   else {
          System.out.println("Executing Subject doAsPrivileged with SecurityManager
checkPermission call." );
          Object o =  Subject.doAsPrivileged( lc.getSubject(),
                  new PrivilegedAction() {
              public Object   run() {
                  SecurityManager sm =
                          System.getSecurityManager();
                      try {
                              sm.checkPermission(
                                new DemoPermission( "doIt" ) );
                              System.out.println("Did doIt." );
                                sm.checkPermission(
                              new DemoPermission( "doThat" ) );
                          System.out.println("Did doThat." );
                                sm.checkPermission(
                              new DemoPermission( "doItAll" ) );
                          System.out.println("Did doItAll." );
      //
      // in Subject.doAsPrivileged, we can see our Subject
      //
      System.out.println(
                        "In doAsPrivileged.\tSubject: " +
              Subject.getSubject(
                        AccessController.getContext() ) );
          }
                  catch (SecurityException e)  {
                        System.out.println(
                "Sorry, you do not have permission to do that ... " );
                        System.out.println(
                "Subject: " + Subject.getSubject(
                        AccessController.getContext() ) );
```

```
                 System.out.println("Exception: " + e );
                            }
          finally {
             return null;
                    }

                  }
            }
            , null );
  }


//
// outside of the Subject
// doAsPriviledged call, AccessControlContext does not have
// our Subject
//
System.out.println("\nOut of doAsPrivileged.\tSubject: " +
        Subject.getSubject( AccessController.getContext() ) );
}
```

Implementing the CallbackHandler

The `CallbackHandler` implementation is used to manage the events triggered by the login process. The `CallbackHandler` interface defines a single `handle` event, which receives an array of `Callback` references. The handler must interrogate this array and take appropriate actions for the references. What this amounts to in this case is the interaction with the user to get the user name and password. (The interaction of these two objects is illustrated in Figure 9–1, shown earlier in this chapter.)

As shown in the code listing below, the `handle` method takes a single parameter, the array of `Callback` references. We use a `for` loop to iterate through the contents of the array and use conditional statements to test the contents of the array.

The callback array has been populated by the `LoginModule` implementation (which will be shown next). In our case, we have populated the array with a `NameCallback` and `PasswordCallback` references. It is the responsibility of this `CallbackHandler` implementation to populate the contents of these callback references with the appropriate name and password.

If we find an element that is an instance of `NameCallback`, then we need to prompt the user for a name and store the user's response. In our example, we use the text console to prompt for a user name and retrieve the user's input. Similarly, in a GUI implementation, we could have created a modeless dialog to retrieve this information.

The processing of the `PasswordCallback` is performed in the same manner. Though passwords are often retrieved without echoing the characters the user is typing, for brevity we do not go through the calisthenics here that are required to do that.

The `handle` method does not return a value. If there are any problems handling the `Callback` elements, we should throw an exception, preferably an `UnsupportedCallbackException` as shown in the code below.

The MyCallbackHandler Inner Class

```
class MyCallbackHandler implements CallbackHandler {

public void handle( Callback[] callbacks ) throws IOException,
UnsupportedCallbackException {

boolean foundCallback=false;

for (int n=0;n < callbacks.length; n++ ) {

   if ( callbacks[n] instanceof NameCallback ) {
      foundCallback=true;
      NameCallback name = (NameCallback) callbacks[n];
      //
      // prompt for the user name
      //
      System.out.print( "* " + name.getPrompt() + " " );
      //
      // get response
      //
      name.setName((new BufferedReader
                  (new InputStreamReader(System.in))).readLine());
   }

   if ( callbacks[n] instanceof PasswordCallback ) {
      foundCallback=true;
      PasswordCallback password =
         (PasswordCallback) callbacks[n];
      //
      // prompt for the user password
      //
      System.out.print( "* " +
         password.getPrompt() + " " );
      //
      // get response
      //
      String pwd = (new BufferedReader (
        new InputStreamReader(System.in))).readLine();
      password.setPassword( pwd.toCharArray() );
   }

}
```

```
if ( !(foundCallback) ) {
    //
    //  callbacks[] ref is not correct
    //
    throw new UnsupportedCallbackException(
                callbacks[0],
                "No valid callback found." );
}
}


}

}
```

The LoginModule Implementation

The `LoginModule` implementation usually interacts with the `CallbackHandler` to perform the validation of the login information. Optionally, this module could choose to do the work of the `CallbackHandler` and interact directly with the user or other source of login information, but such an approach reduces the modularity of JAAS.

In the first implementation we examine here, the validation of the user input is hardcoded into the class. Though fine for an example, this is not a particularly useful implementation. The second example will show a `LoginModule` that interacts with a database to validate the user information—a more practical approach. Sun Microsystems also provides implementations for JNDI (LDAP, NDIS) login modules, NT and UNIX, and Kerberos-based logins.

The `initialize` method is called by the `LoginContext` implementation when the `LoginModule` implementation is first loaded. In this implementation, we use the `initialize` method to obtain the `Subject` and `CallbackHandler` we will use for our implementation. These parameters are stored in instance members. Other `initialize` parameters are intended to share information with other login modules—for instance, for a custom implementation of a single sign-on login. They are not used in this implementation.

The `login` method is called by the `LoginContext` implementation to perform the login process and returns a boolean true if the login succeeded or a boolean false if the login failed. Our implementation creates a `Callback` array with two elements and instantiates a `NameCallback` and a `PasswordCallback`, which we saw in the previous code listing for the `CallbackHandler`. We populate our array with these references and then call the `handle` method for the `CallbackHandler` reference we received in the `initialize` method.

After calling the `login` method, we proceed to determine whether or not the contents of the `Callback` array (which was passed by reference, so we can check its contents with the same reference we passed). In this example, we hardcode our validation, and if the user entry was valid, we set our boolean flag to true; otherwise, we set the flag to false. We then catch a number of exceptions, and then in the `finally` block we return our boolean flag, which has been set to a value that indicates the success or failure of the login operation.

The DemoLoginModule Class

```
import javax.security.auth.login.*;
import javax.security.auth.*;
import javax.security.auth.callback.*;

import java.util.*;
import java.io.IOException;
import javax.security.auth.spi.*;
import java.security.Principal;

public class DemoLoginModule implements LoginModule {

Subject subject;
CallbackHandler callbackHandler;
Map   sharedState;
Map   options;
     Principal namePrincipal;
     Principal emailPrincipal;
boolean valid = false;
String name;      // user name
String password; // user password

public void initialize( Subject subject,
     CallbackHandler callbackHandler,
     Map sharedState, Map options) {

//
// store the references to the appropriate
// elements
//
this.subject = subject;
this.callbackHandler = callbackHandler;
this.sharedState = sharedState;
this.options = options;

}
// -

public boolean login() {

valid = false;

try {

Callback callbacks[] = new Callback[2];
```

```
callbacks[0] = new NameCallback( "name: " );
callbacks[1] = new PasswordCallback(
                    "password: ", false );

//
// ** call our handler to populate our callbacks
//
callbackHandler.handle(callbacks);

name = ((NameCallback) callbacks[0]).getName();
password = new String( ((PasswordCallback) callbacks[1]).getPassword());

System.out.println( " Values entered: " );
System.out.println( "    Name: " + name );
System.out.println( "    Password: " + password );

//
// hardcode our validation of user input
// only user 'art' is allowed
//
if ( ( name.equals("art")) && ( password.equals("yes") ) ) {
   valid = true;
}
else {
   valid = false;
}


}
catch (IOException e) {
      System.err.println("IOException in login: " + e );
      e.printStackTrace();
}
catch (Exception e ) {
      System.err.println("Exception in login: " + e );
      e.printStackTrace();
}
catch (Throwable e ) {
      System.err.println("Exception in login: " + e );
      e.printStackTrace();
}

finally {
 return valid;
}
}
```

The DemoLoginModule: The commit and abort Methods

The `commit` method is called by the `LoginContext` as part of the two-phase login process to commit the contents of the login operation. As opposed to a database commit operation, we are not expected to write data to a disk, but instead we are expected to complete the population of our subject. This multiphase operation is intended to support a single sign-on type of operation where multiple logins may be processed, and the operation should fail if one or more of the logins fail.

In our implementation of the `commit` method, we test our boolean `valid` flag (an instance member), and if our operation has gone correctly, we create the `Principal` objects that we intend to associate with our `Subject`. The `Principal` objects are stored in the `Subject` in a `Set` collection, which we access using the `getPrincipals` method. We return a boolean true value if we succeeded.

The `abort` method is called by the `LoginContext` if the login operation has failed. We must implement this to clear the `Subject` instance of our `Principal` objects. Our implementation of the `abort` method checks our `valid` flag, and if it is set to false, there is nothing to undo (since nothing has been placed in the `Subject` instance). If, however, the `valid` flag is true, we need to clear the internal `Subject` of `Principal` object references we have added. This method returns a boolean true if it succeeded.

The commit and abort Methods

```
public boolean commit() {

if ( valid )   {
  //
  // add this subject
  //
  namePrincipal = new DemoPrincipal( name );
  subject.getPrincipals().add( principal );

  //
  // principal/user art is also has an email account
  // that is used as a login
  //
  emailPrincipal =
      new DemoPrincipal( "taylorart@zippy.net" );
  subject.getPrincipals().add( principal );
}

//
// clear state
//
name     = null;
password = null;

return valid;

}
public boolean abort() {
boolean retVal = false;
```

```
if ( !(valid) ) {
   //
   // we didn't succeed, nothing to undo
   //
   retVal = false;
}
else {
   //
   // clear all principals
   //
   subject.getPrincipals().remove (namePrincipal);
          subject.getPrincipals().remove(emailPrincipal);
   retVal = true;

   //
   // clear state
   //
   name     = null;
   password = null;
}
return retVal;

}
public boolean logout() {
   //
   // clear all principals
   //
   subject.getPrincipals().clear();

   //
   // clear state and reset flag
   //
   name     = null;
   password = null;
   valid    = false;

   return true;

}

}
```

The UserPropertiesAction Class

The `UserPropertiesAction` class is used in the authorization process to provide a privileged action. Any privileged action executed must be wrapped by an implementation of the `PrivilegedAction` interface or by `PrivilegedExceptionAction` if it throws an exception. These interfaces define a single method, the `run` method, which returns an object reference. (The `PrivilegedAction` interface is often implemented inline as an anonymous object, as shown previously in the `DemoJAAS` class.)

Our implementation of `PrivilegedAction` is fairly simple. It defines a run method, which accesses a system property and returns the value. Since with a `SecurityManager` installed accessing a system property is a privileged action, the `Subject` executing this code will need to have been authorized to perform the action through one if its `Principal` objects.

The UserPropertiesAction Class

```
import java.security.PrivilegedAction;

public class UserPropertiesAction implements PrivilegedAction {

public Object run() {
    String home =System.getProperty("user.home");
    return home;
}

}
```

The JDBCLoginModule

In the previous code example, we were introduced to an implementation of the JAAS `LoginModule`. Ours was a simple version that used a hardcoded validation of the user name and login entry. Though simple, it did introduce us to the nontrivial relationships between the `LoginModule` and the `CallbackHandler`.

In this example, we create a more realistic `LoginModule` implementation, which uses JDBC to interact with a relational database to validate login information. Though the approach to validation is quite different from the `DemoLoginModule` or the `UnixLoginModule` provided by Sun, because of the modular design of JAAS, this module can easily be substituted for authentication without requiring any change to the controlling code.

In fact, that is exactly what was demonstrated in the `DemoJAAS` program shown previously. If you will note, the configuration file showed an entry for a `JDBCJAAS` login configuration, which used the `JDBCLoginModule`. Using a command-line parameter, the `DemoJAAS` program can be executed to load the `JDBCJAAS` implementation and, when doing so, will run the same as with the other implementations.

The code for the `JDBCLoginModule` is shown below. As with the `DemoLoginModule`, this implementation provides an initialize method, which accepts parameters for a `Subject` and `CallbackHandler`. The method then retrieves a `DataSource` from the `DirectoryService` (a code example from this book). The `DataSource` is then used to obtain a database connection, which is stored in an instance member for the `JDBCLogin` class. The `prepareStmts` method is then called to prepare the SQL statement that will be used to retrieve the user login information from the database.

The JDBCLoginModule Class

```
import javax.security.auth.login.*;
import javax.security.auth.*;
import javax.security.auth.callback.*;

import java.util.*;
import java.io.*;
import javax.security.auth.spi.*;
import java.security.Principal;

import java.sql.*;
import javax.sql.*;

import javax.naming.directory.*;
import javax.naming.*;

import service.DirectoryService;


public class JDBCLoginModule implements LoginModule {

private Subject subject;
private CallbackHandler callbackHandler;
private Map  sharedState;
private Map  options;
boolean valid;

private String name;
private String password;
private String userEmail;

private Connection        connection;
private PreparedStatement getUserStmt;

public void initialize( Subject subject, CallbackHandler callbackHandler, Map
sharedState, Map options) {

this.subject = subject;
this.callbackHandler = callbackHandler;
this.sharedState = sharedState;
this.options = options;

try {
  //
  // get a DataSource connection
  //
```

```
    DirectoryService directory = new DirectoryService();
    DirContext context = (DirContext) directory.getContext(
        "o=jdbc, o=general-application-objects, dc=movies, dc=com" );
    DataSource moviesDS = (javax.sql.DataSource) context.lookup( "cn=movies" );
    connection = moviesDS.getConnection();

    //
    // prepare the SQL statement
    //
    prepareStmts();

}
catch( NamingException e ) {
    System.err.println("SQLException : " + e );
}
catch( SQLException e ) {
    System.err.println("SQLException : " + e );
}

}
```

The JDBCLoginModule Class: The login Method

The login method for the JDBCLoginModule class is shown below. This method is similar to the same method in the DemoLoginModule class. A Callback array is declared, and elements are created for a NameCallback and a PasswordCallback. The handle method of the CallbackHandler is then called to prompt the user for a user name and password.

Once the CallbackHandler has interacted with the user and provided entries for the user name and password, they are stored in the member variables for the class. The user name is then used to set a JDBC PreparedStatement parameter for the user name. The PreparedStatement is then executed and a ResultSet (the row) from the query is retrieved. We expect only one row to be retrieved and the password and email address are retrieved from this row.

Since it is entirely possible that an invalid user name or password has been entered, we need to allow for that contingency. The password as retrieved from the database (dbPassword) was set to a null value at the start of the method. If this variable still has a null value, then we assert that the user name was not found in the database, and we set the valid flag to false. If we have retrieved a password from the database, we compare that password to the password the user has entered. In this example, both passwords are strings and can be compared using the equals method. If the passwords match, the valid flag is set to true. If they do not match, then the valid flag is set to false. In the finally block of the method, the valid flag is returned. If all has gone well, we can be sure it was set to true and the login method will return true.

The JDBCLogin Class: The login Method

```
public boolean login() {

valid = false;
String dbPassword = null;
userEmail   = null;

try {

Callback callbacks[] = new Callback[2];
callbacks[0] = new NameCallback( "name: " );
callbacks[1] = new PasswordCallback( "password: ", false );

callbackHandler.handle(callbacks);

name = ((NameCallback) callbacks[0]).getName();
password = new String( ((PasswordCallback) callbacks[1]).getPassword());

try {
    getUserStmt.setString( 1, name );
    ResultSet results = getUserStmt.executeQuery();
    //
    // this should have returned a single row
    //
    if ( results.next() ) {
        dbPassword = results.getString( "password" );
        userEmail = results.getString( "email" );
    }
}
catch (SQLException e ) {
        System.err.println("SQLException e: " + e );
}

//
// if password is null, the user name wasn't found
//
if ( dbPassword == null ) {
    valid = false;
}
else {
    if ( dbPassword.equals( password ) ) {
        valid = true;
    }
    else  {
        valid = false;
    }
}

}
catch (IOException e) {
        System.err.println("IOException in login: " + e );
```

```
}
catch (Exception e ) {
      System.err.println("Exception in login: " + e );
}
catch (Throwable e ) {
      System.err.println("Exception in login: " + e );
}

finally {
   return valid;
}
}
```

The JDBCLogin Class: The prepareStmts and commit Methods

Since it is more efficient to prepare a SQL statement before it is used, the `initialize` method in the `JDBCLogin` class makes a call to the `prepareStmts` method to prepare the SQL statement used to retrieve the login information.

This method uses the `java.sql.Connection` object that was created in the initialize method and calls the `prepareStatement` method to prepare the SQL statement. The results of this call are stored in the `getUserStmt`, a `PreparedStatement` reference that is an instance member. This object is used in the login method to retrieve the user login information.

The commit method shown below is called by the `LoginContext` when it believes the login information should be saved. In our code, we take the information on the user name and store that in a principal (a `DemoPrincipal` instance). We also take the user email address and create a principal for that. Both principals are saved as part of the `Subject`.

The `logout` and `abort` methods both perform the same set of operations: clearing the instance members of user-specific values and then clearing the `Subject` member of `Principal` objects.

The JDBCLoginModule: The prepareStmts, commit, abort, and logout Methods

```
private void prepareStmts() {

try {

   getUserStmt =  connection.prepareStatement(
            "select login_name, password, email " +
            " from logins, users " +
          " where login_name = ?  and " +
          " logins.user_id = users.user_id "
                                    );
}
catch (SQLException e ) {
```

```
        System.err.println("SQLException : " + e );
}

}

public boolean commit() {

// add this subject
if ( valid   ) {

   DemoPrincipal principal = new DemoPrincipal( name );
   subject.getPrincipals().add( principal );

   // principal/user also has an email account that is used as a login
   principal = new DemoPrincipal( userEmail );
   subject.getPrincipals().add( principal );

}

// --
public boolean abort() {

name      = null;
password  = null;
userEmail = null;

valid = false;

subject.getPrincipals().clear();

return true;

}

// --
public boolean logout() {

name      = null;
password  = null;
userEmail = null;

valid = false;

subject.getPrincipals().clear();

return true;

}
```

The Security Policy File for the JAAS Examples

The security policy file contains the Java security entries used by JAAS to perform authorization. This file also contains the entries that allow the JAAS package to be used with the Java security manager.

The first entries shown grant system permissions that allow JAAS to create a login context (the `LoginContext`) and modify principals. Additionally, we need to have the ability to execute privileged code by executing the `Subject doAsPrivileged` method. We use the `getSubject` method in the `LoginContext` class and the `Subject` class to examine the subject, and we use the reference to execute privileged code.

We also need to grant access to network ports for the LDAP server and the relational database used to retrieve login information with the `JDBCLoginModule`. These network sockets are part of library code, which is not identified specifically in the grant statement (in a production environment it should) and instead grants permission to connect to these ports to all Java code that uses this `security.policy` file.

Several different sets of authorizations are then established. Different principals are used to demonstrate that the JAAS authorization mechanism does distinguish between the specific `Principal` implementation being used. To demonstrate that JAAS distinguishes between principal implementations (as it should), not all principals are granted all permissions.

The security.policy File

```
//
// grant these permissions only to code in our package
//
grant  codebase "file:./-" {
  permission javax.security.auth.AuthPermission "createLoginContext";
  permission javax.security.auth.AuthPermission "modifyPrincipals";
  permission javax.security.auth.AuthPermission "doAsPrivileged";
  permission javax.security.auth.AuthPermission "getSubject";
};


//
// any service can access these ports
//
grant {
  permission java.net.SocketPermission
          "localhost:3306", "connect,accept";
  permission java.net.SocketPermission
          "localhost:389", "connect,accept,resolve";
};


//
// authorizations
//
```

```
grant  Principal com.sun.security.auth.UnixPrincipal "art"  {
  permission java.util.PropertyPermission "user.home", "read";
  permission DemoPermission "doIt";
  permission DemoPermission "doThat";
  permission DemoPermission "doItAll";
};

grant  Principal DemoPrincipal "art" {
  permission java.util.PropertyPermission "user.home", "read";
  permission DemoPermission "doIt";
  permission DemoPermission "doThat";
  permission DemoPermission "doItAll";
};

grant  Principal DemoPrincipal "fred" {
  permission java.util.PropertyPermission "user.home", "read";
  permission DemoPermission "doIt";
};

grant  Principal DemoPrincipal "cary" {
  permission java.util.PropertyPermission "user.home", "read";
};
```

Application Execution

Executing the application returns differing results depending on the user who was authenticated since different users (and their subjects) have different permissions.

As we saw in this chapter, the JAAS package is by design highly configurable. The JAAS configuration file for the execution of our demonstration program is as follows.

The DemoJAAS Configuration File

```
TextJAAS {
      DemoLoginModule required debug=true;
};

TestJAAS {
      DemoLoginModule required debug=true;
};

DemoJAAS {
      com.sun.security.auth.module.UnixLoginModule required debug=true;
};
```

```
JDBCJAAS {
      JDBCLoginModule required ;
};
```

Each of these `LoginModule` configurations is referenced and used in the `DemoJAAS` program as arguments to the `LoginContext` constructor.

In the first example, user `art` is logged in using JAAS. If you recall, according to the `security.policy` file, we are using, user `art` is granted permission to execute all the methods (`doIt, doThat, doItAll`). The pertinent fragment of that `security.policy` file is shown below.

Security Policy File Fragment

```
// authorizations
grant  Principal com.sun.security.auth.UnixPrincipal "art"  {
  permission java.util.PropertyPermission "user.home", "read";
  permission DemoPermission "doIt";
  permission DemoPermission "doThat";
  permission DemoPermission "doItAll";
};

grant  Principal DemoPrincipal "art" {
  permission java.util.PropertyPermission "user.home", "read";
  permission DemoPermission "doIt";
  permission DemoPermission "doThat";
  permission DemoPermission "doItAll";
};

grant  Principal DemoPrincipal "fred" {
  permission java.util.PropertyPermission "user.home", "read";
  permission DemoPermission "doIt";
};

grant  Principal DemoPrincipal "cary" {
  permission java.util.PropertyPermission "user.home", "read";
};
```

This would be run from the command line using the following:

```
java -classpath . -Djava.security.policy==./security.policy -Djava.security.manager
-Djava.security.auth.login.config=./DemoJAAS.config DemoJAAS
```

Running the program with this set of commands, and using the login for user `art`, the following output would be generated.

Execution of Sample Application with User art Login

```
Values entered:
   Name: art
   Password: yes
Login successful.
Principals loaded:
       Principal: art
       Principal: taylorart@zippy.net

Executing Subject doAsPrivileged ...
Privileged action completed. Value Returned: /home/art

Executing Subject doAsPriviledged with SecurityManager checkPermission call.
Did doIt.
Did doThat.
Did doItAll.
In doAsPrivileged.    Subject: Subject:
       Principal: TestPrincipal: art
       Principal: TestPrincipal: taylorart@zippy.net


Out of doAsPrivileged. Subject: null
```

User `fred`, however, does not have permission to access `doThat` and `doItAll`. The application therefore throws an exception when the `SecurityManager` `checkPermission` call is made for `doThat`, as shown below.

Application Execution Output for User fred

```
Login successful.
Principals loaded:
       Principal: fred
       Principal: freddy@zippyone.net

Executing Subject doAsPrivileged ...
Privileged action completed. Value Returned: /home/art

Executing Subject doAsPriviledged with SecurityManager checkPermission call.
Did doIt.
Sorry, you do not have permission to do that ...
Subject: Subject:
       Principal: TestPrincipal: fred
       Principal: TestPrincipal: freddy@zippyone.net

Exception: java.security.AccessControlException: access denied (DemoPermission
doThat)

Out of doAsPrivileged. Subject: null
```

User `cary` has an even more restrictive set of permissions. User `cary` only has permission to retrieve the user properties and does not have any of the privileged permissions, as this listing indicates.

Application Execution Output for User cary

```
Login successful.
Principals loaded:
        Principal: cary
        Principal: carry@zippyone.net

Executing Subject doAsPrivileged ...
Privileged action completed. Value Returned: /home/art

Executing Subject doAsPriviledged with SecurityManager checkPermission call.
Sorry, you do not have permission to do that ...
Subject: Subject:
        Principal: TestPrincipal: cary
        Principal: TestPrincipal: carry@zippyone.net

Exception: java.security.AccessControlException: access denied (DemoPermission doIt)

Out of doAsPrivileged. Subject: null
```

Using the operating system to provide authentication is a useful mechanism that can provide a single sign-on solution. As far as the policy file permissions are concerned, the specific principal class being validated, and not some superclass, must be identified in the policy file. In this case, using UNIX, the principal class is `com.sun.security.auth.UnixPrincipal`. The following listing is the result of user art performing using UNIX for authentication.

Output for UnixLoginModule JAAS Login

```
        [UnixLoginModule]: succeeded importing info:
                uid = 501
                gid = 501
                supp gid = 501
                supp gid = 0
                supp gid = 22
                supp gid = 43
                supp gid = 80
                supp gid = 81
                supp gid = 504
        [UnixLoginModule]: added UnixPrincipal,
                    UnixNumericUserPrincipal,
                    UnixNumericGroupPrincipal(s),
                to Subject
Login successful.
Principals loaded:
```

```
          Principal: art
          Principal: 501
          Principal: 501
          Principal: 0
          Principal: 22
          Principal: 43
          Principal: 80
          Principal: 81
          Principal: 504


Executing Subject doAsPrivileged ...
Privileged action completed. Value Returned: /home/art

Executing Subject doAsPriviledged with SecurityManager checkPermission call.
Did doIt.
Did doThat.
Did doItAll.
In doAsPrivileged.     Subject: Subject:
        Principal: UnixPrincipal: art
        Principal: UnixNumericUserPrincipal: 501
        Principal: UnixNumericGroupPrincipal [Primary Group]: 501
        Principal: UnixNumericGroupPrincipal [Supplementary Group]: 0
        Principal: UnixNumericGroupPrincipal [Supplementary Group]: 22
        Principal: UnixNumericGroupPrincipal [Supplementary Group]: 43
        Principal: UnixNumericGroupPrincipal [Supplementary Group]: 80
        Principal: UnixNumericGroupPrincipal [Supplementary Group]: 81
        Principal: UnixNumericGroupPrincipal [Supplementary Group]: 504


Out of doAsPrivileged. Subject: null
```

Running this program and attempting a login as user sam would generate a
set of exceptions that would produce the following output.

Program Execution for User sam (Invalid User)

```
name: password: LoginException: authentication failed:
javax.security.auth.login.LoginException: Login Failure: all modules ignored
javax.security.auth.login.LoginException: Login Failure: all modules ignored
        at javax.security.auth.login.LoginContext.invoke(LoginContext.java:768)
        at javax.security.auth.login.LoginContext.access$000(LoginContext.java:129)
        at javax.security.auth.login.LoginContext$4.run(LoginContext.java:599)
        at java.security.AccessController.doPrivileged(Native Method)
        at javax.security.auth.login.LoginContext.invokeModule(LoginContext.java:596)
        at javax.security.auth.login.LoginContext.login(LoginContext.java:523)
        at DemoJAAS.main(DemoJAAS.java:66)
name: password: LoginException: authentication failed:
javax.security.auth.login.LoginException: Login Failure: all modules ignored
javax.security.auth.login.LoginException: Login Failure: all modules ignored
```

```
        at javax.security.auth.login.LoginContext.invoke(LoginContext.java:768)
        at javax.security.auth.login.LoginContext.access$000(LoginContext.java:129)
        at javax.security.auth.login.LoginContext$4.run(LoginContext.java:599)
        at java.security.AccessController.doPrivileged(Native Method)
        at javax.security.auth.login.LoginContext.invokeModule(LoginContext.java:596)
        at javax.security.auth.login.LoginContext.login(LoginContext.java:523)
        at DemoJAAS.main(DemoJAAS.java:66)
name: password: LoginException: authentication failed:
javax.security.auth.login.LoginException: Login Failure: all modules ignored
javax.security.auth.login.LoginException: Login Failure: all modules ignored
        at javax.security.auth.login.LoginContext.invoke(LoginContext.java:768)
        at javax.security.auth.login.LoginContext.access$000(LoginContext.java:129)
        at javax.security.auth.login.LoginContext$4.run(LoginContext.java:599)
        at java.security.AccessController.doPrivileged(Native Method)
        at javax.security.auth.login.LoginContext.invokeModule(LoginContext.java:596)
        at javax.security.auth.login.LoginContext.login(LoginContext.java:523)
        at DemoJAAS.main(DemoJAAS.java:66)
Login failed.

Executing Subject doAsPrivileged ...
Exception in doPrivileged.
exception: java.security.AccessControlException: access denied
(java.util.PropertyPermission user.home read)
java.security.AccessControlException: access denied (java.util.PropertyPermission
user.home read)
        at
java.security.AccessControlContext.checkPermission(AccessControlContext.java:270)
        at java.security.AccessController.checkPermission(AccessController.java:401)
        at java.lang.SecurityManager.checkPermission(SecurityManager.java:542)
        at java.lang.SecurityManager.checkPropertyAccess(SecurityManager.java:1291)
        at java.lang.System.getProperty(System.java:572)
        at UserPropertiesAction.run(UserPropertiesAction.java:7)
        at java.security.AccessController.doPrivileged(Native Method)
        at javax.security.auth.Subject.doAsPrivileged(Subject.java:436)
        at DemoJAAS.main(DemoJAAS.java:101)
Executing Subject doAsPriviledged with SecurityManager checkPermission call.
Sorry, you do not have permission to do that ...
Subject: null
Exception: java.security.AccessControlException: access denied (DemoPermission doIt)

Out of doAsPrivileged. Subject: null
```

Summary

Java has always provided strong security features for Java applications. The JAAS package continues that trend and expands on the security features of Java to provide authentication and authorization features that work with existing Java security features to provide added application security.

As J2EE developers, we need to understand the JAAS package to be able to capitalize on its features. This chapter examined the JAAS package and provided examples that demonstrated how it can be used to provide authentication and authorization and how it can be customized to provide specific features as required by your application.

Next, we'll take a look at some additional J2EE packages that can provide additional security for applications. We will take a look at JSSE which provides SSL support, and JCE which provides cryptography facilities.

The Java Secure Sockets Extension: JSSE

INTRODUCTION

While the Internet has done much to create a flexible wide area network open to all, this remnant of Arpanet and academia also leaves gaping security holes for hackers to exploit. The most significant downside of the Internet is that network traffic on the Internet travels from node to node, so even the relatively unskilled hacker can sniff the clear text packets on the network and determine what is being passed.

For any enterprise concerned about moving sensitive data over this open network, these security weaknesses could be a serious issue. In response to these issues, very early in the adoption of the Internet, Netscape developed a standard for secure network socket connections known as Secure Sockets Layer (SSL). This standard has been refined to work in concert with HTTP using the HTTPS (HTTP with SSL) protocol.

The Java Secure Sockets Extension provides an API for creating and using SSL connections with Java. This chapter provides a description of the API and several examples of its usage.

THE JSSE API

The JSSE API is designed to allow Java applications to use SSL connections. The SSL protocol was developed by Netscape in 1994 with input from the technical community. In no small part due to its strong security, flexibility, and ease of use, it has become the de facto standard of secure transmissions over the Web.

The SSL protocol uses a number of cryptographic strategies to provide security, combining the various approaches to create an easily deployed, secure communication strategy. The SSL standard is now under the control of the Internet Engineering Task Force (IETF), which has renamed the protocol Transport Layer Security (TLS). The current release of TLS is 1.0 and is very similar to the commonly supported SSL version 3.0.

Secret Key and Public Key Cryptography

Cryptography is the science of encryption of information. In essence, encryption allows information to be transmitted over open channels, in open view of those who want unauthorized access to the information. Encryption scrambles the information being transmitted in such a way that descrambling that information is so difficult and would take such a large amount of time and CPU power that it is practically impossible for the unauthorized user to gain access to the information.

Secret key cryptography involves two parties communicating with encrypted messages that are encrypted and decrypted with the same key. Communicating parties must agree on the key and cryptographic algorithm before the encrypted messages can be sent.

The problem with secret key cryptography is that the key must be disseminated before encrypted communication can begin. But once the secret keys have been deployed, this type of encryption, which is also known as *symmetric encryption*, can be fast and efficient.

Public key cryptography uses a public key and a private key. Both a public key, which can be openly transported, and a private key, which is kept private by the party transmitting the public key, are used. Any party wishing to receive encrypted data can send its public key over the network. The public key can then be used by the sender to encrypt data. The interesting aspect of this cryptography is that only the party that provided the public key, the party that wishes to receive the encrypted data, can decrypt the data using the secret key. This means that if a hacker managed to intercept a message with the public key, he or she would still not be able to decrypt any message encrypted using that same public key because the hacker doesn't have the corresponding private key.

This type of cryptography is also known as *asymmetric cryptography*. It does require the distribution of public keys to all potential participants. This could be managed by physically distributing a set of public keys to all clients. But if the network is large and the clients unknown, this approach becomes difficult. When a client receives a public key, how does the client know that the public key is from the correct source? Perhaps some hacker is trying to intercept the message traffic between the client and the server.

The solution to this problem is the introduction of a certificate authority (CA). The CA is a trusted third party that provides authentication that a public key certificate that is being passed from peer to peer is in fact an authentic certificate.

While public key cryptography does manage to avoid the logistical issues with secret key cryptography, it requires extensive calculations and can hammer a CPU fairly quickly. Thus, CPU resource consumption tends to restrict the use of asymmetric cryptography.

What is interesting about the SSL protocol is that it uses both symmetric and asymmetric security combined in a sort of best-of-both approach. SSL manages to gain the deployment advantages of the public key cryptography and the performance advantages of secret key cryptography by a clever process of handshaking and support for multiple encryption algorithms. The following sections provide additional details on the SSL protocol.

THE SSL PROTOCOL

The SSL protocol involves several processing steps known as a *handshake protocol* to establish the secure communication channel. Should any of these steps fail, the channel will not be established and the connection will fail. These steps are as follows:

1. Determine the cipher suite to use.
2. Optionally authenticate the server.
3. Agree on an encryption mechanism.
4. If necessary, exchange secret keys using a public key.
5. Begin encrypted communication.

The ability for the client and server to negotiate to determine the cipher suite to use is one of the flexibility features of SSL. A number of cipher suites are available, and this handshake protocol allows the client and server to mutually determine the best protocol to use.

The process of authentication of the server is optional but provides an added layer of trust for applications. One of the security ploys possible over the Internet is for a hacker to pretend to be another server. An e-commerce application is especially vulnerable to this type of attack, known as spoofing, since the e-commerce server can request and receive critical information such as a user's credit card number, information a hacker would love to have.

The process of authentication is performed using security certificates. A public key certificate is presented to the client. The client must determine whether or not the certificate is from a trusted source or a source validated by a CA. If the client can't validate the certificate, it may optionally prompt the user with a warning about the failed validation attempt and allow the user to choose whether or not to continue.

The bulk of the data transmitted with SSL is encrypted using secret key or symmetric encryption. The reason for this is performance; symmetric encryption is faster than asymmetric or public key encryption. The persistent problem with symmetric encryption is deployment, since the client must have the secret key of the server.

The SSL protocol cleverly gets around this problem by using public key encryption to exchange the secret key. The public key encryption does not require the client to have the private key of the server; the client only needs the server's public key. The client encrypts its secret key, using its private key and the server's public key, and sends it to the server. The server decrypts the secret key using its private key.

Once this has been done, the client and the server hold a secret key to be used for symmetric encryption, thus being able to avoid the overhead of asymmetric encryption. This encryption is further augmented using a digital signature appended to the message. The digital signature is used to validate that the contents of a document have not been changed since the document was signed.

The digital signature is a checksum or message digest computed using a one-way hash function. It is not an effort to encrypt the contents of the document—the contents may even be in clear text. Instead, the process for creating the message digest involves the sender computing the digest and then encrypting the result of the operation and appending it to the document, effectively signing the document.

The recipient of the document then retrieves the signature and decrypts it to get the hash value. The recipient then recomputes the hash value on the document he or she has received and compares the results to the hash value stored in the document. If the two values do not match, then the document has been tampered with and should be rejected.

JSSE INSTALLATION

As of version 1.4.0, SSL is included in the JDK. Prior to this version, SSL was an optional package and required a separate download. The appropriate JAR files must be in the program's or server's classpath. The Java Runtime Environment (JRE) must also be configured to recognize the SSL provider. Entries must be made in the `java.security` file for the JRE to identify the providers. The security providers use the following format:

```
<security.provider.name>.<priority>=<className>
```

The security provider name should be an appropriate name for the provider. The class name should identify the Service Provider Interface (SPI) class for the JSSE implementation. The priority indicates the order in which the providers are searched for an appropriate implementation, starting at 1. The class specified is the provider's subclass of the `java.security.Provider` abstract class. For the JDK 1.4.0, the following are the entries that identify the SSL providers for the installation.

```
security.provider.1=sun.security.provider.Sun
security.provider.2=com.sun.net.ssl.internal.ssl.Provider
security.provider.3=com.sun.rsajca.Provider
security.provider.4=com.sun.crypto.provider.SunJCE
security.provider.5=sun.security.jgss.SunProvider
```

Public Key Certificates and Trust

The certificate used by SSL must be a *trusted* certificate, which requires that it be signed either by a CA or via some type of self-signing mechanism. JSSE applications use a Java keystore, a database of trusted certificates, to store and access an appropriate security certificate.

Self-Signed Certificates

The `keytool` utility (covered in Chapter 8) provides the ability to self-sign a certificate. This requires that all clients be sent a copy of the self-signed certificate and append the certificate to their list of security certificates they trust. This process may be adequate for a small set of applications on a local network, but it is virtually impossible for large distributed applications with a large number of users.

For large applications, a certificate could be created and then sent to a trusted CA; the CA would sign the certificate and return it. Such a certificate could then be placed in the server's keystore. The clients do not need a copy of the server certificate (which contains the private key). The clients will receive a public key certificate from the server (which has been signed by the CA) and will be able to verify that certificate with the CA. This avoids the logistical nightmare of sending a large number of certificates to all potential clients (for instance, e-commerce sites on the Internet).

Creating the Certificates

In order to run JSSE, a certificate *keystore* must be provided. This keystore is used by the server and the client to provide the secret keys and public keys it will use for secure communication.

The Java `keytool` is a command-line utility that provides a number of options that can be used for creation of certificates. The `keytool` stores the certificates in a file known as a keystore, effectively a database for security certificates. To create a certificate named `mykey`, you could use the following on the command line:

```
keytool -genkey -alias mykey -keystore keystore
```

This generates a certificate named with the alias `mykey` to be placed in the keystore named `keystore`. If the certificate is not going to be sent to a CA to be signed, then it must be *self-certified* in order to be trusted by the client. The following `keytool` command performs that function.

```
keytool -selfcert -alias mykey -keystore keystore
```

This command self-certifies the certificate with the alias name of `mykey` in the keystore database named `keystore`. This certificate is now available for use by the server. When a JSSE SSL server is used, it can be told to read the keystore database named `keystore` and use that database to supply certificates to clients.

An SSL client must trust a certificate in order to begin SSL communication. Trusting a certificate means that the client must be able to validate that the server is who it says it is and that the certificate is valid. In order to use the certificate created in the previous example for the server in the client, the certificate must be exported and then provided to the client as a list of certificates the client will trust. This is accomplished using the Java `keytool` with the following command:

```
keytool -export -alias mykey -keystore keystore -file mykey.cert
```

This command exports the certificate with the alias `mykey` to the file specified: `mykey.cert`. The certificate is extracted from the keystore database named `keystore`. Once extracted, the certificate must be imported into the keystore database for the client, using the following command.

```
keytool -import -alias mykey -keystore truststore -file mykey.cert
```

This command imports the certificate in the file `mykey.cert` into the keystore database with the name `truststore`. The certificate is provided the alias name `mykey`.

All of the previous `keytool` commands require one or two passwords. One password is required to access the keystore database, and another password may be required to access the certificate. If the passwords are lost or forgotten, the certificates in the keystore cannot be accessed.

THE JSSE PACKAGE

The JSSE package contains the classes and interfaces that implement SSL with Java. This package was not intended to replace the Java socket implementation, but instead was designed to augment the package. The primary classes in the JSSE package are listed in Table 10–1.

Table 10–1   *Classes/Interfaces in JSSE*

Class/Interface	Description
SSLContext	Represents the SSL implementation and acts as a factory for secure sockets.
KeyManager	Manages the key material used to authenticate the SSL socket.
TrustManager	Manages the trust material used when making trust decisions.
KeyManagerFactory	Acts as a factory class for the KeyManager class.
TrustManagerFactory	Acts as a factory for the TrustManager class.
SSLSocketFactory	Acts as a factory for the SSLSocket class.
SSLServerSocket	Extends java.net.ServerSocket and provides SSL-specific features.
SSLSocketFactory	Acts as a factory class for the SSLSocket class.
SSLSocket	Extends java.net.Socket and provides SSL-specific features.

The JSSE package uses the factory design pattern to manage the creation of the various components used to implement SSL. JSSE was designed to work with Java sockets. The JSSE socket and server socket are subclasses of the java.net Socket and ServerSocket classes, so code developed for java.net sockets can be seamlessly integrated into a JSSE solution, as demonstrated in this chapter.

The JSSE socket is encapsulated in the SSLSocket class, and the JSSE server socket is encapsulated in the SSLServerSocket class. While the underlying network implementation is the TCP/IP socket, the process of creating an SSL connection requires several steps, as outlined in the previous sections. Since SSL servers require secure keys, a KeyManager class is used to manage the process of accessing these keys. An SSL client must trust the key certificates received from the server and therefore requires a database of trusted certificates; a TrustManager class is used to manage the access to this database. In keeping the factory design pattern paradigm, factory classes can be accessed to create instances of the classes. Table 10–2 identifies these classes.

Table 10–2	JSSE Factory Classes

Class/Interface	Description
KeyManager	Manage the key material that is used to authenticate credentials. Key material may be a certificate or provider-specific material.
KeyManagerFactory	Used to create KeyManager references.
TrustManager	Manage the trust material that is used to authenticate a socket. Trust material may be a certificate or provider-specific material.
TrustManagerFactory	Used to create TrustManager references.
SSLSocket	Represents a secure socket connection.
SSLSocketFactory	Creates references for secure socket connections.
SSLServerSocket	Represents a server for secure SSLSocket connections.
SSLServerSocketFactory	Creates references for SSLServerSocket connections.

The process of creating the SSL connections requires a number of steps, which, though not trivial, are not prohibitively difficult. When compared with the efforts necessary to establish an encrypted peer-to-peer network connection without using the SSL protocol, JSSE is clearly the easier alternative.

JSSE Code Sample

The following code sample builds on a socket-based application developed with the java.net package. The application accepts special orders for a fictitious movie store. Since the special order can be made using a credit card number and can be made over the Internet, the communication channel should be secure.

The server and client use a protocol specified in a Request class, as shown below. This class defines several request types that may be sent to the server and responses that will be returned from the server. The Request object will contain an integer type member that will indicate the type of request being sent and a String member that will contain the contents of the message. Public get and set methods are available to manipulate the contents of the Request object.

The Request Class

```
package movies.control;

public class Request implements java.io.Serializable {
private int type;
```

```
private String message;

// Request Types
public static final int ORDER_REQUEST = 1;
public static final int ORDER_CANCEL  = 2;

// responses
public static final int ACKNOWLEDGE        = 3;
public static final int PROCESSING_FAILED  = 4;
public static final int BACK_ORDERED       = 5;

// accessors and mutators
public String getMessage() {
    return message;
}
public int getType() {
    return type;
}

public void setMessage(String message) {
    this.message = message;
}
public void setType(int type) {
    this.type = type;
}

public String toString() {

    return "Request" + "\n" +
                "type: " + getType() + "\n" +
                "message: " + getMessage() ;
}
}
```

An `OrderRequestProcessor` class used by the server to manage the request received from the client and is shown below. This class obtains the socket connection established by the SSL server and then creates an `ObjectInputStream` and `ObjectOutputStream` on the socket connection. The `ObjectInputStream` is then used to read the `Request` object from the input.

The `Request` object contains a type member that indicates the type of message being sent. The `OrderRequestProcessor` class examines this member (using the `getType` method) to determine what work is required.

If an order request (`Request.ORDER_REQUEST`) has been received, then the message is passed to the `OrderProcessing processOrder` method. The `processOrder` method has been overloaded accept either an XML-formatted string containing the order or an `OrderDAO` object reference. This example has passed an XML string containing the order, and that is what is passed to the `processOrder` method.

The request processor will continue to read from the input as long as there is a request found. If an I/O error occurs during an attempt to read from the input stream, an exception is quietly handled and the loop is exited.

The OrderRequestProcessor Class

```
package movies.control;

import java.net.*;
import java.io.*;
import movies.control.OrderProcessing;

public class OrderRequestProcessor implements Runnable {
Socket socket;
OrderProcessing processor;

public OrderRequestProcessor( Socket socket ) {
        this.socket = socket;
        processor = new OrderProcessing();
}
public void run() {
Request request = null;
try {
  //
  // Connection received. Get an input and output  stream
  //
  ObjectInputStream  in  = new ObjectInputStream(
                                 socket.getInputStream() );
  ObjectOutputStream out = new ObjectOutputStream(
                                 socket.getOutputStream() );

  //
  // read from the stream
  //
  request = (Request) in.readObject();
  while ( request != null ) {

      if ( request.getType() == Request.ORDER_REQUEST ) {

      System.out.println( "Order request received.");
      System.out.println( "message: " +
                     request.getMessage() );

      //
      // we know the message contains the
      // order in XML format We let the OrderProcessing
      // instance process the order
      //
      processor.processOrder( request.getMessage() );
```

```
       //
       // send a response
       //
       Request r = new Request();
       r.setType( Request.ACKNOWLEDGE );
       r.setMessage( "Order request has been received.");
       out.writeObject( r );
       out.flush();
       }

   if ( request.getType() == Request.ORDER_CANCEL  )  {

       System.out.println(
           "Order cancel request received.");
       System.out.println( "message: " +
           request.getMessage() );


     //
     // cancel the order
     //

       //
       // send a response
       //
       Request r = new Request();
       r.setType( Request.ACKNOWLEDGE );
       r.setMessage(
           "Order cancel request has been received.");
       out.writeObject( r );
       out.flush();

   }

  // read another request if it's there
  try {
     request = (Request) in.readObject();
  }
  catch (IOException e ) {
   // just exit on failed read
   break;
  }
}
  //
  // now go away
  //
  socket.close();
}
catch (IOException e) {
     System.out.println("IOException in run(): " +  e );
```

```
        e.printStackTrace();
}
catch (ClassNotFoundException e) {
        System.out.println("ClassNotFoundException in run(): " +  e );
        e.printStackTrace();
}


}


}
```

THE SSLSERVER CLASS

The `SSLServer` class creates a socket server and then listens for connections from clients. This class behaves much as a standard socket server implementation would in relation to the socket connection. It listens for a connection, and when a connection is received, it spawns a new thread to manage the connection. The thread started is an instance of the `OrderRequestProcessor` class, as shown previously. This class manages the details of the communication protocol and uses an instance of the `OrderProcessing` class to process the request.

A single instance member is declared for an `SSLServerSocketFactory` reference. As we will see shortly, the constructor performs the task of creating this reference.

Within the `main` program block, an instance of the `SSLServer` class is created, thus calling the `no-arg` constructor defined in the class and creating a reference for the `SSLServerSocketFactory` (`ssf`) instance member. The `SSLServerSocketFactory` instance member is then used to create a `ServerSocket` on port 1500 on the local machine. Though the underlying connection created on port 1500 is a TCP/IP socket, the SSL security wraps neatly around the port to provide secure communication. This highlights the flexibility of this approach—that the result of this effort is a standard (though very secure) TCP/IP server socket.

The server program then initiates a `while` loop and begins listening for connections on port 1500 using the `ServerSocket` accept call. Once a connection is established, a new Java thread is started using a new instance of the `OrderRequestProcessor` class shown previously. The constructor for the `OrderProcessor` class is passed the reference to the socket that was received from the accept method, which is the client connection that must be processed. (Though the `while` loop uses a boolean control parameter, it is not used in this implementation; this is essentially a perpetual loop which continues until the program is shut down.)

The SSLServer Class

```
package examples.jsse;

import java.net.*;
import javax.net.*;
import javax.net.ssl.*;
import java.security.*;
import java.security.cert.*;

import java.io.*;

import java.security.KeyStore;
import javax.security.cert.X509Certificate;

import movies.control.OrderRequestProcessor;


public class SSLServer {

private SSLServerSocketFactory ssf;

public static void main( String[] args ) {


SSLServer sslServer = new SSLServer();

try {
  //
  // create a server socket on port 1500
  //
  ServerSocket ss = sslServer.ssf.createServerSocket(
                      1500 );

  System.out.println(
            "Secure socket created. Listening ... " );

  //
  // listen for connections
  //
  boolean loop = true;
  while ( loop ) {
      Socket socket = ss.accept();

      //
      // start a thread to handle this
      //
      Thread t = new Thread(
            new OrderRequestProcessor( socket ) );
      t.start();

  }
```

```
}
catch ( IOException e) {
 System.err.println("IOException in main: " + e );
}

}
// —
...
```

THE SSLSERVER CLASS CONSTRUCTOR

The SSLServer class constructor does the work necessary to create the SSL connection. Within this constructor, the KeyManagerFactory must be created to provide the keys necessary to allow encryption and to provide clients to the server some assurance that we are who we say we are.

In this example, the keys are stored in a keystore in the form of X.509 certificates. We therefore require a password to our keystore, which we've chosen to embed in our code in plain text. (More sophisticated and secure implementations would store this password in encrypted form in a hidden file or database.)

An SSLContext is used to obtain our SSLServerSocketFactory instance, so the static getInstance method is called to obtain a new SSLContext for our use. We request an instance of a TLS factory (as stated earlier, TLS is for Transport Layer Security, the new name for SSL).

A KeyManagerFactory is then created to provide access to the keystore. The getInstance method is passed a string indicating that X.509 certificates will be stored in the keystore.

Finally a KeyStore reference is created. The factory getInstance method for this class specifies that a Java keystore (JKS) will be used to store and retrieve keys. The contents of the keystore database are loaded into the KeyStore object, which is then used to initialize the KeyManagerFactory.

The final step is to initialize the SSLContext using the init method, which takes three arguments: an array of KeyManager instances being used, an array of TrustManager instances being used, and a SecureRandom instance to use. In our case, we are a server and we are concerned only with the KeyManager, which will be passed as our first argument. We implicitly trust clients, so a TrustManager argument is not provided (a null reference is passed). The final argument is for a secure random-number generator, an important tool for strong encryption. We choose to use the default generator provided with Sun's implementation of JSSE.

The initialized `SSLContext` is then used to create an instance of an `SSLServerSocketFactory`. This reference will be used to create the `ServerSocket` created in the `main` program block.

SSLServer Class Constructor

```
public SSLServer() {

try {
  //
  // our keystore password as a byte array
  //
  char[] passphrase = "password".toCharArray();

  //
  // get an instance of an SSLContext
  //
  SSLContext context = SSLContext.getInstance("TLS");

  //
  // get an instance of our X509 key manager
  //
  KeyManagerFactory keyManagerFactory =
            KeyManagerFactory.getInstance("SunX509");

  //
  // get an instance of our keystore
  //
  KeyStore keyStore = KeyStore.getInstance("JKS");

  //
  // load our keystore and initialize
  //
  keyStore.load(
        new FileInputStream("keystore"), passphrase);
  keyManagerFactory.init(keyStore, passphrase);

  //
  // initialize our SSL context using our key managers
  //
  context.init(keyManagerFactory.getKeyManagers(),
              null,
              null);

  //
  // create a server socket factory and store reference
  // in our instance member
  //
  ssf = context.getServerSocketFactory();
}
```

```
catch ( IOException e) {
 System.err.println(
     "IOException in main: " + e );
}
catch ( KeyStoreException e) {
 System.err.println(
     "KeyStoreException in main: " + e );
}
catch ( KeyManagementException e) {
 System.err.println(
      "KeyManagementException in main: " + e );
}
catch ( NoSuchAlgorithmException e) {
 System.err.println(
     "NoSuchAlgorithmException in main: " + e );
}
catch ( CertificateException e) {
 System.err.println(
        "CertificateException in main: " + e );
}
catch ( UnrecoverableKeyException e) {
 System.err.println(
         "UnrecoverableKeyException in main: " + e );
}
}
}
```

THE SSLCLIENT CLASS

The SSLClient class is used to demonstrate the SSL server program shown previously. This class uses the JSSE package to create a SSLSocket, a client socket that connects to the server socket specified.

The work required to create the SSLSocket is performed in the constructor of the class. In the main program block, the no-arg constructor for the SSLClient class is called. The reference returned contains a reference to the SSLSocketFactory class which is used to make a call to the createSocket method. This method returns a SSLSocket opened on port 1500 on the host localhost.

Unlike the standard java.net Socket, the SSLSocket must start the handshaking process that will initiate SSL security. This is done with a call to the startHandshake method. If the startHandshake method fails, an IOException will be thrown. The IOException will be caught, an error message will be displayed, and the program will exit.

If the SSL handshake process succeeds, the program will continue and call the doProcessing method, passing the socket connection being used. The `doProcessing` method is code that was written for a `java.net.Socket` connection. It can be used here because the `SSLSocket` is a subclass of the `java.net.Socket` class.

The SSLClient Class

```java
package examples.jsse;

import java.io.*;

import javax.net.*;
import javax.net.ssl.*;
import java.security.KeyStore;

import java.security.*;
import java.security.cert.CertificateException;

import movies.control.OrderRequestProcessor;

public class SSLClient extends examples.net.Client {

private SSLContext context;
private SSLSocketFactory factory;

public static void main( String[] args ) {

try {
    SSLClient client = new SSLClient();

    SSLSocket socket = (SSLSocket)
            client.factory.createSocket("localhost", 1500);

    System.out.println( "Starting handshake ... " );
    socket.startHandshake();

    //
    // use our processing method inherited
    // from examples.net.Client
    //
    client.doProcessing( socket );
}
catch (IOException e) {
     System.err.println("IOException in main: " + e );
}

}
...
```

The SSLClient Class Constructor

The SSLClient class constructor contains the details of obtaining the SSLSocketFactory reference. The SSLSocketFactory must be initialized using three arguments: the keystore to be used, the truststore to be used, and the SecureRandom class reference to use.

As was done in the SSLServer constructor, the password is created as a character array. The getInstance factory method for the KeyStore is then created using the JKS format. The KeyStore is then loaded, passing both the password and the InputStream for the keystore file to the load method. In this case, the truststore file is read from the directory in which the program is run.

A TrustManagerFactory is then created using the default encryption algorithm. The TrustManagerFactory is initialized using the keystore (for the truststore file) as an argument. An array of TrustManager references is then retrieved from the TrustManagerFactory.

An instance of the SSLContext is then retrieved for the TLS protocol (which will provide SSL). The context is initialized using the TrustManager array instance and null values for the KeyStoreManager array and the SecureRandom instance. Once initialized, the SSLContext is used to create the SSLSocketFactory, which is used in the main program block to create the SSL communication socket.

The SSLClient Constructor

```
...
public SSLClient() {

try {
    KeyManagerFactory keyManagerFactory;
    KeyStore keyStore;

    //
    // our password as a byte array
    //
    char[] password = "password".toCharArray();

    //
    // assign our truststore. these are certificates we trust
    //
    keyStore = KeyStore.getInstance( "JKS" );
    keyStore.load( new FileInputStream( "truststore"), password  );
    TrustManagerFactory trustManagerFactory =
            TrustManagerFactory.getInstance(
                TrustManagerFactory.getDefaultAlgorithm() );
    trustManagerFactory.init ( keyStore );
    TrustManager[] trustManagers =
            trustManagerFactory.getTrustManagers();
```

```
    //
    // create an SSLContext
    //
    context = SSLContext.getInstance("TLS");

    //
    // initialize our context using the keymanagers
    //
    context.init(null, trustManagers, null);

    //
    // create an SSL socket factory from our context
    //
    factory = context.getSocketFactory();

}

catch ( IOException e) {
 System.err.println("IOException in main: " + e );
}
catch ( NoSuchAlgorithmException e) {
 System.err.println("NoSuchAlgorithmException in main: " + e );
}
catch ( KeyStoreException e) {
 System.err.println("KeyStoreException in main: " + e );
}
catch ( UnrecoverableKeyException e) {
 System.err.println("UnrecoverableKeyException in main: " + e );
}
catch ( CertificateException e) {
 System.err.println("CertificateException in main: " + e );
}
catch ( KeyManagementException e) {
 System.err.println("KeyManagementException in main: " + e );
}
}
}
```

THE CLIENT SUPERCLASS

The `SSLClient` class shown previously was a subclass of the `Client` class shown below. This class works with standard Java network connections and was pressed into usage for the SSL code to demonstrate the interoperability between standard sockets and SSL. The `main` program block just contains a test harness for the program and a facility for testing a `java.net.ServerSocket` implementation to which the program would be connecting.

What should interest us is the `doProcessing` method, which was called in the previous code example to perform processing against an SSL socket. As we can see here, the `doProcessing` method takes as an argument a `java.net.Socket`. Within the body of the method, an `InputStream` and `OutputStream` are created on the socket. Since the method will be implementing a protocol, both input and output will be required.

A `createOrderRequest` method is then called to create an order and place the contents of the order in a `Request` object (as shown previously in this chapter). The `Request` object reference returned is then written to the `OutputStream` (an `ObjectOutputStream`), and the response from the server is immediately read from the `InputStream` (an `ObjectInputStream`). The results of the object read operation are written to the console. The process is then repeated for an order cancel request. Once all processing is complete, the socket is closed.

The `createOrderRequest` method creates test data for testing the socket programs. This method loads an `OrderDAO` object and then creates a `Request` object. The `Request` object type parameter is then set to `ORDER_REQUEST`, and the contents of the `String` message member is set to an XML version of the `OrderDAO` object.

The `cancelOrderRequest` method takes the order number to cancel passed into the method. The order number is then wrapped in an XML format, placed into the message `String` of a `Request` object, and returned to the calling method.

The examples.net.Client Class

```
package examples.net;

import java.io.*;
import java.net.*;

import movies.control.Request;
import xmlutil.ObjectToXML;

public class Client {
private ObjectOutputStream out;
private ObjectInputStream  in;

public static void main( String[] args ) {

try {

   Client client = new Client();
   //
   // create a SSL socket connection to our server
   //
   Socket socket = new Socket( "localhost", 1500 );
```

```
        System.out.println( "Socket created. Processing ... " );

        client.doProcessing( socket );

}
catch (IOException e ){
        System.err.println("IOException in main: " + e );
}

}

protected void doProcessing( Socket socket ) {

try {
    //
    // get the input and output
    //
    out = new ObjectOutputStream(
                  socket.getOutputStream() );
    in  = new ObjectInputStream(
                  socket.getInputStream()  );
    //
    // send an order request
    //
    Request r = createOrderRequest();
    out.writeObject( r );

    //
    // read a response
    //
    r = (Request) in.readObject( );
    System.out.println( "received: " + r );

    //
    // send an order cancel
    //
    String orderNumber = "293093";
    r = createCancelRequest( orderNumber );
    out.writeObject( r );

    //
    // read a response
    //
    r = (Request) in.readObject( );
    System.out.println( "received: " + r );

    //
    // now go away
    //
    socket.close();
}
```

```java
catch ( IOException e) {
 System.err.println("IOException in main: " + e );
}
catch ( ClassNotFoundException e) {
 System.err.println(
        "ClassNotFoundException in main: " + e );
}


}

protected Request createOrderRequest( ) {

    //
    // create an order
    //
    CCOrderDAO order = new CCOrderDAO();

    //
    // just insert some test data
    //
    // first the credit card information
    //
    order.setNumber("2099-3909-3909-8897");
    order.setExpires("08/01");
    order.setType( "MC");

    //
    // billing, shipment information
    //
    order.setShipToID( "09309393-A" );
    order.setBillToID( "1109393-A" );
    order.setOrderNumber("09039093");
    order.setQuantity(12);
    order.setMovieID(1332);
    order.setUPC("Z2AA-3355");

    Request r = new Request();
    r.setType( Request.ORDER_REQUEST );
    r.setMessage( ObjectToXML.convertToXML( order ) );

    return r;

}

// —
protected Request createCancelRequest( String orderNumber ) {

    Request r = new Request();
    r.setType( Request.ORDER_CANCEL );
    r.setMessage( "<order-cancel><order-number>" + orderNumber + "</order-
number></order-cancel>" );
```

```
    return r;

}

}
```

SUMMARY

One of the strongest and most popular security mechanisms in place today is the SSL security standard. This widely supported security mechanism is neatly layered on top of TCP/IP network sockets so that an application implemented to work with sockets can be easily converted to work with SSL.

This chapter examined the JSSE package, which allows Java applications to use this security mechanism. We first examined the API and then, since an example is worth a thousand words, we provided an example that demonstrated the use of JSSE.

CHAPTER 11

Using Cryptography with Java

INTRODUCTION

The Internet is like a phone line with millions of listeners—the ultimate party line. Anyone connected to the Internet could, with the right connection and the right equipment, listen to others connected at the same time. This is called *packet sniffing* and does not require a high degree of technical expertise.

For a large percentage of Internet traffic, this may not be an issue. But as businesses increasingly turn to the Internet for business-to-business commerce traffic, some higher level of security may be needed.

Fortunately, Java provides packages that allow Java programs to use state-of-the-art encryption techniques. The Java Cryptography Extensions (JCE) provide Java language access to common cryptography algorithms, and the JSSE package provides access to Secure Socket Layer (SSL) communications as we saw in Chapter 10. In this chapter we take a look at the JCE package.

The JCE API

The JCE package provides access to Java cryptography. On the surface, cryptography seems to solve a number of the secure communications issues. Data is encrypted, and only those parties with permission to use, and with the key to decrypt, can access the data. But cryptography comes with a price.

Encrypting and decrypting data can consume CPU resource. How much resource is consumed depends on the algorithm and on the amount of data to be encrypted and decrypted. Given the ever-increasing CPU speeds of modern computers, CPU resource may not be the show-stopping issue it used to be. But for some extremely saturated servers, adding encryption to the processing load may be too much.

Using the Internet to move business data is an attractive, inexpensive alternative for many enterprises. But as the chapter introduction pointed out, the generally weak security of the medium is a significant consideration.

Encryption is a necessary security measure when the content, the data, is an important information asset that should only be seen by the selected parties. Alternatively, if it is just a matter of ensuring that data is not manipulated in transmission, then adding a digital signature to the data document may be an adequate alternative which will require much less CPU resource then encrypting the entire document.

PACKAGE DESIGN

JCE allows symmetric, asymmetric, block, and stream ciphers with support for secure streams and sealed objects. The API supports this set of algorithms using a relatively small set of classes. The specifics of the various algorithms are managed by providers with a default set of supported algorithms provided with the JDK (as of JDK 1.4).

To use JCE, you must understand the specific properties required by the form of encryption being used. The properties required for various implementations of JCE tend to vary depending on the algorithm being used. JCE providers are identified in the Java security properties file, usually named `JAVA_HOME/jre/lib/security/java.security`.

Using JCE, the process of encrypting or decrypting data is referred to as a *transformation*. The commonly used `Cipher` class encapsulates the functionality of a cryptographic cipher. A separate `Cipher` object is created for each transformation.

JCE is designed using a factory design pattern. The `getInstance` method of the `Cipher` class is used to create `Cipher` objects. This method is overloaded to take arguments for the transformation to use or for both the transformation and provider to use, as shown in the code fragment below.

```
...
// use the blowfish algorithm
Cipher cipher = Cipher.getInstance( "Blowfish" );


...
// use the DESede algorithm
Cipher cipher = Cipher.getInstance( "DESede/CBC/PKCS5Padding");
...
```

The transformation is specified using a string that includes the name of the transformation algorithm to use and optionally a mode and a padding scheme. The values are provider-specific but should take the form of <algorithm-name> or <algorithm-name>/<mode>/<padding-scheme>. If no mode or padding scheme is provided, then the provider's defaults will be used. If a block-cipher is being used in stream mode, then the number of bits for each processing cycle may also be specified by appending the bits to the mode name.

If a provider is not referenced in the constructor, then JCE will load all providers specified for the installation and scan each to see which one can provide the transformation needed. If there is more than one that can provide the transformation, then JCE will try to determine which is the preferred provider.

A Cipher object must be initialized before it is used. This initialization will start any of the algorithms that are being used to provide the encryption/decryption services. Exactly how the initialization will be performed and the arguments provided to the initialization vary depending on the algorithm being used. The Cipher class instance will be set to one of four modes (see Table 11–1).

Table 11–1   *Cipher Class Modes*

Mode	Description
ENCRYPT_MODE	Encryption of data.
DECRYPT_MODE	Decryption of data.
WRAP_MODE	Wraps a key into bytes for secure transportation.
UNWRAP_MODE	Unwraps a previously wrapped key.

Not all initialization parameters must be specified. According to the JCE specification, if parameters are not specified, then it is the responsibility of the underlying implementation to provide those parameters through default values or random selections. If that cannot be done, then the implementation should throw an exception. As a developer, you should be familiar with the parameters of a particular algorithm being used, since different parameters (padding, key length) can affect the strength and efficiency of an algorithm.

JCE EXAMPLE

A common implementation of secret key cryptography is application password encryption and decryption. There are two problems often associated with secret key or asymmetric cryptography. One is the requirement that both encryption and decryption require the same key, so the receiver of an encrypted document must somehow be given the key of the party that encrypted the document. The other is that if an unauthorized third party were to obtain access to the secret key, he or she could decrypt the messages or impersonate the sender and encrypt messages, so the physical security of the secret key is important.

Password encryption applications are a good fit for secret key encryption because they usually reside on only a few servers, which are under the control of IT. Therefore, the secret key does not need to be distributed, and the servers usually have a higher level of physical security.

The following code example demonstrates password encryption. The first example is of the utility class that provides the encryption services.

The JCETool Class

The `JCETool` class is a utility class that provides encryption and decryption services. The class handles the details of selecting the encryption algorithm and obtaining the JCE components to manage the encryption process. It exposes two methods to perform encryption and decryption.

In order to perform encryption/decryption, we need an instance of the `Cipher` class. The `JCETool` class shown below performs the task of creating the `Cipher` class and initializing it. We obtain an instance of the `Cipher` class in the constructor and then initialize it with the appropriate parameters for the type of secret key cryptography we will use. Two methods are declared in the class to provide encryption and decryption services, named appropriately `encrypt` and `decrypt`.

We begin by importing the various classes we need, including the local services we use to access logging, our directory server, and our JDBC data source. We declare two `Cipher` instance members, one for decryption (`decrypt`) and one for encryption (`encrypt`). Within the main programming block, we then have a small test harness that demonstrates the operation of the class methods.

The `main` program block creates an instance of the `JCETool` class and then creates a string, which will be the target of the encryption process. Both the `encrypt` and `decrypt` methods return a Java byte array. The target encryption string is first encrypted using the `encrypt` method. The resulting byte array is then displayed to the console. The `decrypt` method is then called to decrypt the string, and the result of that operation is output to the console after converting the byte array to a Java `String`.

The JCETool Class

```
package examples.jce;

import java.security.*;
import javax.crypto.*;
import javax.crypto.spec.*;

import java.io.*;
import org.apache.log4j.*;

// import our service packages
import service.*;

public class JCETool {

private Cipher encrypt;
private Cipher decrypt;
private static Category logger;

public static void main( String args[] ){

try {

  JCETool tool = new JCETool();

  String target = "The answer is: 42";
  System.out.println("before: " + target );
  byte[] encrypted = tool.encrypt( target );
  System.out.println("encrypted : " + encrypted );
  byte[] decrypted = tool.decrypt( new String( encrypted ) );
  System.out.println("decrypted : "  + new String( decrypted ) );

}
catch (Exception e) {
    logger.error("Exception caught in main: " + e );
}

}
```

JCETool Constructor

As shown in the code listing below, our constructor for the `JCETool` class performs the work of creating the `Cipher` instances used, finding the secret key or creating the secret key if one is not available, and then initializing the `Cipher` objects.

The current implementation of this program looks for the secret key in the local directory in a file named `.key`. If the file is not found, then we need to perform the work to create the key and write the results out to a file. This allows us to avoid the overhead of key generation each time the `Cipher` is used.

Creating a key requires a `KeyGenerator` instance which we then use to generate the key. We then obtain a byte array for the key and write the results out to the key file (`.key`). If the file storing the key already exists, we open it and read the contents into a byte array. The secret key is then used to create the `SecretKeySpec` (secret key specification) we will use to initialize the `Cipher`. We then create two `Cipher` instances. One for encryption and one for decryption. As you might expect, we then initialize the encrypt `Cipher` in `ENCRYPT_MODE` and the decrypt `Cipher` in `DECRYPT_MODE` using the secret key specification we created earlier.

The JCETool Class (continued): The Constructor

```
JCETool() {

byte[] bytes = new byte[10]; // limit the key to 10 bytes

 //
try {

  logger = LoggingService.getLogger( "JCETool" );

    //
    //currently we just look in our local directory for a secret key
    //
  File file = new File( ".key" );

  if ( !(file.exists()) ) {
     FileOutputStream out = new FileOutputStream( file );

     // get a key generator and create the key
     KeyGenerator kgen = KeyGenerator.getInstance( "Blowfish" );
     SecretKey secretKey = kgen.generateKey();

     // write the key out to a file for later retrieval
     //
     bytes = secretKey.getEncoded();
     out.write( bytes );
     out.close();
  }
  else {  // the file with the secret key exists
     FileInputStream in = new FileInputStream( file );
     in.read( bytes );
  }

   //
   // create the spec key
   //
  SecretKeySpec specKey = new SecretKeySpec( bytes, "Blowfish" );

   //
```

```
// create the Cipher
//
encrypt = Cipher.getInstance( "Blowfish" );
decrypt = Cipher.getInstance( "Blowfish" );

 //
 // initialize the Cipher
 //
encrypt.init( Cipher.ENCRYPT_MODE, specKey );
decrypt.init( Cipher.DECRYPT_MODE, specKey );

}
catch (InvalidKeyException e ) {
    logger.error( "InvalidKeyException in constructor: " + e );
}
catch (FileNotFoundException e ) {
    logger.error( "FileNotFoundException in constructor: " + e );
}
catch (IOException e ) {
    logger.error( "IOException in constructor: " + e );
}
catch (NoSuchAlgorithmException e ) {
    logger.error( "NoSuchAlgorithmException in constructor: " + e );
}
catch (NoSuchPaddingException e ) {
    logger.error( "NoSuchPaddingException in constructor: " + e );
}
}
```

The encrypt and decrypt Methods

We have created two methods to perform the basic operations of encryption and decryption, as shown below. Since most of the specifics of the cryptography have been identified in the initialization of the Cipher, these methods are fairly simple.

The encrypt method encrypts a string passed into the method. This method accepts a string (since data is usually manipulated using strings, not byte arrays) and returns a byte array for the encrypted data. It simply calls the Cipher doFinal method on the encrypt instance member (a Cipher object) and returns the result, catching various exceptions in the process. The decrypt method performs the same type of operation, but decrypts the data string passed into the method.

JCETool Class (continued): The encrypt and decrypt Methods

```
byte[] encrypt(String target) {

byte[] bytes = null;
try {
    bytes = encrypt.doFinal( target.getBytes() );
```

```
}
catch (BadPaddingException e) {
    logger.error( "Exception in encrypt: " + e );
}
catch (IllegalBlockSizeException e) {
    logger.error( "IllegalBlockSizeException in encrypt: " + e );
}
finally {
   return bytes;
}


}
// -

byte[] decrypt(String target) {

byte[] bytes = new byte[100];

try {
   bytes = decrypt.doFinal( target.getBytes() );
}
catch (BadPaddingException e) {
    logger.error( "Exception in encrypt: " + e );
}
catch (IllegalBlockSizeException e) {
    logger.error( "IllegalBlockSizeException in encrypt: " + e );
}
finally {
   return bytes;
}


}


}
```

Using Encryption and Decryption with JAAS Logins

As mentioned previously, a logical application of encryption and decryption is with the use of passwords. We would prefer to store our passwords in encrypted form, since this provides the contingency that even if the contents of the password storage facility were compromised, the passwords would have no value without the secret key.

The following code listing shows an implementation of the JAAS LoginModule, which performs the operation of authenticating a user. The sections pertinent to our discussion are shown here; the complete listing is shown with the JAAS discussion in Chapter 9.

This authentication process is commonly performed using a user name and password. The process of collecting the user name and password is performed by another class (an implementation of `CallbackHandler`) and is not germane to this discussion.

This particular implementation of the `LoginModule` uses a JDBC connection to connect to a database and obtain the user login name and password. Since the passwords are stored in an encrypted form, they must be decrypted to determine whether or not they match the user's entry (which is in a plain text string).

The code shown below demonstrates the process of using JCE in an application. The lines specific to the use of JCE are in bold text. The `initialize` method of the `LoginModule` is called by the JAAS `LoginContext`, a controlling class for the login process. In this case we have the `initialize` method create an instance of the `JCETool` class shown previously in this chapter. This object, stored as a class instance, provides access to the `decrypt` method we need to decrypt the password.

The `login` method is called by the `LoginContext` to perform the login process. In this example, the `CallbackHandler` instance is expected to interact with the user and obtain strings for a user name and password. The `login` method then uses the user name to obtain a row from the database containing the user name, password, and email address. The password from the database (`dbPassword`) must be compared to the password the user has entered. But before the comparison can be done, the password must be decrypted. This is done using the `JCETool decrypt` method. If the result of the decryption operation matches the password string the user entered, then the password is valid and a boolean true is returned. If the password is not valid, then a boolean false is returned by the login method.

One obvious caveat for this process is that the secret key used for decryption at this point must be the same secret key used to encrypt the password.

Partial JDBCLoginModule Class

```
package service;

import javax.security.auth.login.*;
import javax.security.auth.*;
import javax.security.auth.callback.*;

import java.util.*;
import java.io.*;
import javax.security.auth.spi.*;
import java.security.Principal;

import java.sql.*;
import javax.sql.*;

import javax.naming.directory.*;
import javax.naming.*;
```

```java
import service.*;

import org.apache.log4j.*;

public class JDBCLoginModule implements LoginModule {

private Subject subject;
private CallbackHandler callbackHandler;
private Map  sharedState;
private Map   options;
boolean valid;

private String name;
private String password;
private String userEmail;

private JCETool jceTool;

private static Category logger;

private Connection        connection;
private PreparedStatement getUserStmt;

public void initialize( Subject subject, CallbackHandler callbackHandler, Map
sharedState, Map options) {

this.subject = subject;
this.callbackHandler = callbackHandler;
this.sharedState = sharedState;
this.options = options;

try {

  // get a logger
  logger = LoggingService.getLogger( "GeneralDAO" );

  // get a DataSource connection
  DirectoryService directory = new DirectoryService();
  DirContext context = (DirContext) directory.getContext(
    "o=jdbc, o=general-application-objects, dc=movies, dc=com" );
  DataSource moviesDS = (javax.sql.DataSource)
                      context.lookup( "cn=movies" );
  connection = moviesDS.getConnection();

  // prepare the SQL statement
  prepareStmts();

  jceTool = new JCETool();
```

```
}
catch( NamingException e ) {
     logger.error("SQLException : " + e );
}
catch( SQLException e ) {
     logger.error("SQLException : " + e );
}
catch( Exception e ) {
     logger.error("Exception : " + e );
}

}

public boolean login() {

valid = false;
String dbPassword = null;
userEmail  = null;

try {

Callback callbacks[] = new Callback[2];
callbacks[0] = new NameCallback( "name: " );
callbacks[1] = new PasswordCallback( "password: ", false );

callbackHandler.handle(callbacks);

name = ((NameCallback) callbacks[0]).getName();
password = new String( ((PasswordCallback) callbacks[1]).getPassword());

try {
    getUserStmt.setString( 1, name );
    ResultSet results = getUserStmt.executeQuery();
    //
    // this should have returned a single row
    //
    if ( results.next() ) {
        //
        // if the password is encrypted, we need to decrypt it
        //
        dbPassword = new String(
            jceTool.decrypt( results.getString( "password" ) ));
      userEmail = results.getString( "email" );
    }
}
catch (SQLException e ) {
     logger.error("SQLException e: " + e );
}

//
```

```java
// if password is null, the user name wasn't found
//
if ( dbPassword == null ) {
   valid = false;
}
else {
     if ( dbPassword.equals( password ) ) {
          valid = true;
     }
     else  {
          valid = false;
     }
}


}
catch (IOException e) {
     logger.error("IOException in login: " + e );
}
catch (Exception e ) {
     logger.error("Exception in login: " + e );
}
catch (Throwable e ) {
     logger.error("Exception in login: " + e );
}

finally {
   return valid;
}
}

private void prepareStmts() {

try {

   getUserStmt =  connection.prepareStatement(
                  "select login_name, password, email " +
                  " from logins, users " +
              " where login_name = ?  and " +
              " logins.user_id = users.user_id "
                                                );
}
catch (SQLException e ) {
    logger.error("SQLException : " + e );
}

}
...
```

SUMMARY

In today's world of wide open networks such as the Internet, being able to encrypt data allows us to 'hide information in plain site'. The JCE package provides the tools to do this with minimal effort. Even though there are a number of different encryption algorithms that could be used, the JCE package manages to provide a convenient yet flexible abstraction of the common aspects of the encryption process. The package allows different implementations from different providers to be substituted in a plug-and-play fashion.

In this chapter we saw firsthand how to use the JCE package. JCE was used to create a `JCETool` class, which provides private key encryption services. This class was then used with a JAAS `LoginModule` implementation to provide for the decryption of user passwords stored in a database.

Using a Naming Service with Java: The JNDI Package

INTRODUCTION

The Java Naming and Directory Interface (JNDI) API provides a uniform, standard method of accessing resources in the form of objects. These resources can be accessed using a naming service that allows lookups to be performed, mapping a name to an object reference.

JNDI builds on the existing technology of name servers and directory servers, and creates a standardized Java API for accessing the resources provided by these servers. Naming services have been in existence for some time. The servers that provide these resources are referred to by various names, including directory servers (LDAP, NDS), registries (RMI registry, Windows/NT registry), and name servers (DNS). These lightweight databases have increased in popularity over the past few years, providing fast, inexpensive, read-intensive access to certain types of enterprise information.

JNDI is used extensively in J2EE to provide access to various resources such as DataSource objects or message queues. In this chapter we will take close look at JNDI, focusing on how a J2EE developer would use this API.

JNDI and Naming Services

JNDI provides access to a *naming service*, which allows various objects to be retrieved using a name which has been associated (or bound) with the object. The naming service and its underlying system determine the syntax that will be used to access its resources. This syntax is referred to as the *naming convention*. For instance, in UNIX the forward slash character (/) denotes separate components (directories). With the Domain Name Service (DNS) servers, a dot (.) character identifies separate components (network domains). The Lightweight Directory Access Protocol (LDAP) standard uses a more complex system of commas (,) and name–value pairs separated by equals (=) signs.

Within the naming service, bindings create names that are then organized into a group called a *context*. More robust naming services allow multiple contexts to be created, usually in a hierarchical fashion. A context provides a facility for retrieving objects in the context through a lookup operation. The naming service may also allow objects in the context to be listed and unbound (removed). The use of contexts allows entries to be neatly organized into specific groups and simplifies the process of retrieving the resources in the naming service.

The set of names accessible by a naming service is known as a *namespace*. The association of a name to an object is known as a *binding*. Using JNDI, a Java application can create a *federated* or combined space for multiple namespaces spanning multiple servers.

JNDI supports a number of different types of naming services. A *name server*, specifically a domain name server, maps a name (an arbitrary string) to an IP address.

Directory servers have traditionally been used to store query intensive information, information that is not updated on a constant basis and remains relatively static over a period of time. An example of this is employee information such as user name and password, or email addresses or corporate building addresses. A large number of directory servers use the LDAP protocol for communications, but other protocols are also used.

Using an appropriate schema, a *directory server* allows a name to be associated with an arbitrary object and allow various attributes to be associated with the object. Using a package like JNDI, these objects can be retrieved easily using the name which has been associated (bound) to the object.

Where JNDI really provides value is in providing a common interface to the various disparate servers it is used to access. The JNDI package supports the multiple naming services from multiple vendors through the inclusion of an implementation provided by the vendor. This is known as the service provider interface (SPI). If multiple SPIs are available, then JNDI supports the creation of a *federated namespace*, thus allowing access to one or more naming services through a single JNDI connection and name space.

THE CONTEXT

JNDI works with one or more *contexts*. A context is effectively a *namespace,* and within a namespace are resources that are identified by a key. A resource is an object that is stored or bound into the namespace using a key and can be retrieved by the key. Namespaces can optionally form a hierarchy much like a directory hierarchy, so that a series of entries relating to computer servers could be organized as follows.

```
/regional
        /corporate_it
        /corporate_backup
/national
        /north
                /local
                        /departmental
                                /accounting
                                /finance
                                /human_resources
        /south
                /local
                        /departmental
                                /accounting
                                /finance
                                /human_resources
```

Using this example, a *fully qualified path name* for a server in the national north region expressed using a forward slash to separate the contexts and reading left to right would be expressed as follows.

```
/national/north/local/departmental/human_resources
```

But not all namespaces use the same syntax. Directory servers using the LDAP protocol use a syntax as follows.

```
o=south, o=sales-regions, o=movies-sales, dc=movies, dc=com
```

This LDAP syntax describes a path within its hierarchy. The path described is read from right to left, so that the path above has com at the top of the hierarchy, movies below com, movies-sales below movies, and so on. Expressed as a common file system hierarchy using a forward slash, this would be expressed as follows.

```
/com/movies/movies-sales/sales-regions/south
```

Some namespaces do not even support hierarchies. These are *flat* namespaces and allow binding only for key (name) and corresponding values (for example, the RMI registry service provider that Sun distributes uses a flat namespace).

DIRECTORY SERVERS

As described earlier, directory servers are a specific type of naming service that provide access to a hierarchical namespace where resources may be stored. These servers have their roots in the hierarchical databases of old, but are now widely used as a low-cost, fast server for query-intensive data.

While we tend to describe directory servers in terms of storing 'resources', what they are really storing under the covers is data. This is information that could be stored elsewhere, perhaps in a relational database. Given the robust capabilities of modern relational databases and the various tools and APIs for accessing this data, this begs the question, Why store data anywhere else?

The reason for using directory servers is largely cost and efficiency. The features and capabilities of relational databases come with a cost. They have a fairly large system footprint, with installations often taking more than 600 megabytes of disk space just for the binary files. These database systems also absorb a large chunk of system resources, spawning heavyweight processes or multiple light-weight threads to manage their workload.

Directory servers are generally lightweight, meaning they carry a small system footprint in terms of installation size and system resource consumption. But despite their small size, they are usually very fast at read operations, often surpassing even the high-end relational databases for a wide range of queries.

Directory servers have found their niche in serving specific types of information. They are heavily used for system administration, storing information on machine resources, and making that information available throughout the enterprise. They are also used to store user information, most commonly email addresses and other information about employees using the computer system (called *identity management* in the latest tech lingo). This information includes the user name, email address, department, phone number, and password. By storing this information in a central location, the various systems operating on the network have access to it, thus greatly reducing the system management nightmare of dispersing informational files (for example, password files) through the various machines in the enterprise. Reading the user name and password from a directory server (most of which now support SSL connections) is a common practice in J2EE applications.

One of the most common common protocols used on directory servers is the LDAP server. LDAP was designed at the University of Michigan and is a simplified version of Directory Access Protocol (DAP), a protocol used to access information in an X.500 directory service, which defines a global directory service. The X.500 standard defines a protocol for a client to access the directory, the DAP, which is itself layered atop the Open Systems Interconnect (OSI) protocol stack. Per the specification, the information is stored in a directory information base (DIB), and entries are arranged in a directory information tree (DIT). An attribute has a defined attribute type and one or more values. A schema is used to define which attributes are mandatory and which are optional.

Because it is an open standard, LDAP servers are platform-independent—they do not belong to a particular vendor. LDAP works on top of TCP/IP and servers are interoperable. LDAP can work with other naming service protocols using a bridge.

LDAP Basics

LDAP servers support a series of entries stored in a hierarchy. An entry can contain attributes. The attributes and whether or not they are required for an entry are stored in one or more schemas being used by the server. The 'type' of the entry is identified with the *'object class* being used to establish a type for an entry (this is not the same as a Java class).

The fully qualified name to a location in the directory hierarchy is created through the *distinguished name,* abbreviated with *'dn'*. A fairly flexible filter mechanism allows filters to be constructed using a base distinguished name, a scope specifier that indicates how far in the hierarchy tree the search will be conducted, and a filter indicating which attributes will be searched and the criteria for the search.

THE JNDI API

Using JNDI, all naming service lookups are performed using a context. On connection to the naming service, an *'initial context'* is provied. Using this intial context, we can gain access to other contexts in the namespace by performing a lookup for the context. A general lookup operation is provided to find and retrieve a resource in one step.

The classes in the JNDI API reflect this approach to resource access. Five packages provide the classes used in JNDI. These packages are described in Table 12–1.

| Table 12–1 | *JNDI Classes* |

Package	Description
javax.naming	The main package for the API. Contains the classes for connecting to naming services and performing lookup operations for resources.
javax.naming.directory	Adds functionality for accessing directory servers.
javax.naming.event	Adds classes and services to support event notification with naming and directory services.
javax.naming.ldap	Contains interfaces and classes to support LDAP v3 operations and controls.
javax.naming.spi	Contains the classes and interfaces that allow service providers to implement JNDI.

The `javax.naming` package contains the core classes for creating a connection to naming service. The most commonly used class in this package is the `InitialContext` class, which represents an initial context within the namespace being accessed. The `InitialContext` class implements the `Context` interface, which describes the core behavior for accessing a naming service context.

The `javax.naming.spi` package contains the interfaces and classes that must be implemented by a service provider for a naming service. These are primarily the factory classes and state management classes. The developer would generally not use these classes or interfaces but would need to ensure that the classes were visible within the class path.

The JNDI API uses the `InitialContext` to establish communication with the naming service. There are a number of properties concerning the naming service that vary depending not only on the naming service but on the local environment where the naming service is running. The constructor for the `InitialContext` must therefore be aware of the context factory that will be used to create the resources (objects) returned by the JNDI implementation, and of the specifics of connecting to and communicating with the naming service.

This information can be provided to the `InitialContext` in one of several ways. In the following code fragment, a `java.util.Hashtable` is created, and entries are added for the `INITIAL_CONTEXT_FACTORY` (the class to manage the initial context or namespace). We must also be able to communicate with a directory or naming service in order to use the service, so we need a URL for accessing the service. In this example, the `PROVIDER_URL` (where JNDI will connect to access the service) is also placed in the `Hashtable`. The `Hashtable` is then passed into the constructor for the `InitialContext`, thereby making the constructor aware of the context factory and the location and communication mechanism for the naming service provider.

...

```
//
// add environment entries for the initial
// context
//
Hashtable env = new Hashtable();
   env.put(Context.INITIAL_CONTEXT_FACTORY,
   "com.sun.jndi.rmi.registry.RegistryContextFactory" );
   env.put(Context.PROVIDER_URL,
   "rmi://localhost:1099");

   //
   // get the initial context
   //
   InitialContext ctx = new InitialContext( env );
```

...

But this approach to obtaining the initial context inserts details about the directory server into the code and would require the code to change should the location or vendor of the directory server change. An alternative approach is to place the details of the JNDI service into a properties file named `jndi.proper-ties`. If this properties file is in the CLASSPATH for the application, it will be read, and if the appropriate properties for the initial context are provided, they will be used to obtain the initial context. If a JNDI properties file is available, then the no-argument constructor for the `InitialContext` can be used as shown in the following code snippet.

```
...
//
// initial context is retrieved
// from the "jndi.properties" file.
//
InitialContext ctx = new InitialContext( );
...
```

At a minimum, in order to obtain the initial context, the `jndi.properties` file must contain the following lines.

```
java.naming.factory.initial:com.sun.jndi.rmi.registry.RegistryContextFactory
java.naming.provider.url: rmi://localhost:1099
```

If the naming service provider is not a local resource, then a security manager may be required. The `jndi.properties` file would then contain an entry for the `java.naming.rmi.security.manager` property. Appropriate security manager entries would be required to grant the applications that will be using the SPI permission to connect and dynamically download classes. The application itself would need appropriate security manager settings in the security policy file to connect to the naming service provider (as detailed in Chapter 8). (If using JNDI from within a J2EE container, container security would manage the access to the JNDI resource, and specific Java security manager settings would not be required for the component.)

Once the initial context is obtained, we can begin using JNDI. The resources available through the JNDI server can be any arbitrary type. The `lookup` method is used to retrieve the resource (the value) stored using the key (or name). The `lookup` method returns an `Object` reference (since the value can be any arbitrary type) and therefore requires a cast to convert the `Object` reference to the correct reference for the stored value, as shown in the following example.

```
...
//
// get the DataSource for the movies DB
//
DataSource ds = (DataSource) ctx.lookup("movies");
...
```

When using JNDI from within a J2EE component—a servlet or EJB—the default `InitialContext` should provide access to the naming service provided by the J2EE container in which the component (JSP, EJB, servlet) is operating. What this means is that there should not be a need to establish the provider URL or naming factory for the JNDI connection.

JNDI CODING EXAMPLES

The most common use of JNDI in Java applications is to access resources in a naming service. Since JNDI allows access to a variety of naming services, the resource access can be one of a number of different types of resources. The resource could simply be a string or other primitive data type containing some important program property, such as a closing date for an accounting transaction, the name of a server that contains a resource, or a standard discount rate for a transaction. Or more commonly, the resource could be an object that encapsulates access to a service such as a database or a message queue.

The JDBC `DataSource` object is the method of choice for accessing a database. The `DataSource` contains the information needed to create a connection to a database and may add capabilities such as connection pooling and distributed transactions. The following code snippet provides an example of using JNDI to obtain a JDBC `DataSource`.

```
1.import java.sql.*;
2.import javax.sql.*;
3.import javax.naming.*;
4.import java.util.*;
5.import com.codestudio.sql.PoolMan;
6.
7.public class BasicExample5 {
8.
9.
10.public static void main( String args[] ) {
11.
12.Connection con=null;
13.try {
14.
15.      // Can set these here, or in a "jndi.properties"
16.      // properties file in the classpath
17.      //
18.      Hashtable env = new Hashtable();
19.      env.put(Context.INITIAL_CONTEXT_FACTORY,
20.        "com.sun.jndi.rmi.registry.RegistryContextFactory" );
21.      env.put(Context.PROVIDER_URL, "rmi://localhost:1099");
22.
23.      // get the initial context
24.      InitialContext ctx = new InitialContext( env );
25.
26.      // get the DataSource from the JNDI name server
27.      DataSource ds = (DataSource) ctx.lookup("movies");
28.
29.      // get the connection from the DataSource
30.      con = ds.getConnection( );
31....
```

In this code example, the `java.sql` package is imported for the JDBC API, and the `javax.sql` package is imported for the JDBC 2.0 standard extensions whch include the `DataSource` interface we will use. Additionally, the `java.io` package is imported for the `Hashtable` created on line 19. On line 5, the `Poolman` package is imported and used to provide the various JDBC capabilities that the current PostgreSQL driver does not support (`DataSource`, JNDI lookup, connection pooling, and scroll cursors).

On line 18, a `Hashtable` is created, and two entries are added to the `Hashtable`. These entries are needed to create the JNDI `InitialContext` that will be used to find the `DataSource`. Two key/value entries are added into the `Hashtable` on lines 19 and 21: The initial context factory, used for creating the initial or topmost context for the directory server, is set, and the provider URL for making the connection to the directory server provider is added. For local resources, which this example demonstrates, these two entries are required to create the `InitialContext`.

On line 24, a call is made to the constructor for the `InitialContext`. This call is passed the `Hashtable` created and loaded on lines 18 and 21. Using the `Context` object returned by the constructor, a call is made to the `Context` `lookup` method on line 27. The lookup method looks for bindings in the name-space of the naming service and, if it finds a match, returns an appropriate object reference. As we know, the `lookup` method returns an `Object` reference and it must be cast to the correct object type that has been returned. In our case, we know we have returned a `DataSource` reference and we cast the object to that type on line 27.

Once we have a `DataSource` object, we can call the `getConnection` method to make a connection to the underlying database, which is done on line 30. Since the `DataSource` object encapsulates the connection details, we do not need to specify the properties for our database connection in our `getConnection` call.

The previous example demonstrated JNDI access through a flat namespace (the RMI registry, to be exact). The name provided to access the `DataSource` was simply `movies`. While this may not be a problem when dealing with a handful of resources, in a complex application with dozens of resources to manage in the naming service, it is preferable to have a namespace hierarchy and to organize the hierarchy logically based on the needs of the organization.

In J2EE servers, a specific syntax for the lookup URL is used. The JDBC-related names are stored in a subcontext of the namespace named `jdbc`. The J2EE servers support using a URL with the lookup call, which starts with `java:`, and then provides a standard `comp` namespace. Under the `comp` namespace there is the `jdbc` namespace, and within the `jdbc` namespace the JDBC `DataSource` objects are stored. To reference the `movies DataSource` using this syntax, the following format is used.

```
...
//
// get the DataSource from the JNDI name server
//
DataSource ds = (DataSource)
      ctx.lookup("java:/comp/jdbc/movies");
...
```

Client Access of J2EE Resources Using JNDI

Client applications in J2EE access EJBs using J2EE. The syntax in this case is basically the same except that the object returned by the `Context` lookup call must be manipulated. Because of the potential use of the RMI-IIOP protocol to communicate with J2EE servers, and because of the need for backward compatibility with CORBA applications, the object returned from the lookup method requires some special coercion to become the object we need. The following code snippet provides an example of this.

```
...
Hashtable env = new Hashtable();
env.put( "java.naming.factory.initial",
         "org.jnp.interfaces.NamingContextFactory");
env.put( "java.naming.provider.url",
         "jnp://localhost:1099");
env.put( "java.naming.factory.url.pkgs",
         "org.jboss.naming:org.jnp.interfaces");

    //
    // get the Context implementation
    //
    Context init = new InitialContext( env );

System.out.println("Initial context found ... ");

    MoviesFacadeHome home = (MoviesFacadeHome)
        PortableRemoteObject.narrow(
            init.lookup("ejb/MoviesFacade"),
            MoviesFacadeHome.class );
...
```

In this example, the JBoss J2EE server is contacted by a J2EE client, and the `MoviesFacade` bean is requested using the `InitialContext lookup` method. The lookup method returns a Java object, which is then passed to the `PortableRemoteObject.narrow` method. This method will manipulate the object if necessary and return an object of the requested class if it is capable of doing so. The `PortableRemoteObject.narrow` method takes two arguments: the object reference to manipulate and the `Class` member of the Java class that it must return.

Using an LDAP Server with JNDI

Using JNDI with an LDAP server involves many of the same calls used for basic JNDI naming service access. But since an LDAP server is a special type of naming sevice, a *directory server*, the JNDI API provides an additional package with additional classes and interfaces to interact with a directory server.

The `javax.naming.directory` packages contains these classes and interfaces. These classes and interfaces provide directory-specific capabilities such as allowing attributes to be defined for an entry. In addition to the `javax.naming.directory` package, there is a `javax.naming.ldap` package, which specifically addresses some of the capabilities of LDAP servers, such as searches with controls.

The following code provides an example of using JNDI with LDAP servers. This example performs a search of a specific node in the namespace of an LDAP server and then outputs the results of that search.

```java
package examples.jndi;

import javax.naming.*;
import javax.naming.directory.*;
import javax.naming.ldap.*;

import org.apache.log4j.Category;

// our classes
import service.LoggingService;
import service.DirectoryService;

public class LdapSearch {


private static Category logger = LoggingService.getLogger();

public static void main(String args[] ) {

LdapSearch ls = new LdapSearch();

try {

DirectoryService directory = new DirectoryService();
InitialDirContext context = (InitialDirContext)
                    directory.getContext();

//
// create a SearchControl
//
SearchControls constraints = new SearchControls();
constraints.setSearchScope(
        SearchControls.SUBTREE_SCOPE );
String search = "objectclass=person";

//
// perform the search and output the results
//
NamingEnumeration results = context.search( "dc=movies, dc=com", search, constraints
);

while ( results != null && results.hasMore() ) {
      SearchResult r = (SearchResult) results.next();
      Attributes attr = r.getAttributes( );
      System.out.println("Common Name: " +
                          attr.get( "cn" ));
      System.out.println("Surname: " +
                          attr.get( "sn" ));
}


}
```

```
catch (Exception e) {
    logger.error("Exception caught: " + e );
}


}


}
```

In this example, we have encapsulated the functionality of obtaining access to the directory server in a class. We simply call the constructor for the `DirectoryService` class and then call the `getContext` method to retrieve our initial directory server context (`javax.naming.InitialDirContext`). The `InitialDirContext` class extends the `InitialContext` class and, among other modifications, adds a number of methods that support the identification of attributes for directory entries.

The code in this example first obtains an instance of the `Directory Service` class. This class is used to manage the specifics of accessing the directory service. Within this class (which is shown below), the environment to access the naming service is specified, including the specific environment parameters required to access the LDAP server. Encapsulating this behavior in a single class provides development benefits. Should the specific access requirements for the server change, the code modification required is localized.

The next step in the application is to create the various objects required to perform a search. A `javax.naming.directory.SearchControls` object is required to define the scope of the search and, in some cases, detail the specifics of what will be returned. In this case, the `SearchControls` object is merely used to indicate that the search will have subtree scope; that is, all subtrees below the current entry will be searched.

A search string is then specified to indicate the filter criteria for the search. This example uses a fairly simple filter, identifying that the `objectclass` of the entries returned should be a person. More complex queries can be executed using the syntax defined in RFC 1558 (*http://www.ietf.org/rfc/rfc1558.txt*).

The context (in this case, an `InitialDirContext` instance) provides a search method, which is called. This method returns a `NamingEnumeration` (`javax.naming.NamingEnumeration`, which extends `java.util.enumeration`), which is then iterated through using a `while` loop. Each element of the enumeration returns a `SearchResult` object, and for each object, the attributes of the object are retrieved in an `Attributes` (`javax.naming.directory.Attributes`) object. This class provides a `get` method, which allows retrieval of an attribute using an attribute ID. The `get` method returns an `Attribute` (an instance of `javax.naming.directory.BasicAttribute`), which is displayed using the overridden `toString` method of the `Attribute` class.

The DirectoryService Class

The `DirectoryService` class wraps the process of creating initial context creation to a naming service provider, in this case an LDAP server. This involves accessing the environment parameters and credentials needed to make the first connection and returning a context for the connection. It extends this basic functionality with a `getContext` method, which takes as an argument a subcontext of the initial context, thus avoiding the step of accessing the `InitialContext` and using that to obtain a subcontext.

The isolation of directory service access has the added benefit of localizing any change required to perform the access. Should some coding change be required, the change could be made in one location rather than in many programs or components that comprise an application.

The application below contains test code in the `main` program block, which demonstrates the access of entries in an LDAP server. The program accesses a logging device when the class is loaded (through a static logger variable initialization). The program then creates an instance of the `DirectoryService` class. This instance is used to retrieve a context, which is in fact a subcontext of the main context for the LDAP server. The specific LDAP syntax (`"o=south, o=sales-regions, o=movies-sales, dc=movies, dc=com"`) is required.

Once the context has been obtained, a series of calls are made to retrieve specific entries within our context. The LDAP syntax (`"cn=<entry_name>"`) is required to perform the lookup operations. In this example, the return value from the lookup is cast as a Java string. This is technically not required in this example, since we could have left them as objects and just passed them to the `System.out.println` method will call the `toString` method of the object returned. The class name for each entry is displayed to highlight the fact that Java types preserved as objects are persisted into the directory server.

DirectoryService.java

```
package service;

import java.util.*;
import java.text.*;
import javax.naming.*;
import javax.naming.directory.*;

import org.apache.log4j.*;

public class DirectoryService {

//
// use our logging service
//
private static Category    logger =
```

```
                    LoggingService.getLogger( "DirectoryService" );

private InitialContext init;

public static void main( String args[] ) {

DirectoryService ds = new DirectoryService();
ds.logger = LoggingService.getLogger(
                "DirectoryService" );

// get context to our subcontext
DirContext context = (DirContext) ds.getContext(
 "o=south, o=sales-regions, o=movies-sales, dc=movies, dc=com" );

try {
System.out.println(" Displaying values ... " );

System.out.println( "OrderQueueName class name: " +
context.lookup( "cn=OrderQueueName").getClass().getName() );
System.out.println( "OrderQueueName value: \t"  +
                    context.lookup( "cn=OrderQueueName" ));

System.out.println( "OrderInfoServiceURL class name: " +
     context.lookup( "cn=OrderInfoServiceURL" ).getClass().getName() );

System.out.println( "OrderInfoServiceURL value: \t"  +
     context.lookup( "cn=OrderInfoServiceURL" ));

System.out.println( "StandardDiscountRate class name: " +
     context.lookup( "cn=StandardDiscountRate" ).getClass().getName() );

System.out.println( "StandardDiscountRate value: \t" +
     context.lookup( "cn=StandardDiscountRate" ));

System.out.println( "SpecialDiscountRate class name: " +
     context.lookup( "cn=SpecialDiscountRate" ).getClass().getName() );

System.out.println( "SpecialDiscountRate value: \t" +
     context.lookup( "cn=SpecialDiscountRate" ));


Object obj =  context.lookup( "cn=Q1ClosingDate" );
String s =
     DateFormat.getDateInstance().format( ((Calendar) obj).getTime() );
System.out.println( "Q1ClosingDate: \t" +  s );

}
catch ( NamingException e) {
     if ( ds.logger == null ) {
         System.err.println( "NamingException in main: " +
                           e );
         e.printStackTrace();
```

```
        }
        else
            ds.logger.error("NamingException in main: " + e );
    }

}
```

THE DIRECTORYSERVICE CLASS: THE getCONTEXT METHOD

The getContext method with no arguments is used to retrieve the base context or the InitialContext for the naming service. As shown in the next listing, the over-loaded version of that method accepts a string parameter and firsts tests to see whether or not the instance member for the InitialContext has been set; if it has, there is no attempt to create it. But if it has not been set, then the getContext method is called to retrieve the InitialContext. This is cast as an InitialContext in this example, but the true type of the reference is an InitialDirContext a subclass of InitialContext (and the reason the cast works).

The next step is to call the InitialContext lookup method to retrieve the specific subcontext being sought. This context is preserved and returned by the method in the finally block.

DirectoryService Class: the getContext Method

```
public Context getContext( String subContext ) {
Context context = null;

try {

    //
    // if we don't have the InitialContext, retrieve it
    //
    if ( init == null )
        init = (InitialContext) getContext();

    //
    // use the initial context to get the local context
    //
    context = (Context) init.lookup( subContext );

}
catch ( NamingException e ) {
        if ( logger == null ) {
            System.err.println(
                "NamingException in getContext: " + e );
            System.err.println(
```

```
                "Attempting to access:   " + subContext );
        }
        else {
            logger.error(
                "NamingException in getContext: " + e );
            logger.error( "Attempting to access: " +
                subContext );
        }
    }
}
finally {
    return context;
}

}
```

The no-argument version of the `getContext` method retrieves the `Initial Context` for the naming service. This method starts by retrieving the environment to use to create the context using the static method of the `Environment` class. This class (as shown below) contains the specifics needed to create the connection to the naming service.

Once the `Hashtable` containing the environment has been created and loaded, it is passed to the `InitialDirContext` constructor to create the initial context for the LDAP namespace. Any exception is logged, but since the `LoggingService` depends on the `DirectoryService` (which in turn relies on the `LoggingService`—the chicken and the egg conundrum), this code allows for a failure to create the logger and alternatively logs to standard error.

The getContext Method

```
public Context getContext() {
//
// retrieve the InitialContext
//
InitialContext init=null;

Hashtable env = new Environment().getEnvironment();

try {

init = new InitialDirContext( env );

}
catch (NamingException e) {
        if ( logger == null )
            System.err.println(
                "NamingException in getContext: " + e );
        Else
            logger.error(
```

```
                    "NamingException in getContext: " + e );
}
finally {
    return init;
}


}


}
```

THE ENVIRONMENT CLASS

The `Environment` class shown below is intended to encapsulate the details of the local environment for the JNDI server. In this particular example, all information is retrieved through the program, but this is information that could just as easily have been retrieved from a properties file, an XML document, or a database. Since we regard the location of the directory server to be relatively static information (moving or renaming the host for a directory server to a new name would have a significant impact on the network), retrieving this information from a localized class should not present a problem.

This class does the majority of its work in the constructor. It creates a `Hashtable` and loads it with the correct parameters to create an `InitialContext` instance to connect to the local naming service. A `getEnvironment` method then returns that `Hashtable` to the caller.

The Environment Class

```
package service;

import javax.naming.*;
import java.util.*;

public class Environment {

private Hashtable env;

public Environment() {

env = new Hashtable();

env.put( Context.INITIAL_CONTEXT_FACTORY,
         "com.sun.jndi.ldap.LdapCtxFactory" );
env.put( Context.PROVIDER_URL, "ldap://localhost:389");
env.put( Context.SECURITY_AUTHENTICATION, "simple");
env.put( Context.SECURITY_CREDENTIALS, "secret");
env.put( Context.SECURITY_PRINCIPAL,
```

```
                "cn=movies,dc=movies,dc=com");
}
public Hashtable getEnvironment() {
      return env;
}

}
```

The ListContext Class

The `ListContext` class demonstrates the retrieval of data from the naming service. This class uses the `Context` list method to retrieve a `NamingEnumeration` of the entries in a context. The program uses the `DirectoryService` to return a `DirContext` (which is a `InitialDirContext`) and then calls the `display Context` method.

The `displayContext` method takes a single parameter, a string, which is the context to list. The method then calls the `list` method and retrieves a `Naming Enumeration`. It then iterates through the `NamingEnumeration`, listing the values in the enumeration.

The ListContext Class

```
package examples.jndi;

import java.sql.*;
import javax.sql.*;
import javax.naming.*;
import javax.naming.directory.*;

import java.util.*;

import service.DirectoryService;
import service.LoggingService;

import org.apache.log4j.*;


public class ListContext {

private static Category    logger =
            LoggingService.getLogger( "ListContext" );
private DirContext context;


public static void main( String args[] ) {
ListContext lc = new ListContext();

try {
```

```
DirectoryService directory = new DirectoryService();

//
// get the initial context
//
lc.context= (DirContext) directory.getContext( );

System.out.println("Listing contexts ... " );

lc.displayContext( "dc=movies, dc=com" );
lc.displayContext( "o=inventory, dc=movies, dc=com" );
lc.displayContext(
        "o=north, o=sales-regions, o=movies-sales, dc=movies, dc=com" );

}
catch (Exception e) {
  lc.logger.error("Exception e: " + e );
}


}


public void displayContext( String contextName ) {

try {

 NamingEnumeration ne = context.list( contextName );
 System.out.println( "Listing context: " + contextName  );

 while ( ne.hasMore() ) {
        System.out.println( "Node: " + ne.next() );
 }
}
catch (Exception e) {
  logger.error("Exception in displayContext: " + e );
}

}

}
```

The BindValues Class

Even though the naming service is expected to contain fairly static, query-intensive information, there are still instances where the data in the naming service must be updated. Data must somehow be placed into the directory server. This process is referred to as *binding* the data into the naming service.

Many software vendors provide tools to input data to the server. Performing this operation using some type of GUI input program or using a Web browser is easier than using a programming API. Nevertheless, the JNDI package provides the ability to bind values into the directory server. The `BindValues` class demonstrates this process.

As you will see from this program, this is accomplished using the `Context` `bind` method, which takes three arguments: the name to associate with the object, the object to bind, and the attributes for the object.

This class begins by using the `DirectoryService` class (shown previously) to obtain a `Context` to use in the namespace of the LDAP server. Specifically, it requests a subcontext of the main context with the path of `"o=south, o=sales-regions, o=movies-sales, dc=movies, dc=com"`. (Viewed as a file system path, this would be `/com/movies/movies-sales/sales-regions/south`.)

The object we are adding into the LDAP namespace must have a set of attributes associated with it. Specifically, it must have an `objectClass` attribute that provides enough information to the server so that the server knows how to manage the object. The `objectClass` we define here will identify the object as a top-level object and as an `extensibleObject` (a Java object).

Attributes are associated with the object we are adding by way of the `BasicAttribute` class (`javax.naming.directory.BasicAttribute`). In the program, a `BasicAttribute` instance is created for the `objectClass` attribute. Two values are then added to the attribute: `extensibleObject` and `top`.

The `BasicAttribute` class is then instantiated, and the `BasicAttribute` containing `objectClass` entries is added to the `BasicAttributes` instance. The `BasicAttribute` instance is added as an attributes value when the name and value are added to the directory server database.

Names, their associated values, and their attributes are added using the `bind` or `rebind` method, as defined in the `DirContext` interface. If it is possible that the value may already have been added, then the `rebind` call may be a better choice. If the name already exists, then the rebind method will silently update the previous value. (If the name already exists and the `bind` method is used, the method call will throw an exception.)

The `BindValues` class will bind several names and values into the south sales region area. These values include two string values and two Java `Double` values. A `Calendar` object will also be bound. The only requirement placed on the objects that may be added using the directory server SPI is that they are `Serializable` objects (objects that implement the `java.io.Serializable` interface).

The final section of the `BindValues` class adds a series of data sources to the directory server. To keep the contents of the server organized, the `DataSources` are placed in the `jdbc` subcontext. The code for this class is shown below.

The BindValues Class

```
package examples.jndi;

import javax.naming.*;
import javax.naming.directory.*;
import javax.naming.ldap.*;

import java.text.DateFormat;
import java.util.Calendar;

import org.apache.log4j.Category;

import service.DirectoryService;
import service.LoggingService;

public class BindValues  {

private static Category logger =
      LoggingService.getLogger(
                          "BindValues" );

public static void main(String args[] ) {

BindValues binder = new BindValues();

try {

DirectoryService directory = new DirectoryService();

//
// use the South region subcontext
//
DirContext ctx = (DirContext) directory.getContext(
      "o=south, o=sales-regions, o=movies-sales, dc=movies, dc=com");

BasicAttribute attribute = new BasicAttribute(
                              "objectClass" );
attribute.add( "extensibleObject");
attribute.add( "top");

BasicAttributes attributes = new BasicAttributes(true);
attributes.put( attribute );

//
// bind several application properties into this node
//
ctx.rebind( "cn=OrderQueueName",
            "Memphis", attributes );

ctx.rebind( "cn=OrderInfoServiceURL",
            "http://Alexandria/OrderStatus",  attributes );
```

```
ctx.rebind( "cn=StandardDiscountRate",
            new Double(".12"),  attributes);

ctx.rebind( "cn=SpecialDiscountRate",
            new Double( ".14" ),  attributes);
//
// create a new Calendar and set the date
//
Calendar c = (Calendar.getInstance());
c.set( 2001, Calendar.DECEMBER, 25 );
ctx.rebind( "cn=Q1ClosingDate",  c, attributes );

//
// Create DataSources for demo programs
//
System.out.println(
        "Creating DataSource object for movies ... " );

org.gjt.mm.mysql.MysqlDataSource mySQLDS =
            new org.gjt.mm.mysql.MysqlDataSource();

mySQLDS.setUser( "art" );
mySQLDS.setPassword( "YES" );
mySQLDS.setServerName( "localhost" );
mySQLDS.setDatabaseName( "movies" );
mySQLDS.setPort( 3306 );

//
// poolman - postgresql
//
com.codestudio.sql.PoolManDataSource psqlDS =
     new com.codestudio.sql.PoolManDataSource( "stock",
                                       "stock-psql");
//
//jndi name
//
System.out.println(
  "Creating DataSource object for knowledgebase ... " );
org.gjt.mm.mysql.MysqlDataSource mySQLKB =
  new org.gjt.mm.mysql.MysqlDataSource();

mySQLKB.setUser( "art" );
mySQLKB.setPassword( "YES" );
mySQLKB.setServerName( "localhost" );
mySQLKB.setDatabaseName( "knowledgebase" );
mySQLKB.setPort( 3306 );

org.gjt.mm.mysql.MysqlDataSource mySQLTest =
            new org.gjt.mm.mysql.MysqlDataSource();
mySQLTest.setUser( "art" );
mySQLTest.setPassword( "YES" );
```

```
mySQLTest.setServerName( "localhost" );
mySQLTest.setDatabaseName( "test" );
mySQLTest.setPort( 3306 );

//
// put these in a general subcontext for business objects
//
DirContext context = (DirContext) directory.getContext(
    "o=jdbc, o=general-application-objects, dc=movies, dc=com" );

//
//
System.out.println( "Binding DataSources ... " );

context.rebind("cn=moviesmysql", mySQLDS, attributes);
context.rebind("cn=movies-mysql", mySQLDS, attributes);

//
// bind PostgreSQL through poolman
//
context.rebind("cn=stock-psql", psqlDS, attributes);

//
// bind knowledgebase and test dbs
//
context.rebind("cn=knowledgebase", mySQLKB, attributes);
context.rebind("cn=test", mySQLTest, attributes);

//
// put this in a general-application area
//
context = (DirContext) directory.getContext(
          "o=logging, o=general-application-objects, dc=movies, dc=com" );

context.rebind("cn=loggingConfigFile",
               "file:/lin/home/art/log4j.xml",
               attributes );

}
catch (NamingException e) {
   binder.logger.error("NamingException caught: " + e );
}


}


}
```

SUMMARY

The JNDI package is a key package to J2EE. A J2EE-compliant application server must provide a naming service. That naming service is used to access EJB components and the J2EE resources residing in the application server. Access to all of the resources of the EJB application server is through the JNDI API.

As we saw in this chapter, access to a JNDI naming service is relatively simple, involving just a few calls. More complex operations, such as binding objects into the naming service and accessing directory servers, were also demonstrated in this chapter but are used much less frequently.

Using Logging with J2EE

INTRODUCTION

The process of application logging has rarely been at the forefront of project design. On many projects, modules to write log files were eventually created, but often the format, consistency, and frequency with which the logs were used varied depending on the developer. Different development groups often used different logging APIs. In addition to the sometimes inconsistent usage, there has always been a debate concerning logging. Many developers feel that logging can slow an application.

Using a good, consistent, and efficient standardized logging API can help prevent these problems. Several good logging APIs are now available for use with the Java language. The Apache Jakarta project has spawned two good APIs: the log4j logging API and the Apache Commons logging API. Sun Microsystems has also delivered a logging API with version 1.4 of the JDK. This chapter takes a look at the log4J API and the `java.util.logging` package that is now being shipped with the Sun JDK.

The Benefits of Logging

Logging can be used to debug an application and determine the root cause of a failure, or to track program and user activity, and to provide a journal of the work being performed with a program for security reasons.

While there are not many who suggest that logging is unnecessary, there are those who argue there are better techniques for debugging than producing excessive log output. There is also the question of when to turn on debugging log output and what is involved in doing that. In its most primitive form, a series of output statements can be written into a Java application to debug the program, as shown below. Removing debugging would then require that all modules with the output statements would need to be removed—a tedious and error-prone process.

```
...
// debug output
System.out.println(
 "Starting input parsing. Status flag is : " + status );
...
```

A more sophisticated approach would use a debug flag, a global value that triggers output based on its value. This debug flag could be a boolean, but in more flexible approaches would be a value indicating the level of log output to use. This would allow various levels of logging to be maintained in the application, depending on how the program was being run (integration testing, production).

Beyond the need to control the logging output in an application, there is a requirement to be able to support multiple output devices for a log. A single flat file for log output is no longer enough. Many applications need to log to a database or one or more log files. Java logging APIs now support some or all of these features.

The log4j API

The first logging package we will examine is the log4j package from the Apache Jakarta project. This is a mature logging API that provides a rich feature set for formatting and controlling logging activity. Logging output can be directed to one or more logs based on severity levels, the name of the component performing the logging, or any arbitrary filter criteria.

The log4j logging package is flexible. Logging output can be directed to a file (either `OutputStream` or `Writer`), a remote log4j server, the UNIX `Syslog`, or the NT event logger. Various configuration parameters can be changed; for example, you can use different logging devices or log different severity levels. Most configuration changes do not require changes to the code performing the logging.

Inefficient logging can severely impact application performance and is often an excuse for eliminating robust logging from application code. But the log4j package is efficient. Using log4j does incur some overhead, but the overhead has been kept to a minimum. A centralized logging configuration file is used to provide the details on how logging is to be performed. We will examine this shortly.

Package Design

The log4j API uses several classes to control the bulk of logging activity. Through interaction and appropriate configuration, these components interact to provide control over how logging is performed and which log messages are output. These components are `Loggers`, `Appenders`, and `Layouts` (see Figure 13–1).

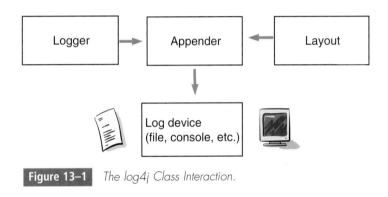

Figure 13–1   *The log4j Class Interaction.*

The *logger,* as the name implies, controls the logging process and is represented by the `Logger` class in the `org.apache.log4j` package. Log messages are output using a `Logger` class instance.

The logger object is referenced by a case-sensitive name, which follows a hierarchical naming pattern using a dot separator. Using this standard, the `class1.class2` logger is a descendant of the `class1` logger. There is a root logger, the parent of all loggers, which always exists and can be retrieved with a call to the static `getRootLogger` method in the `Logger` class.

The loggers are assigned logging levels, which effectively filter output to the logs based on a level parameter, as defined in the `Level` class. The log level implies information about the severity or significance of the log message. The levels are, in order of priority, FATAL, ERROR, WARN, INFO, and DEBUG. A Level of OFF is provided to turn off all logging, and ALL is provided to turn on all logging. A level could be added to the system by subclassing the `Level` class.

Setting a log level is the same as setting a threshold; all log output at a lower level is ignored. All log output at the same level or greater is output. If a logger is not assigned a level, it inherits the level of its nearest ancestor.

There are two different ways to create log message output with a logger. One form of output involves using the print methods defined in the `Logger` class for each of the logging levels. The method names correspond to the log levels (in lowercase) and are `debug`, `info`, `warn`, `error`, and `fatal`. The following code snippet demonstrates log output using these methods.

```
Logger logger = Logger.getLogger("myClass");
...
logger.warn("This is a warning");
...
logger.error("An error has occurred.");
...
```

If a logger is not set to a level equal to or greater than the level being attempted for output, then the attempt to log the message will fail quietly. The log level can be set in the configuration file for log4j, or it can be set programmatically. The `setLevel` method in the `Logger` class can be used to change the log level threshold as follows.

```
...
Logger logger = Logger.getLogger("myClass");
...
//
// we will now log at the info level - ignore
// debug messages
//
logger.setLevel( Level.INFO );
logger.info("Starting main processing thread.");
...
```

The preferable method for setting the log level is in the configuration file where it can be changed without modifying code. Since log messages can appear in numerous source files, the process of modifying various log message calls can be tedious. It is best to use a disciplined approach to logging and leave level and filter settings to be made in the log4j configuration file where they are easy to change.

Loggers are usually named after the software component or class in which they are being used, but that is not required. The name is assigned in the call to the `Logger` class `getLogger` method. Programmers are free to name loggers as they see fit.

The Log Appenders

The job of the log appender is to see to it that the log message is sent to the correct log device. In this respect, the appender represents a destination. A destination can be a console, a file on the local file system, a remote socket, an NT event logger, a Java Messaging Service (JMS) topic, or the UNIX Syslog.

Appenders can also log asynchronously, logging events to a bounded buffer that, when filled, is then written to its associated output device. In some instances this can improve performance, but that is not always the case.

Appenders are associated with a logger. This association is consummated using the `addAppender` method of the `Logger` class (inherited from the deprecated `Category` class). Multiple appenders may be attached to a logger.

Appenders perform filtering and determine the layout for the log message, but the details of these tasks are left to related objects (specifically, instances of the `Layout` class and the `Filter` class).

The Layout Class

The `Layout` class provides formatting of the log message for the output device. Layouts may be in text format according to a pattern, or a layout may optionally be in XML format where it can later be transformed into a more useful, readable format (such as HTML).

The `PatternLayout` class provides facilities for creating a transformation pattern using special characters. This string of characters is then used to produce the log message for output to the logging device.

A great deal of useful information may be output to a log file. But not without a cost. Outputting a large amount of logging information not only makes it tedious to monitor the logs, but can have a serious impact on performance. Additionally, what is referred to as *location* information, information on the line number and method where the program is currently executing, exacts a severe performance penalty; outputting this information (`%M` for method, `%L` for line number) should be limited to debugging or tracking information on an exception that is thrown rarely.

Configuring the log4j Package

A good logging package is only useful if it allows a great deal of configurability without requiring changes to application code. The log4j package provides a large, flexible set of configuration options, which can be changed without touching the application code.

Configuration information can be placed in a Java properties file or an XML-formatted configuration file. By default, the package will look for a file named `log4j.properties` in the program's classpath to load configuration properties.

Optionally, these same properties can be loaded programmatically using the `PropertyConfigurator` class as follows. But before we look at a configuration file, let's take a look at the use of log4j in an application.

A LOG4J CODE EXAMPLE

The following code example demonstrates the process for using logging with the log4j package. This program begins by importing the `org.apache.log4j` package. This package is not part of the standard JDK and must be downloaded from the Jakarta/Apache site (*http://jakarta.apache.org/log4j*). Within the package downloaded is a JAR file (for version 1.2, it is named `log4j-1.2.jar`) that must be made visible to the Java Runtime Environment (JRE) of the application using the package (in the classpath or in the `$JAVA_HOME/jre/lib/ext` directory).

This code example loads the log4j configuration using a URL (in string format), which is used to set the value of the `log4j.configuration` System property. This value could also have been set on the command line with the -D parameter but is placed in the code to make the configuration process more visible. (A later example will demonstrate retrieving the configuration file location from a naming service, providing additional flexibility in locating the file.)

Once the `log4j.configuration` System property has been set, the `log4j` package is now aware of where to load its configuration. The constructor for the `LoggingLog4j` class is called. In the constructor, the static `Logger` `getLogger` method is called to retrieve an instance of a `Logger`. This method is passed the class of the currently executing class. The `log4j` `Logger` retrieves the name of the class and uses that to name the logger. Standard format output uses the name of the class in its output, making it easy to identify the component that generated the log message. The `getLogger` method is overloaded to also accept arbitrary strings as logger names.

At this point, we are able to use our logger to make log entries. We have made the logger reference public, so it is in scope throughout the entire class. We call the `testIt` method, which will write a series of log entries of various levels using the various print methods in the `Logger` class.

The LoggingLog4j Class

```
package examples.logging;
import org.apache.log4j.*;
public class LoggingLog4j {

private Logger logger;

public static void main( String args[] ) {
String loggingConfigFile = "file:/lin/home/art/log4j.xml";
```

```
//
// set the system property to get the configuration file
//
System.setProperty( "log4j.configuration", loggingConfigFile );

LoggingLog4j logTester = new LoggingLog4j();

logTester.testIt();

}

public void testIt() {
//
// Log some information
//
logger.info("Just some information.");
logger.debug( "This is debugging output.");
logger.error( "This is an error.");
logger.warn( "This is an warning.");

//
// Can also use these methods for log output.
// This would provide easier conversion to Sun's logging API (and
// vice-versa)
//
logger.log( Level.INFO,
            "This is another informational message." );
logger.log( Level.DEBUG,
            "This is a debug message." );
logger.log( Level.ERROR,
            "This is an error message." );
logger.log( Level.WARN,
            "This is a warn message." );

}

public LoggingLog4j() {
  //
  // Get the Logger
  //
  logger = Logger.getLogger( LoggingLog4j.class.getName() );

}

}
```

As the previous example showed, it is fairly trivial to program logging into a Java application using log4j. The application code required to start logging can take as little as one or two lines of code. But there is more to successful logging than making the correct calls in the program. The log4j package provides a great deal of flexibility, which would imply that there are a number of decisions to be made and then communicated to the log4j package. Those decisions are made and then entered in the log4j configuration file.

The configuration file allows appenders to be created. In configuring an appender, a layout (output format) may be selected, and the output device (file, socket, syslog, NT event log) is also selected. Loggers may then be assigned to one or more specific appenders, thus allowing logging output to be controlled indirectly through the associations made for the logger.

The log4j configuration file usually contains a mix of appender and category entries. The following listing shows a log4j configuration file named `log4j.xml` (the XML extension should be used to make the `PropertyConfigurator` aware that this is an XML-formatted file). The file begins with several appenders being declared. Each appender contains parameters appropriate for the class of the appender being used. For the general appender (which will be used to log most entries), a `FileAppender` is created. The value of the `name` parameter (an attribute of the `param` element) is `/tmp/general.log`—this is where the log output will be written. An `append` element is used to indicate that the file will be appended. If this had been set to false, then the file would have been overwritten each time the program started.

An output format for the log entry is established by specifying the layout class (a subclass of the `Layout` class) for the appender. The layout chosen in this example is the `PatternLayout`. This layout allows a string pattern to be used to specify what will be written to the log. A series of special characters is identified in the Javadoc for the `PatternLayout` class. The pattern to be used for this appender is specified in the `ConversionPattern` parameter, as shown below, where the `value` attribute specifies the pattern to be used.

An appender named `debugOutput` is also declared. This appender also uses a `FileAppender` class and a `PatternLayout` log formatter. But the `ConversionPattern` used for this appender is different. In this `ConversionPattern`, location information on where the logger was called is specified. The `%M` and `%L` patterns are used to indicate the Java method and the program line number where the logger was called, respectively. As discussed previously, it is expensive for the appender to gather this information, but given its usage here, for debug output only, we would not expect to use this appender with production code, so the performance impact should only be experienced during testing where it should not be an issue.

The configuration file also contains a number of `category` definitions. These provide definitions for *categories* (in log4j versions prior to 1.2, this was the name used for the `Logger` class). These entries indicate that if a logger has the name specified by the name attribute, then the elements within the body of the `category` element apply. So, for the `examples.jaxp.XMLDemo3` category (the logger name), the priority (or the level) is set to `info`. This means that all entries below `info` in the level hierarchy will not be printed. This includes `debug` and all (which turns on all logging), so this setting effectively turns off all debug logging and allows other log messages to be logged.

The category element also contains an appender-ref element whose attribute identifies the appender that will handle the log entries for this logger. The final entry in the file provides properties for a root logger. This logger is the parent of all other loggers. The root logger contains an element for priority (level), which is set to debug, indicating all log level entries for debug and higher will be written and sent to the general appender. This has the effect of sending all log entries to the appender named general. These entries are shown in the following listing.

log4j Configuration file

```xml
<?xml version="1.0" encoding="UTF-8" ?>
<!DOCTYPE log4j:configuration SYSTEM "log4j.dtd">

<log4j:configuration xmlns:log4j="http://jakarta.apache.org/log4j/">

    <appender name="general"
            class="org.apache.log4j.FileAppender">
        <param name="File"    value="/tmp/general.log" />
        <param name="Append" value="true" />
        <layout class="org.apache.log4j.PatternLayout">
            <param name="ConversionPattern"
                value="%d [%c-%t] %-5p - %m%n"/>
        </layout>
    </appender>

    <appender name="debugOutput"
            class="org.apache.log4j.FileAppender">
        <param name="File"    value="/tmp/debug.log" />
        <param name="Append" value="true" />
        <layout class="org.apache.log4j.PatternLayout">
            <param name="ConversionPattern"
                value="%c [%M:%L] %-5p - %m %n"/>
        </layout>
    </appender>

    <!-- debug is turned off for now -->
    <category name="examples.jaxp.XMLDemo3">
      <priority value="info" />
      <appender-ref ref="general" />
    </category>

    <!-- debug is turned on -->
    <category name="examples.jaxp.XMLDemo4">
      <priority value="debug" />
      <appender-ref ref="general" />
    </category>
```

```
<category name="LogTest">
  <priority value="info" />
  <appender-ref ref="general" />
</category>

<category name="SendingServlet">
  <priority value="debug" />
  <appender-ref ref="general" />
</category>

<category name="MovieInfoService">
  <priority value="debug" />
  <appender-ref ref="general" />
</category>

<root>
   <priority value ="debug" />
   <appender-ref ref="general" />
</root>
```

`</log4j:configuration>`

The output from the execution of this program using the configuration file shown previously is shown below. This was created using the `PatternLayout` class with the pattern specified in the configuration file (`value="%c [%M:%L] %-5p - %m %n"`).

Logging Output from the LoggingLog4j Program

```
2002-05-17 17:58:48,608 [LoggingLog4j-main] INFO  - Just some information.
2002-05-17 17:58:48,618 [LoggingLog4j-main] DEBUG - This is debugging output.
2002-05-17 17:58:48,619 [LoggingLog4j-main] ERROR - This is an error.
2002-05-17 17:58:48,620 [LoggingLog4j-main] WARN  - This is an warning.
2002-05-17 17:58:48,621 [LoggingLog4j-main] INFO  - This is another informational
message.
2002-05-17 17:58:48,622 [LoggingLog4j-main] DEBUG - This is a debug message.
2002-05-17 17:58:48,623 [LoggingLog4j-main] ERROR - This is an error message.
2002-05-17 17:58:48,624 [LoggingLog4j-main] WARN  - This is a warn message.
```

This output includes several useful pieces of information concerning where the logging entry was made. This includes the date and time when the log entry was made, the module (class) and method (or code block in the case of `main`) where the logging request was made, the logging output level and the error message.

Alternatively, the `HTMLLayout` class could have been specified using the following entry.

```
<layout class="org.apache.log4j.HTMLLayout">
```

The results of using this `Layout` class would be all of the log entries in the log file in HTML format, as shown in Figure 13–2.

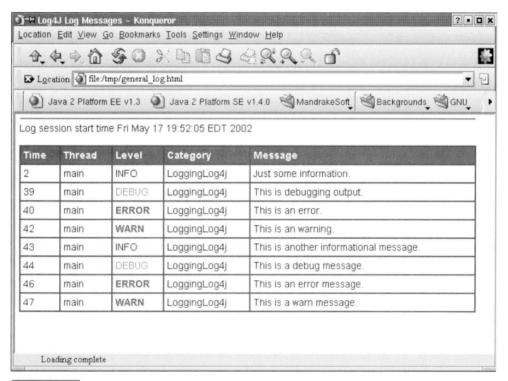

Figure 13–2   *HTML formatted log output.*

Yet another alternative for reading log files is the `Chainsaw` log viewer, as shown in Figure 13–3. This GUI program (written in Java Swing) is part of the log4j package (as of 1.2). This program can read an existing log4j log output file that has been written in XML, or it can communicate with a log4j logging server and accept logging output. The program allows log entries to be filtered by logger (category), level (priority), and other log properties. Highlighting a log entry provides additional details about the log in the text pane on the bottom of the window.

The java.util.logging Package

In an effort to extend the utility of the Java development environment and to address some of its shortcomings, a logging package has been added to the JDK as of version 1.4. This package, while not as feature rich as the log4j package, does provide some flexibility and features that create a foundation for application logging. The core classes and interfaces in this package are listed in Table 13–1.

As you might expect, there are similarities between the this logging package and the log4j logging package. Both packages have a `Logger` class to provide basic logging control and a `Level` class to indicate the level or priority of the logging message. But where the log4j package has an `Appender` class to provide for the output of logging messages, the `java.util.logging` package uses a `Handler` class. A `Handler` is similar to the log4j appender. Its job is to direct the log message to an output device. And instead of a using a `Layout` class to describe the format of log output, the `java.util.logging` package uses a `Formatter` class.

The Sun logging package uses several levels to define the severity of logging output. These levels, in order of priority, are listed in Table 13–2.

Table 13–1   *Java.util.logging Core Classes*

Class/Abstract class/Interface	Description
Logger	This class is used to make logging calls.
LogRecord	This class is used to pass logging requests between individual log handlers.
Handler	Directs LogRecord objects to various locations or output devices. A Llocation can be memory, output streams, consoles, files, and sockets.
Level	Defines standard logging levels that control logging output and control what is output.
Filter	In addition to the logging levels, this class provides control over what gets logged.
Formatter	Allows LogRecord objects to be formatted.

Table 13–2   *Logging Levels*

Level	Description
SEVERE	A severe error has occurred. The application cannot recover.
WARNING	A warning of potential problems.
INFO	General informational warning.
CONFIG	A description of static information concerning the operation of a program for debugging purposes.
FINE	A finely grained debug output message. Detailed tracing information for debugging.
FINER	A even more finely grained debug output message. Detailed tracing information for debugging.
FINEST	The very finest grained debug output message. Detailed tracing information for debugging.

Using the `Logger` class, a log message level could be set programmatically. Alternatively, the level could be set in a configuration file (the preferable method). Once a level has been set for a logger, all log messages with levels below that level will be ignored. For convenience, there is an ALL level defined that can be used to set a logger to log all messages of all levels. There is also an OFF level that will stop all logging.

An instance of the `Handler` class is used to designate where the output for the logger will go. Multiple `Handler` objects can be assigned to a single logger, thus allowing logging output to be logged in multiple locations. The `Handler` class is an abstract class; concrete implementations have been provided for file output (`FileHandler`), console output (`ConsoleHandler`), memory (`MemoryHandler`), and sockets (`SocketHandler`).

JAVA JDK LOGGING CODE SAMPLE

The following code sample demonstrates the use of the Java JDK logging facility. This example defines a logger using a logging configuration file and directs the logger to log messages to a file. The program then sends a series of log messages to the logger, which outputs (or publishes) the log messages to the file.

A `Formatter` instance is then added as a handler. The purpose of this object is to format the output of the logger as a single line of text. (By default, the `SimpleFormatter` class outputs a head and tail, or two separate lines of text plus the log message for each log message written.)

This sample program creates a logger as a static member of the class in which it will be used. This is the recommended method of loading a logging device since the logger is loaded when the class is loaded. In this way the logger is available as soon as the class is used and is able to log errors that may pertain to class loading.

The `main` program block shown below is then used to output a series of log messages. The messages are output in order of their severity level. Since the output level or threshold for the logger is set to INFO in the configuration file used by the program, all messages with severity levels below the INFO level would be ignored. This would mean that in the example below, the output messages for the CONFIG, FINE, FINER, and FINEST levels (generally used for debug statements) would fail quietly.

The log level is then reset to the FINEST level, using the `Logger` class `setLevel` method and log messages are sent to the `Handler` again. This time, because the level has been changed, the `Handler` will allow all log messages to be sent to the assigned location.

Next in the program, we add a new `Handler` to the `Logger` class instance. In this case, it is a `FileHandler`, which will direct output to an additional log file. (This does not reset existing `Handler` objects that have been defined in the configuration file.) Several log entries are written using the new `FileHandler`.

Next, we add another `FileHandler` to the logger, and this time we add our own special implementation of a `Formatter`, the `SingleLineFormatter` class (shown below). This class provides concise log output, taking the log message and summarizing it in a single line of text.

The new `FileHandler` is created first, identifying a file to be used for log output. The `SingleLineFormatter` object is then created and added to the `FileHandler` object, using the `setFormatter` method. The `FileHandler` object is then added to the logger, using the `addHandler` method. Two additional log messages are then sent to the logger. These messages are output to the new `FileHandler`, using the `SingleLineFormatter`, as well as the other `Handler` objects currently attached to the logger.

The LoggingJDK Class

```java
import java.util.logging.*;
import java.io.*;

public class LoggingJDK {

public static Logger logger = Logger.getLogger( "LoggingJDK" );

public static void main( String args[] ) {

logger.info("Hello Logging world.");


//
// configuration properties file is set to INFO, so
// all messages below the INFO level will be ignored
//
logger.log( Level.SEVERE, "This is severe.");
logger.log( Level.WARNING, "I'm warning you.");
logger.log( Level.INFO, "This is just information.");
logger.log( Level.CONFIG, "Configure this.");
logger.log( Level.FINE, "This is FINE.");
logger.log( Level.FINER, "This is FINER.");
logger.log( Level.FINEST, "This is FINEST.");


//
// reset the level and try logging messages again
//
logger.setLevel( Level.FINEST );
logger.info( "** LOG LEVEL HAS BEEN RESET **" );
logger.log( Level.SEVERE, "This is severe.");
logger.log( Level.WARNING, "I'm warning you.");
logger.log( Level.INFO, "This is just information.");
logger.log( Level.CONFIG, "Configure this.");
logger.log( Level.FINE, "This is FINE.");
logger.log( Level.FINER, "This is FINER.");
```

```
logger.log( Level.FINEST, "This is FINEST.");

try {

//
// add a file handler for logging with an append flag set to TRUE
//
logger.addHandler( new FileHandler( "AnotherLogFile.log", true ) );
logger.info( "** LOG FILE HAS BEEN ADDED **" );
logger.log( Level.INFO, "This is just information.");
logger.log( Level.FINEST, "This is FINEST.");

//
// create a file handler and use our formatter
//
FileHandler fh = new FileHandler(
      "AConciseLogFile.log", true );

//
// SingleLineFormatter is our class
//
fh.setFormatter( new SingleLineFormatter() );
logger.addHandler( fh );

//
// now log with our new formatter
//
logger.log( Level.INFO,
  "This is just some more pertinent information, in case you were wondering." );
logger.warning(
    "Danger Will Robinson. Danger Will Robinson." );

}
catch (IOException e) {
    logger.warning( "IOException in main: " + e );
}

}


}
```

The SingleLineFormatter Class

The `SimpleFormatter` class in the JDK logging package uses three lines of text to produce a log entry. The previous example demonstrated the use of a custom log output formatter. To produce a more concise log output message, the `SingleLineFormatter` class we develop here is used to format a message that uses only a single line of text. Attaching a formatter to a `Handler` object requires an object which implements the `Formatter` abstract class. For convenience, we choose to extend the `SimpleFormatter` class, which provides a concrete implementation of the `Formatter` abstract class, and we extend only the methods whose behavior we wish to alter. The code for this class is shown below.

We first create a class declaration, which extends the `SimpleFormatter` class. Producing the output for the log message requires that a long integer representing a millisecond time value for the time the message was logged be formatted into a human readable date-time value. We can convert an integer representation of time with a `DateFormat` object. To provide an efficient implementation, we will create the `DateFormat` object once as an instance member and then reuse it as needed.

The `format` method receives a `LogRecord` parameter containing the pertinent information for the current log message. Within the body of the method, we create a `StringBuffer` (more efficient for multiple appends than a `String` variable). As we can see here, there are a number of `getXXXX` methods in the `LogRecord` class, which we can call to retrieve the information in the log record. The `LogRecord` `getMillis` method retrieves the time of the log entry in milliseconds. This integer value is passed to the `DateFormat` object we created as an instance member. In this example, it will return a short format date.

We must also provide an implementation for `getHead` and `getTail`. These methods return a `String` reference for the *header* and *tail*, two lines that are used to wrap messages using the `SimpleFormatter` class. Since we do not want a header and tail in our output (after all, we are being concise), both of these methods are overridden to return a blank (not null) value. (Returning a null reference would confuse other methods in the logging package call chain.)

The SingleLineFormatter Class

```
package examples.logging;
import java.util.logging.*;
import java.util.Date;
import java.text.DateFormat;

public class SingleLineFormatter extends SimpleFormatter {

//
// store our Date/Time formatter
//
DateFormat df = DateFormat.getDateTimeInstance( DateFormat.SHORT, DateFormat.SHORT
);

public String format( LogRecord record ) {

StringBuffer output = new StringBuffer( 124 );

//
```

```java
// output the level
//
output.append( record.getLevel().toString().trim() + " - " );


//
// output the class and method name
//
output.append(
    record.getSourceClassName().trim() + " : " +
    record.getSourceMethodName().trim() + " : " );

//
// output the date/time the message was received
//
output.append(
  df.format( new Date( record.getMillis() ) ) + " - " );

output.append( record.getMessage() );
output.append( "\n" );

return output.toString();

}

public String getHead( Handler h ) {

 //
 // we don't want to wrap the message in a head and tail
 //
 return "";

}

public String getTail( Handler h ) {

 //
 // we don't want to wrap the message in a head and tail
 //
   return "";

}

}
```

The output of using the `SingleLineFormatter` class is demonstrated in tthe log file shown below.

Logfile Output for AConciseLog.Filelog

```
INFO - LoggingJDK : main : 5/16/02 10:35 PM - This is just some more pertinent
information, in case you were wondering.
WARNING - LoggingJDK : main : 5/16/02 10:35 PM - Danger Will Robinson. Danger Will
Robinson.
```

CREATING A CONVENIENCE METHOD
TO IMPLEMENT LOGGING

Both of the logging packages we have demonstrated here required a configuration file. These configuration files contain a number of flexible settings which detail how logging should be performed. In a production environment where logging is being used to track the progress of critical programs or to log potentially serious warnings and errors, it is important that logging be done correctly. To make logging work correctly it is important that a centralized set of one or more configuration files be managed and controlled by staff responsible for system administration and maintenance.

To facilitate this process of maintaining centralized control over the set of configuration files, the location of these files could be stored as an application property and could be retrieved by applications from a centralized location. In a J2EE environment, the naming services provided by a JNDI provider facilitate access to a centralized naming service and are the tool of choice for providing access to centralized application properties such as this.

An application design technique for ensuring consistent access to this naming facility is to create a convenience method to wrap the process of performing a lookup in the naming service and retrieving the correct resource. The `LoggingService` class shown below acts as a service for the retrieval of the `Logger` class instance used to perform logging in the application. This class conceals the details of the lookup and retrieval of the logging resource and manages any exceptions that may be encountered in the process of retrieval.

In the `LoggingService` class, the `getLogger` method is used to retrieve a logger to be used for logging services. This class performs a lookup using the naming service to find the name of the logging configuration file to use. Once this entry is found, the configuration property for the logging package is set and the logger is returned to the caller.

The `directory` and the `context` variables used are instance members, which are set on the first pass through the method. The program code examines them to determine whether or not they are a non-null value. If they are non-null, the program code can assert that they have been set and can be used, thus avoiding the overhead of creating them on each pass.

The code shown here is not inherently thread-safe. Since we are using static members in this code, we have the potential that multithreaded applications might become deadlocked on these resources. Multithreaded applications would either have to synchronize when accessing this object or add a `synchronized` block to the `getLogger` method.

The LoggingService Class

```
package service;

import org.apache.log4j.*;
import javax.naming.directory.*;
import javax.naming.*;

import java.net.*;

import service.DirectoryService;


public class LoggingService {
//
//private static Category logger;
//
private static DirectoryService directory;
private static DirContext context;
private static String loggingConfigFile;

public static void main( String args[] ) {

}

public static Logger getLogger( String loggerName ) {
Logger logger = null;

try {

if ( directory == null )
   directory = new DirectoryService();

if ( context == null )
   context = (DirContext) directory.getContext(
     "o=logging, o=general-application-objects, dc=movies, dc=com" );

//
// be sure to use the correct config file
```

```
//
loggingConfigFile = (String) context.lookup(
                    "cn=loggingConfigFile" );

//
// set the System property to configure our URL
//
System.setProperty( "log4j.configuration", loggingConfigFile );


logger = Logger.getLogger( loggerName );

logger.debug("Using log config file: " + loggingConfigFile );

}
catch (NamingException e) {
    System.err.println(
        "NamingException in getLogger" + e );
}
finally {
    return logger;
}

}
// --

public static void setConfig() {

try {
   PropertyConfigurator.configure( new URL( loggingConfigFile ) );
}
catch (MalformedURLException e) {
    System.err.println("MalformedURLException in getLogger" + e );
}

}

}
```

SUMMARY

Logging is an essential part of any application, small or large. While sometimes ignored in small applications, using a good logging service can save hours of development time by helping debug developing applications and helping to isolate problems in deployed production applications. Logging becomes even more important when using distributed programming, since a problem could originate in one application tier and not be discovered until later execution on another tier. Using logging trace can help isolate these problems quickly.

This chapter demonstrated two choices that are available to Java developers: the log4j package from Jakarta Apache, or the Sun Java logging package that has been added to JDK 1.4 (`java.util.logging`). Both packages provide a number of features that can prove useful to the Java programmer, both for debugging during the development process and trouble shooting in a production environment.

Java and XML: Introduction to XML

INTRODUCTION

When the Extensible Markup Language (XML) was first standardized there were many who felt that this was it, finally the silver bullet that would allow all applications to interoperate. Many felt that this standard and its related technologies (which at the time were largely incomplete) would revolutionize data interchange and easily solve all existing problems.

XML is used to encode data, to take some information and surround it with tags which describe the contents. But while XML did provide significant benefits for data interchange, it didn't necessarily solve many long-standing problems with schema incompatibilities and the corresponding semantic issues that data modelers had been struggling with for years.

As we will see in this chapter, XML alone is of little use. It is the parsers that provide the value. Parsing involves taking the XML document and processing its contents. The output of this parsing process is commonly the same information as the original encoded document, but presented in a different format, a process known as *transformation*.

Despite some shortcomings, the technologies surrounding XML have had an immense impact on the IT field. As a standard markup language, it is free, flexible, and easy to learn. The documents described with XML, to varying degrees, can be *self-describing* and *self-validating*. The related parsing tools are also available for free and have a short learning curve.

Adding to the value of using XML are corresponding transformation standards for XSLT (Extensible Stylesheet Language for Transformation). The emerging standards for Web Services, most notably SOAP, also build on these toolsets to provide for both point-to-point and asynchronous messaging using XML documents.

In this chapter we will examine the XML standard and related standards. We will see how to describe data using XML and a DTD and examine examples of XML documents. Successive chapters will demonstrate how to use XML documents to write parsers using the Document Object Model (DOM) and the Simple API for XML (SAX). Transformation of XML documents will also be demonstrated using XSLT. Chapter 22 and 23 revisit XML and demonstrate applications using SOAP.

Uses of XML

XML is used for a variety of purposes wherever data must be defined in an open, platform-neutral, and application-neutral manner. XML is also language-independent and can be used with C, C++, Visual Basic, or any other language that has the required parsing and transformation libraries.

XML is now widely used to exchange information in business-to-business (B2B) applications and for formatting data for presentation. It has also become something of a standard for configuration files, describing properties for an application (for example, the configuration file for log4j as we saw in Chapter 13, and the properties file for EJB deployment with J2EE).

XML allows a data document to be formatted once and then presented using different formats. For instance, an XML formatted document of data containing a catalog of books could be formatted as HTML for display in a Web browser, or formatted as text for report output.

This approach allows for further abstraction of presentation information, providing a loosely coupled architecture for the presentation tier. The XSLT and XPATH standards described in this chapter provide the tools for creating this type of architecture. We will demonstrate applications that use this approach in Chapter 16 and in examples later in the book.

What It is and What It Isn't

XML and its related technologies certainly have made their mark in the IT world and will no doubt continue to transform the industry. But it is not and never has been a single solution to all of IT's data interchange ills. Applications must have some knowledge of the data being interchanged to be able to use it, and often proper use of that knowledge involves subtleties in the data that must be managed in the application. Semantics issues (e.g., closing date, date of closing, and closed date may or may not mean the same thing), data formatting issues, and locale issues are just some of the problems that are not solved by the XML standard.

XML is also not HTML. HTML is an Standard Generalized Markup Language (SGML) extension that is used to describe the formatting of Web pages. It is not extensible or case-sensitive, and it allows improperly structured pages—pages that don't conform completely to the HTML syntax—to be displayed. Whitespace (non-printing characters) is not preserved in the formatted output.

XML, however, is an extensible markup language and is not limited to the tags that have been defined. XML is case-sensitive, and documents must be well-formed, conforming to the syntax of XML. Documents that are not well-formed, with balanced end-tags and without interleaved tags, should not be parsed by XML parsers. Whitespace in XML documents is preserved in the parsed output.

XML: Applying Order to Data

XML is a markup language that provides information about data in a document. This information is conveyed through a series of tags that are spread throughout the document. These tags are structured in a hierarchical format. This structure, in concert with the tags themselves, conveys meaning about the data.

For instance, information about a customer would include a name and address for the customer. But the customer may have more than one address: a home address and a billing address. The information about the customer could also include the customer's billing information and the customer's buying history. All of this information could very succinctly be described in a hierarchical fashion. The customer could represent the outermost part of this structure, with the address information being nested within the customer information. The address information could also contain nested information for the two customer addresses: the home address and the business address. The customer's billing information could also involve nested information, containing cash purchase billing information and credit purchase information, as shown in Figure 14–1.

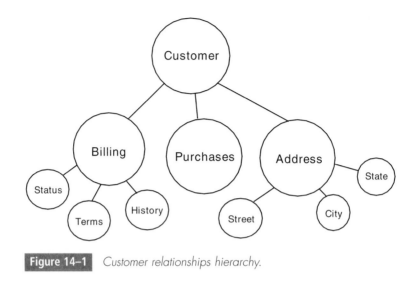

Figure 14–1   *Customer relationships hierarchy.*

XML tags use the same basic format as HTML with an open tag symbol, the tag name, tag attributes, tag values and content, and a closing tag. XML documents are self-describing and may optionally be self-validating, partially through that structure and partially through the use of document type definitions (DTDs). Though somewhat limited in their current capabilities, DTDs can be used to provide some validation of an XML document. DTDs are explained in more detail later in this chapter.

XML documents must be well-formed, meaning the document conforms to the syntax of XML: In essence, it has beginning and end tags, is organized in a hierarchical structure, and does not have nested tags. Additionally, a document may be considered valid if it has a DTD and conforms to the syntax and structure defined in that DTD. An XML parser may optionally validate an XML document against a DTD. Such a parser would be considered a *validating parser*. But XML parsers are not required to perform validations (and many XML documents do not use DTDs), so many parsers are nonvalidating parsers and do not validate an XML document against a DTD (though most provide a choice).

Certainly, a very good way to understand an XML document is to examine one. The following document provides just such an example.

ResultSet Output XML Document

```
<?xml version="1.0" encoding="ISO-8859-1"?>
<!DOCTYPE ResultSet FILE "rs.dtd">
<resultSet run_date="01-02-2001" user="fred">
  <row>
   <column>
```

```
  <name>movie_id</name>
  <table owner="admin">movies</table>
  <type>LONG</type>
  <data>1</data>
</column>
<column>
  <name>movie_name</name>
  <table owner="admin">movies</table>
  <type>VARCHAR</type>
  <data>Stamping Out the Evil Null Reference</data>
</column>
<column>
  <name>release_date</name>
  <table owner="admin">movies</table>
  <type>DATE</type>
  <data>2001-01-01</data>
</column>
<column>
  <name>movie_desc</name>
  <table owner="admin">movies</table>
  <type spec="true">BLOB</type>
  <data>** not provided **</data>
</column>
<column>
  <name>special_promotion</name>
  <table>movies</table>
  <type>TINY</type>
  <data>1</data>
</column>
<column>
  <name>update_date</name>
  <table>movies</table>
  <type>DATE</type>
  <data>2002-01-14</data>
</column>
<column>
  <name>category</name>
  <table>movies</table>
  <type>VARCHAR</type>
  <data>Comedy</data>
</column>
</row>
<row>
 <column>
  <name>movie_id</name>
  <table>movies</table>
  <type>LONG</type>
  <data>801</data>
</column>
<column>
  <name>movie_name</name>
  <table>movies</table>
```

```
      <type>VARCHAR</type>
      <data>Crazy/Beautiful</data>
   </column>
   <column>
      <name>release_date</name>
      <table>movies</table>
      <type>DATE</type>
      <data>2000-05-23</data>
   </column>
   <column>
      <name>movie_desc</name>
      <table>movies</table>
      <type>BLOB</type>
      <data>Clever, witty, slow paced</data>
   </column>
   <column>
      <name>special_promotion</name>
      <table>movies</table>
      <type>TINY</type>
      <data>1</data>
   </column>
   <column>
      <name>update_date</name>
      <table>movies</table>
      <type>DATE</type>
      <data>2002-01-28</data>
   </column>
   <column>
      <name>category</name>
      <table>movies</table>
      <type>VARCHAR</type>
      <data>Comedy</data>
   </column>
   </row>
</resultset>
```

This example represents data retrieved from a database containing information on movies. The information has been retrieved by executing a query against a table containing a series of fields containing information on the movie.

Using JDBC, the results of executing this query have been stored in an object of type ResultSet, as described in Chapter 7, "JDBC: Preparing SQL Statements and Examining Results." This document demonstrates how XML can be used to encapsulate the information gained from executing a query against a database table.

Even without knowing the specifics of XML, it is possible to read this document and gain some understanding of the contents. Based on the indentation of the rows and the names of the tags, and the nesting of the tags it appears that some type of hierarchy exists in the document. Between the start tags and end tags, there is tag body content, which relates to the tags. In all, this represents a rather clean expression of data encoding compared to other more complex and arduous methods that preceded XML.

Rather than attempting to dissect this document at this point, the following sections will explain XML documents in more detail. Following these sections, the contents of this document will become clearer.

XML Standards

The XML standard was created by the World Wide Web Consortium (W3C) which created the specification based on input from a number of individuals and organizations. Additional standards have been developed which complement the XML standard and loom large in any discussion of using the technology. These standards are listed in Table 14–1.

The complete description of XML and the tools used for XML processing are beyond the scope of this text. We will focus on the more common usage of XML in a J2EE application: data description and formatting. This entails coverage of the XML parsing and transformation APIs: XML, XSL, and XPATH. These APIs and standards are described and demonstrated in this chapter.

Table 14–1   *XML and Related Standards*

Standard	Description
XML	Document markup language;. hierarchical description of the enclosed data.
XML Namespaces	Namespace definition for elements of an XML document.
XSL-FO	Document and page description formatting definition for XML.
XSL	XML style sheet language;. describes how to transform an XML document.
XPATH	A language definition for describing a path to a location in the hierarchy of the XML document.
XLinks	Describes the linkages of XML documents.
XPointer	In combination with XLINKS, describes how XML data in other documents can be linked.
XMLSchema	DTD for an XML document.

Java XML Packages

The capabilities of XML lend it to a number of tasks, from messaging to informational registries. In order to use XML correctly, we also require class libraries to help perform some of the common tasks required, such as describing data correctly and parsing and transforming XML data to more useful structures. The various Java XML packages currently or soon to be available provide these capabilities (see Table 14–2).

Table 14–2 *Java XML Packages*

Package	Description
JAXP	XML parsers and transformation libraries.
JAXB	Conversion of XML to data program structures.
JAXM	XML for messaging (SOAP).
JAXR	XML for registries.
JAX-RPC	XML for messaging using remote procedure calls (RPC). Provides Web Services using this mechanism.

The JAXP package provides the ability to read and understand the contents of an XML document, an important step to any XML processing. The JAXP package provides two types of parsers—event-based and object-based—and transformation APIs that understand XSL stylesheets which can be used to transform documents into any format needed by the developer.

The JAXB package provides classes and tools that translate a DTD into corresponding Java classes. The resulting Java classes can parse XML documents described by the DTD and produce objects representing the parsed data as described in the DTD. The class can also handle the details of formatting an XML document based on the contents of the object.

The JAXM package allows Java applications to participate in XML messaging using SOAP. A SOAP server can be created to receive SOAP messages, or a Java application can generate a SOAP message, which can be sent to a SOAP server.

An XML registry is an information repository containing information on available Web Services. The JAXR package provides access to a variety of XML registries, using a unified interface.

The JAX-RPC package allows XML messaging to be performed using the RPC protocol and SOAP. Communication is, as the name implies, over the RPC mechanism.

THE XML DOCUMENT

The XML document or data packet is considered an XML entity. Within the XML document, various tags similar to HTML tags are used to delineate content. These tags represent elements that form a hierarchy. XML has been designed for internationalization so that documents may be represented in different encoding formats. This requires that the case of characters in the document be preserved, so markup in an XML document is case-sensitive.

XML Names

An XML document creates structure, applies order to data. Structures within an XML document are always named, usually using markup tags. Certain rules apply to the choice of names in XML document creation. Names must begin with a letter, underscore, or colon, and must continue with a sequence of characters that are considered valid name characters: letters, underscores, colons, digits, hyphens, and periods. The colon character can be used in a name, but is generally reserved for delimiting *namespaces* (a naming facility that reduces ambiguity in the use of names in an XML document). Parsers make no specific assumption about the use of the colon character in names.

The XML prefix for names in a document is reserved for special syntax. The string literal `"XML"` cannot be used at the beginning of XML names, including both uppercase and lowercase versions of the string.

XML Document Parts

An XML document is composed of three parts:

- A prolog
- A body
- An epilog

Only the body of the document is required—all other parts are optional. The parts must appear in order.

The optional prolog contains processing instructions and encoding information about the document. These instructions usually just the version of XML used and possibly identification of a DTD to use during parsing, as follows. An example of this is shown below.

```
<?xml version="1.0"?>
<!DOCTYPE ResultSet SYSTEM "file:/processing/transform/resultset.dtd">
```

The body contains the elements of the XML document structured as a hierarchy of elements and may also contain character data. The optional epilog may include comments, processing instructions, or whitespace that follows the elements of the document. The epilog or miscellaneous section is considered a design error by some and should not be included in a document unless absolutely necessary, since forward compatibility may be an issue.

ELEMENTS IN AN XML DOCUMENT

Elements are used to define the structure of an XML document. Elements are the basic unit of markup in XML and are defined by tags. They must form a hierarchy. Elements in turn may contain other elements, character data, processing instructions, or CDATA (character data) sections.

Elements are identified using *tags,* which contain a tag name within the current namespace. The syntax of tag representation is similar to that of XML, as shown in the document fragment below.

```
<book>
   <title>Hello World and Other Stories</title>
   <publisher>Small World Press</publisher>
</book>
...
```

XML documents are represented as a hierarchy. This hierarchy is composed of elements and their tags, with a single required root element that represents the document as a whole. This root element is known as the *document entity* (it represents the entire entity). It is also referred to as the *document root.*

The document root contains a child element that is the root of all elements in the XML document. This element is known as the *document element,* and it would have one or more child elements representing the content of the document. Figure 14–2 illustrates this concept.

An element in an XML document must have a *start tag* and an *end tag.* A special form of an XML tag, an empty content tag, can be used as a shorthand to indicate the tag has no content. (Such tags are often used to indicate a flag setting within an application or to convey properties through attributes, as discussed shortly.) Start and end tags must be consistent and balanced—every start tag must have a corresponding end tag.

A document is considered well-formed if, among other requirements, tags are nested correctly and each start tag has an appropriate end tag. An XML document must be well-formed in order to be parsed, indicating that every start tag has a corresponding end tag, as in the following example.

```
<!-- this would fail to parse -->
<tag1>
   <tag2>
```

```
</tag1>
    </tag2>
```

In this example, the `tag1` element has a nested `tag2` element. After the start of the `tag2` element, the innermost element at this point is `tag2`, and `tag2` must have an end tag before an end tag for `tag1` is encountered. That is not the case in the above example, and the document is not well-formed; an XML standards-compliant parser would abort the parsing of this document.

Any text that is not part of the tags used to identify elements, process information, or insert comments into a document is considered to be character data by XML syntax. The XML standard currently has no concept of a numeric data type. This does not mean that numbers cannot be stored in XML documents—they can. It means that XML parser validations will not validate that data is formatted correctly for various primitive data types, such as numbers. Applications parsing the XML documents must manage any formatting exceptions that may occur while parsing the document.

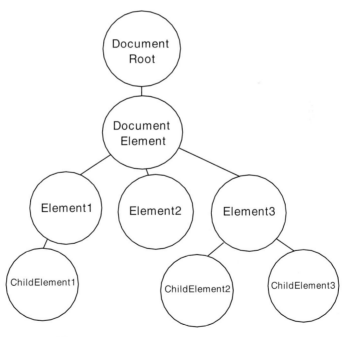

Figure 14–2   *XML document structure.*

Elements may optionally have attributes. Attributes provide property information about an element and use the following form.

```
...
<car color="red" make="Chrysler" model="300 M" mileage="low"/>
...
```

This tag defines an element of car and then provides various attributes to describe the car. Note that this is information that could be conveyed using nested tags, as shown below.

```
...
<car>
    <color>read</color>
    <make>Chrysler</make>
    <model>300 M</model>
</car>
...
```

By definition, XML parsers will preserve whitespace. The term whitespace is usually applied to character data that is used to create formatting in text. Space characters or tab characters are the more common types of whitespace. The XML specification defines the following four hexadecimal characters to be whitespace in an XML document (see Table 14–3).

Table 14–3   *Allowed XML Whitespace Characters*

Character(Hex)	Description
9	Horizontal tab
0A	Line feed
0d	Carriage return
20	ASCII space character

Comments can be placed in an XML document using the same comment tag used in HTML. This tag is shown below.

```
<!-- this is a comment  -->
```

A comment may be extended over multiple lines in the document, but a comment cannot be used in an element tag (within the brackets).

A CDATA section can be declared in an XML document to indicate that the text in that section should not be parsed and should be passed to the output as is. The syntax for a CDATA tag is as follows.

```
<! [CDATA [ this is escaped text ... ]]>
```

Usually, a CDATA section would be used to include text in a document as markup that should not be parsed.

```
...
<! [CDATA   [

Markup should be as follows:

  <customer>
   <name>Fred Flintstone</name>
   <country>US</country>
   <street-address>222 Stony Place Ct</street-address>
  </customer>

]]!>
```

Well-Formed Documents

Any data object that conforms to the XML syntax specification is considered to be a well-formed document, also known as a standalone document. A well-formed document does not require a DTD to be parsed by XML parsers. The criteria for a well-formed document are as follows.

- Syntax is compliant with the XML specification;
- The elements in the document form a hierarchical tree; and
- No references to external entities exist, with the exception of a DTD.

Parsers that read a well-formed document should throw a fatal exception if an error in the well-formed elements is detected. This fatal error should be expected to stop the execution of the application.

XML Parsers

XML documents are converted into a usable form using *parsers*. Parsers take an XML document and, based on how the user has programmed the application, parse the document using the parsing API. XML parsers come in two flavors: *nonvalidating* and *validating*. A nonvalidating parser allows any well-formed document to be parsed and uses no DTD. Alternatively, a validating parser requires access to a DTD for the document and validates the XML document against the DTD. Most parsers provide a method call that allows parsers to alter the validating behavior of the parser to be either validating or nonvalidating.

DESCRIBING THE XML DOCUMENT: THE DTD

As mentioned previously, the XML document is both *self-describing* and *self-validating*. The degree to which the document provides these features can vary, depending partly on whether or not the document identifies a corresponding DTD. The DTD describes the type, order, frequency, and relationship of elements in an XML document. In the current release of the XML-DTD specification, data types are limited to variations of character data.

An XML document is composed of elements in a specific order or structure, a hierarchy. These elements may optionally contain attributes that further describe the elements. The element may also contain corresponding values. We would therefore expect the DTD to allow some or all of this structure to be described.

The DTD uses tags that begin with ' <! ' and then describe some portion of the XML document. The DTD contains two primary tags for describing the XML document: the ELEMENT tag to describe, as you might have guessed, the elements in the document, and the ATTLIST tag to describe the list of attributes for an element.

The DTD specification allows the number of occurrences of an element and the order of any child elements to be described using the ELEMENT tag. An example of this tag is shown below.

```
<!ELEMENT resultset      (row)+>
```

This example shows that the element resultset can contain a child element, which must appear in parentheses: (row). The plus sign (+) after the child element indicates the number of occurrences for this element. In this case, the plus sign indicates that the element may appear one or more times. Other characters placed after an element or group of elements that indicate the number of occurrences are as shown in Table 14–4.

Table 14–4 *DTD Special Characters*

Character	Description
+	one 1 or more occurrences
*	Occurs 0 or more times
?	Occurs 0 or 1 time
<no specification>	Occurs 1 time

The Element Tag

The data type of an element can also be described in the DTD. This is most commonly #PCDATA for text data, as shown below.

```
<!ELEMENT name     (#PCDATA)>
```

An element can be composed of a set of child elements. The order of these elements can be specified as follows.

```
<!ELEMENT name (first, last, middle-initial)>
```

In this case, the name element will be composed of one occurrence of the first, last, and middle-initial elements. Alternatively, the element definition could specify a choice, as follows.

```
<!ELEMENT interior-seat-covers (cloth | leather | vinyl )>
```

The element of interior-seat-covers allows a choice of either the cloth, leather, or vinyl element as a child element. Only one of the set can be used, and there will be only one occurrence of the element. A list can also be specified to indicate that all of the indicated elements should follow the defined element, as shown in the example below.

```
<!ELEMENT name (first, last, middle-initial)>
```

This indicates the a name element will contain one and only one occurrence of the first, last, and middle-initial elements. To indicate multiple occurrences of child elements, the following syntax could be used.

```
<!ELEMENT car (luxury*, mid-size*, sedan*)>
```

In this example, a car element may contain zero or more occurrences of the luxury element, zero or more occurrences of the mid-size element, and zero or more occurrences of the sedan element. Using the syntax shown above, the order specified must be used, or a validating parser would reject the XML document. To provide more flexibility, a set of alternative definitions could be provided, as shown in the listing below.

Car XML Document DTD

```
<!ELEMENT car (( luxury*, mid-size*, sedan*) |
  (mid-size*, sedan*, luxury*) |
  (sedan*, luxury*, mid-size*) |
  (luxury*, mid-size*, sedan*) |
```

```
(luxury*, sedan*, mid-size* ))>
```

This example provides for variations of the `car` element, allowing the order of the child elements to be any of the alternatives listed. The character `|`, which separates the alternatives, indicates that a choice of one of the alternatives is allowed.

The ATTLIST Tag

The `ATTLIST` tag is used to describe attributes for an element. The tag definition allows the tag names and default values to be identified using the following syntax.

```
<!ATTLIST element-name attribute-name element-data-type default-declaration>
```

The data type is usually `CDATA`, and the default declaration can be one of the values listed in Table 14–5.

Table 14–5   *Default Declaration Values*

Default Declaration	Description
#REQUIRED	Attribute and value must always be present in the document.
#IMPLIED	If the attribute is not present, then no value will be used.
'string value'	If the attribute isn't provided, then use the 'string value' provided as a default value.

An example of the use of this tag is as follows.

```
<!ATTLIST resultset run_date CDATA #IMPLIED>
```

In this example, the attribute `run_date` will be provided with the `resultset` element. Since the attribute is identified with the `#IMPLIED` default declaration, then if the attribute is not provided, no value will be used. A complete DTD for the `resultset` XML document is provided in the code example below.

The resultset DTD: resultset.dtd

```
<!-- DTD for ResultSet XML document    -->
<!ATTLIST resultset run_date CDATA #IMPLIED>
```

```
<!ELEMENT resultset    (row)+>
<!ELEMENT row    (column)+>
<!ELEMENT column (name?, table?, type?, data?))>
<!ELEMENT name    (#PCDATA)>
<!ELEMENT table    (#PCDATA)>
<!ELEMENT type    (#PCDATA)>
<!ELEMENT data    (#PCDATA)>
```

This DTD describes the XML document file layout for an XML document that will be used to capture JDBC `ResultSet` output. The DTD indicates that the `resultset` document will contain one or more `row` elements, and a `row` will contain one or more `column` elements, indicated by the + sign following the element name. (Technically, a valid `ResultSet` that was the product of a query that found no rows would contain zero rows, but would not be valid for our purposes.)

Within the `column` element, a number of child elements are allowed in the order specified: `name`, `table`, `type`, and `data`. Per this DTD, the child elements are not required—they may occur zero or one time as indicated by the ? after the element name. The element types are then identified in the DTD as PCDATA, indicating that it is text data.

(The `ResultSet` object type in JDBC represents the results of a query or the execution of a stored procedure directed against a relational database using JDBC. The specifics of a `ResultSet` are not germane to this discussion, but are discussed in detail in Chapter 7.)

SUMMARY

To simply say that XML is important for a Java developer to understand would be an understatement. XML is now the language of choice for data interchange, and since data drives the enterprise, as Java developers we can expect that at some point in the development of an enterprise application, we will be using XML.

XML is more than just a specification for a data description language. It has come to encompass a set of related specifications and tools for working with XML documents. As we learned in this chapter, this includes language parsers, DTDs, conversion to Java objects with JAXB, transformation using XSL, and messaging with SOAP. Successive chapters demonstrate parsing XML documents, transformation, and XML messaging using JAXM.

CHAPTER 15

XML and Java: The JAXP Package

INTRODUCTION

In Chapter 14, "Java and XML: Introduction to XML," we introduced XML and explained how this versatile markup language can be used to describe data in a platform-independent and tool-independent manner. As developers, we need to be able to use the data described by XML in our applications. This involves reading XML-formatted documents from various sources and parsing the documents into a useful representation for our application. With Java, this means that we usually parse these documents into one or more objects in our application. But it is highly probable that our applications will not be limited to the role of only consuming XML-formatted data; our applications will also be required to produce XML-formatted data.

Fortunately, the J2SE (part of J2EE) provides several packages that allow XML data to be manipulated by Java applications. Open-source efforts such as the Apache XML project (`xml.apache.org`) provide the very robust Crimson and Xerces parsers, and the `JDom` parser (`www.jdom.org`) also provides an alternative to those provided with J2SE. These packages are not covered in this text (though the usage is similar). Instead, in this chapter we focus on the packages provided by Sun Microsystems with J2SE in the package known as JAXP.

Two basic approaches to managing XML documents are used: the Document Object Model (DOM), which works with XML documents represented as objects, and the event-driven approach of the Simple API for XML (SAX) parser. In this chapter we examine how both of these approaches can be used to work with XML documents.

PARSING AND TRANSFORMING

XML documents are processed in two ways: parsing and transforming. Parsing involves reading the XML document and interpreting document nodes in a way that is useful for the application. What this may mean is that if the application contains a number of nodes which are not of interest to the application, they will be passed over or ignored. Only the content that is meaningful to the application will be used. An application may use this document content either by placing values into specific member variables, or by creating objects which encapsulate the information from the XML document.

Alternatively, an application may not need to place any of the information in an XML document in the application's state. Instead, the role of the application may be to convert the XML document from one format into another. This is what is known as document transformation and it involves using not only the XML standard, but the Extensible Stylesheet Language (XSL) to provide a script for describing the transformation process, and the XPATH standard to describe how to address specific nodes in the XML document. In this chapter we will examine the parsing of XML documents. Transformation will be covered in Chapter 16.

Both the parsing and transformation packages are contained under the umbrella of JAXP. Support is provided through a number of different Java packages which we will examine next. Once we understand which packages are provided, we will determine how they are used by Java applications to provide the parsing of XML documents.

JAXP OVERVIEW

The classes and interfaces used to support XML processing are divided based on the functionality provided by the package, distinguishing between parsing the XML document and transforming the document into another format. These packages are subpackages of the `javax.xml` package as shown below (see Table 15–1).

Table 15–1	*The javax.xml Packages*

Package	Description
javax.xml.parsers	Provides the basic classes needed to perform XML parsing.
javax.xml.transform	Provides the classes for the transformation of XML documents using XSL instructions.
javax.xml.transform.sax	Provides for the transformation of XML documents using the SAX parser.
javax.xml.transform.dom	Provides for the transformation of XML documents using the DOM parser.
javax.xml.transform.stream	Allows sources and results of transformation processing to be implemented using a Java stream.

Classes are also divided based on the standard that defined them. The classes defined by the World Wide Web Consortium (W3C) XML standards are placed in the org.w3c.dom and org.w3c.sax packages, as detailed in Table 15–2.

Table 15–2	*Additional XML Packages*

Package	Description
org.w3c.dom	Defines the interfaces that must be implemented to use the Document Object Model (DOM)DOM.
org.xml.sax	Defines the interfaces that must be implemented to provide the SAX.
org.xml.sax.ext	Provides extension classes for SAX parsing.
org.xml.sax.helpers	Provides helper classes for SAX parsing.

XML parsers work with a *source*. A source can be either an input source or an output source. Though the input and output sources are commonly different objects, they could conceivably be the same. For XML parsing, the source represents an XML document that provides the input for the parsing operation. With DOM, the result of the parsing operation is an object representation of the XML document. The DOM object contains a hierarchical series of nodes that represents the XML structure of the document, as illustrated in Figure 15–1.

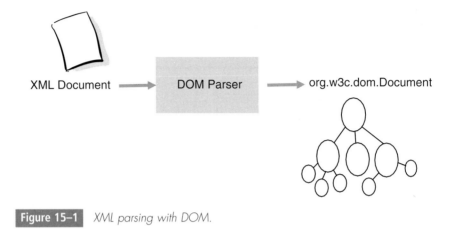

Figure 15–1 *XML parsing with DOM.*

Alternatively, an event-based parser such as SAX could be used. This type of parser is provided an implementation containing methods to handle the events triggered by the parsing operation. As the parser reads the XML document, and as XML nodes are encountered, it calls the various handler methods to manage the content of the XML document. Figure 15–2 illustrates this process.

As we mentioned earlier, in many cases a document is being parsed as a means of converting it from one format, in this case an XML document, into another format. This process is referred to as *transformation* and is often used to convert XML documents into HTML documents (as demonstrated in the next chapter). XML transformations involve the use of a stylesheet to describe the transformation process, as shown in Figure 15–3.

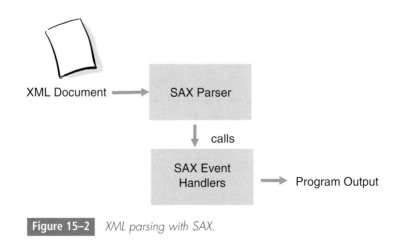

Figure 15–2 *XML parsing with SAX.*

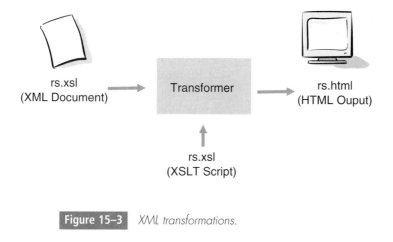

Figure 15–3 *XML transformations.*

XML Parsing and Transformations

To be useful to an application, XML documents are generally converted into another format through either *parsing* or *transformation*. Transformation is effectively the parsing and conversion of a document combined into one process. The result of a transformation is the output of a document in a different format.

Parsing involves the disassembling of a target document into useful elements. Parsing is a common practice in computer processing. A common example is that of parsing a computer program during the compilation process—one of the first steps taken when a computer program is compiled. This involves applying a grammar, a set of rules for the structure of the program. Failure to follow the rules of the grammar result in a failed compilation. Successful parsing will generally move the compilation into the next process where lower level processing instructions are created based on the computer program being compiled. The ultimate output from this process of computer program compilation will be output which can be executed using a runtime environment (with Java or Visual Basic) or a system executable binary.

Parsing an XML Document

A number of parsers are available for parsing XML with Java. As of J2SE version 1.4, parsers are included with the Sun JDK. There are two primary types of parsers available: event-driven parsers and tree-based parsers.

Event-driven parsers process the XML document as a stream and generate events as elements are encountered. Developers must implement event handlers to manage the parsing process. These parsers are fast, efficient, and lightweight.

The most common example of this parser is the SAX, developed by members of the XML-DEV mailing list.

Tree-based parsers take the target document, parse its contents, and create an internal object tree to reflect the contents of the document. Developers must then write code to traverse the object tree to find the content they need or perform the transformation desired. These parsers are not as fast and require more system resources for larger documents than event-based parsers. The most common of these parsers is the DOM, developed by the W3C.

The following sections examine both of these parser types, as provided with the Sun JDK, examining first the DOM parser and then the SAX parser, and using code examples to demonstrate their usage.

Using the DOM Parser API

The DOM parser API included with the JDK provides the implementations of the various abstract classes and interfaces needed to parse a document and obtain output using the DOM parser. The most common classes used are listed in Table 15–3.

Table 15–3   *DOM Classes and Interfaces*

Class	Description
`javax.xml.parsers.DocumentBuilderFactory`	Implements a factory pattern for the creation of `DocumentBuilder` objects. Used to set various attributes for the parser, including its validating behavior.
`javax.xml.parsers.DocumentBuilder`	Provides methods to perform the parsing to create an internal DOM representing the XML document.
`org.w3c.dom.Document`	Represents the *document root* or document entity. An element which contains the constituent (all child) elements of the document.
`org.w3c.dom.Node`	A single node in the document tree. A node can be an element, an attribute, an entity, document, or text node.
`org.w3c.dom.NodeList`	An ordered enumeration of nodes.
`javax.xml.transform.Source`	Represents a location for a source for a parsing or transformation operation.
`javax.xml.transform.Result`	Represents a location for the results of a transformation or parsing operation.

Processing an XML Document with DOM

Processing an XML document with DOM involves creating a small number of objects to manage much of the process. Parsing the document then involves iterating over the various nodes in the document tree to obtain the information needed.

The DOM API makes use of the *factory* design pattern. The DocumentBuilderFactory class allows a number of properties for the parser to be determined and set before the parser is created. This simplifies the use of the resulting parser object. The expectation is that the creation of the factory and the document builder (DocumentBuilder) would be performed once for the duration of the application, since the builder object will retain its properties. The following code example demonstrates the use of the DOM API.

The XMLDemo1 Class: Declarations and main Program Block

This code example executes an SQL statement, which reads rows from a database used to store information about movies. The results of this SQL query are stored in a JDBC ResultSet object (see Chapter 7, "JDBC: Preparing SQL Statements and Examining Results"). The ResultSet object is then converted into an XML document that contains the results of the query. This XML document is stored internally in a string and is then parsed using the DOM API. The JSSE implementation of DOM does not have a facility for parsing the contents of a string directly, but it does provide for parsing a stream input source so we must wrap our string with an input source before it can be parsed.

The program parses the XML document and then calls a method recursively, parsing a node and then parsing all child nodes of that node, until the entire document has been parsed. The results of the parsing operation are written to the console.

The code for this demonstration application is shown below. The program begins by instantiating an instance of itself and then calls its getConnected method. The getConnected method performs the task of looking up and connecting to the DataSource. At this point, the instance members for the JDBC statement (stmt) will have an active reference, and the call to the processQuery method (which will use the stmt reference) will return a valid ResultSet. This ResultSet object reference (rs) is then passed to the JDBCXML toXMLString method to convert the contents of the ResultSet to an XML document. The XML document is stored in the string reference (s). (The JDBCXML class is shown in Chapter 16, "XML Transformation and Creating XML Documents.")

The parse method takes an InputSource object reference as an argument (overloaded versions of the parse method take other arguments, but the InputSource is the most convenient for parsing of this XML document). The

`String` object reference is wrapped with a `StringReader`, which is then wrapped with an `InputSource` object.

For simplicity, the majority of the work involved in creating the parsers is performed in the `main` program block. In practice, this work is best done in a constructor or an initialization method. First, a call is made to get the `DocumentBuilderFactory`. The `DocumentBuilderFactory` instance is then used to create a `DocumentBuilder` object. This is the object that will be used to perform the parsing operation.

The `DocumentBuilder parse` method is then used to parse the `InputSource`. The result of this call is a reference to a `Document` object, represents the *document root* of the parsed document. The `Document normalize` method is then called to simplify the parsing operation and ensure only structure separates text nodes.

The `getDocumentElement` method is then called to retrieve the root element of the document tree; all other elements will reside under this element. The root element is then passed to the `parseNode` method to begin the parsing operation. The code for this section of the application is shown below.

The XMLDemo1 Class: Declarations and main Program Block

```
package examples.jaxp;

import java.sql.*;
import java.io.*;
import javax.naming.*;
import javax.sql.*;
import javax.xml.transform.*;
import javax.xml.parsers.*;
import org.w3c.dom.*;

import org.apache.log4j.Category;

import jdbcutil.JDBCXML;
import service.LoggingService;


public class XMLDemo1 {

private static Category logger = LoggingService.getLogger(
                         "examples.XMLDemo1" );
private Statement   stmt;
private Connection con;

private String pad = "                         ";

public static void main( String args[] ) {
Document doc=null;
```

```
try {

  XMLDemo1 xmldemo = new XMLDemo1();

  //
  // connect to the database
  //
  xmldemo.getConnected();

  //
  // retrieve a JDBC ResultSet
  //
  ResultSet rs = xmldemo.processQuery();

  //
  // convert the ResultSet into an XML document
  // and store it in a string
  //
  String s = JDBCXML.toXMLString( rs );

  //
  // parse the XML document
  //
  // create an InputSource around the string document
  //

  StringReader in = new StringReader( s );
  org.xml.sax.InputSource source =
            new org.xml.sax.InputSource( in );

  //
  // get the DOM Factory
  //
  DocumentBuilderFactory dbf =
                DocumentBuilderFactory.newInstance();
  DocumentBuilder db = dbf.newDocumentBuilder();


  //
  // parse the XML source
  //
  doc = db.parse( source );
  doc.normalize();

  //
  // recursively parse the XML document starting at the root
  //
  org.w3c.dom.Node root = doc.getDocumentElement();
  xmldemo.parseNode( root, 0 );

}
catch (Exception e) {
```

```
    logger.error("Exception e: " + e );
 }
}
```

The XMLDemo1 Class: getConnected and processQuery Methods

The `getConnected` method performs the task of obtaining the `InitialContext` and performing a lookup to obtain the appropriate `DataSource`. A connection to the `DataSource` is then obtained, and a JDBC `Statement` object is created, which is used by the `processQuery` method to execute a query against the `DataSource`.

The `processQuery` method executes a query and returns a `ResultSet` containing the results of the query. It simply calls the `executeQuery` method of the JDBC `Statement` class and captures and returns the `ResultSet` resulting from that operation.

The getConnected and processQuery Methods

```
public void getConnected() {

try {

InitialContext ctx = new InitialContext();
DataSource ds = (DataSource) ctx.lookup( "movies" );

con = ds.getConnection();

stmt = con.createStatement();


}
catch (Exception e) {
 logger.error("Exception e: " + e );
}

}

protected ResultSet processQuery() {

ResultSet rs=null;

try {

rs = stmt.executeQuery("select * from movies");

}
```

```
catch (SQLException e) {
    logger.error("Exception e: " + e );
}

finally {

        return rs;
}

}
```

The XMLDemo1 Class: The parseNode Method

In XML documents, the node name and corresponding value reside in different nodes, so that a node containing a customer name would have a child node containing the value of the customer name in a text node. For this reason, parsing a DOM object involves iterating through various child nodes to find the appropriate content. The `parseNode` method does this using recursion, the ability of a method to call itself using the wonders of program call stacks.

The `parseNode` method performs the parsing operation for this application. It does not look for any specific element names in the document; it merely outputs all node names and node values for any nodes found in the document. The output for the node name and the corresponding value is output on one line.

In many cases, an application would look for specific nodes and their corresponding values and perform processing on those nodes. Other examples in this text will demonstrate that process.

The `parseNode` method outputs each node to the console and indents based on the depth of the node in the document tree hierarchy. For this reason, it accepts two arguments: the node to parse and an integer representing the depth into the hierarchy. A string is used to perform the indentation, padding output using a substring of the string based on the depth into the document hierarchy. This string is created as a local variable for the method, and a substring is created at the start of processing based on the depth into the tree hierarchy.

The `Node getNodeName` method is called to determine the name of the node and to determine whether or not the node is a text node. If the node is not a text node and if it is not a blank character or a null reference, it is output. Note that the `PrintWriter print` method is used to perform the output and not the `println` method which outputs a newline; we do this because we want to control the output of the newline character which is done in the next control block.

If the node is not a text node, then a test is performed to determine whether or not the node contains a valid node name. If it does, the node name is output to the console. Following the test to determine whether or not node content or node name needs to be output, a test is performed to determine if there are any child nodes for this node. If there are, then those nodes must be examined and a call is made to obtain the list of child nodes. Then, for each of the child nodes, a call is made to this same method, indicating that the next level of the hierarchy is being used by passing the depth+1 as a parameter to the method.

The XMLDemo1 Class: The parseNode Method

```
public void parseNode( org.w3c.dom.Node node, int depth ) {

//
// create a string for output padding
//
String outputPad = pad.substring(0, depth*2 );

//
// if this is a text node, it has our value
//

if ( node instanceof Text ) {
    String value = node.getNodeValue();
    //
    // if it isn't whitespace, then print it
    //
    if ( ( value != null ) && ( value.trim().length() > 0 ) )
        System.out.print("- value: " + node.getNodeValue() );
}
else {
    //
    // if this isn't a text node, it may have our node name
    //
    if ( node.getNodeName() != null )
        System.out.print( "\n" +
                            outputPad +
                            node.getNodeName() + ": " );
}

//
// parse any child nodes
//
if ( node.hasChildNodes() ) {
    NodeList list = node.getChildNodes();
    for ( int n = 0; n < list.getLength();n++)  {
        parseNode( list.item(n), depth + 1 ); } }

}

}
```

The result of running the XMLDemo1 program is shown below.

XMLDemo1 Program Output

```
resultset:
  row:
    column:
      name: - value: movie_id
      table: - value: movies
      type: - value: LONG
      data: - value: 1
    column:
      name: - value: movie_name
      table: - value: movies
      type: - value: VARCHAR
      data: - value: Stamping Out the Evil Null Reference
    column:
      name: - value: release_date
      table: - value: movies
      type: - value: DATE
      data: - value: 2001-01-01
    column:
      name: - value: movie_desc
      table: - value: movies
      type: - value: BLOB
      data: - value: ** not provided **
    column:
      name: - value: special_promotion
      table: - value: movies
      type: - value: TINY
      data: - value: 1
    column:
      name: - value: update_date
      table: - value: movies
      type: - value: DATE
      data: - value: 2002-01-14
    column:
      name: - value: category
      table: - value: movies
      type: - value: VARCHAR
      data: - value: Comedy
  row:
    column:
      name: - value: movie_id
      table: - value: movies
      type: - value: LONG
      data: - value: 801
    column:
      name: - value: movie_name
      table: - value: movies
      type: - value: VARCHAR
      data: - value: Crazy/Beautiful
```

```
column:
  name: - value: release_date
  table: - value: movies
  type: - value: DATE
  data: - value: 2000-05-23
column:
  name: - value: movie_desc
  table: - value: movies
  type: - value: BLOB
  data: - value: ** not provided **
...
```

Retrieving the Value of a Specific Node using DOM

The DOM API provides a useful set of classes and methods for moving through a DOM object, but what is lacking are some convenience methods for performing certain operations. For instance, being able to search for a single node and retrieve the corresponding value of that node requires a set of programmatic loops to be executed using the standard DOM API. (Other XML parsers provide better interaction with the Java collection API to provide this functionality.)

Coding a series of loops to retrieve a single value is not always the most convenient way to use DOM. While this may be appropriate for operations where the entire contents of a DOM object must be parsed, it becomes cumbersome when only certain nodes and their values are needed. This is the case when an XML file is being used to store configuration parameters or program properties. In such a case, it is easier to use the DOM object as an object similar to a hashtable where a string key can be passed to a method and a corresponding string value for the key can be returned.

The following static method, getElementValueByName, performs just that type of operation. The method is passed a Node object reference for the Node (or Element) to search and the element name to find in the Node. The method returns a string that corresponds to the first occurrence of a text value of the element name passed. If the element name is not found, then a null reference is returned.

The method expects to be passed a Node or Element that contains the child hierarchy in which the element name requested will be found. For a DOM object, a call to the Document getDocumentElement method returns an Element object reference, which extends the Node interface. Passing a root element object reference to this method will cause the entire document to be searched.

The getElementValueByName method will search for the first occurrence of the element name and then attempt to find the child node that contains the corresponding value (the text node) for that element. Only the first occurrence of the element will be returned. Multiple occurrences of an element name on a separate node within the document tree, which is allowed by XML, will not be returned.

The code for this method is listed below. The method begins by creating a string (`elementValue`) object reference that will be returned by the method. It assigns its value to null. If no occurrences of the element name are found in the document tree, then code execution will fall through and the null value will be returned by the method.

The first conditional statement tests to determine if the node name for the current node is not equal (the condition is negated) to the element name being sought. If it is not, then the child nodes will be searched with a call to the `Node getChildNodes` method, which returns an enumeration-like object that can be used to iterate through child nodes.

For each child node, a conditional test is performed to determine if the node name matches the element name, and if it does, the reference for that node is preserved through a call to the `NodeList item` method and the loop is exited.

If the node does not match the element name, then the else condition is executed. This code block recursively calls the `getElementValueByName` method to search any nodes that may reside below this node and return the value.

The final conditional block tests to determine if the `elementValue` has been set (by a recursive call to the `getElementValueByName` method). If it has not been set, then the code block within the conditional statement attempts to set the `elementValue`. This is done by getting the list of child nodes for the current node and searching for text nodes. If a text node is found, then the `elementValue` is set to the value of the text node. The `finally` block is then used to return the value of the element (`elementValue`), which has been set previously in the method.

The XMLUtil Class

```
package xmlutil;

import org.w3c.dom.*;
import org.apache.log4j.Category;

import service.LoggingService;


public class XMLUtil {

private static Category logger =
          LoggingService.getLogger( "xmlutil.XMLUtil" );

public static String getElementValueByName( Node node, String elementName ) {
//
// Perform a search starting at the current node and
// descending over child nodes until the element name is found.
// Returns the text value of the node if found.
//
// If the element name is not found, returns a null reference.
```

```
//
//
String elementValue = null;
boolean foundElement = false;
try {
//
// if this isn't the node, then search the child nodes
//

if ( !(node.getNodeName().equals( elementName )) )
    if ( node.hasChildNodes() ) {
        NodeList list = node.getChildNodes();
       for ( int n = 0; n < list.getLength(); n++ ) {
          if (
              list.item(n).getNodeName().equals( elementName ) ) {
                node = list.item(n);
               foundElement = true;
                break;
            }
            else {
                //
                // recurse the child nodes
                //
                  if ( node.hasChildNodes() ) {
                      elementValue =
                getElementValueByName( list.item(n), elementName );
                 }
            }
        }
    }


if (elementValue == null ) {

  //
  // if the node name matches, get the value
  //
  if (node.getNodeName().equals( elementName ) ) {
    //

    // get the list of child nodes for this node
    //
    NodeList list = node.getChildNodes();

    for (int n  = 0;
        (node != null) &&
        (node.hasChildNodes()) &&
        (n < list.getLength()); n++ ) {
            node = list.item(n);

            //
            // if this is a text node, get the value
```

```
                  //
                  if ( node instanceof org.w3c.dom.Text ) {
                      elementValue = node.getNodeValue();
                   break;
              }
          }
      }
  }


}
catch (Exception e ) {
    logger.error(
            "Exception in getElementValueByName: " + e );
}
catch (Throwable e ) {
    logger.error(
            "Throwable error in getElementValueByName: " + e );
}
finally {
    return elementValue;
}
```

Using getElementValueByName: The loadXMLDoc Method

The getElementValueByName is a useful method when a series of values must be retrieved from an XML document. In the following example, an Order object is used to represent an order for a movie. An XML document is passed to an order processor control object, which then processes the order using an Order object. As part of the order processing effort, the contents of the XML document detailing the order are loaded into the Order object. The method that performs that operation is named loadXMLDoc and is shown below.

The method begins by creating an InputSource using the XML document string and then parses the document. The getDocumentElement reference retrieves an element that represents the entire document. This element is then passed to the getElementValueByName method to retrieve specific values for elements from the XML document. These values are passed directly into the internal set methods for the Order object.

Note that the integer values must be converted and that the conversion process could potentially fail; XML has no facility for data type validation. This example uses the Integer parseInt method to format integers and makes a point not only to trap the error in the method, but to output the element (which will help the debugging effort). The result of outputting the element will be that the entire document's elements and element values will be output, thus allowing the offending element value to be identified.

The loadXMLDoc Method

```
...
public void loadXMLDoc( String XMLDocString ) {

Element element = null;

try {

//
// get the InputSource
//
InputSource source = new InputSource(
                          new StringReader(
                              XMLDocString ) );
Document doc = docBuilder.parse( source );
doc.normalize();

//
// retrieve the document element
//
element =  doc.getDocumentElement();

//
// set our internal state based on the contents
// of the XML document
//
setOrderNumber(
     XMLUtil.getElementValueByName( element, "ordernumber" ) );
setQuantity(
   Integer.parseInt(
     XMLUtil.getElementValueByName( element,
            "quantity").trim() ) );
setBillToID(
     XMLUtil.getElementValueByName( element, "billtoid" ) );
setShipToID( XMLUtil.getElementValueByName( element,
                                      "shiptoid" ) );
setUPC(
     XMLUtil.getElementValueByName( element, "upc" ) );

setMovieID( Integer.parseInt(
             XMLUtil.getElementValueByName(
                     element, "movieid" ).trim() ));

}
catch (SAXException e) {
     logger.error("SAXException in loadXMLDoc: "
                        + e );
}
catch (IOException e) {
     logger.error("SAXException in loadXMLDoc: "
                        + e );
```

```
}
catch (NumberFormatException e) {
      logger.error(
          "NumberFormatException in loadXMLDoc: " +
          e );
      logger.error("element value: " + element );
}

}
...
```

EVENT-DRIVEN PARSING: THE SAX PARSER

The SAX parser provides a fast, streamlined approach to parsing XML documents. While some feel that SAX is the more complex approach to parsing documents, depending on the requirements of the application, it may in fact represent an easier and faster approach than using a DOM parser.

When the SAX parser is used, the XML document is parsed as a serial stream of content. As the content of the document is scanned, events are triggered. It is the job of the event handlers to either preserve or ignore the content being scanned by the parsers. The more common classes or interfaces used by a SAX parser application are as follows (see Table 15–4).

A complete implementation of the SAX parsing classes and interfaces shown above can provide a very fine-grained control of the parsing process, but not every document parser requires that level of control. Therefore, default implementations and adapters are available. The `DefaultHandler` class can be extended, and only the specific callback methods needed can be overridden. This is the approach used in the example shown below.

SAX Parsing Example

The following example uses an approach similar to the first XML parsing example. A query is executed, which returns a `ResultSet` object, and the `ResultSet` object is converted into an XML document. The XML document is then parsed by the application. This example adds a new twist in that several queries are executed, and their output is converted to XML documents and then parsed and output to different file locations. To make the program's execution dynamic and flexible, the queries and various other program properties are read from a properties file.

The following code block performs the import operations needed to make the appropriate classes and interfaces available to the application. The class declaration for the `XMLDemo4` class is then made to extend the `DefaultHandler` class.

Table 15–4   *Common SAX Classes*

Class/Interface	Description
`org.xml.sax.SAXParserFactory`	Acts as a factory class for the creation of SAX parsers. Allows various parameters to be set for the creation of the parser.
`javax.xml.parsers.SAXParser`	Manages the document parsing. Calls the callback methods as content being scanned triggers events.
`org.xml.sax.XMLReader`	Interface that must be implemented to handle parsing an XML document using SAX.
`org.xml.sax.helpers.DefaultHandler`	A convenience class for SAX applications. Provides the basic callbacks for all of the SAX interfaces.
`org.xml.sax.EntityResolver`	Allows an application to intercept entity resolution. Not commonly used.
`org.xml.sax.DTDResolver`	Allows an application to intercept DTD resolution. Not commonly used.
`org.xml.sax.ContentHandler`	Allows an application to intercept content recognition.
`org.xml.sax.ErrorHandler`	Allows an application to intercept parsing errors.

This allows the class to use default handlers to handle the SAX events that we don't care about and allows us to override the callback methods we do care about.

Two arrays are declared as instance members: the `query` array, which is an array of `String` references used to store the queries to execute, and the `output` array, an array of `String` references used to store the output locations for the parsing operation. A `log4j` (`org.apache.log4j`) log instance is also obtained and used throughout the program to provide logging. The code for this section is shown below.

The XMLDemo4 Class: Declarations and main Program Block

```
package examples.jaxp;

import java.sql.*;
import java.io.*;
import javax.naming.*;
import javax.sql.*;
import java.io.*;
import java.net.*;
import java.util.*;
import javax.xml.transform.*;
import javax.xml.transform.stream.*;
```

```
import javax.xml.parsers.*;
import javax.naming.directory.DirContext;
import org.xml.sax.*;
import org.xml.sax.helpers.*;

import org.apache.log4j.Category;

import jdbcutil.*;
import service.LoggingService;
import service.DirectoryService;


public class XMLDemo4 extends DefaultHandler {

private Statement stmt;
private Connection con;
private Transformer transformer;
private String[] query  = new String[5];
private String[] output = new String[5];
private StringBuffer buffer;
private PrintWriter out;

private String xslTemplate;
private String dataSource;

private static Category logger = LoggingService.getLogger(
                    "examples.jaxp.XMLDemo4" );
...
```

The XMLDemo4 Class: The `main` **Program Block**

The `main` program block is shown next. This program block controls the execution of the application and is used to call the constructor for the class and to gain a connection to the database using the `getConnected` method. As in the previous example, the `getConnected` method will establish the database connection and assign the `Connection` class and `Statement` class references obtained to the XMLDemo4 instance members.

A `SAXParserFactory` is obtained, and the `setValidate` method is used to establish the parser as a validating parser (it uses the identified DTD to validate the document). The `newSAXParser` method is then used to create a `SAXParser` object which is used to obtain an `XMLReader`.

In practice, all of the steps up to and including the creation of the `XMLReader` could be performed before processing begins. All that is needed to parse multiple XML documents is to vary the source document as shown in this example.

A `for` loop is started to loop through three iterations. Within the `for` loop block for each iteration, a new output file is created, a new SQL statement is executed and converted into a new XML document, and the new XML document is parsed using the SAX parser. As we will see below, the callback methods, the methods called by the SAX event handling mechanism, will output the results of the parsing process to the file pointed to by the out instance member.

As in the previous example, the XML document is stored in a string. This string is wrapped in a ByteArrayInputStream by calling the toBytes method of the String class to convert the string into a byte array. This InputStream object is then used to create an InputSource object required by the XMLReader parse method. (Alternatively, the SAXParser parse method could have been called with two arguments: an InputStream and a DefaultHandler object reference.) Once the document has been parsed, the output device for the parsing (the instance member out) is closed.

The XMLDemo4 Class: The main Program Block

```
...
public static void main( String args[] ) {

try {

  XMLDemo4 xmldemo = new XMLDemo4();
  //
  // connect to the database
  //
  xmldemo.getConnected();

  //
  // create our SAX parser and get the XMLReader
  //
  SAXParserFactory sf = SAXParserFactory.newInstance();
  sf.setValidating( true );      // request a validating parser
  SAXParser parser = sf.newSAXParser();
  XMLReader xmlreader = parser.getXMLReader();

  //
  // assign the event handlers
  //
  xmlreader.setContentHandler( xmldemo );
  xmlreader.setErrorHandler( xmldemo );


  //
  // will process 3 XML documents which are generated dynamically
  //
  for ( int n = 0; n < 3; n++ ) {

       logger.info("Processing query: " + n + " - output: " +
                   xmldemo.output[n] );
```

```java
        //
        // open a new output device
        //
        xmldemo.out = new PrintWriter( new FileWriter(
                                        xmldemo.output[n] ));


        //
        // retrieve a JDBC ResultSet
        //
        ResultSet rs = xmldemo.processQuery( n );


        //
        // convert the ResultSet into an XML document
        // and store it in a string
        //
        String s = JDBCXML.toXMLString( rs );


        //
        // get the input reader - our XML document source
        //
        ByteArrayInputStream in = new ByteArrayInputStream(
                                        s.getBytes() );


        //
        // create the input source
        // our source - an XML document file
        //
        InputSource source = new InputSource( in );


        //
        // parse the document
        //
        xmlreader.parse( source );
        xmldemo.out.close();
    }


}
catch (IOException e) {
    logger.error("IOException : " + e );
}
catch (ParserConfigurationException e) {
    logger.error("ParserConfigurationException : " + e );
}
catch (SAXException e) {
    logger.error("SAXException : " + e );
}


}
```

The XMLDemo4 Class: The Implementation of the error, endElement, and characters Methods

There are several callback methods, methods that will be called by the SAX parser, that we would like to override for our application. (In fact, if we did not override them, then we would not see any output.) One of these methods, the `error` method, is called when a SAX parsing error is encountered. Our implementation simply logs the output to our log device.

The `characters` method is called by the parser when character data is encountered. The characters passed into this method represents the characters in our node values and must be preserved as part of our application state. We do this by appending the content, the character array, to our internal buffer (a `StringBuffer`), using the `append` method.

The `endElement` method is called by the parser when the end of an element is encountered, usually when the end tag is encountered in the parsing operation. In this implementation, the name and value of the element will be output to the device defined by the instance member `out`. The name of the element is obtained from the local name (`localName`) parameter passed into the method, and the value of the element is the value currently stored in the internal `StringBuffer`; both are output using the `println` method.

The `getConnected` and `processQuery` methods perform the same operations as in the previous example. The `getConnected` method establishes a connection to the database (through a `DataSource`), and the `processQuery` method executes a query and returns a `ResultSet`.

```
...
public void error( SAXParseException e) {
    logger.error("SAXParseException : " + e );
}


public void characters( char ch[], int start, int end ) {
  buffer.append( ch, start, end);
}

public void endElement( String uri, String localName, String raw ) {
   //
   // output the current element name and value
   // value is currently stored in our internal StringBuffer
   //
   out.println( "Element name: " + localName +
                " - value: " + buffer.toString().trim() );
   buffer.setLength(0);
}

public void getConnected() {
try {
```

```
  DirectoryService directory = new DirectoryService();
  DirContext init = (DirContext) directory.getContext(
      "o=jdbc, o=general-application-objects, dc=movies, dc=com" );
  DataSource ds = (DataSource) init.lookup( dataSource );

  con = ds.getConnection();

  stmt = con.createStatement();


}
catch (SQLException e) {
  logger.error("SQLException in getConnected: " + e );
}
catch (NamingException e) {
  logger.error("NamingException in getConnected: " + e );
}


}

protected ResultSet processQuery( int n ) {

ResultSet rs=null;

try {

    rs = stmt.executeQuery( query[n] );

}
catch (SQLException e) {
    logger.error("SQLException e: " + e );
}

finally {
      return rs;
}

}
```

The XMLDemo4 Class: The Constructor

The XMLDemo4 class performs a bit of work in its constructor as shown below. To make the application flexible, a properties file is used to load various properties for the application. The application assumes that it may not know the exact location of the properties file, so it uses the classpath to search for the file (using the classLoader). The class loader getResource method searches for the file name specified and returns a URL for the resources. This URL is used to create an InputStream for the properties file.

A properties file is then created, and the properties load method is used to load the contents of the Properties object from the InputStream generated by the URL.

Various SQL statements are then extracted from the properties file and stored in the instance member arrays for the XMLDemo4 class. The DataSource for the movies database is also retrieved from the properties file.

```
public XMLDemo4() {

try {

    buffer = new StringBuffer( 2054 );

    //
    // find the configuration file in the CLASSPATH
    //
    ClassLoader classloader =
          this.getClass().getClassLoader();
    URL url = classloader.getResource(
                "movies.properties" );
    InputStream moviesPropertiesStream =
                url.openStream();

    //
    // load the query from a properties file
    //
    Properties p = new Properties();
    p.load( moviesPropertiesStream );

    query[0] = p.getProperty( "movies.query1" );
    query[1] = p.getProperty( "movies.query2" );
    query[2] = p.getProperty( "movies.query3" );

    output[0] = p.getProperty( "movies.output1" );
    output[1] = p.getProperty( "movies.output2" );
    output[2] = p.getProperty( "movies.output3" );

    dataSource = p.getProperty( "movies.data.source" );

}
catch (IOException e ) {
    logger.error("IOException thrown in constructor: " +
                e.getMessage() );
}

}

}
```

Retrieving Program Properties

As shown below, the properties file for this example demonstrates how program properties that are likely to change can be abstracted out of the program (avoiding the tendency to hardcode them) and retrieved by the program as properties. In this case, a Java properties file was used. Just as easily, as we have seen in these examples, an XML-based properties file could have been used. As we will see later in this text, with Web tier components such as servlets and JSP pages, program properties (attributes) can be placed in a configuration file (`web.xml` for servlets) and accessed using JNDI, an even more flexible approach.

The point being made here, and it is a point that will be made more than once in this text, is that if possible, details that have a tendency to change should be abstracted and made accessible through configuration entries. This avoids the costly process of changing, compiling, and deploying a Java application to implement the change.

The properties file shown below contains entries for the various queries run by the demonstration application, and the names of the files the program will use for output. The name of the JDBC data source is also identified, as well as the XSL script file which we will discuss in the next chapter.

The movies.properties File

```
movies.query1: select salesman as 'Salesmen', sales_date as 'Date',
sales_dollars as 'Dollar Amount' from sales
movies.query2: select movie_id as 'ID', movie_name as 'Movie Name',
release_date as 'Release Date', category as 'Category' from movies
movies.query3: select customer.customer_id as 'ID', first_name as 'First', last_name
as 'Last', address1 + ' ' + address2 as 'Address',              city as 'City',
state as 'State', postal_code as 'Zip' from customer, customer_address where cus-
tomer.customer_id = customer_address.customer_id

movies.output1: rs1.out
movies.output2: rs2.out
movies.output3: rs3.out

movies.xsl.template: rs.xsl

movies.data.source: movies
```

An abridged version of the output generated by running this application is shown below.

Output of XMLDemo4 (rs1.out)

```
. . .
Element name: name - value: Movie ID
Element name: table - value: sales
Element name: type - value: LONG
```

```
Element name: data - value: 3
Element name: column - value:
Element name: name - value: Order Number
Element name: table - value: sales
Element name: type - value: VARCHAR
Element name: data - value: 0.306762085549
Element name: column - value:
Element name: name - value: Quantity
Element name: table - value: sales
Element name: type - value: LONG
Element name: data - value: 2
...
```

SUMMARY

JAXP represents the bundle of classes that we use to parse and transform XML documents. In this chapter we took a look at the JAXP package, specifically at the classes that allow us to parse XML documents.

We found that there are two types of XML parsers available in the JDK: the Document Object Model (DOM) parser and the Simple API for XML (SAX) parser. We first examined the parsing of a document using DOM and then examined how to perform parsing using SAX.

We often have to examine an XML document and retrieve specific values. Rather than scan the entire document for an XML element and its corresponding value, it is easier to provide this capability through a convenience method. Unfortunately, the parsers provided with the JDK do not provide such a convenience method (though other parsers do). In this chapter we provided a code example that created just such a method.

Now that we understand how the JAXP package provides support for parsing, we will examine how to use the same package (and many of the same classes) to transform an XML document. In the next chapter we will write a class that performs transformation of an XML document into HTML format and later in this book we will use that class as part of a demonstration application.

CHAPTER 16

XML Transformation and Creating XML Documents

INTRODUCTION

As we mentioned in the previous chapter, it is often useful to simply convert the contents of an XML document to another form, to *transform* the contents. Applying this approach to multitiered J2EE development, business tier components can be developed to output data in XML format and the presentation tier can then perform the appropriate transformation to create the presentation needed, whether that presentation is an HTML page or a Swing GUI.

The `javax.xml.transform` package and its subpackages contain the classes and interfaces that provide for XML transformation. In this chapter we examine the process of transformation and provide an example of using the transformation API.

In developing applications, we also have the need to create XML documents. In this chapter we examine the different approaches to creating XML documents, including creating an object by creating a concatenated string of XML elements, and using the Java Reflection API and object accessors to determine the contents of an object and to output its contents as an XML document.

Transforming XML Documents

The task of converting or transforming an XML document is not trivial. It involves finding a path to specific elements in the document, parsing the document elements and values and mapping them to new values, and potentially applying decision logic at many points along the way.

Fortunately, there are some very useful XML tools available for transformation of documents. APIs such as Saxon provide transform capabilities, and a transform API is part of JAXP. These APIs make use of the Extensible Stylesheet Language for Transformation (XSLT) scripting language to describe the transformation process. This concise language, in combination with the XPATH descriptive syntax, provides a flexible facility for describing XML transformation.

The XSLT language describes the logic and flow of control involved in performing the transformation and includes any new or substituted content to be placed in the output stream. The XPATH language (syntax that is part of XSLT) describes in a very concise fashion how to reach a specific node in an XML document and the XSLT script then describes the action to take and the output to produce at that node (see Figure 16–1).

XSLT combines with XPATH to create what is known as a template that describes the transformation process. Any content in the template that does not contain the `xsl` namespace prefix is placed onto the output stream as is. This allows for a simple syntax that describes the transformation, not the output. The output is simply authored in place in the template. The following listing is an example of an XSLT script.

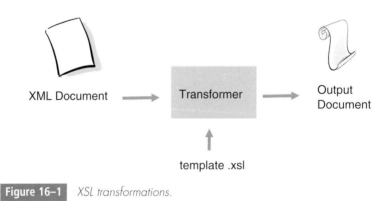

XML Document ⟶ Transformer ⟶ Output Document

↑

template .xsl

Figure 16–1   *XSL transformations.*

The rs.xsl XSL Template

```
<html
 xmlns:xsl="http://www.w3.org/1999/XSL/Transform"
 xsl:version="1.0">
 <body>
        <table width="100%" border="2">

            <tr>
                <xsl:for-each select="resultset/row[1]/column">
                    <td bgcolor="#E0E0E0">
                        <xsl:value-of select=".//name"/>
                    </td>
                </xsl:for-each>
            </tr>

         <xsl:for-each select="resultset/row">
             <tr>
               <xsl:for-each select=".//column">
                   <td><xsl:value-of select=".//data"/></td>
                 </xsl:for-each>
             </tr>
           </xsl:for-each>
        </table>
   </body>
 </html>
```

As you can see, the XSL template allows for simple substitution of the syntax of the resulting transformation output document. In this example, the transformation output is an HTML document, so the initial line in the template identifies HTML as the output.

The template document then contains a number of standard HTML tags, which identify the creation of an HTML table. Within the HTML `<tr>` tag, which identifies a table row, an `<xsl:for-each>` tag indicates the start of an iteration, a control loop for each element in the namespace identified in the foreach select attribute (using XPATH syntax). There are three iterations identified in the XSL template.

The first `select` attribute for this iteration tag identifies `"resultset/row[1]/column"` as the location in the document hierarchy. This indicates that the for-each iteration will be done for each column tag encountered and that the column tag specifically will be located under the row element, which is in turn under the resultset element.

Within the for-each loop, a `<td>` tag is used to set the background color for the table data rows, and then an `<xsl:value-of>` tag is used to insert the contents of the name element at that point in the output stream. The syntax for this tag is `<xsl:value-of  select=".//name"/>`. The select attribute within this tag uses XPATH syntax, which directs the parser transform routine to the name element and returns the value of that element. A closing <td> tag is also output within the for-each loop. Thus, the product of executing this portion of the XSL template will be to output a table data (<td>) section for the value of the name element for each of the columns in the first row element encountered in the XML document.

The syntax for the row element is row[1], which indicates that the contents of the for-each loop should only be executed when the first row is encountered; after that it should not be executed. The reason this syntax is used is that the for-each loop is used to print the column headers for an HTML table. The column headers appear in the output for each row, but they only need to be displayed in the table once. This syntax allows that to be done.

The second for-each loop executes for each row element (XPATH = "resultset/row"). For each row element encountered (not just the first), the XSL template directs a table row tag (<tr>) to be written to the output stream. An <xsl:value-of> tag then directs the value of the name element to be output using the <xsl:value-of select=".//data"/> XPATH syntax. (The leading period (.) in the select attribute indicates that the current node in the hierarchy will be substituted for the path selection.) This output will be placed between table data (<td>) tags, having the effect of outputting the data within a row in a series of table data cells. A closing table row (<tr>) tag is output at the end of the inner for-each loop and before the end of the outer for-each loop. The end result of this execution is an HTML table containing the XML document data.

Now that we know how to write the XSLT script file for the transformation, we need to know how to execute the transformer within our application. We will determine how to do this in the next section.

Programming XML Transformations

Programming XML transformations involves creating an object instance of the Transformer class. The Transformer object will be responsible for reading the XSLT instructions, reading the XML source document, and producing the output.

The creation of the Transformer object must be done through the TransformerFactory class. The TransformerFactory class can create the Transformer object directly, using the XSLT script as a parameter, or else a Templates object can be created using the XSLT script and then the Transformer object can be created using the Templates object. The second approach has the advantage of convenience and creates a thread-safe implementation of the template class.

The code example shown below uses the same approach demonstrated in XMLDemo4. A properties file is used to store a set of queries and output files. The properties file also stores entries for the transformation script and the DataSource to use. The differences in the two programs are minor and generally involve a reduction in Java code that is possible because of the transformation process. To highlight the coding differences required for the transformation process, the code used to perform the transformation is set in boldface in the following code listing.

In the declarations section for the code, a `Transformer` object is declared (`transformer`). This object is used at the end of the `for` loop in the `main` program block to perform the transformation. The `transform` method takes arguments for the source XML document and the result, in this case an output file, although any valid `javax.xml.transform.Result` implementation will do (for example, a DOM or SAX object or various Java I/O streams).

Highlighted in the constructor for the `XMLDemo3` program are the entries used to create the `Transformer` object. As you might expect in an API that implements the factory design pattern, a `TransformerFactory` instance is obtained. A `StreamSource` object is used to wrap the `InputStream` that references the XSLT script file to be used for the transformations. This `StreamSource` is then passed to the `TransformerFactory` `newTemplates` method to create the `Templates` object. The `Templates` object is then used to create the `Transformer` object used to perform the transformations.

The remainder of the program is identical to `XMLDemo4`, so a detailed explanation would be redundant. It is, however, included here for completeness.

The XMLDemo3 Class

```
package examples.jaxp;

import java.sql.*;
import java.io.*;
import javax.naming.*;
import javax.sql.*;

import java.io.*;
import java.net.*;
import java.util.*;

import javax.xml.transform.*;
import javax.xml.transform.stream.*;
import javax.xml.parsers.*;

import javax.naming.directory.DirContext;
import org.w3c.dom.*;
import org.apache.log4j.*;

import jdbcutil.*;
import service.LoggingService;
import service.DirectoryService;

public class XMLDemo3 {

private Statement stmt;
```

```
private Connection con;
private Transformer transformer;

private String[] query  = new String[5];
private String[] output = new String[5];

private String xslTemplate;
private String dataSource;

private static Category logger = LoggingService.getLogger(
                        "examples.jaxp.XMLDemo3" );

public static void main( String args[] ) {
Document doc=null;

try {

  XMLDemo3 xmldemo = new XMLDemo3();

  //
  // connect to the database
  //
  xmldemo.getConnected();

  for ( int n = 0; n < 3; n++ ) {

      logger.info("Processing query: " +
                  n + " - output: " +
                  xmldemo.output[n] );

      //
      // retrieve a JDBC ResultSet
      //
      ResultSet rs = xmldemo.processQuery( n );

      //
      // convert the ResultSet into an XML document
      // and store it in a string
      //
      String s = JDBCXML.toXMLString( rs );

      //
      // get the input reader - our XML document source
      //
      StringReader in = new StringReader( s );

      //
      // create the input source
      // our source - an XML document file
      //
      StreamSource source = new StreamSource( in );
```

```
            //
            // our result - an output file
            //
            Result result = new StreamResult(
                    new FileOutputStream( xmldemo.output[n] ));
            xmldemo.transformer.transform( source, result );
        }

    }
    catch (IOException e) {
        logger.error("IOException e: " + e );
    }
    catch (TransformerException e) {
        logger.error("TransformerException e: " + e );
    }


    }

    public void getConnected() {

    try {

    DirectoryService directory = new DirectoryService();
    DirContext init = (DirContext) directory.getContext(
      "o=jdbc, o=general-application-objects, dc=movies, dc=com" );
    DataSource ds = (DataSource) init.lookup( dataSource );

    con = ds.getConnection();

    stmt = con.createStatement();


    }
    catch (SQLException e) {
     logger.error("SQLException e: " + e );
    }
    catch (NamingException e) {
     logger.error("NamingException e: " + e );
    }

    }

    protected ResultSet processQuery( int n ) {
    ResultSet rs=null;

    try {
        rs = stmt.executeQuery( query[n] );
    }
    catch (SQLException e) {
        logger.error("SQLException e: " + e );
    }
```

```
finally {
     return rs;
}


}

public XMLDemo3() {
URL url=null;

try {

    //
    // look for configuration files
    // in our CLASSPATH
    //
    ClassLoader classloader =
          this.getClass().getClassLoader();
    //
    // find the properties file and open an InputStream
    //
    url = classloader.getResource(
          "movies.properties" );
    InputStream moviesPropertiesStream =
          url.openStream();

    //
    // load the query and other info.
    // from a properties file
    //
    Properties p = new Properties();
    p.load( moviesPropertiesStream );

    query[0] = p.getProperty( "movies.query1" );
    query[1] = p.getProperty( "movies.query2" );
    query[2] = p.getProperty( "movies.query3" );

    output[0] = p.getProperty( "movies.output1" );
    output[1] = p.getProperty( "movies.output2" );
    output[2] = p.getProperty( "movies.output3" );

    dataSource = p.getProperty( "movies.data.source" );
    xslTemplate = p.getProperty(
          "movies.xsl.template" );

    //
    // find the XSL template and open an InputStream
    //
    url = classloader.getResource( xslTemplate );
    InputStream xslTemplateStream = url.openStream();

    //
    // create an XML transformer
```

```
        //
        TransformerFactory tf =
                TransformerFactory.newInstance();
        StreamSource templateSource = new StreamSource(
                                xslTemplateStream );
        Templates template = tf.newTemplates(
                                templateSource );
        transformer = template.newTransformer();

}
catch (IOException e ) {
    logger.error("IOException thrown in constructor: " +
                e.getMessage() );
}
catch (TransformerConfigurationException e ) {
    logger.error(
 "TransformerConfigurationException thrown in constructor: "
        + e.getMessage() );
}
catch (Throwable t ) {
    logger.error("Throwable thrown in constructor: " +
                t.getMessage() );
    t.printStackTrace();
}
}
}
```

The output from running the XMLDemo3 class is a transformed version of the ResultSet XML document. The transformation is used to create an HTML document which describes the creation of an HTML table as shown below.

Output from XMLDemo3 (rs2.out)

```
<html>
<body>
<table border="2" width="100%">
<tr>
<td bgcolor="#E0E0E0">ID</td><td bgcolor="#E0E0E0">Movie Name</td><td
bgcolor="#E0E0E0">Release Date</td><td bgcolor="#E0E0E0">Category</td>
</tr>
<tr>
<td>1</td><td>Stamping Out the Evil Null Reference</td><td>2001-01-
01</td><td>Comedy</td>
</tr>
<tr>
<td>801</td><td>Crazy/Beautiful</td><td>2000-05-23</td><td>Comedy</td>
</tr>
<tr>
<td>601</td><td>The Last Compile</td><td>2000-01-11</td><td>Comedy</td>
</tr>
<tr>
```

```
<td>3</td><td>The Final Test</td><td>1997-01-22</td><td>Thriller</td>
</tr>
<tr>
<td>4</td><td>One Last Try Before the Lights Go Down</td><td>1998-01-
11</td><td>Comedy</td>
</tr>
<tr>
<td>501</td><td>Trying Again</td><td>1992-03-01</td><td>Comedy</td>
</tr>
<tr>
<td>2</td><td>The Cold Coffee Cup</td><td>1993-04-05</td><td>Thriller</td>
</tr>
<tr>
<td>903</td><td>J2EE Under Fire</td><td>2002-01-03</td><td>Action</td>
</tr>
<tr>
<td>5</td><td>The Missing Man</td><td>2000-03-01</td><td>Action</td>
</tr>
<tr>
<td>902</td><td>American Outlaw</td><td>2000-01-23</td><td>Action</td>
</tr>
<tr>
<td>901</td><td>J2EE for Fun and Profit</td><td>2002-01-05</td><td>Action</td>
</tr>
</table>
</body>
</html>
```

When displayed in a browser, the output produces an HTML table, as shown in Figure 16–2.

CONVERTING OBJECTS TO XML FORMAT

There are several methods for creating an XML document. One of the simplest methods is to write a program to create a string with the XML tags and corresponding content for the document. While effective and efficient, this approach has its limitations. One notable limitation is that it would require each XML document to be created and coded separately so you would need to write a method or an application for each XML document.

Another limitation is the potential for error should the developer make a coding error, which would lead to mismatched tags and the creation of a document that is not well-formed. This limitation could be overcome by creating a generic object-to-XML method to create XML documents from any Java object that conforms to a certain set of rules.

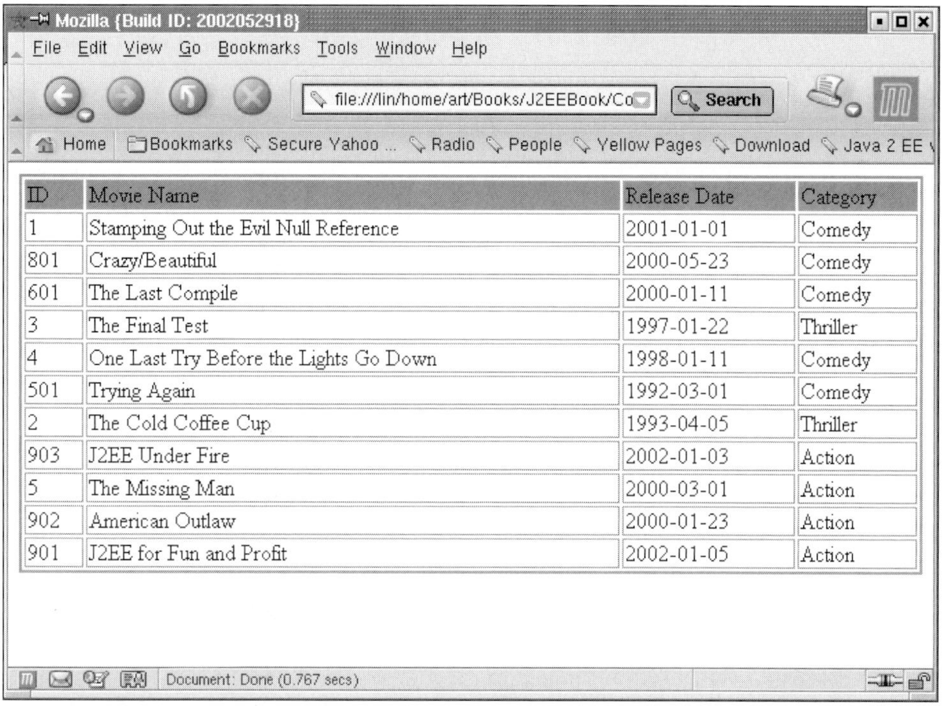

Figure 16–2   *HTML output generated by XMLDemo3.*

Another alternative is to use the DOM API to create the XML document. The DOM API provides methods for creating an internal object that represents an XML document tree. Methods are available to add nodes and related content to the document. Since any document created with the DOM API will be assured of being well-formed, using the DOM provides an added level of safety to creating an XML document.

The following utility class demonstrates both approaches to XML document creation. A generic object-to-XML method is demonstrated; it uses the Java Reflection API to create an XML document that corresponds to the getXXX methods (the accessor methods) within an object. The class also contains a method that uses the DOM API to create a DOM object. When the object is complete, it is transformed to a string, which is then returned by the method. In all, the class contains three static methods, listed in Table 16–1.

The following sections examine each of these methods in detail.

Table 16–1	*Static Methods*

Method	Description
convertToResultSetXML	Takes an object reference argument and converts the contents to an XML document that resembles a JDBC ResultSet format. Uses Java Reflection to extract object information using the accessor methods (getXXX) and builds a string version of the XML document using a StringBuffer. Returns a string containing the XML document.
ConvertToXML	Converts the contents of an object reference to an XML document. Returns a string containing the XML document.
objectToResultSetXML	Converts the contents of an object reference argument to an XML document that resembles a JDBC ResultSet format. Uses Java Reflection to extract object information using the accessor methods (getXXX) and builds a DOM version of the XML document using the DOM API. Transforms the DOM object to a string containing the XML document and returns the string.

Declarations and the convertToResultSetXML Method

This utility class is intended to be used for discrete method calls where all work will be performed within the scope of a single method call. For this reason, the class will not retain any values and there is no reason to declare instance members for that purpose. The only exception to this is the declaration of the logging device.

As explained earlier, the convertToResultXML method shown below takes an object argument and converts the content to a JDBC ResultSet format, containing elements similar to those of a JDBC ResultSet object used earlier in this book.

This method takes an object reference and examines the methods declared within the object. Any getXXX methods are assumed to be accessor methods and are used to identify the name of the XML element and the corresponding text value for the element. We assert that the getXXX method takes no arguments, and we assert that all getXXX methods are of interest whether they are declared in our immediate class or in a superclass (with the exception of the Object class).

The output will be an XML document with the className as the outermost element (the document element). Within the document, a <row> tag is used to represent the set of data elements in the object. A column element represents one of the data elements in the object. A column has within it a name element containing the name associated with the data element, and a value element containing the value of the data. For our purposes, we treat the name of the data element (the column name) as the method name with the `get` portion removed, so that a `getUserID` method would be represented by a `column` element with a `name` element containing the value of `userid`.

We begin the method by declaring a `StringBuffer` to hold the contents of our XML document. We then use the class of the object to determine which methods have been declared within the object, using the `Class getMethods` method. We retrieve all of the methods, including those declared in any superclass. The results are returned in an array of `Method` objects.

We then loop through our list of methods. If the method was declared as part of the `Object` class, it is ignored. If any method begins with the string `get`, we assume it is an accessor method and process it by creating a `column` element and retrieving the name of the column from the method name, shifted to lowercase. The value of the column (the instance member) is retrieved by invoking the method with no arguments (the `args` array has been assigned a null value). When all of the methods have been processed, the corresponding tags are closed and the value of the buffer is returned as a string.

The convertToResultSetXML Method

```
package xmlutil;

import java.io.*;
import javax.xml.transform.*;
import javax.xml.parsers.*;
import javax.xml.transform.dom.*;
import javax.xml.transform.stream.*;
import org.w3c.dom.*;

import java.lang.reflect.*;

import org.apache.log4j.Category;

import service.LoggingService;

public class ObjectToXML {

private static Category logger = LoggingService.getLogger(
                           "ObjectToXML" );


//
// Convert an object with 'getXXXX' methods to an
// XML document. Use JDBC ResultSet type tags to
// all the use of ResultSet XLS transformations
//
// ** use the Reflection API and build document
// with a StringBuffer **
//
```

```java
public static String convertToResultSetXML( Object obj ) {

StringBuffer buffer = new StringBuffer( 1024 );

try {
Method[] m = obj.getClass().getMethods();
Object[] args = null; //

String className = obj.getClass().getName().toLowerCase();
buffer.append( "<" + className + ">\n" );

//
// add 'resultset' tags
//
buffer.append("  <row>\n");

for ( int n = 0; n < m.length; n++ ) {

    // ignore any methods from Object
    if ( m[n].getDeclaringClass().getName().equals(
                            "java.lang.Object" ) ) {
      continue;
    }
    if ( m[n].getName().startsWith("get") ) {

        //
        // this is a 'column'
        //
        buffer.append("    <column>\n");

        //
        // this is the tag name
        //
        String s = m[n].getName().substring(3).toLowerCase();
        buffer.append( "      <name>" + s +
                    "</name>\n" );
        //
        // insert the value
        //
        buffer.append( "      <data>" );
        buffer.append( m[n].invoke( obj, args ) );
        buffer.append( "      </data>\n" );

        //
        // close the column node
        //
        buffer.append( "    </column>\n");
    }
}
```

```
//
// close the last column tag and close the row
//
buffer.append( "  </row>\n");
buffer.append( "</" + className + ">\n" );


}
catch (Exception e) {
      logger.error("Exception e: " + e );
}
finally {
   return buffer.toString();
}


}
```

The convertToXML Method

The `convertToXML` method shown below takes an object reference and converts the object to an XML document. This method is identical to the previous method with the exception of the portion of the `for` loop, which creates the XML document elements.

Unlike the previous method, this method does not treat the object as a row; it simply creates elements using the name of the method as the element name and inserting the value of the instance member (as returned by the `getXXX` method) as the value of the node. The portion of the method that is different is set in boldface.

The convertToXML Method

```
...
//
// Convert an object with 'getXXXX' methods to an
// XML document.
//
public static String convertToXML( Object obj ) {

StringBuffer buffer = new StringBuffer( 1024 );

try {

Method[] methods = obj.getClass().getMethods();
Object[] args = null; // assert a no-args getXXXX method

String className = obj.getClass().getName().toLowerCase();
buffer.append( "<" + className + ">\n" );
```

```
//
// for each 'get' method, output a tag for the element
// and the corresponding value
//
for ( int n = 0; n < methods.length; n++ ) {

    // ignore any methods from Object
    if ( methods[n].getDeclaringClass().getName().equals( "java.lang.Object" ) ) {
        continue;
    }

      if ( methods[n].getName().startsWith("get") ) {

          //
          // this is the tag name
          //
          String elementName =
                  methods[n].getName().substring(3).toLowerCase();
          buffer.append( "<" + elementName + ">" );
          //
          // insert the value
          //
          buffer.append( methods[n].invoke( obj, args ) );

          //
          // close the tag
          //
          buffer.append( "</" + elementName + ">\n" );

      }
}

//
// close the last column tag and close the row
//
buffer.append( "</" + className + ">\n" );

}
catch (Exception e) {
      logger.error("Exception e: " + e );
}
finally {
    return buffer.toString();
}


}
```

The objectToResultSetXML Method

The `objectToResultSetXML` method shown below presents a different twist on the creation of XML documents. This method uses a DOM object to hold the XML document being created. It is clear from this example that this approach does not necessarily reduce the amount of code required but does add some level of safety to the code, since the resulting document is guaranteed to be well formed.

We begin by declaring a `ByteArrayOutputStream` object, which we will use to capture our XML output later in the method. Since we are writing a static method that may be shared by concurrent threads, we need to provide a thread-safe solution. We therefore begin this method by creating a new instance of a `Transformer` object and a `DocumentBuilder` object so that each caller will have its own version of the `Transformer` and `DocumentBuilder`. The `Transformer` instance will be used later. The `DocumentBuilder` instance is used to create a new DOM object representing the XML document we will create.

We then obtain an array of methods within the object and begin looping through the methods. We have obtained a DOM object, a document, through the `DocumentBuilder` instance. We add nodes to the document, adding to the document node using the `appendChild` method. We first add an element for the top-level node, which is the name of the class for the object we are processing.

We then iterate through the methods as before. If we encounter a `getXXX` method, we process it by adding additional child elements to our DOM document. Note that we do not need to explicitly close a node—this is done automatically by DOM.

When the processing loop is complete, we must convert the DOM object into a string. This is done by performing a transformation with the `StreamResult` object, wrapping our `ByteArrayOutputStream` declared earlier. In the `finally` block we convert the `ByteArrayOutputStream` to a string and return it. The code for this method is shown below.

```
...
//
// Convert an object with 'getXXXX' methods to an
// XML document. Use JDBC ResultSet type tags to
// all the use of ResultSet XLS transformations
//
// ** use DOM object to create an string containing the XML
// document **
//
public static String objectToResultSetXML( Object obj ) {

ByteArrayOutputStream out    = null;

try {

Transformer     transformer =
        TransformerFactory.newInstance().newTransformer();
```

```
DocumentBuilder db          =
        DocumentBuilderFactory.newInstance().newDocumentBuilder();
out = new ByteArrayOutputStream();

Document      doc   = db.newDocument();

Method[] methods = obj.getClass().getMethods();
Object[] args = null;

String className = obj.getClass().getName();

Node docNode = doc.appendChild( doc.createElement( className.toLowerCase() ) ) ;

//
// create the top level node - the row
//
Node topNode =
     docNode.appendChild( doc.createElement( "row"  ) );
for ( int n = 0; n < methods.length; n++ ) {

    if ( methods[n].getName().startsWith( "get" ) ) {

        //
        // create the column node
        //
        Node colNode =
          topNode.appendChild( doc.createElement( "column"  ) ) ;

        //
        // get the name of the method = name of the column
        //
        String name = methods[n].getName().substring(3).toLowerCase();

        //
        // create the column node
        //
        Node node = colNode.appendChild( doc.createElement( "name"  ) ) ;
        node.appendChild( doc.createTextNode( name ) );

        //
        // create the value node
        //
        node = colNode.appendChild(
           doc.createElement( "value"  ) ) ;
        node.appendChild(
            doc.createTextNode(
                methods[n].invoke( obj, args ).toString() ) );
    }
}

//
// now transform the doc to a String
```

```
//
Result result = new StreamResult( out );
Source source = new DOMSource( doc );

transformer.transform( source, result );


}
catch (TransformerConfigurationException e ) {
       logger.error(
         "TransformerConfigurationException in objToXML: " + e );
}
catch (TransformerException e ) {
       logger.error(
         "TransformerConfigurationException in objToXML: " + e );
}
catch (IllegalAccessException e ) {
         logger.error("IllegalAccessException in objToXML: " + e );
}
catch (InvocationTargetException e ) {
         logger.error("InvocationTargetException in objToXML: " + e );
}
catch (Throwable e ) {
         logger.error("Throwable in objToXML: " + e );
}
finally {

   //
   // return the output (ByteArrayOutputStream) as a String
   //
   return out.toString();
}


}
```

THE JDBCXML CLASS

The JDBCXML class contains two static methods: the toXMLString method, which takes a JDBC ResultSet object and converts it to an XML document in string form, and the toXMLFile method, which takes a ResultSet object and a Writer object and converts the ResultSet to an XML document, which is then written to the file output. The code for this class is shown below.

The toXMLString method takes the ResultSet argument and obtains a ResultSetMetaData object to gather information about the ResultSet, such as the number of columns in the ResultSet and the names of the columns. It creates a StringBuffer to hold the contents of the XML document.

A loop is started to iterate through the contents of the ResultSet. As long as the ResultSet next method returns true, we have a row to process. For each row, we step through each of the columns in the row (as indicated by the ResultSetMetaData getColumnCount method). To manage the occasional null object reference as returned by the ResultSet getObject method, we retrieve the object reference from the ResultSet column and then test it before processing. Appropriate tags are added for each of the elements being processed.

The toXMLFile takes two arguments: the ResultSet object to convert and the object reference of a java.io.Writer object where the XML document will be output. This method simply creates a BufferedWriter on the writer object passed into the method and then takes the ResultSet object and calls the toXMLString method to create the XML document as a string. The resulting string is then output to the Writer and the output is closed.

The JDBCXML Class

```
package jdbcutil;

import java.sql.*;
import java.io.*;
import db.*;

import org.apache.log4j.Category;
import service.LoggingService;

public class JDBCXML {

private static Category logger = LoggingService.getLogger( "JDBCXML" );

public static String toXMLString( ResultSet rs ) {
StringBuffer buffer = new StringBuffer(1024);
int rows = 0;

buffer.append( "<resultset>\n" );

try {

ResultSetMetaData rsmd  = rs.getMetaData();

while ( rs.next() ) {
rows++;
buffer.append( "  <row>\n");
   for ( int n = 1; n <= rsmd.getColumnCount(); n++ ) {

       buffer.append( "    <column>\n" );

       buffer.append( "      <name>" ).append(
               rsmd.getColumnName(n) ).append( "</name>\n" );
       buffer.append( "      <table>" ).append(
```

```
                    rsmd.getTableName(n) ).append( "</table>\n" );
        buffer.append( "      <type>" ).append(
                    rsmd.getColumnTypeName(n) ).append( "</type>\n" );

        //
        // must manage null object references
        //
        Object o = rs.getObject( n );
        if ( rs.wasNull() ) {
            buffer.append( "      <data>null</data>\n");
        }
        else {
            buffer.append(
    "       <data>").append(o.toString()).append("</data>\n");

        }
        buffer.append( "    </column>\n" );

    }
buffer.append( "  </row>\n");

}
// only write end tag if we processed rows
if ( rows > 0 ) {
    buffer.append( "</resultset>\n" );
}
else  { // no rows, return an empty buffer
    buffer.setLength( 0 );
}

}
catch (SQLException e) {
        logger.error( "SQLException thrown in toXMLString " +
                            e.getMessage() );

}

finally {
if ( buffer != null )
    return buffer.toString();
else
    return null;
}


}


public static void toXMLFile( ResultSet rs, Writer writer ) {
//StringBuffer buffer = new StringBuffer();

try {
```

```
BufferedWriter out = new BufferedWriter( writer );

//
// write the XML document to the output stream and close it
//
out.write( toXMLString( rs ) );
out.close();

}
catch (IOException e) {
        logger.error( "IOException thrown in toXMLString " + e.getMessage() );

}


}


}
```

SUMMARY

The previous chapters explained XML and its related technologies, and demonstrated how to parse an XML document using the classes provided in the JAXP bundle. Being able to parse an XML document is a big part of the XML picture, but it is not the complete picture.

There are some excellent facilities available to transform an XML document from one format to another. In this chapter we saw how XSL templates build on various standards to provide a useful scripting language for describing the transformation process. Using an XSL script file and the various classes in the `javax.xml.transform` package, it is a fairly simple process to perform XML transformations using Java, as we demonstrated in this chapter.

Java applications must also be able to create XML documents. There are several methods for doing this, from creating simple string representations of XML documents to the more complex approaches demonstrated in this chapter.

CHAPTER 17

Java Networking API

INTRODUCTION

The foundation of all distributed programming is the network. The network allows applications to communicate, and through the standards of TCP/IP, the structure of this communication process is virtually the same regardless of whether the communicating applications reside on the same machine, on separate machines on the same local network, or on separate machines separated by thousands of miles.

TCP/IP represents a networking standard that has helped to promote the proliferation of computer networks. But while TCP/IP has been a widely accepted standard for some time, communicating between different computers with different operating systems and different hardware architectures was not an easy task. Managing data being moved between machines was tedious and formed the core subject matter for many networking books. (Simply moving an integer value could require 10 lines of C language code to insure the bit pattern was correct.)

But the Java language has simplified network communications not only with the transmission of primitive data types, but also with the transmission of objects across the network (through object serialization) and, as we will see in this chapter, through the well-designed network sockets API.

As this chapter demonstrates, the Java networking API provides a clean, object-oriented basis for networking communications. Other Java APIs augment the networking API and add additional services (RMI, JMS, EJB), but the networking API still represents a potential lightweight solution for many applications.

We begin by examining the basis for Java networking—the TCP/IP standard. We then examine the Java network sockets API and review using the API with an example that demonstrates a basic protocol to provide a remote order-processing system.

TCP/IP NETWORKING

A network can be considered a series of points along a line. These points are nodes, and the electronic network provides high-speed communication between the nodes. A network provides this communication using a *protocol*, a preassigned language for communication, and a predetermined format for a *data buffer* or information *packet*.

The data buffer or packet is transmitted between nodes and is a combination of the actual data being transmitted and information about the data packet contained in the packet header. To transmit a packet, a node may set a flag in the packet header indicating that the packet is being transmitted to a specific target; the target address may also be included in the header. Once transmitted, a packet may travel to a number of different nodes until it is received at the node where it was sent. The source and destination nodes may exchange additional packets of data to ensure delivery of the data packet. This exchange of additional packets is part of a *handshaking protocol* used to add reliable data flow services to the transmission process.

At any given point, a large number of data packets may be coursing through a network. These packets are sent to their correct destination via *routers*. The routers examine the packet to determine where the packet is bound and then sends the packet on its way (see Figure 17–1).

TCP/IP is the most common protocol for networking. This combination of acronyms stands for Transmission Control Protocol and Internet Protocol and is actually two protocols: TCP and IP. The IP protocol provides routing information on how to find the address of the resource being requested. The IP protocol splits the data into packets and attaches a source and destination address to the packet. This information is then used to route the packet from the source to the destination.

The TCP protocol uses the IP layer protocol to provide routing services. TCP establishes the connection and provides a handshaking mechanism to ensure that

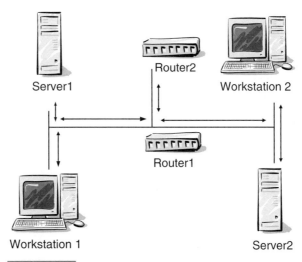

Figure 17–1 *TCP/IP network with routers, servers, and workstations.*

data gets to its destination. TCP provides guaranteed delivery of data (unlike other protocols, which do not) and for this reason provides some level of error correction and integrity for data transmission. TCP/IP networking also uses the User Datagram Protocol (UDP), a simpler protocol that does not provide the reliability guarantee.

With respect to the World Wide Web infrastructure, TCP/IP and HTTP are part of a network protocol layer framework known as the Open Systems Interconnection (OSI) developed by the ISO standards organization. The framework provides for seven layers, and though vendors have implemented parts of this framework, rarely is the entire standard adhered to in a product. TCP/IP combined with HTTP comprise the part of this layer model used in this book (see Table 17–1).

Table 17–1 *Common OSI Layers*

OSI Layer	Type	Description
HTTP	Application	HyperText Transport Protocol
TCP	Transport	Transport Control Protocol
IP	Internet	Internet Protocol
Ethernet, ISDN, PPP, SLIP	Data Link	Network Packet Transmission

At the lowest level, a layer exists to move the network packets from one point to another. This layer has only rudimentary knowledge of the contents of the packets; higher level protocols such as IP provide the routing of the packets. Above IP, the TCP layer provides for the communication between network nodes and ensures accuracy, using the IP layer for routing. And above all other layers, the HTTP layer executes the handshaking between client and server with some knowledge of the information being transmitted.

TCP/IP NETWORK ADDRESSES

IP originally defined network addresses as 32-bit binary addresses generally represented as 3 digit decimal numbers separated by periods. Since each section or *octet* of the address represents an 8 bit byte, the highest number that can be placed in the octet is 255 ($2^8 - 1$).

But not all 32-bit IP addresses are available. Five different types of networks were reserved in the original scheme, referred to as Class A,B,C,D and E networks. These network classes are as listed in Table 17–2.

Table 17–2   *Reserved Network Types*

Class	Range	Max. Networks in Class	Max. Hosts
A	0.0.0.0 to 127.255.255.255	126	over 16 million
B	128.0.0.0 to 191.255.255.255	16384	65534
C	192.0.0.0 to 223.255.255.255	2097152	254
D	224.0.0.0 to 239.255.255.255	<for multi-cast>	n/a
E	240.0.0.0 to 247.255.255.255	<reserved>	n/a

This addressing scheme was conceived before the proliferation of PCs and before the growth of the Internet. At the time, the general consensus was that only very large companies would require the number of nodes in a class A network. Some mid-sized organizations would need the 65,000 hosts in the class B network, and the 2 million plus class C networks would be enough for everyone else.

With the growth of the Internet, it was clear that this network scheme would not be adequate. The IPv6 networking addressing standard provides a larger address space and is slowly being adopted in the industry. As part of the IPv6 standard, however, support for the older addressing scheme is required.

Network addresses are difficult to remember and do not convey any information about the host they represent. For that reason, host names are usually associated with IP addresses. These names are arbitrary, contiguous strings that are mapped to server IP addresses using a naming service such as Domain Naming Service (DNS) or Yellow Pages. Using the naming scheme allows network administrators to change IP addresses as needed while allowing applications and users to continue to use host names they are familiar with. The following figure illustrates the operation of DNS on a network (see Figure 17–2).

A *host* is a network node that usually represents a server that can offer network services. Even though a client machine may not technically be a host, it is still assigned a host address, since it technically offers network services such as socket endpoints for network communications, as discussed below.

A host may also provide network ports, multiple network destinations for the host at the network transport layer. Machines typically offer in the range of 65,535 ports. A portion of these ports, sometimes referred to as the lower 1024, are reserved as *well- known ports*. These are ports used by common network utilities, such as the File Transport Protocol (FTP), gopher, and HyperText Transport Protocol (HTTP). (These ports are also used by hackers to gain access to servers, and for this reason network administrators will generally turn these services off to strengthen security.)

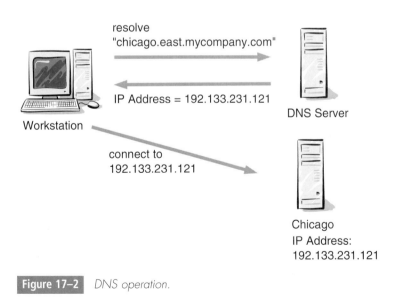

Figure 17–2   *DNS operation.*

NETWORK PROGRAMMING: THE NETWORK SOCKET

The basic TCP/IP network programming facility is the *network socket*. The network socket represents a communication point between two programs. Programs use the sockets for input, output, or both. The socket is identified by a begin point (an IP address) and an endpoint (an IP address and a port number) such that multiple connections can be made to the same server on the same port, as shown in Figure 17–3.

Java provides an API that allows the creation of sockets over TCP/IP networks. This API is integrated with the streams API to provide a clean abstraction of I/O. An application could be written to use a Java `InputStream` to read data. This application could receive the `InputStream` reference from a file on the local machine, or from a network socket, or via a URL using HTTP; the application accepting the `InputStream` reference would work the same either way.

The network socket is an endpoint represented by a combination of IP address and port number. Any socket communications requires two endpoints. One application listens for a connection and is referred to as a server. The other application requests a connection to the server and is referred to as the client.

Once communication between the client and server is initiated, both the client and server can send and receive information over the socket connection. As we will see in the next section, the Java networking API makes it fairly simple to create this connection and then send and receive information using the connection.

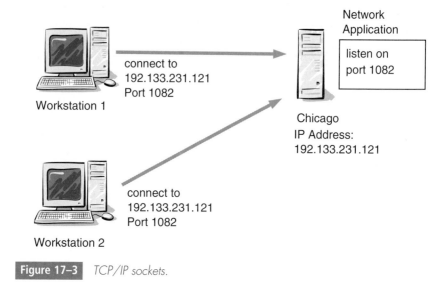

Figure 17–3 *TCP/IP sockets.*

JAVA SOCKETS

Two classes are generally used to create socket connections using Java: `java.net.Socket` and `java.net.ServerSocket`. The server application uses an instance of the `ServerSocket` class, and the client application uses an instance of the `Socket` class.

The `ServerSocket` is created first, identifying a port number where the server will listen for a connection. The `ServerSocket` will only listen for a connection on the host server where it is running.

The client application creates a `Socket` class instance, which accepts a combination of a host name or IP address and a port number as arguments to the constructor. If a successful connection is made, then an instance of the `Socket` class is created. This instance is then used to retrieve an `InputStream` for the socket connection, which is used to perform the communication between the client and the server.

While the `Socket` and `ServerSocket` classes contain a number of methods that allow the connection to be configured, in practice very few of these are used. Instead, a socket connection can be made and used with very few calls, as shown in the following example.

DATA TRANSMISSION AND OBJECT SERIALIZATION

Java has provided for a network I/O interface by allowing a Java socket to return a stream object, either a `java.net.InputStream` or a `java.net.OutputStream`. This means that reading and writing data to the socket is functionally similar to reading and writing data to any other device that can be used with the stream interface—for example, a file with the `FileInputStream` or a byte array (with the `ByteArrayInputStream`). Primitive data types can be transmitted over socket connections without concern for type compatibility across the potentially different machine architectures.

A significant feature of Java socket support is the capability to transmit Java objects over the socket connection. This support is provided not by the Java networking (`java.net`) API but by the Java I/O (`java.io`) streams support, specifically by the `ObjectInputStream` and `ObjectOutputStream` classes. By wrapping one of these objects around the appropriate stream object returned from the socket, performing object I/O in Java is relatively simple.

But the underlying work required to perform object I/O is not a trivial task. Objects exist in program memory as complex collections of their members (primitive data types and other objects) and code (their methods) in what is referred to as an *object graph,* which is usually stored in memory in a noncontiguous fashion, as shown in Figure 17–4. In order to write this information to a stream I/O interface,

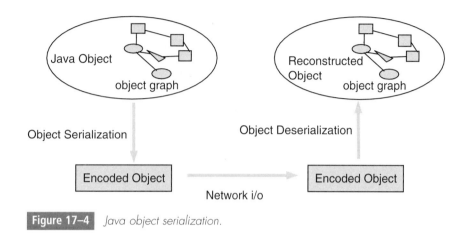

Figure 17–4   *Java object serialization.*

the object information must somehow be converted into a format that can be written to and read from the stream. This is where Java *object serialization* comes into play.

Object serialization allows the state of an object to be serialized. Object serialization converts an object graph into an encoded format with the class signature of the object and all constituent primitive data types and object references. Any object reference contained in the object will also lead to the serialization of the object that is referenced. The resulting encoded format is essentially a stream of bytes that can be written to any supported I/O device. This stream of bytes can later be read from an I/O device, and the object graph can be reconstructed using the same serialization mechanism through what is sometimes referred to as deserialization.

Only objects whose class has been identified as serializable can be serialized. This is accomplished in Java by having the class implement the `java.io.Serializable` interface. This interface is a marker interface and does not require the implementation of specific methods. Any subclass of a serializable class is also serializable. The superclass of a serializable class does not need to be serializable.

The state of all instance members cannot be serialized – there are some exceptions. For instance, references to local files or network addresses cannot be copied to another machine and used. (This makes sense when you consider that these are references to local machine resources which do not exist on the other machine.) These members are referred to as *transient members* and should be identified using the `transient` identifier. Transient members will not become part of the encoded object byte stream and will not be available in the reconstructed form of the object.

Socket Programming Example

The best way to learn the Java network API is through a demonstration. In the following example, a `SocketServer` instance listens for a connection, and when a connection is detected, it starts a thread to manage the connection. This is a fairly efficient method for handling connections, since incoming connection requests do not need to wait while prior connections are handled—all are, theoretically, handled at the same time.

In practice, the spawning of threads would not be open-ended and would be limited in some way to avoid overloading the system with processing. In this example, for brevity, we do not show that code.

The Server Application

The server application represents a server for order processing. As requests are received, a thread is started to manage the request. In the `main` programming block, the `ServerSocket` constructor is called with the name of the port on which the server will listen. This creates a socket listener on the local host on the designated port.

Once the `ServerSocket` instance has been created, a `while` loop is started, and within the `while` loop, the `accept` method is called to listen for connections on the designated port. The Java application blocks on the `accept` call, effectively waiting until either a connection is made or an exception is thrown.

If a connection is received, then execution drops to the next line in the application, which creates a new instance of the `OrderRequestProcessor` using the socket that was created previously. This new instance of the `OrderRequestProcessor` class instance, which is shown later, is used to manage the specifics of the request. Any exception thrown will exit the `while` loop, generate an error message, and then exit the program.

The Server Class

```java
package examples.net;

import java.net.*;
import java.io.*;

import movies.control.Request;
import movies.control.OrderRequestProcessor;

public class Server {

public static void main( String[] args ) {

Server Server = new Server();
```

```
try {
  //
  // create a server socket on port 1500
  //
  ServerSocket ss = new ServerSocket( 1500 );

  System.out.println("Socket created. Listening ... " );

  //
  // listen for connections
  //

  boolean loop = true;
  while ( loop ) {
      Socket socket = ss.accept();

      //
      // start a thread to handle this
      //
      Thread t = new Thread(
          new OrderRequestProcessor( socket ) );
      t.start();

  }

}
catch ( IOException e) {
 System.err.println("IOException in main: " + e );
}

}

}
```

The Client Application

The client application shown below takes advantage of Java object serialization to easily move objects over the network. This allows us to encapsulate our request as an instance of our Request object (shown below) and pass information to and from the server application using this object.

    This application creates an instance of the Socket class using a constructor that attempts a connection on the localhost to the port number where the server application is attached (as identified in the constructor to the ServerSocket class in the previous example). This connection, represented as a Socket instance, is then passed to the doProcessing method of this class. It is this doProcessing method that performs the bulk of the work.

The `doProcessing` method begins by creating an `ObjectInputStream` and `ObjectOutputStream` on the socket connection that it has received as a parameter. These streams are used to read and write objects to and from the server.

This application uses a custom `Request` class to encapsulate the request being sent to the server. This class contains a message type attribute and a message attribute. The `Client` class contains two methods that create, populate, and return a `Request` class instance: the `createOrderRequest` method and the `CreateCancelRequest` method. The first of these methods called, the `createOrderRequest` method, returns a `Request` object, which is written back to the server. The server (which has delegated the communication process to an `OrderRequestProcessor` thread) responds with a message in the form of a `Request` object. This message is read and written to the console to demonstrate that it has been received by the server.

Next, the `createCancelRequest` method is called. This method creates an order cancel request using an order number. As with the other request, it is written to the server and the response from the server is read and displayed to the console. Finally, when all this processing has been completed, the socket connection is closed.

The `createOrderRequest` method is also shown below. This method creates a credit card order Data Access Object (an instance of the `CCOrderDAO` class) and populates it with sample data. This object is then placed in the `Request` instance, but not as a Java object. Instead, it is converted to XML format using the `ObjectToXML convertToXML` method and added as the message content for the class. The resulting `Request` object is then returned by the method.

The `createCancelRequest` method accepts a string order number and creates an XML-formatted text message that indicates a cancel order is being sent. The text message is placed in the `Request` object instance, and the resulting `Request` object is returned by the method.

The Client Class

```
package examples.net;

import java.io.*;
import java.net.*;

import movies.control.Request;
import db.CCOrderDAO;
import xmlutil.ObjectToXML;

public class Client {
private ObjectOutputStream out;
private ObjectInputStream  in;

public static void main( String[] args ) {
```

```
try {

    Client client = new Client();

    //
    // create a socket connection to our server
    //
    Socket socket = new Socket( "localhost", 1500 );

    System.out.println(
            "Socket created. Processing ... " );

    client.doProcessing( socket );

}
catch (IOException e ){
    System.err.println("IOException in main: " + e );
}

}

protected void doProcessing( Socket socket ) {

try {
    //
    // get the input and output
    //
    out = new ObjectOutputStream(
                    socket.getOutputStream() );
    in  = new ObjectInputStream(
                    socket.getInputStream()  );
    //
    // send and order request
    //
    Request r = createOrderRequest();
    out.writeObject( r );

    //
    // read a response
    //
    r = (Request) in.readObject( );

    //
    // send an order cancel
    //
    String orderNumber = "293093";
    r = createCancelRequest( orderNumber );
    out.writeObject( r );

    //
    // read a response (currently we ignore it)
```

```
    //
    r = (Request) in.readObject( );

    //
    // now go away
    //
    socket.close();
}

catch ( IOException e) {
 System.err.println(
       "IOException in main: " + e );
}
catch ( ClassNotFoundException e) {
 System.err.println(
        "ClassNotFoundException in main: " + e );
}

}

protected Request createOrderRequest( ) {

    // create an order
    CCOrderDAO order = new CCOrderDAO();

    //
    // just insert some test data
    //
    order.setNumber("2099-3909-3909-9932");
    order.setType( "MC");
    order.setExpires("08/01");

    order.setShipToID( "09309393-A" );
    order.setBillToID( "1109393-A" );
    order.setOrderNumber("09039093");
    order.setQuantity(12);
    order.setMovieID(1332);
    order.setUPC("Z2AA-3355");

    Request r = new Request();
    r.setType( Request.ORDER_REQUEST );
    r.setMessage( ObjectToXML.convertToXML( order ) );

    return r;

}

protected Request createCancelRequest( String orderNumber ) {

    Request r = new Request();
    r.setType( Request.ORDER_CANCEL );
```

```
r.setMessage( "<order-cancel><order-number>" +
    orderNumber +
    "</order-number></order-cancel>" );

return r;

}

}
```

The OrderRequestProcessor Class

The `OrderRequestProcessor` class shown next represents what is effectively an implementation of the command design pattern. It encapsulates the processing of a request. As we saw earlier in this chapter, the server class spawns a new thread for each incoming request and leaves it to the `OrderRequestProcessor` class instance to manage the request. This class in turn delegates much of the processing work to the `OrderProcessing` class.

This class contains two instance members: a `Socket` reference and an `OrderProcessing` reference. The constructor used in this example takes a single argument: a `Socket` reference. The `Socket` reference passed in is stored, and an `OrderProcessing` instance is created and assigned to the instance member. Following the execution of the constructor, the two instance members for the class have been populated.

Since the `OrderRequestProcessor` will be invoked as a thread and therefore implements the `Runnable` interface, we must provide an implementation of the `run` method. Within the `run` method, an `ObjectInputStream` and an `ObjectOutputStream` are created. These references are used to communicate with the client connecting to this server thread.

We know that only `Request` objects will be passed to and read from the client, so we read the `Request` object that we assert will be in the input stream. A `while` loop is started, which continues processing requests as long as the `Request` reference is not null. We then check the type of request sent. If the request is an order request, we retrieve the message and display it to the console. We then call the `OrderProcessor processOrder` method to process the order. This method accepts a string argument that can be evaluated as an XML representation of the order object (in this case, a `CCOrderDAO` object).

Once the order has been processed, a response is sent, which simply acknowledges that the order has been received for processing. The response is sent in the form of a `Request` object with the request type of `Request.ACKNOWLEDGE`.

If the request type is a cancel order, we currently have no specific implementation, but we do send a `Request.ACKNOWLEDGE` message indicating the order cancel request has been received.

At the end of the `while` loop, we read another object from the input stream. If we encounter an `IOException` on the read operation, we simply break from the `while` loop. Otherwise, we have a `Request` reference, and execution begins back at the top of the loop where the reference is tested.

The OrderRequestProcessor Class

```
package movies.control;

import java.net.*;
import java.io.*;

import movies.control.OrderProcessing;

public class OrderRequestProcessor
     implements Runnable {
private Socket socket;
private OrderProcessing processor;

public OrderRequestProcessor( Socket socket ) {
      this.socket = socket;
      processor = new OrderProcessing();
}

public void run() {

Request request = null;

try {

  //
  // Connection received. Get an input and output stream
  //
  ObjectInputStream  in  = new ObjectInputStream(
                       socket.getInputStream() );
  ObjectOutputStream out = new ObjectOutputStream(
                       socket.getOutputStream() );

  //
  // read from the stream
  //
  request = (Request) in.readObject();

  while ( request != null ) {

     if ( request.getType() == Request.ORDER_REQUEST ) {

     System.out.println( "Order request received.");
     System.out.println( "message: " +
                           request.getMessage() );
```

```
    //
    // we know the message contains the order
    // in XML format
    //
    processor.processOrder( request.getMessage() );


    //
    // send a response
    //
    Request r = new Request();
    r.setType( Request.ACKNOWLEDGE );
    r.setMessage( "Order request has been received.");
    out.writeObject( r );
    out.flush();
    }

  if ( request.getType() == Request.ORDER_CANCEL   )   {

      System.out.println(
            "Order cancel request received.");
      System.out.println( "message: " +
            request.getMessage() );

    //
    // cancel the order (currently not implemented)
    //

     //
     // send a response
    //
     Request r = new Request();
     r.setType( Request.ACKNOWLEDGE );
     r.setMessage(
        "Order cancel request has been received.");
     out.writeObject( r );
     out.flush();

  }
//
// read another request if it's there
//
try {
   request = (Request) in.readObject();
}
catch (IOException e ) {
 //
 // just exit on failed read
 //
 break;
}
}
  //
```

```
  // now go away
  //
  socket.close();
}
catch (IOException e) {
      System.out.println("IOException in run(): " +
                             e );
      e.printStackTrace();
}
catch (ClassNotFoundException e) {
      System.out.println(
        "ClassNotFoundException in run(): " +  e );
      e.printStackTrace();
}


}


}
```

The Request Class

We create our own custom request class to encapsulate the requests that will be sent to and from the order-processing server. This class represents a generic request that will be moved to and from the server. Since object instantiations will move over a network, it is also declared to implement `java.io.Serializable`.

The `Request` class contains an instance member for an integer representing the request type and a string for storage of the message. Accessor and mutator (`getXXXX` and `setXXXX`) methods are created for each of the instance members, and integer constants are defined for the request types.

The Request Class

```
package movies.control;

public class Request implements java.io.Serializable {
private int type;
private String message;

// Request Types
public static final int ORDER_REQUEST = 1;
public static final int ORDER_CANCEL  = 2;

// responses
public static final int ACKNOWLEDGE        = 3;
public static final int PROCESSING_FAILED  = 4;
public static final int BACK_ORDERED       = 5;

// accessors and mutators
```

```java
public String getMessage() {
   return message;
}
public int getType() {
   return type;
}

public void setMessage(String message) {
   this.message = message;
}
public void setType(int type) {
   this.type = type;
}

public String toString() {

   return "Request" + "\n" +
              "type: " + getType() + "\n" +
              "message: " + getMessage() ;

}

}
```

SUMMARY

Networking is obviously the basis for any distributed programming. This chapter provided an overview of the TCP/IP standard and examined the Java network. Sockets are one of the more common networking facilities used, and in this chapter we reviewed an example that used a request object to encapsulate an order-processing request. A simple protocol was implemented, which accepted a request, submitted an acknowledgment, and performed any processing needed.

As we will see in later chapters, this concept of remote processing is expanded in Java using Remote Method Invocation (RMI), Java Messaging Services (JMS), and Java for XML Messaging (JAXM). Later chapters examine these packages and provide examples of their usage, examples that are strikingly similar to the example seen in this chapter. This similarity is no accident, since these technologies are commonly used to provide remote processing services for client applications, as we demonstrated here with the TCP/IP sockets.

CHAPTER 18

Using Remote Method Invocation

INTRODUCTION

Enterprise applications are by definition distributed applications that disperse processing across a number of application components, which may reside on one machine or across several machines at an installation. An application developed in this fashion does not perform all processing in a single application component (as with the *monolithic* approach to running applications) but instead allows a number of application components to work together to perform the tasks required. Applications running in this fashion must have some means of interprocess communication between application components. It is this interprocess communication between application components which is critical; it should allow the distributed components of the application to communicate easily just as though they were object methods within an application, passing application information between components as needed with very few restrictions. Though most distributed component environments provide some type of communication facility, in the past these facilities were difficult to use and had a number of restrictions.

J2EE provides a number of different facilities that provide communication between distributed components, including Enterprise JavaBeans (EJBs), network sockets with object serialization, remote procedure calls (Java-RPC), and Remote Method Invocation (RMI). Each have their advantages and drawbacks, and deciding which J2EE technology to use and when to use it is an important part of architecting good solutions with J2EE.

RMI builds on the networking capabilities of Java, such as platform-independent primitive data types and object serialization, and extends these features by not only allowing Java objects to be transmitted over the network but also allowing their methods to be invoked over the network. RMI is also an enabling technology, forming the foundation for important Java technologies such as EJBs and Jini.

In this chapter we will examine Java RMI and discuss some of the reasons why this technology can make a good choice in developing a J2EE solution. We will discuss the pros and cons of RMI versus other solutions, and detail the development of an RMI application through the course of several examples.

THE CONCEPT OF REMOTE OBJECTS

The notion of remote objects is not new. Remote objects are an extension of remote communication, allowing two applications or components to communicate using a network layer. While remote procedure calls (RPCs) also allow communication, they do not map neatly into an object-oriented environment. Java RMI was designed to work with Java objects and build on such Java features as object serialization, Java type safety, Java security mechanisms, and garbage collection with the RMI-Java Remote Method (JRMP) protocol.

Using remote objects incurs a cost. Network communications can be expensive, and there are security issues involved. It is imperative that we apply some control over this process. This is accomplished with RMI by using a proxy object to manage the details of the communication process. This is an effective implementation of the proxy design pattern, which, as we will see shortly, involves the use of a generated *stub* class to provide access to our communication surrogate, our proxy.

Java RMI provides a mechanism that not only allows objects to communicate (which can be done without RMI just using network sockets) but allows objects to invoke methods on other objects. The methods being invoked may be objects or Java primitive data types, and can return objects or primitive data types. The design of Java RMI was to make this process as similar to the manipulation of local objects as possible.

The ability to send and receive objects in a type-safe environment is significant. While other languages may provide this capability, they generally require additional coding and data type translations to allow it to be done in a platform-independent manner. But the design of the Java environment greatly simplifies the process of object communication with Java objects.

THE RMI FRAMEWORK

Before we take a look at using RMI, it is useful to understand the underlying framework of RMI and how the communication protocol fits into this framework. Understanding this framework will help in understanding the development process for RMI applications.

RMI applications work with what are commonly referred to as a *stub* and *skeleton*. Though the skeleton has become optional following the JDK 1.2, it is still a useful part of the RMI discussion (see Figure 18–1).

The stub acts as a proxy and implements what we refer to as a *proxy design pattern*. The stub contains all of the methods that the remote object is exposing. The client can call the methods on the stub just as if the remote object were a local object. The stub handles the details of the network communication, the security, and the serialization of parameters and return values. Specifically, the stub performs the following actions when a remote method is invoked.

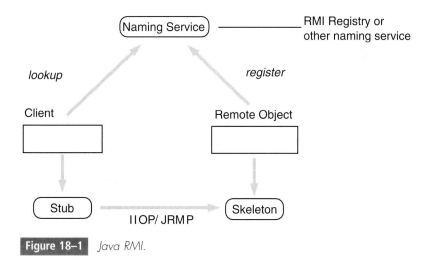

Figure 18–1 *Java RMI.*

- Initiates the connection to the remote object, if required.
- Serializes any object parameters.
- Writes parameters to the network connection for the remote object.
- Listens for response from the remote object.
- Reads return values.
- Deserializes any object parameters.
- Returns values to the client.

(The process of serializing and transmitting any parameters or return values is sometimes referred to as *marshalling* and *unmarshalling* of parameters.)

When the RMI client executes remote communication, it merely invokes a method on an object reference. It is clear from viewing the list of actions above that the work performed by the RMI technology is nontrivial.

As we can see from Figure 18–1, we have two major participants in this discussion: the *RMI client* representing the consumer of the remote object's services and the *RMI remote object server* representing the remote object the client wishes to use. Other participants are the naming service, which provides the client with a remote reference to the RMI remote object, and possibly a proxy server for accessing remote objects behind a firewall.

The RMI remote object is a distributed object that exposes some or all of its methods as remote services. These services can be invoked remotely by clients wishing to access those services through a remote reference as implemented by the RMI stub.

The RMI client accesses the services of the remote object using a proxy, the RMI stub. The client may either load the reference to the stub through a lookup to the RMI registry, through some naming service, or using some other programmatic feature such as reading a serialized version of the remote reference from a disk file.

The RMI registry provides the client with the remote object proxy, the RMI stub, which it needs to access the remote object. Sun Microsystems provides a default (and minimal) implementation of a naming service (`rmiregistry`), which allows object binding and lookups, but this implementation is not particularly robust; the use of a better naming service, such as LDAP or NDIS, is supported by RMI and is recommended.

RMI currently supports two communication protocols: JRMP and the Internet Inter-ORB Protocol (IIOP). The IIOP protocol support was added after the initial release of RMI to provide better interoperability with the Common Object Request Broker Architecture (CORBA) object servers and to make it easier for application server vendors (most of whom supported IIOP) to implement EJBs (which are based on RMI). Sun has committed to supporting both protocols in the future.

Objects passed to remote methods using RMI are passed by value with the exception of remote references (references to other remote objects). This can be problematic for an application that has taken advantage of the Java pass-by-reference mechanism for object references. (Technically, the object reference is passed by value, but one could argue that the instance members of the object are being passed by reference.) Developers should be aware of this difference in behavior and program accordingly.

BUILDING AN RMI APPLICATION

Unlike the other J2EE APIs we've examined before RMI, creating and running an RMI application is a multistep process that requires creating classes and interfaces, generating skeletons and stubs and running the remote object server. The steps involved are as follows.

- Create an interface that extends the `Remote` interface.
- Code the server to extend the appropriate RMI server object (`RemoteObject` or `UnicastRemoteObject`) and implement the `Remote` interface we've extended in the previous step.
- Code the client to use the interface created in step 1.
- Compile all classes.
- Run `rmic` to create stubs and possibly create skeletons.
- Start RMI registry or naming service and bind `Remote` objects into registry.
- Start RMI remote object (the server).
- Run RMI client object.

In the following sections we will examine each of these steps and ultimately demonstrate RMI through a code example which uses RMI to provide information on the status of orders at a fictitious movie store.

Create a Remote Interface and Code the Remote Object Server

The first step is to create an interface that identifies the remote methods that will be called by the application. This implies that we have identified the methods of a server class (which is implied in the steps outlined above) and we know which of these methods we wish to expose remotely. Note that not all server methods must be exposed remotely; only those methods that the client must call need to be exposed. The declaration for a remote interface is as follows.

```
public interface MyRemote extends java.rmi.Remote {

public String doSomething( String something )
```

```
        throws RemoteException;
...
```

The remote interface must extend the `java.rmi.Remote` interface. Any method parameters declared in the remote interface must be Java primitive data types or must be serializable objects (`java.lang.String` is serializable). Any method return values have the same requirements.

The remote object server must then be coded. This Java class must extend the appropriate class in the `java.rmi.server` package: `UnicastRemoteObject`, `RemoteObject`, `Activatable` (as of JDK 1.2), or `RemoteServer`. The most common approach is to extend `UnicastRemoteObject`. The `RemoteServer` and `RemoteObject` classes are abstract classes, which require specific methods be implemented. These classes are useful when the behavior of these methods must be customized—for example, when providing a custom implementation of `RemoteServer getLog` method to customize logging operations for a remote object. Logically enough, since it is expected to provide a remote implementation of these methods, the remote object class should also implement the remote interface declared in step 1. An example of the declaration for the remote object server is as follows.

```
public class MyRemoteObject extends java.rmi.UnicastRemoteObject implements the
MyRemote {
...
```

Code RMI Client to Use the Remote Interface

An RMI client class does not have any specific design requirements. The only requirement is that it must obtain a remote object reference for the remote object it wishes to access. This reference will be used in the class with the type of the interface created in step 1. The most common approach to obtaining the remote reference is to use a naming service. An example of using the RMI naming service is shown below.

```
...
    MyRemote remote = (MyRemote)
        Naming.lookup("//localhost:1099/myRemote");
    System.out.println( remote.doSomething( "Art" ) );
...
```

In this example, the stub for the `MyRemote` class, which is a Java class file, must be in the classpath of the remote client. Once the remote object reference has been obtained by the client class, the methods in the object can be invoked just as though they were being executed by the local object.

Compile All Classes and Run the RMI Compiler to Create Stubs and Skeletons

All classes must then be compiled using the Java compiler. This will result in a set of classes files that must then be compiled using the RMI compiler (`rmic`). The RMI compiler is commonly run against the remote object class using the following command-line argument (shown for a class declared in the default package).

```
rmi MyRemoteObject
```

Running this command would generate a class file named `MyRemoteObject_Stub.class` and a class file named `MyRemoteObject_Skel.class`. (The RMI compiler takes a number of different arguments, which are beyond the scope of this discussion.)

The stub class must be made available to the RMI client application in order for the client to be able to use the remote object. This class can either be passed to the client by the naming service (as we will see shortly), or it can be available to the client by being located in the client's classpath. The operation of the RMI codebase property affects how this stub class is loaded and is one of the more interesting aspects of RMI, which will be covered later in Chapter 19, "Additional RMI Concepts."

Start the Registry and Bind Remote Objects

Before a remote object can be accessed by the RMI client, the remote object reference must be available to the client. This reference is usually obtained by the client through a naming service, as shown previously. Before the naming service can provide the remote reference, it must be bound into the namespace. With the RMI registry, this binding can be accomplished by writing a Java application that contains the following code.

```
...
MyRemoteObject myRemote = new MyRemoteObject();
Naming.rebind( "myRemote", myRemote );
...
```

Other naming services can be used for accessing RMI remote objects. The process for binding remote objects into these servers will be shown in Chapter 19.

To state the obvious, the naming service must be running in order to be able to bind the remote object into the sever. For the RMI registry naming service on UNIX, this would entail running the `rmiregistry` program in the background.

Start the RMI Remote Object and Run the RMI Client

Before the remote client can access the remote object, the remote object must be running along with the naming service or the RMI registry. The client is then run against the remote object. As mentioned previously, the RMI stub class must be visible to the client application.

USING JAVA RMI

Invoking a remote object requires information to be gathered about that remote object. Rather than require that information to be deployed with every component that wishes to invoke the remote object, Java RMI allows a remote object to be located in a registry and the information about the object—itself encapsulated in an object—can be retrieved from the registry. Retrieving an object may involve not just serializing the object and its members, but loading classes that are not local to the client invoking the remote object. For this reason, Java RMI allows remote classes to be loaded as part of the object retrieval process.

To create a remotely invoked object, the server and client interfaces for the objects must be identified. Since we assume that remote network communication will be performed between the two objects (as opposed to local network communication), we need to make an effort to communicate efficiently. With network communications, this means minimizing the chatter between two objects and communicating in large, efficient blocks rather than in a series of small blocks. Using this approach, it would be better to make a single remote call to retrieve a Java collection with the entire results of a query than to make a series of remote calls on the `get` and `set` methods of an object to retrieve the same results.

Java RMI makes the use of remote objects very similar to the manipulation of local objects, but there are a few notable differences. They are as follows.

- Objects passed to and returned from remote methods are passed by value, with the exception of remote objects, which would conceptually be passed by reference.
- The client interaction with the remote object will be indirect, through a proxy; the client will not be communicating directly with the remote object and thus will not have direct access to any of its members. The client interaction with the server will be through method calls on the proxy.
- The remote object will operate in a different virtual machine than that of the client.

Remote objects are invoked by the client based on a client-side *stub* class. The client can execute the methods of the remote object by proxy using the stub. Any classes required to execute the method are accessed locally (where the JVM will search first), and if the classes are not found there, a codebase property (`java.rmi.server.codebase`) of the remote object is used to search for classes, which are then dynamically downloaded to the client as needed. The codebase is a URL which indicates where classes may be located, a remote version of the local CLASSPATH. (Dynamic downloading of the classes requires an appropriate security policy on the client.)

The process for creating an RMI application involves first identifying the client and remote class. This will most likely be a natural extension of the design process where services are identified and isolated. For a number of these services, which will no doubt be implementing the business logic of the enterprise and controlling access to important resources, remote invocation by client applications is an attractive architectural approach. RMI provides a facility for this remote deployment. (EJBs provide another and will be discussed in Chapters 24, 25 and 26.

RMI CLASSES AND INTERFACES

The Java RMI API consists of a relatively small number of classes, interfaces, and exceptions. Of these classes and interfaces, developers will most likely work with only a very few to create remote objects. The packages that comprise Java RMI and a description of their contents are listed in Table 18–1.

Table 18–1   *Java RMI Packages*

Package	Description
java.rmi	The core package for Java RMI. Contains the Remote interface and a number of the exceptions thrown by RMI applications.
java.rmi.activation	Provides the capability to persist a Java remote object (RMI) and recall the object.
java.rmi.dgc	Provides the ability for RMI to track object usage in the client and invoke distributed garbage collection when the object is no longer in use.
java.rmi.registry	Classes and interfaces that provide access to a registry of remote objects.
java.rmi.server	Provides classes and interfaces that provide the ability to create and access an RMI server.

The java.rmi Package

Of these packages, the most commonly used are the `java.rmi` and the `java.rmi.server`. The `java.rmi` package contains the core classes and interfaces used to implement Java remote objects and clients. The classes and interfaces in this package are listed in Table 18–2.

Table 18–2   *Interfaces and Classes in the java.rmi Package*

Interface/Class	Description
Remote	An interface that is extended and used to mark the remote methods that will be invoked by the RMI server object.
Naming	This class provides access to the registry naming service to allow access to references to remote objects.
MarshalledObject	This class represents the serialized representation of an object transferred using RMI.
RMISecurityManager	This class implements a security manager, which can be used to secure RMI applications.

As mentioned previously, in developing an RMI application, we must create an interface that identifies the methods that will be invoked remotely. This Java interface is identified by extending a common interface, the `java.rmi.Remote` interface. This interface is a marker interface and does not require the implementation of any methods.

The `Naming` class provides access to the simple naming service that supports Java RMI: the registry. This class provides methods to bind, rebind, and unbind names and associated remote objects into the namespace. A registry may be shared among a number of users, or a remote object may create its own registry and provide object access through that registry. RMI can also be used with other naming services.

The `MarshalledObject` class is used internally in RMI to represent the objects transferred (by value) using remote method invocations and in establishing the RMI activation system. The `RMISecurityManager` provides a security manager that will, if the appropriate security permissions have been set, allow classes to be downloaded from remote locations. Downloading classes over networked connections significantly increases the potential for a security compromise, since downloaded classes will execute on the local machine. As usual, Java defaults to restrictive security and will not allow this security hole to exist unless the user specifically allows it to exist. To allow remote class loading, a `SecurityManager` (extends `java.lang.SecurityManager`), which potentially allows this action, must be loaded by the client, and the security policy file must contain an entry that specifically allows the network connection and class loading. The `java.rmi.RMISecurity` manager provides this capability, as will be demonstrated later in this chapter.

The java.rmi.server Package

The `java.rmi.server` package contains the classes and interfaces used to create a remote object server, an object that will allow connections and remote execution of its methods. The interfaces listed in Table 18–3 are part of the `java.rmi.server` package.

Table 18–3 *The java.rmi.server Interfaces*

Interface	Description
RemoteRef	An interface which represents the handle for a remote object.
RMIClientSocketFactory	An interface which, when implemented, is used by RMI to obtain client sockets.
RMIFailureHandler	An interface which can be implemented and registered to handle certain RMI failures.
RMIServerSocketFactory	An interface implemented to provide server sockets for the RMI runtime.
ServerRef	An interface that represents a reference to the server side of a remote object implementation.
Unreferenced	If implemented, this interface allows the object to receive notification that no more clients have references to the object.

The majority of the interfaces identified above are implemented by the RMI provider and usually are not used by the developer in creating RMI remote objects and clients. In some cases specific implementations of these interfaces can be used to provide customized behavior to RMI applications. For example, to control the selection of communication ports by RMI, implementations of the `RMIServerSocketFactory` and `RMIClientSocketFactory` can be provided, which select from a set of one or more previously designated ports.

The `java.rmi.server` package contains the classes and interfaces used to implement the RMI remote object server. These classes are listed in Table 18–4.

Table 18–4   *The java.rmi.server Classes*

Class	Description
ObjID	A final class which provides an ID which identifies a remote object that has been exported.
RemoteObject	An abstract class, which is the base class, similar to the java.lang.Object class, for remote objects.
RemoteServer	An abstract class which is the superclass for RMI server implementations.
RemoteStub	An abstract class which is the common superclass of all remote interface objects in RMI.
RMIClassLoader	Contains static methods which support dynamic class loading using RMI.
RMIClassLoaderSpi	An abstract class whose implementation is responsible for loading the classes specified.
RMISocketFactory	An abstract class whose implementation is used to obtain client and server sockets for RMI.
UID	Generates a unique ID, which can be returned as a string or integer hashcode value.
UnicastRemoteObject	Represents a remote object, which is valid as part of a corresponding server. This class is extended to create RMI server objects.

The UnicastRemoteObject class is the most commonly used of these classes and is extended to create an object server class, which then accepts connections from client objects. Methods exist to export the object and make it available either on an anonymous port as selected by the RMI subsystem or on a specific port.

Other classes in this package are used only to alter the default behavior of RMI, such as in the selection of ports for communication. By default an RMI server chooses a random port to create its connection to client objects. This can be problematic on servers where firewall protection severely limits the ports available for connections. To change this behavior, the RMISocketFactory class could be extended and used to provide connections only on specific ports. An example of this approach is shown in the next chapter.

RMI Examples

Coding services in RMI is simpler than developing similar solutions with RPCs or simple network sockets, but it is unfortunately not a simple one-step process. As we discovered previously, at the very least, three separate Java source files must be created to implement RMI for an object. They are as follows.

- An interface that identifies the methods to be invoked remotely
- A class whose instance will implement the remote methods
- A client who will call the remote methods

The process of completing these steps is best shown through an example. To keep it simple and focus on the basics of RMI, the familiar "Hello World" example is used in the following section.

The Hello World RMI Example

The code shown below is the remote interface definition for our first RMI example. As we explained previously, this interface must declare the remote methods that will be exposed to client objects. This example declares a single method, the `helloThere` method, which takes a string argument for a name (which will be used in the response). The method returns a string value and must be declared to throw a `RemoteException`. The arguments to and the return values from any method declared in this interface can be Java primitive data types or objects that are serializable (implementing `java.io.Serializable`), and must conform to the restrictions of serializable objects. The interface itself must extend the `java.rmi.Remote` interface, which is essentially a marker interface and requires no method implementations. Other exceptions may be thrown as needed.

Remote object methods declared in this file must declare that they throw a `RemoteException`. Any program exceptions must be serializable and will be caught by the skeleton and sent to the remote object reference, the proxy, where it is thrown back to the application.

A checked exception will not kill the server object. Throwing an exception or error will not kill the server object, but of course an error rethrown on the client will shut down the client, which will terminate the connection to the server.

The Hello Interface

```
package examples.rmi;

import java.rmi.*;

public interface Hello extends Remote {
```

```
    public String helloThere( String name ) throws RemoteException;
}
```

The Remote Object for Hello World

The remote object class for our first RMI example will act as an object server, exposing a method (a service) to client objects. The interface declared previously identifies those methods. The server class must declare the implementation for those methods. Additional methods may also be declared and used in the server class as needed, but the class must implement the interface shown previously (the remote interface) and of course must implement the methods identified in that interface to create a concrete class. The most common approach to creating a server object is shown here with the extension of the java.rmi.server.UnicastRemoteObject class to provide the functionality needed to create a remote RMI server object. The code example below shows the server object declaration for the "Hello World" example.

In the example shown here, the class extends UnicastRemoteObject and implements the Hello interface, which requires an implementation for the helloThere method. The helloThere method simply accepts the single string argument for the name and returns a salutation with the name concatenated on the salutation string. Note that even though the method is declared to throw a RemoteException, it does not need to do this explicitly, as the exception will be thrown by the RMI runtime environment.

The RMIHello Class

```
package examples.rmi;

import java.rmi.*;
import java.rmi.server.*;
import java.io.*;

import RMIExample.*;

public class RMIHello extends UnicastRemoteObject implements Hello {

public RMIHello() throws RemoteException { super(); }

public String helloThere( String name ) throws RemoteException {

        return "Hello there, " + name + ".";

}

}
```

Binding Remote Objects

Before the client can access the remote object, it must be bound into the RMI registry. This is accomplished using the few lines of code shown below.

```
...
System.out.println("binding RMIHello");
RMIHello hello = new RMIHello();
Naming.rebind( "hello", hello );
...
```

The server objects must be bound into the registry each time it is used. For this reason, when using the registry server, it is useful to create a bootstrap program to bind all required objects into the registry server. Alternatively, an RMI application can call the `LocateRegistry createRegistry` method to create its own registry and bind its remote objects as needed, or an RMI server could implement RMI activation in which case the object server would be launched as they are requested (RMI activation is demonstrated in chapter 19).

The Client Object for Hello World

The client object for the "Hello World" example must somehow obtain a reference for the server object. This involves using a simple naming service provided by the RMI package. The objects provided through this service are not persistent; that is, they do not retain state information. (The `java.rmi.activation` package does provide a mechanism for managing remote object persistence.)

In the code listing shown below, the first step is to install a security manager, which will allow class downloading from remote hosts (as mentioned previously, Java does not allow this by default). The code first checks to see if a security manager is installed, and if none is installed, it installs the `RMISecurityManager`.

The reference to the remote object is retrieved from an RMI naming service, a registry that associates names with remote object references. The `java.rmi.Naming` class provides access to this registry and can be used to locate the remote object using the `lookup` method. This method is passed a URL with the following format,

```
//host:port/remote_object_name
```

where the host name (or the IP address) is provided along with a specific port where the connection to the naming service will be made. The name of the remote object is any arbitrary name assigned to the object when it is bound into the RMI registry (which will be discussed soon). The reference to the remote object is retrieved, and since the `Naming lookup` method is defined to return an `Object` reference, which is not particularly useful, the reference is cast to the remote inter-face type, the `Hello` interface. The type being returned is what was bound into the RMI registry, a type that must extend the `java.rmi.Remote` interface. Once this example has retrieved the reference to the remote object, the reference is used as any other Java object would be used to invoke a method using the reference, the `helloThere` method.

The RMIClient Class

```
package examples.rmi;

import java.rmi.*;

public class RMIClient {

public static void main( String args[] ) {

// get hello Object through naming service
try {

if ( System.getSecurityManager() == null ) {
    System.setSecurityManager( new RMISecurityManager() );
}

Hello hello = (Hello) Naming.lookup("//localhost:1099/hello");
System.out.println( hello.helloThere( "Art" ) );

}
catch (RemoteException e) {
   System.out.println("RemoteException in main: " + e.getMessage() );

}

}

}
```

The policy file used by the client that is invoking the `RMISecurityManager` must contain an entry granting specific network permis-sions. A standard Java security policy is used, which identifies the hostname (or IP address) for the connection and the port or ports that will be used for the connec-tions. (The Java security policy file was discussed in Chapter 8, "Java Security.") This example allows TCP/IP socket access on the `sunwise` host on ports greater than 1024. Permission is granted to accept connections, to listen for connections, and to connect to the specified host on the specified ports. (The permission to resolve the host name is implied by connect, accept, and listen.)

Security Policy File

```
grant {
      permission java.net.SocketPermission
            "sunwise:1024-", "accept, listen, connect";
};
```

To have the Java application use this policy file, it must be identified on the command line as the security policy file to use. The syntax for doing that is as follows.

```
java -Djava.security.policy=security.policy
```

Alternatively, the application could be allowed to default to the security policy file in its home directory (usually named .java.policy), or the application could be directed to load a security policy file by using the System setProperty method within the application (if the installed security manager allows system properties to be changed), as shown in the code fragment below.

```
...
//
// set a specific and restrictive security policy
// for this application
//
System.setProperty(
      "java.security.policy", "network_security.policy" );
...
```

USING THE RMI REGISTRY

Any client object using RMI must be able to locate the remote object server. This can be accomplished in several ways. One approach is to use the RMI registry, which is the approach used in the previous examples. The RMI registry is a program included with the JDK named rmiregistry. This program is invoked from the command line using the following syntax.

```
rmiregistry <runtime_options> <port>
```

The runtime options are options that are passed to the Java runtime environment. The port is the port where the registry will listen for connections. The default port for the RMI registry is 1099. To have the RMI registry listen on port 1100 instead of port 1099, the following could be issued from the command line.

```
rmiregistry 1100
```

The code listing below shows the process of binding several remote objects into the registry. Since the RMI registry does not create persistent references, this bootstrap process must be done each time the RMI registry is started. An alternative is to use the RMI activation system, where various properties for RMI are stored and then activated (registered) when the RMI registry system is started.

In this example, an object is instantiated for each of the remote objects that will be bound in the RMI naming service. The objects are then passed into the `Naming rebind` methods as the second argument. The first argument to this method is the name that will be used by clients to retrieve the remote object.

The objects are automatically cast to the required type as method arguments, and in this case, the `Naming rebind` method requires the second argument, the object reference, to implement the `java.rmi.Remote` interface.

These examples use a shortened URL to identify the RMI registry. The name being associated with the remote objects as the first argument to the `Naming rebind` method is a URL without the host name and port (`//hostname:port./remote_object_name`). When these entries are eliminated from the URL, the default host (local host) and the default port (port 1099) are used.

The bindObjs Class

```
package examples.rmi;

import java.rmi.Naming;
import java.rmi.RemoteException;
import java.net.MalformedURLException;

import RMIExample.*;

public class bindObjs {

public static void main( String args[] ) {

try {

  //
  // binding the RMIHello remote object
  //
  RMIHello hello = new RMIHello();
  Naming.rebind( "hello", hello );

  //
  // bind the OrderStatusServer
  //
  OrderStatusServer orderStatus =
     new OrderStatusServer();
   Naming.rebind( "orderStatus", orderStatus );
```

```
    //
    // bind the OrderStatusThreadServer
    //
    OrderStatusThreadServer orderStatusThreads =
                new OrderStatusThreadServer();
    Naming.rebind( "orderStatusThreadServer",
                orderStatusThreads );

}
catch (RemoteException e) {
  System.out.println(
            "RemoteException in main: " + e.getMessage() );
}
catch (MalformedURLException e) {
  System.out.println(
            "RemoteException in main: " + e.getMessage() );
}

} // end main

}
```

AN RMI ORDER STATUS SERVER

RMI allows service objects to be created and made available to one or more Java applications that may require that service. One possible application of RMI is to use it as an informational gateway, providing simplified access to what may be a complex subsystem. The following application demonstrates such a solution.

The example shown below uses an RMI server object to expose an order status information object, which when passed an order number, returns an object that encapsulates the order status information for that order.

The single method exposed to client objects is identified in the Java interface shown below. The OrderStatus object returned is part of the movies.control package (an example developed for this book) and implements the java.io.Serializable interface.

OrderStatusIntf.java

```
package examples.rmi;

import java.rmi.*;

import movies.control.OrderStatus;

public interface OrderStatusIntf extends Remote {
```

```
public OrderStatus getOrderStatus( String orderNumber )
       throws RemoteException;

}
```

The OrderStatusServer Class

The `OrderStatusServer` class performs the work necessary to respond to the service request from the client: to return order status information for the order number specified. This remote object implementation delegates the work to determine the order status to an `OrderProcessing` object, which contains the business logic and database access code to determine the order status. The `OrderProcessing` object is instantiated in the `OrderStatusServer` constructor when the remote object is created.

The `getOrderStatus` method accepts a string argument for the order status to retrieve and then calls the `OrderProcessing` `getOrderStatus` method to return the order status in an `OrderStatus` object. Note that we place the call to the `getOrderStatus` method in a `synchronized` block. This is because the RMI specification does not guarantee thread safety of invoked methods. An invoked method may or may not be run in a separate thread, so calls on the same object method from different clients may run concurrently, and object state could become compromised. This class has delegated the processing of order status to the `OrderProcessing` class, which is not thread-safe (it was written assuming that each client class would obtain a separate copy of the object). We must therefore guarantee thread-safe access or our `OrderProcessing` information by using a `synchronized` block around the critical method invocation.

The constructor for the server first calls the superclass constructor (an important step here, since the `UnicastRemoteObject` superclass must establish this object as a remote object). Next it creates the `processor` object, an instance of the `OrderProcessing` class.

The class constructor for the `OrderProcessing` class performs a bit of work, creating connections to two databases and preparing several database queries, so it is worthwhile to create this object once, before it is used, and to then reuse it each time the remote object is called.

OrderStatusServer.java

```
package examples.rmi;

import java.rmi.*;
import java.rmi.server.*;
import java.io.*;

import org.apache.log4j.Category;
```

```
import movies.control.OrderStatus;
import movies.control.OrderProcessing;
import service.*;

public class OrderStatusServer extends
        UnicastRemoteObject implements OrderStatusIntf {

private static Category logger =
        LoggingService.getLogger( "OrderStatusServer" );
private OrderProcessing processor;

public OrderStatus getOrderStatus( String orderNumber ) throws RemoteException {

    //
    // the OrderProcessing service object will
    // determine the order status
    //
synchronized (this) {
    return processor.getOrderStatus( orderNumber);
}

}

public OrderStatusServer() throws RemoteException {
  super();

  //
  // create our OrderProcessing object
  //
  processor = new OrderProcessing();
  //
  // log our start message
  //
  logger.info( "OrderStatusServer has started." );
}

}
```

The OrderStatusClient Class

The OrderStatusClient class accesses the OrderStatusServer remote object and requests the status information for a particular order. The main program block contains the code to create an RMISecurityManager and then executes the naming lookup call to retrieve the reference to the remote object. The object reference returned is cast as an OrderStatusIntf object, the interface that defines the method signature for the getStatus method.

The reference returned from the `lookup` method (the server object) is then used to retrieve the status information using the `getStatus` call—`server.getOrderStatus( "112233" )`—which is output to the console.

OrderStatusClient.java

```
package examples.rmi;

import java.rmi.*;

import movies.control.*;

public class OrderStatusClient  {

public static void main(String[] args ) {

try {

if ( System.getSecurityManager() == null ) {
    System.setSecurityManager(
        new RMISecurityManager() );
}

OrderStatusClient client = new OrderStatusClient();

OrderStatusIntf server = (OrderStatusIntf)
        Naming.lookup( "//localhost:1099/orderStatus" );

System.out.println(
        "Current order status for order 112233: \n" +
        server.getOrderStatus( "112233" ) );
System.out.println(
        "Current order status for order 223344: \n" +
        server.getOrderStatus( "223344" ) );
System.out.println(
        "Current order status for order 445566: \n" +
        server.getOrderStatus( "445566" ) );

}
catch (RemoteException e) {
      System.out.println("RemoteException in main: " + e);
}
catch (NotBoundException e) {
      System.out.println(
          "NotBoundException in main: " + e);
}
catch (java.net.MalformedURLException e) {
      System.out.println(
          "MalformedURLException in main: " + e);
}
```

```
}


}
```

   The return value from the `getOrderStatus` method is an `OrderStatus` object. The `toString` method for the `OrderStatus` class has been overridden to provide meaningful output, which is shown below.

```
Current order status for order 112233:
        Order number: 112233
        Ship date: 2001-02-03
        Status code: SHIPPED
        Ship to ID: S235
        Quantity: 20

Current order status for order 223344:
        Order number: 223344
        Ship date: 2001-02-04
        Status code: BACKORDERED
        Ship to ID: S333
        Quantity: 40

Current order status for order 445566:
        Order number: 445566
        Ship date: null
        Status code: CANCELLED
        Ship to ID: null
        Quantity: 0
```

SUMMARY

As we saw in this chapter, RMI is a mature technology that provides basic distributed object facilities. Using RMI, you can create an object that can be invoked remotely by one or more client programs.

In this chapter we discussed the framework for RMI and how this framework is used to provide the ability to access an object's methods over a network. We saw that RMI remote method parameters must either be primitive data types or serializable objects. After discussing the process for building an RMI application, we demonstrated the basic capabilities for using RMI first with an academic demonstration followed by a more complex, business-oriented sample application.

But RMI can do still more, as we will see in the next chapter, where we examine RMI callbacks, remote objects that create their own registries, RMI activation and the use of the codebase parameter with RMI.

CHAPTER 19

Additional RMI Concepts

INTRODUCTION

In the previous chapter we were introduced to Java RMI. We reviewed the framework of RMI framework and the interaction between the RMI client and the remote object it is using. But RMI is not limited to simple invocation of objects. As we will demonstrate in this chapter, an RMI remote object can make calls back to the client which invoked it, and it can provide its own registry services or export its remote reference to a naming service other than the default RMI registry.

The RMI implementations we saw in the previous chapter had to be running in order for the client to retrieve the reference for the object and invoke its methods. But for some RMI implementations this may not be the optimal approach. RMI activation, as demonstrated in this chapter, allows an RMI object to be started based on client calls to the object.

USING RMI CALLBACKS

Most remote object invocations use one-way invocation; the client obtains a remote object reference and makes calls on the methods of that remote reference. But sometimes it is convenient to provide two-way communication with a server object, allowing a client to make a call on a server object and having the server object respond to the client using a *callback* method. An efficient implementation of such a remote server would use internal multithreading to manage the clients. The following example demonstrates such an approach.

In this example we have a client application that would like to monitor orders as they are shipped. To implement this solution, we will register the client applications with the server to receive status updates. In order for the server object to notify the clients of status updates, the server will need to execute callbacks on the client application (see Figure 19–1).

To provide status updates, the server object runs a thread that executes a query to examine the state of all existing orders by examining two tables in the stock database. The results of this query are then sent to the various clients who have registered with the server. An internal thread within the server waits for a predetermined interval and then scans the list of clients and distributes order status information to the clients in the list.

As we know from the previous chapter, there are several class files that need to be written for the RMI object. We will examine these class files in the following sections.

The StatusClientThreadIntf Class

Since we have a server that interacts with a client, we need an interface for the remote object (the server) and the client that receives callbacks from the server. The code sample below shows the interface for the client callback in this example. This exposes the `sendStatus` method, which the remote object server uses to send the order status results to the client.

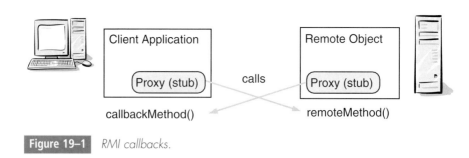

Figure 19–1   *RMI callbacks.*

The StatusClientThreadIntf Class

```
package examples.rmi;

import java.rmi.Remote;
import java.rmi.RemoteException;
import java.util.Collection;
import movies.control.OrderStatus;

public interface StatusClientThreadIntf extends Remote {

public void sendStatus( Collection status )
                    throws RemoteException;

}
```

The OrderStatusThreadIntf Interface

The server also exposes a remote interface, as shown below. This interface expos-es a single method, the setRemote method, which is used to identify the remote client (the client that receives the callback from the server). This method accepts a single argument, the remote reference to the client program.

The OrderStatusThreadIntf Class

```
package examples.rmi;

import java.rmi.*;

import movies.control.OrderStatus;

public interface OrderStatusThreadIntf extends Remote {

public void setRemote( StatusClientThreadIntf client )
            throws RemoteException;

}
```

The OrderStatusThreadServer Class

The server class for this example is the OrderStatusThreadServer as shown in the code listing below. This class becomes the remote object that accepts calls from clients to register to receive order processing updates. Since the code also uses Java multithreading, it implements the Runnable interface.

The object accepts calls from the client through the setRemote method, which is passed a single argument: the reference to the client instance (an object reference that implements the `StatusClientThreadIntf`). The method adds this reference to an internal collection of client references. The method code then tests to see if the internal processing thread has been created, and if it has not, it is created and the internal thread is started.

The OrderStatusThreadServer Class

```
package examples.rmi;

import java.rmi.RemoteException;
import java.rmi.server.UnicastRemoteObject;

import java.util.Vector;
import java.util.Collection;
import org.apache.log4j.Category;
import movies.control.OrderStatus;
import movies.control.OrderProcessing;
import service.LoggingService;

public class OrderStatusThreadServer
            extends UnicastRemoteObject
                implements OrderStatusThreadIntf, Runnable {

private static Category logger =
            LoggingService.getLogger(
                                "OrderStatusServer" );


private OrderProcessing processor;

private long sleepInterval = 5000;

private StatusClientThreadIntf client;
private Vector clients = new Vector();
private Thread clientThread;

public void setRemote( StatusClientThreadIntf client ) {

clients.add( client );

//
// if we haven't started the thread, then start it
//
if ( clientThread == null ) {
    clientThread = new Thread( this );
    clientThread.start();
}


}
```

The OrderStatusThreadServer Class: The run Method

The run method is called by the Java runtime to execute a thread within the object. In our example, as shown in the code listing below, this method is used to first get the current order status information and then update the various clients connected to the remote object.

The method declares a boolean variable that is used to control an enclosing while loop. As long as the boolean tests true, the while loop (and the thread controlling processing and posting of order status) will continue. Any failure, either a RemoteException or an InterruptedException, will end the processing loop.

Within the while loop, the Thread sleep method is called. This method is passed a long integer, which represents the number of milliseconds to sleep (stop execution) before continuing. In this example, a parameter of 5,000 milliseconds, roughly five seconds, is passed to the sleep method.

When the thread wakes from its sleep state, the current order status information is retrieved using the OrderProcessing getOrderStatus method. This method retrieves the status of all orders currently entered in the system. This information is returned in a Collection object (a Vector class instance, which is serializable).

The client's object is a Vector that stores all current clients that have requested updates of order status information. For each element in the Vector, the get method is called to retrieve the object reference stored in the vector. This reference is cast as a StatusClientThreadIntf (the remote interface for the client callback method), and the client sendStatus method is called. This sends the status information back to the client.

The constructor for the OrderStatusThreadServer is also shown below. This constructor is used to call the constructor for its superclass (the UnicastRemoteObject class). Then, an instance of the OrderProcessing class is created, and an entry is written to the log indicating that processing for the remote object has been started.

The OrderStatusThreadServer Class: The run Method

```
public void run() {

boolean continueProcessing = true;

while ( continueProcessing ) {

   try {

      Thread.sleep( sleepInterval );
      //
      // get the current order status
```

```
      //
      Collection status  = processor.getOrderStatus();

       //
       // update our clients with the current status
       //
       for ( int n = 0; n < clients.size(); n++ ) {

               StatusClientThreadIntf client =
                  (StatusClientThreadIntf)
                       clients.get( n );

               //
               // execute the client callback method
               //
               client.sendStatus( status );

          }
      }
      catch (RemoteException e) {
        logger.error( "RemoteException: " + e );
        continueProcessing = false;
      }
      catch (InterruptedException e) {
        logger.error( "InterruptedException: " + e );
        continueProcessing = false;
      }

   } // end while


   public OrderStatusThreadServer() throws RemoteException {
      super();

      processor = new OrderProcessing();

      logger.info( "OrderStatusServer has started." );

   }

   }
```

The OrderStatusClientThread Class

The `OrderStatusClientThread` class communicates with the object server (the `OrderStatusThreadServer` remote instance) and requests that it be made a client (effectively a remote object) for the server object. This client program then starts a thread to monitor for updates with the remote object server. When an update of the order status is received, it displays the output of the order status.

The output from this application is written to the console. A possible implementation, not shown here for brevity, would be to output the results of the monitor operation to a GUI application (Java Swing, Applet, Web Start) or update the session information for a Java servlet.

The main program block in the listing below contains the code that calls the Naming lookup method to retrieve the remote reference to the OrdersStatusThreadServer remote object. The program then creates an instance of the OrderStatusClientThread.

The server reference is then used to call the setRemote method, passing the client reference (the reference to this object) to the remote object. The remote object stores the reference in its internal collection and later uses the reference to make a callback to the client.

OrderStatusClientThread Class

```
package examples.rmi;

import java.rmi.Remote;
import java.rmi.RemoteException;
import java.rmi.NotBoundException;
import java.rmi.server.UnicastRemoteObject;
import java.rmi.Naming;
import java.util.Collection;
import java.util.Iterator;

import org.apache.log4j.Category;

// local
import movies.control.OrderStatus;
import service.LoggingService;


public class OrderStatusClientThread extends UnicastRemoteObject
   implements Runnable, Remote, StatusClientThreadIntf, java.io.Serializable {

private static Category logger = LoggingService.getLogger( "OrderStatusClientThread"
);

private Collection status;
private long sleepInterval = 5000;
private String clientName;

private boolean received;

public static void main(String[] args ) {

try {

  //
```

```
   // lookup the remote object
   //
   OrderStatusThreadIntf server =
              (OrderStatusThreadIntf) Naming.lookup(
       "//localhost:1099/orderStatusThreadServer" );

   //
   // get an instance of us
   //
   OrderStatusClientThread client = new
             OrderStatusClientThread();

   //
   // register this object reference with
   // the remote server
   //
   logger.info( "Registering as a client with server." );
   server.setRemote( client );

}
catch (RemoteException e) {
      logger.error("RemoteException in main: " + e);
}
catch (NotBoundException e) {
      logger.error("NotBoundException in main: " + e);
}
catch (java.net.MalformedURLException e) {
      logger.error("MalformedURLException in main: " + e);}

}
```

The OrderStatusClientThread Class

The `sendStatus` method shown below is the callback method provided to the remote object reference for dispersal of order status information. Depending on the setting of the interval in the remote object server, this method is called periodically to update the order status information.

The `sendStatus` information receives a collection object, which contains all `OrderStatus` records for the current set of orders in the stock database. In this example the information collected is output into the console.

The OrderStatusClientThread Class: The sendStatus and run Methods

```
//
// This is the remote method provided to the 'server'
// remote object
// for callbacks.
//
```

```
// Will be called by the server every 5 seconds to display
// the status of all orders.
//
//
// this will be called by the server every few seconds to update
// the status of all orders
//
public void sendStatus( Collection status )
        throws RemoteException {


//
// assign this as our current order status
//
this.status = status;
this.received = true;

Iterator i = status.iterator();
while ( i.hasNext() ) {
        System.out.println( "Order status: \n" + (OrderStatus) i.next() );

}
```

The output of running the previous program is shown below. The program lists the contents of the OrderStatus object for each order that has been posted to the stock database.

Output of the OrderStatusClientThread Program

```
Order status:
        Order number: 112233
        Ship date: 2001-02-03
        Status code: SHIPPED
        Ship to ID: S235
        Quantity: 20

Order status:
        Order number: 223344
        Ship date: 2001-02-04
        Status code: BACKORDERED
        Ship to ID: S333
        Quantity: 40

Order status:
        Order number: 445566
        Ship date: null
        Status code: CANCELLED
        Ship to ID: null
        Quantity: 0

Order status:
```

```
Order number: 112233
Ship date: 2001-02-03
Status code: SHIPPED
Ship to ID: S235
Quantity: 20
```

```
Order status:
Order number: 223344
Ship date: 2001-02-04
Status code: BACKORDERED
Ship to ID: S333
Quantity: 40
```

```
Order status:
Order number: 445566
Ship date: null
Status code: CANCELLED
Ship to ID: null
Quantity: 0
```

The OrderProcessing Object

The `OrderProcessing` object takes responsibility for executing the business logic involved in determining the status of existing orders. The `getOrderStatus` method shown below retrieves the order status information, loads the information into the `OrderStatus` objects, and loads the `OrderStatus` objects into a collection. Ultimately, the collection is returned by the method. The `OrderStatus` information is retrieved using a JDBC prepared statement, which returns all orders regardless of date. (A more production-oriented solution would filter by date or some other criteria.)

In the `getOrderStatus` method a `Vector` object and a reference to hold the order are created. The prepared statement, which will query the database, is then executed and the `ResultSet` representing the results is retrieved.

A `while` loop is then used to iterate through the results, and for each row in the `ResultSet`, an `OrderStatus` object is created and loaded with the contents of the row. Once the `OrderStatus` object has been loaded, it is added to the `Vector` object, which is then returned by the method.

The OrderProcessing Class: The getOrderStatus Method

```
...
public Collection getOrderStatus(  ) {
//
// retrieve the status of ALL orders
// return a null reference if not found
//
Vector returnAll = new Vector();
```

```
OrderStatus status = null;
try {

ResultSet rs = pstmtOrderStatusAll.executeQuery();

while ( rs.next() ) {    // we have results
    status = new OrderStatus();

    //
    // load the order status object
    //
    status.setOrderNumber( rs.getString( "order_number" ) );
    status.setShipToID( rs.getString( "ship_to_id" ) );
    status.setQuantity( rs.getInt( "quantity" ) );
    status.setShipDate( rs.getDate( "ship_date" ) );
    status.setStatusCode( rs.getString( "status_code" ) );

    returnAll.add( status );

}

}
catch (SQLException e ){
    logger.error(
        "OrderProcessing: SQLException in getOrderStatus: " + e );
// ** rollback trans **

}
catch ( Exception e ) {
    logger.error(
        "OrderProcessing: Exception in getOrderStatus: " + e );
    e.printStackTrace();
}

finally {
    return returnAll;
}

}
...
```

Creating RMI Registries in the Remote Object

As indicated previously, one solution to running RMI remote objects requires the RMI registry to be running on the server where the remote object will be requested (where the lookup operation will be performed). The rmiregistry and the remote object must be on the same machine.

The registry entries are not persistent, so each time the registry is started, all remote objects that will be offered through the registry must be bound again. This is usually accomplished using an RMI bootstrap program/script, which starts the RMI registry and then executes a Java program that performs the necessary bindings.

An alternative to using a single registry (rmiregistry) to contain entries for all RMI remote objects to be offered on a system is to have a remote object create its own registry and bind its remote references into that registry. This provides a convenience mechanism that involves running a single program to provide access to a remote service. The code example below demonstrates this process.

This class extends UnicastRemoteObject, as with the previous examples. Where it differs is in the call to the LocateRegistry createRegistry method to create a registry. This call is passed a port number where the registry will listen for connections.

The RMIHello1 Class

```java
package examples.rmi;

import java.rmi.*;
import java.rmi.server.*;
import java.rmi.registry.*;
import java.io.*;

import RMIExample.*;

public class RMIHello1 extends UnicastRemoteObject implements Hello {

public static void main( String args[] ) {

try {

RMIHello1 server = new RMIHello1();

//
// create a registry on port 1100
//
LocateRegistry.createRegistry( 1100 );

//
// bind this remote object there
//
Naming.rebind( "//localhost:1100/RMIHello1", server );

}
catch (RemoteException e) {
    System.err.println(
        "RMIHello1: RemoteException in main: " + e );
}
catch (java.net.MalformedURLException e) {
    System.err.println(
```

```
        "RMIHello1: MalformedURLException in main: " + e );
}

}
// --

public RMIHello1() throws RemoteException {
super();

}

public String helloThere( String name ) throws RemoteException {

        return "Hello there, " + name + ".";

}

}
```

The client class that connects to the `RMIHello1` server looks like previous client classes with one exception: The URL to connect to the server now specifies a different port, port 1100, as shown below. As with the previous examples, this call retrieves the remote reference and then makes the remote method call.

RMIClient1 Class

```
package examples.rmi;

import java.rmi.*;

public class RMIClient1 {

public static void main( String args[] ) {

// get hello Object through naming service
try {

if ( System.getSecurityManager() == null ) {
    System.setSecurityManager(
            new RMISecurityManager() );
}

Hello hello = (Hello) Naming.lookup("//localhost:1100/RMIHello1");
System.out.println( hello.helloThere( "Fred" ) );

}
catch (Exception e) {

  System.out.println("Exception in main: " +
                    e.getMessage() );
```

}

}

}

Restricting RMI to Specific Ports

By default, RMI remote objects listen for connections on a specified port (which can be designated) and then establish return communications through a random port. On secure machines with firewalls, this use of random port numbers may not be possible, since TCP/IP connections may be restricted to a limited number of ports for security reasons. If this is the case, then it may be necessary to limit the ports RMI uses. Fortunately, this can be accomplished with very little pain by providing custom server connection factory and client connection factory implementations when the remote object is exported. The server connection factory is used to provide `java.net.ServerSocket` connections where the server will listen for connections. The client connection factory is used for the creation of socket connections to the client. The `java.rmi.server` package contains classes that must be implemented to gain control over the creation of these sockets. The `RMIServerSocketFactory` interface defines how `ServerSocket` connections will be made, and the `RMIClientSocketFactory` interface defines how client socket connections will be made.

The `java.rmi.server` package contains the `RMISocketFactory` class, which implements both the `RMIServerSocketFactory` and the `RMIClientSocketFactory` interfaces. For convenience, and to avoid implementing a number of methods that we need to alter, the solution presented here simply extends the `RMISocketFactory` class (which implements both `RMIServerSocketFactory` and `RMIClientSocketFactory`) and provides specific implementations for the methods that control the creation of sockets.

The code for the server that uses the remote object with a custom socket factory to limit socket access is shown below. This code reuses the "Hello World" example for simplicity and performs its own bootstrapping operation, exposing the remote object and binding the name into the RMI naming service. Note that the class does not extend `UnicastRemoteObject` in its declaration. This is because it will explicitly export the remote object (an instance of itself) with specific entries for server socket and client socket factories.

The class begins by creating an instance of itself, and then creates a single instance of our custom socket factory. As we will see later in this section, this custom socket factory (the `RestrictiveSocketFactory` class) implements both `RMIServerSocketFactory` and `RMIClientSocketFactory`, and will therefore be used as both a server socket factory and a client socket factory. The `UnicastRemoteObject exportObject` method is called to export the remote object. This static method takes arguments as follows.

```
UnicastRemoteObject exportObject(
            Remote <server_object>,
            int <port_number>,
            RMIClientSocketFactory <client_socket_factory>,
            RMIServerSocketFactory <server_socket_factory>);
```

This method call allows a server object to be exported or exposed on a specific port using specific factory implementations to provide sockets. Since we would like to provide custom socket implementations to restrict port selections, this method provides the control we need.

The `exportObject` method returns a reference to our stub class. This stub object reference reflects the customizations we have performed on our remote object, so it is important that we bind this reference into the RMI namespace.

We create a registry for the object on port 1100 using the `LocateRegistry` `createRegistry` method. A reference to the registry is then retrieved, and the reference is bound to the name `RMIHello2`. As with the previous "Hello World" example, an implementation of the `helloThere` method is provided. This is the method that will be called remotely.

The RMIHello2 Class

```
package examples.rmi;

import java.rmi.*;
import java.rmi.server.*;
import java.rmi.registry.*;

import java.io.*;
import java.net.*;

import RMIExample.*;

public class RMIHello2 implements Hello {

public static void main( String args[] ) {

try {

//
// create our server
//
RMIHello2 server = new RMIHello2();

//
// create our restrictive socket factory
//
RestrictiveSocketFactory sf = new RestrictiveSocketFactory();

//
```

```
// export our remote object to a specific port (1100) and identify
// a client socket factory and server socket factory
//
Hello stub = (Hello) UnicastRemoteObject.exportObject(
                                    server, 1100, sf, sf );

//
// create a registry on port 1100
// and control selection of ports
//
LocateRegistry.createRegistry( 1100 );
Registry registry  = LocateRegistry.getRegistry(1100);

//
// bind our stub object
//
registry.rebind( "RMIHello2", (Hello) stub );

}
catch (RemoteException e) {
      System.err.println("RMIHello2: RemoteException in main: " + e );
      e.printStackTrace();
}

}


public String helloThere( String name ) throws RemoteException {

      return "Hello there, " + name + ".";

}

}
```

The RestrictiveSocketFactory Class

The RestrictiveSocketFactory class shown in the following provides the implementations for the RMIServerSocketFactory and the RMIClient SocketFactory interfaces. This class provides those implementations by extending the RMISocketFactory class, which provides implementations for both interfaces.

Two instance members are declared to identify the ports to be used to provide server sockets and client sockets. These members are assigned default values, which can be overridden using one of the class constructors.

Two methods are called to create sockets for the RMI object server: the createServerSocket method and the createSocket method for the server socket and client socket respectively. Both methods are overridden by this implementation to control the selection of ports.

The `createServerSocket` method accepts an argument with the port number for the server socket to create. This port number is simply ignored, and the method attempts to create a server socket using the value of its member variable (`serverSocket`). If it cannot create the server socket, a null value is returned.

The `createSocket` method takes two arguments: the host name for the socket connection and the port number. The host name is used, but the socket number is ignored in lieu of the value of the instance member (`clientSocket`). If it cannot create the connection, it returns a null reference.

A no-argument constructor is provided, which calls the superclass constructor. An overloaded constructor that takes arguments for the client and server socket numbers is also provided and also calls the constructor for the superclass.

The RestrictiveSocketFactory Class

```
package examples.rmi;

import java.io.*;
import java.net.*;
import java.rmi.server.*;

public class RestrictiveSocketFactory extends RMISocketFactory implements
java.io.Serializable {

private int serverSocket = 1101;
private int clientSocket = 1101;

//
// create the server socket
//
public ServerSocket createServerSocket( int port ) {
//
// ignore the port number and use a specific port
// allowed on our firewall
//
ServerSocket ssocket = null;

try {

    //
    // we will only work with specific port
    //
    ssocket = new ServerSocket( serverSocket );

}
catch (IOException e) {
    System.err.println("IOException : " + e );
    e.printStackTrace();
}
```

```
catch (SecurityException e) {
      System.err.println("SecurityException : " + e );
      e.printStackTrace();
}
finally {
    return ssocket;
}


}
//
// create the client socket
//
public Socket createSocket( String host, int port ) {

Socket socket = null;
try {

    //
    // only use a specific port
    //
    socket = new Socket( host, clientSocket );

}
catch (IOException e) {
      System.err.println("IOException : " + e );
      e.printStackTrace();
}
catch (SecurityException e) {
      System.err.println("SecurityException : " + e );
      e.printStackTrace();
}
finally {
    return socket;
}


}

public RestrictiveSocketFactory( int clientSocket,
                                 int serverSocket ) {
super();

this.clientSocket = clientSocket;
this.serverSocket = serverSocket;

}

public RestrictiveSocketFactory( ) {
super();
}


}
```

The RMIClient2 Class

The `RMIClient2` class shown below accesses the `RMIHello2` remote object server. Unlike the previous "Hello World" example, this client program must communicate with the server through a restricted set of ports. A security manager is loaded, which loads the security policy (shown below) that identifies the ports allowed. The URL for the `Naming lookup` call also specifies the port to use for the lookup operation.

The RMIClient2 Class

```
package examples.rmi;

import java.net.MalformedURLException;
import java.rmi.Naming;
import java.rmi.NotBoundException;
import java.rmi.RemoteException;
import java.rmi.RMISecurityManager;


public class RMIClient2 {

public static void main( String args[] ) {

try {


//
// load a security manager
//
if ( System.getSecurityManager() == null ) {
        System.setSecurityManager(
            new RMISecurityManager() );
}

//
// get our remote object
//
Hello hello = (Hello) Naming.lookup("//localhost:1100/RMIHello2");


//
// execute a method on our remote object
//
System.out.println( hello.helloThere( "Sammy" ) );

}

catch (RemoteException e) {
   System.out.println(
```

```
            "RemoteException in main: " +
            e.getMessage() );
}
catch (MalformedURLException e) {
  System.out.println(
      "MalformedURLException in main: " +
      e.getMessage() );
}
catch (NotBoundException e) {
  System.out.println(
      "NotBoundException in main: " +
      e.getMessage() );
}


}


}
```

The security policy file shown below specifies the ports that can be accessed by the Java application whose security manager uses the file, which in our case is the `RMIHello2` client program shown previously. The `grant` entry shown specifies a set of socket permissions and indicates the host name, in this case the local host, and a range of port numbers allowed. In this example we allow only two port numbers: port 1100 and port 1101. The network operations allowed on those ports are `accept` (to accept connections on a server socket), `listen` and `connect`.

The security.policy File

```
grant {
      permission java.net.SocketPermission "localhost:1100-1101", "accept, listen,
connect";
};
```

Auto-starting RMI Servers with Activation

By default, RMI applications require a remote object to be running in order to accept connections from client applications. If a client application were to attempt to connect to a remote object server that was not running, it would fail.

RMI activation addresses this issue by providing a mechanism for starting remote objects as they are requested. This reduces the load on system resources that would be consumed by running a number of remote objects that were not being used consistently.

But RMI activation is not for all objects. Starting a remote object can take time and would slow the execution of the client program. For remote objects that are used often, starting the object server before it is used and having it ready to accept connections is probably a better alternative to activation.

RMI activation requires two daemon processes, `rmiregistry` and `rmid`, to be running on a server that will accept lookup calls for RMI objects. Activation also requires a setup program be written to identify the remote objects that will be started with activation. Once the setup parameters for the activation of a remote object is in place, the setup program does not need to be run again—the setup parameters are persistent.

The code sample below demonstrates the process of creating a setup program for RMI activation. The program begins by loading an RMI security manager and then creates a `Properties` object and adds an entry for a Java security policy file. This policy file is used to create an activation group, which is then registered with the RMI activation system. Remote objects are registered with the system using the activation group.

The RMI activation system must know where to look for the class files to activate. Unlike Java programs, the activation system does not depend on the classpath environment variable to determine the location of the class files for activation. Each activation description (`ActivationDesc`) provides information on the location of the class files (effectively, a single classpath), the specific class files to load, and any data (`MarshalledObject`) for initialization.

The `ActivationDesc` instance is then used to register the object with the RMI activation system. This returns a `Remote` (`java.rmi.Remote`) stub, which is then registered with the RMI naming service.

The ActivationSetup Class

```
package examples.rmi;

import java.rmi.*;
import java.rmi.activation.*;
import java.util.Properties;

public class ActivationSetup {

public static void main( String[] args ) {

try {

  //
  // load a security manager
  //
  System.setSecurityManager( new RMISecurityManager() );

  //
  // set the security policy
  //
```

```
Properties properties = new Properties();
properties.put( "java.security.policy",
                "security.policy" );

//
// create an activation group
//
ActivationGroupDesc.CommandEnvironment env = null;
ActivationGroupDesc group = new
          ActivationGroupDesc( properties, env );

//
// get the ID for the application
//
ActivationGroupID id =
      ActivationGroup.getSystem().registerGroup(
                                      group );

//
// the location where the classes reside
//
String location =
            "file:/disk1/J2EE/examples/rmi/";

MarshalledObject data = null;
//
// identify the class to load
//
ActivationDesc desc = new ActivationDesc( id,
                      "examples.rmi.RMIHello3",
                      location, data );

//
// get the stub from the Activatable register operation
// and bind it
//
Hello hello = (Hello) Activatable.register( desc );
Naming.rebind( "RMIHello3", hello );

  }
  catch (Exception e) {
      System.out.println("Exception caught in main: "
                          + e );
      e.printStackTrace();
  }
 }
}
```

The RMI object server used with the RMI activation system is shown below. This class implements the `Hello` interface, which provides the single `helloThere` method and extends the `Activatable` class (not the `UnicastRemoteObject` class).

RMI object servers that are used with activation must provide an implementation of a constructor with two arguments: the `ActivationID` (or a unique ID to represent the object on the system) and object data to be used to initialize the object server (which may optionally be left null). This constructor should call the superclass constructor, as shown in this example.

The RMIHello3 Class

```
package examples.rmi;

import java.rmi.*;
import java.rmi.server.*;
import java.rmi.activation.*;
import java.io.*;

import RMIExample.*;

public class RMIHello3 extends Activatable implements Hello {

public String helloThere( String name ) throws RemoteException {

        return "Hello there, " + name + ".";

}
//
// constructor required for activation
//
public RMIHello3(ActivationID id,
                 MarshalledObject data)
            throws RemoteException {
// register and export the object
super( id, 0); // 0 = anonymous port
}

}
```

The client application for the activation example is shown in the code listing below. This example does as the previous examples have done: It executes a `Naming lookup` method to retrieve a reference to the remote object (or the remote reference or stub).

The RMIClient3 Class

```
package examples.rmi;

import java.net.MalformedURLException;
import java.rmi.Naming;
import java.rmi.RMISecurityManager;
import java.rmi.RemoteException;
```

```
import java.rmi.NotBoundException;

public class RMIClient3 {

public static void main( String args[] ) {

try {

//
// load a security manager
//
if ( System.getSecurityManager() == null ) {
    System.setSecurityManager(
            new RMISecurityManager() );
}


//
// get the remote object from the naming service
//
Hello hello = (Hello) Naming.lookup("//localhost:1099/RMIHello3");

//
// execute a method on the remote object
//
System.out.println( hello.helloThere( "Harry" ) );

}
catch (RemoteException e) {
  System.out.println("RemoteException in main: " +
                        e.getMessage() );
}
catch (NotBoundException e ) {
      System.out.println("RemoteException in main: " +
                            e.getMessage() );
}
catch (MalformedURLException e ) {
      System.out.println("RemoteException in main: " +
                            e.getMessage() );
}

}

}
```

Running an RMI Activation Example

As mentioned previously, to use remote object servers that have been registered with the activation system, two programs must be running: the rmiregistry and the rmid daemon. The rmiregistry is run as it was with the previous examples. Optionally, a port for the RMI registry can be specified on the command line, as follows.

```
rmiregistry 1100
```

This example will start the `rmiregistry` listening on port 1100.

The `rmid` program, which provides an activation daemon for remote objects, must also be running. This program can optionally be run with command-line arguments indicating the security policy file to load, as shown in the following example.

```
rmid -J-Djava.security.policy=security.policy
```

BINDING RMI OBJECTS INTO A DIRECTORY SERVER

The registry that is provided with RMI is fairly simple and limited. It was not intended for production use. It is possible and recommended that the remote objects (the remote object stubs) for a production application be bound into any JNDI naming service where they can then be retrieved by client applications. The following code fragment demonstrates this process.

In this example, a Data Access Object (DAO), an intelligent object for accessing databases, is exposed as a service. This particular DAO has been developed to handle general queries and to store the aggregated results of those queries (similar to the `javax.sql.RowSet` class but without the JDBC syntax for accessing the results).

To bind the remote object into the naming service, the JNDI object for the naming service must be retrieved. This is done using a service we have created to encapsulate the process of obtaining access to the directory server. (See Chapter 12 for details on the `DirectoryService` class and JNDI.)

To bind an object into a directory server, in this case an LDAP server, we must create a valid attribute (as defined by the LDAP schema we are using). Once the attributes have been defined, we obtain a reference to the directory server (of type `DirContext`). (The `DirectoryService` class being used will retrieve the `InitialContext` and then access the context requested.)

Now that we have a reference to the specific context in our directory server, we need to create the reference we would like to bind into the server. This is accomplished by calling the constructor for our object (`RemoteGeneralDAO`) and exporting the object using the `UnicastRemoteObject exportObject` method. This is done by identifying a port on the server where the object will listen.

The `exportObject` method returns a reference to the remote object that has just been bound, a client stub to the server object. It is this remote reference that is used in the rebind call to bind the remote object into the directory server namespace.

Binding Remote Objects to a JNDI Naming Service

```java
package db;

import java.sql.*;
import javax.sql.*;

import javax.naming.*;
import javax.naming.directory.*;
import java.util.*;
import java.io.*;

import java.rmi.*;
import java.rmi.server.*;

import org.apache.log4j.Category;

import db.*;
import service.DirectoryService;
import service.LoggingService;

public class RemoteGeneralDAO implements RemoteDAO, Serializable {

Connection con                    = null;
PreparedStatement preparedQuery = null;
ResultSet              resultSet = null;
ResultSetMetaData      resultMD;

private Category logger = LoggingService.getLogger(
                           "RemoteGeneralDAO" );

GeneralAggregateVO      gvo = new GeneralAggregateVO();

public static void main(String[] args ) {
RemoteGeneralDAO rgdao=null;
try {

//
//
// must be bound each time the object
//   server(RemoteGeneralDAO)is started
//

//
// Create the attributes needed for the directory server
//
BasicAttribute attribute = new BasicAttribute(
                             "objectClass" );
attribute.add( "extensibleObject");
attribute.add( "top");
BasicAttributes attributes = new BasicAttributes(true);
attributes.put( attribute );
```

```
//
// access the directory server with our 'service'
// use our specific subcontext for RMI
//
DirectoryService directory = new DirectoryService();
DirContext context = (DirContext) directory.getContext(
"o=rmi, o=general-application-objects, dc=movies, dc=com" );

//
// create an instance of our remote server object (this class)
//
rgdao = new db.RemoteGeneralDAO();

//
// export this object on a specified port
//
Remote remote = UnicastRemoteObject.exportObject( rgdao, 1201 );

//
// bind the results of the export operation to the
// directory server
//
context.rebind("cn=RemoteGeneralDAO", remote, attributes );

}
catch( RemoteException e) {
     rgdao.logger.error( "RemoteException in main: " + e );
}
catch( Exception e) {
     rgdao.logger.error( "Exception in main: " + e );
}

}
```

As we can see from the code below, accessing the remote object through a client program involves obtaining a reference to the correct context within the directory server, as shown in the following code listing. This context is then used to obtain a reference to the remote object (an instance of `RemoteGeneralDAO`).

The remote object is used to call the `executeQuery` method. This remotely executed method takes a string parameter that is an SQL query, executes the query, and stores the results in an internal value object (a object representation of the data row). (Chapter 32 covers these *Java design patterns* in more detail.) The query is executed on the server, and the results are stored in an instance member of the server object, an *aggregate value object* (a matrix of the data rows retrieved).

The application executing this code uses the value object to display the data returned in Swing GUI table. But rather than make a large number of remote calls to retrieve the data in the value object, the value object is retrieved using the `getGeneralAggregateVO` method and stored in a reference local to the client program.

Client Access to Directory Server Remote Object

```
...
   GeneralAggregateDAO gdao;
...
   //
   // get the remote object from our directory server
   //
   DirectoryService directory = new DirectoryService();
   DirContext context = (DirContext) directory.getContext(
       "o=rmi, o=general-application-objects, dc=movies, dc=com" );
   gdao = (RemoteDAO) context.lookup( "cn=RemoteGeneralDAO" );

   // execute the query and store results
   System.out.println("Executing Query ... " );
   gdao.executeQuery( query );

   //
   // get the aggregated Value Object with our results
   //
   gvo = gdao.getGeneralAggregateVO();
...
```

RMI versus Other Remote Services Solutions

When it comes to accessing remote services in J2EE, RMI is one potential solution. There are of course other remote components available: Enterprise Java Beans, servlets, network socket programs, and Web Services using JAXM. The question arises, Where does RMI fit into this picture?

In terms of functionality and ease of use, RMI is a step up from programming an application using network sockets. RMI is relatively simple to use and offers a natural syntax and a short learning curve for the Java developer. RMI also offers a very low-cost solution that requires very little system resources.

But RMI has limitations, both in performance and usage. If using RMI with activation, there can be some delay in starting a remote object. Once a remote object is running, the RMI implementation may or may not make use of threads. There is no explicit pooling of resources with RMI, so each invocation may require the instantiation of a new object to manage the request.

RMI has no consistent configuration and bootstrap process. RMI activation provides an API for activating remote objects, but there is no corresponding configuration file where this information can be stored and maintained. This leaves the responsibility for bootstrapping or starting RMI applications to developers and administrators who must develop custom programs and scripts to manage the process.

These various limitations are addressed to a large extent with EJBs. EJBs run within a container, which provides services such as life cycle management and security. Within the realm of life cycle management comes the pooling of resources. EJB containers often keep a pool of remote components (instantiations of the remote object) and select from this pool as remote objects are requested. This greatly reduces the work required to manage incoming requests and improves performance.

EJBs also provide consistent and flexible administration. The deployment descriptor contains information on the distributed components, the resources, the security, and the transactional behavior of EJB applications. EJB application server vendors are required to support the deployment descriptor, and most have extended the functionality of the deployment and configuration of EJBs in some way.

DYNAMIC CLASS LOADING WITH RMI

RMI can potentially provide a mechanism for a thin client, a client application with a very small footprint. We would expect an RMI thin client to be easy to deploy and maintain. This RMI client application should therefore require a small number of classes to run. The work required by the RMI client should be performed as much as possible on the RMI object server. Should the client need additional classes to perform some task, we would prefer to be able to dynamically load the required class from a server rather than deploy the class files with the RMI client code. RMI makes this process of dynamic code downloading—dynamically loading the classes from some location—fairly easy to accomplish.

In most cases we would probably want the RMI server to perform the bulk of the work required. This is the main reason for RMI: to be able to execute methods (as part of some class) on a remote server. We can further apply rigor and logic to our effort by using design patterns to guide the design of our distributed application. There are two particularly useful design patterns often applied with RMI: the *proxy* and the *command* design patterns.

The proxy design pattern involves the use of an object that acts as a surrogate for another object. Consider that we have some object that contains methods we wish to execute. The proxy object contains those same methods and is responsible for forwarding requests to the object (see Figure 19–2).

The command design pattern encapsulates the actions of a particular command in an object. A command object would therefore contain the code required to execute a specific command. An interface describes the command object, and the client class does not need to know the specifics of the command being executed; it merely accesses the object to request execution of the command (see Figure 19–3).

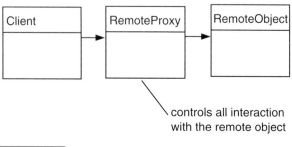

Figure 19–2   *The proxy design pattern.*

With RMI we have applied our *proxy* pattern by using our stub as a proxy to request work of our server (the remote object). Additionally, if we apply the *command* design pattern, we can request some action of the server using a parameter that encapsulates our command object as a member, passing the command object as a parameter to the server. The class for this command object would not need to be available to the RMI client at runtime; it could be located by the server (using its codebase), and loaded and executed to fulfill the requirements of the execute method of the command object.

Downloading classes using RMI is controlled largely based on the setting of the codebase property for the RMI server. A codebase can be considered a source from which classes will be loaded. The classpath can be considered a local codebase where the codebase property for RMI allows remote class loading.

This property is controlled by the setting of the `java.rmi.server.codebase` property. This property contains a string, which contains one or more URLs

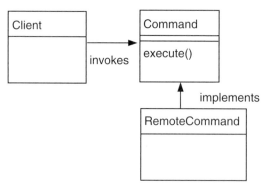

Figure 19–3   *The command design pattern.*

that identify locations where class files may be found. The URL can reference an HTTP server, an FTP server, or a local file system.

The scenario for the dynamic class loading for the server is fairly evident. If the server needs to load a class to be able to reference an object parameter in a method, then the codebase property is similar to a classpath except that it now allows the classes to be loaded from a central server running the HTTP or FTP protocol. But what would be a valid scenario for the RMI client to download a class?

One of the more common cases for downloading code to a client is the downloading of the stub class that allows access to the remote object server. Allowing this class to be downloaded (potentially from a centralized server where it is accessible to a number of remote clients) simplifies the deployment process. Should the stub class change for some reason, it would only need to be deployed to the central location, where it would then be downloaded to any clients that required access to the remote object server.

There are specific rules concerning when the RMI server will download classes and when it will not. If the classes are in the remote object server's classpath (and it does not need to search codebase), then the downloading of classes will not be necessary and will be disabled. Alternatively, setting the `java.rmi.server.useCodebaseOnly` property in the server to true will instruct the remote object server to search for classes using only the codebase property.

It is important to note that the codebase property should be set before the remote object is bound into the RMI registry or into some other naming service. This is because the codebase property setting of the JVM for the remote object's server is the codebase that is stored with the remote object in the remote object reference in the registry.

All of this class loading magic is possible because RMI uses a custom class loader, the `RMIClassLoader`. As a developer, you need to be aware that if the stub class was loaded from the remote object server (via the `RMIClassLoader`), then the RMI subsystem is already aware of the codebase for the stub. If, however, the class was loaded from the classpath (perhaps loaded from the client's local classpath), then the RMI subsystem is not aware of the codebase and will interrogate the `java.rmi.server.codebase` system property.

SUMMARY

In this chapter we learned firsthand that RMI is much more than just the remote invocation of object methods. We examined some of the additional RMI features, such as client callbacks, and the ability to pass a remote object to another remote object and effectively invoke callback methods on the client code.

We know that the RMI registry is not meant for prime time. This tool does not allow remote objects on other machines to be bound into the registry (a curious limitation for a distributed technology). But RMI does allow remote objects to be exported into more robust naming servers, such as LDAP servers. We reviewed an example of that binding operation in this chapter.

Before RMI activation was available we were required to have RMI remote objects running in order for them to be available to clients applications. With RMI activation, an activation daemon can be started and instructed to activate an RMI remote object only when it is needed. Using RMI activation requires a number of steps, which we reviewed in an example in this chapter.

RMI is a core technology for J2EE, and we will see later in this text how other technologies such as EJBs depend on RMI for communication.

CHAPTER 20

Using Messaging with Java: The JMS API

INTRODUCTION

As we discussed in the first section of this book, *tight coupling* between components can create maintenance problems in a distributed application. A small change in one component could lead to numerous changes in other tightly coupled components. These changes could also be difficult to identify and program. With the *loosely coupled* architecture of messaging services these problems can be avoided. Messaging services allow application components to communicate in a loosely coupled fashion.

The Java Message Service (JMS) API provides access to various messaging services. The applications or components using these services can communicate peer-to-peer in a *loosely coupled* fashion. Messages may be sent even if the recipient is not currently available; this is referred to as asynchronous messaging.

With messaging, the sender of the message and the receiver of the message can be on completely different platforms in remote locations and can have been developed with different software—they can still communicate using messaging as long as they use the correct message format and the correct message addresses.

481

In this chapter we will examine the JMS API, the J2EE API which allows Java applications to access messaging services. We will look at the two variations on messaging supported by JMS, point-to-point messaging and publish and subscribe, and demonstrate their usage with several programming examples.

THE JMS API

The JMS API was designed to allow Java programs to communicate with messaging systems from a variety of vendors. The API provides for *asynchronous* messaging, where a client can send a message and does not have to wait for the recipient to receive the message and process it.

The most familiar example of asynchronous messaging is email. When an email is sent, if we are the sender we do not expect the recipient to be sitting at their computer waiting to receive the message as soon as we send it. We don't even expect the recipients computer to be turned on. In fact, we know that the message will most likely be sent to a number of different locations where it will be routed to its final destination, ultimately arriving in the mailbox of our recipient.

The processing of messages is similar. It is unlikely that a message sent using JMS will be routed directly to the target messaging system. More than likely it will be routed to one or more locations before finally arriving at the messaging system which will perform the processing.

Such a loosely coupled architecture creates potential processing issues for developers. How do we know that the message finally reached its intended recipient? What happens if one of the links in the message routing fails? If there are multiple recipients that can receive and process the message, how can we be sure that the message is only processed once.

The JMS API also supports reliable transactions, where message services can ensure that a message is delivered once and only once. Though available in many messaging servers, this level of service is not a requirement; less rigorous delivery strategies can be used if the application can manage their results.

Recent developments have made messaging services even more attractive alternatives for information interchange. The use of XML as message content (or *payload*) reduces the necessity of programming for multiple message formats. Knowledge of the XML schema is all that is required to parse a message.

Messaging requires a messaging server. J2EE compliant application servers provide these servers and they must support both message queues and message topics which we will examine in more detail shortly. The JMS API provides access to both of these server types and reduces the learning curve needed to learn how to access a specific messaging service. If the messaging service has provided a JMS service provider interface (most major vendors have), then programming for a TIBCO messaging service is virtually identical to programming for an IBM MQSeries messaging service.

WHEN MESSAGING IS A GOOD CHOICE

Using a messaging service makes sense when the application either never requires information back from a request or could wait some time before getting information back about a request—for example, when requesting inventory replenishment from a supplier. The application or component requesting the inventory does not need to know when the request is made if the inventory is available. It is not uncommon for supplies to be backordered, and it may be perfectly acceptable to wait several days before the information about the backordered supply replenishment order is received.

Some products are assembled on request (for instance, furniture). These assembly orders often take weeks or months to fulfill and are sometimes delayed for various reasons. The component or application making the request will most likely not be able to determine when the order will be fulfilled.

Using a messaging service would make sense for both of these applications. A message could be sent to the supplier concerning the supply replenishment order. If the order were backordered, notification could be emailed to personnel responsible for monitoring the stock status. A product assembly request message could be sent for a furniture order, and if the assembly process were delayed for some reason, the customer could be contacted directly with the bad news.

Messaging systems also provide an access point for legacy applications that would otherwise require complex APIs to access. Using messaging provides access to these applications that would otherwise require expensive programming with a proprietary API (and the expensive programmer that knows the API).

The JMS API is a required part of the J2EE 1.3 platform, providing both JMS message queue access and integration with Enterprise Java Beans (EJB) in the form of message-driven beans (MDBs). Clients and components can both use JMS messaging services and participate in distributed transactions when using the services. An MDB component can be created to act as a message consumer, processing messages that have been applied to a message queue or topic.

Basic Concepts

The JMS API manages the processing of messages using a clean object-oriented design. The core components of this API are listed in Table 20–1.

Provider

The provider represents an implementation of a messaging server and the corresponding drivers for JMS. This is the vendor or open-source solution that provides the messaging server, effectively the service provider interface, which allows JMS to work. The major players in the J2EE server market, such as BEA, Iplanet, and WebSphere, provide solid JMS implementations, as does JBoss, the leading open-source solution.

| Table 20–1 | *Basic JMS Components* |

Component	Description
Provider	An implementation of a messaging system interface in JMS.
Client	Produces messages and distributes them to message consumers. Alternatively, a client could be simply a consumer of messages.
Message	Objects that encapsulate the information exchanged between JMS clients.
Administered objects	Objects that are required by clients in order to use JMS. These are destinations and connection factories.

Client

The client is the user of the messaging system and so can be either a provider of messages or a consumer of messages. A client could be an end-user software program, a distinct application, or a component in a J2EE server. Since messaging is a loosely coupled solution, a provider could also be a non-Java application or component, such as a Distributed Component Object Model (DCOM) component running on a Windows machine, or a mainframe application that retrieves and processes product orders.

Message

The message is an abstraction that encapsulates the information being exchanged between clients through the messaging system. A message could be a text message, or if both the client and consumer are Java applications, the message could be a binary message or an arbitrary Java object (which must be serializable), or a Java map collection. A text message could contain any type of valid textual content, including XML, an increasingly popular format, which is demonstrated in the example in this chapter.

Administered Objects

Administered objects are the portion of the messaging system that require maintenance in order to support the messages. These are commonly the destinations (the queues and topics) for the messages and connection factories that allow connections to be created. The messaging system administrator must create these objects, and developers creating messaging clients must address their messages correctly to arrive at the queues.

JMS Message Domains

Message-processing systems over the years have used a variety of techniques to manage the receipt and dispersal of messages. In developing the JMS API, the most common methods in use at the time were modeled in the API. These domains or types of message-processing paradigms are *point-to-point* messaging and *publish and subscribe* messaging. The following sections discuss these two approaches in more detail.

Point-to-Point

A point-to-point approach to messaging involves the use of message queues to store messages for later retrieval. Message queues are used by senders and receivers. Senders send messages to the message queues where they will be stored (or queued) and delivered at a later time. Receivers access a message queue and retrieve messages.

Receivers and senders use specific queue names to control the transmission and consumption of messages. By using named queues, a client application posting a product order would direct the order document, packaged as part of a message, to a message queue named *'orders'*. The client receiving or consuming the message would access the named *'orders'* queue and process any orders that had been placed in the queue.

There are specific rules relating to the use of JMS message queues. A message may have only one consumer, so that once a message has been retrieved from a message queue by a consumer, it is deleted from the message queue.

The consumer of the message is also allowed to retrieve messages whether or not the consumer was running when the message was delivered. And finally, the receiver may acknowledge successful retreat of a message. See Figure 20–1.

Since this approach specifies that each message will have one consumer, it is best used by applications where a one-to-one relationship exists between a message and consumer. The diagram in Figure 20–1 demonstrates this with consumer1 connecting to the queue and obtaining Message1, and consumer2 connecting to the queue and obtaining Message2 and Message3; each message has been consumed only once.

Publish and Subscribe

With the publish and subscribe approach to messaging, the publishing client addresses messages to a topic. A subscriber client may then retrieve the messages from that topic. Topics are deleted once they have been delivered to one or more subscribers.

As with message queues, there are certain rules applied to publish and subscribe messaging. One rule, or lack of restriction, is that each message may have

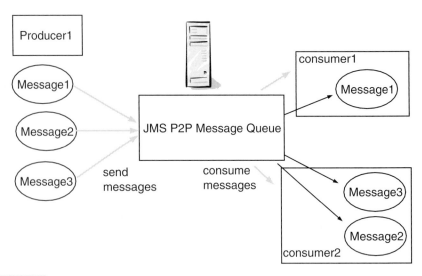

Figure 20–1   *Point-to-Point Message Queue*

multiple consumers. Another rule creates a default timing dependency between the publisher and subscriber. A subscriber may only consume messages delivered after they have initiated their subscription, and the subscriber must remain active to consume messages. Since this rule can be restrictive, it is relaxed in JMS, which allows for *durable subscriptions,* which can receive messages even while subscribers are not active. See Figure 20–2.

As the diagram in Figure 20–2 demonstrates, using a publish and subscribe messaging paradigm involves one or more client applications sending messages directed to specific targets and one or more client applications subscribing to those topics and consuming messages for those topics. In this diagram one client publishes messages directed to two specific topics. Two message-consumer clients are connected to the messaging service and subscribe to two different topics. The messaging service then distributes the messages to all subscribers of the topic. In this case, Consumer2 consumes messages for both Topic1 and Topic2. Consumer1, however, consumes messages only for Topic1. The end result of this approach is that the messages for Topic1 are consumed twice. While this may seem counterintuitive at first, this approach does have the benefit of providing built-in replication of the message consumption. For example, if we had a series of servers running copies of an inventory system and we wanted each to be kept synchronized, we would have each separate system consume the messages (inventory transactions) for the inventory topic.

Message consumption with JMS may be either asynchronous or synchronous. Asynchronous communication can be achieved by registering a listener with an asso-

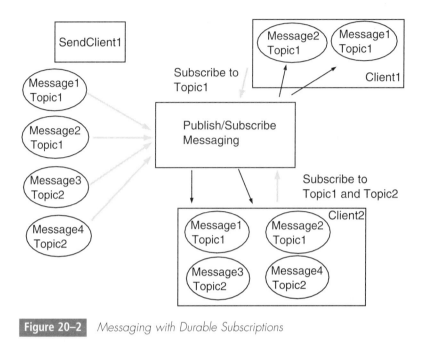

Figure 20–2 *Messaging with Durable Subscriptions*

ciated consumer. As messages arrive, the messaging service delivers the message to the client by calling the `onMessage` method in the associated queue consumer. Synchronous communication with the message server is provided using the `receive` method. The receive message blocks until a message arrives or optionally times out. The following sections demonstrate these two approaches to processing messages.

USING JMS WITH A MESSAGE QUEUE

In the following example, a message queue is used to process orders for sales of movies. A queue has been established in the JBoss message queue with the JNDI name of `queue/movie-orders`. The client application inserts a set of orders into the queue. An order listener is created to listen to the queue and, when orders are available, retrieves the orders and processes them. Order processing is performed using helper classes.

Since these examples use a message queue and expect to perform asynchronous messaging, there is no timing requirement between the client and the recipient. If the recipient of the message is not connected to the queue, the message is stored (persisted) until some point in the future when a process connects to the queue and retrieves the message. Additionally, because we use a message queue, we can be assured that only one process will consume an order message, so an order will be processed only once. After an order has been retrieved from the queue (by the listener), the order is deleted from the queue.

An order class is used that represents an application of a Java Data Access Object (DAO) design pattern (discussed in Chapter 32). This DAO contains a convenient method that converts the contents of the DAO into an XML document using a schema that is specific to the order DAO. This effectively converts the binary representation of the data into XML format for data interchange.

The code examples we will examine first would run external to a J2EE application server – they are not J2EE components. But as mentioned previously, as of J2EE 1.3, the *message driven bean* was added to the arsenal of EJBs. An MDB can (and will, later in this chapter) take the place of the messaging service listener application. Likewise, an EJB, most likely a session bean, or a Web-tier component could act as the producer client and add messages to the message queue.

Posting Messages to the Message Queue

The code in the following sections demonstrates a client application that connects to a message queue running within the JBoss J2EE server. To demonstrate the capabilities of working with message queues, this application randomly generates a set of orders, which are applied to the message queue.

As the following code demonstrates, the process of connecting to the queue is not that complicated. We are able to request the queue resource, the connection factory for the queue, from the JNDI naming service running in the J2EE server. A `Hashtable` is created, and the various parameters needed to connect to the JBoss naming service are inserted into the `Hashtable` and then passed into the constructor for the server.

The `InitialContext` is used to first access the `QueueConnectionFactory`, which is used to create a `QueueSession` object (`javax.jms.QueueSession`). The session is created without transactions and with auto-acknowledgment of message receipt. (In production systems, obviously, a higher level of data integrity would entail using transactions and tracking receipt of messages and the context environment would not be hardcoded.)

Next, the queue resource itself is retrieved from the naming service using the queue name of "`queue/movie-orders`". At this point we have a queue and a session object; we now combine the two to create a sender (`javax.jms.QueueSender`) object, which allows us to send messages to the queue. The `QueueSession` object is used to do this with the `createSender` method.

A `for` loop is then started to post 10 messages to the message queue. Within the `for` loop, an `order` object (`OrderDAO`) is created and random values are added to the object. The contents of the object are converted to XML format and added to the message, and the message is then sent to the queue using the `QueueSender send` method, which is passed arguments for the message to be sent and the queue where the message should be posted.

```java
package examples.jms;

import java.util.Hashtable;
import javax.naming.*;
import javax.jms.*;
import db.*;

public class JMSClientQueue {

public static void main( String args[] ) {

//
// connect to JBoss Message queue
//
Hashtable ht  = new Hashtable();
ht.put( Context.INITIAL_CONTEXT_FACTORY,
          "org.jnp.interfaces.NamingContextFactory" );
ht.put( Context.PROVIDER_URL,
        "jnp://localhost:1099" );
ht.put( URL_PKG_PREFIXES,
        "org.jboss.naming:org.jnp.interfaces" );

try {

   InitialContext context = new InitialContext( ht );

   QueueConnectionFactory factory =
      (QueueConnectionFactory) context.lookup(
                                "QueueConnectionFactory");
   QueueConnection connection = factory.createQueueConnection();

   QueueSession session =
           connection.createQueueSession( false,// no transactions
                      Session.AUTO_ACKNOWLEDGE);// auto-ack

   Queue queue = (Queue) context.lookup( "queue/movie-orders" );

   QueueSender sender  = session.createSender( queue );
   TextMessage message = session.createTextMessage();

   //
   // queue is ready ... now add messages
   //
for ( int n = 1; n < 11; n++ ) {

   //
   // load the order object
   //
   OrderDAO order = new OrderDAO();
   order.setOrderNumber(
         Integer.toString(
             new Double( Math.random() * 10000 ).intValue()) );
```

```
    order.setQuantity( n*2 );
    order.setMovieID( n*3 );
    order.setShipToID( "2039093" );
    order.setBillToID( "9023983" );
    order.setUPC( "UXA9883983" );

    //
    // convert the order object to an XML string
    //
    message.setText( order.toXMLString() );

    //
    // send the message ... add it to the queue
    //
    sender.send( queue, message );

}


}
catch (NamingException e) {
        System.out.println("NamingException e: " + e );
}
catch (Exception e) {
        System.out.println("Exception e: " + e );
}
}
}
```

Retrieving Messages: The Queue Listener

In order to retrieve messages from a message queue, a listener class must be created. It is the job of the listener class to connect to the queue and wait (or listen) for messages. This is done by creating a class that implements the MessageListener (javax.jms.MessageListener) interface and providing an implementation for the onMessage method. Once the class has been established as a listener on the queue, the onMessage method in that class will be called when a message is received for that queue.

The listener is responsible for processing the order on the queue. It is good design to let the specifics of order processing be managed by another object and have the listener remain focused on managing the access to the message queue. For that reason, an OrdersProcessing object (shown later) is used to manage the order.

The Queue Listener: The main Program Block

In the code listing shown next, as in the previous example, we obtain the QueueConnectionFactory, the QueueSession object and the Queue object are obtained from the naming service.

The queue object and the session object are then combined using the QueueSession createReceiver method to create a receiver object. The receiver object returned by this method allows us to identify a listener for the queue using the createMessageListener method. In order to start listening to messages on the queue, we must call the QueueConnection start method, which is the final action in this block of code.

The OrdersListener Class: The main Program Block

```
package examples.jms;

import java.util.*;
import javax.jms.*;
import javax.naming.*;

import db.*;
import movies.control.*;

public class OrdersListener implements MessageListener {

OrderDAO order;
OrderProcessing processor;

public static void main( String args[] ) {

OrdersListener listener = new OrdersListener();

//
// connect to the JBoss message queue
//
Hashtable ht  = new Hashtable();
ht.put( "java.naming.factory.initial",
        "org.jnp.interfaces.NamingContextFactory" );
ht.put( "java.naming.provider.url",
        "jnp://localhost:1099" );
ht.put( "java.naming.factory.url.pkgs",
        "org.jboss.naming:org.jnp.interfaces" );

try {

    listener.processor = new OrderProcessing();

    InitialContext context = new InitialContext( ht );

    //
    // get the QueueConnectionFactory and create a Session
    //
    QueueConnectionFactory factory =
        (QueueConnectionFactory) context.lookup(
                          "QueueConnectionFactory");
```

```
    QueueConnection connection = factory.createQueueConnection();
    QueueSession    session    = connection.createQueueSession(
              false,                           // no transactions
              Session.AUTO_ACKNOWLEDGE); // auto-acknowledge

    //
    // get the message queue
    //
    Queue queue = (Queue) context.lookup( "queue/movie-orders" );

    //
    // create a message receiver
    //
    QueueReceiver receiver = session.createReceiver( queue );

    //
    // add an instance of this class as a listener
    //
    receiver.setMessageListener( listener );

    //
    // must start the connection to begin receiving messages
    //
    connection.start();

}
catch (NamingException e) {
    System.out.println( "NamingException e: " + e );
    e.printStackTrace();
}
catch (Exception e) {
    System.out.println( "Exception in main: e: " + e );
    e.printStackTrace();
}

}
```

The Queue Listener: The onMessage Method

The onMessage method shown below is called by the message listener facility when a message is received. This method is passed an argument, which is the message currently being processed. Since we know the message being received is a text message, we can cast the Message (javax.jms.Message interface) as a text message and call the getText method. The onMessage method then delgates the work of processing the message to the OrdersProcessor object by calling the OrdersProcessor processOrder method.

The OrdersListener Class: The onMessage Method

```
public void onMessage( Message message ) {

try {

    //
    // retrieve the message body - a text message
    //
    String messageText  = ((TextMessage) message).getText();

    processor.processOrder( messageText );

}
catch (JMSException e) {
    System.out.println("JMSException thrown in onMessage: " + e );
}

}
}
```

The OrderDAO Class

The `OrderDAO` class is a DAO that encapsulates the data involved in processing an order for the movies sales example used in this text. There is no single relational database table behind this example, which is not uncommon for a DAO, but in fact two tables in two separate databases must be accessed to execute the order.

This object contains members relating to the data elements that must be captured for the movies orders. As shown below, various `getXXXX` and `setXXXX` methods are used to query and modify the object's state.

OrderDAO Class: getXXXX and setXXXX Methods

```
package db;

import java.io.*;

import javax.xml.transform.*;
import javax.xml.transform.stream.*;
import javax.xml.parsers.*;

import org.xml.sax.*;
import org.w3c.dom.*;

import xmlutil.*;

public class OrderDAO {
```

```
private   String orderNumber;
private   int movieID;
private   String UPC;
private   String shipToID;
private   String billToID;
private   int quantity;

DocumentBuilder docBuilder;

public void setOrderNumber( String orderNumber ) {
    this.orderNumber = orderNumber;
}
public void setMovieID( int movieID ) {
    this.movieID = movieID;
}
public void setQuantity( int quantity ) {
    this.quantity = quantity;
}

public void setShipToID( String shipToID ) {
    this.shipToID = shipToID;
}
public void setBillToID( String billToID ) {
    this.billToID = billToID;
}
public void setUPC( String UPC ) {
    this.UPC = UPC;
}

// ---
public int getQuantity( ) {
    return this.quantity;
}
public String getOrderNumber( ) {
    return this.orderNumber;
}
public int getMovieID( ) {
    return this.movieID;
}

public String getShipToID( ) {
    return this.shipToID;
}
public String getBillToID( ) {
    return this.billToID;
}
public String getUPC( ) {
    return this.UPC;
}
```

Orders Class: The toXMLString Method

The orders DAO has the ability to convert itself into an XML document. This is accomplished through the `toXMLString` method, which creates an XML document based on the internal state of the object and returns the XML document as a string. Since a great deal of string appends are required to perform this transformation, the more efficient `StringBuffer` class is used to append the appropriate tags onto the string buffer which is then converted to a `java.lang.String` and returned as shown below.

The Orders Class: The toXMLString Method

```
public String toXMLString() {
StringBuffer buffer = new StringBuffer( 255 );

// ** insert XML header **
buffer.append("<?xml version=\"1.0\" ?>\n");

buffer.append("<movie-order>\n");

buffer.append("<order-number>\n");
buffer.append( getOrderNumber()   );
buffer.append("</order-number>\n");

buffer.append("<order-quantity>\n");
buffer.append( getQuantity()   );
buffer.append("</order-quantity>\n");

buffer.append("<movie-id>\n");
buffer.append( getMovieID()   );
buffer.append("</movie-id>\n");

buffer.append("<ship-to-id>\n");
buffer.append( getShipToID()   );
buffer.append("</ship-to-id>\n");

buffer.append("<bill-to-id>\n");
buffer.append( getBillToID()   );
buffer.append("</bill-to-id>\n");

buffer.append("<upc>\n");
buffer.append( getUPC()   );
buffer.append("</upc>\n");

buffer.append("</movie-order>\n");

return buffer.toString();

}
```

A Generic Alternative to the toXMLString Method

While the toXMLString method provides a valid solution for converting the contents of the object to an XML document, it does require some tedious coding. By applying some general rules to the creation of the object, a more generic solution can be coded.

As most experienced Java programmers are aware, a general object-oriented approach to coding suggests that fields or members of the object be private or protected data that is manipulated through the accessors and mutators, the friendly get and set methods. If objects are created using this standard, and if it is possible to discover the get methods in an object and to invoke those methods and retrieve the underlying values, then it is possible to eliminate the task of coding a toXMLString method for every object we created. The following code demonstrates this approach using what is referred to as Java *reflection*.

The convertToXML method shown below takes an object reference as an argument and converts the object to a corresponding XML representation of the object. The object's class name is the top-level node of the XML document (the root node), and the contents/members of the object represent distinct child tags with the values of the members as text data for those tags. In order to determine the methods available in the object that has been passed into the method, the Java reflection API is used.

The Class class (not a typo) contains two methods to determine the method in a class. One returns all methods, including the inherited methods; the other returns only those methods that are members of the immediate class. Since we want only the get methods declared in the object passed into the method, we make a call to the getDeclaredMethods method to return an array of java.lang.reflect.Method objects.

This method iterates through the array of methods and tests to determine if the name of the method begins with the string get. If a match is found, a substring of the method is taken and shifted to lowercase. The result is used as the name of the element for the XML tag.

Next, the value of the member must be retrieved. We assert that the method takes no arguments and returns a single object argument with a valid toString implementation. Based on this assertion, we can use Java reflection to call the method, using the java.lang.reflect.Method invoke method and passing an argument which indicates the method does not require parameters. The StringBuffer append method takes the object argument, which is the result of the invoke method call, and calls the toString method on the object reference. The element name is then used to create a closing tag, and when the for loop completes for all methods in the object, the class name is used to create a closing tag.

The ObjectToXML Class: The convertToXML Method

```
package xmlutil;

import java.lang.reflect.*;

public class ObjectToXML {
//
// Convert an object with 'getXXXX' methods to an
// XML document. Use JDBC ResultSet type tags to
// all the use of ResultSet XLS transformations
// public static String convertToXML( Object obj ) {

StringBuffer buffer = new StringBuffer( 1024 );
try {

    Method[] methods = obj.getClass().getDeclaredMethods();
    Object[] args = null; // no parameters/arguments

//
// assert a no-args getXXXX method
//
String className =  obj.getClass().getName().toLowerCase();
buffer.append( "<" + className + ">\n" );

//
// for each 'get' method, output a tag for the element
// and the corresponding value
//

for ( int n = 0; n < methods.length; n++ ) {
    if ( methods[n].getName().startsWith("get") ) {
    //
    // this is the tag name
    //
    String elementName =
               methods[n].getName().substring(3).toLowerCase();
    buffer.append( "<" + elementName + ">" );

    //
    // insert the value
    //
    buffer.append( methods[n].invoke( obj, args ) );

    //
    // close the tag
    //
    buffer.append( "</" + elementName + ">\n" ); } }

    //
    // close the last column tag and close the row
```

```
    //
    buffer.append( "</" + className + ">\n" );

}
catch (Exception e) {
      System.out.println("Exception e: " + e );
}
finally {
   return buffer.toString();
}

}

}
```

The Orders Class: The loadXMLDoc Method

The `loadXMLDoc` method shown below allows the DAO to be loaded from the contents of an XML document. It takes an XML document as an argument, converts the document to Java primitives and objects, and loads them into its internal state. This requires the creation of a parser, in this case a DOM parser. The string passed into the method that contains the XML document is wrapped with a `StringReader` and then wrapped with an `InputSource` object. This `InputSource` object is passed to the parser, which returns the document element, the top-level element for the XML document that encompasses all child elements.

The remainder of the method makes heavy use of the `XMLUtil` `getElementValueByName` method, a method that will search for an element name in all child nodes and then return its value.

Note that the integer values use the `String trim` method to remove whitespace before and after the integer value. This prevents common parse and conversion errors generated by the `Integer parseInt` method.

The Orders Class: The loadXMLDoc Method

```
public void loadXMLDoc( String XMLDocString ) {

Element element = null;

try {

InputSource source = new InputSource(
                  new StringReader( XMLDocString ) );
Document doc = docBuilder.parse( source );
doc.normalize();

element =  doc.getDocumentElement();
```

```
setOrderNumber(
    XMLUtil.getElementValueByName( element, "ordernumber" ) );
setQuantity(
    Integer.parseInt(
      XMLUtil.getElementValueByName(
                    element, "quantity").trim() ) );
setBillToID(
    XMLUtil.getElementValueByName( element, "billtoid" ) );
setShipToID(
    XMLUtil.getElementValueByName( element, "shiptoid" ) );
setUPC( XMLUtil.getElementValueByName( element, "upc" ) );
setMovieID(
    Integer.parseInt(
      XMLUtil.getElementValueByName(
                    element, "movieid" ).trim() ));

}
catch (SAXException e) {
      System.out.println("SAXException in loadXMLDoc: " + e );
}
catch (IOException e) {
      System.out.println("IOException in loadXMLDoc: " + e );
}
catch (NumberFormatException e) {
      System.out.println(
          "NumberFormatException in loadXMLDoc: " + e );
      System.out.println("element value: " + element );
}

}
```

The Orders Class: The Constructor

The constructor for the Orders class is shown next. This constructor merely creates the DocumentBuilderFactory and the DocumentBuilder object. These are used to perform the XML parsing done in the loadXMLDoc method shown previously.

The Orders Class: The Constructor

```
public OrderDAO() {

try {

//
// get a parser factory
//
DocumentBuilderFactory dbf = DocumentBuilderFactory.newInstance();
docBuilder = dbf.newDocumentBuilder();
```

```
}
catch (ParserConfigurationException e) {
    System.out.println("ParserConfigurationException e:" + e );
}


}


}
```

The OrdersProcessor Class

As mentioned previously, the `OrdersProcessor` class performs the work of processing an order that has been posted to the message queue. As the code in this class demonstrates, this involves the insertion of records into two separate databases.

The OrdersProcessor Class: The processOrder Method

The `processOrder` method performs the actual processing of the order; this is the method that is called from the message queue listener method (`onMessage`). This method has been overloaded to accept either an `OrderDAO` object argument or a string that is an XML document that represents an order. Within the body of the method, two database updates must be performed. One database update is to the sales database where the sales transaction should be recognized, and the other is to the stock database where the shipment of the inventory is requested through a database transaction.

The first `processOrder` method takes an `OrderDAO` object as an argument. It then uses the contents of the object to set the values of a JDBC `PreparedStatement` object. Once all appropriate elements have been updated in the `PreparedStatement` object, the `PreparedStatement executeUpdate` method is called to update the `movies` database. The same work is performed for the stock database, after which the `PreparedStatement executeUpdate` method is called to update that database.

The overloaded version of the `processOrder` method is passed a string, which is an XML document representing the order. This method first creates the internal `OrderDAO` object if it hasn't been created yet, then calls the `OrderDAO loadXMLDoc` method to load the members of the `OrderDAO` object to the value of the order in the XML document. Once the order object has been loaded, the other overloaded version of the `processOrder` method is called and passed the order object.

The OrdersProcessor Class

```
package movies.control;

import java.sql.*;
```

```
import javax.sql.*;
import javax.naming.*;

import java.util.*;

import db.*;

public class OrderProcessing {

Connection conMovies;
Connection conStock;
PreparedStatement  pstmtMovies;
PreparedStatement  pstmtStock;

private OrderDAO order;

public void processOrder( OrderDAO order ) {
int rows = 0;
try {
//
// process order from an Order DAO
//

// ** start transaction **

//
// update the sales table in the movies database
//
pstmtMovies.setInt( 1,     order.getMovieID()  );
pstmtMovies.setInt( 2,     order.getQuantity() );
pstmtMovies.setString( 3,  order.getOrderNumber() );
rows = pstmtMovies.executeUpdate();

//
// update the orders table in the stock database
//
pstmtStock.setString( 1, order.getOrderNumber() );
pstmtStock.setString( 2, order.getShipToID() );
pstmtStock.setString( 3, order.getBillToID() );
pstmtStock.setString( 4, order.getUPC() );
pstmtStock.setInt( 5, order.getQuantity() );
rows = pstmtStock.executeUpdate();

// ** commit  trans **

}
catch (SQLException e ){
      System.out.println(
          "SQLException in processOrder: " + e );
      e.printStackTrace();

// ** rollback trans **
```

```
}
catch ( Exception e ) {
     System.out.println("Exception in processOrder: " +
                          e );
     e.printStackTrace();
}


}


public void processOrder( String orderXMLDoc ) {
//
// process order from an XML doc
//

if ( order == null ) {
    order = new OrderDAO();
}

//
// parse the XML doc and load it
//
order.loadXMLDoc( orderXMLDoc );

//
// process the order
//
processOrder( order );

}
```

The OrdersProcessor Class: Prepare SQL Statement

If a SQL statement is going to be executed multiple times, it is always best to *prepare* it before it is used. This provides more convenient access and can help achieve more efficient database performance.

The `prepareStockStatements` method is used to prepare the SQL insert statement for the update of the `stock` database. The `prepareMoviesStatements` performs the same task for the `movies` database.

The OrdersProcessor Class: Prepare SQL Statements

```
public void prepareStockStatements() {
try {

pstmtStock = conStock.prepareStatement(
```

```
        "insert into orders (order_number," +    // 1
        " ship_to_id, " +      // 2
        " bill_to_id, " +      // 3
        " UPC, "          +    // 4
        "  quantity ) " +      // 5
        " values ( ?,?,?,?,?) " );
}
catch (SQLException e) {
        System.err.println("SQLException in prepareMovieStatements: " + e);
}


}

// --

public void prepareMoviesStatements() {
try {

    pstmtMovies = conMovies.prepareStatement(
            "insert into sales   " +
            " (movie_id, quantity, order_number) " +
            " values ( ?,?,? ) " );
}
catch (SQLException e) {
        System.err.println(
        "SQLException in prepareMovieStatements: " + e);
}
}
```

The OrdersProcessor Class: The Constructor

The constructor for the `OrdersProcessor` class obtains connections to the two databases used to perform the order transaction: the `stock` database and the `order` database. This is done by retrieving the appropriate `DataSource` object through the JNDI naming service and then requesting a connection to the underlying database for the `DataSource`. If the connection to both databases has been successful, then the respective methods are called to prepare the `stock` and `movies` database SQL statements for use.

The OrdersProcessor Class: The Constructor

```
public OrderProcessing() {

try {

InitialContext init = new InitialContext( );
```

```
//
// connect to the movies database
//
DataSource moviesDS = (DataSource) init.lookup(
                        "movies-mysql" );

if ( moviesDS != null )
    conMovies = moviesDS.getConnection();
else
    System.out.println(
        "Error obtaining connection to movies-mysql.");

if ( conMovies != null )
   System.out.println(
        "Connected to the movies-mysql DataSource ... ");

//
// connect to the stock database
//
DataSource stockDS = (DataSource) init.lookup(
                "stock-psql" );
if ( stockDS != null )
   conStock = stockDS.getConnection( );
else
    System.out.println( "Error obtaining connection to stock-psql.");

if ( conStock != null )
    System.out.println(
        "Connected to the stock-psql DataSource ... ");

if (( conStock != null ) && ( conMovies != null ) ) {
    prepareStockStatements();
    prepareMoviesStatements();
}

}

catch (SQLException e) {
      System.err.println("SQLException in OrderProcessing: " + e );
}
catch (NamingException e) {
      System.err.println("NamingException in OrderProcessing: " + e );
}
catch (Exception e) {
      System.err.println(
          "Exception in OrderProcessing: " + e );
}
}
}
```

USING PUBLISH AND SUBSCRIBE MESSAGING

As discussed at the beginning of this chapter, publish and subscribe messaging provides an alternative method of loosely coupled component interaction. In the following example, a message client sends a request for information on particular movies. As shown previously with the message queue example, the message is in an XML format, so parsing and processing the message is made simpler.

Creating a publish and subscribe client is similar to creating a message queue client. But instead of sending the message to a queue, we will *publish* it to a topic. The following code example demonstrates this process.

The JMSClientPS Class

```
package examples.jms;
import java.util.*;

import javax.naming.*;
import javax.jms.*;


public class JMSClientPS {

public static void main( String args[] ) {

Hashtable ht   = new Hashtable();

ht.put( Context.INITIAL_CONTEXT_FACTORY,
         "org.jnp.interfaces.NamingContextFactory" );
ht.put( Context.PROVIDER_URL,
         "jnp://localhost:1099" );
ht.put( Context.URL_PKG_PREFIXES,
         "org.jboss.naming:org.jnp.interfaces" );

try {

  InitialContext context = new InitialContext( ht );

 TopicConnectionFactory factory =
         (TopicConnectionFactory) context.lookup(
                          "QueueConnectionFactory");
 TopicConnection connection = factory.createTopicConnection();

 TopicSession session = connection.createTopicSession(
                false,   // no transactions
Session.AUTO_ACKNOWLEDGE); // auto-acknowledge sessions

 Topic topic = (Topic) context.lookup( "topic/movie-info" );

 TopicPublisher publisher = session.createPublisher( topic );
```

```
TextMessage message = session.createTextMessage();

for ( int n = 1; n < 11; n++ ) {

    //
    // create a dummy request for test purposes
    //
    message.setText( "<movie-info-request>" +
                     "<movie-id>" + n + "</movie-id>" +
                     "<customer-id>" + n*3 + "</customer-id>" +
                     "</movie-info-request>" );

    publisher.publish( topic, message );

}

}
catch (NamingException e) {
    System.out.println("NamingException e: " + e );
}
catch (Exception e) {
    System.out.println("Exception e: " + e );
}

}

}
```

In this example, a topic connection factory (`javax.jms.TopicConnectionFactory`) is first created, and a connection to the topic is created from the factory. The connection is then used to create a session object, and the session is used to create a text message for publishing to the topic.

The topic is looked up via the naming service, and then the topic and session are combined using the `TopicSession createPublisher` method to create a publisher (`javax.jms.TopicPublisher`) object. A `for` loop is then used to generate a series of movie information requests, which are published to the topic.

Publish/Subscribe: Listener

The publish and subscribe listener connects to the topic via a subscription. The subscription is then used to obtain messages for the subscription. By default, there is a timing requirement that the listener must be subscribed to the topic to receive the message. Optionally, a *durable queue* could be used to provide messaging services, which would allow this timing requirement to be relaxed.

The listener class shown next performs the work necessary to subscribe to a topic and then uses the TopicSession setMessageListener method to identify an instance of itself (JMSListenerPS class) as a listener for that subscription. The listener class must implement the MessageListener interface in order to subscribe to a topic. Once the listener has been registered, the TopicConnection start method is called to begin receiving messages.

The onMessage method processes the message passed into the method by extracting the message and displaying the information to the console. A production implementation would take the message and delegate processing to another object. In this case processing would involve the generation of an email message to the client containing the information on the movie the client has requested in the message.

The JMSListenerPS Class

```
package examples.jms;

import java.util.Hashtable;
import javax.jms.TopicConnectionFactory;
import javax.jms.TopicConnection;
import javax.jms.TopicSubscriber;
import javax.jms.TopicSession;
import javax.jms.MessageListener;
import javax.jms.TextMessage;
import javax.jms.Topic;
import javax.jms.Session;
import javax.jms.Message;
import javax.jms.JMSException;
import javax.naming.Context;
import javax.naming.InitialContext;
import javax.naming.NamingException;

public class JMSListenerPS implements MessageListener {

public static void main( String args[] ) {

//
// connect to the JBoss message queue
//
Hashtable ht  = new Hashtable();
ht.put( Context.INITIAL_CONTEXT_FACTORY,
        "org.jnp.interfaces.NamingContextFactory" );
ht.put( Context.PROVIDER_URL, "jnp://localhost:1099" );
ht.put( Context.URL_PKG_PREFIXES,
        "org.jboss.naming:org.jnp.interfaces" );
```

```
try {

    JMSListenerPS listener = new JMSListenerPS();

    InitialContext context = new InitialContext( ht );

    TopicConnectionFactory factory = (TopicConnectionFactory)
                context.lookup( "TopicConnectionFactory");
    TopicConnection connection = factory.createTopicConnection();
    TopicSession session = connection.createTopicSession(
            false,                      // no transactions
            Session.AUTO_ACKNOWLEDGE); // auto-acknowledge sessions

    //
    // get the message queue
    //
    Topic topic = (Topic) context.lookup( "topic/movie-orders" );

    //
    // create a message receiver
    //
    TopicSubscriber subscriber = session.createSubscriber( topic );

    System.out.println("Subscribed to topic ... ");

    //
    // add an instance of this class as a listener
    //
    subscriber.setMessageListener( listener );

    System.out.println("Starting connection ... ");

    //
    // must start the connection to begin receiving messages
    //
    connection.start();

}
catch (NamingException e) {
    System.out.println( "NamingException e: " + e );
    e.printStackTrace();
}
catch (Exception e) {
    System.out.println( "Exception in main: e: " + e );
    e.printStackTrace();
}

}

public void onMessage( Message message ) {

try {
```

```
    System.out.println("Processing message ... " );

    //
    // retrieve the message body - a text message
    //
    String messageText   = ((TextMessage) message).getText();

    System.out.println("received message id: " +
        message.getJMSMessageID() + " - value: " + messageText );

    processor.processMessage( messageText );

}
catch (JMSException e) {
    System.out.println("JMSException thrown in onMessage: " + e );
}

}

}
```

SUMMARY

We know that tight coupling between components can create maintenance issues in an application, issues where a small change in one component can have an impact on other associated (or *coupled*) applications. Messaging therefore provides an extremely valuable facility for allowing distributed components to communicate in a loosely coupled fashion, thus improving the maintainability of an application.

Java provides the JMS package to allow Java applications to interact with messaging services. Common approaches to messaging include message queues and publish and subscribe message topics. The JMS package allows for interaction with both of these services, as we saw in this chapter.

CHAPTER 21

The JavaMail API

INTRODUCTION

As we saw in the previous chapter, messaging provides one facility for loosely coupled communication between components. With messaging, components don't communicate directly via method calls (as they do with EJBs); instead they communicate using a message, usually one with a predefined format that allows it to be parsed and processed by listeners.

Another facility often used for simple messaging is email. Though email servers often lack many of the controls of messaging servers (delivery acknowledgment, transactions), they do provide a low cost, easy to implement solution for applications which do not require these controls. Email could be used to send and receive formatted messages or for providing automated communication between an application and its users. Email is also a convenient facility for allowing an application to communicate with users (for example, sending an automated "your product has been shipped" message) or to allow an application user to communicate with the application administrator about an application problem (for example, emailing an administrator that "the sales reports are not current").

The JavaMail provides these capabilities for Java applications. This package allows Java applications to access email servers using common email protocols. But to use JavaMail you need to have some understanding of the underlying email protocols. In this chapter we provide an overview of email protocols, the JavaMail API, and provide an application example of using JavaMail to send email.

ELECTRONIC MAIL

Electronic mail has been around for almost as long as the semiconductor-based computer. Early electronic mail systems were proprietary and text-based, and allowed communication between parties on a private network. Arpanet, later the Internet and some standardized email protocols expanded on this by allowing a large number of users to communicate using the same type of service.

Email requires the use of an email server to store and forward email messages and an email program to provide user access to the server and to allow the user to send, receive, and delete messages (see Figure 21–1). Today these email servers use common, widely supported protocols such as POP3 (Post Office Protocol 3) and IMAP (Internet Messaging Access Protocol) to process messages.

Both IMAP and POP3 protocols use the Simple Mail Transfer Protocol (SMTP) to transfer and receive messages. While POP3, IMAP, and other protocols

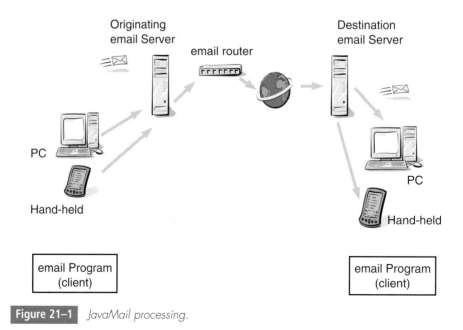

Figure 21–1   *JavaMail processing.*

define how to interact with the email server, the previously mentioned SMTP describes the format of the email message and the message transfer agent (MTA).

Users connect to the server by logging in with a user name and password. Though commonly used, the POP3 protocol has limitations. This protocol does not allow users to specify a subset of messages to download, nor are they allowed to read only mail headers. Instead POP3 users must download all pending messages to their email program. Though this is a simple protocol for the server to implement, it leads to additional network traffic and additional work for the mail program running on the client.

The IMAP protocol provides more flexibility than POP3. Users log into the server with a user name and password, and are then allowed to archive mail in folders and selectively read only message headers.

Originally, email was used only for text messages, but now non-text is commonly sent with email (and is in fact the source of many a nasty email virus). Using the Multipurpose Internet Mail Extensions (MIME) allows a document to be described and encoded for transmission (as text) and then later decoded using one of two encoding methods. The widely supported MIME has now become the standard method of transmitting non-text data via email. MIME messages are sent as email attachments.

Email traffic is now a common and widely accepted facility for communicating globally, with email messages currently measured in the trillions worldwide. The alternative, ground mail, is now derisively referred to as *snail mail* and is reserved only for what cannot be somehow placed into electronic format.

Security Risks with Email

Email is sometimes routed only through the local network, but in most cases it is directed over the Internet. This means that the information in the email is visible to the world at large. If what is being transmitted should not be visible to others, then the information should be encrypted. If what is being transmitted can be read by others, but the receiver would like to be certain it has not been tampered with and that it was in fact sent by a known party, then a digital signature can be used to validate the sender and the integrity of the contents. (Both encryption and digital signatures can be created with JCE as covered in Chapter 11)

Speed and Delivery Certainty

As with messaging, email is asynchronous—the sender does not wait for an immediate response from the recipient but instead simply passes the message off to a mail server for processing and routing.

But unlike point-to-point messaging using a set of internal messaging servers, using Internet email subjects the message process to the whims of the Internet. Performance of intermediate email servers between the sender and the receiver on the Internet is generally an unknown. Problems anywhere along the network could delay the delivery of the message or even cause the delivery to fail.

This sometimes faulty delivery mechanism coupled with the proliferation of "junk-email" that clogs the recipients inbox has impacted the usefulness of email. As developers, we must weigh these factors against the requirements of the application before choosing email as a messaging option.

Using the JavaMail Package

Since a variety of email protocols are in use today, Java we require a Java API that can support these multiple protocols. The JavaMail API meets this requirement by using an abstraction of an email service *provider,* described in the `Provider` class, to act as a container for the classes that support the email protocol to be used. The functionality of the email message itself is encapsulated in an implementation of the `Message` abstract class. The communication with the sending email server is provided using an implementation of the `Transport` abstract class, and the communication with the receiving server is provided using an implementation of the `Store` abstract class. Figure 21–2 diagrams the process flow using these classes.

There are a number of other classes available in the JavaMail package that provide access to mail attachments and allow filtering of email messages to be retrieved by the mail program client. These classes are listed in Table 21–1.

Complete coverage of JavaMail is beyond the scope of this chapter, but it is within scope to demonstrate one of the more useful implementations of JavaMail in an application. The following code example demonstrates an implementation of a mail service class to allow an application to communicate with a user using email. This class allows this communication to be achieved using a small set of calls to a convenience method exposed by the mail service class.

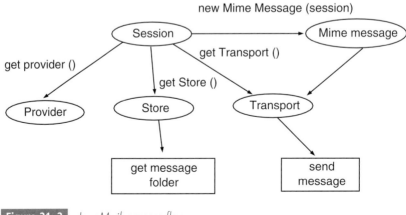

Figure 21–2   *JavaMail process flow.*

Table 21–1   *JavaMail Classes*

Class	Description
Address	Represents an address in an email message.
Authenticator	Indicates that an object can obtain authentication for a network connection.
BodyPart	One constituent part of a multi-part form.
FetchProfile	Used to list the message attributes to pre-fetch from the server for a range of messages.
Flags	A set of flags (Flags.Flag) on a Message.
Flags.Flag	Inner class representing an individual flag.
Folder	An abstraction of a folder for mail messages. A folder can contain messages or other folders.
Message	An abstraction of an email message.
Message.RecipientType	Defines the types of recipients allowed by the message.
MessageContext	Encapsulates information about the environment of the message.
Multipart	An abstract class that acts as a base class for the content holder for multipart documents.
PasswordAuthentication	A repository for the user name and password.
Provider	Encapsulates the implementation of a protocol.
Provider.Type	Defines the type of provider.
Service	Provides the functionality of the messaging service.
Session	Encapsulates a mail session.
Store	Provides an encapsulation of a message store.
Transport	An encapsulation of a message transport that provides the ability to send an email message.
URLName	Contains a URL name and functionality to parse the name.

A JavaMail Example: The MailService Class

The MailService class shown next encapsulates the functionality of connecting to a known SMTP host and sending a text email message. It exposes this functionality using a sendMessage method. An overloaded makeMessage method is used to create the MimeMessage to be sent. This makeMessage method can optionally be called with no arguments, in which case default settings will be used to create the MimeMessage. The method allows defaults to be overridden to create the MimeMessage allowing the 'to' and 'from' addresses to be specified along with the email 'subject' and 'message.'

Alternatively, only the 'to' and 'from' addresses can be specified to create the message, and the `MimeMessage` methods can then be used to set the `to` and `from` fields for the message. The main program block for this class contains test code and is shown below.

The MailService Class

```
package examples.javamail;

import java.util.Properties;
import javax.mail.Session;
import javax.mail.Address;
import javax.mail.Transport;
import javax.mail.Message;
import javax.mail.MessagingException;
import javax.mail.internet.MimeMessage;
import javax.mail.internet.InternetAddress;

import service.Constants;

public class MailService {

private Session session;  // this can be shared

public static void main( String args[] ) {

MailService mailer = new MailService();

//
// create the message to send
//
MimeMessage message = mailer.makeMessage(
        "taylorart@zippy.net",    // from address
        "taylor003a@zippy.com" ); // to address

try {
  message.setSubject("Nothing Important.");
  message.setText( "This is an email message.");
}

catch (MessagingException e) {

      System.out.println( "Exception in main: " + e );
  }

//
// send the message
//
mailer.sendMessage( message );
```

```
//
// send another message
//
mailer.sendMessage (
        mailer.makeMessage( "taylorart@zippy.net",
                             "taylorart@zippy.com",
                    "The subject",
                    "The message." ) );

}
```

This block of code contains the imports and declarations for the class, including a declaration for a `javax.mail.Session` object, which can be shared among multiple invocations of users. The first invocation of the `makeMessage` method takes arguments for the 'from' address and the 'to' address. This implementation creates a `MimeMessage` for the current session (created by the constructor) and sets the 'to' and 'from' addresses. The message retrieved is then used to set the 'subject' and text 'message' for the email. Once the email message is complete, the `sendMessage` method of the `MailService` class is called to send the message.

The code for the various implementations of the `makeMessage` method are shown next. As we will see in the next section, this convenience method can be called with up to four arguments: one for the 'from' address, one for the 'to' address, and parameters for an email 'subject' and 'message'.

The makeMessage Method

The job of the `makeMessage` method is to create a `MimeMessage` based on the session being used by the `MailService` instance. The various implementations of this overloaded method are shown in the code listing below.

```
public MimeMessage makeMessage( ) {
        return new MimeMessage( this.session );
}

public MimeMessage makeMessage( String from, String to ) {
        MimeMessage message =
                    new MimeMessage( this.session );
try {

    Address[]  address = { new InternetAddress( from ) };
    message.addFrom( address );
    message.addRecipient(
            Message.RecipientType.TO,
            new InternetAddress( to )
            );
}
```

```
catch (MessagingException e ) {
    System.out.println(
        "MessagingException in makeMessage: " + e );
}
finally {
  return  message;
}


}

public MimeMessage makeMessage( String from, String to, String subject, String msg )
{

MimeMessage message = makeMessage( from, to );
try {

        message.setSubject( subject );
        message.setText( msg );

}
catch (MessagingException e ) {
    System.out.println(
        "MessagingException in makeMessage: " + e );
}
finally {
  return  message;
}


}
```

The first `makeMessage` shown takes no arguments. This method creates a default email message for the session and returns the reference to the message.

The next implementation takes two arguments: one for the 'from' address and one for the 'to' address. This implementation creates and returns a `MimeMessage` for this session. Since an email can have come from multiple email addresses, the 'from' element of the email message is created as an array, in this case a single element array since we assert a single 'from' address, and is added to the message with a call to the `message.addFrom` method. The 'recipient' for the email is added with a call to the `addRecipient` method, which takes arguments for the recipient type and the recipient address. Multiple calls to the `addRecipient` method will create an email addressed to multiple recipients.

The final implementation of the `makeMessage` method shown here takes arguments for the 'from' address, the 'to' address, the 'subject', and the 'message'. This method calls the `makeMessage` method with the 'from' address and 'to' address to create a `MimeMessage`, and then calls the `setSubject` and `setText` methods to set the 'subject' and 'text' for the email message.

The sendMessage Method

The `sendMessage` method shown next is a convenience method which allows an email message to be sent using the current email session (which it asserts has been properly created). This method takes an argument, which is the email message to send and uses the current session to create a transport and send the message, as shown in the code listing below.

```
public void sendMessage( MimeMessage message ) {

try {
  Transport transport = session.getTransport( "smtp" );
  transport.connect( Constants.SMTP_HOST,
                     Constants.SMTP_PORT,
                     Constants.SMTP_USER_ID,
                     null); // password

  transport.send( message );
}
catch ( MessagingException e ) {
    System.out.println( "MessagingException in makeMessage: " + e );
}

}
```

The method creates a transport using the `Session getTransport` call and specifying the `smtp` transport type. The `Transport connect` method (inherited from the `Service` class) is called with arguments specifying (using constants defined for this example) the SMTP port (usually 25) and the user ID for the SMTP host to use to log into the mail server. The final argument for this method is the password to use to log into the server.

The MailService Constructor

The `MailService` constructor shown below is used to create a `Session` object to be used to provide the email services. This is done by creating a `Properties` object and identifying an SMTP host. The static `Session getInstance` method is then used to create an instance of the `Session` object. The second argument is for an authenticator object used to authenticate mail sessions via a callback. Since that is not used in this implementation, we pass a null value. The `Session` object returned is saved in a member instance.

```
public MailService() {

  Properties props = new Properties( );
  props.put( "mail.smtp.host", Constants.SMTP_HOST );
```

```
this.session = Session.getInstance( props, null );

}

}
```

The Constants Class

The Constants class is just used to define several string constants used in the example. The contents of this class is shown below.

```
package service;

public class Constants {

public static final String SMTP_HOST =  "pop.zippy.net";
public static final int SMTP_PORT    =  25;
public static final String SMTP_USER_ID =  "art";

}
```

SUMMARY

The JavaMail package provides access to common email protocols for Java applications. This provides yet another facility for creating loosely coupled J2EE components or for simply providing an application user with access to email. In this chapter we demonstrated some of the basic facilities for using JavaMail and provided a demonstration of coding a set of convenience methods for accessing an email service with the JavaMail API.

CHAPTER 22

JAXM: Java Web Services

INTRODUCTION

Probably no other technology has generated so much interest in the past few years than Web Services. Web Services provide a convenient mechanism for businesses to exchange information. While this task, the simple exchange of information, may sound simple to those outside of the IT industry, anyone who has ever struggled with data formats and protocols to move data from application to application knows this is not a trivial task. Moving data from one application to another within the same enterprise has its own significant set of difficulties. Moving information from one application to another application in another enterprise running on a different platform is even more difficult.

Web Services were meant to smooth over the difficulties of data interchange and in the process introduce a new facility for delivering services. Since these services were designed to be delivered using the HTTP protocol, they have been dubbed *web services*.

This chapter examines the world of Web Services and identifies, at least for the purposes of this text, where Web Services fits into the J2EE architecture. We will use several examples to demonstrate the process of creating and using a Web Service.

Why We Need Web Services

Large enterprises have a great deal of information to work with. For instance, a large clothing retailer may capture 300 gigabytes of information per year. Some portion of this information must be exchanged with suppliers and other divisions. For example, shipping must notify stores of shipments. Stores must notify inventory control of orders (see Figure 22–1).

This exchange of information is complicated by the presence of numerous specialized software applications, some of which may have been developed in-house. These specialized applications often provide something of a competitive edge for the enterprise, so eliminating them to implement some large, integrated application may not be desirable.

Exchanging data between systems running on different platforms is one problem. Managing the proprietary formats for the data is yet another problem. The XML standard has alleviated a large number of the platform-specific issues. The wide availability of XML parsers allow an XML document to be exchanged easily between applications as long as the applications have been made aware of the schema (layout) of the XML document.

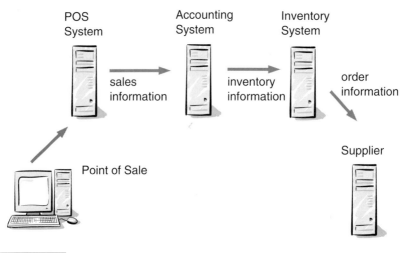

Figure 22–1   *Information flow in the large enterprise.*

But the ease of exchange of XML data solves only part of the problem. Applications must still define a protocol for the exchange of information. And since these applications may be complex and proprietary, we would prefer to have the components communicate in a loosely coupled manner. This is where using Web Services provides benefits.

WEB SERVICES DEFINED

Web Services are Web-based applications that interact in a dynamic fashion with other Web applications. This interaction takes place using a variety of open standards, which we have already seen in this text, including XML and HTTP. Added to these open standards are the newly defined protocols and formats for Web Services: Simple Object Access Protocol (SOAP), Universal Description, Discovery, and Integration (UDDI), and Web Services Description Language (WSDL).

As we saw in Chapter 14, "Java and XML: Introduction to XML," using XML provides a convenient method for describing data being exchanged between applications—data interchange. We can refer to the information being exchanged as *business documents*. These business documents are part of a message that can also be referred to as a *business message*. An application that consumes business documents in a previously agreed-upon format and produces business documents as a response is considered a *business service*. Performing these same functions over the World Wide Web is referred to as a *Web service*.

All of this is essentially business-to-business (B2B) messaging. Web Services provide this messaging using an HTTP communication protocol with XML message formats. SOAP provides the framework for the message. WSDL allows the Web Service to describe its capabilities. And the UDDI standard describes a universal business registry that allows applications to discover and use each others' Web Services.

These standards can be combined into an architecture where services that are to be exposed using SOAP register with a UDDI registry. Clients that interact with the UDDI registry process WSDL, which describes the services available. Once client applications are aware of the services available, they may optionally choose a service and interact with it using SOAP, as shown in Figure 22–2.

The specifics of using UDDI and WSDL offer an attractive possibility for the open use of Web Services over the Internet, but various data format standards and security issues must be resolved before these standards are widely used. The SOAP protocol has met with some success on corporate intranets and is the focus of the examples in this chapter. These standards are described in more detail in the following sections.

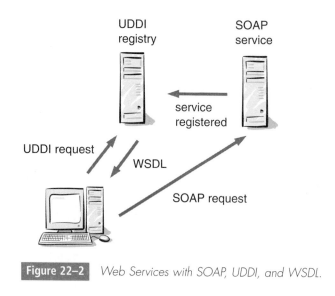

Figure 22–2 *Web Services with SOAP, UDDI, and WSDL.*

SOAP

The SOAP specification provides a framework for the message, which uses three parts: an envelope describing what is in the message and how to process it, rules for encoding application-defined data types, and a process for executing remote procedure calls and responses.

SOAP is a protocol for information interchange. Since it uses messaging, it is a loosely coupled approach which allows participants to be dispersed geographically and still easily exchange information. It uses XML for information encoding, thereby providing a convenient mechanism for describing the data in the message. The SOAP messaging specification does not specify the protocol to use but it does describe bindings for using SOAP with HTTP and the HTTP extension framework.

WSDL

WSDL is a protocol and format description that allows a Web Service to describe its capabilities. It was developed by IBM and Microsoft to be used in combination with the UDDI. WSDL descriptions can be stored in a UDDI directory where they can be retrieved by potential clients. The Web Services Flow Language is a related protocol from IBM that describes the workflow between services.

UDDI

The UDDI standard is part of an industry initiative for defining a universal business registry. Created through the combined efforts of Ariba, IBM, Microsoft, and others, this standard is designed to allow applications to automatically discover and use each others' services over the Internet. The information in the UDDI directory is also available in a human-readable format, allowing users to scan the directory for potential services. The UDDI specification contains provisions for white pages (addresses and contacts), yellow pages (industry classifications), and green pages (descriptions of services). The current specification also provides the Document Type Definition (DTD), the XML version, and the type of encryption used.

The stated goal is to use the UDDI discovery mechanism to register a service on the Internet. This would allow any application to search the directory, find the service, determine the format of the data delivered by the service, and then interact with the service. It is assumed that this approach would also provide a mechanism through which the service provider could charge a fee for the service.

THE SOAP MESSAGING STANDARD

At the core of the Web Services story lies the SOAP message standard. The SOAP message is composed of several parts: a header, an envelope, and a body (see Figure 22–3). These elements are used together to create, send, and process a SOAP message.

The SOAP header provides a generic mechanism for describing the message and provides some mechanisms for defining who should process the message and how features should be managed. Within the SOAP header, a `mustUnderstand`

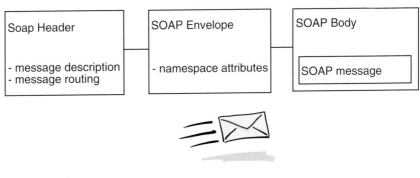

Figure 22–3   *The SOAP message.*

attribute may be declared to indicate what elements must be understood by the recipient in order to process the message. An optional actor attribute may also be used to indicate how and by whom the message will be processed.

A SOAP envelope represents the top level of the message document. It may contain namespace attributes and additional declarations, and is generally used to provide some description of the document. This description will be used by the recipient to make decisions on how to process the document.

The SOAP body is effectively the container for the information being sent in the message. Only one element is defined for the SOAP body: the Fault element, which describes and reports errors that have occurred in processing the message. A body may contain a number of XML entries as needed to provide the contents of the message.

JAVA AND WEB SERVICES

J2EE supports Web Services through the Java Web Services development pack. Specifically as of this writing, it supports the SOAP 1.1 specification and the SOAP with attachments specification. The API implements synchronous messaging using a request–response cycle or implements asynchronous one-way messaging using a provider. It is possible to create a standalone client using the API as long as the JAXM class files are visible to the client.

Two communication paradigms are possible using SOAP: *point-to-point* and *remote provider* communication. The difference between these two approaches is essentially that of synchronous versus asynchronous messaging.

A point-to-point model involves direct communication between the client, the sender of the SOAP message, and the recipient. The message goes directly to the recipient using a direct communication link is made between the sender and the recipient (see Figure 22–4).

The remote provider communication model is more akin to a messaging server. Messages are sent to a *remote provider* which may optionally acknowledge receipt of the message. The remote provider then delivers the message to the application (or component) that is responsible for processing the message. The application that will process the message need not be active when the message is received (see Figure 22–5).

The exchange of SOAP messages is divided into five categories in the JAXM specification. These categories are detailed in Table 22–1.

These message categories are explained in more detail in the following sections.

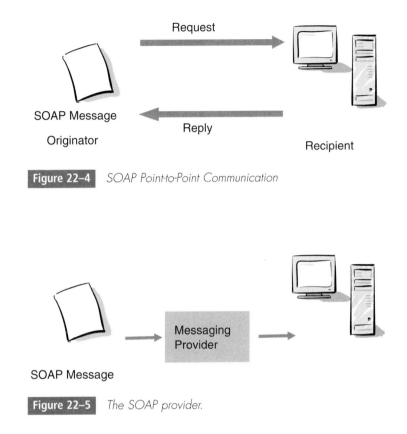

Figure 22–4   *SOAP Point-to-Point Communication*

Figure 22–5   *The SOAP provider.*

Table 22–1   *Categories of SOAP Messages*

Category	Description
Asynchronous inquiry	Sender sends message without waiting for a response. A reply is sent at some later time.
Asynchronous update with acknowledgment	Reception of acknowledgment indicates the earlier request has been completed. Acknowledgment must reference the request.
Synchronous request	Sender sends request and must wait for a response before proceeding.
Synchronous inquiry	Sender receives a response that the message was received. Response need not reference the request.
Fire and forget	Sender does not expect a response to the message that was sent.

Asynchronous inquiry

With asynchronous inquiry, the sender sends a message to a SOAP recipient. The sender does not wait for an immediate reply and can continue processing. The recipient can send a reply to the sender or can wait for an indeterminate period of time before replying. There is currently no contingency for a timeout parameter waiting for a reply from this type of SOAP transaction.

Asynchronous Update with Acknowledgment

This is similar to the previous type of transaction except that the recipient of the SOAP message is required to generate a reply on successful completion of the message transaction. The reply generated must be able to be matched to the message that was sent. The specifics of how the request is matched to the reply is left to the JAXM implementation.

Synchronous Request

This represents a completely synchronous transaction between the sender and the SOAP recipient. The sender cannot proceed until it receives an acknowledgment response from the message which was sent. The acknowledgment response received by the sender must correlate to the message that was sent. A possible response to an update would be to indicate that the update had been successfully completed.

Synchronous Inquiry

The synchronous inquiry is similar to the synchronous request except that the response is not an acknowledgment response. The requirements for the response from the SOAP recipient to the sender have been relaxed. A response is sent to the message sender by the SOAP recipient, but this response does not necessarily match the message that has been sent; its purpose is only to unblock the sender so that the sender may proceed.

Fire and Forget

With the fire-and-forget strategy of SOAP messaging, a message is sent to a SOAP recipient and the sender continues processing. The sender does not expect a response from the recipient.

JAXM PACKAGES

Java provides two packages that allow SOAP messages to be manipulated. The most commonly used package is the `javax.xml.soap` package, which contains the core classes for creating and manipulating messages. The packages and their classes are described in Table 22–2 and Table 22–3.

Table 22–2   *JAXM Packages*

Package	Description
javax.xml.messaging	Used to manage one-way (message server) messaging with SOAP messages.
javax.xml.soap	Used for the creation and transmission of SOAP messages

The javax.xml.soap package contains some of the core classes to create and manipulate SOAP messages. These classes are shown in Table 22-3 below.

Table 22–3   *JAXM Packages*

Class	Description
AttachmentPart	Represents an attachment for a SOAP message.
MessageFactory	A factory for the creation of a SOAPMessage object.
MimeHeader	Contains the MIME header name and its corresponding value.
MimeHeaders	Contains a set of MimeHeader objects representing the MIME headers in the MIME portion of the message.
SOAPConnection	Used to create the point-to-point connection for sending messages directly to a SOAP recipient. Does not require the use of a SOAP provider.
SOAPConnectionFactory	A factory for the creation of SOAP messages.
SOAPElementFactory	A factory for the creation of SOAP elements.
SOAPMessage	Represents the root object for all SOAP messages. The various SOAP elements are attached to this object.
SOAPPart	Contains the various SOAP elements that comprise the message. Is a MIME part and contains MIME headers.

A SOAP message is ultimately composed of a set of logically associated objects as shown in Figure 22–6. One part of this set is aptly named the `SOAPPart`. This object in turn contains the `SOAPEnvelope`, which contains a header (`SOAPHeader`) and a body (`SOAPBody`). The header and body in turn contain one or more elements of type `HeaderElement` and `BodyElement`.

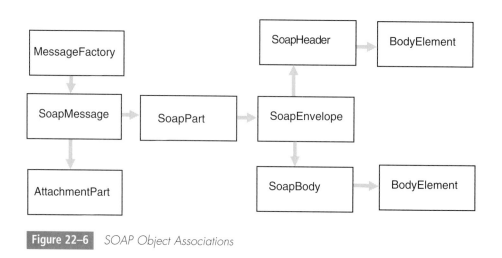

Figure 22–6   *SOAP Object Associations*

The factory design pattern is applied throughout the SOAP API. A `MessageFactory` is required to create SOAP messages, and a `SOAPConnectionFactory` is used to create a `SOAPConnection`. There are also a number of interfaces in the JAXM package implemented by the SOAP provider and listed in Table 22–4 .

The `SOAPFault` object would contain a `Detail` object and one or more `DetailEntry` objects, which describe the error that occurred during the processing or routing of the message.

The `SOAPHeader` object provides information about the messag and allows `SOAPElement` objects to be added to the header to describe the message. Usually, these would be `SOAPHeaderElement` objects set to indicate that they are an actor element or a `mustUnderstand` element. The `SOAPHeaderElement` is set using the `setActor` method, which accepts a string that resolves to the URI, providing information about the current processing and routing of the SOAP message.

Table 22–4   *Interfaces in the javax.xml.soap Package*

Package	Description
Detail	An interface that represents a container for DetailEntry objects.
DetailEntry	An interface that represents the content for a Detail object, which provides details concerning a SOAPFault.
Name	Represents an XML name and contains methods to determine the local and name space qualified names.
Node	Represents a node in a DOM representation of the document.
SOAPBody	Contains the contents of the SOAP body
SOAPBodyElement	An element of the SOAP body. A collection of these represents the SOAP body.
SOAPConstants	Various constants defined as part of the SOAP 1.1 protocol.
SOAPElement	Represents the contents of a SOAP body. A base class (interface) for a number of the interfaces used to define the SOAP object.
SOAPEnvelope	Contains the SOAP header and SOAP body of the SOAP part.
SOAPFault	An element in the SOAP body object that contains information on errors that have occurred or on current status information.
SOAPFaultElement	The contents of the SOAPFault object.
SOAPHeader	An interface that represents the SOAP header.
SOAPHeaderElement	An interface that represents an element in the SOAP header.
Text	An interface that represents a text node in the SOAP message.

The `setMustUnderstand` header element is set to indicate the message processing behavior, which relates to the handling of header entries that have the `mustUnderstand` attribute set. If the `mustUnderstand` attribute is set to true for a header entry, then the recipient processing the message must understand the header entry and be able to process it. If the recipient does not know how to process the element, the recipient must discard the message.

The javax.xml.messaging Package

The `javax.xml.messaging` package contains the classes and interfaces used to access a SOAP messaging provider. These classes allow an endpoint or destination for the message to be specified and provide access to the connection factory provided by the provider. Table 22–5 identifies these classes.

Table 22–5	Classes in the javax.xml.messaging Package

Class	Description
Endpoint	Represents the endpoint of a SOAP transaction.
ProviderConnectionFactory	A factory for the creation of provider connections.
URLEndpoint	A variation of the Endpoint class that allows direct, point-to-point communication between a consumer and a SOAP recipient.

The `Endpoint` represents the target for a SOAP message. Conceptually, this is a business entity with the URI representing a logical name and the URL representing the physical name.

When using JAXM profiles, an endpoint is not required because the profile will contain the endpoint information, and additional URI-to-URL mapping (to the physical destination) will be done when configuring the provider. For point-to-point messaging, however, the specification of an endpoint is required as a parameter to the call method that distributes the message to its target. Endpoints can be created programmatically or looked up in a naming service, which provides a more flexible approach.

The listener interface is implemented by the provider to provide for the processing of the message. Table 22–6 details the interfaces used to create JAXM listeners and providers.

The `OnewayListener` is implemented to create a component for processing messages from a sender without providing a response to the sender. These are referred to as *one-way* or asynchronous messages, since the sender does not need

Table 22–6	javax.xml.messaging Interfaces

Interface	Description
OnewayListener	An interface implemented by components that will receive and consume one-way, asynchronous messages.
ProviderConnection	Represents an active connection to a messaging provider.
ProviderMetaData	Allows the retrieval of information about a messaging provider
ReqRespListener	An interface implemented by components that will be used for request–responses (point-to-point) SOAP messages.

to wait for the message to be processed but may continue processing immediately after sending the message. The interface provides for an `onMessage` method, which must be implemented by the developer.

The `ReqRespListener` is implemented to allow point-to-point messaging in which a sender will send a message to a recipient and wait for the recipient to respond to the message before continuing processing. The interface provides an `onMessage` method, which the developer must implement to provide for the processing of the message.

The `ProviderConnection` and `ProviderMetaData` interfaces must be implemented by messaging providers to allow JAXM access to their systems. The implementations of these interfaces are used by client applications or components to send SOAP messages to the provider and to access metadata information on the provider connection.

Using JAXM: Sample Applications

Developing a SOAP application using JAXM is a fairly straightforward process. The SOAP message contains a number of parts, and understanding how those parts work together is important. Once that knowledge has been gained, the processes of creating and sending a message, and of receiving and processing a message, are not complicated.

The following example works with a fictitious movie database. What is needed is a service component that can receive a movie ID, a unique identifier for a movie, and return information about the movie. The application sending the request for the information ultimately outputs the information to a Web browser, so at some point the information needs to be formatted as HTML. This requirement makes using XML as an interchange format a natural choice.

Since the information requested is going to be used to create a display, this must be a synchronous, point-to-point request. The information is retrieved from a relational database, so the JDBC API is used to access the data in the database. Since we would like to use XML as the interchange format, we must convert the results of the SQL query to XML format.

The following code example demonstrates a service component that processes a SOAP request. Since SOAP identifies HTTP as a protocol, this is a special case of a Java Web tier component, in this case a servlet. The servlet we define here is a `JAXMServlet`, which extends the `HTTPServlet` class and adds additional behaviors and members to support SOAP transactions. Additionally, this class implements `ReqResponseListener`, an interface which identifies the class as a server participant in a request–response SOAP transaction. This interface requires the implementation of the `onMessage` method, which is invoked by the servlet container when a SOAP message has been received for this servlet.

Various class members are used to hold values that will be initialized in the `init` method and should be constant across all instances of the servlet (so that sharing instance members among sessions does not create a problem).

The servlet `init` method is used to initialize various instance members that will be used to handle the SOAP message. Within the body of the `init` method, a servlet initialization parameter is used to retrieve the query to be used to retrieve the information from the database. (This is a value stored in the `web.xml` file, which can be retrieved when the servlet executes./ This allows the query to be changed without requiring a code change.

The `init` method then creates a `SOAPConnectionFactory` and from that creates a `SOAPConnection`. This is saved in an instance member for use in the `onMessage` method. Next, a transformer factory is created and will be used to process the message content received: an XML document that contains the movie information requested. A message factory for the creation of `SOAPMessage` is also created and saved in another instance member.

The `DirectoryService` class is then accessed as shown below. This accesses an LDAP directory server being used to store various resources. A context containing JDBC resource references (`DataSource` references) is selected, and the `movies-mysql DataSource` is requested. Finally, a JDBC connection is created, and a JDBC statement is created from the connection. Various exceptions are logged using the logging service.

MovieInfoService Servlet Class: Class Declarations and init Method

```
package examples.webservices.movieinfo;

import java.io.StringReader;
import javax.servlet.ServletConfig;
import javax.servlet.ServletContext;
import javax.servlet.ServletException;
import java.sql.PreparedStatement;
import java.sql.ResultSet;
import java.sql.Connection;
import java.sql.SQLException;
import javax.sql.DataSource;
import javax.xml.messaging.JAXMServlet;
import javax.xml.messaging.ReqRespListener;
import javax.xml.soap.MessageFactory;
import javax.xml.soap.SOAPPart;
import javax.xml.soap.SOAPHeader;
import javax.xml.soap.SOAPBody;
import javax.xml.soap.SOAPEnvelope;
import javax.xml.soap.SOAPException;
import javax.xml.soap.SOAPMessage;
import javax.xml.soap.SOAPConnection;
```

```
import javax.xml.soap.SOAPConnectionFactory;
import javax.xml.soap.SOAPBody;
import javax.xml.transform.stream.StreamSource;
import javax.xml.transform.Transformer;
import javax.xml.transform.TransformerFactory;
import javax.xml.transform.Source;
import javax.xml.transform.dom.DOMResult;
import javax.naming.InitialContext;
import javax.naming.NamingException;
import javax.naming.directory.DirContext;
import org.w3c.dom.Document;
import org.w3c.dom.NodeList;

// our packages
import jdbcutil.JDBCXML;
import service.DirectoryService;
import xmlutil.SOAPXML;

public class MovieInfoService
     extends JAXMServlet
     implements ReqRespListener {

private ServletConfig  config;
private ServletContext context;

private String query;

private Transformer transformer;

private String to    = null;
private String data = null;

private ServletContext servletContext;

// Connection to send messages.
private SOAPConnection soapcon;

private Connection      con;
private Statement       stmt;

private MessageFactory messageFactory;

public void init(ServletConfig servletConfig ) throws ServletException {
  super.init( servletConfig );

  context = servletConfig.getServletContext();

  try {

      //
```

```
    // get a SOAP connection
    //
    SOAPConnectionFactory cf = SOAPConnectionFactory.newInstance();
    soapcon = cf.createConnection();

    //
    // create a transformer
    //
    TransformerFactory tf =
            TransformerFactory.newInstance();
    transformer = tf.newTransformer();

    //
    // Create a message factory.
    //
    messageFactory = MessageFactory.newInstance();


    } catch(Exception e) {
        logger.error("Exception in init: " + e);
    }

if ( con == null ) {
        //
        // use our directory server to access resources
        //
        DirectoryService directory = new DirectoryService();
        DirContext init = (DirContext) directory.getContext(
"o=jdbc, o=general-application-objects, dc=movies, dc=com" );
        javax.sql.DataSource ds =
        (javax.sql.DataSource) init.lookup( "cn=movies-mysql" );

        //
        // create the DataSource connection
        //
        con  = ds.getConnection();

        //
        // get the query to execute
        //
        query = context.getInitParameter( "movies-query" );

        //
        //
        // create the PreparedStatement
         stmt = con.prepareStatement( query );

      }
    }
    catch (SQLException e) {
          logger.error("Exception in init: " + e );
    }
```

```
catch (NamingException e) {
      logger.error("NamingException in init: " + e );
}

}
```

The MovieInfoService Class: `onMessage` **Method**

This servlet must provide an implementation for the methods defined in the `ReqRespListener` interface. That interface defines a single method, `onMessage`, which is defined as receiving a single parameter, a `SOAPMessage`, and returning a single parameter, a `SOAPMessage`. This method is effectively used as an event handler for messages received by the SOAP recipient. The SOAP message sent from the sender is received as a parameter, and since this is a synchronous message transaction, the SOAP message returned as a reply to the sender is the value returned by this method. (The `OnewayListener` interface provides a listener for asynchronous transactions and defines an `onMessage` method with no return parameters.)

Because this service has been designed to be sent only one type of message, it does not need to discern between multiple message types. For this reason, it does not need to examine the SOAP envelope or any other parts of the message that might contain information about the message. Instead, it can go directly about the business of retrieving the content of the message.

This is done by extracting the `SOAPPart` from the message (`msg.getSOAPPart`) and from the `SOAPPart` retrieving the content of the message with the `getContent` call. The result of these calls is a `Source` (`javax.xml.transform.Source`) object.

The `Source` object must be transformed before we can extract content from it. Once the transformation has taken place, we retrieve the top-level node (the document node) from the `Result` object (an instance of `javax.transform.dom.DOMResult`). From this node we then retrieve a list of elements with `movie-id` tag, and since we know there is only one, we retrieve the value stored for this tag. This is done using the call as follows.

```
Integer.parseInt( list.item( 0 ).getFirstChild().getNodeValue());
```

This call retrieves the first element in the `NodeList`—`list.item(0)`—and retrieves the first child node of that node—`getFirstChild()`. This has taken us to the text node that contains the value we need, and we can simply call the `getNodeValue` method to retrieve its value.

At this point we have the movie ID for the movie the sender has requested. The next few lines go about the business of constructing the SOAP message we will use for reply. This involves creating the message using a message factory and then creating the SOAP part, envelope, and header for the message. Then the SOAP body is retrieved from the envelope using the `getBody` method.

Now that we have a SOAP message and a message body, we need to create the content for our reply. We have the movie ID the user has requested; now we need to extract the information for that movie ID from the database and prepare the data as an XML document. A call to the `getInfo` method (shown below) extracts the information for the movie from the database and converts the information into an XML document.

We would like to make our XML document part of our SOAP message, but there is a restriction with SOAP messages that requires the message body, the content of a SOAP message, to be not just an XML document, but a specific type of XML document: a SOAP message XML document. This does not drastically change the information we are returning; it merely involves wrapping the XML document we have created with the tags required to create top-level nodes for the SOAP message XML document so our XML document will be encapsulated within the SOAP message XML document. This is accomplished using the `SOAPXML` `makeSOAPMessageXML` method.

Now that our XML document is the correct type of XML document, we can call the `setContent` method to add our document as the content of the SOAP message. But the `setContent` method needs a `StreamSource` argument. We provide this by wrapping the string, which is our XML document, with a `StringReader` object and passing the `StringReader` object to the constructor for a `StreamSource`.

At this point the SOAP message contains the XML document as the content for the message. In the `finally` block of the method, we return the SOAP message document we have created and populated to the caller.

Note that there is no attempt to manage any exceptions that may have occurred; it is up to the caller to determine whether or not the content in the reply message is useful. The method does set the message reply to null, which will serve as an indication to the caller that an error has been encountered.

MovieInfoService: onMessage Method

```
public SOAPMessage onMessage(SOAPMessage msg)

int movie_id = 0;
SOAPMessage reply=null;
try {

    // get the request parameters from the message
    Source source = msg.getSOAPPart().getContent();
    DOMResult result = new DOMResult();

    // transform the content (source) into a DOM object (result)
    transformer.transform( source, result );
```

```
    Document doc = (Document) result.getNode();

    NodeList list = doc.getElementsByTagName("movie-id");
    // get the movie id from the incoming message
    // order is guaranted by the DTD
    movie_id =
        Integer.parseInt(
            list.item( 0 ).getFirstChild().getNodeValue());

    // Create a message from the message factory.
    reply = messageFactory.createMessage();

    // create a SOAPPart
    SOAPPart soappart = reply.getSOAPPart();

    // get the envelope from the soap part
    SOAPEnvelope envelope = soappart.getEnvelope();

    // Create a soap header from the envelope.
    SOAPHeader header = envelope.getHeader();

    // Create a soap body from the envelope.
    SOAPBody body = envelope.getBody();

    //
    //  build the reply message
    //  return the movie information for this movie_id
    //  as an XML document
    //
    String movieInfo = getInfo( movie_id );

    //
    // wrap the message as a SOAP message XML document
    //
    movieInfo = SOAPXML.makeSOAPMessageXML( movieInfo );

    //
    // the information as an XML document is part of
    // our return message
    //
    soappart.setContent(
            new StreamSource( new StringReader( movieInfo ) ) );

}

catch (SOAPException e) {
    logger.error("Exception in onMessage: " + e );
    reply = null;
}

catch (Exception e) {
    logger.error("Exception in onMessage: " + e );
```

```
      reply = null;
}
finally {
    //
    // send the reply
    //
    return reply;

}

}
```

The MovieInfoService class: The getInfo Method

In the code shown previously, the `getInfo` method is responsible for retrieving the movie information from the database and formatting it into an XML document. This is accomplished using several standard JDBC method calls and using a custom utility class to format the JDBC `ResultSet` data as an XML document

The `getInfo` method first sets the single placeholder parameter in the prepared statement (`java.sql.PreparedStatement`) class to the integer value passed into the method. The prepared statement is then executed, and the results are stored in a `ResultSet`.

In the `finally` block of the `try/catch` block in the method, the `ResultSet` object is passed into the `JDBCXML.toXMLString` method to convert the contents of the `ResultSet` into an XML document. The resulting XML document is returned to the caller as a Java `String`.

The getInfo Method

```
private String getInfo( int movieID ) {

ResultSet rs = null;

try {

  //
  // set the prepared statement parameter
  //
  pstmt.setInt( 1, movieID );

  //
  //execute the statement
  //
  rs = pstmt.executeQuery( );

}
catch (SQLException e) {
```

```
    logger.error("SQLException in getInfo: " + e );
}
finally {
  //
  // format the ResultSet as an XML document
  //
  return JDBCXML.toXMLString( rs );
}

}
```

Consumers of Web Services: RequestMovieInfo Client

The `SendingServlet` represents the client for the Web Services provided by the `MovieInfoService` shown above. This servlet uses the information retrieved from the service immediately, so a synchronous call, one that returns results immediately, is required. The results returned from the SOAP transaction are XML documents, so the servlet uses an XSL template to transform the results into an HTML table for display to a browser.

The `init` method is used to create many of the objects that will be used in the `doGet` method. A `SOAPConnectionFactory` is used to create a connection and send the point-to-point SOAP message. A template is used to perform the XML transformation; that template is loaded as part of the initialization process being carried out.

The RequestMovieInfo Class

```
package examples.webservices.movieinfo;

import javax.servlet.http.HttpServletRequest;
import javax.servlet.http.HttpServletResponse;
import javax.servlet.http.HttpServlet;
import java.io.StringWriter;
import java.io.InputStream;
import java.io.PrintWriter;
import java.net.URL;
import javax.servlet.ServletException;
import javax.servlet.ServletConfig;
import javax.servlet.ServletContext;
import javax.xml.messaging.*;
import javax.xml.soap.SOAPPart;
import javax.xml.soap.SOAPHeader;
import javax.xml.soap.SOAPBody;
import javax.xml.soap.SOAPEnvelope;
import javax.xml.soap.SOAPException;
import javax.xml.soap.SOAPMessage;
import javax.xml.soap.SOAPConnection;
import javax.xml.soap.SOAPConnectionFactory;
```

```java
import javax.xml.soap.SOAPBody;
import javax.xml.soap.SOAPBodyElement;
import javax.xml.soap.MessageFactory;
import javax.xml.transform.stream.StreamResult;
import javax.xml.transform.stream.StreamSource;
import javax.xml.transform.Transformer;
import javax.xml.transform.TransformerFactory;
import javax.xml.transform.Source;
import javax.xml.transform.Templates;
import javax.xml.transform.dom.DOMResult;
import javax.naming.InitialContext;
import javax.naming.NamingException;
import javax.naming.directory.DirContext;

public class RequestMovieInfo extends HttpServlet {

    String to = null;
    String data = null;
    ServletContext context;

    Transformer templateTransformer;
    Transformer basicTransformer;

    //
    // Connection to send messages.
    //
    private SOAPConnection con;

    public void init(ServletConfig servletConfig)
            throws ServletException {
        super.init( servletConfig );
        context = servletConfig.getServletContext();

        try {
            SOAPConnectionFactory scf =
                    SOAPConnectionFactory.newInstance();
            con = scf.createConnection();

            //
            // create a transformer factory
            //
            TransformerFactory tf = TransformerFactory.newInstance();

            //
            // use this template for transformation
            //
            //InputStream xslTemplate =
                new URL( "file:/lin/home/art/data/rs.xsl").openStream();

            String xsl = context.getInitParameter(
                    "XSL-template" );
            if ( xsl == null ) {
```

```
        logger.error(
            "XSL-template parameter is missing in web.xml" );
        xsl="file:/lin/home/art/data/rs.xsl";
    }
    InputStream xslTemplate =
            new URL( xsl ).openStream();

    Templates template = tf.newTemplates(
            new StreamSource( xslTemplate ) );
    templateTransformer = template.newTransformer();
    basicTransformer =  tf.newTransformer();

    context.log(
        "SendingServlet: servlet has been initialized." );

} catch(SOAPException e) {
    context.log(
        "SendingServlet: Unable to open a SOAPConnection" + e);
} catch(Exception e) {
    context.log(
        "SendingServlet: Exception in servlet: " + e);
}


}
```

The RequestMovieInfo Class: The doGet Method

The doGet method is used to process the HTTP Get request for the servlet that sends the SOAP request. This method creates and sends the SOAP message and retrieves the response. The response will be a SOAP message containing the data we would like to display in XML format. The doGet method will take the XML document and transform it into an HTML table which will be sent to the response stream for the servlet.

The method begins by obtaining the PrintWriter output stream for the servlet. A message factory is then created, and a SOAP message is constructed. The SOAP message sent by this servlet must contain the movie ID of the movie we would like information for.

A SOAPMessage is created, and then a SOAPPart is created and the SOAPEnvelope is retrieved. Then the SOAPHeader and the SOAPBody are both retrieved from the SOAPEnvelope.

Since we would like to specify the movie ID of the movie to receive information for, we store that information as an element in the SOAPBody. This is done by first adding a body element named movie-info where we will store our request information. The movie ID for the request is then retrieved from the request parameters passed to the servlet, an element named movie-id is added to the `movie-info` element, and a text node is added with the value of the movie ID. Next, the endpoint for the SOAP transaction is added to the document. This is the `movieInfoService` servlet shown previously.

Once all of this work is complete, the `SOAPConnection call` method is called with two arguments: the message we have created and the endpoint (the target URL) of the SOAP message recipient. This `call` method is synchronous and will block until a response is received from the recipient. This reply is itself a SOAP message. In our case, this message should be the information we have requested.

The next few lines of code are used to retrieve the SOAP message from the response, the content in the `SOAPPart` of the body, and the envelope and header (which are not used in this example).

The content of the `SOAPPart` of the body is an XML document representing our results. We then transform this document into HTML and output it to our HTTP response, producing the HTML table shown in Figure 22–7.

The code for the `doGet` method is shown below.

Figure 22–7   *Movie Information Response*

The SendingServlet Client: The doGet Method

```
public void doGet(HttpServletRequest req, HttpServletResponse resp)
throws ServletException {

    String retval ="<html> <H4>";

    try {

        //
        // get the output stream
        //
        PrintWriter out = resp.getWriter();

        //
        // create a soap message
        //
        MessageFactory mf = MessageFactory.newInstance();

        SOAPMessage msg = mf.createMessage();

        SOAPPart soapPart      = msg.getSOAPPart();

        SOAPEnvelope envelope = soapPart.getEnvelope();

        SOAPHeader hdr          = envelope.getHeader();

        SOAPBody bdy            = envelope.getBody();

        //
        // create the message body
        //
        SOAPBodyElement gltp
        = bdy.addBodyElement(envelope.createName("movie-info",
                                "info",
                                "http://wombat.stuff.com"));

        //
        // this servlet should be called with a
        // parameter for the movie-id
        //
        String movie_id = req.getParameter( "movie-id" );

        //
        // the movie-id that we would like information for
        //
        gltp.addChildElement(
            envelope.createName("movie-id")).addTextNode(
                                    movie_id );

        //
```

```
    // set the endpoint
    //
      String to =
        "http://localhost:8080/J2EE_Beyond/movieinfoservice";

      URLEndpoint urlEndpoint = new URLEndpoint(
        "http://localhost:8080/J2EE_Beyond/movieinfoservice" );


     //
    // Send the message to the provider service
     //
      SOAPMessage reply = con.call(msg, urlEndpoint);


    //
    // get the information from the synchronous reply
     //
    Source source     = reply.getSOAPPart().getContent();
     SOAPEnvelope env = reply.getSOAPPart().getEnvelope();
     SOAPBody body     = env.getBody();

    //
    // transform the raw xml into an html table
     //
     StringWriter stringOutput = new StringWriter() ;
    StreamResult result = new StreamResult( stringOutput );
     templateTransformer.transform( source, result );


    //
    // result of transform is an html table
    // with information about the movie in the table
     //
     out.println( stringOutput.toString() );


  } catch(SOAPException e) {
     logger.error("Exception in doGet:" + e);
  } catch(Exception e) {
     logger.error("Exception in doGet:" + e);
  }


  }


}
```

The web.xml File

The two servlets shown in this example were both deployed in the same Web application. The `web.xml` file that describes these servlets maps both servlet names back to their respective Java classes as follows.

```
<?xml version="1.0" encoding="ISO-8859-1"?>

<!DOCTYPE web-app
    PUBLIC "-//Sun Microsystems, Inc.//DTD Web Application 2.2//EN"
    "http://java.sun.com/j2ee/dtds/web-app_2_2.dtd">

<web-app>

        <context-param>
            <param-name>XSL-template</param-name>
            <param-value>file:/lin/home/art/data/rs.xsl</param-value>
        </context-param>

        <context-param>
            <param-name>movies-query</param-name>
            <param-value>select * from movies where movie_id = ? </param-value>
        </context-param>

    <servlet>
        <servlet-name>
            movieinfoservice
        </servlet-name>
        <servlet-class>
            examples.webservices.movieinfo.MovieInfoService
        </servlet-class>
        <load-on-startup>
            1
        </load-on-startup>
    </servlet>

    <servlet>
        <servlet-name>
            movieorderservice
        </servlet-name>
        <servlet-class>
            examples.webservices.movieinfo.MovieOrderService
        </servlet-class>
        <load-on-startup>
            1
        </load-on-startup>
    </servlet>

    <servlet>
        <servlet-name>
            sendorder
```

```xml
        </servlet-name>
        <servlet-class>
                examples.webservices.movieinfo.SendOrder
        </servlet-class>
    <load-on-startup>
        1
    </load-on-startup>
</servlet>

<servlet>
    <servlet-name>
        sendingservlet
    </servlet-name>
    <servlet-class>
            examples.webservices.movieinfo.SendingServlet
    </servlet-class>
    <load-on-startup>
        1
    </load-on-startup>
</servlet>

<servlet-mapping>
    <servlet-name>
            movieinfoservice
    </servlet-name>
    <url-pattern>
            /movieinfoservice
    </url-pattern>
</servlet-mapping>

<servlet-mapping>
    <servlet-name>
        sendingservlet
    </servlet-name>
    <url-pattern>
            /sender
    </url-pattern>
</servlet-mapping>

<servlet-mapping>
    <servlet-name>
            sendorder
    </servlet-name>
    <url-pattern>
            /sendorder
    </url-pattern>
</servlet-mapping>

<servlet-mapping>
    <servlet-name>
            movieorderservice
    </servlet-name>
```

```
    <url-pattern>
        /movieorderservice
    </url-pattern>
</servlet-mapping>

</web-app>
```

Summary

Web Services provide a convenient mechanism for applications and components to interact using standard protocols. The emerging standards of SOAP, UDDI, and WSDL create an architecture that allows services to be registered, queried, and used in a dynamic fashion. Currently it is primarily the SOAP standard that is used, providing XML document interchange using HTTP but over time other services may become more widely used.

The JAXM package allows Java applications to create specialized servlets to perform point-to-point synchronous SOAP transactions. This chapter demonstrated one such application. In the next chapter, we examine the use of JAXM to create remote providers to allow asynchronous SOAP transactions.

CHAPTER 23

Using a Remote Provider: SOAP-RP

INTRODUCTION

In the previous chapter we learned the benefits of using SOAP with point-to-point protocols. Even though the use of a point-to-point protocol is relatively simple to implement, this direct synchronous interaction between components is not always needed and is often not possible. Instead, asynchronous interaction between components, and the loose coupling it provides, is more appropriate. SOAP-RP provides this asynchronous service.

Using a SOAP-RP remote provider is similar to using a messaging server. In this chapter we will examine the process of developing a SOAP-RP service to handle the "move information" request shown in the previous chapter. We will provide some information on how a SOAP-RP service operates and then demonstrate the creation of a SOAP-RP service using an example.

SOAP REMOTE PROVIDERS

Using SOAP with a *remote provider* provides many of the features of using a messaging service, including asynchronous dispatch of messages and queuing of messages at the provider. Various options such as the number of retry attempts and logging and retry time intervals can be configured for the provider.

JAXM allows other protocols to be added to SOAP by message providers using *profiles*. These profiles are implemented on top of the SOAP protocol. For instance, ebXML provides features that do not exist in SOAP, so a provider could support ebXML as a profile and accept SOAP messages that contain the required ebXML parts. A provider may implement multiple profiles, but a message can use only one at a time.

With a messaging provider, a message may be sent to more than one destination. These intermediate destinations are referred to as *actors* and are specified in the `SOAPHeader`. Specific attributes must be added to the header to provide information about the actors.

The client.xml File

Without a messaging provider, a SOAP client is limited to point-to-point message transactions. All transmissions to the SOAP recipient must be request–response transactions. The recipient must be available when the transmission is sent, and the client must block until a response is received from the recipient. While this may be adequate for some business transactions, such as the get movie information transaction shown in Chapter 22, this would not be the case for all business transactions. For instance, posting an accounting transaction to a journal and processing a purchase order are activities that would usually require some time to complete, so waiting for a response to validate completion is not a good option for the client application that initiated the business transaction. Using an asynchronous or *fire-and-forget* type of transaction is the preferable technique and with JAXM this requires the use of a SOAP remote provider.

SOAP-RP requires a number of configuration files. One of these which is used by the SOAP client, the `client.xml` file, contains information on the disposition of SOAP messages created and transmitted using JAXM. This is an XML file containing various elements that detail client configuration, as shown below.

client.xml

```
<?xml version="1.0" encoding="ISO-8859-1"?>
<!DOCTYPE ClientConfig
    PUBLIC "-//Sun Microsystems, Inc.//DTD JAXM Client//EN"
    "http://java.sun.com/xml/dtds/jaxm_client_1_0.dtd">
<ClientConfig>
    <Endpoint>
```

```
        http://www.wombats.com/movie-order/process
    </Endpoint>
    <CallbackURL>
        http://localhost:8080/jaxm-soaprp/receiver
    </CallbackURL>
    <Provider>
      <URI>http://java.sun.com/xml/jaxm/provider</URI>
      <URL>http://127.0.0.1:8080/jaxm-provider/sender</URL>
    </Provider>
</ClientConfig>
```

The entries in this file provide important information specific to Web Services, which explains why the entries are not part of the `web.xml` file. The `<Endpoint>` element indicates the URI of the message target. The `CallbackURL` indicates the location the recipient will use to receive the results of the transmission. The `<Provider>` element is used to indicate the URI/URL of the message provider.

THE PROVIDER.XML CONFIGURATION FILE

The current Reference Implementation of the Java Web Services contains a messaging provider implementation that runs within a servlet container. This implementation uses a `provider.xml` configuration file to direct how a message will be delivered as shown in the following listing.

The provider.xml File

```
<?xml version="1.0" encoding="UTF-8"?>
<ProviderConfig>
  <Profile profileId="ebxml">
    <Transport>
      <Protocol>http</Protocol>
      <Endpoint type="uri">
        <URI>http://www.wombats.com/remote/sender</URI>
        <URL>http://localhost:8080/jaxm-provider/receiver/ebxml</URL>
      </Endpoint>
      <ErrorHandling>
        <Retry>
          <MaxRetries>5</MaxRetries>
          <RetryInterval>2000</RetryInterval>
        </Retry>
      </ErrorHandling>
      <Persistence>
        <Directory>ebxml/</Directory>
        <RecordsPerFile>10</RecordsPerFile>
      </Persistence>
```

```
    </Transport>
    <Transport>
      <Protocol>https</Protocol>
      <Endpoint type="uri">
        <URI>jaxm.dummy.uri</URI>
        <URL>https://localhost:8443/jaxm/dummy/</URL>
      </Endpoint>
      <Persistence>
        <Directory>ebxml-https/</Directory>
        <RecordsPerFile>10</RecordsPerFile>
      </Persistence>
    </Transport>
  </Profile>
  <Profile profileId="soaprp">
    <Transport>
      <Protocol>http</Protocol>
      <Endpoint>
            <URI>http://www.wombats.com/movie-order/process</URI>
        <URL>http://localhost:8080/J2EE_Beyond/movieorderservice</URL>
      </Endpoint>
      <Endpoint type="uri">
        <URI>http://www.wombats.com/soaprp/sender</URI>
       <!-- <URL>http://localhost:8080/jaxm-provider/receiver/soaprp</URL> -->
       <URL>http://127.0.0.1:8080/J2EE_Beyond/movieorderservice</URL>
      </Endpoint>
      <ErrorHandling>
        <Retry>
          <MaxRetries>3</MaxRetries>
          <RetryInterval>2000</RetryInterval>
        </Retry>
      </ErrorHandling>
      <Persistence>
        <Directory>soaprp/</Directory>
        <RecordsPerFile>20</RecordsPerFile>
      </Persistence>
    </Transport>
    ...
```

These entries and their descriptions are defined in Table 23–1.

JAXM PROVIDER EXAMPLES

The following example demonstrates the use of a SOAP messaging provider to process an order. A movie order is sent to the SOAP recipient within the SOAP provider environment where it is processed. The client sending the request does not wait for a response and does not receive a response. The assumption is that the order will be processed correctly or that some other process will determine the failure and respond to it.

Table 23–1	JAXM Provider Configuration Entries

Element	Description
Transport	Contains the elements that describe how to handle a request.
Protocol	The protocol to be used to handle the request.
Endpoint	The destination of the message.
ErrorHandling	The number of times the provider will try to send the recipient the message.
Persistence	Where the messages will be stored before they are delivered.

The `MoviesOrderService` component is used to process the request. This Java component is a Java servlet, which subclasses `JAXMServlet` (which in turn subclasses `HttpServlet`) and implements `javax.xml.messaging`. Since it is running in a provider and will not return a response for the order being processed, it implements the `OnewayListener` interface. This interface requires an implementation of the `onMessage` method, which, as you would expect, returns no value. The code for this component is shown below.

The approach used in this example is to encapsulate the contents of the order in a Java object. The Java object is converted into XML and sent as an XML document in the body of the SOAP message. When received by the `MoviesOrderService` component, the XML document that represents the movie order is retrieved from the message and transformed into a stream where it is then passed to an order-processing object to process the order.

In the listing below the declarations and the `init` method are shown. The `init` method is merely used to create a `Transformer` object to transform the incoming XML document (as part of the SOAP message) and to create an instance of the order-processing object.

The MoviesOrderService Class

```
package examples.webservices.movieorders;

import java.io.ByteArrayOutputStream;
import javax.servlet.ServletConfig;
import javax.servlet.ServletContext;
import javax.servlet.ServletException;
import javax.xml.messaging.JAXMServlet;
import javax.xml.messaging.OnewayListener;
import javax.xml.soap.SOAPMessage;
import javax.xml.soap.SOAPConnection;
```

```java
import javax.xml.soap.SOAPException;
import javax.xml.soap.MessageFactory;
import javax.xml.transform.Transformer;
import javax.xml.transform.TransformerFactory;
import javax.xml.transform.TransformerException;
import javax.xml.transform.stream.StreamResult;
import javax.xml.transform.Source;

import movies.control.OrderProcessing;
import db.OrderDAO;

public class MovieOrderService
    extends JAXMServlet
    implements OnewayListener {

private ServletConfig  config;
private ServletContext context;

private String query;

Transformer transformer;

private ServletContext servletContext;

// Connection to send messages.
private SOAPConnection soapcon;

private OrderProcessing processor;

private MessageFactory messageFactory;

public void init(ServletConfig servletConfig ) throws ServletException {
  super.init( servletConfig );

  context = servletConfig.getServletContext();

  try {

      //
      // create a transformer
      //
      TransformerFactory tf = TransformerFactory.newInstance();
      transformer = tf.newTransformer();

      processor = new OrderProcessing();

  }
  catch(TransformerException e) {
          context.log(
            "MovieOrderService: TransformerException in init: " +
            e );
  }
```

```
finally {

context.log(
"MovieOrderService: MovieOrderService has been initialized.");

}
```

THE MOVIESORDERSERVICE CLASS: THE ONMESSAGE METHOD

The onMessage method shown below is used to handle the incoming messages for movies orders. The method receives the SOAP message as a parameter. By making a call to retrieve the SOAP part of the message and to retrieve the content of the message, we are able to retrieve an XML document that represents the message. Embedded within this XML document (as a subtree) is the XML document which represents our movies order.

Four lines of Java code are then used to convert the source object, an object that implements javax.xml.transform.Source, into a string representation of the XML document. This is done by creating a ByteArrayInputStream and wrapping it with a StreamResult (javax.transform.stream.StreamResult) object and making the StreamResult object the target of the transform operation. The string resulting from that operation is then passed into the processOrder method of the OrdersProcessing class, which executes the order.

The MoviesOrderService Class: the onMessage Method

```
. . .
}

public void onMessage(SOAPMessage msg) {

try {

    context.log( "MovieOrderService: processing order. ");

    // get the order, in XML format, from the body content
    //
    Source source = msg.getSOAPPart().getContent();

    //
    // transform the DOM XML body content into string format
```

```
//
ByteArrayOutputStream out = new ByteArrayOutputStream();
StreamResult streamResult = new StreamResult( out );
transformer.transform( source, streamResult );

//
// convert the ByteArrayInputStream into a string
//
String xmlDoc = out.toString();

//
// pass the XML document to the order processor
//
processor.processOrder( xmlDoc );

context.log( "MovieOrderService: order has been processed. ");
}
catch (TransformerException e) {
    context.log(
"MovieOrderService: TransformerException exception in onMessage: " + e );
}
catch (SOAPException e) {
    context.log(
        "MovieOrderService: SOAPException exception in onMessage: " +
        e );
}

finally {
    context.log(
        "MovieOrderService: onMessage completed successfully.");
}

}
```

Sending a Message to a SOAP Messaging Provider

The process of sending a message to a messaging provider is similar to using point-to-point SOAP communication. As with the point-to-point example, a SOAP message must be prepared. The process of preparing the message is the same, though the process of addressing the message is slightly different.

As you might expect, the process of establishing communication with the message recipient is also different. The SOAPConnection object is not used to establish the connection; instead, a ProviderConnection factory, most likely retrieved from a JNDI naming service, is used to create a connection to the messaging provider.

In this client example as shown below, we use a Java servlet to send the SOAP message to the remote provider. The servlet `init` method shown below establishes a connection to a `ProviderConnectionFactory`. In practice, this would be done using JNDI to provide access to this resource. The connection factory is then used to create a connection to the SOAP provider.

The SendOrder Class: The init Method

```java
package examples.webservices.movieorders;

import java.io.PrintWriter;
import java.io.StringReader;
import java.io.IOException;
import java.net.URL;
import java.io.ByteArrayOutputStream;
import javax.servlet.ServletConfig;
import javax.servlet.ServletContext;
import javax.servlet.ServletException;
import javax.servlet.http.HttpServlet;
import javax.servlet.http.HttpServletRequest;
import javax.servlet.http.HttpServletResponse;
import javax.xml.messaging.JAXMServlet;
import javax.xml.messaging.JAXMException;
import javax.xml.messaging.ProviderConnectionFactory;
import javax.xml.messaging.ProviderConnection;
import javax.xml.messaging.ProviderMetaData;
import javax.xml.messaging.URLEndpoint;
import javax.xml.soap.SOAPMessage;
import javax.xml.soap.SOAPPart;
import javax.xml.soap.SOAPEnvelope;
import javax.xml.soap.SOAPBody;
import javax.xml.soap.SOAPBodyElement;
import javax.xml.soap.SOAPException;
import javax.xml.soap.MessageFactory;
import com.sun.xml.messaging.soaprp.SOAPRPMessageImpl;
import javax.xml.transform.stream.StreamSource;

import movies.control.OrderProcessing;
import db.OrderDAO;
import xmlutil.SOAPXML;
import xmlutil.ObjectToXML;

public class SendOrder extends HttpServlet {

    private ServletContext context;

    private ProviderConnection con;

    public void init(ServletConfig servletConfig)
            throws ServletException {
```

```
      super.init( servletConfig );

try {

      //
      // get the servlet context
      //
      context = servletConfig.getServletContext();

      //
      // create a provider connection factory
      //
      ProviderConnectionFactory pcf =
              ProviderConnectionFactory.newInstance();

      //
      // create a connection handle to the provider
      //
      con = pcf.createConnection();

   }
   catch( JAXMException e) {
       context.log("Exception thrown in init: " + e );
   }
   catch( Throwable e) {
       context.log("Exception thrown in init: " + e );
   }
   finally {
       context.log( "SendOrder: Initialization complete. " );
   }

}
```

The SendOrder Class: The doGet Method

The doGet method shown below is used to perform the processing for the servlet. The servlet expects to receive several request parameters: a movie ID; the quantity of movies to process; and the ship-to ID and the bill-to ID, which indicate where to ship the product and who to send the product to respectively.

The doGet method begins by creating a MessageFactory using a profile. The profile specified in this example is the soaprp profile. This creates a message factory, which creates messages with a number of the headers (used to route the message and define its contents) preset to the correct values.

The message factory is then used to create a message that is cast to the type of SOAPRPMessageImpl. This creates a message that will be routed correctly to the SOAP remote provider. The message body and envelope are created using the resulting message (msg) object.

The request parameters relating to the movies order are then retrieved and used to set the the values for the `OrderDAO` object that has been created. The resulting `OrderDAO` object is then converted into XML format using the `ObjectToXML convertToXML` method.

At this point we have an XML document that represents our order, but it is not in the correct format for insertion into a SOAP document. The `SOAPXML makeSOAPMessageXML` method is called to create the entries that allow the document to represent the SOAP message content (essentially wrapping the movies order XML document with XML document tags for a SOAP document).

The XML document resulting from this operation must now be converted into a `Source` object. This is accomplished by wrapping the XML document with a `StringReader` and passing that to the constructor for the `StreamSource` method. The object which results from this operation is then passed to the `setContent` method for the SOAP part of the existing message.

The `to` and `from` endpoints for the message are then set. These entries correspond to entries in the `client.xml` file for the component. Finally, the message is sent to the messaging provider using the provider connection.

The doGet Method

```
...
public void doGet(HttpServletRequest req, HttpServletResponse resp)
    throws ServletException {

        String retval ="<html> <H4>";

        try {

            PrintWriter out = resp.getWriter();

            context.log( "SendOrder: preparing order." );
            ProviderMetaData pmd = con.getMetaData();

            MessageFactory mf = con.createMessageFactory(
                            "soaprp" );

            //
            // create a SOAP message for a provider
            //
            SOAPRPMessageImpl msg =
                (SOAPRPMessageImpl)mf.createMessage();

            SOAPPart soapPart = msg.getSOAPPart()
            SOAPEnvelope envelope = soapPart.getEnvelope();
            SOAPBody body = envelope.getBody();

            //
            // get request parameters and create an order
```

```
   //
   OrderDAO order = new OrderDAO();
     order.setMovieID(
       Integer.parseInt(
          req.getParameter( "movie-id" ).trim()  ) );
     order.setQuantity(
                Integer.parseInt(
           req.getParameter( "movie-units" ).trim() ) );
     order.setShipToID(
          req.getParameter( "ship-to-id" ).trim() );
     order.setBillToID(
        req.getParameter( "bill-to-id" ).trim() );
     order.setOrderNumber( req.getParameter(
                               "order-number" ).trim() );
     order.setUPC( req.getParameter( "upc" ).trim() );

    //
// convert order object and convert to an XML document
//
String xmlOrder = ObjectToXML.convertToXML( order );

    //
   // take the XML document that is the order
   // and format it as a SOAP XML document
   //
    String soapOrder = SOAPXML.makeSOAPMessageXML(
               xmlOrder );

   //
   // make the XML document the SOAP Part content
   //
    soapPart.setContent(
      new StreamSource( new StringReader( soapOrder ) ) );

    //
    // create the message body
    //
    SOAPBodyElement bodyElement
         = body.addBodyElement(envelope.createName(
                "movie-order",
                "process",
                "http://www.wombats.com"));
    //
// set the to and from end points
//
    msg.setTo( new URLEndpoint(
        "http://www.wombats.com/soaprp/sender" ) );
    msg.setFrom( new URLEndpoint(
         "http://www.wombats.com/movie-order/process") );

    con.send( msg );
```

```
            context.log( "SendOrder: processing completed." );

            out.println(
"<html><body><p>Movie order has been sent.</p></body></html>" );

        } catch(SOAPException e) {
            context.log("Exception in doGet:" + e);
        } catch(Exception e) {
            context.log("Exception in doGet:" + e);
        }

    }
```

SUMMARY

This chapter described using JAXM with SOAP remote providers. From the client's perspective, the functionality is similar to that of using point-to-point protocols. But using remote providers involves creating a specialized servlet, which is invoked each time a SOAP message is received.

As we demonstrated in this chapter, the end result of this approach is the creation of a messaging server for processing SOAP messages. For the right type of transaction, this loosely coupled, asynchronous approach to communication between objects may be the best approach to communication. Using SOAP for the protocol provides interoperability not only with other J2EE applications and components, but with components developed using other technologies (for example, .NET).

CHAPTER 24

Enterprise JavaBeans:
An Introduction

INTRODUCTION

Enterprise JavaBeans (EJBs) are one of the principal technologies of the J2EE architecture. They represent the middleware component specification for Java.

Following the release of the first EJB specification, the specification was quickly embraced and implemented by a number of application server vendors, and at last count, there were over 20 J2EE application servers available with varying costs and compliance levels (not all 20 are J2EE-certified by Sun Microsystems). A number of these servers are from open source efforts which provide an extremely low cost (practically no cost) entry point for implementing the technology and avoid the *vendor-lock* of vendor developed servers.

Note that not all J2EE applications require EJBs. In fact, a large number are deployed with no EJBs at all. But architecturally, EJBs represent one of the three core technologies of J2EE and provide a very robust mechanism for handling the business logic of an application. Whether or not an application needs the features provided by EJBs depends of course on the application. These next few chapters will detail those features and demonstrate how EJBs are used.

In this chapter, we will explain the important features of EJBs and detail how they operate in a J2EE application server. We will use a simple, minimal implementation example to demonstrate how they are used. The following chapters will discuss security and transactions with EJBs and will demonstrate how to use them to manage the business logic of the application.

THE JAVA MIDDLEWARE ARCHITECTURE

EJBs represent the middleware technology for the multitiered J2EE architecture. As such, it is useful to review where this technology fits within the overall multi-tiered technology we are developing.

Ultimately, the goal of EJBs is to provide a distributed software component—a remote object that can be accessed or invoked by remote clients. These components operate within a container which provides a specific set of services for the component. These services, as detailed in the next section of this chapter, represent the value added to this basic remote object invocation capability by J2EE.

The J2EE specification provides for EJB components. These components are special Java objects that can be invoked and run remotely by a client application. The communication mechanism for these components is based on RMI (as covered in Chapters 18 and 19).

EJB components run within a *container* that provides various services for the components and represents the runtime environment for the component. The J2EE specification for EJBs details the services the container is expected to provide, though it does not detail how the container will provide the services.

This use of distributed software components is not new; the ability to create those components with a standard API and a standard, widely adopted, cross-platform language is new. Many of the features J2EE-compliant application servers provide for EJBs would need to be developed with custom, proprietary code if another component technology were used.

Flavors of EJBs

EJBs come in three flavors as of the EJB 2.0 specification: *session beans, entity beans,* and *message-driven beans* (MDBs). Each has its specific benefits and is discussed in the following sections.

Session Beans

Using a service design model of distributed components, a client application communicates with a distributed component in a conversation. In the course of this conversation the client requests services of the component. These services execute business logic, access databases and other resources, and generate results. EJB session beans represent a session between a client and an EJB component, known as a *client conversation*.

This communication between the client process and the bean may or may not require the EJB to retain state information between invocations. If a session bean retains client state between invocations, then it is considered a *stateful session bean*. If a session bean does not retain client state between invocations, then it is considered a *stateless session bean*. (A stateless session bean can contain state in the form of instance variables, but since the stateless session bean is shared among clients, these instance variables are shared and there is no specific *client state*.)

State information is maintained in EJB components using instance members. Any stateless session bean, since it does not retain client state between invocations, should not use instance members for this purpose, because they will not be guaranteed to have sensible values, values specific to a client session, between invocations. In this vein, the most common processing cycle for a stateless session bean would be to receive a request, perform all work necessary to complete the request, and then return results for the request, all within the space of the invocation (the remote method call on the stateless session bean).

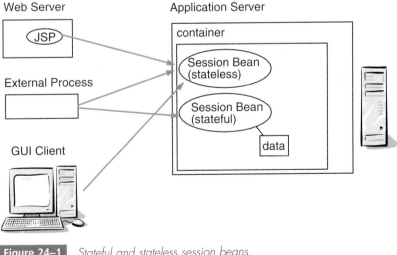

Figure 24–1   *Stateful and stateless session beans.*

Entity Beans

Entity beans (see Figure 24–2) represent a unique element in a persistent data store. They represent persistent data, and in relational database terms, they are said to represent a conceptual row in a database table (or potentially a unique record composed of a join across multiple tables).

Entity beans represent business data, and as such, they do not belong to a client session. Entity beans are usually accessed by other business tier components and are not (and should not) be accessed directly by a presentation tier or client tier component. A facade design pattern is recommended, to provide a layer of code logic between the client tier component and the business data. If multiple sessions attempt to access an entity bean using the same primary key, that entity bean will be shared amongst the multiple sessions.

Since it represents a unique relation in a persistent data store, an entity bean is represented by a *primary key,* a unique identifier for the entity bean. A primary key can be represented by one or more columns in the underlying table or tables.

An entity bean does not need to be mapped into a relational database. An entity bean could be mapped into a legacy database system or even into a set of files, though the most common implementation is that of *object-relational* mapping, using the entity bean to represent some portion of a relational database.

Entity beans must remain synchronized with the persistent data store. This synchronization is managed by the container by calling specific methods on the entity bean component.

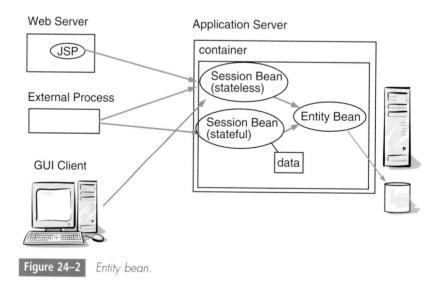

Figure 24–2   *Entity bean.*

These methods must be implemented by the entity bean (methods defined in the `EntityBean` interface). Specifically, the `ejbLoad` method is used to load the bean from the database, and the `ejbStore` method is used to synchronize the bean with the database.

Either an entity bean developer can write the code for the `ejbLoad` and `ejbStore` methods (and a few others) or the application server vendor can provide a tool that writes the code for these methods. If the developer provides the code for the entity beans database synchronization, then the bean is using *bean-managed persistence* (BMP). If the developer allows the application server tool to create the code for the entity bean persistence, then the entity bean is using *container-managed persistence* (CMP).

As part of the EJB 2.0 specification, additional features have been added to entity beans to improve performance, address some of the limitations of the previous specification, and enhance the implementation of CMP. A query language has also been added (EJB-QL), which allows internal selects and the navigation of related beans, values, and dependent objects using an application server and database server independent mechanism.

Message-Driven Beans

Message-driven beans (see Figure 24–3) were added to the EJB specification with the 2.0 revision. These beans represent a useful integration of the Java Messaging Service (JMS) and EJB technologies, providing a mechanism for delivering loosely coupled services using J2EE application server components.

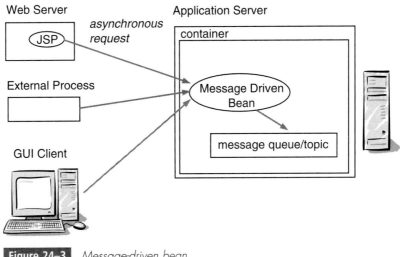

Figure 24–3 *Message-driven bean.*

Unlike session beans and entity beans, which submit a request (through method invocation) and expect an immediate response, message-driven beans allow an asynchronous request to be posted in the form of a message with no immediate response required. The message-driven bean is stateless and is invoked by the container upon the arrival of a message. (JMS, the underlying technology for MDBs, is covered in Chapter 20.)

The EJB Container

With EJBs, the container is implemented by what is commonly called an *application server*. Application server vendors and development groups may add additional services above and beyond the EJB specification and have some discretion on how services are implemented, but in order to be compliant, they must provide a core set of services as follows:

- security
- transactions
- naming
- scalability
- life-cycle management

These services and some background information on how they may be implemented are discussed in the following sections.

Security

EJB application servers must implement a specific role-based security model and must provide a role reference facility that allows a role reference name to be established for the role. Role permissions are then associated with methods and can be assigned to all methods within a component.

EJB security does not deal with authentication—the expectation is that this is managed in the presentation tier or the client tier. EJB security is concerned with the user's role and whether or not the user has permission to perform the action he or she is attempting to perform (executing a method in a component or accessing a resource).

Transactions

The EJB specification provides for transactions related to components and for transaction managers that transparently manage transactions with a single data source or with multiple data sources combined. Transactions can be managed either by the container, using *container-managed transactions* (CMTs), or programmatically through specific method calls, using *bean-managed transactions* (BMTs).

Components may run within a transaction and may propagate transactions down the call chain. This means that a method may have one transaction mode and call another method. The method being called may elect to use or not use the transaction of the method that called it, depending on the configuration of the component. This provides an easy mechanism to manage transactions based on component boundaries.

The transactional rules for entity beans are more stringent than for session beans. Entity beans must run within a transaction, so only CMTs may be used for entity beans. (Using BMTs would allow a programmer to eliminate transactions for an entity bean through exclusion of transaction code, and that is not allowed by the specification.)

Naming

The naming services provided by the EJB application server allow the component to use a JNDI name server to access resources. These resources could be an EJB component, a data source, or an environment entry that provides configuration information for the component. The naming service allows entries to be retrieved as `object` references, which may be cast, or *narrowed*, to their specific Java type.

Scalability

The *scalability* of an application represents the application's ability to handle an increase in usage without a significant drop in performance. For instance, an application that can manage a workload of 500 simultaneous users can double its usage level and increase the user load to 1,000 simultaneous users while experiencing only a 10 percent performance decrease (instead of a linear 50 percent decrease).

The EJB server should provide scalability features, which should be realized by the components transparently. The EJB specification does not provide details on what these scalability features should be or how they should be implemented (though it does specify that pooling of EJB components may be done and provides callback methods to allow some control over the process). Virtually all EJB application servers provide some type of scalability feature, though the type and sophistication varies.

Contributing to the feature of scalability is that of *load balancing*. The process of load balancing involves using a dispatcher, which dispatches requests over one or more servers. Load balancing is discussed in more detail in a later section.

Life-Cycle Management

The EJB server should provide life-cycle management services for the component. This means that the application server should find the bean when it is requested and should be able to return a home `object` reference for the bean. When the home object attempts to create or locate the bean, the application server should create or access the remote `object` reference and return it to the client that requested the component.

Life-cycle management also includes the *passivation* of EJBs. If an EJB component has not been accessed for some time, the application server can elect to passivate the bean. When the EJB component is later requested, the application server must be able to find the bean and restore its state.

EJBs can be instantiated before use and kept in a *pool*. Then, when an EJB is requested by a client, it is simply retrieved from the pool and made available to the client, thus avoiding the overhead of object instantiation (for the EJB) at runtime. See Figure 24–4.

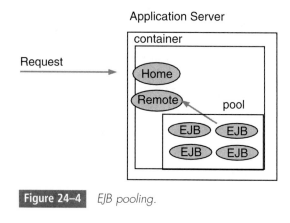

Figure 24–4   *EJB pooling.*

In addition to those mentioned above, application servers provide additional features and functionality. A few of the more important features that are not addressed directly by the EJB specification are server clustering and component failover, as detailed in the next section.

SERVER CLUSTERS AND FAILOVER CAPABILITIES

In order to provide both failover and additional scalability, application server vendors allow clusters or groups of hardware servers running the same software to be addressed as a *server cluster* (see Figure 24–5). This server cluster appears as a single server to external clients, which continue to make requests of a single application server host.

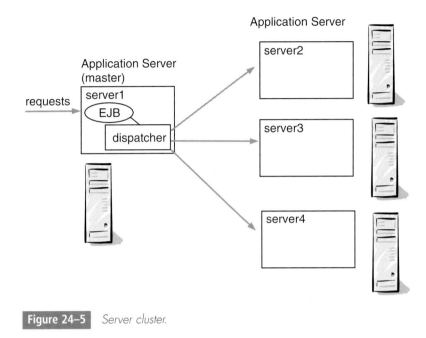

Figure 24–5   *Server cluster.*

The operation and management of the server cluster is completely under control of the EJB container. The implementation of the server clustering is transparent to the EJB component. Application server vendors provide configuration and tuning for the clustering, but this varies from vendor to vendor and is not addressed by the EJB specification.

Through clustering, both scalability and component failover are addressed. Implementation includes a dispatcher that is aware of all the servers in the cluster and distributes requests to the servers based on both availability information and various performance factors. Should one of the servers in the cluster no longer be available, the dispatcher would need to know about that.

Should there be a difference in performance metrics between the servers in the cluster, the dispatcher would also need to know about that. For example, several of the servers have a large amount of memory and extremely fast CPUs. This performance information is usually relayed to the dispatcher in the form of configuration settings, which are read when the server starts, but with some J2EE application servers, performance metrics are actually captured in real time and relayed to the dispatcher. Using this real-time data, the server can make intelligent decisions about load-balancing incoming requests, as we will see in the next section.

Load-Balancing Requests

As requests are made of a J2EE application server, the container implementation dispatches the requests to the appropriate component. As we have already been informed, if a client application has a reference to a session bean running on an application server, they don't communicate directly with the session bean. Instead they communicate with a remote reference to the session bean. This remote reference has both a client implementation (which is an RMI stub) and a remote reference running in the application server. The container implementation of the remote reference is responsible for interacting with the container and in so doing can provide additional features such as load balancing. As requests are directed to the container through these EJB remote references, the container can use an internal subsystem to determine where to direct the request. On servers with load-balancing features, this dispatch subsystem would be aware of server clusters and would use one or more load-balancing algorithms to determine where to direct the request among available servers.

Load balancing can be done using various algorithms, from a simple *round-robin* algorithm, where requests are distributed evenly among all available servers, to a *weighted average* form of load balancing, where requests are distributed among servers based on some statistical weight.

Even more complex load-balancing algorithms are used by some servers. As mentioned previously, some load-balancing algorithms evaluate the load on the servers in the cluster in real time and load-balance according to the actual system load rather than using static configuration parameters.

Request Failover (High Availability)

Application server clustering can also be used to provide high availability services for an application. If one of the servers in a cluster fails, obviously all of the EJB components being provided by that server will also fail. Using clustering, components may be available across multiple servers, so should one server be unavailable, the access to the component could be provided by another server. See Figure 24–6.

Providing a failover capability with a component like the stateless session bean is relatively easy to manage. Should a request fail on one server (because the hardware went down), the dispatcher can simply direct the same request to another server. Since there is no session bean state information required to provide the service that has been requested, fulfillment of the request can simply be provided by another server.

But providing failover for the EJB components, which contain state information, is more problematic. State information must be stored off the server where

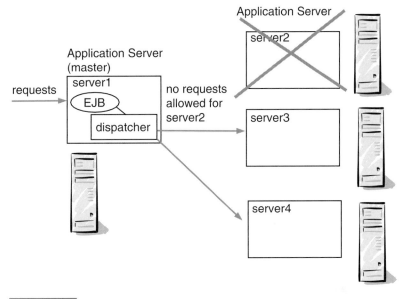

Figure 24–6 *Application server cluster with failover.*

the component is being executed. If the server where the component is being executed fails, then the state information for the failed components must be moved to another server that can execute the bean. All of this adds overhead to the operation of the application server. Maintaining and monitoring state information between application servers requires additional network bandwidth and uses additional CPU resources. The benefit is that for critical operations that require state information, a high degree of availability can be obtained using this feature.

Failover capabilities are required to be transparent to the component. The component does not need to make a specific method call or implement a certain interface to obtain this capability. There are, however, some coding restrictions. Since the component will be moved to another hardware server, local references such as file handles and network sockets would no longer be valid. This means that the EJB component that may be used to failover to another server should not open a file, make a network connection, or use an RMI object. Using native code (which has its own set of restrictions and issues beyond the scope of this chapter) should also not be used by components that may potentially failover to another server.

All EJB components, including session beans and entity beans, are candidates for failover. It is up to the application server implementation to provide the capability and identify any additional restrictions.

EJB DEPLOYMENT

Unlike other application development paradigms, EJB components are not simply compiled and then run. The J2EE application server must be made aware of the components to be run in the application server and the properties of those components. The properties or attributes of these components can be used to express useful information about the behavior of the components in the process, increasing the flexibility and reuse capabilities of J2EE applications. This process of making the application server aware of the components is known as *deployment* (see Figure 24–7).

J2EE applications are required to use a deployment descriptor to provide information about the EJB components to be deployed. This deployment descriptor allows *declarative programming* to replace what would previously require traditional programming techniques to provide important information about the EJBs, including the security and transactional properties of the components.

The class files that represent the EJB components to be deployed into the application server are packaged into a JAR file, which includes the deployment descriptor, an XML document describing the properties of the components.

Specifically how a J2EE application server will provide deployment is not defined in the EJB specification. Some vendors allow the JAR file of components to be placed in a directory and then deployed (known as *directory deployment* or

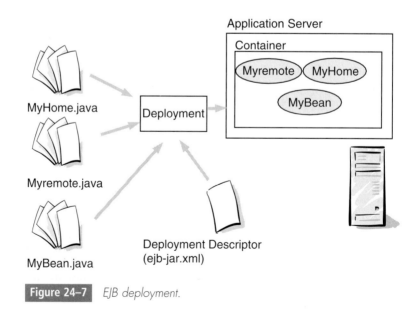

Figure 24–7 *EJB deployment.*

auto-deployment). Others provide a graphical tool that allows constituent class files to be selected and component properties described. Most Java integrated development environments (IDEs) provide the ability to build EJB JAR files, and many are integrated into specific J2EE application servers.

Unfortunately, this fast deployment feature is not universal, and changes to a deployment that do not require a new class to be installed (changing the deployment descriptor, for example) are not always recognized without restarting the application server.

EJB RUNTIME OPERATION (HOW EJBS WORK)

As mentioned in the discussion of RMI, RMI is a foundation technology that forms the basis for other Java technologies. RMI is an enabling technology for EJBs. Alternatively, EJBs conceptually extend RMI and add additional capabilities. In fact, EJBs build on and use a number of Java capabilities and technologies, which are reflected in Figure 24–8

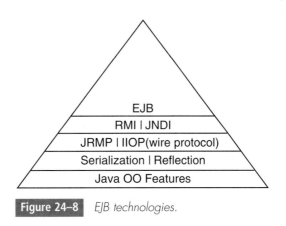

Figure 24–8 *EJB technologies.*

Client applications that access EJBs do not access the EJB directly; they access the bean indirectly through a *proxy* object. A client application uses a naming service to look up the home interface (an `EJBHome` implementation) for the EJB. Once the home interface object is obtained, it is used to access a remote object for the EJB. Using this remote object, the client application can then interact with the EJB by calling the business methods of the EJB using the object. In this way, the client uses the EJB indirectly via the remote object, the proxy for the actual EJB. See Figure 24–9.

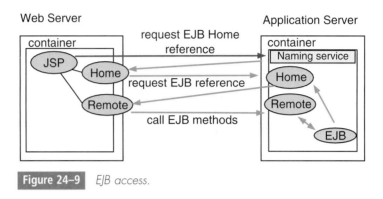

Figure 24–9   *EJB access.*

We can summarize this information into a three-step process used by a client to connect to and use an EJB `SessionBean` or `EntityBean` as follows.

1. Performing a lookup using a naming service to obtain a home reference for the EJB component.
2. Use the home reference to obtain a remote reference for the EJB by creating the reference for a session bean, or finding an entity bean.
3. Using the EJB remote reference, invoke the exposed component methods as needed.

The process for having a client use a `MessageDrivenBean` is a different matter. A `MessageDrivenBean` is accessed by remote clients by posting a message to a message queue or topic. The process for creating and using these beans is covered in a later section. For now, just note that clients access these beans differently than they would a `SessionBean` or `EntityBean`.

EJBS AND TRANSACTIONS

One of the services provided by the EJBs container is transactional control. Transactions can be controlled either programmatically by the developer or declaratively by the container. If transactions for a bean are controlled by the container, they are considered *container-managed transactions* (CMTs) and are declared by making entries in a configuration file used to deploy the EJB application. If the transactions for a bean are controlled by programmatic instructions, then they are considered *bean-managed transactions* (BMTs).

Since entity beans are guaranteed to be synchronized with a persistent data store, they are considered transactional by nature. With session beans, transactions are optional, but with entity beans, transactions are required. Therefore, entity beans must be defined to use CMTs.

Developing EJBs

What should be noted about EJBs is that an application server is required to develop and deploy these components. The Sun J2EE download from its Web site includes a development version of an application server, but this is not considered appropriate for a production environment. Application servers range in price from nothing for open-source products (JBoss) to mid-range prices (JRun and Orion) to high range (IPlanet, WebLogic and WebSphere). (The Web site *www.flashline.com* has a very good application server matrix, which includes a comparison of application servers, their EJB compliance, their prices, and most importantly, user reviews.)

Not all application servers that support the development of EJBs are considered EJB-compliant. Compliance is important in providing portability of EJBs so that an EJB developed and deployed on the application server of one vendor can easily be deployed onto another vendor's application server.

This is not to say that an application server that has not been certified by Sun as J2EE compliant are not viable solutions. The JBoss open source J2EE application server is not J2EE compliant certified largely due to the high cost of certification which Sun charges, but it represents an excellent choice implementing a significant portion of the J2EE application server specification.

The EJB API

The classes used to create EJB applications are contained in the *javax.ejb* package included as part of the J2EE SDK. This package includes the classes and interfaces listed in Table 24–1.

As we know from our previous explanation of EJB processing, EJB components require a home interface and a remote interface. These interfaces are provided by the `EJBHome` interface for the home interface, and by the `EJBObject` interface for the remote object interface, or using the the local counterparts (`EJBLocalObject`, `EJBLocalHome`) with EJB 2.0.

Prior to the EJB 2.0 specification, all EJB components were accessed using a network interface. This was not a problem if beans were being accessed by a remote client across a network, but when an EJB accessed another EJB in the same container, the same network interface would be used. Even though the interface was what is known as a *local loopback* interface, the communication process still incurred additional network overhead in the communication process, overhead that was technically not necessary, since the components were most likely running on the same machine in the same application server container.

With the EJB 2.0 specification, the concept of *local beans* was introduced. Local beans could be identified using specific interfaces, and the container implementation would presumably provide a faster, more efficient communication interface for the components. Local beans are identified with the `EJBLocalHome` interface for the home interface and the `EJBLocalObject` interface for the remote interface.

Table 24–1   *EJB Interfaces*

Class/Interface	Description
EJBContext	Provides access to the information the container carries about the EJB instance.
EJBHome	Represents the home instance for the EJB. This is returned by the lookup operation for the bean and is used to access the remote reference for the bean.
EJBLocalHome	Similar to the EJBHome interface, but this interface allows bean communication to be performed locally, within the same EJB container.
EJBLocalObject	Represents the base interface for all local EJB local component references. This interface is extended by the remote interface for the local EJB component (local to the same container).
EJBMetaData	An instance of the EJBMetaData interface provides information about EJB components. Primarily used by tool vendors.
EJBObject	The base interface for all remote EJB components. This interface is extended by the remote component and used to provide communication witht the EJB component.
EnterpriseBean	The base interface for all EJB remote components. The SessionBean, EntityBean, and MessageDrivenBean interfaces extend this interface.
EntityBean	The interface that must be implemented by an EntityBean.
EntityContext	The instance of this interface provides access to the container's interaction with the EntityBean instance.
Handle	A handle for the EJB component that allows storage of the remote reference to the component.
HomeHandle	A handle for the EJB home reference that allows storage of the reference to the home component.
MessageDrivenBean	The interface that must be implemented by a MessageDrivenBean component.
MessageDrivenContext	The implementation of this interface provides access to container information about a MessageDrivenBean instance.
SessionBean	The interface that must be implemented by a SessionBean.
SessionContext	The implementation of this interface provides container information about a SessionBean instance.
SessionSynchronization	An implementation of this interface allows a SessionBean instance to be notified by its container of its transaction boundaries.

Prior to EJB 2.0, parameter passing using the EJB remote reference (`EJBObject`) was performed using *call by value* and parameters needed to be serialized (just as with RMI); local beans remove this restriction and allow *call by reference* with Java object references. (Note that this does not bypass the EJB proxy mechanism; the remote reference still represents a proxy to the EJB.)

A remote client reference would most likely obtain the home interface as returned using a naming service `lookup` call. A J2EE-compliant application server must provide a naming service that can return an `EJBHome` reference. Using JNDI, a call is made to the `lookup` method. Alternatively, a reference to the home object could have previously been created and stored as a `HomeHandle` reference, in which case it could simply be retrieved and used to obtain the home reference.

The home reference is used to create or find the remote reference for the EJB. For session beans, this is accomplished by calling the `create` method on the `EJBHome` interface implementation. The J2EE container is required to provide a valid remote reference for the bean that is referenced by the home interface. This does not necessarily require a bean to be instantiated, since the container implementation may optionally be using bean pools. If an appropriate remote reference is available in the bean pool, the container may return that remote reference to the client executing the `EJBHome create` method for the session bean, or by performing a lookup using an entity bean finder method.

The remote reference for the bean provides the proxy access to the EJB. Once this reference has been obtained, calls can be made on the EJB methods as though the bean were an object reference local to the client program.

As we know, the container takes responsibility for providing a number of services to for the components under its control. The container can provide many of these services because of the proxy access to the components.

The EJB client does not access the EJB component directly; method calls are routed through the container. This allows the container to intercede in the remote call process and provide the various services required of a J2EE application server.

The container interacts with the EJB component using a number of *callback methods* identified in the extended implementations of the various interfaces EJB components must provide. As the container is intervening in the communication process, it has the opportunity to direct a request to another location to manage transactions, provide security, and effectively provide the various services the J2EE application server is expected to provide.

As developers, we need to extend and implement specific EJB interfaces. The following example provides a simple EJB implementation which helps illustrate this process.

EJB Code Sample

Because EJBs are special objects (components) which run within a container, they require a very specific development and deployment process. An EJB component must implement a set of interfaces correctly and be deployed into an application server before it can be used. The following example demonstrates the process of creating an EJB and how multiple beans can communicate.

The myBean class shown below is developed as a session bean and therefore must implement the javax.ejb.SessionBean interface. This bean in turn will access the Cust bean to retrieve customer information.

The ejbCreate method is required for the implementation, and in this example is an empty-body method. For session beans, this method is called by the container when the bean is instantiated by the container. Were there some initialization activity that needed to be done when the bean was started, the code for that intitialization could go in this method, though good coding practice dictates that per session initialization should be located elsewhere (see note).

NOTE Note that the use of EJB pooling leads to the possibility that the ejbCreate method will always be called by the container each time a client creates or finds a bean. For this reason, the setSessionContext or setEntityContext may be the better location for initialization code since these methods are called each time the container is asked to create or find a remote reference for an EJB. This is where client session specific initialization should be located. Alternatively, if some type of initialization only needed to be performed once (perhaps to access tax rates for all clients or local configuration parameters) that initialization could logically be located in the ejbCreate method.

The ejbPassivate method is called when the bean is passivated and is potentially sent to the ready pool, a pool of available EJB components. Likewise, the ejbActivate method is called when the bean is retrieved from the ready pool and is set to the appropriate state (its instance members are set to the appropriate value) for the bean. In this example, since there is no specific code for this bean to implement before it is passivated or when it is activated, these methods have a blank body. However, if the bean were managing a database connection, we may want it to make a call to the close method of the Connection class when the bean is passivated and the ejbPassivate method is called, and have it establish a new connection in the ejbActivate method when the bean is activated. Also, if there are any variables that you do not want saved during the passivation process, they should be set to null in the ejbPassivate method.

The SessionContext is used to implement programmatic security and for programmatic management of transactions. The setSessionContext method is called and passed a parameter for the `SessionContext` for the EJB. It is good practice to save this reference for future use as shown here.

The `ejbRemove` method is called when the `remove` method is executed on the home interface or when the bean no longer has any active connections and the container is removing the resources associated with the EJB. This is where the component may want to clean up its environment and close any open resources. The implementation shown here does not require any clean-up processing, so it has an empty body.

The myBean Class

```
import javax.ejb.*;
import javax.naming.*;
import javax.rmi.*;

public class myBean implements SessionBean {
SessionContext sc;

// SessionBean interface methods

public void ejbCreate() { }
public void ejbPassivate() { }
public void ejbActivate() { }

public void setSessionContext( SessionContext sc )
  {
     this.sc = sc;
}

public void ejbRemove() {}
```

The myBean Class: The getCustData Method

The `getCustData` method implements the business logic for the retrieval of customer information. This bean in turn delegates the retrieval of the customer information to another EJB component.

As shown below, this method uses a `lookup` method call to access another EJB and is therefore an EJB which is a client to another bean. This method obtains the `InitialContext` (using default parameters for finding the naming service as detailed in Chapter 12) and then performs a lookup to obtain the home object for the `Cust` bean. The object reference obtained by the `InitialContext` cannot simply be cast to the appropriate type (this is because of the underlying implementation for the `lookup` call and for backwards compatibility with existing CORBA middleware). The `PortableRemoteObject narrow` method must be used to convert the `object` reference obtained to the appropriate type.

Once the home object has been converted into the correct type, that of the CustHome class, the home object can be used to create references for the remote object for the Cust bean, acting as a factory for the bean, which is what is done in this method. The remote object reference is then used to call the getCustData method on the Cust bean and return the results to the client bean that accessed myBean. The code for this method is shown next.

Note that in this example, for simplicity, we access the remote object reference for the CustHome EJB on each call to the getCustData method.

```
public String getCustData() {

CustRemote cr       = null;
CustHome    ch      = null;
String      retval = null;

try {

//
// get the InitialContext
//
InitialContext ic = new InitialContext();

//
// lookup our home object
//
Object obj = ic.lookup("Cust");

//
// special cast for home object
//
ch = (CustHome) PortableRemoteObject.narrow( obj,
                                    CustHome.class );
//
// create our remote object
//
cr = ch.create();

//
// call our 'business method'
//
retval = cr.getCustData();

}
catch (NamingException e) {

System.out.println("NamingException caught in getData(): " +
                                    e.getMessage() );
throw new EJBException("naming exception");

}
```

```
catch (Exception e) {

System.out.println("Exception caught in getCustData(): " +
                                        e.getMessage() );
throw new EJBException("naming exception");

}
finally {

    return  retval;

}
}

}
```

The myHome Interface

As discussed previously, EJBs being accessed remotely require that a home and remote interface be defined. The EJBHome interface represents an implementation of the Factory design pattern, since this interface controls the creation of remote objects for the EJB. This interface extends java.rmi.Remote and as you recall from our discussion of RMI, RMI requires remote methods to be declared to throw a RemoteException. Using the home interface allows the container to intercede in the creation process and manage pooled resources and perform other house-keeping operations for the bean.

The EJB developer must create a specific interface that extends the EJBHome interface, as shown in the following code. A signature for the create method must be declared to return the type of the remote interface for the EJB.

You, the developer, do not provide the implementation for this interface. It is the responsibility of the application server vendor to provide the implementation which is usually done during the deployment process.

The myHome Interface

```
import javax.ejb.*;
import javax.naming.*;
import java.rmi.*;

public interface myHome extends EJBHome {

public myRemote create() throws CreateException,
                                RemoteException ;

}
```

The myRemote Interface

A remote interface must be declared for the EJB to extend the `EJBObject` interface. This interface must provide signatures for all of the business methods in the EJB class that are to be accessed from the client. As with the `EJBHome` interface, it is the responsibility of the application server vendor to provide an implementation for this interface during deployment. The remote interface for this example is shown next.

The myRemote.java Interface

```
import javax.naming.*;
import javax.ejb.*;
import java.rmi.*;

public interface myRemote extends EJBObject {

public String getCustData() throws RemoteException;

}
```

Deploying the EJB

Once the interfaces and classes for the EJB have been declared, they must be *deployed* into the application server. This deployment process reads a deployment descriptor, an XML-encoded document that describes various properties of the EJB. These properties include but are not limited to transactional behavior, whether a session bean is stateful or stateless, and whether an entity bean is using CMP or BMP.

The application vendor is expected to provide a tool that will perform the deployment process. The EAR (Enterprise Application Resource) file specification places all resources for the EJBs into one archive. This file includes the deployment descriptor which describes the deployment process for the EJBs (discussed in more detail in the next two chapters) and any additional classes needed by the components. Deployment may be done implicitly, by simply placing the EAR file in a specific directory being monitored by the application server. When the application server becomes aware of the EAR, it will open it and attempt to deploy the application. The deployment process will include reading the deployment descriptor, finding the classes and interfaces, possibly generating implementation code for the interfaces, and making entries into the name server.

EJB Client Code

The client application for an EJB must obtain two `object` references to be able to access the EJB. The first reference it must obtain is the *home* object, the implementation of the `EJBHome` interface for the EJB. Once it has a reference to the home object, it can call the `create` method on the home object (or possibly the `findByPrimaryKey` or other *finder* method if using an entity bean) to receive a reference to the *remote* object. The remote object is an implementation of the `EJBObject` interface that will provide a proxy to the actual EJB running on the application server. For all practical purposes, it is used as though it were a reference to the actual EJB.

The home `object` reference is usually found using the *name server* provided as part of the J2EE-compliant application server. This name server allows name/value pairs to be stored in a lightweight, hierarchical database. The J2EE specification provides that this name server will be provided by the application server vendor, and access to the name server will be provided using JNDI.

The name/value pairs that can be stored in the name server include the ability to store references to objects. Part of the deployment of an EJB application involves placing a JNDI lookup name and the `object` reference for the home interface into the JNDI namespace.

In this code example, a command-line parameter is optionally passed in to provide the lookup name for the home interface. If a name is not supplied on the command line, then a default name is supplied.

The usual process for an EJB client is to obtain an *initial context* using a call to the `InitialContext` method. This provides access to the name server and allows the `lookup` method to be called, passing a string that corresponds to the name for the home interface (as declared during the deployment process).

The `InitialContext lookup` method will return an `object` reference that must be converted into the appropriate type for the home interface of the EJB. Because of the nature of the underlying communication mechanism for EJBs, the `PortableRemoteObject.narrow` method is used to perform the conversion of the object reference to the type of the home interface.

Now that the home interface has been obtained, a call can be made to the `create` method of the home interface. The `create` method returns a reference to the remote object for our EJB. Once we have this remote object, we can make calls to the business methods of our EJB. The code for this client program follows.

The TestClient Class

```
import javax.naming.*;
import java.rmi.*;
import javax.rmi.*;

public class testClient {
```

```java
public static void main( String args[] ) {

//
// home object
//
myHome mh = null;

//
// remote object
//
myRemote mr = null;

try {

//
// may pass the bean name on the command line
//
String lookupName =null;
if (args.length > 0 )
    lookupName=args[0];
else
    lookupName = "myBean";

//
// get the InitialContext
//
InitialContext ic = new InitialContext();
System.out.println("InitialContext found. " );

//
// get the bean name
//
Object obj = ic.lookup(lookupName);
System.out.println(
        "myBean found. Performing narrow ... " );

//
// get the home object
//
mh = (myHome) PortableRemoteObject.narrow( obj, myHome.class );

//
// create the remote object from the home object
 //
mr = mh.create();
System.out.println("Customer Data: " + mr.getCustData() );

}
```

```
catch (Exception e) {
    System.out.println("Exception in main: " + e.getMessage() );
}

}

}
```

When to Use EJBs

EJBs have their place in server-side development. For applications that require high scalability and some level of session failover capabilities, EJBs are a good fit. This includes sites with a heavy user load and/or the need for transactions to failover transparently to the end user. Also for applications that are inherently transactional or that require distributed transactions. But for sites that don't have these requirements, the need for using EJBs is not as clear.

EJBs provide the capability to create an application with components that can then be accessed fairly easily from remote locations. Using EJBs, a client application running on a modest hardware platform can access a complex, expensive processing routine and, through the architecture of EJBs, the processing routine will run on the remote hardware platform (where the EJBs are deployed). With this architecture, the resource-intensive processing will be done on the remote machine, which will have the hardware processing to manage the load; it will not be done on the modest client machine.

Many would argue that the centralized, middleware architecture of EJBs provides a better development and deployment paradigm for software in general. Using this architecture, the information technology department maintains a high degree of control of the development and deployment of the component software. Since the EJBs will reside on a centralized platform, the IT department will have control over these machines and the development and runtime environment. Client applications, such as Web applications, can have a much smaller footprint, since they will not need to carry the complex code that will reside in the EJBs on the central server. The messy process of deploying software to client machines is minimized or, depending on departmental responsibilities, possibly even eliminated.

Counter to this argument would be that the deployment of a Web application with JSPs, servlets, and JavaBeans has the same low deployment cost profile as the same application with an EJB application server and does not incur the expense of installing and running the application server.

SUMMARY

EJBs are the distributed software component for the Java language and are at the core of the J2EE specification. These components run within an abstract container implementation provided by an application server. Application servers that are J2EE-compliant provide a complete set of services that now represent the standard, the basic set of services expected of application servers.

Before we can really understand how to use EJBs, we must understand how they work together. This chapter provided a brief summary of EJBs and discussed how these components are developed with Java. A brief minimal implementation sample application was used to demonstrate this process.

In the next chapter we take a closer look at security and transactions with EJBs and provide a more involved example of their usage.

CHAPTER 25

EJBs: Deployment, Security, and Transactions

INTRODUCTION

As we have seen, EJBs provide distributed components in a manner similar to that of RMIs and RPCs, but they add to this capability a set of services. In addition to providing these services, EJBs allow certain component properties to be described at deployment time, promoting extensibility and flexibility. Specifically, the security and transactional properties for an EJB can be described through entries in the DD. This allows the transactional or security properties for components from disparate sources (vendors, development groups) to be set easily and appropriately for an application through the entries in the EJB DD. Alternatively, if a more finely grained control is needed, then the EJB API provides methods for controlling security and setting transactional boundaries.

Ultimately, the goal is to create a cohesive yet dynamic application by combining EJB components. To understand how to do this, we must first understand the source document that describes deployment properties: the EJB deployment descriptor (DD). Once we have explained the DD and how the deployment process works with EJBs, we examine how security works with EJBs and how protection domains can be built, which extend from the presentation tier where authentication is performed to the business tier where we execute business logic and determine authorization.

Transaction control is one of the more important services provided by J2EE application servers. J2EE application servers come bundled with a transaction monitor, which provides the ability to create distributed transactions across multiple data resources. The boundaries for these transactions can be controlled using declarative programming by making entries in the DD, which describes the components and methods that represent the transaction boundary. Alternatively, once again providing a more finely grained approach, a programmatic approach can be used. The EJB API provides access to methods that can set transaction boundaries and explicitly commit or roll back a transaction. In the following sections we examine how EJB transactions can be set and controlled in the DD or through the EJB API.

EJB ROLES

The EJB specification defines six roles for EJB development. As with other parts of the EJB specification, there was a distinct effort to make it possible to provide code reuse, portability, and interoperability with both existing and future technologies. To that end, these roles define responsibilities and input and output work units. In practice, these roles may be combined, and one individual or group could take on the work of several roles (in fact, that is usually the case). These roles are as follows.

- bean provider
- application assembler
- deployer
- EJB container provider
- EJB server provider
- system administrator

The bean provider creates the constituent class and interface files required to create one or more EJB components. The output, the result of the provider's efforts, are the JAR files (`ejb-jar`) containing the EJBs and the DD for the components. (The bean provider is also sometimes referred to as the bean developer, but the EJB specification is fairly consistent in referring to this role as the bean provider, or *provider* for short.)

The provider is responsible for providing the appropriate EJB classes and interfaces, as identified previously, and for providing a DD with the structural information about the beans. The information about the beans includes the names and types of resources the bean uses, and basic information about the bean such as its type (for example, session bean or entity bean), its home and remote interfaces, and any local resources it may use.

Because of the architecture of EJBs, the provider is not required to understand or program services such as transaction control or security for the application. Instead, he or she can be focused on the domain-specific issues of the components and simply code the business logic required.

The programming of the security and transaction control are tasks that can be left to another individual to complete at some later point. If the component has been programmed correctly, then these additional services can be programmed into the components without affecting the operation of the component. One of the real values of EJBs is that it is a relatively easy task to program these services using DD entries.

> Providing security and transaction properties for an EJB component in the DD make it easier for an independent software vendor (ISV) to develop components for resale. An ISV could develop an EJB component that defers security and transactions to assembly and deployment. This component could then be purchased by a development team, which could integrate the component into an application using DD assembly instructions. These assembly instructions could be modified further, depending on the installation. For example, for a business application, security properties could be very restrictive at remote offices where IT has little control over the operation of the application, but could be relaxed at headquarters where IT can verify (perhaps by login or using security certificates) that only authorized individuals are running the application.

The application assembler takes the pieces of the EJB and combines them into a larger, more complete piece. The assembler takes as input the JAR files of the existing components and adds assembly instructions to the DD.

The most important part of this task is the assignment of security roles and links. Whereas the bean provider did not need to be concerned with security or transactions, the application assembler does need to have some knowledge of the requirements for these services and must be able to define these requirements in the DD. The application assembler does not need to have specific knowledge about the implementation of the components, but obviously must understand the application security and transaction model.

Application assembly is often described as occurring before deployment, but this is not a requirement. Application assembly instructions may optionally be added and changed after deployment.

The deployer takes the JAR files for the components and the DD and deploys the EJBs into a specific application server and container. The deployer is responsible for ensuring that all external dependencies for the beans are resolved and that all application assembly instructions can be followed. (Most application servers will not allow the application to be deployed if the DD is not correct.) The deployer is ultimately responsible for the installation of the enterprise beans and required classes into the application server. Once the process of deployment is complete, the application server can be started and the bean components can be invoked.

The EJB server provider and EJB container provider are one and the same. The EJB server provider is the vendor or open source group that provides the operating environment for the EJBs. The application server must have a valid implementation of the EJB container to be able to deploy and run components.

The system administrator is responsible for the installation and operation of the application server environment. He or she is also responsible for ensuring the beans operate correctly when the server is running.

THE EJB DEPLOYMENT DESCRIPTOR

At the center of all declarative programming is the DD. As a developer, we need to be aware of the instructions that can be made through this document so it is worthwhile to take a look at these entries at this point. The following sections detail the DD entries based on the EJB roles that should be making the entry.

Bean Provider Entries

Per the EJB specification, various pieces of structural information, basic information about how the application server should create the bean, should be entered by the bean provider. The more common of these entries are listed in Table 25–1.

Table 25–1   *Common EJB Structural DD Elements*

Entry	Element	Description
EJB name	`ejb-name`	The name of the EJB. Note that this is the name the EJB will be referenced by, using the application server vendor's tools; this is not necessarily the name that will be used by the client to perform a naming service lookup to obtain the bean's home reference.
home interface	`home`	The Java interface file containing the extended `EJBHome` interface for the bean.
remote interface	`remote`	The Java interface file containing the extended `EJBObject` interface for the bean.
local home interface	`local-home`	The Java interface file containing the extended `EJBLocalHome` interface for the bean.

Table 25–1   *Common EJB Structural DD Elements (cont.)*

Entry	Element	Description
local interface	`local`	The Java interface file containing the extended `EJBLocalObject` interface for the bean.
EJB type	`session, entity, message-driven`	The type of bean:. Currently, one of session bean, entity bean, or message-driven bean (MDB).
session bean management type	`session-type`	How (or if) the session bean will maintain state information: currently one of stateful or stateless.
environment entries	`env-entry`	Optionally specify various environment entries (application properties) for the EJB. These are values that can later be retrieved and used by the EJB.
resource environment references	`res-ref-name`	For any resource factories to be used, this entry must declare references to the administered objects that are used as resources.
EJB references	`ejb-ref-name`	This entry is used to declare references to remote homes of other EJBs.
EJB local references	`ejb-local-ref`	This entry is used to declare references to local homes of other EJBs.
security role references	`security-role`	This entry is used to declare references to security roles (mapping one security role to another).
message driven bean's destination	`message-driven-destination`	This is the type (queue or topic) to which a message-driven bean (MDB) should be assigned and an optional entry concerning whether or not the subscription will be durable.
message driven bean's message selector	`message-driven-selector`	A JMS message selector, which may be declared to determine which messages should be directed to the EJB message bean.
message driven bean's acknowledgment mode	`acknowledge-mode`	The acknowledgment mode to be used with a MDB using transactions.
session or MDB transaction type	`transaction-type`	This indicates whether or not transactions are managed by the container or managed programmatically.

Because the entity bean has a number of special properties associated with it, there are several additional entries that apply to entity beans as detailed in Table 25–2.

Table 25–2   *Entity Bean DD Entries*

Entry	Element	Description
re-entrancy indication	`reentrant`	This is used to indicate whether or not the entity bean is re-entrant.
entity bean's persistence type	`persistence-type`	A required entry which indicates how the entity bean will be persisted to the underlying data store. This is either bean-managed, meaning the bean provider has written the code to manage this, or container-provided, meaning the container has provided facilities to perform this function.
entity bean's primary key class	`prim-key-class`	This is the fully qualified class name for the primary key class for the bean. This is a required entry.
entity bean's abstract schema name	`abstract-schema-name`	With container-managed persistence (CMP) in version 2.0, this identifies the abstract schema name.
container-managed fields	`cmp-field`	Entity beans that use CMP must identify the container-managed fields, the fields where the container will manage the persistence. Nested `cmp-field` elements are used to identify the fields to be persisted.
container-managed relationships	`n/a`	Using CMP with EJB 2.0, this is used to specify the relationships managed by the container.
finder and select queries	`n/a`	Using CMP with EJB 2.0, finder and select queries can be identified using the nested query element to specify the EJB-QL finder and select queries.

Application Assembler-Related Entries

An application assembler may make changes to the various entries that have been made by the bean provider. Obviously, important structural information like the type of bean (entity bean, session bean, message-driven bean) or the transaction type (container-managed or bean-managed) should not be changed by the application assembler, since the bean has been programmed with the expectation that it will exhibit the properties associated with the bean type or transaction type. But there are other entries which can be changed by the application assembler. These entries are detailed in Table 25–3 and they concern how the component will be integrated with other components that comprise the application.

Table 25–3 *Application Assembler Entries*

Entries	Description
environment entries	These entries concern application properties that must often be adjusted as part of the application configuration process. The application assembler participating in this process would make changes accordingly.
description fields	Since the EJB component does not access any of the description fields in the DD, changing these fields will not have any effect on the application. These fields should be changed to reflect the application being assembled by the application assembler.
relationship names	Any references to other beans or resources must be resolved by the application assembler through relationship names.
MDB selector	The application assembler may refine this entry, which is used to determine which selector will provide access to the message-driven bean.

The application assembler should not change the name of the entity bean's abstract schema name, since EJB-QL queries depend on the name. We do, however, expect the application assembler to refine any security or transaction entries that have been made since it is the role of the application assembler to complete the description of the security and transactional behavior for the application. This would involve changing security roles, security role references, and transaction entries in the DD.

The DD is an XML document. More specifically, it is a well-formed and validated XML document that must conform to the DTD detailed in the EJB specification.

Additionally, the content of the DD elements is quite often case-sensitive, so any entries in the DD should be verified for correct case.

SECURITY WITH EJBS

As we already know, EJB security can be managed either programmatically using method calls in the application, or declaratively by making entries in the DD. Using EJBs a security role can be defined. This security role represents a grouping of permissions, which are associated with one or more methods. This means that EJB application security roles are granted permission to execute one or more methods. No distinctions are made pertaining to reading or writing information using an EJB; permissions are associated with method execution only.

Being able to execute a method implies that parameters may be passed to the method and values may be returned from the method. Permissions may be assigned to specific method signatures so that overloaded versions of a method may be identified. Alternatively, permissions may be assigned to a method and all of its overloaded versions.

EJBs are business tier components and are not expected to interact directly with a user. For this reason, authentication, verifying that a user is who he or she claims to be, is not included in the EJB specification. Authentication is assumed to have been performed by some other component; as EJB developers we assume that the user or caller has been authenticated when the call to the EJB is made.

The EJB caller is assigned a principal, and it is this principal that is the focus of EJB security. The principal is mapped to a security role using some proprietary mechanism provided by the application server (for example, a GUI application or an XML configuration file). The DD allows the security role to be mapped to another security role if necessary and allows it to be assigned to EJBs and their methods using a flexible syntax (see Figure 25–1).

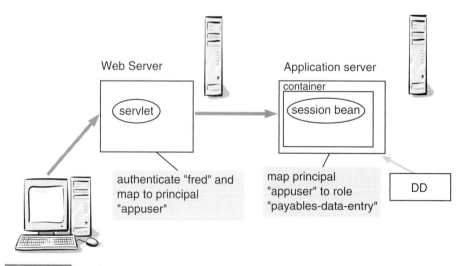

Figure 25–1   *Authentication credentials passed to the business tier.*

Declarative Security Programming

Declarative security programming is the most flexible and by far the preferred method of implementing a security policy using EJBs. The EJB specification provides very detailed information about how security roles should be assigned in the DD, but it does not provide details on the mapping of principals to the security roles. This mapping operation is left entirely to the application server provider. The application server provider is expected to provide a tool that details a security view, allowing available principals to be listed and mapped to security roles.

In practice, most application server provide a mechanism for authentication on the Web tier and mapping the authentication and assignment of a principal back to the business tier (the application server). These tools are often GUI tools that make the process relatively straightforward.

To avoid straying off-topic, we will focus on what the EJB specification does define. In the following section we will demonstrate how security roles are defined and mapped to EJB methods in the DD.

Deployment Descriptor Examples

Assuming that we are developing an accounts payable module for an accounting system, we would create a series of security roles to reflect the users of the system. For the sake of simplicity, let's assume that we have three types of users: managers who should be allowed to perform all functions, data entry clerks who should only be allowed to enter specific information, and vendors who should be allowed to query the system to see if their checks have been created. This would potentially lead to the definition of the following security roles as shown next.

```
<assembly-descriptor>
              <security-role>
                      <description>
                       The manager is allowed to do everything.
                      </description>
                      <role-name>payables-manager</role-name>
               </security-role>

              <security-role>
                      <description>
                              Payables entry clerk.
                      </description>
                      <role-name>payables-data-entry</role-name>
               </security-role>

              <security-role>
                      <description>
                          Vendor who wants to know if the
                          check is in the mail.
                      </description>
```

```
                       <role-name>payables-vendor</role-name>
              </security-role>
       ...
</assembly-descriptor>
```

Since these roles are expected to be assigned as part of the responsibilities of the application assembler, they are defined as part of the `assembly-descriptor` element in the DD. In this example, we first create a security role for a `payables-manager`. As the description shown next indicates, this security role is granted a broad set of permissions in the system effectively being allowed to execute any method in the `AccountsPayable` EJB.

The entries shown next define a role for a `payables-clerk` and a `payables-vendor`, both of whom are granted a much more narrow set of permissions. The `payables-clerk` is only allowed to execute the `payablesInput` method, and the `payables-vendor` is only allowed to execute the `vendorQuery` method.

```
...
<method-permission>
    <role-name>payables-manager</role-name>
    <method>
        <ejb-name>AccountsPayable</ejb-name>
        <method-name>*</method-name>
    </method>
</method-permission>

<method-permission>
<role-name>payables-clerk</role-name>
<method>
        <ejb-name>AccountsPayable</ejb-name>
        <method-name>payablesInput</method-name>
</method>
</method-permission>

<method-permission>
    <role-name>payables-vendor</role-name>
    <method>
        <ejb-name>AccountsPayable</ejb-name>
        <method-name>vendorQuery</method-name>
         <method-params>
                <method-param>java.lang.String</method-param>
                <method-param>java.lang.String</method-param>
                <method-param>int</method-param>
         <method-params>
    </method>
</method-permission>
...
```

As we can see in the previous set of sample entries, we map a series of accounts payable security roles to specific methods for a bean. These entries are made using the DD `method-permission` element. Within the method-permission element, the `role-name` element designates the security role, and the `ejb-name` is the name of the bean we are mapping to. The `method-name` element is then used to identify the method we are mapping to. In the first `method-permission` entry, we map the `payables-manager` role to the `method-name` *. This syntax indicates that the `payables-manager` role will be mapped to all methods in the `AccountsPayable` bean. Since we would like the payables manager to have broad permissions, this is acceptable.

For the `payables-clerk` role, we would like to assign more limited permissions. For this security role, we identify a single method to access—the `payablesInput` method.

We know that the vendor just needs to be able to query the system to see whether or not checks have been sent out. This requires access to the `vendorQuery` method, but the `vendorQuery` has been overloaded. We want the vendor to be able to query for only a single version of the method. We can use the `method-param` element to identify the method signature for the method the `payables-vendor` role is allowed to call.

It is possible, though it was not shown here, for a method to be mapped to more than one security role. For example, if the `AccountsPayable` `payablesUpdate` method were to be accessed by both the `payables-clerk` role and the `accounts-manager` role, then the following entry would be used.

```
<method-permission>
<role-name>payables-clerk</role-name>
<role-name>accounts-manager</role-name>
<method>
        <ejb-name>AccountsPayable</ejb-name>
        <method-name>payablesUpdate</method-name>
. . .
```

Programmatic Security

If a developer uses programmatic security and references a security role in the application code (i.e., the developer has hardcoded the name), the security role name used in the application should be referenced in the DD using a `role-link`. This provides some additional flexibility by allowing hardcoded role names to be mapped to existing security roles. This is accomplished using the `role-link` entry, as demonstrated in the example below.

```
. . .
 <enterprise-beans>
     <entity>
```

```
        <ejb-name>AccountsPayable</ejb-name>
        <ejb-class>com.book.examples.AccountingBean</ejb-class>
        <description>
                    This is a sample.
        </description>
        <security-role-ref>
            <description>
                        This is a role name ref.
            </description>
          <role-name>ap-manager</role-name>
        <security-role-ref>
      </entity>
    </enterprise-beans>
```

In this example, the `AccountsPayable` bean is identified as having used programmatic security to reference the `payables-manager` security role. This information is provided in the `security-role-ref` element in the DD, which is itself nested in the `enterprise-beans` element.

The `role-name` that was used in the application was `ap-manager`. Now that we've identified the role, we must relate this role name to an active security role. (This must be done even if the role name reference and the security role have the same name.) This is accomplished using a `role-link` element, as demonstrated in the following example.

```
<enterprise-beans>
    <entity>
        <ejb-name>AccountsPayable</ejb-name>
        <ejb-class>com.book.examples.AccountingBean</ejb-class>
          <description>
                Map the ap-manager name to the payables-manager
                security role.
          </description>
            <security-role-ref>
              <description>
                    This is a  role name ref.
              </description>
              <role-name>ap-manager</role-name>
              <role-link>payables-manager</role-link>
        </security-role-ref>
      </entity>
    </enterprise-beans>
```

This DD entry will map or link the `ap-manager` security role reference to the `payables-manager` security role, an active security role that was shown in the previous example. We can assume that some authentication mechanism will map a user to a principal and that the principal will be mapped by the container to the security role of `payables-manager`. Then when the `AccountingBean` method which uses the `ap-manager` security role is executed, the container will automatically map the `ap-manager` to the `payables-manager` role and the programmatic authorization will succeed.

The run-as Capability

The EJB security architecture also allows a component to be called with one security role to run with another security role. This is accomplished using the `run-as` element in the DD. Using the `run-as` element, the specified security role will be used in place of the security role of the caller. The following example demonstrates this capability.

```
<enterprise-beans>
        ...
        <session>
          ...
          <ejb-name>AccountLookupService</ejb-name>
            ....
            <security-identity>
              <run-as>
                  <role-name>accounting-manager</role-name>
              </run-as>
            </security-identity>
          </session>
        </enterprise-beans>
    ...
```

In this example, any caller executing a method in the `AccountLookupService` will execute the method using the `accounting-manager` security role. This effectively lets a caller with one role assume a potentially more permissive role for the purposes of the call (see Figure 25–2). This addition to the DD was necessary for components like MDBs which have no explicit principal context associated with them. (MDBs are not run directly by a user session but are instead executed based on the presence of messages on the queue or posted to a topic.) The `run-as` capability should be used sparingly, carefully, and only when necessary.

> If MDBs are being used with the `run-as` facility, the functionality of those components should be reviewed, and if necessary, some sort of the validation mechanism (for example, digital signatures or a vendor-specific mechanism) should be employed to validate that the message has not been tampered with by some unauthorized third party.

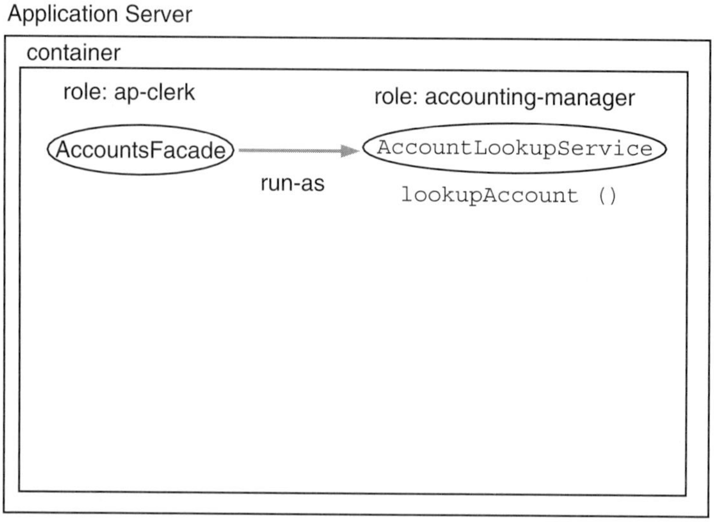

Application Server

Figure 25–2   *Security role run-as capability.*

Though EJBs have the ability to change the security role that is being propagated from one method to another, they do not provide this capability with principals. The principal is conceptually assigned to a session within the container and does not change from call to call. The EJB specification does not provide for the alteration of the assigned principal.

Who Does What

The deployer is expected to perform the bulk of the security assignment work. He or she is responsible for assigning principals or groups of principals to specific security roles that have been identified by the application assembler. The deployer is also expected to identify any `run-as` identities required by the application.

The EJB specification provides no specific guidance on the principal identity used to access the underlying OS. The specifics of this are left to the application server provider and obviously can vary depending on the implementation.

As always with EJBs, using OS-specific capabilities or depending on a particular application server implementation reduces the portability of the application and should be avoided.

If there is no other choice but to use the OS feature, then the usage should be abstracted out to a specific set of classes using a proxy pattern to control access to the feature. This will make the process of porting the application to other application servers and other operating systems easier.

The deployer may also need to alter the mapping of security roles to methods. This is work that may have originally been done by the application assembler but because of the manner in which components are being deployed (for example, the application is being deployed at a new site with different security requirements), may require the deployer to make changes to the assignment of security roles.

Programmatic Security Using the EJB API

Though EJB does provide a robust facility for implementing role-based security through entries in the DD, there may be occasions when programmatic access to security information is required. Two methods available through the EJBContext can provide this access as shown in Table 25–4

Table 25–4   *EJBContext Methods*

Method	Description
getCallerPrincipal(): Principal	Returns the java.security.Principal of the current caller.
isCallerInRole(String role): boolean	Returns a boolean true if the caller is in the role passed.

The getCallerPrincipal method returns a java.security.Principal object, which, if the program requires it, can be compared with another Principal object or string using the Principal getName method.

Since the principal has been mapped to a security role through the application server's security facility, we could also use the isCallerInRole method to test for a specific security role that the caller is currently assuming.

```
...
AccountsPayableBean implements SessionBean {

EJBContext context;
...
public void validateSession() {
       if ( context.isCallerInRole( "payables-manager") ) {
       //
       // valid user who is allowed to make our secure method
       // call
       //
       payablesUpdateProcessing();
else
       {
```

```
            throw new Exception( "Action cannot be performed." );
        ...
}
}
```

Assuming that we are using the accounts payable session bean shown in the previous examples, we now choose to validate the caller role using the `isCallerInRole` method. This method accepts a string, which is the name of the role to test. If the caller is in the role identified, a boolean true is returned and in this example we call the `payablesUpdateProcessing` method, a method which allows various privileged business activities to be performed. If the caller is not in the role specified, a boolean false is returned and we throw an exception indicating the action cannot be performed.

The `EJBContext` `getCallerPrincipal` method returns some useful information concerning the `java.security.Principal` assigned to the caller. In some cases this information may be used internally by the application, as shown in the following code snippet.

```
...
AccountsPayableBean implements SessionBean {

EJBContext context;
...
public void doPrincipalSearch() {
        //
        // search for records for our Principal name
        //
    String principalName =
            context.getCallerPrincipal().getName();
        //
        // lookup related records in the database
        //
        ...


}
```

In this example, the name of the caller principal is retrieved from the `EJBContext` and is stored in a local string. This string will later be used to perform a database lookup to retrieve records related to the principal name.

TRANSACTIONS WITH EJBS

Transactions involve grouping multiple database update operations into a single, self-contained, atomic update. Since J2EE applications often involve the integration of multiple legacy systems, database updates can involve the updates of multiple databases from different database vendors. For this reason, the EJB specification requires application servers to provide a transaction manager to manage the updates between the databases and provide for a *distributed transaction,* a transaction that can be maintained across multiple database resources.

In real-world applications, database update activity can become very complex very quickly. Having the ability to simply roll back and undo a set of complex database updates, even across different databases from different database vendors, provides significant value. With a distributed transaction, a failure of an update to one of the databases in the transaction would lead to a rollback of the updates to all of the databases thus returning the databases to a consistent, valid state (see Figure 25–3).

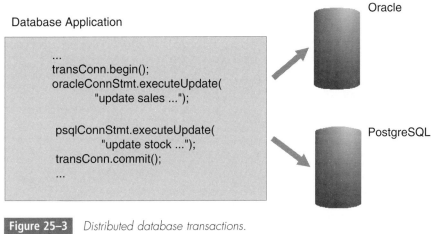

Figure 25–3   *Distributed database transactions.*

As with security, EJBs provide both a programmatic and declarative approach. Each EJB is identified as using either bean-managed transactions (programmatic) or container-managed transactions (declarative).

Transactions boundaries are associated with the methods in the EJB. A transaction may start in one method and potentially be propagated to other methods called by the EJB, depending on the transaction properties of the EJBs. This means that a transaction started in one method could be the controlling transaction for work performed in other methods (see Figure 25–4).

How transactions are propagated from one method to another, or even if they are propagated at all, can be configured in the DD. The two types of transaction control with EJBs are referred to as *bean-managed transactions* (BMT) and *container-managed transactions* (CMT). The type of transaction control to be used by a bean is declared in the DD using an entry as shown below.

Application Server

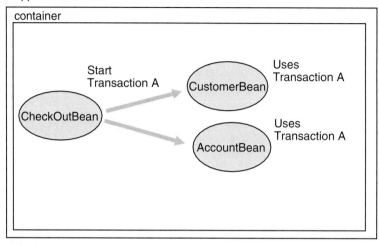

Figure 25–4 *EJB transaction propagation.*

```
<application>
...
<enterprise-beans>
    <session>
     <ejb-name>Email</ejb-name>
     <ejb-class>accounting.utilities.EmailBean</ejb-class>
     <home>accounting.utilities.EmailHome</home>
     <remote>accounts.payables.EmailRemote</remote>
     <session-type>Stateless</session-type>
     <transaction-type>Bean</transaction-type>
    </session>
```

This entry declares the session bean `EmailBean` as using bean-managed transactions. This would require the bean code, and thus the bean developer, to manage transactions through calls to the Java Transaction API (JTA). Session beans and message beans may both elect to use BMTs using the `transaction-type` attribute.

Alternatively, if we would like to have a session bean use CMTs, we could make the following declaration.

```
<application>
...
<enterprise-beans>
```

```
<session>
 <ejb-name>AccountsPayable</ejb-name>
 <ejb-class>AccountsPayableBean</ejb-class>
 <home>accounting.payables.AccountsPayableHome</home>
 <remote>accounts.payables.AccountsPayableRemote</remote>
 <session-type>Stateful</session-type>
 <transaction-type>Container</transaction-type>
</session>
```

The choice of using CMT or BMT apply only to session beans and MDBs. Entity beans are required to be under transaction control at all times; CMT is implied for these beans.

Stateless session beans may use transactions but must complete the transaction within the scope of the method being called. Since a transaction requires a transaction context to be saved between invocations, a stateless session bean has no means of saving a transaction context, since it effectively does not exist between calls. For this reason, the stateless session bean cannot have a transaction that spans multiple method invocations.

The availability of CMT and BMT leave us with an option to choose. The advantages of using CMT are obvious: the ease of use and the flexibility of being able to change transaction control using the DD. But CMT limits the transaction boundary to the method block, and there are times when the more finely grained control of BMT may be required. The following sections discuss these two approaches.

Container-Managed Transactions

Using CMT allows the container to control transactions based on method block boundaries. The method represents the transaction demarcation. This is markedly different from BMT, where the arbitrary occurrence of the `begin` and `commit` methods represent the transaction boundary.

This means that with CMT, each method represents a potential transaction boundary. But with CMT, transaction boundaries are not limited to a single method block and can extend over multiple methods by allowing transactions to be propagated from the calling method to the called method.

Transaction Attributes

How these transactions are propagated is under the direct control of the application assembler (or the EJB developer who may commonly be assuming that role). The EJB defines a number of transaction attributes that apply directly to this transaction propagation. These attributes are listed in Table 25–5.

Table 25–5	EJB Transaction Attributes

Attribute	Description
NotSupported	This defines a method that does not support transactions.
Required	This defines a method that must be executed with a transaction context.
Supports	This defines a method that may or may not run within a transaction.
RequiresNew	Defines a method that will always run within a new transaction context.
Mandatory	Defines a method that must be called with a transaction context.
Never	Defines a method that will never run within a transaction.

Using the NotSupported transaction attribute, if the method is called by a caller with a transaction context active, the container suspends the transaction while the method executes and resumes the transaction when the method exits.

With the Required transaction attribute, if the method is called by a caller with a transaction context, that transaction context is used by the method. If the method is called by a caller without a transaction context, then a transaction is started for the duration of the method and completed at the end of the method.

Using the Supports transaction attribute, if the method is called by a caller with a transaction context, the method is executed within the context of the caller. If the method is called by a caller without a transaction context, then the method executes without a transaction.

With the RequiresNew transaction attribute, if the caller has a transaction context, it is suspended and a new transaction started and completed by the end of the transaction. If the caller has no transaction context, a new transaction is started and completed at the end of the transaction.

If the Mandatory transaction attribute is used and the method is called without a transaction context, then an exception is thrown. If the method is called by a caller with a transaction context, then the method is executed within that transaction.

With the Never transaction attribute, if the caller has a transaction context, the container throws an exception. If the caller has no transaction context, then the method is executed without a transaction.

MDBs may only use the NotSupported or Required transaction attributes. Any other attribute is meaningless, since there is no explicit caller and therefore no transaction attribute to propagate.

Transaction Rollback and Commit Operations

By default, with no other instructions to the contrary, the container will commit a CMT on the method boundary. If a method has called other methods and propagated its transaction, the transaction is committed on return from all called methods. This behavior can be changed with a call to the `EJBContext` `setRollbackOnly` method. A call to this method identifies the transaction for rollback and on completion of the call to the enclosing method, the container informs the transaction manager that the method transaction should be rolled back. Note that merely throwing an exception will not guarantee a rollback; exception handling must explicitly call the `setRollbackOnly` method.

We must define transaction attributes for each of the methods in our EJB. Fortunately, syntax has been defined to make declarations for multiple methods in a single entry. The application assembler can define the transaction attributes for the methods in the bean as follows.

```
<assembly-descriptor>
...
     <container-transaction>
            <method>
               <ejb-name>AccountsPayable</ejb-name>
               <method-name>*</method-name>
            <method>
            <trans-attribute>Required</trans-attribute>
     <container-transaction>

     <container-transaction>
            <method>
               <ejb-name>AccountsPayable</ejb-name>
               <method-name>updateCriticalRecords</method-name>
            <method>
            <trans-attribute>RequiresNew</trans-attribute>
     <container-transaction>

</assembly-descriptor>
...
```

In this example, the `AccountsPayable` bean has several methods that we would like to execute under a single transaction. This is accomplished by describing the transactional properties of the bean using transaction attributes. Since we want all code in the bean (and therefore all methods) to execute under a transaction, the first entry declares all methods in the bean to have the `Required` transaction attribute.

Next, we would like the `updateCriticalRecords` method to operate in its own transaction, so we declare it to have a transaction attribute of `RequiresNew`; this entry overrides the previously declaration of the `Required` transaction attribute, which was declared for all methods, including this one.

Though it may appear that a transaction attribute of `RequiresNew` is creating a *nested transaction*, that is not the case. Nested transaction implementations in robust database systems allow one or more *savepoints* to be declared in a set of transactions so that rollbacks may be conducted back to a specific point. A rollback to one savepoint can optionally require the rollback of other savepoints and invalidate previously declared savepoints.

The EJB transaction implementation is more limited than these nested transaction implementations and is considered a *flat-transaction* implementation, meaning that only one transaction at a time is active.

BEAN-MANAGED TRANSACTIONS

Using BMT, the transaction is controlled programmatically in the code surrounding the update operations. BMT allows transaction demarcation, the selection of transaction boundaries, to be any arbitrary location in the code, as shown in the following example.

```
...
    javax.transaction.UserTransaction ut;
    javax.ejb.EJBContext            context;

    ...

    try {
      //
      // establish the connections and create the
      // statements
      //
      InitialContext init = new InitialContext();
      DataSource accountingDS = init.lookup(
                    "java:comp/env/jdbc/accounting");
      DataSource legacyAccountingDS = init.lookup(
                    "java:comp/env/jdbc/accountingL");

      java.sql.Connection conAcctg =
                    accountingDS.getConnection();
      java.sql.Connection conLegacy =
                    accountingDS.getConnection();

      java.sql.Statement stmtUpdAccounts =
                    conAcctg.prepareStatement("...");
      java.sql.Statement stmtUpdLegacy =
                    conLegacy.prepareStatement("...");
    }
    catch ( java.sql.SQLException ) {
```

```
        ...
      }

   //
...

   //
   // now perform our distributed transaction
   //

   //
   // get our current transaction context
   //
   ut = context.getUserTransaction();

   //
   // save and test our update count
   //
   int     updCount = 0;

   //
   // begin the transaction
   //
   ut.begin();

        updCount =
             stmtUpdAccounts.executeUpdate();

        if ( updCount > 0 ) {

            updCount = stmtUpdLegacy.executeUpdate();

        }

        //
        // if this second update failed to update any
        // rows, we have a problem and should rollback
        if ( updCount == 0 ) {
            ut.rollback();
        }


   }
   catch (java.sql.SQLException e ) {
      //
      // a problem with the updates ... rollback
      //
      System.out.println("Exception caught: " + e );

      //
      // rollback if we have an active transaction
      //
```

```
    if ( ut.getStatus() ==
        javax.sql.transaction.Status.STATUS_ACTIVE ) {
        try {
          ut.rollback();
        }
        catch (java.sql.SQLException e) {
            System.out.println("Could not rollback. " +
                                " Exception caught: " + e );
        }
    }
}
finally {
  //
  // if we still have an active transaction,
  // let's commit it
  //
    if ( ( ut.getStatus() ==
            javax.sql.transaction.Status.STATUS_ACTIVE ) )


  {
      try {
          ut.commit();
      }
      catch (java.sql.SQLException e ) {
          System.out.println( "Could not commit. Exception: " +
              e );
      }
  }

}
```

In this code snippet, we obtain a connection to two separate resources, in this case databases. One database represents a database for our current accounting system and the other some legacy accounting system database that is still in use to provide unique challenges for the IT department. Connections are obtained on the two databases and a set of prepared statements are created for the separate connections.

Next, the EJBContext is used to provide the current transaction context by calling the getUserTransaction method. This method returns a reference to a javax.transaction.UserTransaction instance representing the current transaction context.

Once the UserTransaction has been obtained, the UserTransaction begin method is called to mark the start of the transaction. A set of updates is then performed and the update count retained. Since it is not an error to update 0 rows no exception will be thrown, so this return value must be checked to determine if updates were actually performed. If, after performing the updates on both statements, the value is 0 indicating no updates were performed, we roll back all work.

If an exception is thrown, we test to determine whether or not we currently have an active transaction. If we do, then we perform a rollback. Note that since the `rollback` method is a critical operation, it may throw an exception, and the exception must be managed by the Java code; in this example we create a small `try/catch` block to handle the exception.

If we arrive at the finally block we test to determine whether or not we still have an active transaction. This is done with a call to the `UserTransaction` `getStatus` method. If the status is active, then we commit the transaction which requires a `try/catch` block to catch the `SQLException` that may be thrown by that operation.

As this code demonstrates, we do have some flexibility with the management of our transactions. With complex distributed transactions that require a great deal of business logic to determine whether to commit or roll back, the use of BMT may be the best option.

Summary

EJBs are designed to provide flexibility, allowing an existing EJB to be easily integrated into an existing set of components. In order to be able to perform this integration, we need to allow an EJB's security and transaction control to be modified to conform to the needs of the application it is being integrated into. EJBs allow this to be done using several different methods.

As we saw in this chapter, the EJB developer does not need to be concerned with security or transaction control when programming the component. The developer can focus on programming the business logic of the component and leave the security and transaction decisions to those responsible for integrating the component into the application. Using declarative programming, these security and transaction properties for an EJB can be placed in an XML configuration file (the DD) and read at deployment time.

Alternatively, if a more finely grained security model must be implemented, then the security and transactions for the component can be controlled programmatically by the developer.

Now that we have explained EJBs and their architecture and we have described how transactions and security can be be programmed into EJBs, we will now turn our attention to the development of EJBs. The next chapter will provide a set of examples of EJBs, and will demonstrate the process of accessing these business tier components from the presentation tier using program examples.

CHAPTER 26

Programming with EJBs

INTRODUCTION

Enterprise JavaBeans (EJBs) provide a facility for creating a component-based application with Java. EJB components operate within a logical environment, a *container*, which is implemented by an application server. The application server implements the container, which provides the runtime environment for the component.

TYPES OF ENTITY BEANS

As we learned in Chapter 24, "Enterprise JavaBeans: An Introduction," entity beans manage persistence in one of two ways: bean-managed persistence (BMP) or container-managed Persistence (CMP).

An entity bean that is declared to use CMP allows the container to control persistence, letting the container determine how the runtime content of the bean will be read from or written to the database. With this approach, the developer will not need to provide any code for the persistence. Instead, the application server provides a tool to describe how this persistence is managed. In EJB 1.1, there were some distinct limitations to CMP that limited its applications. In EJB 2.0, these limitations have been largely overcome with the ability to track dirty data and perform lazy loading from the database.

An entity bean may also be declared to use BMP, where the developer must write the database code to manage persistence for the bean. Using this type of persistence, developers must create instance members for the bean and must write the code to load data from the database and to write updated instance members to the database.

If CMP works well, then there is no compelling reason to write database access code for an entity bean. But there is a catch. As application queries grow more complex, it is likely that CMP tools, which provide the object-relational mapping for the application, will fail or will result in sluggish performance. For this reason, it is not uncommon to use BMP in EJB applications.

CONNECTING EJBs TO PRESENTATION TIER COMPONENTS

Design patterns provide useful abstractions to help guide the development process. These patterns represent proven solutions for recurring problems. One pattern that has proven useful in the development of EJB solutions is the *session facade* design pattern. Using this design pattern, the EJB session bean provides a layer of control between the objects it works with and the client code accessing it. The EJB client invokes the session bean and submits requests. The session bean is responsible for gathering any resources needed, using various helper objects. The facade object also plays a controller role, managing the workflow and formatting the results to return to the client. See Figure 26–1.

The following example illustrates the use of the *session facade* design pattern using a session bean that provides access to business objects, which return information back to the presentation tier. In this example, we use our `knowledgebase` database (a message system) to gather information on the status of a support help desk for the movies e-commerce system. The presentation tier is comprised of a servlet, which is used to create the help status page with the help of XML and XSLT. The ultimate output of executing this servlet is shown in Figure 26–2.

The session bean in this example exposes a simple interface, a single method, which is accessed by the client servlet. Much of the work being performed by the EJB has been isolated in the helper objects so that ultimately the code needed to create the session facade EJB is relatively simple. The following sections provide an explanation of the code for the session bean and its interfaces and for the helper class used in the example.

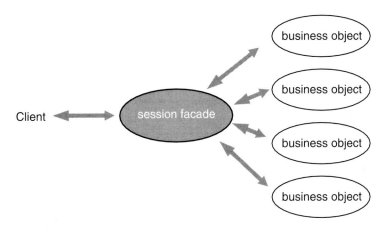

Figure 26–1   *Session facade design pattern.*

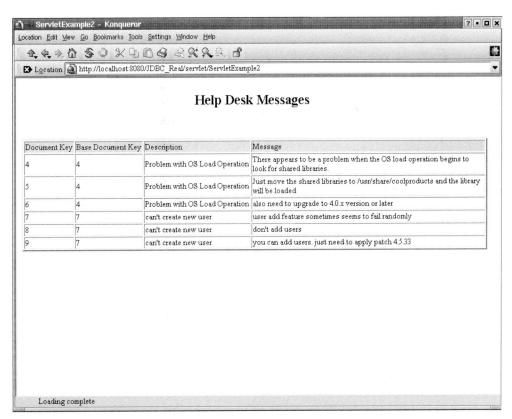

Figure 26–2   *ServletExample2 output.*

THE SERVLETEXAMPLE2 CLASS DECLARATION

The `ServletExample2` servlet receives an XML document and uses the Saxon transformation API to transform the XML document into an HTML table. It uses an EJB component to access the database and encode the data as an XML document. The first code block, shown here, simply declares the class and various instance members needed to perform its work.

The ServletExample2 Class: Class Declaration

```
package ServletExamples;

import java.io.*;
import java.text.*;
import java.util.*;
import javax.servlet.*;
import javax.servlet.http.*;


import java.sql.*;
import java.net.*;
import java.io.*;

// j2ee
import javax.ejb.*;
import javax.naming.*;
import java.rmi.*;
import javax.rmi.*;
import java.io.Serializable;

// our packages
import db.*;
import jdbcutil.*;
import movies.ejb.*;

// saxon
import com.icl.saxon.trax.*;
import org.xml.sax.*;

public class ServletExample2 extends HttpServlet {

ServletConfig        config;
ServletContext       context;

MoviesFacadeRemote moviesEJB;

//
// for Saxon XML transformations
//
```

```
Processor    processor;
Templates    templates;
Transformer transformer;

String           defaultStyleSheet = "file:/stylesheets/xslt/rs.xsl";
...
```

The ServletExample2 Class: doGet Method

The next code block shows the implementation of the doGet method for the servlet. This method is called by the servlet container to respond to the HTTP GET request. The code sample shown here obtains the PrintWriter object from the response and displays some HTML formatting elements to the output writer. The getQueryResults method is then called and returns an XML-formatted document as a string containing the results of the query.

Once the XML document has been returned, it is transformed into an HTML table. The transform method accepts the XML document as a Reader (java.io.Reader) by wrapping the string with a StringReaderPrintWriter as a Result (part of the Saxon API) class.

The ServletExample2 Class: The doGet Method

```
    public void doGet(HttpServletRequest request,
                        HttpServletResponse response)
        throws IOException, ServletException
    {
        PrintWriter out = response.getWriter();

        out.println("<html>");
        out.println("<head>");

      out.println("<title>ServletExample2</title>");
        out.println("</head>");
        out.println("<body bgcolor=\"white\">");

        try {

        //
        // retrieve the query results as an XML document
        //
        String xmlDoc = getQueryResults();

        //
        // transform the XML to the format for our
        // output (an HTML table)
         //
          Transformer transformer = templates.newTransformer();
          transformer.transform(   new InputSource(
```

```
                              new StringReader( xmlDoc ) ),
                          new Result( out ) );


            out.println("</body>");
            out.println("</html>");
        }
      catch (Exception e) {
            log( "Exception in doGet: " + e.getMessage() );
      }


    }
```

ServletExample2 Class: The getQueryResults Method

The getQueryResults method is called in the doGet method to return an XML document and calls the getHelpDeskStatus method. Within the getQueryResults method, the EJB (moviesEJB) is accessed. This returns a string containing the XML-formatted document, which is returned to the calling method.

```
...
public String getQueryResults() {
String retVal = null;
try {
    retVal = moviesEJB.getHelpDeskStatus();
}
catch (RemoteException e) {
        //context.log(
        "RemoteException in ServletExample2.getQueryResults: " +
         e.getMessage() );
        System.out.println(
         "RemoteException in ServletExample2.getQueryResults: " +
         e.getMessage() );
}
finally {
  return retVal;
}

}
...
```

The ServletExample2 Class: The init Method

The init method is responsible for initializing the servlet to be used in the application. This method is called once when the servlet is first loaded and will not be called again. The init method is, as the name implies, a good location to perform initialization work, work which for performance reasons we do not want to be doing each time the servlet is invoked. The code for this method is shown next.

```
public void init( ServletConfig config ) {

Hashtable env = new Hashtable();

        this.config = config;
       this.context = config.getServletContext();

         //
         // get the location of the xslt stylesheet from a
             // context parameter
         //
         String styleSheet = context.getInitParameter(
                             "XsltStyleSheet" );

try {
         //
         // build the URL for the stylesheet
         //
         if ( styleSheet == null )
            styleSheet = defaultStyleSheet;
            else
            styleSheet = "file:" + styleSheet;

            //
         // create the objects we need for the XSL transformation
         //
         processor = Processor.newInstance("xslt");

            //
         // get an InputStream from the URL
            //
         templates = processor.process(new InputSource(
                         new URL( styleSheet ).openStream() ) );

         transformer = templates.newTransformer();

            //
            // get a connection to the EJB server
         //
            // We hardcode the naming service parameters here.
            // in production code, we would get these from the
            // servlet context (context-param or init-param)
            // or from a properties file.
            //
            env.put( "java.naming.factory.initial",
                     "org.jnp.interfaces.NamingContextFactory");
            env.put( "java.naming.provider.url",
                     "jnp://localhost:1099");
            env.put( "java.naming.factory.url.pkgs",
                     "org.jboss.naming:org.jnp.interfaces");

        InitialContext init = new InitialContext( env );
```

```
        //
        // get the home object
        //
        Object obj =    init.lookup("ejb/MoviesFacade");

        //
        // perform a special 'cast' on the home object
        //
        MoviesFacadeHome home = (MoviesFacadeHome)
              PortableRemoteObject.narrow( obj,
                                            MoviesFacadeHome.class );

        //
        // create our remote reference
        //
        moviesEJB = home.create();
}
catch (ProcessorException e) {
        System.out.println(
            "ProcessorException in ServletExample2.init: " +
            e.getMessage() );
}
catch (NamingException e) {
        System.out.println(
            "NamingException in ServletExample2.init: " +
            e.getMessage() + " - " + e );
}
catch (Exception e) {
        System.out.println(
            "Exception in ServletExample2.init: " +
            e.getMessage() );
}

    }

    }
```

In the `init` method, the XSLT stylesheet is chosen and the transformer, template, and processor are created. Since we must initiate communication with an EJB, we must create a connection to the naming service for the EJB container as provided by the application server where the EJBs are running. This means that we need to contact the naming service running in the application server. But if we call the `InitialContext` constructor without any parameters we would get the naming service for the servlet container where the servlet is running.

In order to access the correct naming service, we need to pass a `Hashtable` with the correct parameters to access the JBoss application server. These environment entries are stored in a `Hashtable`, which is then passed into the `InitialContext` constructor as a parameter. For simplicity, and to highlight the fact that we must access a naming service outside of our servlet container, we hardcode the initialization parameters required to access the naming service. To maximize flexibility in a production application, we would load these parameters from some other source such as the servlet context (in the `web.xml` file) as an `init-param` or `context-param`, or read them from a properties file.

Once the `InitialContext` is obtained, the `lookup` method is executed to find the home object for the `MoviesFacade` bean. For backwards compatibility and to maintain portability, this home object must be cast using a special method, the `PortableRemoteObject narrow` method. The result of the `narrow` call is the appropriate home object for the `MoviesFacadeBean` EJB.

This home object for the bean then acts as a factory for obtaining references to the remote object for the `MoviesFacadeBean` EJB. The `create` method for the home object acts as the factory method, returning an `object` reference for the remote object (`moviesEJB`).

The remote object is technically a proxy and is not the EJB, since that is running on the server. Despite this distinction, the remote object gives us complete access to the EJB through the methods we have exposed to client code by defining them in the remote interface (`MoviesFacadeRemote`), which we will examine shortly.

Session Beans: The MoviesFacadeBean Class

The `MoviesFacadeBean` class contains a set of business methods for the movies application. Since it is a session bean, it must implement the `SessionBean` interface. Because of the internal operation of the helper class for the session bean, we need to declare it to be a *stateful* session bean in the deployment descriptor.

The methods in any class implemented as an EJB can perform a wide range of operations, but for maximum portability, they should not access local resources (disk files, open network connections), should not use threads, and should have serializable arguments if they are going to be exposed to client code by defining the signature in the remote interface. The code for the `MoviesFacadeBean` class is shown next.

MoviesFacadeBean Class: The Class Declaration

```
package movies.ejb;

import javax.ejb.*;
import java.rmi.*;
import java.io.Serializable;

import java.sql.*;
```

```
import javax.sql.*;
import javax.naming.*;

import db.*;
import jdbcutil.*;

public class MoviesFacadeBean implements SessionBean {

EJBHome     ejbHome;
Handle      ejbHandle;

DBUtil      dbutil;

StatusDAO statusDAO;

PreparedStatement statusQuery1;

SessionContext context;
...
```

The MoviesFacadeBean Class: Method Declarations

This EJB class contains a single method definition that is exposed to the client code: the getHelpDeskStatus method, as shown in the following code example. The *helper object*, the statusDAO DAO, is used to retrieve general status information for a hypothetical help desk. Since the getGeneralStatus method of the statusDAO object retrieves all active help desk messages, it does not require any parameters to be passed to express filter criteria.

The getGeneralStatus method of the StatusDAO class returns a ResultSet. Since we have created a servlet that uses an XSLT transformer to render output based on XML input, we would prefer to have the results formatted in an XML document. This is accomplished through the use of a helper class, the JDBCXML class. The ResultSet returned from the statusDAO object is passed to the JDBCXML toXMLString method, which returns a string containing an XML encoded document containing the data in the ResultSet.

The ejbCreate method, which is invoked each time a session bean is created, is used to create the statusDAO object, passing in to the statusDAO constructor an argument for the name of the DataSource to use.

The setSessionContext method is called when the session bean is created and at other times during the life of the bean. This associates the bean with the container in which it is running. The common practice is to save the context to an instance member, as shown in this example. The SessionContext object is used to access security information, obtain a home object reference, and obtain a transaction control object. The code for these methods is shown next.

The MoviesFacadeBean Class Methods

```
//
// return XML formatted string of help desk status
//
public String getHelpDeskStatus() {

        // getGeneralStatus returns a ResultSet which we
        // will convert/transform to an XML formatted string
        //
        return JDBCXML.toXMLString( statusDAO.getGeneralStatus() );
 }

public void ejbCreate() throws CreateException {

  //
  // give constructor the name of the DataSource to use
  //
  statusDAO  = new StatusDAO(
          "java:comp/env/jdbc/knowledgebase" );

}

public void setSessionContext(SessionContext sc) {

      //
      // store the SessionContext
      //
      this.context = sc;
}

// ** required for compilation, but not used **
public void remove() {}
public void ejbPostCreate() { }
public void ejbRemove() { }
public void ejbActivate() { }
public void ejbPassivate() { }

public MoviesFacadeBean() {}

}
```

The MoviesFacadeBean Helper Objects: The StatusDAO

Using the session facade design pattern, the session facade object is responsible for marshaling and coordinating the resources needed to accomplish its task. In this example, this is accomplished using a single DAO to perform the low-level specifics of data access.

The StatusDAO class represents a simple business object, a specific implementation of a Data Access Object design pattern. In this example, the DAO provides the help desk status information to the facade bean, which then returns that information to the client object which requested the information. The DAO effectively abstracts the database access operation; the client components need not be aware of the details of database access.

There are other approaches to abstracting the database access operation such as using an Entity bean (shown later in this chapter), using a generic DAO implementation, or using Java Data Objects. As of this writing, the JDO specification was not complete (though an early access release was available) and was not part of the J2EE package. For our purposes in this example the DAO serves the purpose of hiding the details of the database access from the client components.

The StatusDAO class approaches the execution of the status query in a manner similar to that shown in previous examples. The actual query to be executed is not hardcoded into the program but is instead stored in an EJB environment entry that can be easily retrieved by the component. Thus, changing the query does not require the component (the MovieEntityBean EJB) to be changed and redeployed.

The constructor for the StatusDAO class establishes a connection to the database using a helper class, which abstracts many of the details of database access using SQL. The InitialContext is then accessed to obtain the environment entry for the status query to execute. These environment entries are available through the naming service for the application server. In this example, we retrieve the value of the query as a string and store it in an instance member.

The final step in the constructor is to call the prepareQueries method. As shown in the code listing below, this prepares the single query that has just been stored in the instance member.

The getGeneralStatus method, the method called by the MoviesFacadeBean to retrieve the help desk status, executes the internal prepared statement and returns the result as a ResultSet. Because this method expects to have an active PreparedStatement reference (it expects the underlying connection for the PreparedStatement to be active), the session bean must be declared to be a stateful session bean, meaning that the container will ensure that the state of the member variables of the session bean are retained even if the bean has been passivated. Since the MoviesFacadeBean contains an instance of the StatusDAO class and expects to be able to use it after it has been created (in the ejbCreate method of the bean), then we must ensure that the container restores the proper reference for the StatusDAO class when the MoviesFacadeBean is invoked; defining the bean as a stateful session bean will accomplish this.

The StatusDAO Class Definition

```
package db;

import java.sql.*;
import javax.naming.*;

public class StatusDAO {

DBUtil                              dbutil;
PreparedStatement   generalStatusQuery;

String statusQuery1;

public StatusDAO( String dataSourceName ) {

try {

    //
    // DBUtil is a helper class for database
    // access
    //
    dbutil =  new DBUtil( dataSourceName );

    //
    // get the query from an environment entry
    // - don't hardcode it
    //
    InitialContext ctx = new InitialContext();
    statusQuery1 = (String)
        ctx.lookup("java:comp/env/statusQuery1");

    //
    // create a prepared statement for the query
    //
    prepareQueries();

}
catch (Exception e) {
    System.out.println("Exception in StatusDAO.constructor: " +
                        e.getMessage() );
}

}

private void prepareQueries() {

try {

    generalStatusQuery = dbutil.createPreparedStatement(
                                statusQuery1 );
```

```
}
catch (Exception e) {
    System.out.println(
            "Exception in StatusDAO.prepareQueries: " +
            e.getMessage() + " - " + e );
}


}

public ResultSet getGeneralStatus( ) {
//
// return a ResultSet with the results of the general
// status query
//
ResultSet rs = null;

  try {

      rs =   generalStatusQuery.executeQuery();

    }
    catch (SQLException e ) {
        System.out.println(
        "Exception caught in StatusDAO.prepareQuery: " +
            e.getMessage() );
    }
    finally {
        return rs;
    }

  }

}
```

The MoviesFacadeHome and MoviesRemote Interfaces

The home and remote interfaces for the `MoviesFacadeBean` are shown below.
These interfaces are required to create the EJB. The methods identified in the
remote interface are the methods that will be visible to the client. The home interface for session beans declares the `create` methods for the bean and can optionally declare `create` methods with multiple arguments, though that is not done
here. Each `create` method declared in the home interface must have a corresponding `ejbCreate` method declared in the session bean class.

The MoviesFacadeHome Interface

```
package movies.ejb;
```

```
import javax.ejb.*;
import java.io.Serializable;
import java.rmi.RemoteException;

public interface MoviesFacadeHome extends EJBHome {

  MoviesFacadeRemote create() throws RemoteException, CreateException;

}
```

The MoviesFacadeRemote Interface

```
package movies.ejb;

import javax.ejb.*;
import java.io.Serializable;
import java.rmi.RemoteException;

public interface MoviesFacadeRemote extends EJBObject {
    public String getHelpDeskStatus() throws RemoteException;
}
```

ACCESSING AN ENTITY BEAN

As we know, an entity bean is an EJB that represents a unique instance of an entity in a permanent data store. Each entity bean is represented by a unique ID: a primary key. Unlike session beans, which are usually created for use, an entity bean represents persistent data and is therefore usually found and retrieved from the data store.

The previous example showed the use of JDBC in a helper object for a session bean. The helper object implemented the Data Access Object (DAO) design pattern, which isolates and encapsulates the data access activity into a coarse-grained object. By using this design pattern, the details of the data and the data access are isolated from the session facade bean.

DAOs can also have utility when used with entity beans, specifically entity beans using BMP. With this approach, the entity bean simply *wraps* the DAO. The following code sample demonstrates this approach.

The `ListMovies` JSP page used the `MoviesBean JavaBean` to access an entity bean. In this example, the `MoviesBean` acted as a presentation tier *business object*. The business object is sometimes referred to as a *business object design pattern*. This is a generalized category for an object that takes on the responsibility of managing business logic, thus removing that responsibility from some other object or component.

As we explained in the section on J2EE architecture, we want to maintain a separation of roles. On the presentation tier, where we have JSPs and servlets creating the presentation for the user, it is useful to remove business logic from these components and allow their development to be focused on creating a presentation. This is just what was done with the ListMovies JSP page as shown below.

Using the MoviesBean object, the only Java code exposed on the JSP page was a call to the MoviesBean loadBean method, which was passed the movie_id for the bean to load. All other interaction with the JavaBean on the JSP was through JSP useBean tags. This keeps the JSP page focused on creating a presentation, and does not add complexity to the page with management of EJB components.

The ListMovies JSP Page

```
<HTML>
<BODY bgcolor="white">

<jsp:useBean id="moviesBean" class="movies.beans.MoviesBean" scope="session" />

<!-- load the bean with the request parameter -->
<% moviesBean.loadBean( request.getParameter( "movie_id" ) ); %>

<br>
<font face="Helvetica, Sans-serif" size=+3 >
<center>
<b>Movie Information for "<jsp:getProperty name="moviesBean" property="movie_name"
/>"  </b>
</center>
</font>
<br>
<br>

<center>
<table border=1 cellpadding=2 bgcolor="white">
<tr>
<td>
<img src="http://localhost:8080/JDBC_Real/servlet/BlobView/?movie_id=<%=
request.getParameter("movie_id") %>" name="Box Picture" align=center >
</td>
</tr>
</table>
</center>

<br>
<br>
<br>

<center>

<font face="Helvetica, Sans-serif" size=+2 color="blue">

<table border=1 cellpadding=2 bgcolor="white">
```

```
<tr>
<td bgcolor="#C0D9D9">Movie ID</td>
<td bgcolor="#C0D9D9">Movie Name</td>
<td bgcolor="#C0D9D9">Release Date</td>
<td bgcolor="#C0D9D9">Movie Description</td>
<td bgcolor="#C0D9D9">Special Promotion</td>
<td bgcolor="#C0D9D9">Update Date</td>
<td bgcolor="#C0D9D9">Category</td>

</tr>

<tr>
<td> <jsp:getProperty name="moviesBean" property="movie_id" /> </td>
<td> <jsp:getProperty name="moviesBean" property="movie_name" /> </td>
<td> <jsp:getProperty name="moviesBean" property="release_date" /> </td>
<td> <jsp:getProperty name="moviesBean" property="movie_desc" /> </td>
<td> <jsp:getProperty name="moviesBean" property="special_promotion" /> </td>
<td> <jsp:getProperty name="moviesBean" property="update_date" /> </td>
<td> <jsp:getProperty name="moviesBean" property="category" /> </td>

</tr>

</table>
</font>
</center>

<br>
<br>

<br>
<br>

</HTML>
</BODY>
```

THE MOVIESBEAN JAVABEAN

The MoviesBean JavaBean (shown previously) is shown here again just to identify the portions of the class that pertain to the retrieval of entity beans.

The MoviesBean JavaBean

```
package movies.beans;

import java.rmi.*;
import javax.naming.*;
```

```
import javax.rmi.*;
import javax.ejb.*;
import java.util.*;

import db.*;
import movies.ejb.*;

public class MoviesBean extends MoviesVO {

private InitialContext context;

private MoviesEntityRemote movies;
private MoviesEntityHome   moviesHome;

public MoviesBean() {

try {
    Hashtable env = new Hashtable();

    //
    // get a connection to the EJB server (Jboss)
    //
    env.put( "java.naming.factory.initial",
             "org.jnp.interfaces.NamingContextFactory");
    env.put( "java.naming.provider.url", "jnp://localhost:1099");
    env.put( "java.naming.factory.url.pkgs",
               "org.jboss.naming:org.jnp.interfaces");
    context = new InitialContext( env );

    //
    // get the movies entity bean
    //
    moviesHome = (MoviesEntityHome) PortableRemoteObject.narrow(
                   context.lookup("ejb/MoviesEntityBean"),
                                      MoviesEntityHome.class );

}
catch (NamingException e) {
      System.out.println(
            "NamingException in MoviesBean constructor: " +
            e.getMessage() );
}
catch (Exception e) {
      System.out.println("Exception in MoviesBean constructor: " +
                            e.getMessage() );
}

}

public void loadBean( String movie_id ) {

try {
```

```
    //
    // lookup this movie_id
    //
    movies = moviesHome.findByPrimaryKey(new Integer( movie_id ));

    //
    // set this object to look like the VO populated by the lookup
    //
    MoviesVO vo = movies.getMoviesVO();

    //
    // set our Value Object to look like the
    // value object returned  by the getMovies method
    //
    setMoviesVO( vo );

}
catch (RemoteException e) {
      System.out.println("RemoteException in MoviesBean loadbean: " +
                              e.getMessage() );
}
catch (FinderException e) {
      System.out.println("FinderException in MoviesBean loadbean: " +
                              e.getMessage() );
}
catch (Exception e) {
      System.out.println("Exception in MoviesBean loadbean: " +
                              e.getMessage() + " - " + e  );
}
catch (Throwable e) {
      System.out.println("Exception in MoviesBean loadbean: " +
                              e.getMessage() + " - " + e  );
}

}

}
```

The MoviesBean constructor calls the InitialContext constructor, using various environment entries to indicate how to access the name server of the JBoss application server. This is required because the JSP page will be executing inside the Tomcat Web server and the default InitialContext will not access the JBoss server. (Other application servers or Web servers, and the use of JBoss with the embedded Tomcat server, may offer a federated namespace that does not require the environment to be set or that sets the environment using different entries; the access of the InitialContext shown here is in no way universal.)

The MoviesEntityBean home object is then obtained through a call to the InitialContext (which is accessing the JBoss server namespace). For reasons explained previously, the home object must be narrowed in order to be accessible as a normal Java object. The constructor then stores the home object reference in an instance member for the entity bean.

The loadBean method, the method called from the ListMovies page, calls the findByPrimaryKey method of the home object (referred to as a *finder* method). The method call returns the remote object for the entity bean, specifically for the entity bean referenced by the movie_id passed into the findByPrimaryKey method.

This remote object is stored in an instance member and is then used to call the getMoviesVO method on the entity bean. This will return a reference to the internal value object of the entity bean, but since this is being done with remote object communication, the value object will be passed by value and copied into the local JVM memory space. The value object reference is then passed to the setMoviesVO method for the MoviesBean class (which is a subclass of MoviesVO). This method will set the internal members of the MoviesBean class to those of the value object of the entity bean, thus synchronizing the MoviesBean to the entity bean.

At this point, the internal members of the MoviesBean (as inherited from the MoviesVO value object) are set to the correct values. The MoviesBean is ready to be accessed by the ListMovies page through the JSP useBean tags. When the JSP page is invoked, the occurrences of the useBean tags on the page will be mapped to the MoviesBean object.

ENTITY BEANS: THE MOVIESENTITYBEAN CLASS

The MoviesEntityBean class provides an entity bean wrapper for the MoviesDAO class, which implements the DAO design pattern. As with previous examples, the details of the data access are encapsulated in the DAO. The implementation of the entity bean class merely maps the entity bean methods called by the application server (the callback methods) to the appropriate MoviesDAO methods. The code listing for the class declaration and findByPrimaryKey method is shown next.

The MoviesEntityBean Class Declaration and findByPrimaryKey Method

```
package movies.ejb;

import javax.ejb.*;
import java.rmi.*;
import java.io.Serializable;

import java.sql.*;
import javax.sql.*;
```

```
import javax.naming.*;

import db.*;
import jdbcutil.*;

public class MoviesEntityBean implements EntityBean {

EJBHome    ejbHome;
Handle     ejbHandle;

EntityContext context;

MoviesDAO moviesDAO;
MoviesVO   moviesVO;

//
// return XML formatted string of help desk status
//
public Integer ejbFindByPrimaryKey( Integer movie_id) throws FinderException {

Integer retVal = null;

try {
        // getGeneralStatus returns a ResultSet which we
        // will convert/transform to an XML formatted string
        //

  //
  // load our DAO using this movie_id
  //
  if ( moviesDAO == null ) {
      moviesDAO = new MoviesDAO("java:/moviesmysql");
      moviesVO  = new MoviesVO();
   }

   moviesDAO.loadDAO( movie_id.intValue() );

  //
  // if the movie_name has not been set, then no movie
  // was found for this primary key
  //
  if ( moviesDAO.getMoviesVO().getMovie_name()!= null )  {
      retVal = movie_id;
  }

  }
  catch (Exception e) {
          System.out.println("Exception in findbyPrimaryKey: " +
                             e.getMessage() + e );
  }

  finally {
```

```
//
// return the primary key
//
return retVal;
    }


}
```

The class declaration for the `MoviesEntityBean` class provides instance members for a `MoviesDAO` DAO and a `MoviesVO` value object. A reference for the `EntityContext` is also declared.

The `ejbFindbyPrimaryKey` method takes an integer argument for the primary key of the movie to find. The purpose of this method is simply to establish whether or not the record exists in the database. It verifies whether or not the record exists, and if the record does not exist, it returns a null reference. If the record does exist, it returns the primary key for the record.

The method code checks to determine whether or not the `MoviesDAO` exists. If it does not, then a `MoviesDAO` object is created and assigned to the instance member for the entity bean, and an instance of the `MoviesVO` object is also created.

Since the DAO we have defined does not have a specific `locate` method, we simply call the `loadDAO` method and attempt to load the DAO for the `movie_id` that has been passed. After loading the DAO, we test the `movie_name` for a null value. If the `movie_name` field is not null, then we assert the DAO has been loaded and the primary key for the entity bean does exist. (A more efficient implementation would simply do a quick database lookup or select a count of records from the database to determine the records' existence.)

Note that a call to the `ejbFindByPrimaryKey` method is not expected to load the entity bean; the `ejbLoad` method will be called by the container to perform that function.

The MoviesEntityBean Class: The getMoviesVO and ejbCreate Methods

The `getMoviesVO` method performs the simple task of returning the internal value object for the entity bean. The `setMoviesDAO` method takes a `MovieVO` object reference as an argument and calls the `MoviesDAO loadDAO` method to set the internal value object for the `MoviesDAO` to the values of the `MoviesVO` value object passed as an argument.

The `ejbCreate` method performs the work of adding a new movie record to the persistent data store for the method parameters that have been passed in. The method code creates a new `MoviesDAO` object and a new `MoviesVO` object and assigns the `MoviesVO` instance members to the values that have been passed into the method. (This example does not set all fields of the movie record.)

The `MoviesDAO loadDAO` method is then called to set the members of the `MoviesDAO` to the values of the value object. The `insertDAO` method is then called to insert the contents of the DAO into the database. The code for these methods is shown next.

The MoviesEntityBean Class: The getMovies Method

```
public MoviesVO getMoviesVO() {
//
// return the internal Value Object
//

   return moviesDAO.getMoviesVO();

}

public void setMoviesVO( MoviesVO moviesVO) {

   //
   // set the internal value object for the DAO
   // to that of the value object being sent
   //
   moviesDAO.loadDAO( moviesVO );

}

public Integer ejbCreate(int movie_id, String movie_name, String category) throws
CreateException {
//
// create a record for this primary key in the permanent data store
//

try {

    //
    // this is a new entity, so we require a new DAO
    //
    moviesDAO = new MoviesDAO("java:/moviesmysql");
    moviesVO  = new MoviesVO();

    //
    // set our elements to the parameter being passed in
    //
    moviesVO.setMovie_id( movie_id );
    moviesVO.setMovie_name( movie_name );
    moviesVO.setCategory( category );

    //
```

```
        // set the DAO to match our Value Object
        //
        moviesDAO.loadDAO( moviesVO );

        //
        // insert into the database
        //
        moviesDAO.insertDAO();

}
catch (SQLException e) {
        System.out.println("Exception in ejbCreate: " + e.getMessage() );
}
finally {
        return new Integer( movie_id );
}

}
```

The MoviesEntityBean Class: The ejbLoad and ejbStore Methods

The `ejbLoad` and `ejbStore` methods are called by the container when it determines it needs to synchronize the bean with the database. Exactly when the methods will be called is implementation-specific, but the developer can be assured they will be called to perform database synchronization.

The `ejbLoad` method loads data from the permanent data store (the database) to the entity bean. The `ejbLoad` method shown below simply maps the call to the `MoviesDAO loadDAO` method after checking to be assured that there is in fact an active instance of the DAO to use. The code in the method should not assume that the primary key value of the current state is the correct primary key. Good coding practice uses the primary key value as made available through the entity context. Since the primary key has been defined to be an instance of `java.lang.Integer` and the `loadDAO` method expects an integer primitive, we call the `intValue` method of the `Integer` class to get the correct form for the method argument.

The `ejbStore` method writes the current contents of the entity bean to the database. This method can assume that the current values of the entity bean are set correctly, and it simply needs to write its contents to the database. This is done by calling the `MoviesDAO updateDAO` method.

The ejbLoad and ejbStore Methods

```
public void ejbLoad() {
//
// load the entity bean from the database
//
try {

if ( moviesDAO == null ) {

    //
    // DAO constructor receives name of DataSource to use
    //
    moviesDAO = new MoviesDAO("java:comp/env/movies");
    moviesVO  = new MoviesVO();

}

    //
    // synch with the database using the primary key value
    // passed as a parameter
    //
    moviesDAO.loadDAO(
        ((Integer) context.getPrimaryKey()).intValue() );
}
catch (Exception e) {
    System.out.println("Exception in ejbLoad: " +
                        e.getMessage() + " - " + e );
}

}


public void ejbStore() {
//
// store the contents of the Entity Bean in
// the permanent data store
//
try {

    //
    // assert our current state is correct
    //
    moviesDAO.updateDAO();

 }
 catch (SQLException e ) {
     System.out.println("Exception in ejbLoad: " + e.getMessage() );
 }

}
```

The MoviesEntityBean Class: The ejbRemove and ejbPostCreate Methods

The `ejbRemove` method is called when the `remove` method of the home object is called by client code; it is not called indirectly by the container. The result of executing this method is to remove the corresponding record for the entity bean from the database.

The implementation of `ejbRemove` shown here maps to the `MoviesDAO` `deleteDAO` method. This method takes an argument for the primary key of the movie to delete. This method cannot be sure that the state of the bean contains the correct primary key, so the primary key is retrieved from the `EntityContext`.

The `ejbPostCreate` is called by the container after the entity bean has been created. Since there is no specific action required for this entity bean, this implementation is left empty.

The MoviesEntityBean Class: The ejbRemove and ejbPostCreate Methods

```
public void ejbRemove() {
//
// remove the record in the permanent data
// store which relates to this entity bean
//
try {

    moviesDAO.deleteDAO(
        ((Integer) context.getPrimaryKey()).intValue() );

}
catch (SQLException e ) {
    System.out.println( "SQLException in ejbRemove: " + e.getMessage() );
}


}

public void ejbPostCreate(int movie_id,
                          String movie_name,
                          String category) throws CreateException { }
```

The MoviesEntityBean Class: The ejbActivate, ejbPassivate, unsetEntityContext, and setEntityContext Methods

The `ejbActivate` and `ejbPassivate` methods are called when the bean is moved in and out of the pool of available entity beans. Since we require no specific action to be taken for this bean, we do not need to provide an implementation.

Following good EJB coding practice, the setEntityContext method is used to perform initialization for the bean. The ejbCreate method is called by the container if a new entity bean is being created, but since entity beans are usually located with a finder method (to find an existing record or records) ejbCreate may not always be called. The setEntityContext method however er is called before most other callback methods are called. This is therefore a good place to locate initialization code for an entity bean.

The code for this example tests for whether or not the MoviesDAO and MoviesVO instance members have been created. If they have not been created, then they are instantiated. The method also stores the EntityContext passed into the method in an instance member.

The unsetEntityContext is available to perform certain actions before an entity context is removed from the active list in the container. This could be used to release database resources or perform similar actions. Since we have no specific resources to release, we do not provide an implementation for this method.

The ejbActivate, ejbPassivate, unsetEntityContext, and setEntityContext Methods

```
public void ejbActivate() { }
public void ejbPassivate() { }

public void setEntityContext(EntityContext ec) {
//
// perform our initialization here.
//

    //
    // create the Data Access Object and Value Object
    //
    if ( moviesDAO == null ) {
        moviesDAO = new MoviesDAO( "java:/movies" );
      moviesVO  = new MoviesVO();
    }

    //
    // store the session context
    //
    this.context = ec;

}

public void unsetEntityContext( ) {}

}
```

The MoviesEntityBean Home Interface

The home and remote interfaces for the MoviesEntityBean are shown next. The home interface defines all of the create methods and finder methods the entity bean will be exposing to the client. This example uses a single finder, the findByPrimaryKey method, and a single create method. The remote interface extends the EJBObject interface and contains the one method this entity bean exposes to the client: the getMoviesVO method.

The MoviesEntityHome Interface

```
package movies.ejb;

import javax.ejb.*;
import java.io.Serializable;
import java.rmi.RemoteException;

public interface MoviesEntityHome extends EJBHome {

    public MoviesEntityRemote create(int movie_id,
                                     String movie_name,
                                     String category )
            throws RemoteException, CreateException;

    public MoviesEntityRemote findByPrimaryKey(
            Integer movie_id ) throws RemoteException,
                                      FinderException;

}
```

The MoviesEntityRemote Interface

```
package movies.ejb;

import javax.ejb.*;
import java.io.Serializable;
import java.rmi.RemoteException;

import db.*;

public interface MoviesEntityRemote extends EJBObject {

    public MoviesVO getMoviesVO() throws RemoteException;
}
```

MESSAGE-DRIVEN BEANS

MDBs are a new addition to J2EE. As mentioned previously, these beans provide a mechanism for providing a messaging server within the application server using EJB components. Prior to the inclusion of MDBs in the J2EE specification, application server vendors provided their own messaging services. While having a messaging service available was useful, what was really needed was a facility to perform messaging processing in the context of the EJB container. MDBs provide that capability using the JMS package interface.

The following code provides an example of a minimal implementation of an MDB. The client application creates a message, locates the message queue, and then sends the message. The server component, the MDB, is awakened by the J2EE container when there are messages to process. It reads the message from the message queue, processes the message, and then stops running until it is awakened again by the container. The code for the MDB is shown next.

The UsersMDB Class

```
package examples.ejb;

import javax.jms.MessageListener;
import javax.jms.Message;
import javax.jms.MapMessage;
import javax.jms.JMSException;
import javax.ejb.MessageDrivenBean;
import javax.ejb.EJBException;
import javax.ejb.MessageDrivenContext;
import javax.ejb.CreateException;
import javax.naming.Context;
import javax.naming.InitialContext;
import javax.rmi.PortableRemoteObject;

public class UsersMDB implements MessageDrivenBean, MessageListener {

  private MessageDrivenContext ctx;

  public void ejbCreate() throws CreateException {

  }
  public void ejbRemove() {
  }

  public void setMessageDrivenContext(MessageDrivenContext messageDrivenContext) {
    ctx = messageDrivenContext;
  }

  public void onMessage(Message message) {
```

```
//
// only process a MapMessage
//
if (message instanceof MapMessage) {
  MapMessage msg = (MapMessage) message;
  try {
    System.out.println("message received ... " );
    System.out.println( "First name: " +
              msg.getString("first_name"));
    System.out.println( "Last name: " +
              msg.getString("last_name"));
    System.out.println( "Address1: " +
              msg.getString("address1"));
    System.out.println( "Address2: " +
              msg.getString("address2"));
    System.out.println( "City: " +
             msg.getString("city"));
    System.out.println( "State: " +
             msg.getString("state"));
    System.out.println( "Postal Code: " +
             msg.getString("postal_code"));

  //
  // process the message
  //
  // ** not implemented **

  } catch (JMSException e) {

      //
      // if this is CMT, set this bean for rollback
      //
      ctx.setRollbackOnly();

      //
      // should log the message to our logging device
      //
      System.out.println(
         "Ignoring invalid message. Error: " + e);
    }
  }
}

}
```

As with other EJBs, it is a good idea to capture the bean context for later use. The value of the MDB context is captured, in this example, on calls to the setMessageDrivenBean method. We will use this reference to rollback our transaction if an exception is thrown.

The `onMessage` method is called by the container when there is a message to process, and it receives the message to process as a parameter. This method is where we perform the processing of our message. In this example, we simply extract the message information and output it to the console. In a complete implementation, we would take the message contents and pass it to another object for processing. (For example, an order message would be passed to an order-processing object as we demonstrated in Chapter 20.)

In this example, we assume we are using CMT and we flag the bean for a transaction rollback in the event an exception is thrown. This would have the effect of placing the message back into the message queue where it would be available to be processed.

EJB MDB Client

The MDB client sends a message to the queue, which is processed at some later time by the MDB. The code in the client looks very much like the code we would expect to see in any messaging client. It creates an `InitialContext` connected to the naming service and then requests a reference to the `QueueConnection` factory. The `QueueConnectionFactory` is then used to create a `QueueConnection`, which is then used to create a `QueueSession`. (The message queues or subscription topics would have been created previously by an administrator.)

Now that we have a session, we need to obtain a reference to the specific queue for the MDB. the naming service returns the reference to the queue. The connection is then used to create a `session`, which is used to create a `QueueSender` to transmit the message, and a `MapMessage` to contain the message. The `MapMessage` is then populated with the message information, and the sender is used to send the information to the message queue, which will ultimately be delivered to the MDB.

```
package examples.ejb;

import java.util.Hashtable;

import javax.naming.InitialContext;
import javax.naming.Context;
import javax.naming.NamingException;

import javax.jms.QueueConnectionFactory;
import javax.jms.QueueConnection;
import javax.jms.Queue;
import javax.jms.QueueSession;
import javax.jms.QueueSender;
import javax.jms.MapMessage;
import javax.jms.Session;
```

```
import javax.jms.JMSException;

public class MDBClientQueue {

public static void main( String args[] ) {

//
// these are harcoded here for simplicity.
// in production, we would read them from a properties
// file
//
Hashtable ht  = new Hashtable();
ht.put( Context.INITIAL_CONTEXT_FACTORY,
        "org.jnp.interfaces.NamingContextFactory" );
ht.put( Context.PROVIDER_URL,
        "jnp://localhost:1099" );
ht.put( Context.URL_PKG_PREFIXES,
        "org.jboss.naming:org.jnp.interfaces" );

try {

  //
  // get the initial context which points
  // for the messaging server
  //
  InitialContext context = new InitialContext( ht );

  //
  // get the queue connection factory
  //
  QueueConnectionFactory factory = (QueueConnectionFactory) context.lookup(
                      "jms/QueueConnectionFactory");

  //
  // get the connection
  //
  QueueConnection connection =
              factory.createQueueConnection();

  //
  // create a session with this connection
  //
  QueueSession session = connection.createQueueSession(
            false,   // no transaction
            Session.AUTO_ACKNOWLEDGE); // auto-ack

  //
  // access our queue
  //
  Queue queue = (Queue) context.lookup(
                "jms/UsersMDBQueue" );
```

```
    QueueSender sender = session.createSender( queue );

    //
    // create a Map message
    //
    MapMessage message = session.createMapMessage();

    //
    // populate the message with customer information
    // for 'Fred' the user
    //
    message.setString("first_name", "Fred" );
    message.setString("last_name", "Freehoffer" );
    message.setString("address1", "Freehoffer" );
    message.setString("address2", "Freehoffer" );
    message.setString("city", "Newark" );
    message.setString("state", "NJ" );
    message.setString("postal_code", "NJ" );

    System.out.println(
              "Queue ready. Sending message ... " );

    //
    // add Fred the user
    //
    sender.send( queue, message );

    System.out.println("Message sent ..." );

}
catch (NamingException e) {
      System.out.println("NamingException e: " + e );
}
catch (JMSException e) {
      System.out.println("JMSException e: " + e );
}

}

}
```

The vendor must provide a facility for providing the name for the naming service to identify the resource. In this case, the MDB is identified with the name `UsersMDBQueue`, and the name of the destination queue (the queue which the client will send the message to) is set to `jms/UsersMDB`. (This naming represents the current convention for naming J2EE messaging services, but is not a requirement.) With JBoss, an XML configuration file is used to establish these names as shown below.

```
<jboss>
```

```
        <enterprise-beans>
             <message-driven>
              <ejb-name>UsersMDB</ejb-name>
  <destination-jndi-name>jms/UsersMDBQueue</destination-jndi-name>
             </message-driven>
...


        </enterprise-beans>
</jboss>
```

The Deployment Descriptor

As we learned in the previous chapter, the EJB *deployment descriptor* (DD) is an XML document that provides configuration, deployment, and assembly information on EJB components. J2EE-compliant application servers must provide support for DDs.

The DD provides basic information about the EJB components, the beans being deployed. This information includes the name of the bean and the collection of classes that comprise the bean. If the EJB is a session bean, the DD must indicate whether or not the bean is stateful or stateless.

Environment entries can also be made in the DD. These values can be retrieved (but not modified) by beans that have been invoked within the container. The entire DD for the EJBs in this chapter is shown below.

EJB Deployment Descriptor

```
<?xml version="1.0" encoding="ISO8859_1"?>
<!DOCTYPE application PUBLIC '-//Sun Microsystems, Inc.//DTD J2EE Application
1.2//EN' 'http://java.sun.com/j2ee/dtds/application_1_2.dtd'>
<application>
  <display-name>JDBC_Real</display-name>
  <description>Demonstration EJBs for JDBC book</description>
  <enterprise-beans>

    <session>
     <ejb-name>MoviesFacade</ejb-name>
     <ejb-class>movies.ejb.MoviesFacadeBean</ejb-class>
     <home>movies.ejb.MoviesFacadeHome</home>
     <remote>movies.ejb.MoviesFacadeRemote</remote>
     <session-type>Stateful</session-type>
     <transaction-type>Bean</transaction-type>

     <env-entry>
      <env-entry-name>statusQuery1</env-entry-name>
      <env-entry-value> select knowledge_base.doc_key, base_doc_key, doc_name, mes-
sage_txt
```

```
        from knowledge_base, knowledge_messages
        where knowledge_base.doc_key = knowledge_messages.doc_key
        order by knowledge_base.doc_key, base_doc_key </env-entry-value>
       <env-entry-type>java.lang.String</env-entry-type>
      </env-entry>

    </session>

    <entity>

       <ejb-name>MoviesEntityBean</ejb-name>
       <ejb-class>movies.ejb.MoviesEntityBean</ejb-class>
       <home>movies.ejb.MoviesEntityHome</home>
       <remote>movies.ejb.MoviesEntityRemote</remote>
       <persistence-type>Bean</persistence-type>
       <prim-key-class>java.lang.Integer</prim-key-class>
       <reentrant>False</reentrant>

    </entity>

  </enterprise-beans>

<message-driven>

            <ejb-name>UsersMDB</ejb-name>
            <ejb-class>examples.ejb.UsersMDB</ejb-class>
            <message-selector></message-selector>
            <transaction-type>Container</transaction-type>
            <acknowledge-mode>Auto-acknowledge</acknowledge-mode>
            <message-driven-destination>
                 <destination-type>javax.jms.Queue</destination-type>
            </message-driven-destination>

</message-driven>

  <assembly-description>
            <container-transaction>
             <method>
              <ejb-name>MoviesEntityBean</ejb-name>
                 <method-name>*</method-name>
             </method>
             <trans-attribute>Required</trans-attribute>
       </container-transaction>
    </assembly-description>
</application>
```

As we would expect, this DD contains entries for the session bean and entity bean shown previously. These entries identify the bean type, the home and remote reference interface, and the class that represents the actual EJB implementation. Other pertinent information about the bean is included in these entries.

Also included in these entries is the environment entry for the query that will be run to deliver the help desk status information. By placing this entry here in the DD, we can change the query executed by the EJB without having to change the EJB or redeploy the bean. Instead, each time the bean is started, the value of this DD entry is bound into the naming service of the EJB container into the namespace of the container (which may require the EJB server to be restarted with some application servers).

The DD also contains entries for the MDB. These entries include (but are not limited to) the MDB name and the class which manages the destination queue. Note that the DD does not contain entries for home and remote interfaces, since the client does not connect directly to the MDB. The transaction property of the entity bean is also declared in the DD with the entry that identifies the transaction attribute as `Required` for the EJB.

MESSAGE DRIVEN BEANS: SECURITY AND TRANSACTIONS

Since MDB clients do not communicate directly with the MDB, the processing of security and transactions is different. When an MDB is invoked, it is invoked by the container for the client, there is no real caller. The container is not aware of the client's principal, security role or transaction mode. While the message may contain some information in its headers about where it originated, the message may have been passed through a number of intermediate servers which can optionally change this message information so the validity of the headers could be dubious. If assuring the validity of the sender is important, then you should consider using digital signatures in the message to verify its authenticity.

As discussed in the previous chapter (Chapter 25), EJB servers provide a `run-as` facility which can be used to indicate that the bean will assume a certain security role when it is run. Considering the nature of messaging and the potential security risks, you should set this security role appropriately for the task required. This means that the security role should be adequate for the task required, and provide no additional security privileges. The `run-as` identity is set in the DD presumably by the deployer or the assembler.

Transaction execution for MDBs is also different than with other EJB components. MDBs support both CMT and BMT. With CMT, since there is no caller with a transaction context, the transaction of the caller cannot be assumed. For this reason, there are two appropriate transaction modes for MDBs: `Required` and `NotSupported`. With `Required`, the container will execute the `onMessage` method within the context of a transaction, and with `NotSupported` the `onMessage` method will not execute within a transaction.

If the `onMessage` method is called with the `Required` transaction attribute and the transaction aborts (the `MessageDrivenContext setRollbackOnly` method has been called as shown in the previous example), then the message will be returned to its queue or topic to be processed again. This provides some level of reliability for message processing but also raises the possibility of creating an endless error loop (a *poison message*). Should the error which raised the exception to begin with recur, then the message could continually fail, be returned to the queue or topic and be processed again only to fail again. Obviously, the developer must code the MDB so that repetitive errors do not occur. One potential solution would be to post the message (with the addition of an error flag and description) to a *stagnant* or problem queue where it would be processed at some later point when the problem is resolved; this would be done in-lieu of aborting the message process and forcing a rollback.

The JMS server as implemented by the J2EE container will commit the transaction for the MDB when the `onMessage` call returns without throwing an exception; this is true when using asynchronous processing with auto-acknowledge mode. Other acknowledgment modes are available which provide varying degrees of transactional integrity. When an MDB is used with the `Required` transaction mode, the auto-acknowledge is ignored for responses and acknowledgment will be performed when the bean completes and is committed.

Note that other resources (JDBC sessions for example) do not participate in MDB transactions. If a JMS/MDB messaging must be used together with JDBC or EJB activity by the client, then Java Transaction API (JTA) should be used to group the actions. This could be done in the client by obtaining a reference to JTA implementation within the server as follows.

```
Context context = new InitialContext();
UserTransaction ut = (UserTransaction)
context.lookup("javax.transaction.UserTransaction");

// start the transaction
ut.start();
// perform transaction activities

// JDBC updates

// message post
...
ut.commit(); // commit the work
...
```

On commit, the messages will be enabled for delivery and the JDBC resource will be notified that the database records can be committed to the database. Alternatively a rollback will reset the state of both the message queue or topic and the database back to the state before the work was performed (before the `UserTransaction start` call was made). This means that the messages will not be posted for delivery and the database records will not be written to the database.

Summary

This chapter provided examples of a number of different EJBs. The session bean, the entity bean, and the message-driven bean were all explained with programming examples.

We saw how a session bean can be used to implement a session facade pattern—an object which is responsible for controlling access to other objects. An how an entity bean is used to encapsulate access to data resources. We demonstrated the use of a DAO with an entity bean, allowing the lower level details of data access to be managed by the DAO and allowing the entity bean to provide transactional and life cycle services through the EJB container.

MDBs allow the J2EE application server to provide messaging services in the context of an EJB. As we saw in this chapter, MDBs are not accessed directly by the client as session beans and entity beans are, but are instead accessed as a messaging service. As was shown in this chapter, messages can be posted to a message queue (or published to a topic). The J2EE application server will then provide the services of the messaging server and notify the appropriate MDB that there are messages to process through a call to the `onMessage` callback method.

CHAPTER 27

Using Java Servlets

INTRODUCTION

J2EE provides not one but two technologies for creating dynamic Web page content: servlets and Java Server Pages (JSP). Historically, Java servlets came first and in fact JSP is built on top of servlet technologies. It is useful (but not entirely necessary) to know Java servlets before discussing JSP, so we will start our discussion there.

Both JSPs and servlets operate over networks, so in order to really understand how to write a Web application, you need to understand networking and HTTP. Once we have developed an understanding of the networking foundation of servlets, we focus our discussion on servlets, and explain the technology using several examples.

THE NETWORK: TCP/IP

Though we may not know the specifics, we all know that the World Wide Web is just a network—a rather extensive and pervasive network, but just a network nevertheless. A Web application runs on a network. The network is the *wire* through which the application operates, and if it were not present, the Web application, which requires remote users to connect to a Web server, would not run. (A Web application can be run locally on a machine and not use a physical network, but it will nevertheless be using local network loopback mechanisms to mimic the operation of the network on the local machine.)

Networks are composed of a series of *nodes* or points on the network (see Figure 27–1). Networks provide high-speed data communications between the nodes using a *protocol*, a predetermined language for communication, and a predetermined format for a *data buffer* or information *packet*. The protocol is used by the two nodes in the communication process to determine what information is being conveyed. The data buffer or packet is what is transmitted between the two nodes and is a combination of the actual data being transmitted and information about the data packet contained in the packet header. To transmit a packet, a node may set a flag in the packet header indicating that the packet is being transmitted to a specific target; the target address is also included in the header. The packet is then transmitted and may travel to a number of different nodes until it is received at the node to which it was sent. The source and destination nodes may exchange additional packets of data to ensure delivery of the data packet; this exchange of additional packets is part of a *handshaking* protocol used to provide some control over the transmission process.

At any given point a large number of data packets may be coursing through a network. These packets are sent to their correct destination via *routers*. The routers examine the packet and try to make a determination about where the packet is bound.

The World Wide Web uses TCP/IP for communication. This combination of acronyms stands for Transmission Control Protocol and Internet Protocol, and represents one of the most common protocols for network communication.

TCP/IP is actually two protocols: TCP and IP. IP provides routing information—information on how to find the address of the resource being requested. IP splits the data into packets and attaches a source and destination address to the packet. This information is then used to route the packet from the source to the destination.

TCP uses the IP layer to provide routing services. TCP establishes the connection and provides a handshaking mechanism to ensure that data gets to its destination. TCP provides guaranteed delivery of data (unlike other protocols, which may not) and for this reason provides some level of error correction and integrity for data transmission.

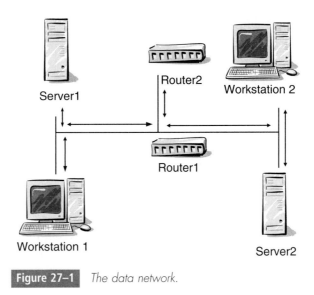

Figure 27–1 *The data network.*

But TCP/IP communication alone does not make the Web. HTTP provides a layer of communication above the TCP/IP layers. This protocol was designed to use a number of handshaking directives to provide access to resources over an open network.

TCP/IP and HTTP are part of a network protocol layer framework known as the Open Systems Interconnection (OSI) developed by the International Standards Organization (ISO). The framework provides for seven layers, and though vendors have implemented parts of this framework, rarely is the entire standard adhered to in a product. TCP/IP combined with HTTP comprise the Application and Transport layers of this model used in this book (see Table 27–1).

Table 27–1 *TPC/IP and HTTP as Network Layers*

OSI Layer	Type	Description
HTTP	Application	HyperText Transport Protocol
TCP	Transport	Transport Control Protocol
IP	Internet	Internet Protocol
Ethernet, ISDN, PPP, SLIP	Data Link	Network packet transmission

At the lowest level, a layer exists to move the network packets from one point to another. This layer has only rudimentary knowledge of the contents of the packets; higher level protocols such as IP provide the routing of the packets. Above IP, the TCP layer provides for the communication between network nodes and ensures accuracy, using the IP layer for routing. And above all other layers, the HTTP layer executes the handshaking between client and server with some knowledge of the information being transmitted. It is this HTTP layer that we work with as Web developers.

THE NETWORK: HTTP

HTTP is one of several network protocols the common Web browser uses. When a Web browser requests a page, it makes this request in the form of a Uniform Resource Locator (URL). This URL contains important information about the resource being requested, using the following syntax.

```
<protocol>://<server name>[ :<port number>] /<location>
```

The *protocol* requested can be one of many different protocols, but most commonly is either HTTP, ftp for *file transfer protocol*, or file for a file on the local machine. Table 27–2 provides a more complete list of protocols that most browsers will accept.

Table 27–2   *Network Protocols*

Protocol	Description
http://	World Wide Web server
ftp://	FTP server (file transfer)
https//	Secure HTTP
news://	Usenet newsgroups
mailto://	e-mail
wais://	Wide Area Information server
gopher://	Gopher server
file://	file on local system
ldap://	directory server request
telnet://	applications on network server
rlogin://	applications on network server
tn3270://	applications on mainframe

The server name can alternatively be an IP address. This identifies for the browser the server that will manage the request it is going to submit. Optionally, this designation of the server can include a network port number. If the URL designates the protocol as http, and the server name portion of the URL contains a port number, the browser will attempt a connection for HTTP services on the designated server at the specified port number. If no port number is specified, then the browser will attempt communication with the server at the default port for HTTP communications, port 80.

Name Resolution

When a server name is specified in a URL, this name alone is not adequate to achieve a connection to the server. The name must be resolved to an IP address. The resolution of the server name involves either retrieving the name from a local `hosts` file, which contains a list of server names and related IP addresses, or more commonly, the use of a *name server*, or *domain name server.*

The job of the name server, which usually resides on the local network, is to take a query for a server name and return an IP address. Since the Internet is large and dynamic, the process of determining the correct IP address for an Internet domain name can involve querying several name servers on the Internet. To avoid the overhead of Internet name resolution, local name servers often make an effort to *cache* Internet domain names so that the name can be resolved on the local network rather than on the external Internet.

Note that if the use of a name server is required, the network software where the browser is running must be configured to use the domain name server or else the request for the URL will fail. Alternately, a local configuration file (usually named `hosts`) can be configured to map domain names to IP addresses, but since it can be problematic to keep these distributed files current, DNS or the use of some other name resolver is preferred (see Figure 27–2).

HTTP transactions operate in a *request/response* cycle. Once an HTTP request is sent, it will course through the network, whether it be an internal intranet or the Internet, and ultimately arrive at a server. An HTTP request is commonly processed by an *HTTP server* (Apache, IIS) or a *Web server,* which would be listening for a connection on a well-known port (port 80 for HTTP). The Web server will accept the connection and then retrieve the URL for processing.

In its simplest form, processing a request is a simple task for an HTTP server, a task which involves little more than retrieving the HTML page and returning it to the client prepending HTTP headers in the process.

But it is not uncommon for a Web server to provide additional services. For instance, Web servers usually provide some form of authentication service, which

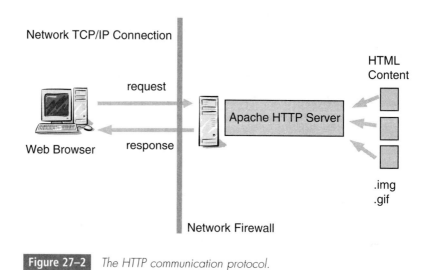

Figure 27-2   *The HTTP communication protocol.*

requires a user to enter a user name and password to access a portion of the Web site. It can also map short names for directories within a site into full directory paths and provide the capability to run Web components such as servlets, or perform the processing required to transform JSPs into HTML.

The processing of requests and responses within the Web server is a stateless transaction. Once a request is sent by a browser to a Web server, the connection to the Web server is usually not retained. Each request to a Web server requires another connection.

This type of request/response cycle is efficient for the server. A Web server can handle a large number of users because it does not need to maintain physical connections to each of the users. Since the Web server is delivering a page to the client browser, the page delivered to the browser by the Web server is considered *self-sustaining* in that the page sent to the client does not need to communicate with the server while the user is processing the page. This relatively low network overhead allows Web servers to manage a heavier user load relative to the more heavyweight network access required by traditional client/server.

THE HTML STANDARD

HyperText Markup Language (HTML) is the language used to develop web pages. HTML is not a procedural programming language and as such has been sorely stretched to perform the work necessary to create complete applications on the Web. HTML is a *presentation language* derived from Standard Generalized Markup

Language (SGML) and is comprised of tags that define how the text they surround will be rendered. These tags, combined with links, the ability to input data into data entry forms, and the ability to execute external programs with Common Gateway Interface (CGI), provide some level of functionality and thus provide the ability to create working applications that operate over the Web. But this combination of tools and components (HTML, links, and CGI) has distinct limitations. Implementing business logic is difficult and clumsy, and the performance of CGI solutions has generally been poor.

In extending the capabilities of the Web architecture, vendors sought a solution which would avoid the cost of replacing Web browsers. This meant that extending or even replacing the Web browser and HTML it could process were not considered a viable solution. What was considered viable was extending extending HTML on the server, and then parsing and executing the extended HTML before it was returned to the browser. Using this solution, what would ultimately be returned to the browser would be plain HTML.

These server-side scripting solutions usually used tag extensions that were embedded into the HTML page and executed at the server (not the browser client). To implement these solutions, the infrastructure of the Web was also extended, often adding an application server to manage the execution of the vendor's server-side script. This application server worked together with the HTTP server to parse, execute, and serve the HTML page to the browser.

THE WEB APPLICATION

As we know, the J2EE specification addresses the broad topic of building applications across multiple conceptual tiers. Java servlets and JSPs are part of what we referred to in our architecture discussion as the *presentation tier* or as it is sometimes referred to as, the *Web tier*. Applications created for the Web tier are considered *Web applications* and the servlet specification details how these applications can be packaged.

A Web application can be composed of a number of different components, not only servlets and JSPs, but HTML pages and any graphic files those pages may require, in addition to various class files the servlets and JSPs may need. But that may not be all. In addition to these components, various XML configuration files and possibly even Java property files may be needed for Taglibs, servlets and other classes. Given this broad collection of components and files we can see that it would be useful to have a mechanism for pulling all of these files together in a single package which can be easily deployed into a Web server or application server.

The Java Web Application aRchive (WAR) can be used to pull all of these components together. Under this specification, a specific directory structure is packaged into an archive which can be deployed into any compliant Web server.

Since any given Web server may have a number of different Web applications, each application can be considered a separate *context* within the Web server. For Java Web applications, this directory structure would include a WEB-INF and META-INF directory. Within the WEB-INF directory would be a `web.xml` configuration file for the context, and below the WEB-INF directory would be a `classes` directory which would contain the various classes which comprise the servlet classes (including the servlet classes) or the classes used by the JSPs.

THE EXECUTION OF JAVA SERVLETS

Java servlets are instances of a Java class that operate as a Web component. They are invoked to manage an HTTP request and can optionally generate a response to the request.

Java servlets operate within a *container*, an operating environment for the component which provides various services. This container is usually provided by the Web server or application server.

The design of the servlet environment reflects the stateless nature of HTTP. The servlet is essentially stateless; there is no guarantee that any instance members of the servlet class will retain their values from one client invocation to the next, so client session information should not be stored in servlet instance members. Java servlets do provide facilities for maintaining session state within servlets and they are the preferred method of maintaining client state.

The servlet component operates within a container which is responsible for providing certain services to the servlet, such as lifecycle management, security, and maintenance of context properties. With lifecycle management, the container is responsible for creation of the component and makes the component available to manage a request. This may involve the creation of a pool of instantiated servlet instances which are used to handle incoming requests.

The container also manages the security for the components, and restricts component access to the local operating environment and optionally provides authentication services, verifying a users identify. The container is also responsible for mapping a request to a servlet component and provides access to a set of developer-defined environment entries.

As multiple requests are handled by the servlet container, multiple threads of activity are executing servlet code. As developers, we need to be aware of both the lifecycle and state activities of the servlet container in this multithreaded environment and to program accordingly. Thread-safe issues can often lead to coding errors with inexperienced servlet developers. If you are aware from the start that certain portions of servlet code are not thread-safe, then these coding errors can be avoided.

The Servlet API

The servlet API reflects the HTTP protocol with which these components will be used. Each component is subject to the lifecycle imposed by the container and is initialized once and then invoked multiple times to handle incoming requests. The Web server maps the URLs to servlets through the servlet container. When the container determines that the servlet is no longer needed (usually through a timeout parameter), the servlet is destroyed.

As Figure 27–3 shows, there are servlet methods called by the container for each of these lifecycle events. The classes in the servlet API reflect a delineation between a generic servlet and a servlet that will operate under HTTP. The class diagram in Figure 27–3 describes these relationships.

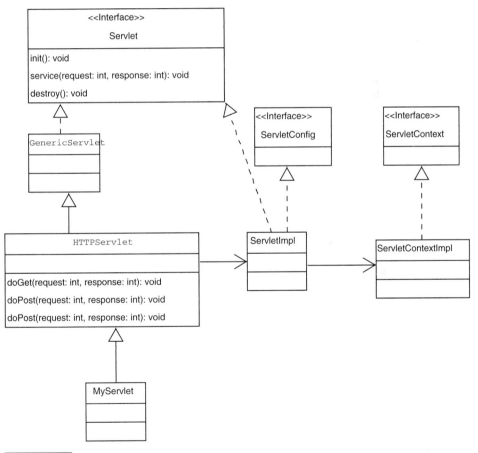

Figure 27–3 *UML diagram of servlet classes.*

The init Method

The `init` method is called to initialize a servlet component. This method is called only once by the container before any requests are handled by the servlet and is usually used in a manner similar to that of a constructor, performing the various initialization tasks that a component may require before it is used. These tasks usually include accessing any resources that may be needed by the servlet and initializing servlet state—for instance, creating a JDBC connection to use or loading an XML translation template.

The `init` method is overloaded to include an `init` method with no arguments and an `init` method with a `ServletConfig` argument. Since the `GenericServlet` and the `HTTPServlet` both implement `ServletConfig`, there is technically no reason to obtain a reference to the `ServletConfig` being used by the servlet, though this is sometimes done for programming clarity. The `init` method with no arguments is a convenience method that is often used to perform initialization.

The `init` method is overridden if initialization tasks need to be performed by the servlet. Since most servlets need to perform some type of initialization, it is not uncommon to see this method overridden. Any `HTTPServlet` implementation overriding the `init` method with the `ServletConfig` argument should be sure to call the superclass `init` method (`super.init(ServletConfig)`), since the `GenericServlet` implementation needs a reference to the `ServletConfig` object.

The service Method

The service method is called by the container to dispatch an incoming request. This method usually calls the `doGet` or `doPost` method, depending on the method being used by the sender. This method could be overridden by an implementation in order to provide some form of custom processing, but that is not usually done. It is more common to override the `doGet` or `doPost` method and take whatever actions are necessary in those methods.

The destroy Method

The `destroy` method is called by the container when it is preparing to destroy the servlet component and free the resources being used by the servlet. This method would be overridden to free any resources used by the servlet that the container was not aware of, such as a JDBC database connection or a message queue reference.

Initialization Parameters

The J2EE servlet specification provides for initialization parameters. These parameters are static values that can be retrieved by a servlet but cannot be set. This provides a very useful mechanism for setting various application properties, such as the URL of an error page for a specific type of error or the email address of the Web administrator. The values of the parameters are set in the servlet web.xml configuration file, as shown below.

Two types of parameters are available: servlet initialization parameters and servlet context parameters. Servlet initialization parameters are defined in the servlet configuration file as part of the servlet initialization and are thus only visible to the servlet for which they were defined. The following provides an example of the declaration of a servlet initialization parameter in the web.xml file.

```
...
<servlet>
  <servlet-name>MyServlet</servlet-name>
   <servlet-class>MyServlet.class</servlet-class>
   <init-param>
          <param-name>site-name</param-name>
          <param-value>Movies-R-Us</param-value>
   </init-param>
</servlet>
...
```

This example declares a parameter named site-name for the servlet MyServlet. Within the body of the MyServlet class, a call to the getInitParameter method could be used to retrieve the value of the site-name parameter as follows.

```
...
   String siteName = getInitParameter( "site-name" );
...
```

Alternatively, a servlet context parameter is defined as part of the context for the servlet, a portion of the Web application. This parameter is thus visible to all servlets within that context, not just to a single servlet, as with the servlet initialization parameters. The following provides an example of the declaration of a context parameter in the web.xml file.

```
<web-app>
   <context-param>
          <param-name>stock-server</param-name>
          <param-value>delaware</param-value>
   </context-param>

  <servlet>
   <servlet-name>AServlet</servlet-name>
          ...
```

In this `web.xml` fragment several parameters are defined for the context in which one or more servlets are defined. In the body of any of those servlets, the following code could be used to retrieve the context parameter `stock-server`.

```
...
  server = getServletContext().getInitParameter(
                               "stock-server");
...
```

The ServletConfig Implementation

The `ServletConfig` implementation of the `ServletConfig` interface provides access to initialization parameters for the servlet, the servlet name, and the `ServletContext`. The methods in this class are commonly used to retrieve the initialization values for the servlet and to access the `ServletContext`. The `ServletConfig` instance being used for a servlet is passed into the `init` method for the servlet and can be stored at that time. Or, since the `GenericServlet` and the `HTTPServlet` implement this interface, the methods defined in the interface can be called directly from the servlet component.

The ServletContext Implementation

The `ServletContext` implementation contains methods that provide access to global attributes, values that can be retrieved by any servlet running in the container. As with any global variable, these attributes should be used sparingly. The general rule of thumb about using the narrowest scope available still applies with servlets. In many cases, a context parameter could be used in place of a `ServletContext` attribute. Also note that these attributes are not thread-safe.

The `ServletContext` also provides access to the logging facility for the context. A string message may be passed to the `log` method, which has also been overloaded to accept a string message and a corresponding object, which implements the `Throwable` interface.

The `GenericServlet` abstract class provides the methods for retrieving the `ServletContext` and the `ServletConfig`: the `getServletContext` `getServletConfig` methods respectively.

Maintaining Session State

Even though HTTP is a stateless protocol, it is possible for a servlet to maintain state information for a session. This is provided through an implementation of the `HttpSession` interface, which is obtained through the request being processed— the `HttpServletRequest` reference which is passed by the container to the methods used to perform request processing (`doGet` for example).

A servlet may store any arbitrary object of interest using the `HttpSession` reference, the *session object*. As long as the session is active, the corresponding session object is available. Objects are stored with the session object through a call to the `setAttribute` method as shown in the following code fragment.

Saving a Session Attribute

```
...
public void doGet( HttpServletRequest request,
                   HttpServletResponse response )
    throws IOException, ServletException  {
...
//
// create a Hashtable of customer shopping cart information
//
java.util.Hashtable customer = new java.util.Hashtable();

customer.put( "customer-name", "Fred Fleller" );
customer.put( "customer-number", "139039" );
customer.put( "customer-shopping-cart-number",
              "333909339" );

request.getSession().setAttribute( "customer-info",
                                   customer );
...
```

Retrieving the session object can be done using the `HttpServletRequest` `getSession` method. Since the `getSession` method returns an object, a cast is required to provide a useful reference, as shown below.

Retrieving a Session Attribute

```
...
//
// get the session object
//
HttpSession session = request.getSession();

//
// retrieve our Hashtable
//
Hashtable customerInfo = (Hashtable)
        session.getAttribute("customer-info");
....
out.println("<p>customer-name: " +
            customerInfo("customer-name"));
```

The session information is visible only to servlets within the current session. These values are not visible to servlets in another context. Additionally, the client may choose to implement features which restrict the container's ability to create a session. A servlet can determine that the container cannot maintain a session by calling the `isNew` method. If a servlet is trying to retrieve a value placed by a previous servlet in the `isNew` method and this method returns true, then the value will not be available (since a session is not active).

A container implementation may elect how to manage session information. A common implementation is to use cookies to store a reference number for the client and have the container create an internal `Hashtable` to store the session information with the reference number as the key.

Since not all browsers accept cookies, URL rewriting is another approach to managing session information. This approach has the client send a session ID as a request parameter with each request. If a container is using this approach, we must be certain to use the `encodeURL` method of the `HttpServletResponse` class to be sure that any forwarded requests will contain the session ID if it is needed.

Yet another approach to maintaining session information is to use cookies to store all of the relevant session information. This is a relatively simple approach, but for security reasons not all clients allow this. As developers, we need to be aware that cookies stored on a client machine may be accessible to the determined hacker.

As touched on previously in this section, a safer approach to using cookies is one that does not store the actual information on the client's machine and instead stores a reference ID. The relevant information is stored elsewhere in a secure environment and can be retrieved only by specific servlets using the session ID.

For instance, a reference ID could be a customer ID that references a customer record on a server or a shopping cart ID that references a shopping cart stored on the server. If valuable account information were stored on the client machine and the malicious hacker were able to access that information, we would have a serious security breach. Alternatively, we could just store a reference (not the actual) to the client's account ID in a cookie on the machine. While a hacker may be able to get the reference ID from the cookie on the client's machine, the ID is of little use to the hacker.

You should be aware that there is a limit to the number of cookies a browser will store for a server (a domain)—usually around 20 per Web server. And the size of the cookie is usually restricted to less than 4KB each.

The client cookie is available through the request and response objects passed to the servlet doXXX methods. The cookie can be set using the `addCookie` method of the `HttpServletResponse` implementation, and it can be retrieved using the `getCookie` method of the `HttpServletRequest` implementation.

A cookie is represented by the `Cookie` object (`java.servlet.http.Cookie`). This class contains methods to get and set various relevant parameters for the cookie, such as the value and age (expiration time) of the cookie. Cookie values are always represented as strings. To set a cookie for a client session, the following code could be used.

```java
...
public void doGet( HttpServletRequest request,
                   HttpServletResponse response )
    throws IOException, ServletException {

...
response.addCookie( new Cookie( "customer-id", "093092309" ) );
...
```

Cookie retrieval requires a little more work, as demonstrated in the following code snippet.

```java
...
public void doGet( HttpServletRequest request,
                   HttpServletResponse response )
    throws IOException, ServletException {

...
response.addCookie(
        new Cookie( "customer-id", "093092309" ) );
...

Cookie[] cookieArray = request.getCookies( );

// load our cookies into a Hashtable
java.util.Hashtable cookies = new Hashtable();

//
// if we didn't get any cookies, we'll get
// a null reference
//
if ( cookieArray != null ) {
    for ( int n = 0; n < cookieArray.length; n++ ) {
        cookies.put( cookieArray[n].getName(), cookieArray[n] );
    }
}

//
// output our customer ID
//

String customerID = null;
if ( cookieArray != null ) {
    if ( cookies.get("customer-id" ) != null ) {
        customerID =
          ((Cookie) cookies.get( "customer-id" )).getValue();
```

```
        response.getWriter().println(
             "<p>Customer ID: " + customerID );
    }
}
if ( customerID == null) {
    response.getWriter().println(
          "<p>Could not retrieve customer ID." );
```

We must retrieve the cookies as an array of all the cookies sent with the request. Since we prefer to examine only specific cookies instead of constantly iterating the entire array, we load the array into a `Hashtable`, which associates the cookie name with the cookie reference (and through that, the cookie value). After storing our cookies in the `Hashtable`, we use the `get` method to retrieve the appropriate cookie and display its value.

Thread Safety and Concurrency Management

As servlet developers, we need to be aware of the process flow for servlets. By default, any given servlet may be executed by one or more clients so that the code for the servlet is effectively shared among clients. This behavior allows multiple clients to concurrently execute code within a servlet `service` method.

This standard behavior can be overridden using the `SingleThreadModel` (`javax.servlet.SingleThreadModel`) interface. Any servlet that implements this interface is guaranteed that no two clients will execute its `service` method concurrently. Since this can hinder server performance, this approach is used sparingly.

We also need to be aware of what is thread-safe and what is not thread-safe. Table 27–3 illustrates the attributes that are available to developers and indicates whether or not they are considered thread-safe by default.

Table 27–3   *Thread Safety of Attributes and Variables*

Attribute/Variables	Thread-Safe
request attributes	yes
session attributes	no
context attributes	no
instance members	no
class variables	no
local variables	yes

As we can see, it is fairly easy to remember what is thread-safe and what is not. Other than request attributes and local variables, all other attributes and variables are not thread-safe by default.

Session attributes are not thread-safe within the context of the client session. Session content is not accessible to other threads from other clients, so there is no risk of that. But should a client session have multiple browser windows open on the same page, there is the possibility session information could become corrupt. This can be prevented by disallowing multiple browser windows for the same page. (A simple check of the session attributes could be used to determine this.)

Any information that may change over the client session should be manipulated in local variables and then stored in the session object, where it can be retrieved later by other servlets participating in the session.

Servlet Exception Handling

The servlet is somewhat restricted in the exceptions it can throw. In fact, it can throw only two exceptions: an `IOException` and a `ServletException`. This is not a very restrictive requirement when you consider that the client accessing the servlet (the browser) is really not expected to handle any exceptions. Exceptions are ultimately caught in the service method where they are handled by branching to a named error page or generating an error page. A robust application should handle exceptions by producing useful log entries and returning a user-friendly error page to the client.

Any checked exception generated by the execution of a servlet must be wrapped in a `ServletException` before execution returns to the `service` method. This requirement suggests the exceptions should be handled locally in the method whenever possible and log entries should be generated at that point. Once that processing is complete, a `ServletException` should be thrown to the caller.

A servlet will generate a default error page if none is declared. An entry can be declared in the `web.xml` file to allow error handling to be directed to another page. The error-page element allows error pages to be identified to handle specific checked exceptions, with one page declared for each exception type.

Application Security

There are two types of security we are concerned with in servlet programming: authentication and authorization. With authentication, we need to determine that a user is who he or she claims to be. This is usually done with some type of password security. With authorization, we need to determine that an authenticated user is allowed to perform the action he or she is requesting.

A user is considered a principal, and once authenticated, a principal may be mapped to certain roles. The security in the servlet ultimately maps certain permissions to certain roles. Consequently, a facility is required that maps the principal (our authenticated user) to a role.

Table 27–4   *Servlet Authentication Techniques*

Authentication	Description
BASIC	HTTP Bbasic authentication. Sends an 'authenticate' request to the browser, which displays a user name/password dialog box to the user. The password is returned as a base64- encoded string; it is not encrypted.
DIGEST	HTTP digest authentication. Sends an authenticate request to the browser, which displays a user name/password dialog box to the user. The password is returned in encrypted form. (Not widely used. Containers are not required to support this form of authentication.)
FORM	An HTML form is used to request a user name and password. Password is returned unencrypted. User name field must be named `j_username`, and user password field, `j_password`.
CLIENT-CERT	Uses SSL over HTTP (HTTPS), which requires the use of public key certificate. Only servlet containers that are J2EE-compliant are required to support this protocol.

The servlet security realm matches a user (principal) to a role. Exactly how the security realm is implemented is vendor-specific. Common implementations in use today use a database to provide authentication information or allow an LDAP server to provide this information. Authentication can take one of the forms listed in Table 27–4.

HTTP basic security involves widely supported HTTP to have the browser generate a dialog box to query the user for a user name and password. Once the user enters the name and password, the results are sent back to the HTTP server. The problem is that when the results are returned to the server, the password is not encrypted; it is encoded using base64 encoding. Unfortunately, it is a fairly simple task to decode a base64-encoded string.

HTTP basic security by itself is not very secure when used over the Internet. When augmented with a very strong security mechanism like HTTPS (HTTP with SSL), this becomes a much more attractive authentication mechanism. In fact, this is the approach used by a large number of Web sites today.

With HTTP digest security, the server sends the client browser a request to authenticate the user. As with HTTP basic security, the browser displays the password dialog and returns the data results to the server. But unlike basic security, the browser encrypts the password.

HTTP digest security involves a security mechanism that is not as strong has HTTPS and is not widely supported among browsers. Servlet containers are encouraged but are not required to support this type of authentication.

Basic security login involves the use of a simple login dialog (see Figure 27–4). For many users, this dialog may be confusing. Form-based security provides some flexibility in the presentation of the login to the user. With this approach, a login form page and error page are identified for a protected Web resource. When the user attempts to access the secure resource, the login form is sent to the client. When the login form is posted back to the server, the user name and password are retrieved and validated. If an error is encountered (the user name or password are invalid), then control is forwarded to an error page.

Figure 27–4   *Basic security login.*

The final form of authentication specifies the use of strong security using SSL with HTTP. SSL combines both symmetric and asymmetric security, in a sense providing the best of both worlds. It is widely supported, relatively simple to implement, and highly secure. Using this approach requires the server to obtain a valid certificate, which may need to be signed by a certificate authority to be useful.

Programmatic and Declarative Application Security

Application security can be handled programmatically or declaratively. With *programmatic security* management, method calls can be made to determine whether or not a user is in a specific role. Application code can then restrict the user to certain actions. Programmatic security provides a very finely grained level of security. Certain actions within a servlet or within a class used by a servlet can be restricted based on a role.

But the programmatic approach is also prone to error. A programmer who misplaces a curly bracket could leave an application with a gaping security hole. Alternatively, with declarative security entries in a deployment descriptor (web.xml) relate roles to secure resources (as referenced by a URL) and allows security to be described more clearly.

SERVLET EXAMPLE

The following example demonstrates the process of creating a simple servlet to perform an XML transformation that ultimately produces an HTML page, which is returned to the client browser. The role of the servlet in this operation is that of a *controller* object; the real work to access the database, create XML, and transform the XML to HTML is being done by the objects the servlet has created. The result is a servlet focused on the task of creating a presentation component and delivering it to the browser that has generated the request.

The servlet retrieves the query to execute from an initialization parameter in the servlet web.xml file (shown in the next code example). The transformation is performed using an XSLT script located in a local file. The code for this servlet is shown in the sections below.

```
package examples.servlet;

import java.io.StringReader;
import java.io.IOException;
import java.io.PrintWriter;
import java.net.URL;
```

```
import java.util.Hashtable;
import javax.servlet.http.HttpServletRequest;
import javax.servlet.http.HttpServletResponse;
import javax.servlet.http.HttpServlet;
import javax.servlet.http.HttpSession;
import javax.servlet.ServletException;
import javax.servlet.ServletContext;
import java.security.Principal;
import java.sql.Connection;
import java.sql.ResultSet;
import java.sql.PreparedStatement;
import java.sql.SQLException;
import javax.sql.DataSource;
import javax.naming.InitialContext;
import javax.naming.NamingException;
import javax.naming.Context;
import com.icl.saxon.trax.Transformer;
import com.icl.saxon.trax.Templates;
import com.icl.saxon.trax.Result;
import com.icl.saxon.trax.Processor;
import com.icl.saxon.trax.ProcessorException;
import org.xml.sax.InputSource;

import jdbcutil.JDBCXML;

public class ServletExample1 extends HttpServlet {

Private Templates templates;
private PreparedStatement    pstmt;
private Connection           con;
private ServletContext        context;

Private String    defaultStyleSheet =
                    "file:/web/xslt/rs.xsl";

public void doGet(HttpServletRequest request,
                  HttpServletResponse response)
    throws IOException, ServletException
{
PrintWriter out = response.getWriter();

out.println("<html>");

out.println("<head>");
out.println("<title>Movies Listing</title>");
out.println("</head>");

out.println("<body bgcolor=\"white\">");

try {

//
```

```
// only need to prepare the query if it hasn't been
// prepared before
//
if ( pstmt == null ) {      // need to prepare the query

  //
  // get the query from an environment parameter
  //
  String query = context.getInitParameter( "Query2" );

  //
  // prepare the query
  //
  pstmt = con.prepareStatement( query );

}

//
// execute the prepared query and retrieve the results
// results are formatted as an XML document
//
String xmlDoc = getQueryResults();

//
// transform the XML to the format for our output
// (an HTML table)
//
Transformer transformer = templates.newTransformer();
transformer.transform(
    new InputSource( new StringReader( xmlDoc ) ),
                     new Result( out ) );
out.println("</body>");
out.println("</html>");
}
catch (Exception e) {
    log( "Exception in doGet: " + e.getMessage() );
}

}
```

We begin by importing various packages needed for operation, including the standard servlet packages, the JNDI packages, Java I/O packages, and the JDBC packages. Packages used for the Saxon XSLT transformer are also imported, as are various local packages used in the servlet.

As we saw in Chapter 16, the XSLT transformer uses a *processor,* a *template,* and a *transformer* to perform its work. A processor is created from a factory method (newInstance) and is then used to create a template. The template is created based on the transform to be done and receives the name of the transform stylesheet to process. The stylesheet contains the script that indicates how to process the document. Once the template has been created (using the transform stylesheet), a trans-

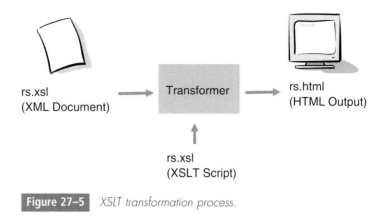

Figure 27–5 *XSLT transformation process.*

former can be retrieved from the template. This transformer is then used to perform the actual transformation of the XML document (see Figure 27–5).

Several instance members are declared in the servlet class: one to hold the XSLT templates reference, the JDBC connection and the JDBC prepared statement. The objects referenced by these variables perform operations which are common to all instances of the servlet, so they are not concerned with client specific state. It is therefor safe to share them among instances. Had they represented some client specific information, they should be declared as local varibles and set within the appropriate method to be called by the servlet engine—for example, the `doGet` or `doPost` method.

Since the servlet is responding to an HTTP request and will respond with the HTTP response, we use declaration parameters that represent the HTTP request (`HttpServletRequest`) and the HTTP response (`HttpServletResponse`). We would like to write our transformed XML document to the response stream, so we obtain the response writer with a call to the `HttpServletResponse getWriter` method.

The code block then contains several statements which HTML statements to format the page. A `try/catch` block is started and the query string for the query to be executed is retrieved with a call to the `ServletContext getInitParameter` method. The value for this parameter is retrieved from the `web.xml` file (shown later in this chapter) declaration for the `context param` entry for `Query2`.

The query is prepared and a `PreparedStatement` object is created. The `getQueryResults` method is then called. This method uses the `PreparedStatement` (`pstmt`) instance member to execute the query and convert the `ResultSet` to an XML document format. If the `pstmt` object is not null (meaning it has been created), then the code to prepare the statement will not be executed.

At this point, the XML document containing the query results is in the string `xmlDoc`. The `Transformer transform` method is then called. This method accepts a `java.io.Reader` parameter and a `Result` (part of the Saxon package) parameter as arguments. The `Reader` argument in this case is created by wrapping a `StringReader` around our `xmlDoc` string, and the `Result` parameter is created by wrapping the `Result` class around the output `PrintWriter` (from our `HttpServletResponse`). This method will use the XSLT transform stylesheet to transform the XML document (in `xmlDoc`) and produce HTML output that will be written to the output `PrintWriter` (`out`). The remaining code in this program block outputs HTML to complete the formatting of the HTML page and provide `catch` blocks for the exceptions that may be thrown in the method.

The ServletExample1 Class: The getQueryResults Method

The `getQueryResults` method performs the task of executing the query and transforming the results into an XML document. The execution of the query simply involves executing the prepared statement that was prepared in the `doGet` method and converting the `ResultSet` into XML format using the `JDBCXML toXMLString` method.

The `executeQuery` method is called in a `try/catch` block, and the conversion to the XML document is performed in the `finally` block, which is used to return the XML document string. Should there be a failure in the execution of the XML statement, the empty or null `ResultSet` will be passed to the `JDBCXML toXMLString` method, which will return an invalid XML document. This will lead to a parser error in the transformation process in the `doGet` method. (Though not shown in this example, a more involved error-checking scheme would determine that the prepared statement execution had failed and return a value to the calling method that would terminate processing at that point.) The code for this method is shown next.

The ServletExample1 Class: The getQueryResults Method

```
public String getQueryResults() {
ResultSet rs = null;
try {
      //
      // execute query statement and return
      // a JDBC ResultSet
      //
      rs = pstmt.executeQuery( );

}
catch (SQLException e) {
      context.log(
 "SQLException in ServletExample1.getQueryResults: " +
  e.getMessage() );
```

```
}
finally {

      //
      // convert ResultSet to XML format
      //
      return JDBCXML.toXMLString( rs );
}

}
```

The ServletExample1 Class: The init Method

As we learned earlier in this chapter, a servlet runs within a container which is responsible for providing various services for the servlet, such as security and a Java Virtual Machine (JVM) to run the class files. When the servlet is first loaded, the `init` method for the servlet class `init` method is called only once by the servlet container.

The `init` method is therefore a good location to provide initialization code for the servlet, much as a constructor is used in a conventional class. As shown below, the `init` method is used to obtain a connection to the database and to prepare the template and create a processor for the XSLT transformation service. The code for this method is shown next.

The ServletExample1 Class: The init Method

```
public void init( ) {
try {

      this.context = config.getServletContext();

      //
      // get the location of the xslt stylesheet
         // from an init parameter parameter
      //
      String styleSheet = context.getInitParameter(
                           "XsltQuery2" );

      //
      // build the URL for the stylesheet
      //
      if ( styleSheet == null )
          styleSheet = defaultStyleSheet;
        else
         styleSheet = "file:" + styleSheet;

         //
       // create the objects we need for the XSL transformation
       //
```

```
        processor = Processor.newInstance("xslt");

        //
        // get an InputStream from the URL
        //
        templates = processor.process(new InputSource(
                        new URL( styleSheet ).openStream() ) );

         transformer = templates.newTransformer();

        //
        // prepare data access
        //
        InitialContext init = new InitialContext( );

        //
        // tomcat 4.02 requires a two step lookup
        //
        Context ctx   = (Context) init.lookup(
                            "java:comp/env/jdbc" );
        DataSource ds = (DataSource) ctx.lookup( "movies" );

        con = ds.getConnection();

}
catch (SQLException e) {
    context.log("SQLException in ServletExample2.init: " +
                        e.getMessage() );
}
catch (ProcessorException e) {
  context.log("ProcessorException in ServletExample2.init: "
                        + e.getMessage() );
}
catch (RemoteException e) {
    context.log("RemoteException in ServletExample2.init: " +
                        e.getMessage() );
}
catch (NamingException e) {
    context.log("NamingException in ServletExample2.init: " +
                        e.getMessage() + " - " + e );
}
catch (Exception e) {
    context.log("Exception in ServletExample2.init: " +
                        e.getMessage() );
}


}

}
```

We use the `init` method to access store a reference to our ServletContext which we use throughout the servlet to write to the log device for our servlet context. We then build the URI name for the stylesheet and a new instance of the Saxon transformation processor is obtained. The processor uses the name of the stylesheet to create a template which is then used to create the transformer reference.

Our last block of code in the `init` method is used to obtain a `DataSource` reference and ultimately a JDBC connection which we use to execute the query used by the servlet.

THE SERVLETEXAMPLE1 CLASS: THE WEB.XML FILE

As defined by the Java servlet specification, the `web.xml` file contains configuration information for a servlet context, or what is also referred to as a Web application. In this example, the `web.xml` file is used to store the initialization parameters used by the servlet, specifically the XSLT stylesheet and the query to execute. The partial contents of this file are shown below.

Annotated web.xml File with Parameters

```
<?xml version="1.0" encoding="ISO-8859-1"?>

<!DOCTYPE web-app
    PUBLIC "-//Sun Microsystems, Inc.//DTD Web Application 2.3//EN"
    "http://java.sun.com/dtd/web-app_2_3.dtd">

<web-app>

        <context-param>
            <param-name>Query1</param-name>
          <param-value>select knowledge_base.doc_key, base_doc_key, doc_name,
message_txt
                from knowledge_base, knowledge_messages
                where knowledge_base.doc_key = knowledge_messages.doc_key
                order by knowledge_base.doc_key, base_doc_key
          </param-value>
        </context-param>

        <context-param>
            <param-name>Query2</param-name>
          <param-value>select  movie_name, movie_id, release_date, category
                from   movies
                order by movie_name
          </param-value>
        </context-param>

        <context-param>
```

```
    <param-name>XsltQuery2</param-name>
    <param-value>/stdApps/Useful/rsQuery2.xsl</param-value>
</context-param>

<context-param>
    <param-name>XsltStyleSheet</param-name>
    <param-value>/lin/home/art/JDBC_Real/Code/Dynamic/rsQ1.xsl</param-value>
</context-param>

<servlet>
    <servlet-name>
        ServletExample2
    </servlet-name>
    <servlet-class>
        ServletExamples.ServletExample2
    </servlet-class>
</servlet>

<servlet>
    <servlet-name>
        ServletExample1
    </servlet-name>
    <servlet-class>
        ServletExamples.ServletExample1
    </servlet-class>
</servlet>

<servlet>
    <servlet-name>
        BlobView
    </servlet-name>
    <servlet-class>
        ServletExamples.BlobView
    </servlet-class>
</servlet>

...

</web-app>
```

The `context-param` tag is used to identify a parameter definition that can be retrieved through a call to `ServletContext getInitParameter`. The definitions boldfaced in the previous listing and used in the `ServletExample1` servlet are for the `XsltQuery2` parameter, which identifies the full path to the XSLT stylesheet, and for the `Query2` parameter, which identifies the SQL `select` query to run.

There are other options for passing parameters into servlets. One common approach is to pass the parameters to the servlet as `request` parameters, meaning that they would appear as part of the URL requesting the servlet, as follows.

```
http://www.asite.com/ServletExamples/ServletExample2?Query2=select+movie_id+from+movi
es&XsltQuery2=/stdApps/Useful/rsQl.xsl
```

As we see in this example, using HTTP parameter passing syntax we can pass parameter values to the servlet for the `Query2` parameter and the `XsltQuery2` parameter. There are obviously a few issues with this approach. The first is that the parameters for the query and the XSLT stylesheet are not expected to change between invocations, so there is no strong, compelling reason to pass them in as parameters. Another issue is that the parameters for a SQL query could quickly become tedious to view and debug when spread across the command line, and certain characters used in SQL queries may not be allowed as part of URLs.

Yet another issue, and a serious issue at that, with passing these parameters as part of the URL is security. The problem with these request parameters is that they expose the data resources of the enterprise to the general user population. As this servlet example stands, any user able to execute the servlet could access any table visible in the database. Opening freely accessible Web applications to generalized queries must be carefully considered.

SUMMARY

This chapter provided an introduction to the J2EE servlet technology. Java servlets represent a robust, useful facility for creating Web components. In this chapter we demonstrated how to program and configure a servlet using an example that performed the transformation of an XML document into an HTML page.

We will come back to Java servlets again in Chapters 33 and 34. For now, we will look at the other Java Web component: the JSP and we will see how this scripting language can be used to create presentation tier components for a J2EE application.

CHAPTER 28

Java Server Pages: The Basics

INTRODUCTION

We have just seen how servlets can be used as presentation tier components. Using servlets we can create Java classes which can interact with Web browsers through a request—response cycle. Since their inception Java servlets have proven to be flexible and efficient components for building Web applications.

But Java servlets require Java programming to produce even the most simple presentation. This one factor has led to a limited acceptance of servlets as a Web site development component. Good Java programming skills are expensive and since other Web development technologies allow a site to be developed without Java programming, these alternative technologies provide a lower cost Web development solution than Java servlets.

But Java Server Pages (JSP) provide an easy-to-use alternative to Java servlets. As we will see in this chapter, JSPs require little or no Java code to create a dynamic Web page. We will start by reviewing the origins of JSPs, the basic syntax of the scirpting the implicit Java objects provided on JSP pages.

WHY JSP?

A large portion of the development of Web pages is now performed by individuals who know nothing of procedural programming languages. These Web page developers often know more about the artistic placement of graphics and text on a page than they do about programming control loops. For these *Web page developers*, developing a Web page involves some knowledge of the HyperText Markup Language (HTML) and the use of GUI development tools to manipulate graphics and text to create an interesting Web page.

Hiring Web page developers is very attractive from an IT management perspective, since it is easier and less expensive to have these individuals build a large portion of a Web site than to find and pay a staff of Java developers to write Java servlet code to run a Web site (and to then maintain the site once it is complete). But the tools do not currently exist to allow Web page developers to develop a truly dynamic site. To create dynamic Web content, some server-side coding is required.

Java servlets provide one method of creating dynamic Web content. With servlets, Java code is created and executed by the Web server in a *servlet container*. When a client (usually a Web browser) references a servlet as a Web page, the servlet container executes the Java code, and the output of the code is the response that will be sent to the client.

Java servlets do a fine job of creating dynamic content, but unfortunately there is no simple solution that allows a Java servlet developer to share work with a Web page developer with no knowledge of Java. Using servlets to develop dynamic content for a site requires Java developers to essentially *own* the development of the dynamic pages they create. Once the servlet is created, any changes to the page require a Java developer.

A more flexible and less expensive development paradigm would have the Java developer write the code (using the required business logic) to create the dynamic content for the site. All other Web page development that concerned the presentation of the content would be the responsibility of the Web page developer. More importantly, once this dynamic page was completed, the Web page developer could perform the bulk of the maintenance on the page.

Using this approach to Web site development, the Web page developer is responsible for the *presentation* of the Web site and the Java developer is responsible for the application of *business logic* and data access. This provides for an attractive *separation of roles,* specifically the roles of the *Java programmer* and the *Web page developer*.

In order for this approach to work, the Web page developer must be able to program business logic and access data using a tool or language that he or she understands. What most Web page developers understand are HTML tags. The Java developer must therefore be able to hide the details of his or her work behind special HTML tags.

Java Server Pages Development

JSP provides the ability to implement the separation of roles in a development effort using an elegant, flexible approach. The Java developer can create a large body of code that is easily accessible through the Web page using special HTML tags. The process for creating access to Java code from within the Web page is simple and straightforward. What is significant is that virtually the complete Java language and the vast majority of the APIs available are accessible through JSP.

This is not to say that servlets do not have their place; they certainly do. When the depth and complexity of the application logic exceeds the description of the visual portion of the page, then execution of a servlet may be preferable—for instance, a dynamic page that creates a report where the dynamic content would control the layout and flow of the page, and where the inclusion and placement of a large number of fields on the page would require the execution of extensive business logic.

Any page where over 50 percent of the page is business logic would be better represented with a servlet or, more appropriately, a servlet and JavaBeans to encapsulate some portion of the business logic. For instance, a page that performs authentication and then makes a decision concerning which view the authenticated user should see could be implemented as a servlet.

If developed correctly, the JSP page would contain minimal Java code and would perform most of the work with Java code off the page (in JavaBeans or through tag libraries). Since the developmental goal is to divide the visual presentation and business logic of the application, the JSP page should be composed primarily of visual aspects of the page: the graphics, fonts, and layout of the page as expressed in HTML. The business logic should reside largely outside of the page, in JavaBeans or some other external component. The actual Java code (referred to as *scriptlets*) on the page should be kept to a minimum.

Another design concept commonly applied to JSP development is that of Model 1/Model 2 architecture. A simple Web application can use a Model 1 architecture which defines a separation of the presentation logic from the business logic from the JSP page, but retains the control flow logic in the application. As applications grow more complex, this control logic, which decides where the application will go next, can become quite complex. Rather than have this logic clutter the JSP page, the Model 2 architecture proposes the use of a control component, most likely a servlet, which makes decisions about what pages the user should be allowed to view and where the user should be directed next.

How JSP Works

The Java servlet technology historically preceded JSPs. This meant that there were vendors and open source projects which had an investment in servlet containers when the JSP specification was being developed. To leverage this investment in technology, JSPs are implemented *on top of* servlet technology. JSP pages are in fact compiled or converted into servlets, which are then run within the servlet container. In the case of the Tomcat server, both the JSP engine and the servlet container are contained within the same server environment. The JSP 1.1 specification requires a servlet container that implements the Java servlets 2.2 specification; the Tomcat server provides both of these and is the *reference implementation* for servlets and JSPs for J2EE (see Figure 28–1).

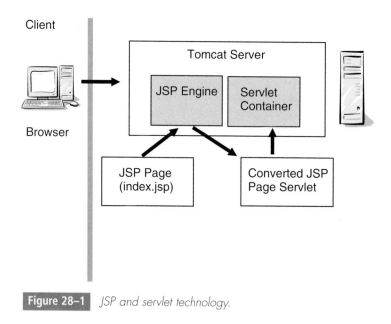

Figure 28–1   *JSP and servlet technology.*

This logically simple approach takes the JSP page and converts the non-Java statements (statements outside of the special JSP tags) into servlet output statements, as shown in the example below.

```
...
<h2> Why JSP is Good </h2>
<p> Of all the important strides made in Web development ...
<h2> Why servlets are Great</h2>
<%
if ( x == 10 ) {
 %>
<p> This is displayed only if x == 10
<% } %>
...
```

These statements would be converted into Java code very similar to the following.

```
...
PrintWriter out = response.getWriter();
out.println("<h2>Why JSP is Good</h2>");
out.println("<p> Off all the important strides made in Web development ...");
out.println("<h2> Why servlets are Great</h2>");
if ( x == 10 ) {
    out.println("<p> This is displayed only if x == 10");
}
```

The *JSP environment* (as distinguished from the servlet *container* within which the JSP page will ultimately run) manages all aspects of processing the JSP page. The Web server handles the initial request for the page, recognizes the page as a JSP page, and then passes the page to the JSP environment for processing. The JSP environment must then process the page and return the results of the page processing to the browser that requested the page.

The initial request for the JSP page, as initiated by the Web browser or some other source, is known as the *request*. The result of processing the requested page is known as the *response*. Output from the response is eventually sent back to the browser that initiated the request (or in some cases, to another destination specified in the initial request).

The JSP pages are converted into servlets, which are then compiled to Java class files (if necessary) and executed. This process of JSP translation to Java code and subsequent compilation is performed only when needed. If the source JSP page has not been modified since the last time the related servlet class file was compiled, then the compiled class file will be executed to satisfy the request (rather than recompiling the JSP page).

Both JSPs and servlets are referred to as *Web components*. Conceptually, these JSP pages are delivered to a *server environment* that provides the necessary processing to convert the page into a valid HTTP response, which is then sent to the browser that requested the page. This server environment provides both the JSP processing and the servlet container. The environment may be a separate thread within the Web server or a complete separate process that communicates with the Web server through a network connection.

The JSP page is effectively converted into a servlet class through a translation phase. The translation phase converts the page first to Java code that supports the servlet API, then compiles the page to a Java class file. This class file represents a servlet that is created at runtime when the page is requested (the resulting servlet will manage the request).

This translation process can be done before the page is requested when the application is deployed or at runtime when the page is requested. Because of the overhead involved in the translation process, the recommendation is that a page be compiled before runtime. The Tomcat server supports both approaches, allowing pages to be compiled before they are deployed or on-demand when the pages are requested. When the Tomcat server receives a request for a JSP page, it makes an effort to determine if the source for the page has been *touched* (modified) since the last translation and compile of the page, and if it has, the page is recompiled before the request is processed.

The JSP page is used to formulate a response, which is ultimately converted into a Java object of type `HTTPServletResponse`. The JSP page itself is a `HttpJspPage` and receives and processes a parameter of type `HttpServletRequest` from the client.

The responsibility of the JSP container during the translation phase is to create a Java class that represents the JSP page, the page that must be used to formulate the response. Per the JSP specification, the container has some freedom in the specifics of this class creation. The translation phase is for the most part transparent to the developer, though the developer must be aware of the nature of the process: specifically, that all Java code in the JSP page will be represented in a single class file and that any scripting variable declared in one section of the page will have scope (be visible) in other sections of the page.

JSP Syntax and Usage

Pages in JSP are conceptually divided into *elements* and *template data*. Elements are data in the JSP page that are directly involved with the JSP processing environment. Conversely, template data is any portion of the JSP page that is not important to JSP. For example, standard HTML tags that concern headers, footers, or links are considered template data within a JSP page.

JSP elements are the tools used to express JSP within the Web page. These elements are either *scripting* elements, *directive* elements, or *action* elements. JSP elements may use attributes and corresponding values to express information about that element. Attribute values must be quoted. These elements are described in more detail below.

Scripting elements, actions, and JavaBean components are used to describe the dynamic content of the JSP page. The prevailing recommendation for development of JSP pages is that scripting elements be kept to a minimum and, wherever possible, custom tags and references to Java Bean components to manage the dynamic content be used. Using such a design strategy results in a JSP page, which concentrates on presentation, while business logic is managed *off-the-page* using other facilities.

THE WEB APPLICATION AND THE SESSION

The Web application, as explained previously, is a combination of *components*, from static HTML, graphic images, text to the dynamic content provided by JSP pages and servlets. When a user accesses a site using their browser, they are accessing any number of these components. Each user access is represented by a request to the Web server. This request is directed to a *location* which results in a response being generated by an HTML page, a JSP page or a servlet. Over the course of a visit to a site, a user may access more than one of these locations over a period of time. This association between the HTTP client (the user's browser) and the HTTP server (the Apache or Tomcat server) is considered a *session*. Though the HTTP protocol does not provide a session (it is in fact a *stateless* protocol and without state you cannot preserve session information) the servers that use this protocol usually provide mechanisms to create a logical session.

Capturing Session Information

These mechanisms usually require a cookie, a state object, to be stored on the client's machine through the browser, implying that the client must support and allow cookies for a session to be maintained with a Web server using the HTTP protocol. Using this approach, a session ID is placed in a cookie in the client's browser and is then sent to the server with each HTTP request. (All active cookies are sent with each request.) The server uses this session ID to access the internal session information that corresponds to the session. This internal session information is then made available to the page being accessed by the request, thus making the maintenance of the session transparent to the page. Alternatives to using cookies to maintain sessions are available but have issues. The most common approach is to use cookies.

The servlet can maintain a logical session through the `HttpSession`, and since a JSP page is based on the Java servlet, it can participate in sessions using the `HttpSession` interface and its representation in the JSP page, the `session` object. The following sections explain the use of this object in more detail.

THE CONCEPT OF SCOPE

The term *scope* applies to the visibility of the programming elements within a program. This term is usually applied to the variables within the program. For Java, variables represent either primitive data types or object references. Java provides eight primitive data types: `byte`, `char`, `short`, `int`, `long`, `float`, `double`, and `boolean`. Everything else in the Java language is an object reference. Since object references can represent any valid Java class, there is a great deal of flexibility and extensibility in this process. Since for all effective purposes, a Java class is a data type, the Java language is type extensible—whatever data type is needed can be created as a class.

All Java references have some form of scope. For Java programs, this scope centers around the notion of the Java *class*. But the JSP page is not a Java program; in fact, the JSP specification refers to the Java code in the JSP page as a page that contains objects and *scriptlets*. Though classes are used to define the objects within the page (and the normal notions of Java scope apply), the page and its contents are not part of a class definition.

Additionally, the JSP page is not executed as a Java application might be. A JSP page is executed as some component of a Web application and would represent only a portion of the application, not the complete application. As such, it must participate with the other components in the application as part of the session or part of the application as a whole.

The JSP page is translated into a class, and the Java code within this page becomes part of that class. All of the code and HTML within the page are converted into code within a single method, the `_jspService` method.

For these reasons, JSP pages have scope attributes that extend those of the Java language. JSP page objects can have a scope attribute of either *page, request, session,* or *application*. An object with page scope is visible only on the page. Once the page has been processed and the request sent back, the object is no longer in scope (i.e., no longer available). References to objects with page scope are stored in the `pageContext` object.

A page declared with request scope is visible throughout the life of the request. In most cases, the request lives for the same duration as the page. But in cases where the request is forwarded to another page, the request object is sent along with the request. The reference to the request scope object is stored in the `request` object. The object reference is released when the request is completed.

A page declared with session scope survives for the duration of the session. A session is considered a succession of request–response operations from the same client, and all pages that are in the same session have access to the same session objects. References to these objects are stored in the `session` object that is created during page activation and are implicitly available to the JSP page. (Note that pages using page scope have access to the session object.)

An object that is declared with *application* scope is available to all pages that are part of a given application. Application objects in another application are not visible to other applications. If a page has chosen not to participate in a session (the session attribute of the page directive is set to false), then the `application` object is still available.

These references are stored in the `application` object created during page activation (as obtained from the servlet configuration object). This object reference is released when the runtime environment reclaims the `ServletContext` object.

Directive Elements

Directives are elements that are interpreted by the preprocessing of the page; they are processed before the JSP page (or resulting servlet page) is executed at runtime. Associated with a directive can be a number of attribute/value pairs. The syntax for directives is as follows.

```
<% directive_name attribute_1 = "value" attribute_2="value" %>
```

A *directive element* is used by the JSP preprocessor as part of the page preprocessing effort. It is used to provide information to the preprocessor about other elements and scriptlets contained within the page. This element is described in more detail in a later section.

Scripting Element

Scripting elements are the syntactical mechanism that allows Java code to be placed in the JSP page. There are three types of scripting elements allowed: *declarations, scriptlets,* and *expressions*. JSP declarations are used to declare elements of the script. The syntax for this element is as follows.

```
<%! declaration %>
```

This construct can be used to declare both variables and methods, as follows.

```
<%!
    int counter = 0;
    public int mkInt(String s) {
        String s1 = s.substring(4, s.length());
        return Integer.parseInt(s1);
    }
%>
```

The first statement in the example above declares an integer variable named `counter` and initializes it to the value of 0. The next declaration declares the method `mkInt` to perform a simple string-parsing operation.

Note that both of these declarations are members of the class that will be created to implement the JSP page. This has implications for variables declared in these blocks. A JSP server may potentially share instances of the JSP page class (a servlet) among multiple requests. Since member variables retain their value in between references (as opposed to local member variables, which are recreated and must be explicitly initialized before each use), member variables could develop unexpected values in this type of environment. For example, in the code shown above, the variable `counter` could be incremented by one session accessing the page; when another user's session accesses the same page, the user will see the incremented value of the `counter` variable, which would be an incorrect value for the session.

Unless there is a compelling reason to create member variables using the declaration element in JSP, it is best to declare variables needed on the page in scriptlets where they are local to the `_jspService` method created for the execution of the page. Since variables declared within the `_jspService` method are local variables, they are destroyed and recreated on each invocation of the page and are thus more inclined to contain expected values. In keeping with the advice to declare variables as close as possible to where they are used, declaring variables within the scriptlet close to their usage is recommended.

Scriptlet blocks provide for Java code within the page. The syntax for these elements is as follows.

```
<%
for (int n=0;n< 10;n++) {
%>
<p> This, that and the other
<% } %>
```

A programming expression is a programmatic expression that is any legal logic statement in the Java language that returns a value that is a valid Java data type. Expressions can be equality statements or method calls. JSP allows expressions in scriptlet code to be directed to the output stream for the response (JspWriter). This is denoted by the following syntax.

```
<%= myVar %>
```

This expression is effectively a shorthand for the following statement.

```
...
out.println( myVar );
...
```

What appears as a variable in this expression can be any Java data type that can be freely converted to a String. This includes all of the primitive Java data types as well as Java object references that have a sensible toString method implementation.

Scriptlets must start and end in the same JSP page; they cannot span pages. Scriptlet variables have scope within a page, so a variable declared in one scriptlet is visible in another scriptlet on the same page. But variables have scope only within that page. To store values that will be visible on other pages, the value must be stored as an attribute of the session or application object shown below, or the value must be passed as a parameter to a new page.

Each JSP page is compiled into a class where the declarations section of the class is a concatenation of all declaration blocks with the JSP page, and the body of the _jspService method in the class is a concatenation of all scriptlets within the page. Concatenation is performed in the order in which the declarations or scriptlets appear in the page.

Element Syntax

JSP *elements* use the syntax of XML tags. They have a start tag, an optional list of attributes and values, an optional body, and either an end tag or closing tag. The following provides an example of this syntax.

```
<specTag attribute1="10" attribute2="20" >
    This is the body of the action element
</specTag>
```

The element name in this example is `specTag`; note that the name is case sensitive. Attributes are set in the start tag and are assigned values that must be quoted. An optional format for an element with an empty body is as follows.

```
<specTag attribute1="20" attribute2="myValue" />
```

In this example, the closing tag is a `/>` set of characters that indicates the end of the element. Note that JSP tags are case sensitive.

Comments in JSP Pages

Comments can be placed in a JSP page either in the HTML portion using an HTML comment or in a JSP element. The syntax for an HTML comment is shown below.

```
<!-- this is a comment -->
```

JSP elements can be placed in an HTML comment using the following syntax.

```
<!-- this is a comment with <%= jspVal %> some JSP data -->
```

Note that since the JSP compiler reads the entire JSP file (including the HTML comments), this JSP element will be parsed, compiled, and executed. Ultimately, the output to the client will contain the HTML comment with the run-time value of the JSP expression. The browser will receive the comment but will not display it unless the user chooses to display the page source at the browser. (In a practical sense, this would only be useful for debugging request output from the JSP page, since reading the comment in the source file would contain only the JSP expression, not the results of the expression.)

To place a comment within a JSP element, use the following syntax.

```
<%!-- this is a JSP comment  --%>
```

Within a scriptlet, the syntax for Java language comments is also valid, as shown below.

```
...
<%
// build HTML list from contents of collection
// peopleList is Iterator for list of participating staff
while (myBean.peopleList.hasNext() ){
%>
<li><%= myBean.i.next() %>

<%
}
%>
...
```

Scripting elements can be quoted with a backward slash (\) character as follows.

```
<% String s = "this is a quoted quote character (\") "; %>
```

If the backward slash character were eliminated, as shown in the following example, then an error would be returned by the JSP preprocessor, as shown below.

```
<!-- this is bad syntax - don't try this at home ... -->
<% String s = "this is a quoted quote character (") "; %>
```

This would result in the following error.

```
Error: 500

Location: /examples/jsp/art/t.jspInternal Servlet Error:

org.apache.jasper.JasperException: Unable to compile
/lin/local/jakarta/tomcat33/work/DEFAULT/examples/jsp/art/t_1.java:62: ';' expected.
          String s = "this is a quoted quote character (") ";
                                                          ^
/lin/local/jakarta/tomcat33/work/DEFAULT/examples/jsp/art/t_1.java:62: String not
terminated at end of line.
          String s = "this is a quoted quote character (") ";
                                                          ^
2 errors                                                  ^
...
```

JSP IMPLICIT OBJECTS

These objects are available implicitly in JSP scriptlet code. Variables are available of the types defined for these objects in the JSP specification. The types (Java classes) for these variables are detailed in the Table 28–1.

Table 28–1   *JSP Objects Implicitly Available*

Object	Class	Description	Scope
request	javax.servlet.ServletRequest	Represents the request from the client.	request
response	javax.servlet.ServletResponse	The response to be formulated for the request.	page
pageContext	javax.servlet.PageContext	Represents the JSP page.	page
session	javax.servlet.HttpSession	Contains session variables and information about session activity.	session
application	javax.servlet.ServletContext	Application information, including application variables.	application
out	javax.servlet.jsp.JspWriter	Provides access to the response output stream.	page
config	javax.servlet.ServletConfig	The servlet configuration for this JSP page.	page
page	java.lang.Object	The instance of this page's class.	page
exception	java.lang.Throwable	Exception object available only on an error page.	page

The request Object

The request object represents the HTTP request that accessed the JSP page and contains information about the request. This object is usually used to access the parameters passed to the request (as part of the query string). For instance, a form that has been filled in on the browser will pass the values of the fields in the form of a request. The following shows an example of using a request object to retrieve parameter values.

```
String custName = request.getParameter("custname");
String custID   = request.getParameter("custid");
```

The string value passed into the getParameter method is the name of the parameter. A string value for the parameter is returned as a Java String. For convenience, parameter names can also be retrieved as an enumeration, as shown in the following example.

```
. . .
Enumeration e = request.getParameterNames();
while ( e.hasMoreElements() ) {
        String s = e.nextElement();
      // process parameters
. . .
```

Additionally, the corresponding values can be retrieved in a String array using the getParameterValues method, as shown below.

```
String[] s  = request.getParameterValues("CheckBox1");
```

The request object can also be used to retrieve information such as the content type, length, and character encoding for the request on the HTTP header. Additionally, a method is available to determine whether or not the request was made on a secure channel such as HTTPS, as shown below.

```
if ( request.isSecure() ) {
   // perform secure processing
   . . .
```

The response Object

The response object represents the output to the client. It is in fact the job of the JSP page to produce this output stream; this happens implicitly in the processing of the JSP page and its constituent scriptlets and tags. This is notably different from the use of servlets which requires explicit output to the response stream. Though this object is used in servlet development to provide output, with JSP pages, output processing is performed differently. JSP pages use the out object, an instance of the jspWriter class, to provide direct access to output.

With servlets, the response object is usually used to obtain the output stream for the response. This output stream can be used for binary or character output, though it is usually used for character output with JSP. To obtain an output stream for character output, the PrintWriter is obtained using the getWriter method, as shown below.

```
PrintWriter pw = response.getWriter();
```

The `response` object is also useful for setting the various headers being returned to the client and thus providing some degree of control of the client-side forwarding, cache control, content expiration, and content type.

The page Object

The `page` object represents an instance of the current page. It is therefore self-referencing to the currently processing page. Within the body of the page, the `page` object reference is similar to the `this` reference within a Java program.

The out Object

The `out` object represents the character response output stream for the current page. The `out` object is an implementation of the `javax.servlet.jsp.JspWriter` interface that is provided by the JSP server (and managed by the corresponding servlet container environment). This object provides the functionality of a `java.io.PrintWriter` or `java.io.BufferedWriter` object in that I/O is buffered and filtered.

Since the JSP scriptlet syntax provides a convenient means of producing output without using a method call (the `<%=` syntax), the use of the `out` object is usually reserved just for certain sections of code where it is simply more convenient to express output using a method call, as shown in the following code.

```
...
<%

for (n = 1, Iterator i = c.iterator();
     i.hasNext(); n++ )   {
    if ( n < 20 )
      out.println("row: " + n " - output: " +
                  i.next() );

...
```

Within the body of a programmatic `for` loop, it is more convenient to insert a method call than it is to close the scriptlet block, perform output using a JSP expression, and then insert another scriptlet block.

Note that while it is possible to perform response I/O processing with the `out` object, it is not recommended. Java scriptlet code within the JSP page should be kept to a minimum, and alternatives to method calls should be used whenever possible. Therefore, the use of the JSP expression for output (`<%= MyVar %>`) is preferable to an `out.println()` method call because it is more understandable to a page developer who knows nothing about Java programming.

The config Object

The `config` implicit object represents the `ServletConfig` (`javax.servlet.ServletConfig`) for the current JSP page. This object can be used to provide information on the underlying servlet, such as the servlet name and the servlet context.

The `ServletContext` is available from the implicit `config` object using the `getContext` method. This method returns a `ServletContext` object. This object contains useful information on the parameters, attributes, and mime type for the servlet. It can also be used to access the log for the servlet using the `log` method which is used to write a string to the servlet log.

The pageContext Object

This implicit object contains a reference to the page context (`javax.servlet.jsp.PageContext`) for the JSP page being processed. This object can be used to explicitly request references to a number of the implicit objects, as detailed in the abbreviated list in Table 28–2.

This pageContext object reference also provides methods to forward to another page and to include another page into the response output stream for the current page. Since these methods all involve manipulation of the presentation logic, it is best to perform this work in the JSP page, using JSP tags whenever possible.

Table 28–2   *pageContext getXXX Methods*

Method	Returns	Type
getOut	Reference to implicit out object.	JspWriter
getPage	Reference to the current page.	Object
getRequest	Returns a reference to the current HTTP request.	ServletRequest
getResponse	Reference to the response for the current request.	ServletResponse
getServletConfig	Reference to the configuration object for the current servlet (converted JSP page).	ServletConfig
getServletContext	Reference to the servlet context.	ServletContext
getAttribute	Returns an object attribute associated with the name passed as a parameter.	Object
getAttributeScope	Passed a scope indicator and returns an enumeration of all attributes for a given scope.	int
getException	Returns the current value of the exception object.	java.lang.Exception
getSession	Returns a reference to the value of the current session object.	HttpSession

The session Object

The implicit `session` object contains a reference to the currently active session (`javax.servlet.http.HttpSession`). The `session` object is generally used to represent a user session across multiple requests. Attributes and corresponding values can be stored within the `session` object during one request, and then retrieved during successive requests. These attributes can be set with calls to the `setAttribute` and `getAttribute` methods, as shown below.

```
...
<% session.setAttribute("custName",
                       request.getParameter("custName")); %>
<% session.setAttribute("custID",
                       request.getParameter("custID")); %>
...
<!-- retrieve the customer name and ID from the session object -->

    <p> Customer Name:  <%= (String) session.getAttribute("custName") %>
    <p> Customer ID: <%= (String) session.getAttribute("custID") %>
...
```

These methods accept and return an object reference, so the `getAttribute` call generally requires a Java cast, as shown in the example above.

The application Object

The implicit `application` object represents the `ServletContext` (`javax.servlet.ServletContext`) for the current servlet/JSP page. This object can be used to gather information about the servlet container and includes methods to set and retrieve attributes for the current servlets and their values, to remove attributes, and to write to a log file for the servlet container. This object can also be used to get the MIME type of a file, to access the request dispatcher (to forward a request to another JSP page, servlet, or HTML page), or to get a list of all attribute names for the servlet.

DIRECTIVES

Directives are elements that are interpreted by the preprocessing of the page; they are processed before the JSP page (or resulting servlet page) is executed at runtime. Associated with a directive can be a number of attribute/value pairs. The syntax for directives is as follows.

```
<%@ directive_name attr1="value" attr2="value" ... %>
```

Table 28–3 lists the directives available in JSP version 1.2.

Table 28–3	JSP Directives

Directive	Description
page	Information about the JSP page that is visible to the user; can provide basic information about the page, the error page to use, whether or not the page is thread-safe, and other information.
include	Include text (not necessarily a JSP page) into the current page. In JSP 1.2, two mechanisms are provided: one to provide includes that will be parsed by the JSP preprocessor and the other to provide runtime includes that will not be parsed.
taglib	Indicates that the page uses a tag library and contains attributes to locate the tag library and to reference the tag library within the page.

The page Directive

A page directive is used to perform certain actions before a page is loaded. This directive can have one of the attributes listed in Table 28–4.

Using the extends Attribute of the page Directive

The JSP container converts each JSP page to a Java class, which is a superclass specified by the JSP container (implementing either the `JspPage` or `HttpJspPage` interface). The `extends` attribute of the `page` directive allows the superclass of the page to be identified. This is not a capability that can be taken lightly, since the JSP container depends on the appropriate implementation of the `JspPage` or `HttpJspPage` interfaces.

The expectation is that the developer of a JSP container will document certain classes that could be used to provide additional capabilities within the page and that these classes will be used as arguments to these attributes.

The taglib facility and the `jsp:useBean` tag can be used to provide additional functionality within a JSP page and, for the average developer, provide a much safer alternative than extending the base class for the JSP page.

More than one `page` attribute can be included with the page directive, as shown in the following example.

Table 28–4 *The page Directive Attributes*

Attribute	Descriptive
import	Java language import directive.
errorPage	The URL of the error page for this page. If an exception is thrown on this page or in one of its helper classes, then this page will be the loaded and returned to the client.
extends	The Java class name that this JSP will extend. (Note that this use of this feature must be carefully considered—see below.)
session	Set to either true or false depending on whether or not this page must participate in a session.
language	The scripting language to be used. (Currently, only Java is supported as the scripting language, but vendors could potentially implement other scripting languages.)
buffer	Set to either none or an integer value indicating the size of the output buffer (where appending 'kb' is mandatory to indicate the buffer size in kilobytes).
autoFlush	Set to either true or false depending on whether or not the buffer will be flushed automatically (note that this requires the buffer attribute be set to some valid value).
isThreadSafe	Set to true or false depending on the level of thread safety in the page.
info	A string entry that can be set to any arbitrary text value and can then be retrieved using the servlet method servlet.getServletInfo.
contentType	Defines the character encoding for the JSP page and the MIME type for the response of the JSP page.
pageEncoding	Defines the character encoding for the JSP page.
isErrorPage	True if this is the error page; false if this is not the error page.

```
<%@ page errorPage="/share/ErrorPage.jsp" info="Standard Customer login page."
isThreadSafe="false" %>
```

The include Directive

The include directive provides the capability to include arbitrary text within a JSP page. This seemingly benign capability provides significant advantages for the developer. The common syntax for this directive is as follows.

```
<%@ include file="file_name" %>
```

This directive is the file specified in the file attribute at the location in the JSP page where the directive was inserted. This form of the `include` directive inserts the file *after* running the file through the preprocessor and is processed (parsed and converted) when the page is translated (see Figure 28–2).

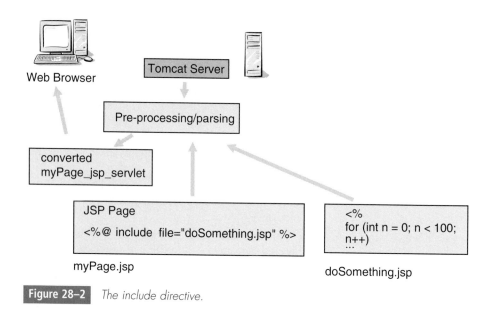

Figure 28-2   *The include directive.*

Alternatively, there is a JSP tag that does *not* translate or preprocess the contents of the included file and performs its operation at the time the JSP page is requested. Using this form of the include operation, the contents of the target page are simply placed on the output stream at the point where the tag is encountered in the page. The syntax for this statement is as follows.

```
<jsp:include page="footer.html" />
```

The difference between the implementation of these two versions of the same directive is the difference between static and dynamic content. If the contents to be included in the page are static—they will not change from the point where the page has been created to the point at which the page is requested—then the first form of the statement is recommended (and will perform better, since it will require less work of the container at request time). This would be useful for including a header and footer in a JSP page or inserting portions of text created and managed by other nondeveloper staff. See Figure 28–3.

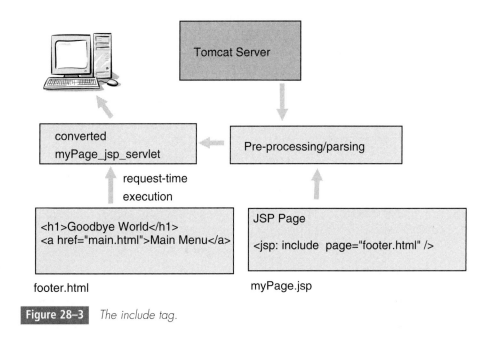

Figure 28–3 *The include tag.*

Alternatively, if the contents to be included change constantly, then the second form of the directive is recommended. This form of the directive will read the contents of the file when the request is made so that the page will always access the most current version of the file. This would be useful for a daily message or for a list of currently relevant news stories and links that should be included in a JSP page.

The taglib Directive

The taglib directive is used to create custom tags that can be used within a Web page. The use of tags is more intuitive for Web page developers not familiar with Java, those commonly responsible for a significant part of Web site development and maintenance. There are a number of tag libraries available both commercially and as open source code.

In order to use tag libraries with JSP, Java code needs to be called using the custom tags, which must be created using a special API. The syntax for the use of this directive is as follows.

```
<%@ taglib uri="libraryURI" prefix="tagPrefix" %>
```

The taglib directive uses two attributes: uri and prefix. The uri attribute identifies the location of the library (the compiled Java code) that implements the custom tag. The prefix that will be used to distinguish a custom action is identified by the `prefix` attribute.

Once a tag library has been identified, the tags contained in the library can be used within the JSP page. The tags can accept arguments from the page and dynamically produce page content by executing the Java code contained in the tag library.

JSP Standard Actions

The JSP container provides a number of useful tags that are referred to in JSP documentation as *standard actions*. These are tags that can be used in the JSP page to set and retrieve properties, reference JavaBeans, include additional content in the page, and perform other functions. These standard action tags are shown in Table 28–5.

Table 28–5   *JSP Standard Action Tags*

Tag	Purpose
jsp:setProperty	To set a property value for a JavaBean.
jsp:getProperty	To retrieve a property value from a JavaBean.
jsp:useBean	To identify a JavaBean to use.
jsp:include	To include a text file in a JSP page. The contents will not be pre-processed and will be retrieved at request time.
jsp:forward	To forward a request to another page. The current request will stop processing.
jsp:param	Pass parameters via a key/value pair. Used with the jsp:include, jsp:forward, or jsp:plugin tags.
jsp:plugin	Allows a browser plug-in to be invoked from the server in order to manage some part of the page to be rendered by the browser.

These tags are explained in more detail in the following sections.

The jsp:useBean Tag

The jsp:useBean tag is used to identify the JavaBean to be used in the JSP page. The attributes of this tag identify the name of the Java class file that contains the Java bean and the ID or name that will be used to identify this bean in the page.

Once a JavaBean has been *included* with the page, all of the members of the object that comprise the JavaBean are available within the Java code used on that JSP page.

The useBean tag must specify a value for either the type or class attribute (Java needs this before it can create the corresponding object to represent the bean). The useBean tag has a number of attributes associated with it (Table 28–6)

Table 28–6   *The useBean Tag Attributes*

Attribute	Description
type	The type of the scripting variable to be created; if this is not the class specified in the class attribute, then it must be a superclass of the class specified.
class	The name of the class for the JavaBean.
beanName	The name of the bean as used by the java.beans.Beans.instantiate() method.
scope	The scope of the bean, one of either page, request, session, or application.
id	The name for the resulting object; also the name of the scripting variable.

If the class and the beanName attribute are not specified, then the object referenced must be visible within the current scope (as specified in the attributes list).

```
<jsp:useBean id="myBean" class="myBean" />
```

In this example, the bean named myBean is loaded using this directive.

```
<jsp:useBean id="myBean" class="tools.myBean">
    <jsp:setProperty name="myBean" property="beanMember" value="Freddy">
</jsp:useBean>
```

In this example, the myBean property beanMember is set to the value of Freddy. The setting of bean properties based on the context of the application (effectively *initializing* the properties) is a common reason for using a body with the useBean tag. Also note that in this example the body of the useBean tag is terminated on the final line of the example.

The jsp:setProperty Tag

The setProperty tag allows a bean property to be set via the value attribute in the tag. The following example demonstrates.

```
<jsp:setProperty name="myBean" property="userName" value="Fred" />
```

In this example, the property `userName` in the Java Bean `myBean` is set to the value specified by the `value` attribute, which in this case is the string value `Fred`. Alternatively, the property value can be set using a request parameter, as shown in the following example.

```
<jsp:useBean id="myBean" class="examples.myBean" />
...
<jsp:setProperty name="myBean" property="userName" param="user" />
```

In this example, the bean named `myBean` has the property `userName` set to the value of the request parameter `user` (`request.getParameter("user")`). (The request parameter is usually passed from an HTML form.) If the attribute `param` is not supplied to the `setProperty` tag and no value parameter is supplied, the JSP container will assume that the `param` name is the same as the property name and it should find a method named `set<param name>` or `get<param name>`. Since most commonly the name of the `getXXX` and `setXXX` methods is the same as the property name, there is no need to use the `param` attribute, and it is not used.

Note that the `param` attribute and the `value` a`ttribute cannot appear in the same tag. The reason for this is obvious: These are mutually exclusive attributes, and values can be retrieved only from one or the other, not from both.

Conversion of the `value` attribute will take place as needed. Since the `value` attribute will initially be passed as a Java `String`, if it is being placed into a `String` in the Java Bean, then no conversion needs to take place. If it is not being placed into a `String`, then conversion must take place using the `valueOf` method of the Java language primitive data type wrapper classes, as listed in Table 28–7.

Table 28–7   *Java Data Type Wrapper Classes*

Data Type	Class
boolean	java.lang.Boolean
byte	java.lang.Byte
char	java.lang.Character
int	java.lang.Integer
long	java.lang.Long
float	java.lang.Float
double	java.lang.Double

The setProperty tag is converted (during the JSP preprocessor stage) into a call that converts the String value into the primitive data type (the data type that is a parameter to the setXXXX method in the Java Bean). The String value is passed to the valueOf method, as follows.

```
...
String s="10";
...
int i = Java.lang.Integer.valueOf( s );
...
```

The valueOf method returns the primitive data type of the wrapper class being used. In this example, the valueOf method returns a Java int data type for the value of the String s.

The jsp:getProperty Tag

The getProperty tag retrieves the value of a bean property and returns it to the output stream of the JSP page. The bean value is first converted to a type String and is then placed on the output stream. Conversion is performed using the Java language classes, which correspond to the primitive Java data types (integer, float, double, short). The format for the getProperty tag is as follows.

```
<jsp:useBean id="myBean" class="examples.myBean" />
...
User Name:   <jsp:getProperty name="myBean" property="userName" />
```

In this example, the getProperty tag is used to retrieve the userName property and return the output into the JSP page. Note that the userName will appear on the page as part of the HTML generated and will appear, appropriately enough, directly next to the User Name: string that appears in the page.

The jsp:include Tag

As mentioned in the previous section, the include tag performs a function similar to that of the include directive. This tag retrieves the text in the file referenced in the attribute of the tag, but unlike the include directive, it does not run the file contents through the preprocessor but instead places the contents directly on the output stream when the JSP page is requested. The included content will not be parsed, as it is with the include directive. The page attribute of the include tag specifies the page to be included. Its argument must be a value that evaluates to a URL string, as shown in the following example.

```
<jsp:include page="/headerPages/header1.html" />
```

In this example, the page `header1.html` is included in the output stream of the current page. Parameters can be specified to be passed to the page using `param` tags within the tag body, as follows.

```
<jsp:include page="headerPages/header1.jsp >
  <jsp:param name="pageTitle" value="User Information">
  <jsp:param name="Date" value=" <%=
  java.text.SimpleDateFormat.getDateInstance( java.text.DateFormat.LONG ).format(
new java.util.Date() ) )  %> " >
</jsp:include>
```

The jsp:forward Tag

The `forward` tag is used to *forward* processing to a specified page. This means that the container running the page (servlet) will terminate processing of the current page and then retrieve the contents of the forward page into the current `ContextManager`. At that point, the processing for the forward page will begin. The syntax for this tag is as follows.

```
...
<jsp:forward page="/jumpPages/jump1.html" />
...
```

The `forward` tag can also include parameters to be passed to the forwarding page by using a tag body containing `param` tags, as shown in the following example.

```
...
<jsp:forward page="/jumpPages/jump1.jsp" >
  <jsp:param name="jumpCount" value=" <%= jumpsCount %>" />
  <jsp:param name="jumpApplication" value=" <%= appName %>" />
</jsp:forward>
...
```

In this example, two parameters are passed to the page `jump1.html`: the `jumpCount` parameter and the `jumpApplication` parameter. These two parameters will be received by the `jump1.html` page as request parameters. Note that the parameters are set using dynamic values (local script variables) in the JSP page.

The jsp:param Tag

The `param` tag is used to set request parameters for an HTTP request to be generated. This element is used in the body of `jsp:include`, `jsp:forward`, and `jsp:plugin` tags, and the request parameters that are set have scope only within that call. Parameters augment or are appended to any existing parameter list. If there is a conflict with parameters, the values set by the param tag take precedence. The syntax for this tag is as follows.

```
. . .
<jsp:forward page="/errorPages/error1.html" >
  <jsp:param name="errorCount" value=" <%= errorCount %>" />
  <jsp:param name="applicationName" value=" <%= appName %>" />
</jsp:forward>
. . .
```

In this example, page execution is being forwarded to an error page named error1.html and is being passed parameter values for errorCount and applicationName, which are set from the values of script variables.

The jsp:plugin Tag

The plugin tag allows a browser plugin to be invoked (from the server side) to manage some part of the page to be rendered by the browser. The use of tag attributes allows parameters to be passed to the plugin. This is commonly used to invoke an applet or a JavaBean component. A <jsp:fallback> tag can be used to indicate an action to be taken if the plug-in cannot be loaded. The syntax for this tag is as follows.

```
. . .
<jsp:plugin type="applet" code="clientCustMaint.class" codebase="/html">
    <jsp:param name="userName" value="<%= userName1 %>"
    <jsp:fallback>
              <b> Unable to start plugin. </b>
    </jsp:fallback>
</jsp:plugin>
. . .
```

In this example, the plugin tag designates the plug-in type to be an applet through the type attribute. The code to be run by the plug-in (the applet) is identified as clientCustMaint.class using the code attribute. The directory where the class will be found is identified as /html using the codebase attribute.

Within the plugin tag block, a single parameter is passed using the param tag. This element is used to set the userName parameter to the value of the userName1 variable. Also within the plugin tag, a fallback tag appears to designate a block of JSP that will be rendered if the plugin cannot be loaded; in this example, a single line of HTML is displayed to indicate that the plug-in cannot be loaded. As of this writing, only arbitrary text can appear in this block.

SUMMARY

This chapter provided an overview of JSP Web tier components and described how JSP implementations are built upon the technology of servlets. JSP pages are converted into servlets and then run in a servlet container. Using existing technology infrastructure in this way has provided a smooth development path for software vendors who already had a servlet container in place. This approach has the added advantage of now having software products that provide two server-side solutions: JSPs and servlets.

The syntax of JSP includes the entire Java language (a powerful feature in itself) and a number of tags and directives that were detailed in this chapter. Using these tags, JSP pages can integrate Java code into the JSP page with minimal Java code. The next chapter continues the coverage of JSPs with code examples of JSP and JSPs using the `taglib` syntax.

CHAPTER 29

JSP Examples

INTRODUCTION

The previous chapter introduced the basics of building an application with Java. The syntax of the JSP language, and the tags, directives, and scriptlets that make up the language were all explained. This chapter builds on the work of the previous chapter by using a series of examples to explain how to develop Web applications using JSP with JavaBeans and custom tag libraries.

Since it is not uncommon for Web applications to require the display of a one-month calendar on a Web page, this chapter provides an example of a JavaBean that can provide this functionality. This provides a useful demonstration of both JSP/scriptlet development as well as the use of custom tags. The conversion of the JavaBean into the custom tag highlights the differences between tag libraries and JavaBeans and demonstrates the relative ease of performing this conversion.

We will first begin with some minimal implementation examples and then progress to more complex examples of JSP involving the creation of a calendar. The use of taglibs provides a nice alternative for simplifying access to business logic. To demonstrate the advantages of tablibs, we will convert the JSP calendar page to a taglib implementation of the same page.

SOME JSP EXAMPLES

We already know that the JSP page includes HTML tags interspersed with special JSP tags. These tags can contain attributes, or a body, which is interpreted by the compiler. The <% tag on the page indicates to the JSP compiler that Java code follows, and a %> indicates to the compiler that this is the end of Java code.

The Java code contained within a block of these tags is not a formal Java class declaration with data members and method declarations; instead it is a fragment of Java code used by the JSP parser to construct the Java code that will be executed when the JSP is accessed. A particular section of the code fragment does not need to be a completed code block, but when the parsing of the JSP is complete, a Java code block should be closed.

Since the code within these JSP code blocks (<%%>) is not complete Java program code, this inserted Java is considered to be a *script*, often referred to as a *scriptlet*. The following fragment contains an example of a JSP scriptlet.

```
<HTML>
<BODY bgcolor="#FFFFFF">

<%@ page errorPage="ErrorPage.jsp" %>

<% for (int n = 0; n < 10; n++ ) { %>

<p> This text will be displayed 10 times.

<% } %>

</BODY>
</HTML>
```

In this example, a directive is used to identify an error page in the event an error is triggered within the page. A Java `for` loop is then started and directed to run for 10 iterations. An opening brace appears on the same line. Note that the entire line of the declaration of the `for` loop, including the starting brace for the `for` loop, is enclosed in a single scriptlet block.

An HTML paragraph element and corresponding text appears on the next line below the `for` loop declaration. Immediately below this line is a scriptlet block with a closing brace; this represents the close of the servlet block.

With this technique, HTML in a JSP page can enjoy the benefits of Java flow-of-control loops. This closing brace is matched with the opening brace on the previous line, and for that reason all HTML text that appears within the `for` loop on the JSP is under the control of the `for` loop. The output of this page is shown in Figure 29–1.

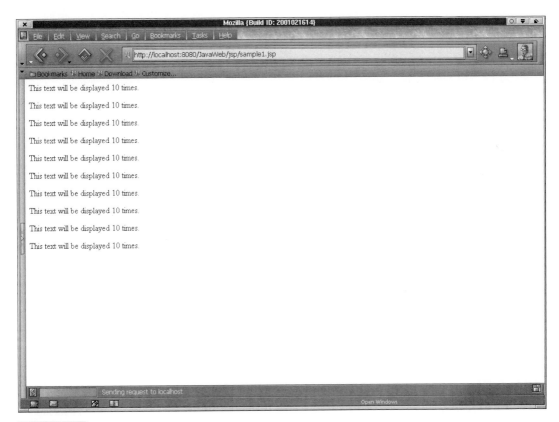

Figure 29–1 *JSP sample1.jsp output.*

JSP also provides convenient access to Java code (or classes) external to the page. This is provided through either an `import` directive, which works like the Java language import statement, or the `useBean` tag.

The `useBean` tag includes JavaBeans in the JSP page and provides a mechanism for associating the JavaBean with a tag within the JSP page. The syntax for the `useBean` tag is shown below.

```
...
<jsp:useBean id="dbutil" class="db.dbUtil" scope="session" />
<jsp:useBean id="kbutil" class="knowledgebase.KBUtil" scope="session" /> ...
```

These tags provide for the inclusion of JavaBeans modules in the JSP, providing for modularized code and code reuse throughout the JSP application. In the example we show here, these tags include modules that are referenced on the JSP page, using the names dbutil and kbutil. The class files for the modules are also specified.

```
...
<!-- table for ResultSet output -->
<table border=0 cellpadding=2 bgcolor="white">

<tr>
<td bgcolor="#C0D9D9"><b>Problem Description<b></td>
<td bgcolor="#C0D9D9"><b>Message<b></td>
<td bgcolor="#C0D9D9"><b>Category<b></td>
<td bgcolor="#C0D9D9"><b>Action<b></td>
</tr>

<!--    // print each column -->
<%
     while ( more ) {
%>

<tr>
<td bgcolor="#E0E0E0"> <%= rs.getString( "doc_name" ) %> </td>
<td bgcolor="#E0E0E0"> <%= rs.getString( "message_txt" ) %> </td>
<td bgcolor="#E0E0E0"> <%= rs.getString( "category" ) %> </td>

<td bgcolor="#C0C0C0"> <a href="viewKB.jsp?pdoc_key=<%= doc_key %>" >View Entry</a>
</td>

<% if ( !request.getParameter( "action" ).equals( "showthread" ) ) { %>

<td bgcolor="#C0C0C0"> <a href="listKB.jsp?pdoc_key=<%= doc_key
%>&action=showthread" >Show Thread</a> </td>
<% } %>

</tr>

<%
     more = rs.next();
     } // end while
%>
</table>
```

In this example, an HTML table is created to display the output of a database query, which is returned in a JDBC ResultSet object. In order to place the contents of the ResultSet object into the HTML table, a Java while loop is executed for each row returned in the ResultSet object.

Note that the while loop is not completed in the first Java code block in the HTML page. Instead, a great deal of HTML is inserted between the sections of the while loop. This is allowed in JSP scriptlets.

At the end of the `while` loop, a call is made to the `ResultSet next()` method to retrieve the next row in the `ResultSet`. If this call succeeds, the script variable `more` is set to the boolean value of true. If the call fails, the script variable is set to false. The boolean value of the script variable `more` is tested at the start of the `while` loop, and if it tests `false`, the `while` loop will not be executed.

This code is intended to show how Java scriptlets can be used to provide control over the dynamic page generation process. But in this example, a portion of the underlying business logic is exposed in the JSP page through the calls to the JDBC `ResultSet`. Since it is exposed, it is visible and can be changed by the same developer who will develop the HTML code within the page. This means that the HTML page developer, who probably knows very little JSP much less Java, could easily become confused and may inadvertently change some critical portion of the Java code. It is therefor better to remove this business logic from the JSP page into a software component which would then be referenced on the JSP page. JavaBeans and/or EJBs provide a convenient facility for doing just that.

JAVA SOFTWARE COMPONENTS: JAVABEANS AND EJBS

To hide the business logic of the application and thus reduce the complexity of the Java code on the JSP page, we need a facility to encapsulate the business logic of the application. This business logic should be encapsulated in the form of software components. The use of these software components fits into *our J2EE architecture,* and Java provides two forms of software components: *Java Beans* and *Enterprise Java Beans (EJBs).*

JavaBeans are a coding facility in Java that allow for the creation of a local component that provides some degree of encapsulation. These components are not as complex as EJBs, and for applications that do not need the features of EJBs, they are more than suitable. Most notably, they do not explicitly support a distributed environment, an environment where the location of the component is not defined; that is, the component could be on the local machine, or the component could be on a machine elsewhere on the network.

As we have learned previously, EJBs provide a number of features that are suitable for a more intensive, robust production environment. EJBs are designed with a notion of *containership.* Just as servlets and JSPs have containers that implicitly provide many of the services needed by those components, an EJB has a container that provides a number of services. EJB containers and their servers provide persistence, location transparency, failure fallback capabilities, and scalability features that heavily used, business-critical applications require.

But this robust feature set comes with a price. EJBs can be difficult to develop and even more difficult to deploy. The servers they require are complex and can be expensive, and can require some level of system maintenance. This is not to say that EJBs should not be used; they have significant value with the right application. But there are simpler, more direct approaches to development that are appropriate for a large number of small to medium-sized applications.

EJBs are generally used on applications that will have a heavy user load, require integration with legacy applications on disparate systems (e.g., a UNIX-based system must use mainframe data), or require a high degree of failover capabilities. For these applications, EJBs provide significant value and are easier to use and more flexible than many of the alternatives available on the market today.

USING JAVABEANS WITH JSPS

JavaBeans are Java classes coded using a set of methods with a standard naming convention. With these classes it is assumed that class data members (or attributes) will be declared with `private` accessibility and will be manipulated using only `get` and `set` methods; the `get` and `set` methods are named with the naming standard `get<attribute_name>` and `set<attribute_name>`, where the attribute name is the name of the attribute or private data member that is to be set.

These `getXX` and `setXX` methods are sometimes referred to as *accessor* and *mutator* methods of the class. JavaBeans do not require the implementation of a Java interface and do not need to be a subclass of any particular class; they are just another Java class with appropriate methods written to manage their attributes. The following provides an example.

```
1.package samples;
2.
3.public class myBean {
4.private int counter;
5.private String name = "MyBean"; // default name
6.
7.public void setCounter( int count ) {
8.this.counter = count;
9.}
10.public void setName( String name ) {
11.this.name = name;
12.}
13.
14.public String getName() {
15.    return name;
16.}
17.
18.public int getCounter() {
19.    return counter;
20.}
21.
22.public void incrementCounter() {
```

```
23.    counter++;
24.}
25.}
```

In this example, a JavaBean named `myBean` is created as a Java class. The JavaBean class has two private data members (or properties): `counter` and `name`, as declared on lines 4 and 5. The four public methods used to access these private members are declared on lines 7 through 20. The `set` methods are used to set the values of these members, and the `get` methods are used to access the values of the members. The `setCounter` method on line 7 is written to set the value of the `counter`, and the `setName` method on line 10 is used to set the value of the `name` member. Likewise, the `getName` method on line 14 is available to retrieve the value of the `name` member. The `getCounter` method on line 18 is available to retrieve the value of the `counter` member.

The `incrementCounter` method on line 22 is an example of how a simple method could be part of a JavaBean. This method increments a counter variable and then returns. The following example demonstrates the use of this JavaBean in a JSP page.

```
1.<HTML>
2.<BODY>
3.<jsp:useBean id="myBean" class="samples.myBean" scope="page" />
4.<jsp:setProperty name="myBean" property="counter" value="1" />
5.
6.<H1>JSP Samples<H1>
7.<p>
8.
9.<% myBean.incrementCounter(); %>
10.
11.<p>Name: <jsp:getProperty name="myBean" property="name" />
12.
13.<p>Counter: <jsp:getProperty name="myBean" property="counter" />
14.
15.</BODY>
16.</HTML>
```

In this sample page, the `useBean` tag on line 3 is identifies the bean to be used and associates the bean with an `id` name in the page. The `useBean` tag uses the `id` attribute to identify the name of the class to load for the bean and the scope attribute to identify the scope of the JavaBean within the JSP page.

The scriptlet on line 9 is used to invoke a method within one of the JavaBeans loaded on the current page or potentially one of the classes available to the servlet built from the page. This scriptlet invokes the `incrementCounter` method to increment the internal counter variable for the JavaBean.

The `getProperty` tags on lines 11 and 13 retrieve the values of the members of the JavaBean class (`counter` and `name`). The values of these members are retrieved and inserted into the HTML page at line 11 after the `Name:` string and at line 13 after the `Counter:` string.

Note that it is not required to write public `get` and `set` methods for all members. Should you wish to hide certain details of the JavaBean, the `get` and `set` methods could be either eliminated or declared private methods, thus restricting access to the methods.

The process of *introspection* is the capability of a Java application to dynamically examine the members of a class and then access the members of that class. This is the facility used by runtime JavaBeans activation and by the JSP container when it implements the `getProperty` or `setProperty` tags on the JSP page.

When a JavaBean is used in a JSP page, the `useBean` tag is used to identify the JavaBean class to load for the bean. The JSP container then finds and loads the class. When a `getProperty` tag is encountered for the JavaBean, the container uses *introspection* to determine whether an appropriate `get<PropertyName>` method is available to call and, if it is available, makes the method call and returns the value. If a `setProperty` tag is encountered, then introspection is once again used to determine whether or not an appropriate `set<PropertyName>` method is available to call. If an appropriate `set<PropertyName>` method is found, it is called and passed the correct value for the call. Note that the property name in the `set<PropertyName>` method must match the `property` attribute of the `jsp:getProperty` tag.

A JSP/JavaBeans Example

A common problem that must be tackled when developing a Web site is to dynamically create Web pages based on the contents of some subset of database tables. Since it is safe to assume we will be retrieving multiples rows of data from the database, we must be able to iterate through these rows. In this situation, a simple set of `getXX` and `setXX` methods that simply retrieve the values of properties contained in the JavaBean will not be adequate.

The JDBC API provides methods that, among other things, execute a query and return an object representing the set of results (a `ResultSet` object). Methods within the `ResultSet` class can then be used to iterate through the results. While we could place this code directly into the JSP page, it would involve placing some portion of business logic into the page where it would be visible (and subject to change) for anyone with access to the page.

It is preferable to encapsulate as much business logic for the application into JavaBeans. In order to accomplish this hiding with JDBC operations, principal JDBC methods must be wrapped with Java code and combined into a small, manageable set of methods.

The process of iterating through the `ResultSet` must include the populating of private members of the `CustBean` class with internal calls to its `set` methods. The `next()` method of the class provides this functionality.

Once this method has been called in the JSP script, the properties of the bean will contain the appropriate value and can be rendered on the page using the `getProperty` tag. The following contains an example of this approach.

The sample1.jsp Page

```
1.<HTML>
2.<BODY>
3.
4.<jsp:useBean id="custBean" class="/classes/CustBean" scope="page" />
5.<jsp:setProperty name="custBean" property="userID" value="<%
request.getParameter("userID") %>" />
6.<jsp:setProperty name="pageID" property="pageID" value="P2023" />
7....
8.<%
9.while ( custBean.getNext() ) {
10.%>
11.
12.<tr>
13.<td bgcolor="#E0E0E0"> <jsp:getProperty name="custBean" property="doc_name" />
</td>
14.<td bgcolor="#E0E0E0"> <jsp:getProperty name="custBean" property="message_text"
/> </td>
15.<td bgcolor="#E0E0E0"> <jsp:getProperty name="custBean" property="category" />
</td>
16.<td bgcolor="#C0C0C0"> <a href="viewKB.jsp?pdoc_key=<jsp:getProperty
name="custBean" property="doc_key" />" >View Entry</a> </td>
17.
18.<% if ( !request.getParameter( "action" ).equals( "showthread" ) ) { %>
19.<td bgcolor="#C0C0C0"> <a href="listKB.jsp?pdoc_key=<jsp:getProperty
name="custBean" property="doc_key" />&action=showthread" >Show Thread</a> </td>
20.<% } %>
21.</tr>
22.<%    } // end while %>
23.</BODY>
24.</HTML>
```

In this example, we need to create a JSP page to display a list of customers. Our goal is to limit the amount of Java code that we must expose in the JSP page and to use HTML/JSP tags as much as possible. Fortunately, we have created a JavaBean that encapsulates the database access activities of retrieving the customer information and allows it to be retrieved using calls to its `getXXX` methods. The bean loads a list of customers (through an internal JDBC `ResultSet`) and then allows clients to iterate through that list. A `getNext` method is also exposed to force the bean to move to the next customer in its internal list.

On line 4 of this example, the JavaBean that is to be used for this page is identified in a JSP `useBean` tag. This tag directs the JSP container to load the bean. On lines 5 and 6, parameters required to perform the retrieval of customer records from the database are set.

By the time the `getNext` method is called on line 9, the information needed to retrieve the data has been loaded into the JavaBean. The call to the `getNext` method positions the data retrieval to the first row of the data set returned and internally sets the properties of the `CustBean` object to the appropriate values for the first row retrieved.

Within the `<td>` tags in the table on lines 13 through 15, a series of `<jsp:getProperty/>` tags are then used to retrieve the data and insert it into the output stream for the HTML table that will be created from this JSP page.

The terminating tag for the `while` loop on line 19 forces execution to branch back to line 9, where the `while` loop calls the `CustBean.next` method again. If there are no rows available, the method returns `false` and the `while` loop terminates. If there are rows available, the method once again internally loads the properties (sets the local data members) for the object.

JSP Example: The Calendar Java Beaning

Many business applications work with calendars, requiring presentation controls that display both a calendar and the current date. While many GUI APIs provide controls (or widgets) to display this information, basic HTML does not provide this capability.

Since static HTML cannot provide this capability, JSP/Java is uniquely suited to this task, providing a calendar API that can retrieve the current date and time for the current time zone of the computer and return information about specific dates that can be used to create a calendar display. Since the purpose of this class is to provide a display *widget*, producing the calendar output at a specified point on the page, it should be invoked with a small number of JSP tags and produce the output necessary.

The Java code that generates the output for these tags is required to send output to the response stream `JspWriter`. While on the surface this may appear to break our rule of having separation of presentation logic appearing only on the JSP page and not in the Java code, given our requirements for this widget, this development approach makes sense. A JSP page that uses a calendar JavaBean to display a calendar is shown below.

The cal1.jsp JSP Page

```
1.<HTML>
2.<HEAD><TITLE>
3.      Calendar
4.</TITLE></HEAD>
5.
6.<%@ page errorPage="ErrorPage.jsp" %>
7.<BODY BGCOLOR="white">
8.
9.<h1> JSP Calendar   </h1>
10.<jsp:useBean id="Cal" scope="page" class="JSPCal.Cal" />
11.<b>Current Date:</b> <jsp:getProperty name="Cal"
```

```
12.                       property="currentDate" />
13.<%
14.Cal.printCal( out );
15.%>
16.
17.</BODY>
18.</HTML>
```

This sample JSP page uses a JavaBean to display the contents of a calendar. A jsp:useBean tag on line 10 locates and loads the JSPCal.Cal class and associates the class with the name Cal to be used within this JSP page. The bean is given page scope, since it will only be used for the current page.

Once the bean is loaded, the getProperty tag on line 11 is used to request the currentDate from the bean. As shown in the code below, the currentDate property has the JSP/servlet engine call the getCurrentDate method, which retrieves the current date from the calendar and displays the date in a text string.

Finally, the printCal method is called on line 14 and is passed the out object, which in a JSP page relates to the JspWriter for the output stream (the response) for the page. The results of this operation is a page that appears as shown in Figure 29–2.

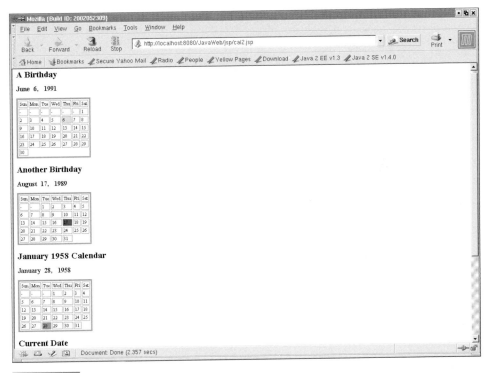

Figure 29–2   *The cal1.jsp page.*

Alternatively, custom tags could be used to display the calendar. Though very similar to the JavaBean approach, the JSP custom tag library provides a cleaner, simpler set of tags to be used in the JSP page, as shown below.

The cal2.jsp Page

```
<html>
<body bgcolor="#FFFFFF">

<%@ taglib uri="/WEB-INF/jsp/TagCal.tld" prefix="tagcal" %>

<H1>A Birthday</H1>
<tagcal:Calendar year="1991" month="6" day="6" highLightColor="pink" />

<H1>Another Birthday</H1>
<tagcal:Calendar year="1989" month="8" day="17"  highLightColor="blue" />

<H1>January 1958 Calendar</H1>
<tagcal:Calendar year="1958" month="1" day="28"  />

<H1>Current Date </H1>
<tagcal:Calendar  />

<H1>Current Date as String</H2>
<H2><tagcal:Calendar dateString="true" /></H2>

</body>
</html>
```

This page loads the tag library using the `taglib` directive, which instructs the JSP/servlet engine to read the `TagCal.tld` to obtain information about how to load the custom tag library class and how to identify the tags. The prefix attribute identifies the prefix to be used when the tags are used on the page.

This tag library uses one tag, the `Calendar` tag, but allows most of the attributes for the tag to be optional. The first use of the tag is to display a specific date (a birthday) specifying a highlight color for the date. The second use of the tag performs the same operation, but this time uses a different highlight color. In the third example, the highlight color is not passed as a parameter (which will cause the tag library to use the default value).

The final use of the `Calendar` tag on this page sets the `dateString` flag to true and does not specify the date for the calendar. The result of using these attributes to invoke the `Calendar` tag (which results in distinct execution of the code) is that the current date is output in text string format. This page produces output as shown in Figure 29–3.

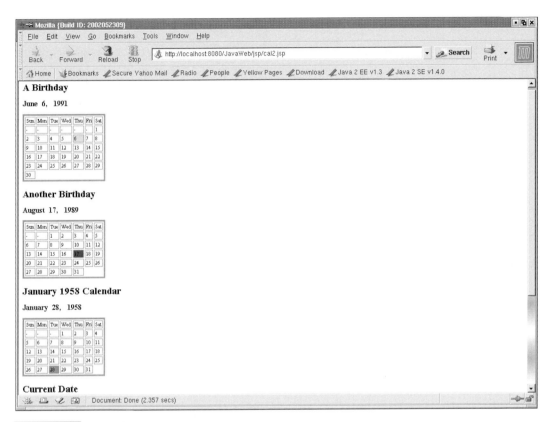

Figure 29–3 JSP cal2.jsp page output.

JAVABEANS VERSUS CUSTOM TAG LIBRARIES

As we can see from these examples, we have two different approaches available to placing content on the JSP page: using JSP scriptlets and tags (getProperty, setProperty) or using custom tags. The differences between the implementation of these two approaches becomes more apparent as we examine the code behind these JSP pages in more detail. While the two approaches share many similarities, there are distinct differences between the structure of the Java code required for each, and later in this chapter we discuss both solutions and provide recommendations on where each is considered appropriate.

The following sections present both approaches, using both the calendar JavaBean and the custom tag library. The first code example uses the JavaBean solution to provide the calendar, and the second example modifies this JavaBean code to create a custom tag to provide the same calendar output.

JSP Calendar: JavaBean Code

The Java code for the calendar bean defines a class named `Cal`, which contains data members and methods to implement the calendar. A series of `getXX` and `setXX` methods within the class are used to access the class methods from JSP `getProperty` and `setProperty` flags.

The `Cal` class uses the `GregorianCalendar` class to create the calendar requested. The `GregorianCalendar` class contains a number of convenience methods to create calendars, including a number of methods to perform date arithmetic and determine the day of the month and day of the week, essential information needed to display a calendar. A number of packages are included in the class, as shown below.

```
package JSPCal;
import java.text.*;
import java.util.*;
import java.io.*;
import javax.servlet.*;
import javax.servlet.jsp.*;
```

Within the body of the `Cal` class, Java `final static` members are created to store the names of the months and the names of the days of the week as well as the abbreviations for the days of the week.

The Cal.java Class

```
...
public class Cal {

// array for months
private static final String[] months = new DateFormatSymbols().getMonths();

// array for days of week in string format
private static String days[] = new DateFormatSymbols().getWeekDays();

// array for day abbreviations
private static String daysAbbrev[] =
  new DateFormatSymbols().getShortWeekdays();
...
```

Locale and Dates

As most Java developers are aware, the display of dates differs depending on the country. Various locales identify a specific country, and Java provides a rich API to support locale-specific formatting. If applications are coded correctly, they can let Java manage this locale-specific formatting for them.

The `Cal` class makes some use of locale by using `java.text.DateFormatSymbols` to generate the array of weekday names. But note that the syntax used here loads these names when the class is loaded (since they are static final variables and thus belong to the class), not at runtime. Since the syntax for the `DateFormatSymbol` constructor does not specify a locale, the locale of the Java runtime environment is used, not the locale of the user accessing the page.

A more robust implementation that needs to support multiple locales based on user logins would need to move the generation of these headings into the constructor for the `Cal` class and then set them based on the known locale of the user, as shown in the code fragment below.

```
...
private static final String[] months;
...
// constructor
public Cal( Locale loc) {
DateFormatSymbols(loc)
months = new DateFormatSymbols(loc).getMonths();
}
```

In this code fragment, the `months` array is declared `static` and `final` (a blank final variable), and must be initialized in the constructor (or all constructors if the constructor is overridden). The constructor is then called with a parameter of type `java.util.Locale`, which is used to set the values of the `months` array. This code assumes that the application has determined the correct locale of the user and passed this information to the constructor.

Internal members are also used to store the month, day, and year of the calendar to be created. A highlight color is defined for the color to use to highlight the current day (and a `setXX` method is available to change this property as needed).

```
// internal date
private int month;
private int day;
private int year;
private String printHighLightColor = "grey";
private Calendar  mCalendar = null;
private JspWriter mOut       = null;
private boolean    dateStringOnly = false;
```

The next block of code defines the bean methods to be used by the bean. A number of `set` methods are defined that can be used via `setProperty` tags in the JSP page. These methods allow the month, day, and year for the calendar to be defined, as shown below.

```
<jsp:setProperty name="Month" value="6" />
<jsp:setProperty name="Day" value="6" />
<jsp:setProperty name="Year" value="91" />
```

The responsibility of the `setXX` methods is to take arguments passed and to apply the value of those arguments to specific local data members (member variables of the class).

```
// Bean methods
public void setMonth( int month ) {
   this.month = month;
}
public void setYear( int year ) {
   this.year = year;
}

public void setDay( int day ) {
    this.day = day;
}
public void setHighLightColor ( String color ) {
    this.printHighLightColor = color;

}

public void setDateString( boolean flag ) {
  this.dateStringOnly = flag;

}

public void setCalDate( int month, int day, int year )
{
    mCalendar = new GregorianCalendar( year,
                                       month,
                                       day );
}
public void setOut( JspWriter out ) {

    mOut = out;
}
```

The `set` method for the current date (`setCalCurrentDate`), as shown below, performs some additional work. The purpose of this method is to get the current date for the system and set the instance of the `calendar` class to that date. (Note that for a Web-based application, this will be the date of the server where the JSPs are running, not the date of the browser that invoked the HTTP request.)

The body of this method begins by creating an instance of `GregorianCalendar` and assigning that to the calendar for the instance. The methods `setDay`, `setMonth`, and `setYear` are then called to set the internal members to these values. Since the `Calendar.month` is zero-based, it is incremented to reflect the use of the month within this class (which is not zero-based but instead starts at the value 1).

```
public void setCalCurrentDate()
{

    mCalendar = new GregorianCalendar();

    setDay(   mCalendar.get( Calendar.DAY_OF_MONTH ));
    setYear(  mCalendar.get( Calendar.YEAR) );
    setMonth( mCalendar.get( Calendar.MONTH )+ 1 );

}
```

The getXX methods are used to wrap the private elements of the calendar and, in the case of the getCurrentDate method, provide convenient access to a date string within a JSP page.

```
// return the Current date (month day, year) as a string
public String getCurrentDate() {

if ( mCalendar == null )
    setCalCurrentDate();

return months[ this.month ] +
               "   " +
               this.day +
               "," +
               "   " +
           this.year;
}
```

The output of this class is a text string with the current date. This could be used in a JSP page as follows. (It should be noted that the output of the Cal.getCurrentDate method is functionally equivalent to DateFormat.getDateInstance(DateFormat.MEDIUM).format(mCalendar.getTime ()), which has the advantage of being non-locale-specific. The approach shown here, however, is intended to take advantage of the internal members of the Cal class.)

```
...
<b>Today's Date:</b>    <jsp:getProperty name="myCal"
property="CurrentDate" />
...
```

The printCal method provides the output to produce calendar output in HTML format. This method takes as an argument the output stream for the response, which with JSP pages is the JspWriter. (This is actually an instance of a class that provides functionality similar to that of the `PrintWriter` class and is not a subclass of `PrintWriter`.) The `printCal` method uses the `JspWriter` output handle to output the resulting calendar. The calendar is produced based on the values of the internal members for the `Cal` class instance.

A local reference is used throughout the method; this is done for convenience and to allow for the easy substitution of a calendar object as a parameter in later revisions of this method. This local reference is first assigned to the internal calendar.

Since the calendar to be output will print all of the days of the month, the `printCal` method starts by setting the internal calendar to the first day of the month using the `set` method of the `GregorianCalendar` class.

```
public void printCal( JspWriter out ) throws ServletException {

Calendar cal = mCalendar;
String printAttr;

// set to the first day of the month
cal.set( Calendar.DAY_OF_MONTH, 1 );
...
```

A `try`/`catch` block is used to catch I/O exceptions for any of the statements that provide output to the `JspWriter` output stream. The output for the calendar is produced within this block.

The first output statement in this block is used to print a header for the calendar. This header displays the date in string format, using the `months` array (which contains the months of the calendar in string format), the `day` member (member variable of the `Cal` instance), and the year of the calendar.

```
...
try {

// print the header
out.println("<H2> " +
            months[ this.month ] +
            "  " +
            this.day +  // day of month
            ", " +
            "   " +
            this.year +
             "</H2>" );
...
```

The next section of the method begins producing an HTML table for the calendar. This section of code currently contains hardcode table attributes, but could be expanded to add additional attributes for the table display.

A table row tag is used to denote the start of a week in the calendar output. Since a table header is needed for the calendar to display the days of the week, a `for` loop is used to loop for seven days (0 to 6 inclusive) and display the days of the week. The days of the week are displayed in text format, using abbreviations stored in the `daysAbbrev` member variable.

```
...
out.println("<table border=3>");

// print the days of the week
out.print("<tr>");
for ( int n = 0; n <= 6; n++ )
    out.print("<td>" + daysAbbrev[n] + "</td>");

out.println("</tr>");
...
```

The next section of code is used to display the days of the week in rows of seven cells (one for each day). Since the first and last rows of output require cells to be produced that may not include a numerical day (i.e., days from the previous month and days from the next month), there is a block of logic that must determine whether or not a numerical day needs to be output. If a numerical day is not displayed, then a dash (-) is output. Additionally, if the day of the week being output is the current day for the calendar (`this.Day`), the day is output using the highlight color attribute. Since Sunday represents the end of the week (in the format used on this calendar), this represents the end of the row and must be output using the table row terminator tag (`</tr>`). Days of the week are represented as integer numbers ranging from 0 to 6.

```
...
// print blanks up to the start day
out.print("<tr>");

// if this is the day of the month highlight the table cell
// using the highlight display attribute
if ( Day == 1 )
    printAttr = "<td bgcolor=" + '"' + printHighLightColor + '"' + ">";
else
    printAttr = "<td>";

if ( cal.get( Calendar.DAY_OF_WEEK) > 1 ) {

    for ( int x = 0;
          x <= ( cal.get( Calendar.DAY_OF_WEEK) - 1);
          x++ ) {

        if ( x < ( cal.get(Calendar.DAY_OF_WEEK )-1) )
            out.print( "<td>" + "-" + "</td>" );
        else
                out.print( printAttr + "1" + "</td>" );
```

```
       if ( x == 6 ) {
           out.println("</tr>");
           out.print("<tr>");
       }
   }
}
else // day_of_week == 1 == 'Sunday'
    out.print( printAttr + "1" + "</td>" );
...
```

The next section of code stores the print attribute for the highlight block for the current day of the month in a string for convenience. A loop is then executed starting from the second element because at least one day of the month (the first day) has been printed in the control previous loop. This control loop continues to process until the value of the loop control variable is greater than the maximum number of days in the month, at which time the loop will terminate.

As in the previous block of code, if the day of the week is the end of the week, as determined by the value of the call to `get ( Calendar.DAY_OF_WEEK)`, then the table row terminator will be printed.

```
...
printAttr = "<td bgcolor=" + '"' + printHighLightColor + '"' + ">";

for ( int n = 2;
      n <= cal.getActualMaximum( Calendar.DAY_OF_MONTH );
      n++ ) {

    if ( n == Day ) // this is the day selected so highlight it
        out.print( printAttr + n + "</td>" );
    else
        out.print( "<td>" + n + "</td>" );

    // print <tr> at end of week
    cal.set( Calendar.DAY_OF_MONTH, n );
    if ( cal.get( Calendar.DAY_OF_WEEK) == 7) {
       out.println( "</tr>" );
       out.print( "<tr>" );
    }
}
...
```

At the end of the processing loop, two tags are output: the table row terminator and the table terminator. An `IOException` catch statement is required for the I/O performed by the `JspWriter` statement.

```
...
out.println( "</tr>" );
out.println("</table>");
```

```
}

catch (IOException e) {

    throw new ServletException("I/O Exception in Cal.printCal() " );

}

}

}
```

Using Custom Tags in JSP

With JSP version 1.1, *custom tag libraries* were introduced. These tag libraries provide a facility for creating custom JSP page tags. They provide a facility in which a common, well-understood approach to page programming, the page tag, can be used to access custom behaviors programmed in Java.

Tags provide a great deal of flexibility and are very effective in hiding the specifics of the operation from the user. For this reason, tags are an excellent mechanism for providing access to business logic to the HTML developer.

These tags resemble HTML tags in the use of a tag name, tag attributes, and a tag body, using the following syntax:

```
<myTag:tagName attribute1="value" attribute2="value">
optional tag body
</myTag:tagName>
```

A tag can be declared that can be inserted into a JSP page. When the JSP container encounters this tag as it preprocesses the page, the underlying code behind the tag is invoked (in the servlet).

Custom tags provide additional value with the ability to perform programming flow-of-control functions within the JSP page. These are operations such as loops or iterations and execution of conditional statements.

Unlike HTML tags, which are just translated into a form that is then rendered on the browser, JSP tags can produce output based on input parameters and can iterate over output, producing various lists and tables in the resulting JSP page.

Coding Tags: Custom Tags and Business Logic

Creating custom tags is more involved than creating a JavaBean and implies some code restrictions. JSP custom tag libraries must implement an interface defined in the `javax.servlet.jsp.tagext` package. While tags offer many significant capabilities to the JSP page, they still do not eliminate the need for scripting. HTML was designed to provide for static page content; it does not provide programmatic flow-of-control statements that are required to perform robust rendering of dynamic content. For this reason, there are many valid purposes for placing scripting elements in a JSP page.

However, the developer must be careful not to confuse the coding of appropriate conditional logic to provide for the creation of the JSP page with the insertion of business logic into the JSP page. Business logic, logic that involves decisions concerning business rules (for example, a rule that indicates that region 1 should be excluded from district 4 totals if this report is for the first quarter), should be placed in *helper classes,* which should, if necessary, be called from within tag code. Decisions that involve the presentation of the page (for example, what color region 1 text should be, what color region 2 text should be) can be included in the page and may require some decision logic. But wherever possible, this logic should be placed in helper classes, thus providing a clear separation of roles and a much more manageable JSP page.

Using a Custom Tag Library: The JSP Calendar Utility

The following section of code uses the calendar creation code shown in the first JSP/JavaBean example to create a custom tag library to display calendar information in a JSP page. Using a JSP tag library requires the implementation of an interface (e.g., `TagSupport`) and the preparation of an XML file, which provides information on the tag library (a `.tld` file). The XML descriptor file is referenced on the JSP page using the `taglib` directive, as shown below.

```
...
<%@ taglib uri="/jsp/TagCal.tld" prefix="tagcal" %>
...
```

This tag indicates that in the `TOMCAT_HOME/webapps/jsp` directory a `.tld` file named `TagCal.tld` is stored. This directs the Tomcat server to read the file and determine how to access the custom tag library that will be referenced on that page, using the `tagcal` prefix. (Note that the `TOMCAT_HOME` directory could instead be the `docBase` directory for the context.)

The tag library descriptor (TLD) file describes the JSP custom tag library to be used by the JSP page. The JSP page is made aware of the TLD by the `taglib` descriptor. Since the TLD is an XML document, there is a corresponding document type definition (DTD) for the document. The first few tags in the document identify this DTD.

```
<?xml version="1.0" encoding="ISO-8859-1" ?>
<!DOCTYPE taglib
 PUBLIC "-//Sun Microsystems, Inc.//DTD JSP Tag Library 1.1//EN"
```

```
"http://java.sun.com/j2ee/dtds/web-jsptaglibrary_1_1.dtd">

<!-- a tag library descriptor -->

<taglib>
...
```

Additional tags are used to indicate the version of tag library being used, the JSP version being used. The short name for the tag library is identified followed by an alternative URI that this tag library may be mapped to. An informational tag provides an entry that describes the tag library.

```
<tlibversion>1.0</tlibversion>
<jspversion>1.1</jspversion>
<shortname>TagCal</shortname>
<uri></uri>
<info>
      Tag library for display of a calendar widget
</info>
```

The next block in the source code file is shown below. This code is used to describe the tag library. This block is identified as the tag block and contains the information most commonly provided by the developer. The tag block contains entries for the name of the tag, the `class` that will be loaded to implement the tag, and some general information about the tag. These entries are made on lines 3, 4, and 5 of the following code listing.

The `class` entry identifies which Java class will be loaded to execute the tag. This class must provide an implementation of `BodyTag` or some other interface in the `javax.servlet.jsp.tagext` package. The name entry identifies the name that will be used to reference the tag.

A large portion of the remaining tag block on lines 7 through 28 is devoted to the various attributes that may be passed to the tag. The attribute is identified followed by a `required` tag, which indicates true or false whether or not the attribute is required for the tag. The example below shows the tags for each of the attributes passed to the `TagCal` calendar example, with tags for the optional attributes of `month`, `day`, `year`, `out` (output), and `dateString` (which sets the boolean `dateString` flag); each of these tags sets the required tag to false, since the attribute is optional. The `bodycontent` tag is used to indicate whether or not the body of the tag will have content. In this example, it is empty.

```
1.
2.    <tag>
3.       <name>Calendar</name>
4.       <tagclass>JSPCal.TagCal</tagclass>
5.       <info> Display calendar</info>
6.
```

```
7.      <attribute>
8.          <name>month</name>
9.          <required>false</required>
10.     </attribute>
11.     <attribute>
12.          <name>day</name>
13.          <required>false</required>
14.     </attribute>
15.     <attribute>
16.          <name>year</name>
17.          <required>false</required>
18.     </attribute>
19.
20.     <attribute>
21.          <name>out</name>
22.          <required>false</required>
23.     </attribute>
24.
25.     <attribute>
26.          <name>dateString</name>
27.          <required>false</required>
28.     </attribute>
29.
30.     <bodycontent>EMPTY</bodycontent>
31.
32.     </tag>
33.  </taglib>
```

The code for the tag library includes a number of `import` statements, which are identical to the JavaBean code, with the exception of the statement to import the `javax.servlet.jsp.tagext` package used to specifically retrieve the tag library interfaces into the class namespace for the program.

```
package JSPCal;

import java.text.*;
import java.util.*;
import java.io.*;

import javax.servlet.*;
import javax.servlet.jsp.tagext.*;
import javax.servlet.jsp.*;
...
```

The major difference between this example and the JavaBean example is in the class definition. A JSP custom tag library must implement one of the interfaces in the `javax.servlet.jsp.tagext` package or extend one of the convenience classes in that package. In this example, the `TagSupport` class is extended, which provides empty body implementations for the methods in the `javax.`

`servlet.jsp.tagext.Tag` interface and thus reduces the amount of work required to create the tag library.

```
public class TagCal extends TagSupport {

// array for months
private static final String months[] = new DateFormatSymbols().getMonths();

// array for days of week in string format
private static final String days[] = new DateFormatSymbols().getWeekdays();

// array for day abbreviations
private static final String daysAbbrev[] = new
DateFormatSymbols().getShortWeekdays();

// internal date
private int month;
private int day;
private int year;

private  String printHighLightColor = "grey";
private Calendar  mCalendar = null;
private JspWriter mOut = null;
...
```

Using Static Variables in JSP Pages

Because many JSP/servlet implementations allow servlet classes to be shared among sessions, the use of `static` variables could potentially create problems, since in Java `static` variables belong to the class, which would in turn be shared among multiple sessions.

But the use of `static` variables in the calendar JavaBean and tag library would not create a sharing conflict, since the variables declared `static` are also declared `final` (which indicate they cannot be changed once they are initialized). They are effectively constants that contain the calendar column headers—the names of the days of the week. As such, they can be shared among multiple objects or multiple JSP/servlet sessions without a problem.

The tag library implementation also adds a boolean flag to indicate the behavior required of the `doStartTag` method. Specifically, this tag is used to indicate that the tag is being used to print the date as a character string and should not print the entire calendar.

```
...
private boolean dateStringOnly = false;
...
```

The `doStartTag` method is the method that is executed when the tag is encountered in the JSP page. The body of this tag is executed *after* the corresponding `setXX` methods have been called for the attributes in tag.

The body of the `doStartTag` method is shown below. This method acts as both a virtual constructor and a `main` program block for the tag. The first few lines of the method check the local members of the tag class to determine whether or not they have been set by the `setXX` methods of the tag (attributes that are not required to be set, as indicated in the TLD). These attributes indicate the date for the calendar to use. If the attributes have not been set, then the tag body assumes that the current date should be used, and the `setCalCurrentDate` method is called. If the attribute values for the date have been set, then the `setCalDate` method is called to set the date for the calendar to the date specified in the attributes. Additionally, if the `JspWriter` output stream has not been specified in an attribute, the output stream is set to the output stream in the page context, as returned by `pageContext.getOut()`.

```
...
public int doStartTag() {

// use the current day as the default date
if ( ( mCalendar == null ) && ( this.month == 0 ) && ( this.day == 0 ) && (
this.year == 0 ) )
    setCalCurrentDate();

if ( ( this.month != 0 ) && ( this.day != 0 ) && ( this.year != 0 ) ) {
    this.month--; // GregorianCalendar expects 0 - based month
    setCalDate( this.month, this.day, this.year );
}

// set the default output stream to the JspWriter in the pageContext
if ( mOut == null )
    setOut( pageContext.getOut() );
...
```

An additional section of this code is shown below. Once all initialization has been done, a simple `if/else` block is used to determine the action to be performed by the tag. If the `dateStringOnly` flag has *not* been set, then the `printCal` method is called to output the HTML calendar for the date specified in the member variables of the calendar. If the `dateStringOnly` flag has been set, then the current date for the calendar (either the current date or the date specified in the attributes) is output as a text string. All of this work is performed in a `try/catch` block, which catches a `ServletException`.

```
...
try {

// print the calendar
if ( !dateStringOnly )
    printCal();
else // print the current date as a string
    mOut.println( getCurrentDate() );

}

catch (ServletException e) {

  System.out.println("TagCal error: " + e.getMessage() );

}
catch (IOException e) {
     System.out.println( "IOException in TagCal: " + e.getMessage() );
}
...
```

When work is complete, the doStartTag method returns a SKIP_BODY flag indicating that processing is complete (there are no additional iterations) and there is in fact no body to process for this tag.

```
...

// the tag shouldn't have a body to process
return (SKIP_BODY);
}
...
```

The class used to turn the calendar JavaBean into a custom tag has an additional method used to set a dateStringOnly flag indicating that the tag should display only the date as a string (and not display the full HTML-formatted calendar). This class data member requires a setXX method to set the value of this flag, as shown below. With the exception of this method, the bodies of the two classes for the JavaBean and the tag library are virtually the same.

```
...
public void setDateString( boolean flag ) {

   this.dateStringOnly = flag;

}
...
```

JAVABEANS OR CUSTOM TAG LIBRARIES: TIPS ON USAGE

JavaBeans and custom tag libraries are two different approaches to the same problem: how to extend the Java code on the JSP page. Since we would like to keep the use of scriptlets on the JSP page to a minimum, we need some mechanism to make use of Java helper classes on the JSP page. JavaBeans provide this capability in such a way that almost any valid Java class could be made into a JavaBean. The only requirement is that any properties accessed using the JSP `getProperty` or `setProperty` tag would require the coding of `get` and `set` methods in the class, using a specific naming convention, but this is not required.

The use of tag libraries with JSP pages is more restrictive in terms of the coding effort but in many ways is more powerful and provides easier access to the library methods on the JSP page. As we have seen here, JSP custom tag libraries require specific Java interfaces to be implemented, and various methods in these interfaces must coded in order for the tag to be executed properly from the JSP page. The integration of existing classes into custom tag libraries would therefore be more difficult than converting the same code into JavaBeans.

One approach to converting existing Java class libraries into custom tag libraries is through the creation of *wrapper classes*, classes that extend the class being converted using methods that consolidate and simplify one or more method call in the class being converted. These wrapper classes can make the conversion process simpler and can make the process of creating a custom tag library easier.

A custom tag library makes sense when there is a requirement to perform an operation repeatedly within an application. This operation could be a general-purpose operation (for example, a calendar) that could be required across multiple applications, or it could be a business-specific operation such as retrieving customer or account information.

Creating a simple custom tag to perform an operation that must be executed repeatedly provides a better solution relative to performing the same operation with several lines of Java code (calling JavaBean methods) in a scriptlet. Essentially, the custom tag approach reduces the lines of Java code (in a scriptlet) that would be required with the JavaBeans approach, and reducing the amount of Java code on a JSP page improves the maintainability of the page and enhances the separation of roles between presentation and business logic. (While it is probably possible to write additional JavaBean methods and reduce the amount of scriptlet code required for a JavaBean approach to this same problem, the custom tag approach would still perform a better job of enhancing the separation of roles.)

The conclusion, then, is that JavaBeans work best with class libraries that map neatly into a `get`/`set` access approach, for instance, providing access to a database record or building a dynamic Web page based on a set of records. And custom tag libraries work best when an operation must be performed repeatedly (as opposed to only once) across many Web pages and the operation does not map easily into a simple `get`/`set` access approach.

MODEL1 AND MODEL2 WEB APPLICATION ARCHITECTURES

Developers of dynamic Web pages quickly realized that coding complex logic into a Web page created development and maintenance problems. This was an issue with early Web page scripting languages even before the introduction of JSP.

The results of early experience with JSP called for a clear delineation of roles for each of the technologies being used. This separation of roles led to some logical conclusions about which technology should be used for which purpose. Because JSP is used in a Web page and a Web page is used for the creation of a presentation, logically JSP should be used just for the creation of dynamic content. Of course, dynamic content can be created using some very complex Java syntax. A JSP can quickly become large and complex just by inserting some control logic to process various request parameters or inserting business logic to handle various business cases. Clearly, some additional direction needed to be provided.

Specifically, this separation of presentation logic from all other logic has led to the creation of several architectural design patterns. The more notable of these design patterns includes the following:

- Model, view, controller
- Model 1, Model 2 architectures
- Java design patterns for Web components

These architectural design patterns are discussed in more detail in the following sections.

Model, View, Controller (MVC)

The model, view, controller (MVC) design pattern dates back to the early days of object-oriented programming to create GUIs. The MVC pattern indicates that components involved in managing a presentation should be created to manage specific tasks. The model component should manage the state information or data used in the creation of the presentation. The view component should manage the interaction with the user and should respond to user actions. The controller should manage the logical flow of the presentation process, processing user actions as returned by the view and sending information to the model so that it can maintain user state (see Figure 29–4).

The MVC pattern is a generic pattern that can be applied to GUI programming with APIs such as Swing but is now frequently used to describe the architecture of Web development frameworks such as Apache Struts. Frameworks are described in more detail in Chapter 33, "Creating a Framework-Based Shopping Cart Application."

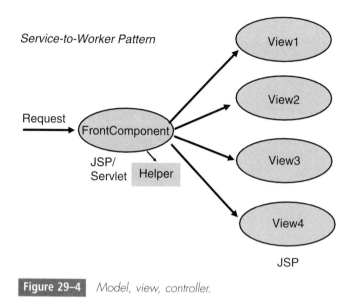

Figure 29–4   *Model, view, controller.*

The MVC pattern has the added benefit of abstracting the view from the control and model; thus the multiple views could potentially share the same model and controller. Using XML and a translation layer can make this possible.

Model 1 and Model 2 Architectures

The Model 1 and Model 2 architectures are applied directly to the task of Web application programming with JSPs and servlets. The Model 1 architecture represents early development with Web page scripting languages, where a great deal of logic was placed in the Web page. A Model 1 architecture JSP page managed the control of the request. The page used some separation of roles in that the management of data and business logic could be managed by JavaBeans or other components, but the management of processing control was handled in the Web page. With simple applications, this did not present a serious problem. But as an application grew more complex, the control processing became more difficult to manage and the JSP quickly became cumbersome and difficult to maintain.

As applications become more complex, the invocation of Web components also becomes more complex. To manage this complexity effectively, and to reuse code as much as possible, Web pages are passed parameters indicating how processing should proceed. The processing of these parameters usually involves a bit of programming logic and could require the use of additional components to make appropriate decisions concerning application state and flow control. It is this processing that the Model 2 architecture addresses.

The Model 2 architecture dictates that a control object be used to manage the flow of a Web application. Usually a servlet, this control object is responsible for parsing any request parameters passed from the client application. The processing of these parameters may require objects to be marshaled, queries to be made, application state to be checked, and the request forwarding location to be indicated; the Model 2 servlet controller is responsible for all of these actions.

This approach to JSP development provides a clearer delineation of presentation logic from business logic. Since the control processing for a Web application can quickly become complex, it is best to move that processing into control components early in the development process. This has the added benefit of centralizing control, making it easier to manage security and application state. Frameworks such as Struts use this architectural approach and provide tools that simplify the creation of the controller. The application demonstrated in Chapters 33, 34 and 35 demonstrate a Model 2 approach to developing a J2EE application.

Java Design Patterns for the Web Tier

There are two Java design patterns for Web application development that provide guidance similar to that of the previous two architectural patterns: the service-to-worker design pattern and the dispatcher view design pattern.

Service-to-Worker Pattern

The `ServicetoWorker` pattern is used to manage applications that must apply a large amount of logic to incoming requests to determine how to process those requests. This pattern is similar to the `DispatcherView` pattern, but differs in the approach to managing the logic. With the `ServicetoWorker` pattern, the logic is processed by the `FrontController` rather than passing that responsibility off to the `View` to make the decisions.

With this design pattern, the request from the client is managed by a `FrontComponent`. The `FrontComponent` evaluates the request and determines which security requirements must be met to handle the request. If business decisions need to be made to manage the request, the `FrontComponent` communicates with a `Helper`, which (playing the same role as a `ViewHelper` in the `DispatcherView` pattern) may in turn interact with a `BusinessDelegate` to accomplish its work (see Figure 29–5).

Once the `FrontComponent` has completed evaluating the logic necessary to make its decision, it forwards the request to the appropriate `View`. The `View` may then refer to a `ViewHelper` to create its dynamic content and build the response for the client.

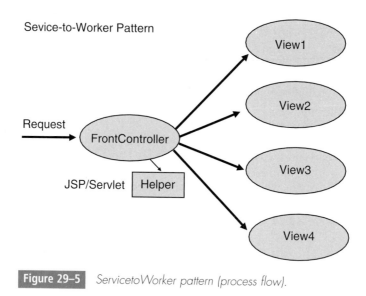

Figure 29–5 *ServicetoWorker pattern (process flow).*

Dispatcher View Pattern

The DispatcherView pattern is applied to applications that require some degree of logic to be applied to the to client requests in order to determine how the client should proceed. With this pattern, a client request is received. This request is examined by a FrontComponent, and decision logic is applied to determine which View should be used to manage the request. Once the View has been chosen, the client request is forwarded to an appropriate View. The View, working with a ViewHelper, is then responsible for generating dynamic content and producing a response to the client request (see Figure 29–6).

Using the Web as our presentation tier, our request is an HTTP request. This request is received and evaluated by the FrontComponent before being forwarded. Since this evaluation process does not involve any presentation to the client (even though it exists on the presentation tier), a servlet is appropriate for this component, though a JSP page could also be used.

Once the FrontComponent has evaluated the request, it forwards the request to an appropriate View. The View has the responsibility of generating the display for the client. It is assumed that this will involve the generation of dynamic content, and therefore the View will require a helper in the form of a component known as a ViewHelper. The ViewHelper performs whatever integration tier or resource tier communication is necessary to formulate the response for the client request. In more simple terms, this means that the View produces the dynamic

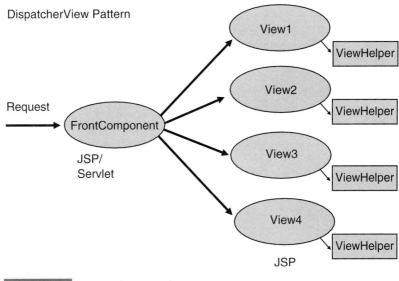

DispatcherView Pattern

Figure 29–6 *Dispatcher view design pattern.*

Web page by using session or application variables and performing database interaction as needed. This will no doubt involve working with other components, which may logically be denoted as belonging to the integration or resource tier in our architecture.

SUMMARY

This chapter covered using JSP to create dynamic Web content. Since we know that we don't want to place too much Java code on the JSP page in scriptlets, we need to have a facility for moving Java code off the page. We have two Java technologies that allow us to do this: using JSP with JavaBeans and using custom tag libraries.

Both approaches to using Java classes on JSP pages were covered in this chapter, using an example that created a set of calendar utilities. The first example used JavaBeans to display an HTML-formatted monthly calendar. Then, to demonstrate the same approach using a custom tag library, the code required to implement the calendar utility as a custom tag library was shown. Finally, we discussed the benefits and drawbacks of each approach and established some guidelines for the use of these two techniques.

The chapter completed with a discussion of Java design patterns which are commonly applied to JSP development. The Model 1/ Model 2 architecture which proposes moving flow-of-control logic out of the JSP view component was also discussed. Chapters 33 through 35 of this text demonstrate an application which uses this approach with the Struts framework.

The next chapter takes a look at a different type of J2EE client application: the Graphical User Interface. This application will be presented as a stand-alone fat client, and then as a thin client which uses an RMI layer to access resources.

CHAPTER 30

Creating Graphical User Interfaces with Java

INTRODUCTION

Up to this point we have focused on using the Web browser to provide the client tier for our J2EE application. While it is clear by now that Web development has distinct advantages especially in the area of deployment, Web applications have their limitations most notably in the quality of the user interface HTML provides. Even with the extensions provided by JavaScript and dynamic HTML (DHTML), the robustness of the interface is simply not as sophisticated as those that can be delivered with a Graphical User Interface (GUI).

Java provides the Swing API which can be used to create GUI clients. In this chapter we will see how to create a GUI that allows a user to enter a database query and then executes the query and displays the results in a table format. But unlike the static presentation of tables with HTML, this application allows the table cells to be resized and the data in the cells to be edited. Application users have the option of committing their changes to the database or optionally resetting their changes and starting over with the editing process.

Java offers several deployment options for GUI applications. The application can be deployed as a standalone GUI, delivered as an applet that will run in a Web browser, or delivered as Webstart client. If an application is written correctly, then it can easily be converted to use these various forms of GUI presentation. In this chapter we will demonstrate the standalone GUI application. In the next chapter we will revisit this example to create a thin client version of the application which uses RMI to implement the database access and then demonstrate the same application implemented as an applet.

THE JAVA GUI

The GUI provides a client interface which uses graphic controls to interact with the end-user. These graphical controls are rendered on the screen as input boxes, check boxes, radio buttons and other objects which make it easier for the user to interact with the computer.

A complete coverage of the Java GUI is beyond the scope of this book and certainly beyond the scope of this chapter. But GUI development does represent a viable alternative for client application development in the J2EE environment and is therefor worthy of some coverage. So that the code examples later in the text are understandable, we will first review some of the basic concepts of a GUI and Java GUI APIs. We will then examine a code example that will bring many of these concepts into focus.

THE ABSTRACT WINDOWING TOOLKIT (AWT)

The Java GUI was developed to be cross-platform and not specific to any particular presentation manager. The presentation environment was abstracted out of the design; thus the name of the toolkit is the Abstract Windowing Toolkit (AWT). The Java GUI has been appended and improved with the introduction of the Swing GUI API, but many of the concepts of the original AWT are still present.

The AWT is centered around the concepts of containers, components, and layouts. A container is an abstract receptacle for components. The component is a high-level abstraction of a GUI object. All GUI objects are a specialization of the component. The AWT provides a `Component` class and most GUI objects are a subclass of this class.

The AWT also provides a `Container` class, which is a subclass of the `Component` class. Containers are used as receptacles for GUI objects. The `Window` and `Panel` classes are subclasses of the `Container` class. The `Window` class provides a free-floating window on the display. The `Panel` component, however, must exist within some other component, such as the `Window`.

Layout managers control the placement of components within a container. Each container has a default layout manager, which can be overridden using the `Container setLayout` method. The class inheritance relationship of the containers and their default layout managers are shown in Figure 30–1.

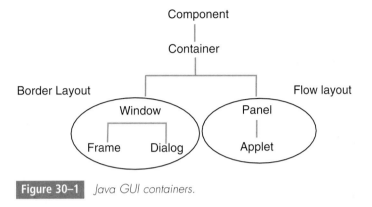

Figure 30–1   *Java GUI containers.*

The Window

The Java window is a primary component of the AWT. A `Window` class instance represents a free-floating window on the display. All `Component` instances for a particular application are placed in the window (using the `add` method) (see Figure 30–1). The layout manager controls specifically where the components will be placed.

The sequence for creating a GUI application is to create a window and then add various frame containers to the window. The components used by the application are then added to the frame containers in the window (see Figure 30–2).

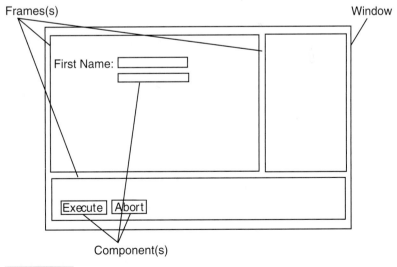

Figure 30–2   *Window construction with containers and components.*

The Layout Manager

GUI presentation managers such as Microsoft Windows, X Windows, and the Apple Macintosh have very specific APIs for controlling the placement of GUI components using specific coordinates in the window or on the screen. To make cross-platform development easier, the Java GUI does not address specific coordinates in the placement of controls but instead using a layout manager to abstract out the details of the GUI environment and provide a simplified facility for component placement.

Layout managers describe where components should be placed in a container and specify the size of the component. Developers can provide general guidelines for the placement of the components and allow the layout manager to manage the details. Java provides five different layout managers as follows.

- FlowLayout
- BorderLayout
- GridLayout
- CardLayout
- GridBagLayout

The *FlowLayout* layout manager places components into the container in a left to right, top to bottom manner. By default, components are displayed with their preferred size and use a centered alignment. These defaults can be changed using the constructor for the layout manager.

The *BorderLayout* layout manager creates sections within the container that roughly correspond to compass points. When components are added to the container, they are added to a specific region. As components are added to a region, they are sized to fill the entire region (see Figure 30–3).

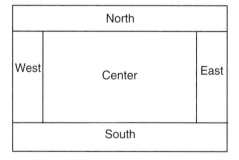

Figure 30–3 *The BorderLayout layout manager.*

The *GridLayout* layout manager divides the container into a grid of evenly sized cells. Components are placed into the cells in the order in which they are added to the container in a left to right, top to bottom manner. When they are added, components are resized to the size of the cell (see Figure 30–4).

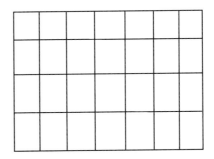

Figure 30–4   *GridLayout layout manager.*

The *CardLayout* layout manager works with a series of components that completely overlap. Only one component in the container can be visible at a time. Applications can move through the card sequentially or can move to a specific card to be displayed.

The *GridBagLayout* layout manager allows for a more finely-grained approach to creating a layout. A rectangular grid of cells is maintained, and components can be placed in one or more cells.

Java GUI Event Handling

When users interact with a GUI application, they perform actions that include but are not limited to moving the mouse around the window, clicking buttons, moving sliders, selecting checkboxes, and entering text into fields. All of these actions must be handled by the application.

To simplify the process of handling these actions, the AWT provides an event-handling mechanism, which has the component generating the event register an event handler for that specific event. These components effectively delegate the responsibility for handling these events to other classes, which is why this approach is referred to as the *delegation model*.

Using the delegation model, the client handlers are registered with the GUI component they are to observe. As the components trigger events (based on user actions), they delegate the handling of those events to the registered handlers. Most components trigger more than one type of event, so multiple handlers are often registered with a component.

THE SWING API

As mentioned previously, the AWT was the original GUI API for Java. Though adequate for some tasks, the AWT had issues such as the somewhat sluggish performance of the components and a lack of some of the more common controls available in other GUI APIs. At a time when PC CPUs were running at a much slower clock rate, the performance of the interpreted Java language running a slow GUI made Java with AWT a difficult choice. While other GUIs provided combo boxes and sliders and 3D buttons—AWT had none of these.

The introduction of the Swing API addressed many of these issues. Swing builds partly on AWT, using the same layout and event-handling framework. But Swing also addresses performance by replacing many of the heavyweight AWT components and containers with more efficient, lightweight versions. Swing includes updated versions of many of the components included in AWT, such as `JFrame`, `JList`, and `JTextField`, as well as new classes such as `JTable`, `JTree`, and `JComboBox`.

THE SWINGGUIDEMO PROGRAM

The following program demonstrates some of the basics of programming with Swing and highlights some of the interesting features of the GUI, such as being able outchange the look and feel of the GUI programmatically. This program generates the window shown in Figure 30–5.

The code for the `SwingGUIDemo` class is shown in the listing below. The `SwingGUIDemo` class extends `JFrame`, allowing us to call `JFrame` methods

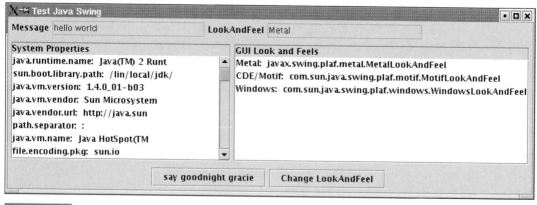

Figure 30–5   *The swing GUI demonstration program.*

directly as instance methods. The application manages the placement of components using the default layout manager for the JFrame the BorderLayout layout manager. In using a common technique for Java GUI programmers, several JFrame instances are created to control the placement of components in that area on the GUI window. These frames are then placed into specific BorderLayout locations in the JFrame container.

The work involved in creating the GUI is encapsulated into a single method. This is accomplished using the go method which creates components and directs their placement in the window using a layout manager. This development approach provides additional flexibility in development and since calling a single method creates the GUI, this also has the benefit of simplifying the process of moving the application to a different GUI delivery medium, such as an applet or Java Webstart application.

The various components used to create the GUI are declared as instance members. This is a convenience mechanism since application code such as event handlers must constantly interact with these components through their object references, having their references easily available as instance members makes the GUI programming process easier.

The main program block shown below we start by creating an instance of the SwingGUIDemo class using the constructor and then calls the go method to create the GUI presentation. The string passed to the constructor will be the name of the window and will appear in the title bar for the window and is simply passed to the superclass (JFrame) constructor.

The go method creates a series of text fields, which cannot be edited by the user (setEditable is called with a boolean false). Several buttons are then created to allow us to demonstrate some user interaction. The buttons are created with a constructor that accepts a single string parameter for the name of the button.

The next step in the creation of the GUI is to populate the list boxes on the page. We do this by generating a list of system properties that are currently in effect. The array returned by the getPropertiesList method (which is part of this class) is used to create a JList component, a GUI list box. This list box is not added directly to the JFrame; it is added to the ScrollPane component, which is added to the JFrame later in this method. The same process is used to create a list box with the names of the currently available look and feel options.

Finally, the scroll panes containing the list boxes are added to the JFrame using the getContentPane method, directing the content to the center of the JFrame.

The next portion of the go method delegates the job of listening and handling events for certain components in the container. We use the addActionListener method to add listeners for the two buttons to be displayed on the JFrame. A window listener is also added using an anonymous object. Since the only action we intend to perform is to close the window when the user chooses the close window button, we simply call the System exit method and close the window.

We then call the `pack` method to pack the components on the frame to make the window presentation more appealing. The `setLocation` method is also called to specify the location of the frame on the display. If this is not done, then the default window location will be used and the window may be placed in a location on the screen where it is difficult to use.

THE SwingGUIDemo Class

```
package examples.clientserver;
import java.awt.*;
import javax.swing.*;
import java.awt.event.*;
import java.util.*;

public class SwingGUIDemo extends JFrame implements ActionListener {

private JTextField   jt1;
private JTextField   jt2;

private JButton      jb1;
private JButton      jb2;
private JButton      jb3;

private JList        jl1;
private JScrollPane js1;
private JList        jl2;
private JScrollPane js2;

private JPanel       jp1;
private JPanel       jp2;
private JPanel       jp3;
private JPanel       jp4;

//
// list of installed LookAndFeels
//
private UIManager.LookAndFeelInfo[] uiList =
            UIManager.getInstalledLookAndFeels();
private int lfIdx;

boolean jtToggle;

    public static void main( String[] args) {
            SwingGUIDemo  g = new SwingGUIDemo("Test Java Swing");
          g.go();
    }
```

```
void go() {

        try {

            //
         // create a text field that cannot be edited
         //
         jt1 = new JTextField( "hello world", 20 );
         jt1.setEditable( false );

         //
         // create a text field and set it to the value
         // of the current look and feel
         //
         jt2 = new JTextField(
                    UIManager.getLookAndFeel().getName(), 20 );
         jt2.setEditable( false );

            //
         // create two buttons
         //
            jb1 = new JButton("say goodnight gracie" );
         jb1.setName("hwButton");
         jb2 = new JButton( "Change LookAndFeel" );
         jb2.setName("lfButton");
         jb3 = new JButton("Close");
         jb3.setName("closeButton");

         //
      // create two list boxes
      // one list box will contain the current values of
         // the system properties
      // the other list box will contain the
         // GUI 'look and feel' packages that can be
         // used (but may not be installed)
      //
         //
      // get a list of system properties
      //
         Object[] propNames = getPropertiesList();
         //
         // create the list box with our list of property
         // names
         //
         jl1 = new JList( propNames );
         //
         // place the list box in our scroll pane
         //
      js1 = new JScrollPane( jl1 );
      js1.setColumnHeaderView(
                    new JLabel("System Properties" ));
```

```
    //
  // get a list of look and feel names
  //
  Object[] lfNames = getLFNames();

    //
    // create a list box with our list of
    // GUI look and feel names
    //
    jl2 = new JList( lfNames );

    //
    // place the list box in our scroll pane
    //
  js2 = new JScrollPane( jl2 );
  js2.setColumnHeaderView(
            new JLabel("GUI Look and Feels" ));

    //
    // add the message text boxes
//
    JPanel jp3 = new JPanel(
            new FlowLayout( FlowLayout.LEFT ) );
    jp3.add( new JLabel( "Message" ));
    jp3.add( jt1  );
    jp3.add( new JLabel( "LookAndFeel" ));
    jp3.add( jt2 );
  getContentPane().add( jp3, BorderLayout.NORTH );

    //
    // display the scroll panes into our first panel
//
    JPanel jp1 = new JPanel( new FlowLayout() );
jp1.add( js1 );
jp1.add( js2 );

    //
    // place the first panel with the list boxes
    // in the center of the frame
    //
    getContentPane().add( jp1, BorderLayout.CENTER );

    //
    // center the buttons by using FlowLayout's
// alignment
//
    JPanel jp2 = new JPanel( new FlowLayout() );
  jp2.add( jb1 );
  jp2.add( jb2 );
    //
    // add the buttons to the bottom of the frame
    //
```

```
        getContentPane().add( jp2, BorderLayout.SOUTH   );


        //
        // listen for button events
        //
        jb1.addActionListener( this );
        jb2.addActionListener( this );


        //
        // quick and dirty way to manage window closing
        //
        addWindowListener(
                new WindowAdapter() {
                        public void
                                windowClosing(WindowEvent e)
                                { System.exit(1); }
                } );

        pack();

        //
        // default location on some systems is
        // upper right hand corner
// so we override that
//
        setLocation(200,200);
        setVisible(true);
        }
        catch (Exception e) {
                e.printStackTrace();
        }

}

SwingGUIDemo( String s ) {
    super(s);
}

SwingGUIDemo() {
    super();
}
```

The Event Handlers

Since the `SwingGUIDemo` class implements the `ActionListener` interface and registers itself as the event handler for the GUI events that will be triggered by the application, all we need to do is declare the method to be called for the event we care about.

We have created two buttons in the application and assigned this object as the handler. As we can see in the code shown next, we need to provide an imple-

mentation of the `actionPerformed` method. This method is passed an
`ActionEvent` object. We then provide a set of conditional statements to evaluate
the `ActionEvent` object to determine which button was pressed and react
accordingly. If the `hwButton` was pressed, we alternately display a "hello world"
or a "goodnight gracie" message using the `setText` method to change the text in
the text field.

If the `lfButton` has been pressed, then application changes the look and feel of
the existing GUI. This is done by setting the look and feel from the current list of look
and feel options available. Then, for each component in the frame, the `updateUI`
method is called to recognize the changes made since they were displayed.

```
//
// event listener for the button events
//
public void actionPerformed( ActionEvent e ) {

    //
    // if the button name was 'hwButton', change the value of the text field
    // toggle to two different values
    //
    if ( ((JButton) e.getSource()).getName().equals("hwButton") ) { // alterna-
tive - e == jb
        if ( !jtToggle ) {
            jt1.setText( "goodnight gracie" );
            jt1.setFont( jt1.getFont().deriveFont( Font.ITALIC ) ); // change
this to italic
            jtToggle = true;
        }
        else {
            jt1.setText( "hello world" );
            jt1.setFont( jt1.getFont().deriveFont( Font.PLAIN ) ); // change this
to italic
            jtToggle = false;
        }

    }

    //
    // if the button name is 'lfButton',
    // then toggle the look and feel of the GUI
    //
    if ( ((JButton) e.getSource()).getName().equals("lfButton") ) {

        toggleLookAndFeel();
            //
        // display the current "look and feel"
        //
        jt2.setText( uiList[lfIdx].getName() );

            //
```

```
            // update the button "look and feel"
            //
            jb1.updateUI();
            jb2.updateUI();

               //
            // update the scroll pane "look and feel"
            //
            js1.updateUI();
            js2.updateUI();

               //
            // update the text fields
            //
            jt1.updateUI();
            jt2.updateUI();
        }

}
```

The getProperties and getLFNames Methods

The getProperties and getLFNames methods shown next create arrays of objects to be used in the list boxes (JList), as shown below. The getProperties method obtains an enumeration of the System properties. The method iterates through the enumeration, and for each property name, it retrieves the value of the system property and stores the value in a Vector (java.util.Vector) object. When this loop is complete, the Vector is converted into an array and returned. The getLFNames loop performs a similar operation, storing data into a Vector and converting the Vector into array (which is what a JList box requires).

The toggleLF method simply maintains a pointer for the current location in the array of valid look and feel names. If the array pointer is too high, it is reset to the first element in the array. When an array element has been selected, the setLookandFeel method is called with the className for the class to be set as the look and feel for the application. Note that this approach does not update the individual components in the JFrame. The individual components must call the updatedUI method to be updated to the appropriate look and feel for the component.

```
//
// return an array of system properties
//
Object[] getPropertiesList() {

    String propName = null;
    Properties  p = System.getProperties();
    Enumeration e = p.propertyNames();
    Vector v = new Vector();
```

```
        String s = null;
        while ( e.hasMoreElements() ) {

            propName = e.nextElement().toString();
            s = p.getProperty( propName );

                //
                // limit the string length of the value to 15 characters
            //
            if ( s.length() < 15 ) {
                 s = s.trim();
             }
             else {
               s = s.substring(0,15);
             }
            v.add( propName + ":   " + s);
        }

        return v.toArray();


    }


    //
    // return an array of GUI 'look and feel' names
    //
    Object[] getLFNames() {
        uiList = UIManager.getInstalledLookAndFeels();
        Vector v = new Vector();

        for ( int i = 0; i < uiList.length; i++ ) {
           v.add( uiList[i].getName() + ":   " +
                    uiList[i].getClassName() );
        }

        return  v.toArray();
    }

void toggleLookAndFeel() {

 try {
        lfIdx++;
        if ( lfIdx == uiList.length ) {
            lfIdx = 0;
        }
         UIManager.setLookAndFeel( uiList[lfIdx].getClassName() );
 }
 catch( Exception e) {
        System.out.println("Error: " + e.getMessage());
 }
}


}
```

SAMPLE APPLICATION: THE TABLE BROWSER APPLICATION

The application demonstrated here uses the Swing API to create a GUI window that displays the results of a query in a tabular format and allows the user to modify those results and apply updates to the database (see Figure 30–6). The user can delete rows from the table display and have those deletes applied to the database table. The user can also insert rows into the table display and have those inserts applied along with other updates directly to the database table.

We will first look at a version of this application as a client/server type of application, where the client works with the data and updates directly to the database using a *data access object (DAO)*.

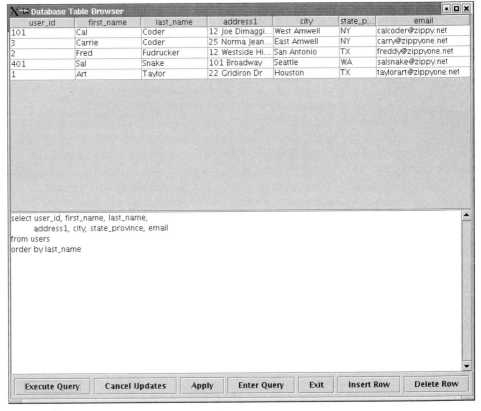

Figure 30–6   *Table browser database application.*

We will trace through the process of converting it to a Remote Method Invocation (RMI)-based application, where the client will retrieve the DAO through RMI and interact with the database through remote calls to the DAO.

Because of the design of the objects we use here, the application is amenable to conversion to an RMI application. The results of the query are aggregated in an object that is passed to the client in one call, thus avoiding network traffic in trying to access the database a row at a time. Updates are then applied to the aggregate value object and applied to the database (through the DAO) all at once, in a *lazy updates* fashion, thereby reducing the network traffic of trying to access the database a row at a time.

The general DAO (GeneralDAO) is used to execute the query and access the database, and the aggregate value object (GeneralAggregateVO) is used to cache the results and updates to the results on the client. (These general design pattern implementations are shown in Chapter 35.)

TECHNICAL APPROACH

The table browser application, for simplicity in presentation and because it is a Swing application, implements both the client and presentation tiers in a single class: the TableBrowser class. This class contains all of the component references needed to display the GUI and to manage the user interaction. This means that all event handlers are contained in this class as inner classes. (At 400 lines, this is not an unmanageable class, but in the development of a production system, you could argue to refactor the inner classes for the event handlers and table data model to external classes.)

Looking at the screen grab in Figure 30–6, you can see the major functions that need to be performed by the application: Enter a query, execute a query, insert data, update data, delete data, apply changes to the database, cancel any pending updates, and exit the application. The advantages of having flexible and robust business objects become clear when you examine the implementation of this demonstration application. Before we begin looking at the code, let's first examine the operation of the application.

Enter Query and Execute Query

The *enter query* option clears any text in the text field in the lower part of the GUI window and allows the user to enter a new query. The *execute query* option reads the text in the lower portion of the window and attempts to execute it as a query using the general DAO (a GeneralDAO) instance. If the query is successful, then the general DAO loads its internal aggregate value object (a GeneralAggregateVO) instance) with the values from the query. The event handler that is managing the execute query option retrieves the aggregate value object from the DAO and uses it to display the GUI tabular window used to display the data.

Insert, Update, and Delete Functions

The insert and update operations are mapped directly to general aggregate value object operations, so they are effectively cached in the aggregate value object until the user decides to apply them to the database (using the apply updates operation). As you will see when you examine the code, the event handlers for the buttons that allow the user to execute these operations simply map to one or two calls in the general aggregate value object.

The delete operation is handled differently. Because of the potential headaches involved in caching delete operations (such as managing an internal phantom row), deletes are handled immediately when the user requests the operation. The user is first prompted whether or not he or she really wants to delete, as seen in Figure 30–7 (we give the user a second chance), and if he or she elects to delete, the delete is performed immediately against the database, using the DAO to perform the operation.

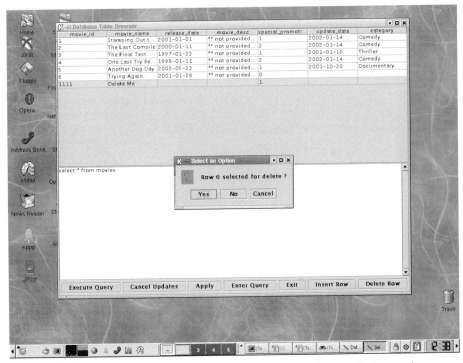

Figure 30–7 *The delete operation prompts the user for confirmation before performing the delete.*

Apply Changes

Once the user chooses the apply changes option, the event handler simply maps the call to a single DAO method to apply the updates in the general aggregate value object to the database. This option does not make any decisions concerning concurrency but simply applies the updates that have been done (they are flagged in the general aggregate value object) to the database.

Clear Updates and Exit

The clear updates option allows the user to clear any updates that have been done in the GUI (and have been automatically reflected in the internal general aggregate value object). The event handler maps this call to the general aggregate value object method to clear its internal flags. This method does not refresh the aggregate value object from the database. The exit option does as the name implies: exits the application. It does not attempt to apply (nor does it check for) any existing updates.

The TableBrowser Class: Class Declaration and Instance Members

Various object references for the GUI components are declared at the start of the TableBrowser class definition. Declaring them here as instance members with visibility throughout the class allows them to be accessed easily. Buttons are declared to allow the user to initiate processing. Buttons are provided for executing the query currently loaded into the table browser, for canceling any updates the user may have entered, for deleting the current row, for inserting a new row, and for exiting the program.

A text area is created and placed at the bottom of the window. A table (JTable) is created and placed at the top of the window. A data table model object (dtModel) reference is declared and used to map the program data (as stored in the aggregate value object) to the GUI table (a JTable instance). The code for this program block follows:

```
package examples.clientserver;
import javax.swing.*;
import javax.swing.table.*;
import java.sql.*;
import java.awt.event.*;
import java.awt.*;

public class TableBrowser {
```

```
//
// store internal data
//
private GeneralAggregateVO gvo;
private GeneralDO          gdo;


//
// query string set to default value
//
private String            query = "select * from movies";

//
// GUI components
//
private JFrame     frame;

//
// buttons
//
private JButton    enterQuery;
private JButton    executeQuery;
private JButton    cancelUpdates;
private JButton    executeUpdate;
private JButton    executeInsert;
private JButton    executeDelete;
private JButton    exitButton;
private JButton    deleteButton;

//
// panels
//
private JPanel     buttonPanel;
private JPanel     contentPanel;

//
// text area for entering a query
//
private JTextArea queryText;

//
// table for data display and update
//
private JTable     table;

//
// store data for JTable
//
dataTableModel dtModel=null;
```

TableBrowser.java: main Program Block

The `main` program block contains a small number of method calls that are used to start the application. The methods retrieve data, load it into the instance members of the `TableBrowser` class instance, and then start the GUI.

A `TableBrowser` instance is created first on line 6. This instance is then used to invoke the `getData` method, which does as the name implies: gets data to be used in the program. Once the data has been loaded, the GUI can be created and used to display the data. This is done through a call to the `buildGUI` method on line 19. The code for this program block is shown next.

```
1.public static void main( String args[] ) {
2.
3.        //
4.        // create table browser
5.        //
6.        TableBrowser tablebrowser = new TableBrowser();
7.
8.        //
9.        // get data from database
10.       //
11.       System.out.println("Loading data ... ");
12.       tablebrowser.getData();
13.
14.       //
15.       // build the GUI, display the data
16.       // and allow user edits
17.       //
18.       System.out.println("Starting GUI ... ");
19.       tablebrowser.buildGUI();
20.
21.}
```

The TableBrowser Class: The getData Method

The `getData` method performs the steps necessary to execute the default query used by the program and uses the results to display the GUI window. This could be a complex process, but fortunately for us, we have a DAO to manage most of the details of this operation.

The method begins by creating a DAO on line 6. This is an instance of the `GeneralDAO` class shown previously. The `GeneralDAO` instance is then used to execute the query on line 11. The `executeQuery` method of the `GeneralDAO` executes the query and loads the results of the query into the internal data members of the `GeneralDAO` instance.

Internally, the `GeneralDAO` instance is using an aggregate value object to store the retrieved data. In this application, we use that aggregate value object, an instance of `GeneralAggregateVO`, within the application to provide for the display of the data and allow updates of the displayed data without having to perform expensive database interaction. For that reason, the internal aggregate value object of the DAO is retrieved and stored in the `TableBrowser` program on line 30 in the internal instance member `gvo`. The code for this example follows:

```
1.protected void getData() {
2.
3.        //
4.        // create general Data Access Object for dynamic queries
5.        //
6.        gdo = new GeneralDAO();
7.
8.        try {
9.            // execute the query and store results
10.           System.out.println("Executing query: " + query );
11.           gdo.executeQuery( query );
12.        }
13.       catch (SQLException e) {
14.
15.               System.out.println(
16.                  "SQLException in TableExample1. Message: " +
17.                  e.getMessage());
18.           JOptionPane.showMessageDialog( null,
19.                     "Database error on load. Message: " +
20.                            e.getMessage(),
21.                            "Error",
22.                            JOptionPane.ERROR_MESSAGE);
23.        }
24.
25.       //
26.       // get the GeneralAggregateVO - aggregate
27.       // Value Object with data and access methods
28.       //
29.       System.out.println( "Retrieving VO ... " );
30.       gvo = gdo.getGeneralAggregateVO();
31.
32.
33.       //
34.       // display dialog box about rows loaded
35.       //
36.       JOptionPane.showMessageDialog( null,
37.                       "Loaded " +
38.                               gvo.getRowCount() + " rows.",
39.                       "Message",
40.                    JOptionPane.INFORMATION_MESSAGE);
41.
42.}
```

The TableBrowser Class: The buildGUI Method

The `buildGUI` method shown next does as you might expect: It builds the GUI. This method makes heavy use of Swing classes. If you are not familiar with Swing, this may seem confusing, but understanding the basic concepts and approach will help you understand how JDBC and database access fit into all of this.

The first few lines of the method on lines 6 through 8 are used to create the frame (an instance of `JFrame`), which is used for the window of the GUI. The `contentPanel` object is used to place the various GUI components used in this window.

On line 13, the data table model is created. This object is used by `JTable` to gather and display the contents (the data) for the `JTable`. This object, which will be shown later, essentially just wraps the aggregate value object returned by the DAO. The table for the display of the data is created on line 16 and passed this same data table model (created on line 13).

The scroll pane is created on line 21. This is a GUI component that allows another component, in our case the `JTable`, to scroll within a region of the window.

On line 27, a window listener is added. This is used to allow the window to close gracefully if the user clicks on the close window button for the window. (Neither Swing nor AWT provide this by default.)

On line 36, a text area is created to provide for the display of the default query string and to allow the user to enter a new query string. Lines 36 through 38 describe the dimensions of the area and the behavior of the component. On lines 43 through 46, a scrolling region is created for the text area.

On line 51, a method is called to create the buttons and button handlers for the various buttons that will populate the bottom of the window.

Finally, starting on line 62, the components are added to the window. Using the layering approach of Swing, components are added to scroll panes or panels, and it is the underlying pane or panel that is added to the window. The window (or `JFrame` instance) uses a default layout manager to display the components. This layout manager is known as the `BorderLayout` layout manager and controls the placement of the components based partly on compass locations (north, south, east, west, and center). Since we have three basic components to add, we can just place them in north, center, and south, and let the layout manager stretch the component to fit the window. We place the data output table in the north, the query text input field in the center, and the buttons in the south. When all of this work is complete, the calls on lines 77 and 78 display the window. The code listing for this method is next.

```
1.protected void buildGUI() {
2.
3.        //
4.        // create the frame and content pane
5.        //
```

```
6.          frame = new JFrame("Database Table Browser");
7.          contentPanel = new JPanel(new BorderLayout());
8.          frame.setContentPane(contentPanel);
9.
10.          //
11.          // load our table model with the data using our object instance
12.          //
13.          dtModel = this.new dataTableModel(   );
14.
15.          // create GUI table
16.          table = new JTable( dtModel );
17.
18.          //
19.          // add the table to the scrollpane
20.          //
21.          JScrollPane scrollpane = new JScrollPane( table );
22.          scrollpane.setPreferredSize( new Dimension( 700, 300 ) );
23.
24.          //
25.          // set the window closing event
26.          //
27.          frame.addWindowListener(new WindowAdapter() {
28.                  public void windowClosing(WindowEvent e) {
29.                          System.exit(0);
30.                  }
31.          });
32.
33.          //
34.          // text area for query input
35.          //
36.          queryText = new JTextArea( query, 5, 80 );
37.          queryText.setLineWrap( true );
38.          queryText.setWrapStyleWord( true );
39.
40.          //
41.          // create a scrollpane for the text area
42.          //
43.          JScrollPane queryPane = new JScrollPane( queryText );
44.          queryPane.setVerticalScrollBarPolicy(
45.                          JScrollPane.VERTICAL_SCROLLBAR_ALWAYS);
46.          queryPane.setPreferredSize(new Dimension(250, 250));
47.
48.          //
49.          // create buttons and handlers
50.          //
51.          createButtonsHandlers();
52.
53.          //
54.          // add all constituent panels and panes to the contentPanel
55.          //
56.
57.          // ** add the components to the window **
```

```
58.
59.       //
60.       // data output
61.       //
62.       contentPanel.add( scrollpane, BorderLayout.NORTH );
63.
64.       //
65.       // query
66.       //
67.       contentPanel.add( queryPane, BorderLayout.CENTER );
68.
69.       //
70.       // buttons
71.       //
72.       contentPanel.add( buttonPanel, BorderLayout.SOUTH ); // buttons
73.
74.       //
75.       // now let's roll ...
76.       //
77.       frame.pack();
78.       frame.setVisible(true);
79.
80.}
```

The TableBrowser Class:
The createButtonHandlers Method

The `createButtonHandlers` method creates the action event handlers for the button-click events; this is the code that is executed when the user presses a button. All of the buttons that appear in the bottom panel of the window are created and then added to the panel in this method. (Not all handlers for the button are handled; this method creates listeners for the most common event, the button click, which causes the GUI to fire the `actionPerformed` event.)

Since this represents a significant portion of the processing done in the program, it is worth covering each handler separately.

The createButtonHandlers Method: Button Declarations

The `createButtonHandlers` method begins by creating the button components to be used in the application. These button components are `JButton` objects, which are declared in sequence in the following code.

```
protected void createButtonHandlers() {

    //
    // create some buttons and corresponding listeners
    //
    enterQuery    = new JButton ( "Enter Query" );
```

```
executeQuery    = new JButton ( "Execute Query" );
cancelUpdates   = new JButton ( "Cancel Updates" );
executeUpdate   = new JButton ( "Apply" );
executeInsert   = new JButton ( "Insert Row" );
executeDelete   = new JButton ( "Delete Row" );
exitButton      = new JButton ( "Exit" );

// button listener/handlers
exitButton.addActionListener( new ActionListener() {
      public void actionPerformed( ActionEvent e) {
            System.exit(0);
      }
  } );
```

The executeInsert Button Handler

The executeInsert button is pressed by the user to insert a new blank row into the table in the GUI window. This method uses the aggregate value object (gvo) to call the appendRow method. This appends a blank row onto the end of the current aggregate value object (which is controlling the display of the table). Once the row has been appended to the aggregate value object, the fireTableStructureChanged method is called to inform the GUI that the table (and the data that supports the table) has changed. This forces the GUI to update the table, which it does by rereading each row of the underlying data object, the GeneralAggregateVO object instance. The aggregate value object now has an additional row with a row of blank columns, which displayed by the GUI window. This method is shown next.

```
// button listener/handlers
executeInsert.addActionListener( new ActionListener() {
      public void actionPerformed( ActionEvent e) {

            gvo.appendRow(); // append a new row
            dtModel.fireTableStructureChanged();

      }
  } );
```

The executeDelete Button Handler

The executeDelete button is used by the user to delete the current row (the row where the cursor is currently located). To avoid much of the confusion that would stem from trying to track deleted rows before performing an update, this method performs delete operations by deleting the row directly from the database, refreshing the aggregate value object by calling the executeQuery method and then informing the GUI table that the data has changed. The end result is that the table will be displayed with the deleted row removed from the table view.

It is always good policy to prompt users before allowing them to actually delete something, and that policy is followed in this example. First, the method obtains the currently selected row by calling the getSelectedRow method of the JTable class. This method returns an integer, which is assumed to be the row the user wishes to delete. If the method returns a value of –1, that means that for some reason, there is no current row. If the getSelectedRow method did return a valid value, then just to be sure, the user is prompted to confirm the delete of the row.

If the user has confirmed that yes, he or she would really like to delete the row, then the row is deleted. Note that the general DAO is used to call the deleteRow method. So, unlike the other operations, which operate on the aggregate value object (gvo) and then apply their updates to the database at some later time, the TableBrowser class applies delete operations immediately and then refresh the TableBrowser class data by executing the query again with a call to the executeQuery method.

At this point, the data in the aggregate value object has been refreshed and can be used for the application. The call to getGeneralAggregateVO is used to set the internal GeneralAggregateVO method to the new value provided by the GeneralDAO.

After the successful conclusion of the updates, a message is displayed to the user indicating that the row selected has been deleted. Finally, the fireTableDataChanged method is called. This forces the GUI to redisplay the table with the new data. The complete code for this example is shown next.

```
// button listener/handlers
executeDelete.addActionListener( new ActionListener() {
     public void actionPerformed( ActionEvent e) {

          // this method will go directly to the database and
          // delete the row and then execute the query again
          // to refresh the data


        //
        // determine which row to delete
        //
     int confirm  = 0;
        int row = table.getSelectedRow();
     if ( row == -1 ) {
             JOptionPane.showMessageDialog(
                         null,
                          "No row selected for delete.",
                          "Error",
                     JOptionPane.ERROR_MESSAGE);
        }
     else {      // we have a row to delete. get confirmation
             confirm = JOptionPane.showConfirmDialog(
                     null,
                 "Row " + row + " selected for delete ?");
```

```
        }

    if ( confirm == JOptionPane.YES_OPTION ) {
      try {
            gdo.deleteRow( row );
            gdo.executeQuery( query );
            gvo = gdo.getGeneralAggregateVO();

    // if at this point, success
        JOptionPane.showMessageDialog( null,
              "Row " + row + " has been deleted.",
              "Message",
          JOptionPane.INFORMATION_MESSAGE);
      }
      catch (SQLException ex) {
          System.out.println(
             SQLException on query execution. Message: " +
                          ex.getMessage() );
          JOptionPane.showMessageDialog( null,
                  "Error on query execution. Message: " +
                    ex.getMessage(),
                    "Error",
                    JOptionPane.ERROR_MESSAGE);
      }
    }
    else {                    // user chose not to delete

        JOptionPane.showMessageDialog( null,
                    "No rows deleted.",
                    "Message",
                JOptionPane.INFORMATION_MESSAGE);
    }

    // this will redraw the table
    dtModel.fireTableStructureChanged();

  }
} );
```

The executeQuery Button Handler

The executeQuery button is used to execute the query currently defined for the application. The action listener uses calls on executeQuery in the general DAO to execute the current query. The listener first calls the queryText textfield to retrieve any query that may be there and passes the resulting query string to the executeQuery method.

Once the executeQuery method has been called, a popup window is displayed with a message indicating the query has been executed. The prompt also displays the number of rows returned by the query, as returned by the getRowCount method of the aggregate value object.

When the user prompt has been completed, the `getGeneralAggregateVO` method is called on the general DAO. This returns the new aggregate value object for the query that has just been executed by the general DAO. Since the table structure has changed (the underlying data has changed), the `fireTableStructureChanged` method is called to redraw the GUI table. The code listing for this handler is shown next.

```java
executeQuery.addActionListener( new ActionListener() {
    public void actionPerformed( ActionEvent e) {
        // use DynamicQuery object to execute the query
        // and process the results
        try {
            gdo.executeQuery( queryText.getText() );
            JOptionPane.showMessageDialog(
                            null,
                            "Loaded " + gvo.getRowCount() +
                            " rows.",
                        "Message",
                    JoptionPane.INFORMATION_MESSAGE);

            //
            // get the new GeneralAggregateVO
            //
            gvo = gdo.getGeneralAggregateVO();
            dtModel.fireTableStructureChanged();
            dtModel.fireTableDataChanged();
        }
        catch (SQLException ex) {
            System.out.println(
              "SQLException on query execution. Message: " +
                ex.getMessage() );

            JOptionPane.showMessageDialog(
                            null,
                            "Error on query execution. Message: " +
                            ex.getMessage(),
                            "Error",
                            JOptionPane.ERROR_MESSAGE);
        }
    }
} );
```

The enterQuery Button Handler

The job of the `enterQuery` button is to allow the user to begin entering a new query in a blank text field. It does this by calling the `setText` method in the `JTextField` class; this clears the text and makes the field ready for input. The code listing for this example follows.

```
enterQuery.addActionListener( new ActionListener() {
    public void actionPerformed( ActionEvent e) {
            queryText.setText( "" );
    }
} );

executeUpdate.addActionListener( new ActionListener() {
        public void actionPerformed( ActionEvent e) {
            //
            // execute all pending updates
          //
        try {
            gdo.applyUpdates( );
            JOptionPane.showMessageDialog( null,
              "Updates applied to database.",
                  "Message",
               JOptionPane.INFORMATION_MESSAGE);
        }
        catch (SQLException ex) {
                System.out.println(
            "SQLException on query execution. Message: " +
            ex.getMessage() );
         JOptionPane.showMessageDialog(
                    null,
                "Error on query execution. Message: " +
                    ex.getMessage(),
                "Error",
             JOptionPane.ERROR_MESSAGE);
        }
    }
} );
```

The cancelUpdates Button Handler and Adding to Panel

The `cancelUpdates` button allows the user to cancel any updates that have been applied to the `GeneralAggregateVO` object. This `actionHandler` simply calls the `clearUpdates` method of the `GeneralAggregateVO` object instance (`gvo`). This clears all update flags in the current object instance.

The final lines of this method are used to add the buttons that have been created to the `buttonPanel`, a blank panel. Button handlers are displayed in the sequence in which they are added to the panel. The code for this listing follows:

```
cancelUpdates.addActionListener( new ActionListener() {
    public void actionPerformed( ActionEvent e) {
            gvo.clearUpdates();
            JOptionPane.showMessageDialog( null,
                    "Updates were cleared.",
                    "Message",
```

```
                        JOptionPane.INFORMATION_MESSAGE);
            }
    } );

    //
    // create a panel for the buttons and add them
    //
    buttonPanel = new JPanel();
    buttonPanel.add( executeQuery );
    buttonPanel.add( cancelUpdates );
    buttonPanel.add( executeUpdate );
    buttonPanel.add( enterQuery );
    buttonPanel.add( exitButton );
    buttonPanel.add( executeInsert );
    buttonPanel.add( executeDelete );

}
```

THE TABLEBROWSER.JAVA APPLICATION:
THE DATATABLEMODEL INNER CLASS

Inner classes in Java provide a very useful syntax to obtain the concise encapsulation of the business logic while still maintaining class scope for the contents of the class. The inner class in this example is used to control the table displayed by the GUI. In this case, the class extends the AbstractTableModel class and overrides certain methods so that they return sensible values for this data model.

The getColumnCount and getRowCount methods return a count of the current number of the rows and columns in the model. These methods map directly to the GeneralAggregateVO object (gvo) stored as an instance member of the application.

The getValueAt method takes an integer row and column argument, and uses the internal general aggregate value object to position to the designated row. The gvo getObject method is then used to retrieve an object reference for the designated column. The code for this example is shown next.

The getColumnName method simply returns the column name for the designated integer column. This implementation maps to the general aggregate value object method to return the column name. The isCellEditable method returns a boolean false if the cell is not editable. In this example, the value is set to return true to facilitate the processing of the example. The getColumnClass method returns the class of the column in the cell. In this example, the class is set to return the class of an Object with each call.

```
class dataTableModel extends AbstractTableModel {

boolean updateFlag = false;  // set true if we have pending updates
```

```
  public int getColumnCount() {
      return gvo.getColumnCount();
  }

  public int getRowCount() {
      return gvo.getRowCount();
  }
  public Object getValueAt(int row, int col) {
      gvo.absolute( row );
      return  gvo.getObject( col );
  }

public String getColumnName( int col ) {
      return gvo.getColumnName( col );
  }

  public boolean isCellEditable( int row, int col ) {
      return true;
}

  public Class getColumnClass( int col ) {
      return new Object().getClass();
  }
```

The dataTableModel Inner Class: The setValueAt Method

The setValueAt method is called by the GUI event loop when a cell is edited. It receives arguments for the value, the row, and the column. These values are passed into the method, which then sets the values of the internal objects to the appropriate values.

The method takes the updateFlag and sets its value to true. This is a flag used by the application to track updates in the dataModel. The generalAggregateValue object is then moved to the current row with a call to its absolute method, using the row value passed into the method. Next, the updateObject method is called and passed the column to update and the corresponding value. Finally, the GUI table is updated using the fireTable CellUpdated method call. The code for this method follows.

```
public void setValueAt(Object value, int row, int col) {

        // set the update flag
        updateFlag = true;

        // update the gvo
        gvo.absolute( row );
        gvo.updateObject( col, value );
        fireTableCellUpdated( row, col ); // update just this row
```

```
    }

        }
}
```

SUMMARY

This chapter introduced the basics of GUI programming with Java. While Web-based development has the notable benefit of making application deployment much easier, it is difficult to create a user interface on a Web application that can approach the robustness of a GUI application developed using Swing.

We first examined the basic nature of GUI development with Java and then learned by example with a simple application that displayed a frame with some common GUI controls. We then progressed to a more complex example that provided a database table browser, allowing the user to enter a SQL query, return the results to a GUI table, and then modify the data and update the database. Our application of Java design patterns abstracted the specifics of database access to data access objects (DAOs), allowing us to keep our GUI application code focused on maintaining the user interface.

In our next chapter we revisit the table browser application and refactor it to be a thinner client by removing the database access code from the local client application and invoking the code using a remote object. We do this using RMI, as shown in Chapter 19, "Additional RMI Concepts"; at the same time, we make some changes to our application to make it more user friendly, adding a menu and eliminating the need to enter a query to populate the GUI table with data.

CHAPTER 31

Using Swing Applications with RMI

INTRODUCTION

As we have know the multi-tiered architecture for J2EE application development contains *client tier* application components that are focused on managing the user interface. This would involve rendering the display for the user and responding to user interaction. The client tier component should not be concerned with database access or any other aspect of the business logic of the application.

But the GUI example shown in the previous chapter did not adhere completely to these architectural rules. This application was essentially a two-tiered application, with the GUI application representing one tier and the database used to store the application data representing the other tier.

A good portion of the GUI application was devoted to managing the user interface, but database interaction, considered business logic, was also included since the DAO and the aggregate Value Object were part of the application. Using our rule of 'separation of roles' we would prefer to have the database interaction and any associated business logic managed in application code that was not on the client tier. We can partially accomplish this with our GUI application by moving the database interaction, which is conveniently encapsulated in the DAO, to another tier. As we have saw in Chapter 18, Java provides a very convenient facility for converting virtually any object into a remote object—RMI.

As we will see in this chapter, because we have applied the DAO design pattern, the process of moving database access (as encapsulated in the DAO) to another tier is relatively simple. We simply need to convert our local DAO to a remote RMI object. This remote DAO exposes the same pertinent methods as our local DAO, but executes those methods remotely (see Figure 31–1).

As we saw in Chapter 18, Java RMI allows us to create a remote object and communicate through that object using a predetermined interface. We do not cover the details of RMI here. Just recall that our remote object will run in a remote location and the local program will communicate with the object by proxy using local stubs.

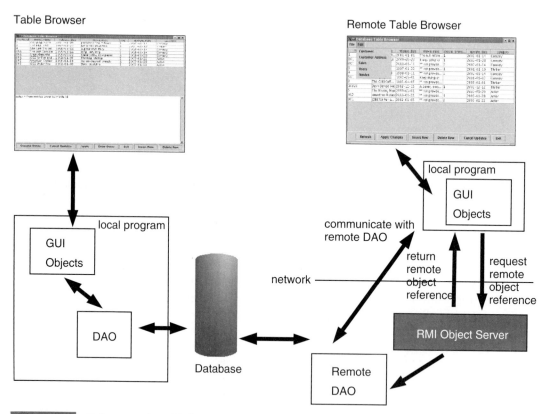

Figure 31–1   *Refactoring the table browser application to use remote objects.*

As part of the effort to refactor this application to use remote objects, we also make the application more user friendly. Instead of requiring the user to type in a SQL query to populate the table, we provide a drop-down menu to allow the user to choose a table (or subject area) for data viewing and editing. This requires us to add a menu to the top of the application frame, remove the scrolling text field from the bottom of the frame, and remove the buttons for clearing, entering and executing the query (see Figure 31–2) shows this modified version of the table browser application.

Database Table Browser

File   Edit

movie_id	movie_name	release_date	movie_desc	special_promo...	update_date	category
1	Stamping Out t...	2001-01-01	The null refere...	1	2002-01-14	Comedy
801	Crazy/Beautiful	2000-05-23	It was either cr...	1	2002-01-28	Comedy
601	The Last Com...	2000-01-11	** not provide...	2	2002-01-14	Comedy
3	The Final Test	1997-01-22	** not provide...	1	2001-01-10	Thriller
4	One Last Try B...	1998-01-11	** not provide...	2	2002-01-14	Comedy
501	Trying Again	1992-03-01	Keep trying an...		2001-01-02	Comedy
2	The Cold Coff...	1993-04-05	** not provide...		2002-01-01	Thriller
10923	Sushi Served Hot	2002-12-15	A clever, plod...	1	2002-12-12	Thriller
5	The Missing Man	2000-03-01	** not provide...		2002-01-20	Action
902	American Outlaw	2000-01-23	** not provide...	1	2003-01-28	Action
901	J2EE for Fun a...	2002-01-05	** not provide...	2	2003-01-22	Action

Apply Changes   **Insert Row**   **Delete Row**   **Cancel Updates**   **Exit**

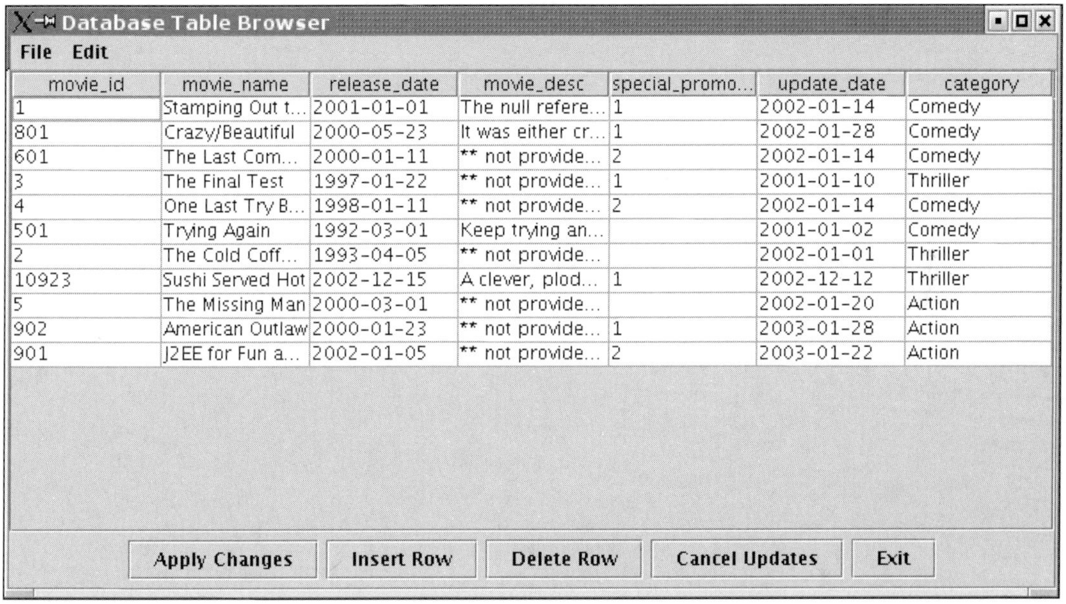

Figure 31–2   *User-friendly table browser application.*

To provide a clear example, this demonstration uses a separate set of classes to implement these changes, but the existing classes could easily have been refactored. For the sake of brevity, only those methods and declarations that have changed are shown.

Creating the Remote DAO

In order to be able to use our remote DAO, we must convert the existing DAO, an instance of the `GeneralDAO` class, to a remote object using RMI. We do this by simply extending the `GeneralDAO` class and overriding the methods we will call remotely, as shown in the following code (and shown in Chapter 35).

The RemoteGeneralDAO Class

```
package db;

import java.sql.SQLException;
import java.rmi.RemoteException;
import common.ValueObjectException;

public class RemoteGeneralDAO extends GeneralDAO implements RemoteDAO {

public void executeQuery ( String query )  {
 try {
   super.executeQuery( query );
 }
 catch (SQLException e ) {
     System.out.println("SQLException e: " + e );
 }
 catch (ValueObjectException e ) {
     System.out.println("SQLException e: " + e );
 }

}

public void applyUpdates ( AggregateVO gvo ) {
//
// apply the gvo before applying the updates,
// to get the two in synch
// this is needed for RMI access of the gdao
//

try {

   //
   // load the general aggregate value object passed in
   //
   this.loadAggregateVO( gvo );

   //
   // apply updates
   //
   this.applyUpdates();
}
catch (ValueObjectException e)  {
      logger.error(
         "ValueObjectException in applyUpdates: " +
          e.getMessage() );
}
catch (SQLException e)  {
      logger.error(
         "SQLException in applyUpdates: " +
          e.getMessage() );
}
```

```
}

public AggregateVO getGeneralAggregateVO() throws RemoteException {

        return gvo;
}

// load aggregate vo
public void loadAggregateVO( AggregateVO  gvo ) {

    this.gvo = gvo;

}

public void deleteRow( int row )   {

  try {

      // delete our current row
      resultSet.absolute( row + 1 );
      resultSet.deleteRow();
  }
  catch ( SQLException e ) {
        System.err.println("SQLException e: " + e );
  }

}

}
```

The `RemoteDAO` interface identifies the methods to be used remotely. It is not necessary to expose all the methods of the DAO remotely; only those that need to be used in the client (the table browser application) need to be identified in the interface. The following code listing shows the interface declaration:

The RemoteDAO Interface Declaration

```
import java.rmi.*;
import java.sql.*;

public interface RemoteDAO extends Remote {

public void executeQuery( String query ) throws RemoteException;

public void applyUpdates( AggregateVO gvo ) throws RemoteException;

public AggregateVO getGeneralAggregateVO() throws RemoteException;

public void deleteRow( int row ) throws RemoteException;

}
```

All remotely accessed methods must throw a `RemoteException`. All parameters passed and values returned must implement the `Serializable` or `Remote` interface. For our purposes, we need only execute the query using the execute query method, apply any updates that the table browser performs using the `applyUpdates` method, return the aggregate value object using the `getGeneralAggregateValue` object method, and delete a row using the `deleteRow` method. You may notice that the `applyUpdates` version used in this remotely accessed DAO example is different from the local DAO version shown previously; this version takes an aggregate value object as an argument. The reason for that is explained shortly.

The code for the table browser client application requires minor modifications. The changes need to be made in the portion of the application that retrieves the DAO. Since this DAO is going to be a remote object, we need to provide the code to retrieve the object correctly. The following code demonstrates this process. The boldfaced portion of the code shows what has changed in the `getData` method. The instance of the `GeneralDataAccessObject`, the object that neatly encapsulates all of our data access, is retrieved using the JNDI name server with a call to the `lookup` method. This returns what we've identified as a reference that implements the `RemoteDAO` interface (not the `GeneralDAO` class type used in the client/server example). (When using RMI, the object returned from the `lookup` call is always treated as an implementation of an interface, not a class.) Once the reference is retrieved from the `lookup` call, the code for accessing and using the DAO is unchanged, with the minor exception of the `applyUpdates` call, shown next.

The RemoteTableBrowser Class: The getData Method

```
protected void getData() {

    try {
    //
    // create general Data Object for dynamic queries
    // do a lookup to retrieve the remote object
    //
    System.out.println("Getting RemoteDAO ... " );
    gdo = ( RemoteDAO ) Naming.lookup( "remote_general_dao" );

        //
        // execute the query and store results
        //
    System.out.println("Executing Query ... " );
        gdo.executeQuery( query );

        //
        // get the GeneralAggregateVO -
        // aggregate Value Object with data and access methods
        //
    System.out.println("Retrieving gvo ... " );
```

```
    gvo = gdo.getGeneralAggregateVO();

}
catch (SQLException e) {

        System.out.println(
    "SQLException in TableExample1. Message: " +
    e.getMessage());
        e.printStackTrace();
        JOptionPane.showMessageDialog( null,
                    "Database error on load. Message: " +
                    e.getMessage(),
                    "Error",
                    JOptionPane.ERROR_MESSAGE);
}
catch (Exception ex) {
        System.out.println(
            "RemoteException in TableExample1. Message: " +
            ex.getMessage());
        ex.printStackTrace();
}
finally {

// print message about rows loaded
if ( gvo != null ) {
    JOptionPane.showMessageDialog( null,
                    "Loaded " +
                        gvo.getRowCount() + " rows.",
                    "Message",
                JOptionPane.INFORMATION_MESSAGE);
}
}
}
```

The RemoteGeneralDAO Class:
The applyUpdates Method

The applyUpdates method is responsible for applying the updates that have been cached in the aggregate value object to the database, using the internal updatable ResultSet of the DAO. When using a remote object server such as RMI, the remote object is running in a separate Java virtual machine (JVM), quite possibly on a completely different server.

   In the previous table browser example, the client application executed a query using the DAO. The DAO loaded the results of the query into an aggregate value object, which was an instance member of the DAO. This aggregate value object was returned as an object reference to the client application—the table browser. The table browser then applied updates to this same aggregate value object, and when it was time to update the database, the table browser application called the `applyUpdates` method.

The `applyUpdates` method requires an aggregate value object to apply the updates, but the method declaration in the DAO did not specify an argument for an aggregate value object. This is because the DAO contained an instance member that was the aggregate value object used to update the database. This reference was appropriately enough the same aggregate value object being updated by the table browser application.

But now we are doing our processing a little bit differently. We are using a remote object server, and any data passed to and from a remote object using method invocations is *passed by value*. This means that a new object reference is being created in the client code to receive the object from the server. For this reason, with the RMI version, the table browser client is working with a *different* aggregate value object reference than the DAO running on the RMI server. So, to apply the updates from the client application, the `applyUpdates` method must be changed to accept an aggregate value object reference, and then that object reference must be used to apply the updates. The following code shows how this was done (see Figure 31–3).

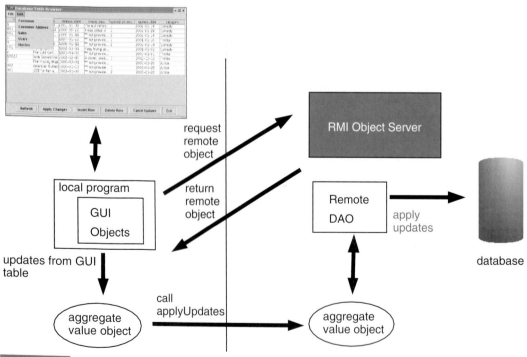

Figure 31–3   *Passing an object reference to the RemoteDAO*

The `applyUpdates` method for the RMI version of the table browser (RemoteTableBrowser) takes the aggregate value object argument (a GeneralAggregateVO instance) and calls the `loadAggregateVO` method with the same argument. After making that call, it calls the `applyUpdates` method with no argument; this method uses the internal aggregate value object (which has just been set to the value of the argument passed in) to apply the updates. The `loadAggregateVO` method, as shown below, simply takes the aggregate value object reference passed in and assigns the internal reference to that value.

The RemoteGeneralDAO Class: The applyUpdates Method

```
public void applyUpdates ( GeneralAggregateVO gvo ) throws SQLException,
RemoteException {
//
// apply the gvo before applying the updates, to get the two in synch
// this is needed for RMI access of the gdao
//

try {

    //
    // load the general aggregate value object passed in
    //
    this.loadAggregateVO( gvo );

    //
    // apply updates
    //
    this.applyUpdates();
}
catch (Exception e)   {
        System.out.println( "Exception in applyUpdates: " + e.getMessage() );
        throw new RemoteException( e.getMessage() );
}

}

public void loadAggregateVO( GeneralAggregateVO  gvo ) throws SQLException,
Exception {

    this.gvo = gvo;

}
```

RemoteTableBrowser: Adding a Menu

As we mentioned earlier in this chapter, in order to make the application more user friendly, we are going to remove the requirement that the user enter and execute a query to populate the browser table and replace that functionality with a series of menu options. These menu options allow the user to simply select the table he or she would like to browse. When the user selects the menu option, a pre-set query is executed to populate the browser table with values. To implement this feature, a MenuBar reference has been added as an instance member to the RemoteTableBrowser class, and a createMenus method has been written, as shown below.

The createMenus Method

```
protected void createMenus() {

    //
    // instantiate a menu bar and assign
    // the reference to our instance member
    //
    menuBar  = new JMenuBar();


    //
    // create our menus
    //
    fileMenu = new JMenu("File");
    editMenu = new JMenu("Edit");

    //
    // populate our menus
    //
    editMenu.add( new CustomAction("Customer") );
    editMenu.add( new CustomAction("Customer Address") );
    editMenu.add( new CustomAction("Sales") );
    editMenu.add( new CustomAction("Users") );
    editMenu.add( new CustomAction("Movies") );

    //
    // add our menus to our menu bar
    //
    menuBar.add( fileMenu );
    menuBar.add( editMenu );

}
```

The createMenus method is called as the GUI is being built. This method creates the menu bar and then creates two menus: a file menu (currently unused) and an edit menu. The argument passed to the add method of the JMenu class must be an object that implements the javax.Swing.Action interface. In this case, we have created a CustomAction class, which implements this interface.

When the menu options are selected at runtime, the actions reference is used to trigger the action for the menu option the user has selected. The code for the `CustomAction` inner class is shown next.

CustomAction Class

```
public class CustomAction extends AbstractAction {
private String name;

public CustomAction( String s) {
          super(s);
          name = s;
      }
public void actionPerformed( ActionEvent e ) {

try {

          //
          // execute the query to populate the table
          // the query is stored in the queries hashtable
          // and referenced by the 'name' of the query
          // we are executing (as stored in our private
          // instance member)
          //
          gdo.executeQuery( (String)
                            queries.get( name ) );

          //
          // retrieve the aggregate value object
          // which stores the results of the query
          //
          gvo = gdo.getGeneralAggregateVO();

          //
          // let the data model know the data
          // has changed
          //
          dtModel.fireTableStructureChanged();
}
catch (RemoteException exception) {
      System.out.println(
          "RemoteException in actionPerformed: " + exception.getMessage());
}
catch (SQLException exception) {
      System.out.println(
          "SQLException in actionPerformed: " + exception.getMessage());
}

}

} // end inner class
```

The `CustomAction` class is declared as an inner class in this example to make it easier to access the various instance members it will need to perform its work. The class is declared to extend the `AbstractAction` class, which provides an implementation of the `Action` interface. The class constructor takes the name of the `CustomAction` passed in, calls the superclass constructor, and then stores the name in an instance member.

The `actionPerformed` event is called by the GUI engine when the user selects a menu option. This method does nothing with the `actionEvent` object reference passed into the method, but instead uses the `name` instance member to determine the name of the query to run. This name is then used to execute the query using the internal DAO used by the `RemoteTableBrowser`. The actual query to execute is stored in a `Hashtable`, which has been populated with the queries to execute (shown next).

Once the query has been executed, we retrieve the aggregate value object used by the DAO and then inform the GUI model that data has been updated. This forces the GUI engine to update the table in the frame.

A `Hashtable` is used to store the queries to be executed by the menu options. These queries are keyed by the query name, which is identical to the name we have associated with the `CustomAction` and stored in the instance member of the `CustomAction` object. The `loadQueries` method provides this functionality, as shown below.

```
protected void loadQueries() {

queries = new Hashtable();

// load the queries that will drive the application
queries.put( "Customer",
             "select * from customer order by last_name");
queries.put( "Customer Address",
             "select * from customer_address");
queries.put( "Users",
             "select * from users order by last_name");
queries.put( "Sales",
             "select * from sales order by order_number");
queries.put( "Movies",
             "select * from movies order by movie_name");

}
```

RMI Binding for the Remote Object

Before the remote object can be used, it must be bound into an RMI registry, as we saw in Chapter 18, "Using Remote Method Invocation." The process of binding the object into the RMI registry provided by Sun Microsystems with the JDK involves the following code. This code instantiates an object reference, which implements the `java.rmi.Remote` interface and the interface with the remotely invoked methods for the DAO we are using. The object is then bound into the RMI namespace using the `naming.rebind` method.

Together, JNDI and RMI provide a number of options for providing access to remote objects; using the RMI registry is only one option. Other options allow objects to be bound into LDAP or other directory servers and the namespaces for those servers integrated into the RMI accessible namespace. These other servers and registries provide additional features and performance benefits that may make them a better choice for RMI than the default registry provided by Sun Microsystems.

bindRemoteGeneralDAO.java

```
package examples.jndi;

import java.rmi.*;
import javax.naming.*;

public class bindRemoteGeneralDAO {

public static void main( String args[] ) {

try {

//
// this object should implement the Remote interface
//
RemoteGeneralDAO rgdao = new RemoteGeneralDAO();

//
// bind the object into a namespace
//
System.out.println( "Binding RemoteGeneralDAO ... " );
Naming.rebind( "remote_general_dao", rgdao );

}
catch (Exception e) {
   System.out.println( "Exception in main: " + e.getMessage() );
}

} // end main

}
```

USING APPLETS

Applets are yet another alternative for developing Web components. One of the major advantages of applets is that the deployment process is greatly simplified. The applet application is deployed automatically and does not reside on the user's machine. When an applet is run, it operates within a *container*. Just as with servlet and EJB containers, this container manages the specifics of the operating system and creates a consistent environment for the applet. (In fact, the applet container was the first Java operating environment container—servlets and EJBs came later.) (See Figure 31–4.)

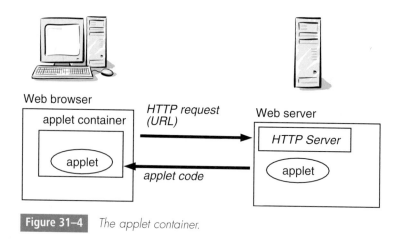

Figure 31–4   *The applet container.*

This container implementation makes the process of running applets across a variety of platforms and environments easier. Since the applet does not need to reside on each machine where it will be used, the person responsible for deploying the application does not need to be concerned with the specific configuration of each machine.

But there is also a downside to using applets. Since the applet does not reside on the user's machine, it must be downloaded each time it is used. This could be a time-consuming process for larger applications. Applets are also designed to run in a fairly restrictive security environment by default and are usually not allowed access to local machine resources. While this promotes security, it does create problems for applications that must have some access to local system resources on the computer where the applet is being run. These restricted local system resources include any peripherals attached to the computer, including the hard disk, the printer, and network connections. This creates interesting problems for applications that must use the network (which includes most database applications). By default, an applet is only able to establish a network connection back to the machine from which it is downloaded.

An applet can be made to run in a less restrictive security environment, but this involves the use of security certificates and digitally signed code (JAR files), which can complicate the deployment process.

In our applet table browser example, the applet must communicate with the remote object, which we assume will be running on another computer (certainly not on the client). This requires a network connection, which we assert will be back to the computer from which the applet was downloaded. The end result is the application that looks like the `RemoteTableBrowser` application and runs within an applet window (see Figure 31–5).

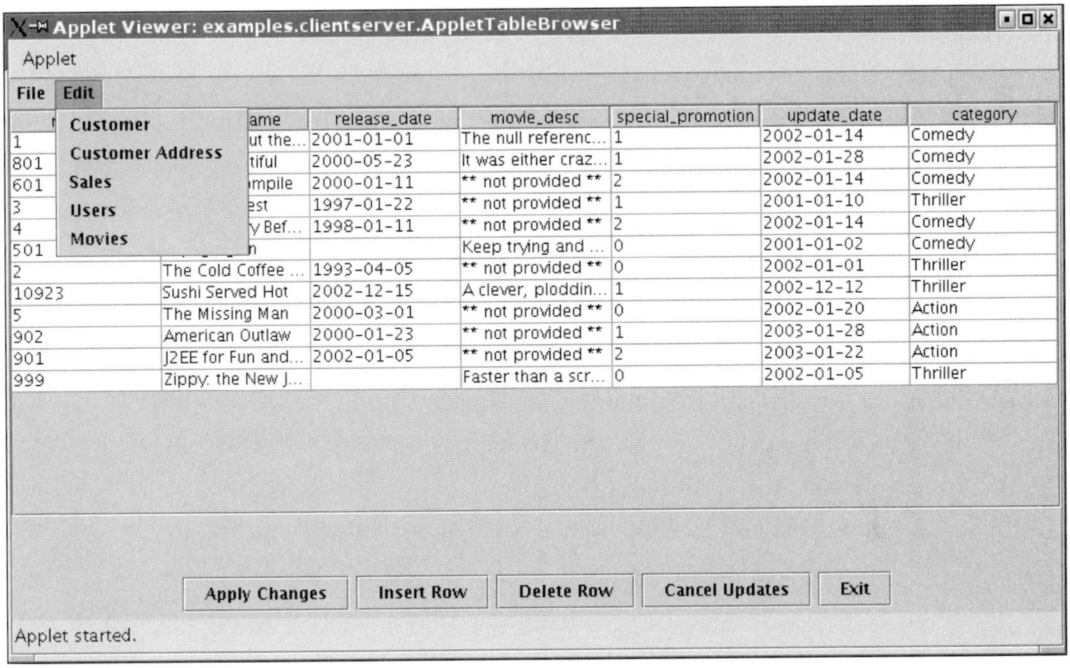

Applet Viewer: examples.clientserver.AppletTableBrowser

Applet

File	Edit							
		ame	release_date	movie_desc	special_promotion	update_date	category
1	**Customer**	ut the...	2001-01-01	The null referenc...	1	2002-01-14	Comedy
801	**Customer Address**	tiful	2000-05-23	It was either craz...	1	2002-01-28	Comedy
601	**Sales**	mpile	2000-01-11	** not provided **	2	2002-01-14	Comedy
3	**Users**	est	1997-01-22	** not provided **	1	2001-01-10	Thriller
4	**Movies**	y Bef...	1998-01-11	** not provided **	2	2002-01-14	Comedy
501		n		Keep trying and ...	0	2001-01-02	Comedy
2	The Cold Coffee ...		1993-04-05	** not provided **	0	2002-01-01	Thriller
10923	Sushi Served Hot		2002-12-15	A clever, ploddin...	1	2002-12-12	Thriller
5	The Missing Man		2000-03-01	** not provided **	0	2002-01-20	Action
902	American Outlaw		2000-01-23	** not provided **	1	2003-01-28	Action
901	J2EE for Fun and...		2002-01-05	** not provided **	2	2003-01-22	Action
999	Zippy, the New J...			Faster than a scr...	0	2002-01-05	Thriller

| Apply Changes | Insert Row | Delete Row | Cancel Updates | Exit |

Applet started.

Figure 31–5   *Table browser application running as an applet.*

For brevity, our discussion focuses only on those portions of the application that have changed. Since we are using the `JApplet` class for our applet, all of the Swing API we have used is valid. The majority of the code that has changed to make this conversion is in the `buildGUI` method, which creates the enclosing frame and places the application controls in the frame.

The first change worth noting is the class declaration for our controlling application. We now identify this class as extending `JApplet`, as shown below. This allows the class to be run within an applet container.

```
public class AppletTableBrowser extends JApplet {
```

The `buildGUI` method is responsible for constructing the GUI. Whereas the previous examples of building this GUI created a frame and then obtained a content pane from that frame, we must manage our content pane differently with an applet. Since the content pane is provided by the applet container and our class type extends `JApplet`, we can simply call the `getContentPane` method to obtain our content pane. We then proceed to add components to our content pane, just as we did with the previous examples. Since we are refactoring our `RemoteTableBrowser`, we will not be placing a scroll area on the page as we did with our first table browser application. We simply add two panels: the scroll panel for the table used to store our data and a panel for our buttons. We then add a menu bar to the enclosing frame. Since the frame is encapsulated in our `JApplet` instance (which is our GUI application), we simply use this reference to call the `setJMenuBar` method.

```
protected void buildGUI() {

    //
    // create the content pane
    //
    Container contentpane = getContentPane();

    //
    // load our table model with the data
    // using our object instance
    //
    dtModel = this.new dataTableModel(  );

    // create GUI table
    table = new JTable( dtModel );

    //
    // add the table to the scrollpane
    //
    JScrollPane scrollpane = new JScrollPane( table );
    scrollpane.setPreferredSize(
              new Dimension( 700, 300 ) );

    //
    // create buttons and handlers
    //
    createButtonsHandlers();
```

```
//
// create the menu
//
createMenus();

//
// add all constituent panels and
// panes to the contentPanel
//
contentpane.add( buttonPanel,
                 BorderLayout.SOUTH ); // buttons
contentpane.add( scrollpane,
                 BorderLayout.NORTH ); // output


//
// add the menu
//
this.setJMenuBar( menuBar );
```

}

In this version of the table browser, as in the RemoteTableBrowser version, we do not require the user to enter and execute a query to populate the data table in the GUI. To implement this change, we need to remove the code in the createButtonsHandlers method, which creates the buttons and their handlers. We show this code as commented out in the code below, though in practice this code would be removed completely.

```
protected void createButtonsHandlers() {

    //
    // create some buttons and corresponding listeners
    //

    // we don't show enterQuery or
    // executeQuery buttons for this version
    //
    //enterQuery     = new JButton ( "Enter Query" );
    //executeQuery   = new JButton ( "Refresh" );
    //

    cancelUpdates = new JButton ( "Cancel Updates" );
    executeUpdate = new JButton ( "Apply Changes" );
    executeInsert = new JButton ( "Insert Row" );
    executeDelete = new JButton ( "Delete Row" );
    exitButton    = new JButton ( "Exit" );

    // button listener/handlers
...
```

We also need to remove the code that places the button handlers onto the button panel, as shown next.

```
...
      //
      // create a panel for the buttons and add the
      // buttons required.
      //
      // We no longer use a refresh or enter query
      // button
      //
      //buttonPanel.add( enterQuery );
      //buttonPanel.add( executeQuery );// refresh
      //

      buttonPanel = new Jpanel();
      buttonPanel.add( executeUpdate ); // apply updates
      buttonPanel.add( executeInsert ); // insert row
      buttonPanel.add( executeDelete ); // delete row
      buttonPanel.add( cancelUpdates ); // cancel
      buttonPanel.add( exitButton );
...
```

The corresponding action listener event is also removed from the code (though without the buttons, it could not be executed by the user). This is done as follows.

```
//
// remove the action listener code for buttons
// we have removed
//
//      executeQuery.addActionListener( new
//                     ActionListener() {
//       public void actionPerformed( ActionEvent e) {
//
//              try {
//                  gdo.executeQuery( query );
...
```

To run the applet, it must be referenced in an HTML file using an applet tag. The following code listing provides a minimal implementation of an HTML page that would launch the `AppletTableBrowser` application.

```
<head>
 <title>Applet Example 1</title>
 </head>
 <body>
```

```
    <hr>
<h1>Applet Example 1</h1>

<!--
   needs to be run with ./examples/clientserver as a
   subdirectory, or from a JAR file
   -->

<applet code="examples.clientserver.AppletTableBrowser" codebase="../.."
height="400" width="800" >

       alt="Your browser understands the &lt;APPLET&gt; tag but isn't running the
applet, for some reason."
       Your browser is completely ignoring the &lt;APPLET&gt; tag!
   </applet>
   <hr>
   <a href="GraphicsTest.java">The source</a>.
</body>
</html>
```

The applet tag describes the codebase for the class file that contains the JApplet implementation. This is similar to the classpath and instructs the applet viewer on where it can find the class files. More commonly, we would package an applet in a JAR file and reference that file as a codebase. The classes referenced in the codebase could be downloaded and then executed.

To run the applet with the applet viewer, the following command is used, assuming that the classes are located in the referenced subdirectory.

```
appletviewer file:./examples/clientserver/appletexample1.html
```

Note that since this applet uses the Java Swing API to run this applet within a Web browser, the Java 2 Plug-in is required.

THE BUSINESS LOGIC

Though we have moved a good portion of the business logic out of the table browser application, we still have some business logic exposed. The menu action code which executes the queries using the remote DAO is hardcoded with the queries to execute. A subsequent refactoring of the application should move this code to a remote object and load the queries from a location where they could be changed without having to alter the program code (for instance, a properties file or as a parameter object in a naming service).

SUMMARY

In this chapter we demonstrated how to take the client-server GUI application from the previous chapter and convert the application to a multi-tiered application. To accomplish this we first refactored the code to use a remote object to implement database access. Using RMI, we created a remote version of our DAO and made some minor changes to accommodate the change in our application. We also changed the application to remove the requirement to enter the query explicitly and added menu items to allow the user to simply choose the table to browse.

One of the major issues with client-server applications is the need for deploying the application. Unlike Web applications which require no deployment (thus the term zero-deployment), Applets provide an attractive alternative for GUI applications. Applets represent a lightweight facility for downloading and executing GUI applications from a remote source. If a Swing application has been coded correctly, as we demonstrated in this chapter, then the conversion from client-server to an applet is fairly straightforward.

CHAPTER 32

Java Design Patterns

INTRODUCTION

As we learned in the first section of this book, J2EE application architecture involves creating components for multiple development tiers. Java design patterns can help provide guidance on how to develop application components for these tiers.

When applied to J2EE, applying these design patterns must take into account the multiple tiers supported by J2EE and the technologies that can be used on those tiers. In this chapter we will examine some design patterns that are commonly applied to the Java development process.

We begin by first revisiting the architectural tiers we discussed in the first section and will then examine various Java design patterns that can be applied to those tiers. The following chapters will then demonstrate the application of several of these design patterns.

The Architectural Tiers

As discussed in the first section of this book, the distributed tiers of a J2EE application are *logical* divisions and do not necessarily relate to physically separate divisions. Components that are distributed across two or three tiers could reside on a single server (see Figure 32–1).

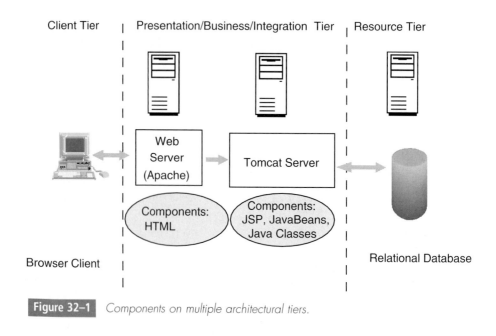

| Client Tier | Presentation/Business/Integration Tier | Resource Tier |

Web Server (Apache)

Tomcat Server

Components: HTML

Components: JSP, JavaBeans, Java Classes

Browser Client

Relational Database

Figure 32–1 *Components on multiple architectural tiers.*

A J2EE application may reside on one or more of these tiers. Table 32–1 briefly describes these tiers. Subsequent sections will provide additional detail.

Client Tier

The client tier logically enough represents the client application. The purpose of this tier is to render the presentation prepared by the presentation tier and to react to the input from the user. The client tier must also communicate with the presentation tier and relay the user's input to that tier. The client tier is usually a Web browser but could be any application that can perform the functions required of the client tier. Using a thin-client architecture, this tier should have a minimal footprint. The goal is to avoid the problems of fat-client architectures, where deploying to the client tier is difficult and expensive.

| Table 32–1 | *J2EE Architectural Tiers* |

Tier	Description
Client	The client-side of the application. This should be a thin client with the responsibility to responsible for rendering the application's visual components, accepting user interaction, and relaying to the results of any interaction to the presentation tier. In our examples, this tier will be represented by a Web browser.
Presentation	The responsibility of this tier is to control the presentation of the application and to relay user interactions to the business tier. For our examples, this tier is synonymous with the Web tier, comprising HTTP servers, JSP environments, and servlet containers.
Business	Components in this tier encapsulate the business logic of the application. Development in this tier is primarily in Java, using JavaBeans, though other components could be used (for instance, Enterprise JavaBeans).
Integration	The responsibility of components in this tier is to provide access to the resource tier. This access usually requires integration with some data resource, usually a relational database but possible a legacy data source such as a mainframe database.
Resource	The resource tier represents the persistent data store for the site, most commonly a relational database. Integration tier components communicate with this tier.

By using a Web browser on this tier, the goal of the thin-client architecture is met. Web browsers provide the client portion of the application by displaying small packets of information—HTML pages. These pages are generated dynamically via a remote connection. There is no need to deploy anything to the client in order to deliver an application (other than an HTML-capable Web browser).

In order to keep this client a thin client, the responsibilities of this tier must be minimized. By minimizing and focusing the responsibilities of this tier, the amount of information that must be sent to the tier is minimized. If we determine that this tier should only render the display and respond to the user's input, then decisions on what to display and how to display it should be left to another tier.

This approach to the client tier has proved effective, allowing the Web browser to do what it does best—display Web pages and collect input. Though it is possible to perform more complex presentation and business logic at the client tier, this work is usually left to other tiers in our architecture.

Presentation Tier

The presentation tier is responsible for the preparation of the output to the client tier. This tier encapsulates the logic required to create the presentation. Since we are usually preparing these pages dynamically, this tier must be able to store and retain information between calls, either in memory or in a data store.

If we are using a Web browser as our client, then the protocol between the client tier and the presentation tier is HTTP. The most logical server for the presentation tier is a server that can perform HTTP, such as Apache. Additionally, we would like the server to be able to manage dynamic content using a robust language such as Java. The Tomcat server provides this capability using servlets and JSP pages.

The components used on this tier are either Java servlets, JSP pages, JavaBeans, or tag libraries. The question we need to answer at the design stage is which type of component should be used. If we want to create components on this tier that require minimal support from Java developers, then JSP should be used to provide the bulk of the presentation logic. JavaBeans and tag libraries could be used to isolate more complex logic, leaving a JSP page that would be familiar and maintainable by most Web page developers.

By maintaining this separation of roles, staff with more specialized skill sets can maintain the presentation tier components. If these components are primarily HTML, then developers familiar with HTML can maintain these pages. Java provides a number of tools that make this approach even more attractive: tag libraries and JavaBean integration into the JSP page. Using these tools, presentation tier logic can be isolated in the JSP page and any additional logic can be moved to back-end components like JavaBeans and tag libraries. The resulting JSP page, composed primarily of HTML elements, can be maintained by an HTML developer. (These HTML page developers are usually available at a lower rate than Java developers.)

Business Tier

The business tier isolates and encapsulates business logic for the application. Logic that could have resided in the presentation tier in Web components, such as JSP pages and servlets, is effectively pushed off and encapsulated in this tier.

The components on this tier can be created using a variety of Java tools: JavaBeans, tag libraries, and Enterprise JavaBeans (EJBs). (Though Java scriptlets in Web pages could be used to manage business logic, this is generally not recommended.)

The business tier should be used to isolate business logic—the business rules of the organization. These are rules such as how to select sales regions for the sales reports, including the usual list of exceptions that always seem to exist for many business rules.

The selection of business tier components should be based on a number of factors, such as performance, availability requirements, and the scalability required for the application. Only when the application requires it based on these needs should EJBs be used.

Business tier components should provide for the retrieval of data from the data store and the application of business rules against this data. This data retrieval is accomplished by communicating with integration tier components, which provide the data retrieval.

The business tier components can, and for our purposes will, operate within the same container as the presentation tier components. The Tomcat server provides the execution of the JSP page and the resulting servlet, and also executes JavaBeans or tag libraries, which contain the business logic of the organization.

Integration Tier

The components on the integration tier are tasked with the retrieval of data from the data store. These components communicate with the business tier to provide the data requested. The purpose of this tier is to encapsulate the data access of the application and to effectively shield the business tier and other tiers from the details of this access.

These components must have knowledge of the location of the data store and the protocol required to retrieve the data. The most common data store in use today is the relational database, and the Java JDBC API provides the means of communicating with this database. But access to other data stores may be required. The Java Connector API will ultimately provide a common, standard method of connecting with these data stores when it becomes available. Both APIs would be used on this tier.

Resource Tier

The resource tier is represented by the data store or persistence engine of the application. For many applications, this layer accesses the relational database engine. The resource tier is responsible for storing the persistent data and maintaining the consistency of the data. Communication with the resource tier is accomplished with a standard API such as JDBC for relational databases.

DESIGN PATTERNS

A *design pattern* is a repeatable solution to a recurring problem in the software development process. Originally, design patterns were applied to physical building architecture, but several prescient individuals felt that these same principles could be applied to the design of object-oriented software. Design patterns can be used to promote consistency in the software development process. They provide a common means of communicating tried and proven solutions to frequently encountered problems.

While design patterns have for a number of years been applied to object-oriented software development, including the development of Java applications, in recent years Sun Microsystems has increased the emphasis on design patterns with Java applications, more specifically on J2EE design patterns. Sun has identified a number of design patterns to be used with J2EE for three tiers: the presentation, business, and integration tiers.

Design patterns are applied to the design of the software components. For the presentation tier, the components would be either JSP pages or servlets. For the business and integration tiers, the components would be either JavaBeans, tag libraries or EJBs. Applying a pattern to these components involves the application of a specified pattern of classes to the design of the components for that tier. Several of the more important patterns for these tiers are identified in the sections below.

Presentation Tier Patterns

Presentation tier patterns provide a means of applying order to the complexities of managing the presentation of the application. These patterns do not provide a means of applying business logic in the presentation tier, since that logic should be applied on the business tier. These patterns are for applications with complexity in the presentation tier, where security or the complexity of the presentation is important. If an application does not have a complex presentation, then the application of this design may not be needed.

Dispatcher View Pattern

The `DispatcherView` pattern (see Figure 32–2) is applied to applications that require some degree of logic to be applied to the client requests in order to determine how the client should proceed. With this pattern, a client request is received. This request is examined by a `FrontController`, and decision logic is applied to determine which `View` should be used to manage the request. Once the `View` has been chosen, the client request is forwarded to an appropriate `View`. The `View`, working with a `ViewHelper`, is then responsible for generating dynamic content and producing a response to the client request.

Using the Web as our presentation tier, our request is an HTTP request. This request is received and evaluated by the `FrontController` before being forwarded. Since this evaluation process does not involve any presentation to the client (even though it exists on the presentation tier), a servlet is appropriate for this component, though a JSP page could also be used.

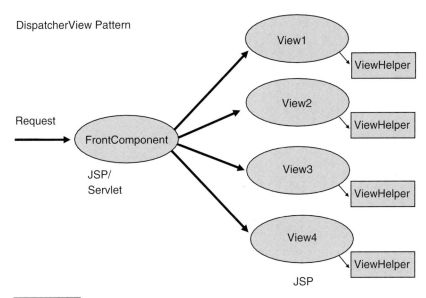

DispatcherView Pattern

Request

FrontComponent

JSP/
Servlet

View1

ViewHelper

View2

ViewHelper

View3

ViewHelper

View4

ViewHelper

JSP

Figure 32–2 *Dispatcher view pattern (process flow).*

Once the `FrontController` has evaluated the request, it forwards the request to an appropriate `View`. The `View` has the responsibility of generating the display for the client. It is assumed that this will involve the generation of dynamic content, and therefore the `View` will require a helper in the form of a component known as a `ViewHelper`. The `ViewHelper` performs whatever integration tier or resource tier communication is necessary to formulate the response for the client request. In simpler terms, this means that the `View` produces the dynamic Web page by using session or application variables and performing database interaction as needed. This will no doubt involve working with other components that may logically be denoted as belonging to the integration tier or resource tier in our architecture.

Service to Worker Pattern

The `ServicetoWorker` pattern (see Figure 32–3) is used to manage applications that must apply a large amount of logic to incoming requests to determine how to process those requests. This pattern is similar to the `DispatcherView` pattern, but differs in the approach to managing the processing logic. With the `ServicetoWorker` pattern, the logic is processed by the `FrontController` rather than passing that responsibility off to the `View` to make the decisions.

With this design pattern, the request from the client is managed by a `FrontController`. The `FrontController` evaluates the request and determines which security requirements must be met to handle the request. If business decisions need to be made to manage the request, the `FrontController` communicates with

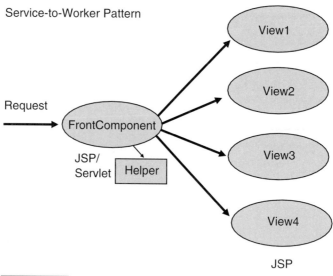

Service-to-Worker Pattern

Request

Figure 32–3　 *Service to Worker pattern (process flow).*

a `Helper` (playing the same role as a `ViewHelper` in the `DispatcherView` pattern), which may in turn interact with a `BusinessDelegate` to accomplish its work.

Once the `FrontController` has completed evaluating the logic necessary to make its decision, it forwards the request to the appropriate `View`. The `View` may then refer to a `ViewHelper` to create its dynamic content and build the response for the client.

Business Tier Patterns

A number of business tier patterns are available to apply order to the construction of business logic components. The main purpose of these patterns is to reduce the interaction or coupling between presentation tier and business tier components. The benefit of this approach is that changes in the business tier components (which is common) should not affect the presentation tier components, thus creating a more flexible (and less *brittle*) application.

The Session Facade Pattern

The `SessionFacade` pattern (see Figure 32–4) works primarily to reduce coupling between the presentation tier component making the request and the business tier component responsible for managing the request. The component on the presentation tier may need to perform a number of business functions in order to complete the request (a dynamic Web page) that must be sent back to the client.

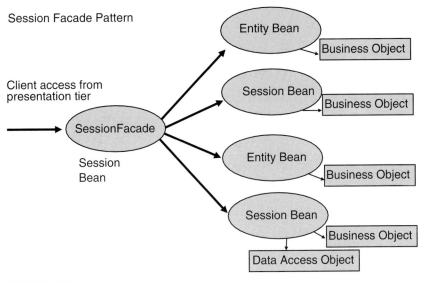

Figure 32–4 *SessionFacade pattern (process flow).*

These functions may involve detailed calls to retrieve data from the integration tier and to apply business logic to the results before producing the response for the client. In order to maintain our division of responsibilities, we would like to encapsulate all of our business logic on the business tier and shield the presentation tier from these details.

Using this pattern, the presentation tier component must execute business logic and possibly retrieve data on behalf of the client. These requests are forwarded to a `SessionFacade` component that will manage the request as needed. The process of managing this request may involve making several additional calls to other components in order to process the request. These other objects could be `BusinessObjects` (which manage the details of access to the integration tier) or `DataAccessObjects` (which are integration tier components that manage the details of access to the persistent data store; the `SessionFacade` object shields the client from these details.) When it has completed its processing, the `SessionFacade` component returns results to the presentation tier component.

Business Delegate Pattern

The `BusinessDelegate` pattern (see Figure 32–5) is used on the business tier to provide access to business tier components using a client-side (presentation tier) object. The `BusinessDelegate` encapsulates any business logic that must be used by the presentation tier component to complete its work. The purpose of this component is to hide the complexity of business tier components from the presentation

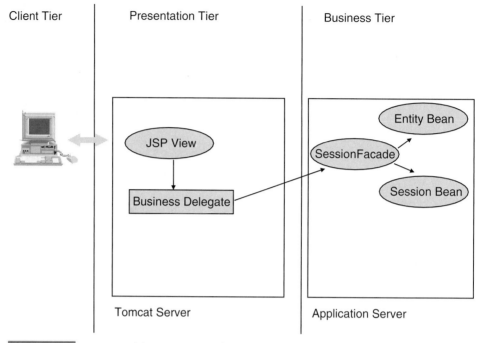

Figure 32–5 *Business delegate (process flow).*

tier, thus reducing the coupling between these two tiers and minimizing the effect of business tier changes on presentation tier components.

This component may be implemented on the Web tier; that is, it may be implemented as a JavaBean or tag library rather than as an EJB. The reason for this is that the `BusinessDelegate` is intended to protect the presentation tier component from the business tier components and may do this by caching data and encapsulating business tier logic on the client side (where the presentation tier is a client for business tier services.)

This also has the effect of reducing the communication traffic between the presentation tier components and the business tier components. While this may not seem significant for components that are operating in the same JVM (which would be the case with servlets/JSP pages, JavaBeans, and tag libraries), this does become a consideration when using EJBs that may be spread over one or more servers in a clustered network configuration.

Value Object Pattern

The `ValueObject` pattern (see Figure 32–6) encapsulates the data elements of a business domain object and provides a means of transporting that information from the business tier to the presentation tier where it can be cached. The

Value Object Pattern

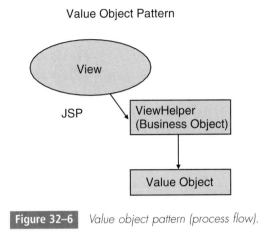

Figure 32–6   *Value object pattern (process flow).*

`ValueObject` contains members that represent the elements of the business domain object and methods to retrieve those members.

The `ValueObject` is generally intended to be immutable, meaning that it is a *read-only* object and the members should not be changed. A `ValueObject` may contain `setXXXX` methods that allow members to be changed, but calling these methods alone will not change the persistent data behind the `ValueObject`; instead, they will only change the `ValueObject` on the presentation tier. It is the responsibility of the `BusinessObject` to manage the persistent data store, and it is therefore the `BusinessObject` that must be called to update the persistent data store by exposing an `update` method to the presentation tier client.

The use of this pattern has the practical benefit of reducing the amount of communication between the presentation tier and the business tier, since only one method call must be made to retrieve all the data required, as opposed to making numerous method calls to the business tier to populate an object on the presentation tier. (Note that the performance benefits of this approach are more significant when using EJBs than when using JavaBean components, but the practical benefits derived during the development process from the reduced coupling and exposure of the presentation tier to the business tier still apply.)

The `ValueObject` is created and loaded via a `BusinessObject` component. The responsibility of this `BusinessObject` component is to instantiate the `ValueObject` and then load the attributes of the `ValueObject` with the correct values. This is performed using a create method that the `BusinessObject` component exposes to the presentation tier.

Integration Tier Patterns

It is the responsibility of the integration tier to provide access to the persistent data store. The responsibility of components on this tier is to abstract the specifics of data access away from the business tier components. This allows developers knowledgeable in the specifics of data access to work on these components and developers who may have little knowledge of the data access operation to work on business tier components and access the integration tier data via a well-defined API.

Data Access Object (DAO) Pattern

The `DataAccessObject` pattern (see Figure 32–7) provides encapsulation of the data access process. The `DataAccessObject` provides the specifics of data access and exposes a simplified API to allow business tier components to access integration tier data.

The component created by this pattern is accessed from the business tier by the business object. The component requests data in the data store using an API method call, which conceals the details of the request. The `DataAccessObject` executes the details of the data access operation, which may involve requesting access to the data source as a specific user, connecting to the data source, performing transactional logic, preparing and executing a query, and retrieving data.

Data Access Object Pattern

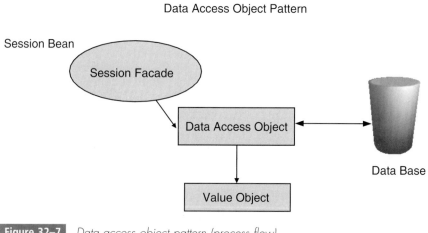

Figure 32–7   *Data access object pattern (process flow).*

SUMMARY

J2EE provides a rich and diverse set of tools that can be used to create applications. But if we don't apply some structure to the development process, we could create an incoherent and jumbled mess.

This chapter provided an overview of some of the more common Java design patterns. In the following chapters we will apply some of those design patterns in the creation of a J2EE application.

J2EE Applied: Creating a Framework-Based Shopping Cart Application

INTRODUCTION

As we have seen in these many chapters, J2EE provides numerous technologies and tools that can be used to create applications: Swing for GUI applications, RMI, servlets, JSPs, EJBs, JMS, JAXM and SOAP, and XML parsers among others. The question you may have formulated through this technology review is how to pull all of this together to build an application.

Previously we have looked at discrete examples of specific J2EE packages at times using them in combination with other APIs. Now we will move beyond that and spend some time looking at examples of complete J2EE applications using a sampling of J2EE packages and applying various Java design patterns in the process.

In this section, we will look at a complete shopping cart application using JSPs, servlets, EJBs and the Jakarta Apache Struts framework environment. Though the shopping cart is a well-worn example these days, it never the less provides a good example of how to use these packages together in a single application. Since the framework component is an essential part of this example, we will begin by explaining the Struts framework and how it is used to bring together the various components which comprise the application.

FRAMEWORKS

Frameworks represent a foundation for building a Web-based application. They provide a common, structured facility for maintaining centralized control over the navigational flow of the application. Since the nature of Web applications is that a large number of components are used to implement user interaction (use cases), maintaining the flow between these components can become difficult. This is not such an issue if there are only a small number of components (perhaps 10), but as the number of components grows and the complexity of their relationships grows, an application without a centralized control mechanism can quickly become complicated and extremely difficult to maintain.

A common expression of this architectural difficulty is the Model 1/Model 2 architecture as applied to Java components. The Model 1 architecture involves the creation of Java Web components to implement use cases. It allowed for the separation of roles that we mentioned earlier, including moving business processes off the JSP page and out of the servlet and having those components remain focused on providing the user view. Data management could also be moved into separate components. So Model 1 could include the application of a number of Java design patterns such as data access objects (DAOs) and session facade objects, but there was no specific contingency for a control object to manage the flow of the application, and as mentioned earlier, this is where the difficulty arises when the number of components increased.

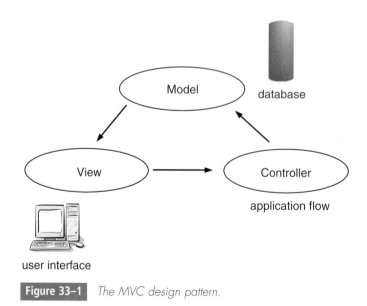

Figure 33–1   *The MVC design pattern.*

The Model 2 architecture addressed this problem by implementing a control object, which managed the flow of the application, the relationships between the Web components. This architecture can also be considered an implementation of an older architectural design pattern, the model, view, controller (MVC) design pattern.

This design pattern was originally applied to the creation of graphical user interfaces (GUIs) with the Smalltalk programming language. Each application component type had a specific purpose, as follows.

Model	Manages the data for the application
View	Manages the user interface
Controller	Manages the flow of the application

Since this design pattern (see Figure 33–1) is an architectural pattern, there would potentially be more than one application component for each component type. The component type stresses the role for the component.

THE STRUTS FRAMEWORK

The Struts framework (`jakarta.apache.org`) provides a facility for implementing a MVC architecture with J2EE Web components: Java servlets and JSP. As you would expect from the previous architectural discussion, Struts provides a controller servlet, which transfers control between Web components by dispatching a request to an appropriate action class. The developer does not need to program the controller servlet; it is provided in the package. The actions taken by the controller servlet are determined by the contents of an XML document, which describes various configuration parameters for the Struts installation, including the flow of the application control.

Struts provides a number of very useful features, including a JSP tag library, facilities for interacting with forms, and a class library that includes a DataSource implementation. The complete description of Struts is beyond the scope of this chapter. The use of Struts in this chapter is to demonstrate the benefits of using a controller servlet, the Model 2/MVC architecture, in the development of a J2EE application. We use the e-commerce shopping cart to demonstrate this architecture. Even though an e-commerce solution may not be your target application, the same principles apply.

THE MOVIES SHOPPING CART APPLICATION

Going back to our fictitious movies store example used in previous chapters, we can assume that the owners of the movie store would like to offer the movies for sale over the Web. In order to allow the user to conduct a sales transaction, we the developers of the application need to be sure that we have the pertinent information on the user before we conduct the sale—information such as the user's name and address, and for some sales, credit card information. This also presents an opportunity to collect useful customer-base information, such as the user's product preferences and other interests. (Many packaged e-commerce solutions provide quite a few value-added features in this area, sometimes referred to as *personalization*.)

For brevity and clarity, we do not demonstrate the collection of a broad spectrum of information from the user or the details of credit-card validation, which would no doubt be done to some extent in a commercial application. Instead, we demonstrate the use of J2EE technology and the Struts package for navigation control and draw on a number of the technologies shown in some detail in the previous chapters, such as XML/XSLT usage and the application of the DAO design pattern.

One of the important aspects of an e-commerce application, common in other Web applications as well, is the need to have the user log in to perform certain functions. This is where the use of a central controller is beneficial. We know that the controller will be executed before each navigational attempt, so we have a central location where we can perform tests to determine whether or not the user has completed the login process.

The use of a security realm provides part of this functionality, but we would also like to have the ability to go beyond the capture of just the basic login information and make sure that before the user attempts certain operations we have populated their session with a collection of personal information. For example, if the user chooses to list all available movies, we can assume that he or she is shopping, and it would be useful to determine whether or not this user has an existing shopping cart. This of course requires that the user perform a login if he or she hasn't already done so, and it requires us to populate the shopping cart information as part of the login process. Having a central controller component, the Struts controller servlet, makes this process easier. If you consider the alternative, maintaining these login checks and the navigation logic in each separate Web component, then it becomes clearer why the Model 2/MVC architecture is so attractive.

The Shopping Cart Application

Our shopping cart application begins with a menu page that includes various options (see Figure 33–2). These options allow (but don't require) the user to log in, shop for movies, enter registration information, and perform other operations.

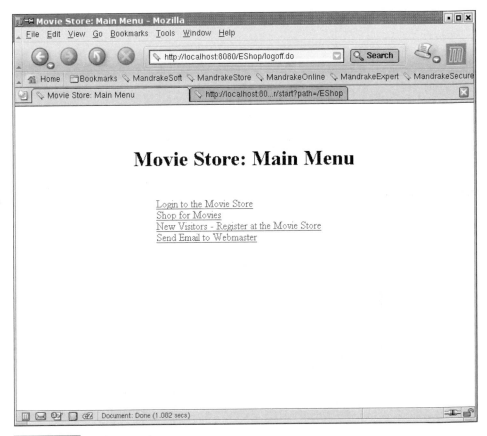

Figure 33–2 *Before user login.*

As we will see shortly, this menu is created dynamically in relation to the user's session environment so that if the user has already logged in, then the option to log in will not be shown.

Once the user has completed the login process, the menu page displays options relevant only to that user's session. This includes examination of whether or not the user has an active shopping cart. If so, then only the option to examine that shopping cart will be shown on this menu. As we will see, the shopping cart page allows the user to add more movies to the shopping cart.

The user login page, as shown in Figure 33–3, allows the user to log in to the Web site. Since we do not know for sure that the user has a login, the page includes a link to the new user registration page. (Though not shown in this example, many sites place a cookie in the user's browser that contains an ID key used to determine whether or not the user has registered with the site.) If the user enters an invalid login, an error page is shown, and he or she is required to log in again.

Figure 33–3   *Login page.*

Once the user has completed the login process, the main menu page is shown again, but this time the menu is different (see Figure 33–4). A message is displayed in the top left corner indicating that the login process has been completed and displaying the name the user has used to login to the system. The menu page also takes into consideration that the user currently has an active shopping cart and provides a link to list the contents of that shopping cart. A link to update user registration and a link to log out of the movie store site are also provided. The link to send email to the Webmaster is always shown on the menu page.

If the user has not registered on the site, then a user registration page is provided (see Figure 33–5). This example allows the user to enter his or her name and address, but could easily be expanded to capture customer preference information.

A page is provided to list all movies in the movie store (see Figure 33–6). This page takes an XML document and, using XSLT transformation, produces the HTML to provide the page. To demonstrate the flexibility of this approach, the same servlet, using a different transformation script, is used to produce three distinct pages: a

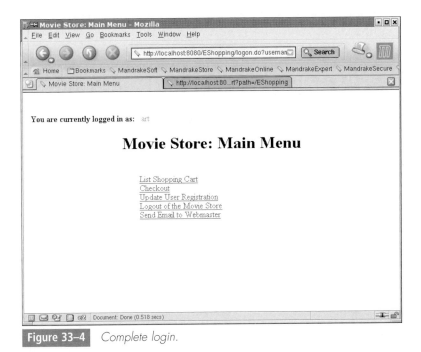

Figure 33–4 *Complete login.*

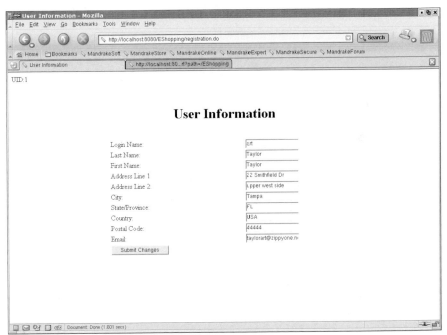

Figure 33–5 *User registration information.*

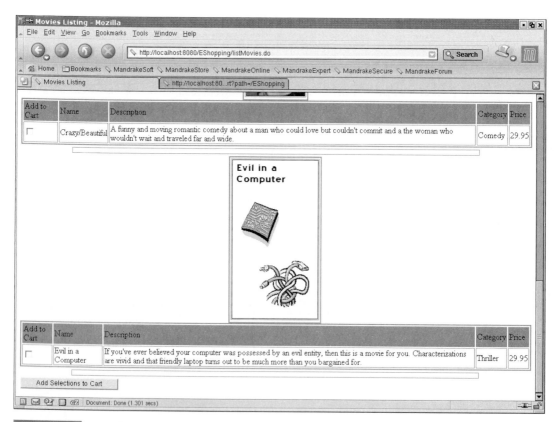

Figure 33–6   *List all movies in the store.*

page that provides a listing of all movies, a listing of the user's shopping cart, and a checkout listing.

The page that lists all movies provides a checkbox on each item row that allows the user to indicate that he or she would like to add the movie on that row to his or her shopping cart.

Since having a shopping cart requires that a user has previously registered at the site, using this page requires that the session has a valid user login. The action servlet that controls access to this page provides that check.

The page that lists the shopping cart provides a listing similar to that of the all movies page but provides a checkbox next to each item to allow the user to remove the item from the cart (see Figure 33–7). A link at the bottom of the page

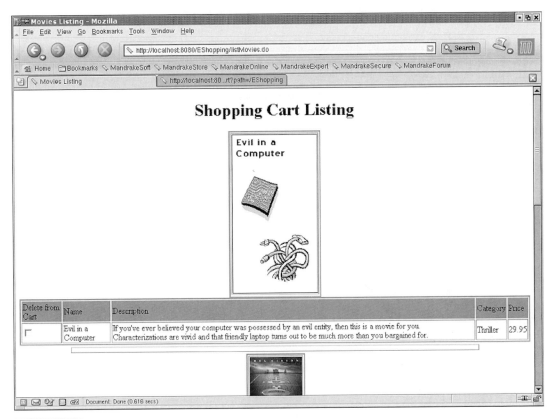

Figure 33–7 *List shopping cart contents.*

allows the user to add more movies to the cart. This link simply invokes the all movies page we examined previously.

For convenience (and to demonstrate the use of the JavaMail package in a Web application), we allow the user to send an email to the Webmaster (see Figure 33–8). While an HTML `mailto` tag could have been used to provide similar functionality, using JavaMail internally gives the developer more control over the operation.

This example takes the e-commerce transaction up to the point of having the user verify the sale information. This page lists the contents of the user's cart and provides subtotal, tax, and grand total information on the bottom of the page (see Figure 33–9).

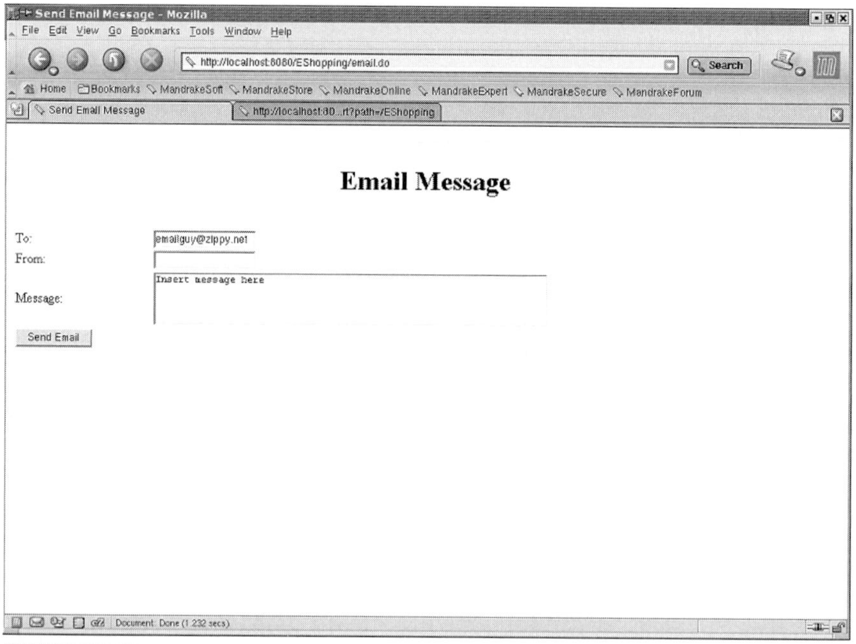

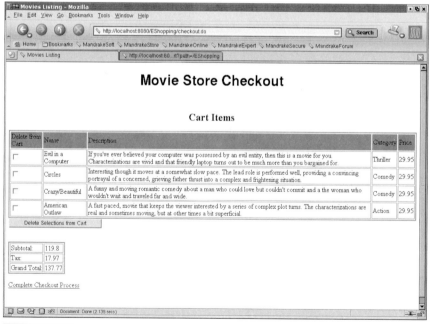

Figure 33–8 Send email page.

Figure 33–9 Shopping cart checkout.

THE STRUTS PACKAGE

The Struts package uses three components to implement the MVC architecture. One of these, the servlet controller, is provided as part of the Struts package. The other components are implemented by the developer by extending Struts base classes. So in architectural terms, the servlet controller represents the MVC controller, JSPs or servlets may represent the MVC view, and business logic is represented using JavaBeans or various helper classes and is considered the MVC model. See Figure 33–10.

With Struts, the servlet controller component receives HTTP requests and routes the request to the appropriate action, a subclass of `org.apache.struts.action.Action` or some type of view in the form of an HTML page, JSP, or servlet. As we will see shortly, the actions themselves perform various validations and preparations, and then pass control on to a view. The views in our example are either a servlet using XML/XSLT to create an HTML page or a JSP page.

The Struts servlet controller uses an XML configuration file, which conveniently provides mappings between HTTP resource requests (in the form of a URI) and the action to be taken. This configuration file provides loose binding between the controller and its mappings, and adds a great deal of flexibility to the applica-

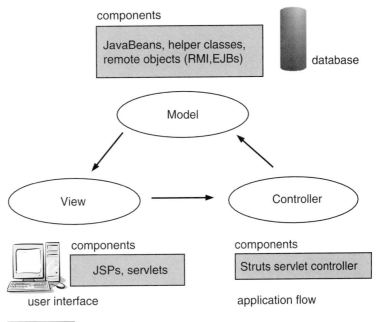

Figure 33–10 *MVC with component interaction.*

tion. Controller mappings can easily be changed during deployment based on the requirements of the installation.

As we demonstrate in this example, the action class provided by Struts allows manipulation of the servlet request session object (`javax.servlet.http.HttpSession`) and thus allows the action to prepare the session environment as needed. This is very convenient for our application, where we need to verify that the user is logged in and has a shopping cart.

THE WEB.XML FILE

As we explained in chapter 27 on servlets, the `web.xml` file is used to provide various configuration parameters for the Web application, or application components, which reside in that context. In the case of our application, we use two queries to drive the creation of the movies list pages. The `carts-totals-query` is defined as a `context-param`, meaning it is part of the context and is available to all Web components in that context.

A number of other entries in the `web.xml` file are for configuring Struts. These entries allow debug levels to be set and other parameters to be configured by the developer or deployer.

The web.xml File

```xml
<?xml version="1.0" encoding="ISO-8859-1"?>

<!DOCTYPE web-app
   PUBLIC "-//Sun Microsystems, Inc.//DTD Web Application 2.2//EN"
   "http://java.sun.com/j2ee/dtds/web-app_2_2.dtd">

<web-app>

      <context-param>
              <param-name>cart-totals-query</param-name>
              <param-value> select cart_items.cart_id, cart_items.movie_id,
sum(items.cost) as subtotal, sum(items.cost*.15) as tax, sum(items.cost*1.15) as
grand_total from items, cart_items where items.movie_id = cart_items.movie_id and
cart_items.cart_id =  ? group by cart_items.cart_id</param-value>
      </context-param>

  <!-- Standard Action Servlet Configuration (with debugging) -->
  <servlet>
    <servlet-name>action</servlet-name>
    <servlet-class>org.apache.struts.action.ActionServlet</servlet-class>
    <init-param>
      <param-name>application</param-name>
      <param-value>ApplicationResources</param-value>
    </init-param>
```

```
<init-param>
  <param-name>config</param-name>
  <param-value>/WEB-INF/struts-config.xml</param-value>
</init-param>
<init-param>
  <param-name>debug</param-name>
  <param-value>2</param-value>
</init-param>
<init-param>
  <param-name>detail</param-name>
  <param-value>2</param-value>
</init-param>
<init-param>
  <param-name>validate</param-name>
  <param-value>true</param-value>
</init-param>
<load-on-startup>2</load-on-startup>
</servlet>
```

Following a number of the Struts entries are servlet entries for our application. We use a servlet named `MoviesChooser` to display movies listings based on SQL queries. This servlet executes the query and returns an XML document containing the results of the query. The servlet performs transformation using an XSLT script file to to describe how to format the page into HTML. The benefits of this abstraction of the presentation (view) are demonstrated in this application by providing code reuse; this same servlet is used by several shopping cart applications to retrieve data and format it using the XML transformation API.

In the `web.xml` file in the block of entries for the `MovieChooser` servlet we provide parameter entries for the XSLT templates to use to format the results of the queries, and we provide the queries to use to retrieve the data as shown next.

```
<servlet>
  <servlet-name>MoviesChooser</servlet-name>
  <servlet-class>examples.struts.MoviesChooser</servlet-class>

  <init-param>
    <param-name>all-template</param-name>
    <param-value>movies_list.xsl</param-value>
  </init-param>

  <init-param>
    <param-name>cart-template</param-name>
    <param-value>cart_list.xsl</param-value>
  </init-param>

  <init-param>
    <param-name>checkout-template</param-name>
    <param-value>checkout.xsl</param-value>
  </init-param>
```

```xml
    <init-param>
            <param-name>all-movies-query</param-name>
            <!-- join to movie_images - currently only want movies with scanned
images -->
            <param-value>select movies.movie_id as 'ID', movie_name as 'Name',
movie_desc as 'Description', category as 'Category', cost from movies, movie_images,
items where movies.movie_id=movie_images.movie_id and items.movie_id=movies.movie_id
order by movie_name</param-value>
    </init-param>

    <init-param>
            <param-name>existing-cart-query</param-name>
            <!-- join to movie_images and join to the shopping cart to only get
the movies in the cart -->
            <!-- this requires a filter clause with the user_id run against the
shopping_cart table. to be added in the servlet   -->
            <param-value>select movies.movie_id as 'ID', movie_name as 'Name',
movie_desc as 'Description', category as 'Category', cost from movies, movie_images,
shopping_cart, cart_items, items where movies.movie_id=movie_images.movie_id and
movies.movie_id=cart_items.movie_id and shopping_cart.cart_id=cart_items.cart_id and
movies.movie_id=items.movie_id </param-value>
    </init-param>

</servlet>

<!-- Standard Action Servlet Mapping -->
<servlet-mapping>
  <servlet-name>action</servlet-name>
  <url-pattern>*.do</url-pattern>
</servlet-mapping>

<servlet-mapping>
        <servlet-name>MoviesChooser</servlet-name>
        <url-pattern>/MoviesChooser</url-pattern>
</servlet-mapping>

<!-- The Usual Welcome File List -->
<welcome-file-list>
        <welcome-file>./mainMenu.do</welcome-file>
</welcome-file-list>

<!-- Example Application Tag Library Descriptor
<taglib>
  <taglib-uri>/WEB-INF/app.tld</taglib-uri>
  <taglib-location>/WEB-INF/app.tld</taglib-location>
</taglib>
-->

<!-- Struts Tag Library Descriptors -->
<taglib>
  <taglib-uri>/WEB-INF/struts-bean.tld</taglib-uri>
```

```
      <taglib-location>/WEB-INF/struts-bean.tld</taglib-location>
   </taglib>

   <taglib>
      <taglib-uri>/WEB-INF/struts-html.tld</taglib-uri>
      <taglib-location>/WEB-INF/struts-html.tld</taglib-location>
   </taglib>

   <taglib>
      <taglib-uri>/WEB-INF/struts-logic.tld</taglib-uri>
      <taglib-location>/WEB-INF/struts-logic.tld</taglib-location>
   </taglib>

</web-app>
```

THE STRUTS CONFIGURATION FILE

The Struts configuration file used for this application is shown in the sections below. This file contains a number of entries which instruct Struts on how to map requests to servlets. Since this example does not use any Struts `form-beans`, so there are no entries in that section and it is not shown here. There are however two definitions for `global-forwards` which map a URI to the path specified as shown next.

Struts Configuration File

```
   <global-forwards>

      <forward    name="logon"   path="/logon.jsp"/>
      <forward    name="index"   path="/index.jsp"/>

   </global-forwards>
```

The `action-mapping` section of the configuration file is where we derive value from using Struts in this application. Even for this relatively simple example, you can see that navigation quickly becomes complex. By providing this configuration file and the controller servlet, Struts allows the navigation to be controlled from a central location using a clearly understood syntax.

As we see in the first entry below, the `action-mappings` section contains a number of action mappings. These mappings specify the path of the mapping, the type (class) of the action class that will be invoked when this path is encountered, the name of the action entry, the scope of the entry, and the input for the entry.

Most importantly, the action entry provides XML elements for the name of the forwarding URI. The `forward` tag contains a name attribute, which is associated with the form URI. This provides some loose coupling and creates a level of indirection. In application code, the forward name is used to identify where navigation should proceed using a method call, as shown below.

```
...
  if ( success ) {
        return (mapping.findForward("success"));
...
```

This means that in the application code, we can indicate the *name* of the resource where navigation can proceed. In the configuration file, we can map the name used in the code to the path. This mapping in the configuration file can be changed as needed without having to touch the code that is performing the forward operation. We have an additional benefit that through the central configuration file, we can clearly see where the pages are being invoked and which action classes are calling them. The entries for our shopping cart application are shown below.

For the main menu action, as we will see when we examine the `MenuAction` class later in this section, we perform some tests to determine whether or not the user is logged in and what information about the user session has been set in the session.

```
<action-mappings>

   <!-- logon action -->
   <action     path="/mainMenu"
               type="examples.struts.MenuAction"
               name="logon"
               scope="session"
               input="/logon.jsp">

    <forward name="success"  path="/index.jsp"/>
    <forward name="failure"  path="/failure.jsp"/>

   </action>

   <!-- logon action -->
   <action     path="/logon"
               type="examples.struts.LogonAction"
               name="logon"
               scope="session"
               input="/logon.jsp">

    <forward name="failure"  path="/failure.jsp"/>
    <forward name="success"  path="/mainMenu.do"/>

   </action>
```

```
<!-- Prepare to list movies and add to the cart.
     Determine whether or not the user is allowed to
     do this  -->

<action    path="/listMovies"
           type="examples.struts.ListMoviesAction"
            name="listMovies"
           input="/listMovies"
           scope="request">

  <forward name="failure" path="/mainMenu.do"/>
  <forward name="list-movies" path="/MoviesChooser"/>

</action>
```

With the registration entry shown next, we choose to allow the registration input page (user.jsp) to perform the forward operation. The submit button on the user.jsp page posts directly to the adduser action. While this may appear to bypass the controller servlet, it does not; since we use the adduser.do URI, we push the control of the post operation through the controller servlet. As we saw previously, the context for our EShopping Web application contains a servlet-mapping entry that maps all servlets with the .do extension to the Struts controller servlet.

```
<action    path="/registration"
           type="examples.struts.RegistrationAction"
            name="registration"
           input="/user.jsp"
           scope="request">

  <forward name="failure" path="/mainMenu.do"/>

  <!-- get the user input.
       The form 'submit' button will POST to adduser.do  -->
  <forward name="success" path="/user.jsp"/>

</action>

<!-- save the registration entries to the database -->
<action    path="/adduser"
           type="examples.struts.AddUserAction"
            name="adduser"
           input="/user.jsp"
           scope="request">

  <forward name="failure" path="/mainMenu.do"/>
  <forward name="success" path="/mainMenu.do"/>

</action>
```

```xml
<!-- save the cart entries to the database -->
<action    path="/submitCart"
          type="examples.struts.SubmitCartAction"
          name="submitCart"
          input="/MoviesChooser"
          scope="request">

  <forward name="failure" path="/mainMenu.do"/>
  <forward name="success" path="/mainMenu.do"/>

</action>

<!-- perform checkout -->
<action    path="/checkout"
          type="examples.struts.CheckoutAction"
          name="checkout"
          input="/submitCart"
          scope="request">

  <forward name="failure" path="/failure.jsp"/>
  <forward name="success" path="/checkout.jsp"/>

</action>

<!-- send email -->
<action    path="/email"
          type="examples.struts.EmailAction"
          name="email"
          input="/email.jsp"
          scope="request">

  <forward name="failure" path="/failure.jsp"/>
  <forward name="success" path="/email.jsp"/>
  <forward name="logon" path="/logon.do"/>

</action>

<action    path="/emailProcess"
        type="examples.struts.EmailProcessAction"
          name="email"
          input="/email.jsp"
          scope="request">

  <forward name="failure" path="/failure.jsp"/>
  <forward name="success" path="/emailProcess.do"/>
  <forward name="logon" path="/logon.do"/>

</action>

<action    path="/logoff"
             type="examples.struts.LogoffAction">
  <forward name="success"                    path="/mainMenu.do"/>
```

```
        </action>

    </action-mappings>

</struts-config>
```

JAVA DESIGN PATTERNS

Two Java design patterns discussed in the previous chapter can also be implemented using the Struts framework. Both the Service to Worker and Dispatcher View design patterns require a controller component, referred to as the *front component* in both design patterns. The Struts controller can be considered the front component for either design pattern.

If the application contains most of its processing logic in the front component, then it can be considered an implementation of the Service to Worker design pattern. Alternatively, if the front component allows more decision logic to be managed by the views (using view helpers), then the design pattern can be considered the Dispatcher View design pattern.

SUMMARY

To demonstrate the use of J2EE technologies and APIs in one cohesive application, we will use a shopping cart example which uses JSPs, servlets and EJBs. A framework provides an extremely convenient mechanism for managing the control of an application. In this chapter we covered the use of Struts frameworks, explaining how these frameworks operate, their architectural foundations, and how the movie store application was developed using this framework. We also examined the pages and the control flow for the ecommerce shopping cart application we will examine in more detail in the next chapter.

CHAPTER 34

J2EE Applied: The Movie Store Application

INTRODUCTION

The previous chapter explained the advantages of using a controller-centric, MVC architectural approach to developing Web applications.

In this chapter we examine a demonstration application developed with a framework. This J2EE application provides an example of an ecommerce site for a Movie Store application which tracks the user interaction at the Web site. The user must logon to the site to perform certain actions. As we will see in this chapter, the user interaction with the site is tracked using various objects which are retained by the application as an attribute of the user's session object.

THE MOVIE STORE APPLICATION

The movie store application as explained in the previous chapter contains a combination of JSP pages which collectively produce the HTML output sent back to the user's browser in the response stream. These JSPs are listed in Table 34–1.

Table 34–1   *Movie Store JSP Pages*

Page	Description
checkout.jsp	Performs the checkout process.
email.jsp	Displays the email page, accepts the user input and submits the email for processing.
failure.jsp	Displays the failure page.
index.jsp	The default index page.
logon.jsp	Provides user login form.
user.jsp	Provides a data entry form for user (customer) registration.

The Struts package uses a controller to manage navigational flow. As the user navigates the application, actions are executed based on user input and entries in the configuration file. Struts applications use *action classes* to process requests. JavaBeans are also used to encapsulate database access. These classes extend the org.apache.struts.action.Action class. The implementations used in the Movies Shopping Cart application are shown below in Table 34–2.

Table 34–2   *Action Classes, Servlets, and JavaBeans for the Movie Store Application*

Action Class/JavaBean	Description
AddUserAction.java	Receives the POST request from the user.jsp page (through the controller) and updates the user JavaBean in the user's session with the new values. Also uses the user JavaBean to update the database with the new values.
CartTotalsBean.java	Generates the totals for the shopping cart. Used on the checkout.jsp page.
CheckoutAction.java	Performs validations to determine whether or not the user is ready to check out. Checks to see that the user has logged in and has a cart, otherwise, a failure condition is indicated and control is passed back to the controller. If the user is ready to check out, this action sets the appropriate session values and forwards control to the success (check.jsp) page through the controller.
Constants.java	Provides various string constants for use in the movies shopping application.

Table 34–2 *Action Classes, Servlets, and JavaBeans for the Movie Store Application (cont.)*

Action Class/JavaBean	Description
EmailAction.java	Validates that the user is logged in before allowing the user to proceed to the email input page.
EmailProcessAction.java	Processes the email using the information posted to the page.
ListMoviesAction.java	The ListMoviesAction class is used to retrieve the action parameter passed and then determines whether or not the user has logged in. If the user has logged in, it then sets the the appropriate session attributes based on the actions passed to the request.
LogoffAction.java	This action removes session attributes for user name, user ID, and shopping cart, and sets session attribute flags indicating the user is not logged in and the user does not have a shopping cart.
LogonAction.java	This action processes the user login, validating the user login name and password. If the login fails, it maps back to an error page, which lets the user retry the login. If the login succeeds, it stores the user name.
MenuAction.java	Performs checks to see if the user has logged in and if they have a shopping cart. Also checks to see if the user is in an administrator role to determine whether or not the user will be forwarded to an administrator page.
MoviesChooser.java	This servlet executes a query, converts the contents of the query to XML, and then translates the XML into HTML to produce a listing of movies. It uses session attributes to determine the query to execute and the XSLT translation script to use.
RegistrationAction.java	Prepares the session for the registration page by ensuring that a user ID is part of the session. No other validations are performed.
ShoppingCartBean.java	Contains the business logic for manipulation of the shopping cart.
SubmitCartAction.java	Prepares the user session for shopping cart submission. Takes the movies the user has selected and adds or deletes them from the cart.
UserBean.java	Encapsulates the data access and business logic for accessing the user table.

Now that we understand how the Struts framework behaves and how our application works, we can examine the code behind all of this. As you will see from the section below, using the framework approach allows us to manage application complexity and keep the application components small, concise, and manageable.

THE LOGONACTION CLASS

The `LogonAction` class shown below is posted to by the logon form through the Struts controller. This action validates the user logon to determine whether or not the user has entered a valid login name and password. If the user has entered a valid login and password, then control is transferred through the Struts controller back to the main menu. At this point the main menu recognizes the login process has succeeded (because the user's session environment has changed) and displays the main menu based on the user's environment.

If, however, the user has not entered a valid user name and password, then control is transferred to a logon error page, which informs the user of the error and allows him or her to either proceed back to the logon form or the main menu.

In this example, the user enters their name and password using the logon form. We chose this approach to effectively open the site to a wider user population and allow users who have not registered (or do not want to bother registering right now) to access the site. Only when the user accesses certain pages do we require them to log in. The code for this class follows.

The LogonAction Class

```
package examples.struts;

import java.io.IOException;
import java.util.Hashtable;
import java.util.Locale;

import javax.servlet.RequestDispatcher;
import javax.servlet.ServletException;
import javax.servlet.http.HttpServletRequest;
import javax.servlet.http.HttpSession;
import javax.servlet.http.HttpServletResponse;

import org.apache.struts.action.Action;
import org.apache.struts.action.ActionError;
import org.apache.struts.action.ActionErrors;
import org.apache.struts.action.ActionForm;
import org.apache.struts.action.ActionForward;
import org.apache.struts.action.ActionMapping;
import org.apache.struts.action.ActionServlet;
```

```
import org.apache.struts.util.MessageResources;

import java.sql.SQLException;
import db.GeneralDAO;
import common.ValueObjectException;

public final class LogonAction extends Action {

    public ActionForward perform(ActionMapping mapping,
                        ActionForm form,
                        HttpServletRequest request,
                        HttpServletResponse response)
        throws IOException, ServletException {

        // Validate the request parameters specified by the user
         ActionErrors errors = new ActionErrors();

         //
         // the user name and password have been posted
         // from the login form
         //
         String username = request.getParameter("username");
         String password = request.getParameter("password");

         //
         // retrieve the userID from the database
         //
         boolean success = false;

try {

//
// validate the password from the database
//
GeneralDAO gd = new GeneralDAO( "movies" );

String query = "select user_id from logins where login_name = " +
            "'" + username.trim() + "'" +   " and " +
            " password = " + "'" + password.trim() + "'";

        gd.executeQuery( query );

        //
        // nothing found, return and display failure page
        //
        if ( gd.getRowCount() == 0 ) {
            success = false;
            System.out.println(
                  "No rows found. LoginFailure ... " );
            return (mapping.findForward("logonFailure"));
        }
```

```
        //
        // if we are here, we have a valid login record
        //
        gd.absolute(0);

        //
        // get the user ID
        //
        Integer userID = (Integer) gd.getObject( "user_id" );

        //
        // Save our logged-in user in the session
        //
        HttpSession session = request.getSession();

        session.setAttribute(Constants.USER_NAME, username);
        session.setAttribute(Constants.USER_ID, userID);

        //
        // create a shopping cart bean and add it to our session
        // this cart persists between sessions
        //
        ShoppingCartBean shoppingCart =
                new ShoppingCartBean( userID );

        session.setAttribute(
                Constants.SHOPPING_CART,
                shoppingCart );

        success = true;

}
catch (SQLException e ) {
        servlet.log( "SQLException : " + e );
        success=false;
        throw new ServletException( "SQLException : " + e );
}
catch (ValueObjectException e ) {
        servlet.log( "ValueOjectException : " + e );
        success=false;
        throw new ServletException( "ValueObjectException : " + e );
}
catch (Throwable t ) {
        servlet.log( "Exception : " + t );
        success=false;
        throw new ServletException( "Exception : " + t );
}

finally {
```

```
if ( success ) {
    return (mapping.findForward("success"));
}
else {
    return (mapping.findForward("failure"));
}

}

}

}
```

As you can see in the code example, we first retrieve the login name and password from the request parameters that have been posted to this servlet. A generic DAO is then created to allow database access, and we perform a quick lookup to determine whether or not the user login name and password combination is in our database. If it is, we add the user name and user ID to the user's session. We also create a new shopping cart bean and add that to the session. The shopping cart bean is instantiated using the user ID parameter, so if the user has a current shopping cart in the database, it will be loaded into the bean.

If the user login is not valid, then control is passed to an error page (see Figure 34–1), which will indicate to the user that they have entered an invalid login. This page provides the user with a link to reenter the login information or to return to the main menu.

Note that we do not demonstrate a high level of security in this example. We do not encrypt the user password in the database (which was demonstrated in Chapter 11), and we do not encrypt the user name and password entered in the login form. A more secure implementation would encrypt the password in the database or use a secure database connection, which would encrypt the communication channel between the database and the application. The password entry form could be secured using an SSL connection with HTTP, otherwise known as HTTPS.

User Registration

Before the user registration page is called, the `RegistrationAction` class is called by the servlet controller. The responsibility of this class is to essentially assure that a user bean object is present in the user's session. If a user bean object is not present, it creates one, assigning it a user ID value of zero, and then allows the user to continue.

Figure 34–1   *Movie store error page.*

RegistrationAction.java

```java
package examples.struts;

import java.io.IOException;
import java.util.Hashtable;
import java.util.Vector;
import java.util.Collection;
import java.util.Locale;

import javax.servlet.RequestDispatcher;
import javax.servlet.ServletException;
import javax.servlet.http.HttpServletRequest;
import javax.servlet.http.HttpSession;
import javax.servlet.http.HttpServletResponse;
```

```
import org.apache.struts.action.Action;
import org.apache.struts.action.ActionError;
import org.apache.struts.action.ActionErrors;
import org.apache.struts.action.ActionForm;
import org.apache.struts.action.ActionForward;
import org.apache.struts.action.ActionMapping;
import org.apache.struts.action.ActionServlet;
import org.apache.struts.util.MessageResources;

import db.GeneralDAO;
import common.ValueObjectException;

public final class RegistrationAction extends Action {

public ActionForward perform(ActionMapping mapping,
                ActionForm form,
                HttpServletRequest request,
                HttpServletResponse response)
        throws IOException, ServletException {

// get our session
HttpSession session = request.getSession();

// make sure we have a session attribute for our userID
if ( session.getAttribute( Constants.USER_ID ) == null ) {
    // add a dummy user id
    session.setAttribute( Constants.USER_ID, new Integer(0) );
}

return (mapping.findForward("success"));

}

}
```

The user registration page is a simple HTML form used to gather information about the user, such as his or her name and address. This form is used for both entering new user information as well as updating existing user information. For this reason, a user JavaBean is used to populate the fields on the form. As you can see in the form below, the user ID is retrieved from the user's session. (Since we don't test for a null value, we assert the user ID is in the session, so the action that is executed before this page is loaded must be sure a user ID attribute exists in the session attributes.)

The user ID is used to load the user JavaBean with a call to the `UserBean` `loadUserID` method. This method call executes a query to search in the database for the user ID. If the user is a new user, the user ID zero is used, no rows are retrieved, and the `getProperty` tags to populate the form returns null values. This behavior is explicitly coded into the user bean, as shown below.

```
...
public String getFirstName() {
String retVal=null;
if ( userDAO.getRowCount() == 0 ) {
    return( retVal );
}
  return (String) user.getObject( "first_name" );

}
...
```

If this method is called and no rows are retrieved by the user bean, a null value for the first name property is returned.

Once the user bean has been populated by the call to the `loadUserID` method, we save it to our session and begin building the input form. As you would expect with an input form, we have a succession of `input` tags. These input tags provide a `value` attribute, which allows a default value to be set for the field. In our case, we would like the default value to be whatever the current value of the corresponding attribute is for our user. Since we have loaded our user bean with our user ID on a previous line, we can be assured at this point that the user bean has been populated with the correct values for our user. We simply set the `value` attribute for the input tag to the value of the corresponding property in our user bean as retrieved using a JSP `getProperty` tag. The code for this JSP page is shown below.

The user.jsp Page

```
<%@page import="examples.struts.Constants"%>
<jsp:useBean id="user" class="examples.struts.UserBean" scope="page" />

<html>

<!-- <body bgcolor="#FFFFFF" background="/JavaWeb/img/bggradient.gif">  -->
<body bgcolor="#FFFFFF" background="/JavaWeb/img/bg2_grey.jpg">

<p>UID:<%= session.getAttribute( Constants.USER_ID ) %>

<!-- assert the userID has been set -->
<% user.loadUserID(
            (Integer) session.getAttribute(
                              Constants.USER_ID ) ); %>

<!-- save this as a session attribute -->
<% session.setAttribute( Constants.USER_BEAN, user); %>

<title>User Information</title>

<center>
```

```
<br>
<h1>User Information</h1>
<br>

</center>

<form method="post" action="./adduser.do">

<table border=0 width=100% >

<tr>
 <td width=5%><br/></td>
 <td width=5%> Login Name: </td>
 <td width=20%>
     <input name="login_name" type="text" value="<jsp:getProperty name="user" proper-
ty="loginName" />"/>
 </td>

</tr>

<tr>
<td width=5%><br/></td>
<td width=5%> Last Name: </td>
<td width=20%>
    <input name="last_name" type="text" value="<jsp:getProperty name="user" proper-
ty="lastName" />"/>
</td>
</tr>

<tr>
<td width=5%><br/></td>
<td width=5%> First Name: </td>
<td width=20%>
    <input name="first_name" type="text" value="<jsp:getProperty name="user" proper-
ty="firstName" />"/>
</td>
</tr>

<tr>
<td width=5%><br/></td>
<td width=5%>Address Line 1 </td>
<td width=20%>
    <input name="address1" type="text" value="<jsp:getProperty name="user" proper-
ty="address1" />"/>
</td>
</tr>

<tr>
<td width=5%><br/></td>
<td width=5%>Address Line 2: </td>
<td width=20%>
    <input name="address2" type="text" value="<jsp:getProperty name="user" proper-
```

```
ty="address2" />"/>
</td>
</tr>


<tr>
<td width=5%><br/></td>
<td width=5%> City:   </td>
<td width=20%>
    <input name="city" type="text" value="<jsp:getProperty name="user"
property="city" />"/>
</td>
</tr>


<tr>
<td width=5%><br/></td>
<td width=5%> State/Province: </td>
<td width=20%>
    <input name="state_province" type="text" value="<jsp:getProperty name="user"
property="stateProvince" />"/>
</td>
</tr>


<tr>
<td width=5%><br/></td>
<td width=5%>Country: </td>
<td width=20%>
    <input name="country" type="text" value="<jsp:getProperty name="user"
property="country" />"/>
</td>
</tr>


<tr>
<td width=5%><br/></td>
<td width=5%> Postal Code: </td>
<td width=20%>
    <input name="postal_code" type="text" value="<jsp:getProperty name="user" proper-
ty="postalCode" />"/>
</td>
</tr>


<tr>
<td width=5%><br/></td>
<td width=5%> Email: </td>
<td width=20%>
    <input name="email" type="text" value="<jsp:getProperty name="user"
property="email" />"/>
</td>
</tr>


<tr>
<td width=10%><br/></td>
<td width=5%>
```

```
    <input name="submit" type="submit" value="Submit Changes" />
</td>

</tr>

</table>

</form>

<br/>
<br/>

</body>
</html>
```

The `user.jsp` page posts to the `adduser.do` action. This sends the request to the Struts controller servlet, which maps the `adduser.do` URI to the `AddUserAction` based on the corresponding entry in the `struts-config.xml` file.

The code for the `AddUserAction` class is shown below. This class retrieves the session object and then retrieves the user bean from the session object. The values that have been posted by the `user.jsp` page are then used to populate the attributes of the user bean using calls to the `GeneralDAO setObject` method. Once the bean has been loaded with the appropriate values, the user bean update method is called to update the values to the database.

The AddUserAction Class

```
package examples.struts;

import java.io.IOException;
import java.util.Hashtable;
import java.util.Vector;
import java.util.Collection;
import java.util.Locale;

import javax.servlet.RequestDispatcher;
import javax.servlet.ServletException;
import javax.servlet.http.HttpServletRequest;
import javax.servlet.http.HttpSession;
import javax.servlet.http.HttpServletResponse;

import org.apache.struts.action.Action;
import org.apache.struts.action.ActionError;
import org.apache.struts.action.ActionErrors;
import org.apache.struts.action.ActionForm;
import org.apache.struts.action.ActionForward;
import org.apache.struts.action.ActionMapping;
import org.apache.struts.action.ActionServlet;
```

```
import org.apache.struts.util.MessageResources;

import db.GeneralDAO;
import common.ValueObjectException;

public final class AddUserAction extends Action {

public ActionForward perform(ActionMapping mapping,
                        ActionForm form,
                        HttpServletRequest request,
                        HttpServletResponse response)
      throws IOException, ServletException {

// get our session
HttpSession session = request.getSession();

UserBean userBean = (UserBean)
         session.getAttribute( Constants.USER_BEAN );

userBean.setLoginName( request.getParameter( "login_name" ));
userBean.setFirstName( request.getParameter( "first_name" ));
userBean.setLastName( request.getParameter( "last_name" ));
userBean.setAddress1( request.getParameter( "address1" ));
userBean.setAddress2( request.getParameter( "address2" ));
userBean.setCity( request.getParameter( "city" ));
userBean.setStateProvince(
         request.getParameter( "state_province" ));
userBean.setPostalCode( request.getParameter( "postal_code" ));
userBean.setCountry( request.getParameter( "country" ));
userBean.setEmail( request.getParameter( "email" ));

userBean.update();

return (mapping.findForward("success"));

}

}
```

DISPLAYING THE MAIN MENU

The MenuAction class, as shown below, is used to prepare the main menu for the user. This involves checking to determine whether or not the user has logged into the movie store and has a cart. Two flags are set to indicate whether or not these conditions are true. These flags are placed in the session object where they are retrieved by the menu page to determine how to display the menu.

The MenuAction Class

```java
package examples.struts;

import java.io.IOException;
import java.util.Hashtable;
import java.util.Locale;

import javax.servlet.RequestDispatcher;
import javax.servlet.ServletException;
import javax.servlet.http.HttpServletRequest;
import javax.servlet.http.HttpSession;
import javax.servlet.http.HttpServletResponse;

import org.apache.struts.action.Action;
import org.apache.struts.action.ActionError;
import org.apache.struts.action.ActionErrors;
import org.apache.struts.action.ActionForm;
import org.apache.struts.action.ActionForward;
import org.apache.struts.action.ActionMapping;
import org.apache.struts.action.ActionServlet;
import org.apache.struts.util.MessageResources;

import java.sql.SQLException;
import db.GeneralDAO;
import common.ValueObjectException;

public final class MenuAction extends Action {

    // --
    public ActionForward perform(ActionMapping mapping,
ActionForm form,
                    HttpServletRequest request,
                    HttpServletResponse response)

    throws IOException, ServletException {

    HttpSession session = request.getSession();

        //
    // is the user logged in ?
        // if so, set a boolean flag indicating true
        //
    if ( session.getAttribute(
            Constants.USER_ID ) != null ) {
        session.setAttribute( Constants.LOGGED_IN,
                            new Boolean( true ) );
    } else {
            session.setAttribute( Constants.LOGGED_IN,
                            new Boolean( false ) );
```

```
        }

            //
        // do they have a cart ?
            //
        if ( session.getAttribute(
                    Constants.SHOPPING_CART ) != null ) {
            session.setAttribute( Constants.HAS_CART,
                                    new Boolean( true ) );
        } else {
            session.setAttribute( Constants.HAS_CART,
                                    new Boolean( false ) );
        }

        return (mapping.findForward("success"));

    }




    }
```

THE MENU JSP PAGE

The main menu is a JSP page, which selectively displays menu options based on the user's current state. If the user has logged in, then the option to log into the movies store is not displayed, and the option to log out of the movies store is displayed. If the user has a shopping cart, then the option to list the shopping cart is shown. If the user has logged in, then the user name is retrieved from the session attribute and displayed to the page. Alternatively, if the user has not logged in, then the option to log into the movies store is displayed and the option to log out is not displayed.

These session values are retrieved using the session object and making a call to the getAttribute method.

The index.jsp Page

```
<%@ page language="java" import = "examples.struts.Constants" %>
<html>
<br>
<title>Movie Store: Main Menu</title>
<body>
<br>

<% if (( ((Boolean)
            session.getAttribute(
            Constants.LOGGED_IN )).booleanValue() ) ){ %>
```

```
  <b>You are currently logged in as:</b>  
                              <font color="red">
              <%= session.getAttribute( Constants.USER_NAME ) %>
                                  </font>
<% } %>

<center>
<h1>Movie Store: Main Menu</h1>
</center>
<br>

<table border=0 width=100% >

<tr>
<td width=30%><br></td>

<td width=40%>

<!-- menuAction will set these -->
<% if (!( ((Boolean)
           session.getAttribute(
           Constants.LOGGED_IN )).booleanValue() ) ){ %>
 <a href="./logon.jsp">Login to the Movie Store</a><br>
<% } %>

<% if ( ((Boolean)
         session.getAttribute(
         Constants.HAS_CART )).booleanValue() ) { %>
 <a href="./listMovies.do">List Shopping Cart</a><br>
 <a href="./checkout.do">Checkout</a><br>
<% } else {   %>
 <a href="./listMovies.do">Shop for Movies</a><br>
<% } %>

<% if (!( ((Boolean)
        session.getAttribute(
        Constants.LOGGED_IN )).booleanValue() ) ){ %>
 <a href="./registration.do">New Visitors - Register at the Movie Store</a><br>
<% } else { %>
 <a href="./registration.do">Update User Registration</a><br>
<% } %>

<% if (!( ((Boolean) session.getAttribute(
        Constants.LOGGED_IN )).booleanValue() ) ){ %>
    <a href="./logoff.do">Logout of the Movie Store</a><br>
    <a href="./email.do">Send Email to Webmaster</a><br>
<% } %>

</td>
<td width=50%><br></td>
</tr>
```

```
</table>

</body>
</html>
```

LISTING MOVIES

The shopping cart application lists movies in a generic way. Movies may be listed either as part of a shopping cart or as a listing of movies available in the store. The current implementation simply lists all movies available; a refinement of this approach could provide search criteria and allow the user to filter on criteria such as title or release date.

Since XML and XSLT are used to perform the final display of the movies information, we can manage the differences in the shopping cart listing and the all movies listing in the XSLT script. The servlet that produces the page and the action class that prepares access to the listing servlet just accepts parameters for the XSLT template script and query, and uses those parameters to produce the listing. The decisions on which script and query to use is made in the action servlet, which is called before the servlet is invoked. This is the `ListMoviesAction` servlet shown below.

The list movies action can optionally be called with a parameter to list all movies regardless of the user's state. This is needed for the user who has a shopping cart but would like to add movies to the cart. The link shown below is provided on the bottom of the shopping cart listing page, which explicitly indicates to this action (through the request parameter) that all movies are to be listed.

```
<a href="./listMovies.do?list-action=list-all">Add New Movies to Cart</a>
```

The action class shown below checks to determine whether or not the user has logged in. If the user has not logged in, then we have a problem. Since the list movies page allows the user to add movies to his or her shopping cart, we do not have a cart to use for the user who has not logged in. (Some sites allow a guest ID to be used at this point, but then require a true registration before final checkout.) This action class redirects the user to the login page if he or she has not logged in.

This action then checks the action request parameter to determine how to set the session values for the SQL query to execute and the XSLT template to use. If the user has an existing cart and it is not empty, then we set parameters to list the contents of their cart. Otherwise, we set parameters to list the all movies in the store.

The ListMoviesAction Class

```
package examples.struts;

import java.io.IOException;
import java.util.Locale;
import javax.servlet.RequestDispatcher;
import javax.servlet.ServletException;
import javax.servlet.http.HttpServletRequest;
import javax.servlet.http.HttpSession;
import javax.servlet.http.HttpServletResponse;
import org.apache.struts.action.Action;
import org.apache.struts.action.ActionForm;
import org.apache.struts.action.ActionForward;
import org.apache.struts.action.ActionMapping;
import org.apache.struts.action.ActionServlet;
import org.apache.struts.util.MessageResources;
import org.apache.struts.util.PropertyUtils;

public final class ListMoviesAction extends Action {


    public ActionForward perform(ActionMapping mapping,
                ActionForm form,
                HttpServletRequest request,
                HttpServletResponse response)
        throws IOException, ServletException {

        HttpSession session = request.getSession();

        String action = request.getParameter(
                        Constants.LIST_ACTION );

        //
        // has the user logged on ? if not, force them to do so
        //
        if ( session.getAttribute(
                Constants.USER_NAME ) == null ) {

            // user name not found. forward to logon page
          return ( mapping.findForward( Constants.LOGON ) );
        }

        // if we have been explicitly requested
           // to list all movies, let's
        // set our parameters to do that
        //
        if (( action != null ) &&
            ( action.equals( Constants.LIST_ALL_MOVIES )) ) {

            // populate the session attributes
                session.setAttribute( Constants.XSL_TEMPLATE,
```

```
                              Constants.ALL_TEMPLATE );
        session.setAttribute( Constants.MOVIES_QUERY,
                        Constants.ALL_MOVIES_QUERY );


        //
        // forward the request - list the movies
        // and let the user choose
        //
        return ( mapping.findForward(
                Constants.LIST_MOVIES ) );
    }



    //
    // do they have an existing cart ?
    // if so, and if it's not empty then we show them the cart
    //
    ShoppingCartBean cart = (ShoppingCartBean)
            session.getAttribute( Constants.SHOPPING_CART );
    if ( ( cart != null ) && ( cart.getItemCount() > 0 ) ) {
        session.setAttribute( Constants.XSL_TEMPLATE,
                        Constants.CART_TEMPLATE );
        session.setAttribute( Constants.MOVIES_QUERY,
                        Constants.SHOPPING_CART_QUERY );
    }
    else {  // no cart or empty cart, show them all movies
        session.setAttribute( Constants.XSL_TEMPLATE,
                        Constants.ALL_TEMPLATE );
        session.setAttribute( Constants.MOVIES_QUERY,
                        Constants.ALL_MOVIES_QUERY );
    }

    // forward the request -
    // list the movies and let the user choose
    //
    return ( mapping.findForward( Constants.LIST_MOVIES ) );

}

}
```

THE MOVIES LISTING SERVLET

The movies are listed using the `MoviesChooser` servlet shown below. This servlet reads values from the session object to get the name of the SQL query to execute and the name of the XSLT template to use. These values relate to the names of `init` parameters in the `web.xml` file for the servlet context where the movie store application is deployed. We retrieve the session values and the corresponding `init` parameter values in the `doGet` method, since the shared servlet code may potentially have different callers from different sessions.

Within the `doGet` method, the query is executed (using the `getQueryResults` method) and the results are returned as an XML document. An XML parser and transformer are then created using the XSLT template we have identified, and the XML document is transformed. The result of that transformation is an HTML document containing an HTML table with the movies the query returned. These results are output directly to the response using the `PrintWriter` for the HTTP response. The servlet `init` method obtains an XML processor to be used by the `doGet` method and creates a DAO, which is used in the `doGet` method to execute the query.

The MoviesChooser servlet

```
package examples.struts;

import javax.servlet.*;
import javax.servlet.http.HttpServlet;
import javax.servlet.http.HttpServletRequest;
import javax.servlet.http.HttpServletResponse;
import javax.servlet.http.HttpSession;
import java.sql.SQLException;
import java.io.InputStream;
import java.io.IOException;
import java.io.PrintWriter;
import java.io.StringReader;

import org.xml.sax.SAXException;
import org.xml.sax.InputSource;
import org.apache.struts.action.ActionServlet;

// our packages
import db.GeneralDAO;
import common.ValueObjectException;

// saxon
import com.icl.saxon.trax.*;

public class MoviesChooser extends HttpServlet {

//
// for Saxon XML transformations
//
private Transformer transformer;
private Templates xslTemplates;
private Processor processor;
private GeneralDAO moviesDAO;

// --
```

```java
public void doGet( HttpServletRequest request,
                        HttpServletResponse response)
  throws IOException, ServletException {
String xmlDoc = null;
PrintWriter out = response.getWriter();

HttpSession session = request.getSession();
out.println("");
out.println("");

try {
//
// get the location of the xslt stylesheet from a parameter.
// The name of the parameter to use has been stored in a
// session attribute by ListMoviesAction.
//
String xslTemplateName = (String) session.getAttribute(
                            Constants.XSL_TEMPLATE );
String xslTemplate = getInitParameter( xslTemplateName );

//
// open the stylesheet template and create a transformer
//
InputSource source = new InputSource(
                MoviesChooser.class.getResourceAsStream(
                                xslTemplate ) );

if ( source == null ) {
    log("Could not open input source: " + xslTemplate );
}

xslTemplates = processor.process( source );
transformer = xslTemplates.newTransformer();
//
// retrieve the query results as an XML document. The name of the
// query to run (as stored as an init parameter) has
// been stored in a session attribute by ListMoviesAction.
//
String queryName = (String) session.getAttribute(
                        Constants.MOVIES_QUERY );
xmlDoc = getQueryResults( queryName );

// retrieve the name of the movies query
//
// transform the XML to the format for our output (an HTML table) //
Transformer transformer = xslTemplates.newTransformer(); transformer.transform(
            new InputSource( new StringReader( xmlDoc ) ),
            new Result( out ) );

out.println("");
out.println("");
```

```
} catch (ProcessorException e) {
    log( "ProcessorException in doGet: " + e );
    e.printStackTrace();
}
catch (TransformException e) {
    log( "TransformException in doGet: " + e );
}
catch (SAXException e) {
log( "SAXException in doGet: " + e );
}
}
// ------------------------------------------------------

public String getQueryResults( String param ) {
String retVal = null;
try {
//
// execute query on each call ... reset state
//
moviesDAO.executeQuery( getInitParameter( param ));
//
// convert to XML format
//
retVal=moviesDAO.toXMLDoc();
}
catch (SQLException e) {
    log("SQLException in Movies Listing: " + e );
}
catch (ValueObjectException e) {
    log("ValueObjectException in Movies Listing: " + e );
} finally {
    return retVal;
}
}

public void init( ) {
try {
//
// create the objects we need for the XSL transformation
//
processor = Processor.newInstance("xslt");

//
// create a DAO for our movies DataSource
//
moviesDAO = new GeneralDAO( "movies" );

} catch (SAXException e) {
    log("SAXException in init: " + e ); }


}
}
```

The XSL Template for the Movies Listing

The results of the movies listing query are converted into an XML document and then processed using XML transformation and an XSL template to describe the transformation process. This template as shown below is similar to the example shown in Chapter 16.

The XML document being processed contains elements which contain information on the database table columns returned by the query, and it contains elements which contain the data contained in those columns. The template processing process scans the XML document and produces HTML output in the form of an HTML table. Unlike the example in Chapter 16, this template requires some complex processing to scan the XML document. Consequently, the XSL template script shown below is far from simple but never the less allows us the opportunity to examine some extremely useful capabilities of XSL scripting.

In this example, instead of each column of data in the XML document being treated the same, processing requires a conditional test based on the name of the column. For instance, the ID column requires special treatment. In our XML document, the column name is contained in the `name` element. Using the syntax shown below, we can scan for the `name` element and then test the text value of that element.

```
<xsl:if test="contains(.//column/name/text(), 'ID')">
```

If the column name is ID, then we know that we are at the node where we can retrieve the movie ID we need. We then extract the value of the movie id which is contained in the data element and store it in an XSL variable using the following syntax.

```
<xsl:variable name="movie_id" select=".//column/data"/>
```

We then use the value of the XSL variable, to create a URL for accessing the `BlobView` servlet (the `BlobView` servlet is shown in the next chapter). The `BlobView` servlet takes the movie_id request parameter and constructs a query to the database table containing the graphic images associated with the movie_id. This graphic image is then returned as part of the HTTP response. (This requires that the response type is set correctly for the MIME type being returned; the `Blobview` servlet manages that detail.) As a result of this processing, the graphic image becomes part of the HTML generated for the response page.

Continuing with the XSL template script shown below, we then perform a conditional test to output the name of the movie in the HTML response. The name of the movie then become part of the response output.

The column headers are then placed in the response. Because of the difficulty of managing these dynamically within the sequence of the XML document, they are hardcoded into the template.

An XSL `foreach` loop is then used to iterate through the columns. An XSL choose block is then created. The movie id is used to create a checkbox in the HTML response, and all other elements are simply placed in the response. As directed in the HTML form tag at the start of the document, the submit button will send ouptut to the `submitCart.do` URL, which will force the response to be directed to the Struts controller servlet for processing.

The movies_list.xsl Template

```
<html
 xmlns:xsl="http://www.w3.org/1999/XSL/Transform"
 xsl:version="1.0">

<body>

    <xsl:text>  <!-- submit results through the controller servlet --> </xsl:text>

    <center> <h1>Movies Listing</h1></center>

    <form method="post" action="http://localhost:8080/EShopping/submitCart.do">

<xsl:for-each select="resultset/row">

 <xsl:if test="contains(.//column/name/text(), 'ID')">
    <table border="2" align="center">
      <tr>
        <xsl:variable name="movie_id" select=".//column/data"/>
        <td>
        <img src="http://localhost:8080/J2EE_Beyond/BlobView?movie_id={$movie_id}"
name="Box Picture" align="center" />
        </td>
      </tr>
      <tr>
        <xsl:if test="contains(.//column/name/text(), 'Name')">
          <td>
              <b><xsl:value-of select=".//column/name/data"/></b>
          </td>
        </xsl:if>
      </tr>
    </table>
 </xsl:if>

        <table width="100%" border="2">

          <!-- the column headers -->
          <tr>
            <td bgcolor="gray">Add to Cart</td>
            <td bgcolor="gray">Name</td>
            <td bgcolor="gray">Description</td>
            <td bgcolor="gray">Category</td>
```

```
            <td bgcolor="gray">Price</td>
         </tr>

      <!-- process the data -->

      <tr>

        <xsl:for-each select=".//column">

          <!-- only write a checkbox for the movie_id. for everything else, output
the data  -->

              <xsl:choose>

                <xsl:when test="contains(.//name/text(), 'ID')">

                    <xsl:variable name="movie_id" select=".//data"/>

                      <td>
                      <input type="checkbox" name="movie_id"
value="{$movie_id}"/>
                      </td>

                </xsl:when>

                  <xsl:otherwise>
                  <td><xsl:value-of select=".//data"/> </td>
              </xsl:otherwise>

               </xsl:choose>

             </xsl:for-each>

          </tr>

      </table>

      <HR size="10" width="80%" align="center" />

   </xsl:for-each>

   <input type="submit" value="Add Selections to Cart"/>

 </form>
 </body>
 </html>
```

ADDING TO THE SHOPPING CART

The page generated by the XSL transformation process is processed by the submit cart action. This is done because the controller servlet will map `submitCart.do` URL to this class based on the information we have entered in the Struts configuration file (`struts-config.xml`). As shown below, this class, run as a servlet, processes the list of movies selected as posted by the movies listing page. These movies are added to a collection that is added to the user's shopping cart by the shopping cart bean. If the user does not have a shopping cart, then an error message is logged and an exception is thrown. Since this action may optionally be used to delete movies from the user's shopping cart, there is logic here to provide that functionality. While flow control logic is clearly expressed in this class, all business logic is left to the shopping cart bean.

SubmitCartAction.java

```
package examples.struts;

import java.io.IOException;
import java.util.Hashtable;
import java.util.Vector;
import java.util.Collection;
import java.util.Locale;

import javax.servlet.RequestDispatcher;
import javax.servlet.ServletException;
import javax.servlet.http.HttpServletRequest;
import javax.servlet.http.HttpSession;
import javax.servlet.http.HttpServletResponse;

import org.apache.struts.action.Action;
import org.apache.struts.action.ActionError;
import org.apache.struts.action.ActionErrors;
import org.apache.struts.action.ActionForm;
import org.apache.struts.action.ActionForward;
import org.apache.struts.action.ActionMapping;
import org.apache.struts.action.ActionServlet;
import org.apache.struts.util.MessageResources;

import db.GeneralDAO;
import common.ValueObjectException;

public final class SubmitCartAction extends Action {

public ActionForward perform(ActionMapping mapping,
                ActionForm form,
                HttpServletRequest request,
                HttpServletResponse response)
```

```
        throws IOException, ServletException {

// Validate the request parameters specified by the user
ActionErrors errors = new ActionErrors();

// get our session
HttpSession session = request.getSession();

// Report any errors we have discovered back to the original form
if (!errors.empty()) {
    saveErrors(request, errors);
    return (new ActionForward(mapping.getInput()));
}

String action = request.getParameter( Constants.CART_ACTION );
if ( action == null ) {
        action = Constants.ADD_MOVIES; // our default action
}

//
// we should receive an array of movie_ids the user has selected
//
String movies[] = request.getParameterValues("movie_id");

//
// get our shopping cart bean and add these movies
//
ShoppingCartBean shoppingCart = (ShoppingCartBean) session.getAttribute(
Constants.SHOPPING_CART );

//
// we must have a cart
//
if ( shoppingCart == null ) {
    servlet.log(
      "Shopping cart has not been found in the session." );
    throw new ServletException(
      "Shopping cart has not been found in the session." );
}

//
// if we need to add or delete movies in the cart, let's do that now
//
if ( movies != null ) {

  //
  // load a collection with the Movies
  //
  Vector v = new Vector();
  for ( int n = 0; n < movies.length; n++ ) {
```

```
        v.add( movies[n] );
    }

    //
    // process the shopping cart changes using the
    // shopping cart bean
    //
    try {

        if ( action.equals( Constants.ADD_MOVIES ) )  {
            shoppingCart.addMovies( v );
        }
        if ( action.equals( Constants.DELETE_MOVIES ) ) {
            shoppingCart.deleteMovies( v );
        }

    }
    catch (ValueObjectException t) {
            servlet.log("ValueObjectException adding/deleting movies in the cart: " + t
);
            return ( mapping.findForward("failure"));
    }
}

//
// set this bean as our current cart
//
session.setAttribute( Constants.SHOPPING_CART, shoppingCart );

return (mapping.findForward("success"));

}
```

THE SHOPPING CART BEAN

The shopping cart bean shown below encapsulates the business processing necessary to maintain the user's shopping cart. The bean contains not only the get and set methods for the shopping cart contents but the addMovies method, used to add a collection of movies to the shopping cart, and the deleteMovies method, which allows a collection of movies to be deleted from the shopping cart.

The ShoppingCartBean uses an internal DAO and value object to manage the shopping bean state. A getItemCount method is used to return the count of items in the shopping cart, used by one of the action classes to determine whether or not the cart is empty. (In Chapter 35 we examine how to implement this as an EJB.)

The ShoppingCartBean Class

```
package examples.struts;

import db.GeneralDAO;
import db.GeneralVO;

import java.util.Collection;
import java.util.Iterator;

import common.ValueObjectException;
import jdbcutil.Unique;
import java.sql.SQLException;
import java.sql.Date;

// --
public class ShoppingCartBean {

private GeneralDAO cartDAO;
private GeneralDAO cartItems;
private GeneralDAO control;

private final String NEW_CART_STATUS = "N";
private final String CHECKOUT_STATUS = "C";

// -- get
public Object getObject( String name ) throws ValueObjectException {
    return cartDAO.getObject( name );
}

public int getItemCount() {
    if ( cartItems == null ) {
        return 0;
    }
    else {
        return cartItems.getRowCount();
    }
}

// -- set
public void setObject ( String name, Object obj ) throws ValueObjectException {
    cartDAO.setObject( name, obj );
}
```

The addMovies method accepts a collection of movie IDs and then iterates through the collection. For each item in the collection, a GeneralVO (value object) is created, and then if the item currently doesn't exist in the cart, it is inserted into the cart.

```
public void addMovies( Collection movies ) throws ValueObjectException {

try  {
     Iterator i = movies.iterator();

     java.sql.Date today = new java.sql.Date(
                          new java.util.Date().getTime() );

     int n = 0;
     while ( i.hasNext() ) {

         Integer movie_id = new Integer((String) i.next());

         //
         // only add an item to the cart (and the DB)
         // if it's not already there
         //
         if ( !(cartItems.contains( movie_id ) ) ) {

             GeneralVO item = new GeneralVO();

             item.setObject( "cart_id",
                             cartDAO.getObject( "cart_id" ));
             item.setObject( "movie_id", movie_id );
             item.setObject( "date_added", today );

             // add a cart item
             cartItems.insertVO( "cart_items", item );

         }

     }

}
catch (Throwable t) {
        System.out.println(
               "Throwable exception in addMovies: " + t );
        t.printStackTrace();
}

}
```

The `deleteMovies` method accepts a collection of movie IDs and builds a query to delete the movies from the database. Only movies currently in the cart are deleted. Once the delete operations have been completed, we need to reload the shopping cart to recognize the deleted movies. (We must build a query to perform the delete operations because the DAO class being used uses an updatable `ResultSet` for database updates. Since the movies being deleted have not necessarily been selected in the `ResultSet` used by the DAO, it would not be possible to delete them through the `ResultSet`.)

```
// delete movies from the cart
public void deleteMovies( Collection movies ) throws ValueObjectException {

//
// the query string used to delete the movies from the cart
//
String query = "delete from cart_items where cart_id = " +
               ((Integer) cartDAO.getObject( "cart_id" )) +
               " and movie_id in ( ";

try  {
    Iterator i = movies.iterator();

    java.sql.Date today = new java.sql.Date( new java.util.Date().getTime() );

    int n = 0;

    // just build a query to perform the deletions
    // execute the query and then reload the cartItems
    // (use the expressive power of non-procedural
    // sql to reduce the work required)
    //
    while ( i.hasNext() ) {

        Integer movie_id = new Integer((String) i.next());

        //
        // only delete an item from the cart (and the DB)
        // if it's already there (it should be)
        //
        if ( (cartItems.contains( movie_id ) ) ) {

            // add a cart item
          //
          //
          if ( n == 0 ) { // first pass
             query = query + movie_id;
          }
          else {     // not first pass
             query =  query + "," + movie_id ;
          }
          n++;
          }
    }
  query = query + ")";

   // delete the items from our cart in the DB
   int rowsUpdated = cartItems.executeUpdate( query );

   if ( rowsUpdated >= 1 ) {
      System.out.println( "No rows deleted in deleteMovies." );
      // try to continue
```

```
    }

    // reload the cart items
    loadCartItems( (Integer) cartDAO.getObject( "cart_id" ) );

 }
 catch (Exception e) {
      System.out.println( "SQLException in deleteMovies: " + e );
 }

}
```

The loadCartItems method is used to load the items in the shopping cart. This method is passed an integer cart ID. We create a DAO for the cart items (the movies). If the user has a cart, then we assert that he or she has cart items, and we load the DAO with those items. If the user does not have a cart, then we create one and load it with the correct fields.

```
protected void loadCartItems( Integer cartID ) {
String query = null;

try {

cartItems = new GeneralDAO( "movies" );
//
// get the items in our existing cart
// assert cartDAO has been loaded and
// if we have a master record, we have children
//
if ( cartDAO.getRowCount() > 0 ) {

    //
    // query the cart_items table for our items
    //
    query = "select * from cart_items where cart_id = " + cartID;
    cartItems.executeQuery( query );

}
else { // no shopping cart ... we need to add one

    GeneralVO newCart = new GeneralVO();

    //
    // set to today's date
    //
    java.sql.Date today = new java.sql.Date(
                   new java.util.Date().getTime() );

    newCart.setObject( "cart_id",
                new Integer( Unique.getUniqueID("cart_id")) );
```

```
        newCart.setObject( "user_id",
                       (Integer) cartDAO.getObject( "user_id") );
        newCart.setObject( "create_date",  today );
        newCart.setObject( "update_date",  today );
        newCart.setObject( "status",        NEW_CART_STATUS );

        cartDAO.appendRow();
        cartDAO.absolute(0);

        // load this cart
        cartDAO.loadVO( newCart );
        cartDAO.applyUpdates();
    }


}
catch (SQLException e ) {
    System.out.println(
          "SQLException in loadCartItems: " + e );
}
catch (ValueObjectException e ) {
    System.out.println(
          "ValueObjectException in loadCartItems: " + e );
}


}
```

The constructor for the shopping cart bean creates the DAOs used and then executes a query to determine whether or not the user has a shopping cart. We execute the query using the user ID to get the shopping cart header record. If the user has a shopping cart, then we load the shopping cart items.

```
public ShoppingCartBean( Integer userID ) {

try {
//
// create a control DAO (to get a cart_id )
//
control = new GeneralDAO( "movies" );

//
// create a new cart DAO (header)
//
cartDAO = new GeneralDAO( "movies" );

//
// create a new Items DAO for the movies in the cart
//
cartItems = new GeneralDAO( "movies" );

//
// does the user currently have a shopping cart ?
```

```
//
String query = "select * from shopping_cart where user_id = " +
                  "'" + userID + "'";
cartDAO.executeQuery( query );
cartDAO.absolute(0);
Integer cartId = (Integer) cartDAO.getObject( "cart_id" );

loadCartItems( cartId );

}
catch ( SQLException e ) {
    System.out.println("SQLException in ShoppingCartBean constructor: " + e );
}
catch ( ValueObjectException e ) {
    System.out.println("ValueObjectException in ShoppingCartBean constructor: " + e
);
}


}

}
```

THE CHECKOUT PROCESS

The checkout process for our movie store example requires us to display the contents of our cart and the display the total cost for the contents of the cart. Since we have been using the movies listing servlet (`MoviesChooser`) to list the contents of our cart, it would be convenient to use this same code in the checkout process. The only thing we would have to add to the output would be the total cost items on the bottom of the checkout page. Unfortunately, we use XSL to produce the output for the movies listing page and the XSL template script language does not have the capability to compute totals. The best way for us to obtain the totals is to create a JavaBean to provide this information, which we do with the `CartTotalsBean` class.

So, our approach to using this page is to use the `MoviesChooser` servlet to output part of the page and use the `CartTotalsBean` to output the bottom part of the page. We will use a JSP page to pull both of these elements together using the JSP `include` tag (as discussed in Chapter 28), we can include output from the `MoviesChooser` servlet on the top of the page and use `jsp:getProperty` tags along the bottom of the page, as shown in the next code listing.

The checkout.jsp Page

```
<%@page language="java" import="examples.struts.ShoppingCartBean" %>
<%@page import="examples.struts.Constants" %>
```

```
<HTML>
<BODY bgcolor="white">

<jsp:useBean id="cartTotals" class="examples.struts.CartTotalsBean" scope="request"
/>

<!-- load the bean using the request parameter -->
<%
    ShoppingCartBean cart = (ShoppingCartBean)
                session.getAttribute( Constants.SHOPPING_CART );
    Integer cartID = (Integer) cart.getObject( "cart_id" );
    cartTotals.loadBean( cartID,
        pageContext.getServletContext().getInitParameter(
                            Constants.CART_TOTALS_QUERY ));
%>

<br>
<font face="Helvetica, Sans-serif" size=+3 >
<center>
<b>Movie Store Checkout</b>
</center>
</font>
<br>
<br>

<!-- output the cart listing -->
<jsp:include page="/MoviesChooser" />

<br>

<!-- output the cart totals -->
<table border="2">

<tr>
<td> Subtotal: </td>
<td> <jsp:getProperty name="cartTotals" property="subtotal" /> </td>
</tr>
<tr>
<td> Tax: </td>
<td> <jsp:getProperty name="cartTotals" property="tax" /> </td>
</tr>
<tr>
<td> Grand Total: </td>
<td> <jsp:getProperty name="cartTotals" property="grandTotal" /> </td>
</tr>

</table>

<br>
<a href="./completeCheckout.jsp">Complete Checkout Process</a>
```

```
<br>
<br>

<br>
<br>

</HTML>
</BODY>
```

The CheckoutAction Class

The CheckoutAction class, as shown next, is called before the checkout listing page is output. This class checks to see that the user has logged in, the user has an existing cart, and the cart is not empty. If the user meets these conditions, then the session attributes for the XSL template and the query to execute for the checkout process are set. If there is an error condition, then control is passed to an error page.

The CheckoutAction Class

```
package examples.struts;

import java.io.IOException;
import java.util.Locale;
import javax.servlet.RequestDispatcher;
import javax.servlet.ServletException;
import javax.servlet.http.HttpServletRequest;
import javax.servlet.http.HttpSession;
import javax.servlet.http.HttpServletResponse;
import org.apache.struts.action.Action;
import org.apache.struts.action.ActionForm;
import org.apache.struts.action.ActionForward;
import org.apache.struts.action.ActionMapping;
import org.apache.struts.action.ActionServlet;
import org.apache.struts.util.MessageResources;
import org.apache.struts.util.PropertyUtils;

public final class CheckoutAction extends Action {

    public ActionForward perform(ActionMapping mapping,
                    ActionForm form,
                    HttpServletRequest request,
                    HttpServletResponse response)
        throws IOException, ServletException {

        HttpSession session = request.getSession();
```

```
String action = request.getParameter(
                        Constants.LIST_ACTION );

//
// has the user logged on ? if not, force them to do so
//
if ( session.getAttribute(
                Constants.USER_NAME ) == null ) {
    return ( mapping.findForward( Constants.LOGON ) );
}

 //
 // an existing cart ? if so, we let them checkout
 //
 ShoppingCartBean cart = (ShoppingCartBean)
        session.getAttribute( Constants.SHOPPING_CART );
 if ( ( cart != null ) && ( cart.getItemCount() > 0 ) ) {
    session.setAttribute( Constants.XSL_TEMPLATE,
                        Constants.CHECKOUT_TEMPLATE );
    session.setAttribute( Constants.MOVIES_QUERY,
                        Constants.SHOPPING_CART_QUERY );
}
else { // no cart or empty cart - can't check out
        // error condition
        System.out.println(
         "Attempting checkout with an empty cart." );
        return ( mapping.findForward( "failure" ) );
 }

  //
  // forward the request -
  // list the movies and let the user choose
  //
  return ( mapping.findForward( "success" ) );
}

}
```

The CartTotalsBean

The checkout process requires that a set of totals be output on the bottom of the page. This requires us to use a `CartTotalsBean` to gather the totals for the current shopping cart. The `CartTotalsBean` shown below exposes the `get` and `set` methods, which are used by the `jsp:getProperty` tags to retrieve the subtotal, tax, and grand total lines for the shopping cart. Each of the `get` and `set` methods checks to see that the bean has been loaded, and if it has not been loaded, the method returns a null value.

CartTotalBean.java

```
package examples.struts;

import db.GeneralDAO;
import db.GeneralVO;
import common.ValueObjectException;

import java.sql.SQLException;
import common.StringUtil;

public class CartTotalsBean {
private GeneralVO   cart;
private GeneralDAO cartDAO;

// get
public Double getSubtotal() {
Double retVal=null;

if ( cartDAO.getRowCount() == 0 ) {
    return( retVal );
}
return (Double) cart.getObject( "subtotal" );

}

public Double getTax() {
Double retVal=null;

if ( cartDAO.getRowCount() == 0 ) {
    return( retVal );
}

return (Double) cart.getObject( "tax" );

}
// --

public Double getGrandTotal() {
Double retVal=null;
if ( cartDAO.getRowCount() == 0 ) {
    return( retVal );
}
 return (Double) cart.getObject( "grand_total" );

}
```

The `loadBean` method of the `CartTotalsBean` is shown next. This method is passed the cart ID for the shopping cart and the query to execute to load the bean. Before the query is executed, the `?` placeholder in the query string is replaced with the cart ID of the shopping cart. (Because of the complexities of handling JDBC prepared statements, the DAO does not expose a prepared statement, and therefore we need to replace the ? instead of creating a prepared statement.)

The constructor for the CartTotalsBean is also shown below. This constructor simply creates the GeneralVO and GeneralDAO objects that are used by the bean.

```
//
// execute a query to retrieve the totals for the
// shopping cart
//
public void loadBean( Integer cartID, String query ) {

try {

  //
  // set our cart_id in the query string
  //
  query = StringUtil.replace( query, "?", cartID.toString());

  cartDAO.executeQuery( query );
  cartDAO.absolute(0);
  cart = cartDAO.getVO();

}
catch (SQLException e ) {
      System.out.println("SQLException in loadBean: "  + e );
}
catch (ValueObjectException e ) {
      System.out.println("ValueObjectException in loadBean: "  +
                          e );
}

}

public CartTotalsBean() {

cart    = new GeneralVO();
cartDAO = new GeneralDAO( "movies" );

}

}
```

SENDING EMAIL

The shopping cart example we have reviewed allowed the user to send an email to the Webmaster for the site. This provides an opportunity to examine the use of JavaMail in a Web application. The JSP page shown next demonstrates how this is done.

The MailService (examples.javamail.MailService) class provides a simplified access to the JavaMail API. We also access the user bean from the session to allow us to fill in the values for some of the fields in the form.

This page is an HTML form and contains various input tags to gather information about the email. The from email address is provided on one of these lines. We use the value attribute for the input tag to set the value to that of the email address of the reader.

The email.jsp Page

```
<%@page import="examples.struts.Constants"%>
<%@page import="examples.javamail.MailService"%>
<%@page import="examples.struts.UserBean" %>

<jsp:useBean id="user" class="examples.struts.UserBean" scope="request"/>

<% user = (UserBean) session.getAttribute( Constants.USER_BEAN ); %>

<html>
<body bgcolor="#FFFFFF">

<title>Send Email Message</title>

<center>

<br>
<h1>Email Message</h1>
<br>

</center>

<form method="post" action="./emailProcess.do">

<table border=0 width=100% >

<tr>
 <td width=5%> To: </td>
 <td width=20%>
    <input name="message_to" type="text" value="emailguy@zippy.net" />
 </td>

</tr>
```

```
<tr>
<td width=5%> From: </td>
<td width=20%>
    <input name="message_from" type="text" value="<jsp:getProperty name="user" prop-
erty="email" />"/>
</td>
</tr>

<tr>
<td width=5%> Message: </td>
<td width=20%>
    <textarea name="message" rows="3" cols="65" wrap>Insert message here</textarea>
</td>
</tr>

<tr>
<td width=5%>
    <input name="submit" type="submit" value="Send Email" />
</td>

</tr>

</table>

</form>

<br/>
<br/>

</body>
</html>
```

The `EmailAction` class as shown below, is used to validate that the user has logged in to the movie store. If they have logged in then the user ID is not equal to 0 (indicating an anonymous user or guest user). If the user has not logged in, they are forwarded to a login page.

The EmailAction Class

```
package examples.struts;

import java.io.IOException;
import javax.servlet.RequestDispatcher;
import javax.servlet.ServletException;
import javax.servlet.http.HttpServletRequest;
import javax.servlet.http.HttpSession;
import javax.servlet.http.HttpServletResponse;

import org.apache.struts.action.Action;
```

```
import org.apache.struts.action.ActionError;
import org.apache.struts.action.ActionErrors;
import org.apache.struts.action.ActionForm;
import org.apache.struts.action.ActionForward;
import org.apache.struts.action.ActionMapping;
import org.apache.struts.action.ActionServlet;

public final class EmailAction extends Action {

public ActionForward perform(ActionMapping mapping,
                    ActionForm form,
                    HttpServletRequest request,
                    HttpServletResponse response)
        throws IOException, ServletException {

// Validate the request parameters specified by the user
//
// get our session
//
HttpSession session = request.getSession();

// Report any errors we have discovered back to the original form
if (!errors.empty()) {
    saveErrors(request, errors);
    return (new ActionForward(mapping.getInput()));
}

//
// is the user logged in
//
Integer userID = (Integer)
                session.getAttribute( Constants.USER_ID );

if ( ( userID != null ) && ( userID.intValue() > 0 ) )  {
    return (mapping.findForward("success"));
}
else { // require them to logon
    return (mapping.findForward("logon"));
}

}

}
```

Processing the Email

The `EmailProcessAction` class shown next performs the task of using the sending the email entered on the `email.jsp` page. This page receives the request parameters from the `email.jsp` page shown previously. A `MailService` class instance (`examples.javamail.MailService` shown in Chapter 21) is delegated the work of creating the email message and sending the email. The `makeMessage` method of this class is used to create a message, and then the request parameter values are used to set the `from` and `to` values of the email message. We then try to set the message subject and message text, and catch any errors that might occur. If we succeed without any errors, the message is sent.

The EmailProcessAction Class

```java
package examples.struts;

import java.io.IOException;

import javax.servlet.RequestDispatcher;
import javax.servlet.ServletException;
import javax.servlet.http.HttpServletRequest;
import javax.servlet.http.HttpSession;
import javax.servlet.http.HttpServletResponse;

import org.apache.struts.action.Action;
import org.apache.struts.action.ActionError;
import org.apache.struts.action.ActionErrors;
import org.apache.struts.action.ActionForm;
import org.apache.struts.action.ActionForward;
import org.apache.struts.action.ActionMapping;
import org.apache.struts.action.ActionServlet;

import javax.mail.MessagingException;
import javax.mail.internet.MimeMessage;

import examples.javamail.MailService;

public final class EmailProcessAction extends Action {

public ActionForward perform(ActionMapping mapping,
                    ActionForm form,
                    HttpServletRequest request,
                    HttpServletResponse response)
       throws IOException, ServletException {

// get our session
HttpSession session = request.getSession();

String messageTo   = request.getParameter( "message_to" );
String messageFrom = request.getParameter( "message_from" );
String messageText = request.getParameter( "message" );

MailService mailer = new MailService();

MimeMessage message = mailer.makeMessage( messageFrom,
```

```
                              messageTo );

try {
  message.setSubject("Movie Store Request");
  message.setText( messageText );
}
catch (MessagingException e) {
    System.out.println("Messaging Exception: " + e );
    return (mapping.findForward("failure"));
}

// send the message
mailer.sendMessage( message );

return (mapping.findForward("success"));

}

}
```

LOGGING OUT OF THE MOVIE STORE

The LogOffAction class shown next is used to log users out of the shopping cart site. When executed, this class removes the user ID, user name, and other user information from the session. It also sets the LOGGED_IN and the HAS_CART session attributes set to false. Once this action is completed, the flow of control is directed back to the main menu.

The LogoffAction Class

```
package examples.struts;

import java.io.IOException;

import javax.servlet.RequestDispatcher;
import javax.servlet.ServletException;n
import javax.servlet.http.HttpServletRequest;
import javax.servlet.http.HttpSession;
import javax.servlet.http.HttpServletResponse;

import org.apache.struts.action.Action;
import org.apache.struts.action.ActionError;
import org.apache.struts.action.ActionErrors;
import org.apache.struts.action.ActionForm;
import org.apache.struts.action.ActionForward;
import org.apache.struts.action.ActionMapping;
import org.apache.struts.action.ActionServlet;
```

```
import org.apache.struts.util.MessageResources;

public final class LogoffAction extends Action {

    public ActionForward perform(ActionMapping mapping,
                      ActionForm form,
                      HttpServletRequest request,
                      HttpServletResponse response)
        throws IOException, ServletException {

        // Validate the request parameters specified by the user
        ActionErrors errors = new ActionErrors();

        HttpSession session = request.getSession();

        session.removeAttribute( Constants.USER_ID );
        session.removeAttribute( Constants.USER_NAME );
        session.removeAttribute( Constants.SHOPPING_CART );

        // we expect these to always exist ... set them to false
        session.setAttribute(  Constants.LOGGED_IN,
                                new Boolean( false ) );
        session.setAttribute( Constants.HAS_CART,
                                new Boolean( false) );


        return( mapping.findForward( "success" ));

}

}
```

THE CONSTANTS

The Constants class only contains string members used as constants throughout
the application. The contents of this class is shown next.

The Constants Class

```
package examples.struts;

public class Constants {

// session attribute keys
public static final String USER_NAME      = "username";
public static final String USER_ID        = "userID";
public static final String SHOPPING_CART  = "shoppingCart";
```

```
// the key to our session attribute
public static final String XSL_TEMPLATE   = "xsl-template";

// our session attribute values. relate to init-params in the web.xml file
public static final String ALL_TEMPLATE    = "all-template";
public static final String CART_TEMPLATE  = "cart-template";
public static final String CHECKOUT_TEMPLATE = "checkout-template";

// the key to our session attribute
public static final String MOVIES_QUERY = "movies-query";
public static final String USER_BEAN    = "user-bean";

// our session attribute values
public static final String SHOPPING_CART_QUERY  = "existing-cart-query";
public static final String ALL_MOVIES_QUERY     = "all-movies-query";

// servlet context parameter key
public static final String CART_TOTALS_QUERY    = "cart-totals-query";

// our forward value for the struts-config.xml file
public static final String LIST_MOVIES = "list-movies";
public static final String LOGON       = "logon";

// request parameter keys
public static final String CART_ACTION = "cart-action";
public static final String LIST_ACTION = "list-action";
public static final String CHECKOUT_ACTION = "checkout-action";

// request parameter values
public static final String LIST_ALL_MOVIES = "list-all";
public static final String ADD_MOVIES      = "movies-add";
public static final String DELETE_MOVIES   = "movies-delete";

// flags for menu building. mapped  to boolean values
public static final String HAS_CART    = "has-cart";
public static final String LOGGED_IN   = "logged-in";

}
```

DEPLOYING AND RUNNING THE APPLICATION

In order to run any J2EE Web application, it must be deployed into the Web server. For this application, the directory structure EShopping must be created under the root context for the server. Within the EShopping directory, there must be a subdirectory structure, as follows.

```
./EShopping
./EShopping/META-INF
./EShopping/WEB-INF
./EShopping/WEB-INF/classes
./EShopping/WEB-INF/classes/examples
./EShopping/WEB-INF/classes/examples/struts
./EShopping/WEB-INF/lib
```

In order to invoke the main menu through the Struts controller, we use the following URL.

```
http://localhost:8080/mainMenu.do
```

Within the `WEB-INF` directory, Struts requires a number of configuration files. The following contains a listing of this directory.

```
classes/
lib/
struts-bean.tld
struts-config.xml
struts-form.tld
struts-html.tld
struts-logic.tld
struts-template.tld
struts.tld
web.xml
```

The `.tld` files are the tag library descriptors, which were not used extensively in this example. The `struts-config.xml` is the Struts configuration file which was shown previously. This file is used to describe the navigational flow for the Struts controller servlet. The `web.xml` file should be familiar to us by now; this is the Web application and servlet configuration file for this context.

The Struts framework requires that the classes in the `struts.jar` classes be available to the Web application. The best location for the JAR file using Tomcat is in the `./lib` directory of the context. We also use a number of other classes in our application—the DAO classes, for instance and we have a JAR file that contains these classes (`J2EE_Beyond.jar`). The contents of our `./lib` directory are as follows.

```
struts.jar
J2EE_Beyond.jar
```

SUMMARY

This chapter explained the implementation of a Model 2/MVC/framework-based application using the Struts package. We examined the code in detail and found useful implementations of the DAO and value object design patterns. We also demonstrated of the use of XML transformations to create HTML output.

In the next chapter we will take a look at some of the servlets and helper classes we saw used in the code shown in this chapter: the `BlobView` servlet and the DAO and value object implementations. We will also examine how to integrate EJBs into this application by implementing the `ShoppingCartBean` shown in this chapter as an EJB.

The Shopping Cart
Application:
Using EJBs and Blobs

INTRODUCTION

In the previous chapter we looked at a movie store application that used two J2EE components, JSP and servlets, to create the application. While it is not uncommon to create an application with only these two J2EE components, we cannot get a complete view of J2EE components without taking a look at using EJBs with this application. In this chapter, we will look at how we can refactor the shopping cart application to use an EJB to implement the `ShoppingCartBean` shown in the previous chapter.

The movie store application also used a servlet to output graphic images (the images of the movie video box) from a database to an HTML page. Storing graphic images in a database has a number of advantages. But to use graphics in a database we need a simple facility for retrieving the image and returning it with the servlet response. We did this in the previous chapter using the `BlobView` servlet and in this chapter we will examine the code behind this servlet.

REFACTORING THE SHOPPINGCARTBEAN

The `ShoppingCartBean` class is used by the action classes and servlets to interact with the user's shopping cart. The main purpose of this component is to provide a mechanism to add one or more movies to the shopping cart or to delete one or more movies from the shopping cart. The movies are selected for addition or deletion to the cart on the two HTML forms generated by the `MoviesChooser` servlet. These forms post to an action class, which compiles the user's selections in a collection that is used by the action servlet (`SubmitCartAction`) to call either the `addMovies` method or the `deleteMovies` method on the `ShoppingCartBean`.

We would like to refactor the `ShoppingCartBean` in a way that has a limited impact on the remainder of the application. If we do this correctly, then the other components in the application will be none the wiser. We will do this by effectively creating a presentation tier proxy for the `ShoppingCartBean` (an implementation of the proxy pattern) using the refactored `ShoppingCartBean`. This presentation tier object will use the remote reference to the shopping cart EJB, basically wrapping the remote object and making calls on it as needed. As we will see in the next section, our shopping cart EJB will simply extend the `ShoppingCartBean` and expose the remote methods needed by the `ShoppingCartBean` running on the presentation tier—the remote client.

The user's shopping cart is referenced by a cart ID, which is in turn referenced by the user ID. The user never sees the cart ID (it is not displayed on any page); it is stored and used internally. In this implementation, the user will have only a single shopping cart, so there is a one-to-one relationship between the user ID and the shopping cart ID. When the `ShoppingCartBean` is created, a user ID is passed into the constructor. This user ID is then used to look up the user's single shopping cart, if there is a shopping cart.

We have left each of the method signatures in this bean the same as in the previous example, since this is the interface it exposes to the action classes. In this way, none of the classes it interacts with will need to change.

The refactored `ShoppingCartBean` is shown next. The constructor for the class obtains a connection to the EJB server and then requests the shopping cart EJB. Once the home reference has been cast and narrowed, the handle for the reference is stored.

The `ShoppingCartBean` is created in the movie store application during the login process. Once the user ID has been obtained by the login process, and after it is determined that it is a valid user login, the user ID is used to create a `ShoppingCartBean`, and the resulting `ShoppingCartBean` is stored in the user's session. By storing the EJB reference handle (`javax.ejb.Handle`), we create a convenient mechanism that allows us to quickly and easily reestablish contact with our EJB.

The Refactored ShoppingCartBean Class

```
package examples.eshop;

import java.util.Hashtable;
import java.util.Collection;

import java.rmi.RemoteException;
import javax.naming.InitialContext;
import javax.naming.NamingException;
import javax.rmi.PortableRemoteObject;

import javax.ejb.EJBHome;
import javax.ejb.Handle;
import javax.ejb.CreateException;

import examples.eshopejb.ShoppingCartSBRemote;
import examples.eshopejb.ShoppingCartSBHome;

import common.ValueObjectException;

//
// wraps the shopping cart EJB
//
public class ShoppingCartBean {

Handle cart;

public ShoppingCartBean( Integer userID ) {

try {

   Hashtable env = new Hashtable();

   //
   // specify a connection to the JBoss EJB server
   // In a production application, we would store
   // these parameters in a properties file, or in
   // servlet context parameters
   //
   env.put( "java.naming.factory.initial",
            "org.jnp.interfaces.NamingContextFactory");
   env.put( "java.naming.provider.url", "jnp://localhost:1099");
   env.put( "java.naming.factory.url.pkgs",
            "org.jboss.naming:org.jnp.interfaces");
   env.put( "jnp.socketFactory",
            "org.jnp.interfaces.TimedSocketFactory" );

   //
   // get the initial naming service context
   //
   InitialContext init = new InitialContext( env );
```

```
//
// get a reference to the MoviesSB bean
//
ShoppingCartSBHome cartHome;

Object o = init.lookup( "ejb/ShoppingCartSB" );
if ( o == null ) {
    System.out.println(
        "Null reference returned by naming service.");
    return;
}
else {

cartHome = (ShoppingCartSBHome)
    PortableRemoteObject.narrow( o, ShoppingCartSBHome.class );
}

// store the handle
cart = cartHome.create( userID ).getHandle();

}
catch ( NamingException e ) {
    System.out.println(
        "NamingException in ShoppingCartBean constructor: " + e );
}
catch ( RemoteException e ) {
    System.out.println(
      "RemoteException in ShoppingCartBean constructor: " + e );
}
catch ( Exception e ) {
    System.out.println(
        "Exception in ShoppingCartBean constructor: " + e );
}
catch ( Throwable t ) {
    System.out.println(
        "Exception in ShoppingCartBean constructor: " + t );
    t.printStackTrace();
}

}
```

Each method in the `ShoppingCartBean` must obtain a remote reference to the EJB. This is because we have not stored a remote reference (which may not be valid across calls) but have instead stored a handle to the EJB. We must make a `getEJBObject` call on the handle to obtain the `EJBObject` for the handle. We then cast down to our `EJBObject` implementation (our remote reference), the `ShoppingCartSBRemote` implementation.

```
// -- get
public Object getObject( String name ) throws RemoteException {
Object o = null;
try {
        o = ((ShoppingCartSBRemote)
            cart.getEJBObject()).getObject( name );
}
catch (RemoteException e ) {
      System.out.println("RemoteException in addMovies: " + e );
}
finally {
      return o;
}

}

public int getItemCount() throws RemoteException {
int i = 0;
try {
      i = ((ShoppingCartSBRemote)
          cart.getEJBObject()).getItemCount();
}
catch (RemoteException e ){
      System.out.println("RemoteException in getItemCount: " +
                              e );
}
finally {
      return i;
}

}

// -- set
public void setObject ( String name, Object obj ) {
try {
      ((ShoppingCartSBRemote)
            cart.getEJBObject()).setObject( name,
                                    obj );
}
catch (RemoteException e ){
      System.out.println("RemoteException in addMovies: " + e );
}

}
```

The addMovies, deleteMovies, and loadCartItems calls use the EJB reference as the other calls do. They pass a collection (movies), which is serializable as required by the EJB specification (and the underlying RMI implementation).

```
public void addMovies( Collection movies ) throws ValueObjectException {
try {

    ((ShoppingCartSBRemote)
```

```
                cart.getEJBObject()).addMovies( movies );
}
catch (RemoteException e ){
        System.out.println("RemoteException in addMovies: " +
                              e );
        throw new ValueObjectException(
                "RemoteException in addMovies: " +
                e );
}


}

public void deleteMovies( Collection movies ) throws ValueObjectException {
try {

    ((ShoppingCartSBRemote)
        cart.getEJBObject()).deleteMovies( movies );
}
catch (RemoteException e) {
        System.out.println("RemoteException in deleteMovies: " +
                              e );
        throw new ValueObjectException(
                "RemoteException in deleteMovies: "
                + e );
}


}

public void loadCartItems( Integer cartID ) {
try {
    ((ShoppingCartSBRemote)
        cart.getEJBObject()).loadCartItems( cartID );
}
catch (RemoteException e ) {
        System.out.println(
                "RemoteException in loadCartItems e: " + e );
}


}

public ShoppingCartBean( ) {
}


}
```

THE SESSION BEAN CODE

The session bean declared for the shopping cart EJB demonstrates object-oriented code reuse by simply extending the ShoppingCartBean class developed for the first example. Since the EJB specification allows EJBs to be part of an inheritance hierarchy (even though they themselves cannot be extended), this use of inheritance is allowed.

The `ejbCreate` method shown next has been overloaded to accept an argument for the `userID`. This integer value is passed to the method and used to set the `userID` for the shopping cart. All other functionality provided by the session bean is in fact provided by its superclass, the `ShoppingCartBean`. Note that any methods exposed in the session bean's remote interface must be declared public (which was not the case in the first example and had to be changed as part of this refactoring).

```
package examples.eshopejb;

import javax.ejb.*;
import java.rmi.RemoteException;
import javax.rmi.PortableRemoteObject;
import java.io.Serializable;

import java.sql.*;
import javax.sql.*;
import javax.naming.*;

import db.GeneralVO;
import jdbcutil.*;

//
//
public class ShoppingCartSB extends ShoppingCartBean implements SessionBean {

SessionContext context;

// remote methods --
public void ejbCreate(Integer userID ) throws CreateException {

        //
        // get the cart for this user
        //
        setUserID( userID );
}

public void setSessionContext(SessionContext sc) {

        //
        // store the SessionContext
        //
     this.context = sc;
}

// ** required, but not used **
public void remove() {}
public void ejbPostCreate() { }
```

```
public void ejbRemove() { }
public void ejbActivate() { }
public void ejbPassivate() { }

public ShoppingCartSB() {
        super( new Integer(0) ); // can't call a no-arg superclass constructor
}

}
```

The Home Interface

The home interface for the shopping cart session bean simply declares the over-loaded `create` method, which accepts the user ID as an argument, for the session bean.

```
package examples.eshopejb;

import javax.ejb.EJBHome;
import javax.ejb.CreateException;
import java.io.Serializable;
import java.rmi.RemoteException;

public interface ShoppingCartSBHome extends EJBHome {

    public ShoppingCartSBRemote create( Integer userID ) throws RemoteException,
CreateException;

}
```

The Remote Interface

The remote interface for the shopping cart session bean declares all of the methods exposed by the `ShoppingCartBean` component and must be made available remotely through the session bean's interface. As required by the EJB specification, all of the arguments passed to the methods and returned by the methods are serializable.

```
package examples.eshopejb;

import javax.ejb.EJBObject;
import java.io.Serializable;
import java.rmi.RemoteException;
import java.util.Collection;

public interface ShoppingCartSBRemote extends EJBObject {
```

```
public Object getObject( String name );
public void setObject ( String name, Object obj );
public void addMovies( Collection movies );
public void deleteMovies( Collection movies );
public void loadCartItems( Integer cartID ) ;
public int getItemCount() ;


}
```

THE BLOBVIEW SERVLET

The BlobView class as shown in the previous chapter, is a servlet that receives a single parameter that represents an ID number for a movie stored in the database. The ID number is used to find the BLOB record in the database, retrieve it, and write it to the output stream for the HTTP response (see Figure 35–1).

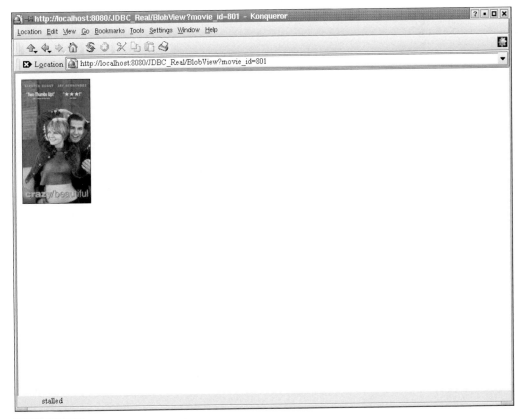

Figure 35–1 *The BlobView servlet*

The movie ID number (`movie_id`) is retrieved from a request parameter, so the URL to call the `BlobView` servlet is as follows:

```
http://serverName/ServletExamples/BlobView?movie_id=801
```

The job of finding and retrieving the BLOB and writing it to the output stream is left to an associated class (`BlobWriter`) so that the servlet is really only responsible for retrieving the request parameter and calling the methods in the associated class to perform the other work required. The code for the `BlobView` servlet is shown in the following example:

```java
package examples.servlets;

import java.io.*;
import javax.servlet.*;
import javax.servlet.http.*;
import java.sql.*;
import java.net.*;
import db.*;
import movies.blobs.*;


public class BlobView extends HttpServlet {

ServletConfig        config;
ServletContext       context;

BlobWriter                blobwriter;


    public void doGet(HttpServletRequest request,
                      HttpServletResponse response)
        throws IOException, ServletException
    {

        //
        // get the output stream for our response
        //
        OutputStream out = response.getOutputStream();

        //
        // set the content type for our graphic file to return
        //
        response.setContentType("image/jpeg");

        try {

            //
```

```
            // this will retrieve the Blob referenced
            // by the movie_id and write it to the
            //OutputStream parameter passed in
        //
        blobwriter.getBlob(
                Integer.parseInt(
                    request.getParameter( "movie_id" ) ), out );


        }
        catch (Exception e) {
                log( "Exception in doGet: " + e.getMessage() );
        }


    }

public void init( ServletConfig config ) {

    //
    // BlobWriter will open the connection and create
    // a PreparedStatement to perform the database i/o
    //
    blobwriter = new BlobWriter( "jdbc/moviesmysql " );

    //
    // save the servlet context
    //
    context  = config.getServletContext();


}


}
```

The `BlobView` servlet uses the `init` method to create a new instance of the `BlobWriter` class, the class that will perform the work necessary to retrieve and display the graphic image. The `BlobWriter` class is passed the JNDI name of the `DataSource` to use to retrieve the images. The servlet context is also obtained in the `init` method.

The `doGet` method retrieves the output stream for the HTTP response by making a call to the `HttpServletResponse getOutputStream` method. The content type for the output is then set to `image/jpeg`, indicating that the response contains a JPEG format graphic image. The `BlobWriter getBlob` method is then called and passed two arguments: an integer for the `movie_id` record to retrieve and the `OutputStream` reference for the response output stream. The work performed by the `getBlob` method is explained in the next section.

THE BLOBWRITER CLASS

The `BlobWriter` class is the utility class used by the `BlobView` servlet. This class contains the methods that perform the task of retrieving the BLOB column for viewing. Unlike some of the other utility classes, this class takes on the responsibility of establishing a connection to the database and creating the prepared statement to use in the database operation. The code for this class is shown in the next few sections.

The BlobWriter Class: The Class Declaration and the main Program Block

The main class declaration for the `BlobWriter` class performs the imports we expect to access JNDI naming services and to use the JDBC API. For convenience, instance members are created for a JDBC `Connection` reference and for a `PreparedStatement` reference.

The `getBlob` method is the method exposed to the client objects. This method takes two parameters: an integer for the `movie_id` record to retrieve and an `OutputStream` reference for the output stream where the BLOB should be written. The `movie_id` is used to set the parameter for the first element in the prepared statement and then executes the `writeBlob` method to perform the task of retrieving the BLOB and writing it.

The BlobWriter Class: Class Declaration and the main Program Block

```
import java.rmi.*;
import javax.naming.*;
import javax.rmi.*;
import java.sql.*;
import javax.sql.*;
import java.util.*;
import java.io.*;

import db.*;

public class BlobWriter {

private Connection                con;
private PreparedStatement   prepStmt;

public void getBlob(int movie_id, OutputStream out ) {

try {

  prepStmt.setInt( 1,movie_id );
  writeBlob( out );
```

```
}
catch (SQLException e) {
      System.out.println("SQLException in getBlob: " +
                           e.getMessage());
      throw new Exception( "SQLException in getBlob: " +
                             e.getMessage());
}
catch (Exception e) {
    System.out.println( "Exception in getBlob: " +
                          e.getMessage());
      throw new Exception( "Exception in getBlob: " +
                             e.getMessage());
}
}
```

The BlobWriter Class: The writeBlob Method

The writeBlob method performs the core work of the BlobWriter class. This private method receives an OutputStream reference where the contents of the BLOB should be written. It creates a byte array buffer with a fixed size (tuned to the size of the graphics we know are stored in the column).

The method executes the query for the prepared statement, and if no rows have been found, it goes no further; a message is displayed indicating the error condition, an exception is thrown, and the method returns (by nature of the exception being thrown).

The getBinaryStream method is then used to obtain an InputStream on the BLOB column (which is column two in the ResultSet). The InputStream is then used in a loop to perform read operations on the stream, reading bytes from the InputStream and writing all bytes read to the OutputStream. This is done until the byte count from the read operation is less than zero (–1). Before the method returns, both the InputStream and the OutputStream are closed. The code for this method follows:

The BlobWriter Class: The writeBlob Method

```
private void writeBlob( OutputStream out )throws Exception {
int byteCount = 0;
byte[] buffer = new byte[1024*5];

try {

//
// execute the query. Throw exception and return if no rows found
//
ResultSet rs = prepStmt.executeQuery();
```

```
if ( !(rs.next()) ) {
    System.out.println("Blob row not found.");
    throw new Exception( "Blob row not found.");
}

//
// get the InputStream for the Blob column
//
InputStream input = rs.getBinaryStream( 2 );

//
// read till bytes read == 0. Write all bytes to the
// OutputStream
//
byteCount = input.read( buffer );
while ( byteCount > 0 ) {

        out.write( buffer );
        byteCount = input.read( buffer );

}

input.close();
out.close();
}
catch( IOException e) {
        System.out.println( "IOException in writeBlob: " +
                              e.getMessage() );
        throw new Exception(  "IOException in writeBlob: " +
                              e.getMessage() );
}
catch( SQLException e) {
        System.out.println( "SQLException in writeBlob: " +
                              e.getMessage() );
        throw new Exception(  "IOException in writeBlob: " +
                              e.getMessage() );
}


}
```

The BlobWriter Class: The prepareStatement Method

The `prepareStatement` method performs the task of preparing the SQL statement to be executed to retrieve the BLOB. In this example, the query is hardcoded into the application code. (A different implementation would potentially store the query in a properties file and extract the value of the query at runtime.) The code for this method is shown next.

```
private void prepareStatement() {

try {
   prepStmt = con.prepareStatement(
                     "select movie_id, movie_image " +
                     " from movie_images " +
                     " where movie_id = ?" );

}
catch (SQLException e ) {
      System.out.println("SQLException in prepareStatement: " +
                           e.getMessage() );
}

}
```

The BlobWriter Class: The getConnected Method

The getConnected method creates, as the name implies, a connection to the database. This method is overloaded using a no-argument version to create a connection to a default DataSource. A version that uses a string parameter allows a specific DataSource name to be specified. This version performs the work of obtaining the InitialContext and executing the lookup method to find the specific DataSource requested. The code for this method is shown next.

The BlobWriter Class: The getConnected Method

```
private void  getConnected() {

 getConnected( "movies" );

}


private void getConnected(String dataSourceName ) {

try {

      InitialContext context = new InitialContext( );

      DataSource ds = (DataSource) context.lookup(
                                        dataSourceName );

      con = ds.getConnection();

   }
catch (SQLException e) {
      System.out.println("SQLException caught in getConnected: " +
```

```
                                          e.getMessage() );
}
catch (NamingException e) {
     System.out.println("NamingException caught in getConnected: "
                             +    e.getMessage() + " - " + e );
     System.out.println("Resolved Name: " + e.getResolvedName()  );

}
catch (Exception e) {
     System.out.println("Exception caught in getConnected: " +
                             e.getMessage() );
}


}
```

The BlobWriter Class: The Constructor

The constructor for the `BlobWriter` class prepares the class for usage by establishing a connection to the data source and preparing the SQL statement. The `getConnected` method is used to obtain the connection to the data source, and the `prepareStatement` method is used to prepare the SQL statement to be used in the servlet. The constructor is overloaded to include a no-argument version that constructs the class with a default data source name. The code for this constructor follows:

The BlobWriter Class: The Constructor

```
public BlobWriter() {
  //
  // create a connection to the database
  // using the default DataSource
  //
  new BlobWriter( "movies" );
}

public BlobWriter( String dataSourceName ) {

  // create a connection to the database
  getConnected( dataSourceName );

  // prepare the sql statement
  prepareStatement();

}

}
```

THE DATA ACCESS OBJECT: THE GENERALDAO CLASS

The data access object encapsulates the specifics of data access in a class design. It is intended to be a coarse-grained object, meaning that the details of the data being accessed (the columns, the data types) are not necessarily understood or managed by the class.

Note that a design pattern is a recommended solution, a desirable approach. A design pattern is not a template, though a template for a class or an interface for a class could result from the implementation of a design pattern. For that reason, there is no template for a data access object; there is just a set of recommendations.

This data access object presents a *generalized* approach to retrieving data. It has not been written to access a single table or a set of tables (which is a common approach to creating data access objects). Instead, it treats data access in a general manner, executing a query and returning a ResultSet, then taking the ResultSet and loading it into an aggregate value object, an aggregation of data rows similar to the ResultSet. The contents of the ResultSet, the specific columns in the rows returned by the ResultSet, are not known, so the data access object is written to read each column in the row as an Object reference and place the reference into the aggregate value object (which will store the reference internally in a Java Vector collection). This will work with virtually all standard SQL data types. More complex types (Blobs, distinct types) are not managed by this implementation. (There are several optional ways to manage this query-result loading operation that allow additional formatting and manipulation of the data and will be discussed when the loadResults method is shown.)

Since this approach treats data in a general manner, the presentation of this example revisits some of the concepts of using dynamic queries with JDBC.

The GeneralDAO Class: The Class Declaration and the executeQuery Method

The GeneralDAO class is shown in the sections below. Since this is a large example, the discussion will be presented by code block in the sequence in which the code blocks appear in the source file.

The source file begins with declarations that you would expect, import statements to include the JDBC API in the class name space for the application (java.sql and javax.sql package) in addition to the javax.naming package for using JNDI. The java.util package is included to provide access to the Java collections classes, and the java.io package is included for file I/O used in the method that reads a database query from a file.

A number of instance members are declared. Since they must be used constantly throughout the life of the GeneralDAO object, we delcare them as instance members. Note that since we are defining a Connection object as an instance member, we expect to have a single connection per data access object. This is also true of the `Statement` and `ResultSet` objects, where we also define a one-to-one relationship between these objects and our class.

An aggregate value object is declared as an instance member of the class (gvo). Once the `loadResults` method of this class has been called, this member will contain the results of the query that has been executed for the data access object.

The `executeQuery` method must be called before the `GeneralDAO` object can be used. The method begins with a call to the `clear` method of the `GeneralAggregateVO` object. This will clear the various internal flags of the `GeneralAggregateVO` object and avoid any confusion when the object is loaded as a result of the `executeQuery` method call.

The `executeQuery` method calls JDBC `prepareStatement` on the `connection` object, then executes the prepared statement. The statement is prepared for performance reasons; the overloaded `executeQuery` method with no arguments will simply execute this prepared statement. The prepared statement is then executed using the `executeQuery` method, and a JDBC `ResultSet` is returned. The `ResultSet` is then passed to the `loadResults` method which will load the contents of the `ResultSet` into the internal aggregate value object.

An overloaded version of the `executeQuery` method for the `GeneralDAO` object appears next. This version of the method asserts that `executeQuery` method for the `GeneralDAO` object has been called previously with a query argument and that the internal prepared statement (`preparedQuery`) has a valid, active prepared statement associated with it.

GeneralDAO.java: The executeQuery Method

```
import java.sql.*;
import javax.sql.*;
import javax.naming.*;
import java.util.*;
import java.io.*;

public class GeneralDAO  {

Connection                    con;
PreparedStatement preparedQuery;
ResultSet                resultSet;
ResultSetMetaData        resultMD;

GeneralAggregateVO       gvo = new GeneralAggregateVO();

public void executeQuery( String query ) throws SQLException {

   // execute the query and store in our local ResultSet
   System.out.println("Preparing and executing query ... ");
   preparedQuery = con.prepareStatement( query );
```

```
    resultSet     = preparedQuery.executeQuery();
    resultMD      = resultSet.getMetaData();

    // store the resultSet in our GeneralVO object
    System.out.println( "Loading results ... " );
    loadResults();

}

public void executeQuery() {

    resultSet     = preparedQuery.executeQuery();
    resultMD      = resultSet.getMetaData();

    // store the resultSet in our GeneralVO object
    System.out.println( "Loading results ... " );
    loadResults();

}
```

The GeneralDAO Class: The Constructor

The constructor for the `GeneralDAO` class performs the task of obtaining a `DataSource` object and connecting to the database. Called with no arguments, it constructs a `GeneralDAO` object with the default `DataSource`, which for purposes of this example is `movies`. If the overloaded version of the constructor is called with a string parameter, the string parameter is used as a `DataSource` name and the various methods and constructors called to create a `DataSource` and connection are used to ultimately create a connection to the `DataSource`.

```
public GeneralDAO() {

    //
    // construct with the default DataSourceName
    //
     this( "movies" );

}
// ---------------------------------------------------

public GeneralDAO( String dataSourceName ) {

try {
     //
     // JNDI startup parameters are stored in the
     // "jndi.properties" file in the classpath.
     //
     InitialContext ctx = new InitialContext( );
```

```
        //
        // get the DataSource from the JNDI name server
        //
        DataSource ds = (DataSource) ctx.lookup( dataSourceName );

        //
        // get the connection from the DataSource
        //
        con = ds.getConnection( );
}
catch (NamingException e ) {
        System.out.println( "NamingException in GeneralDAO: " +
                              e.getMessage() );
}
catch (SQLException e) {
        System.out.println( "SQLException in GeneralDAO: " +
                              e.getMessage() );
}

}
```

The GeneralDAO Class: The getQuery Method

The getQuery method reads a query string from the file name passed as a parameter and returns the string containing the query. This method simply wraps the file access work needed to read the query string from a file.

The method begins by declaring a data buffer for reading the file and a string reference for the return value. The named file is opened and a buffered file reader is associated with the file.

Since we assume we are reading new text with new line delimiters from this file, the readLine method is used to read the first line of text. The readLine method returns a null if it fails to read a line of text, so the controlling while loop tests for a null value.

If the String reference return value (retVal) is null, then we have yet to set this string to a value. This condition is tested and if the value is null, then the string is assigned to the first row read from the file. If not, the return value buffer (retVal) is appended with the current content of the current line. The readLine method is used to read the next line from the file.

When the file read operation is complete and there are no more rows to read, the file is closed and in the finally block the return value string (retVal) is returned by the method.

The GeneralDAO Class: The getQuery Method

```
public String getQuery( String fn ) {
String buffer  = null; // data buffer
String retVal  = null; // query string to return
```

```java
try {
    //
    // create a file reader for the file containing the query
    //
    BufferedReader reader = new BufferedReader (
                    new FileReader( fn ));

    //
    // start reading the file
    //
    buffer = reader.readLine();
    while ( buffer != null ) {

        if ( retVal == null ) {    // this is the first pass
            retVal = buffer;
          }
        else {
            retVal += buffer;      // append
        }
     //
     // continue reading the file
     //
     buffer = reader.readLine();
    }

    //
    // close the file reader
    //
    reader.close();
}
catch (FileNotFoundException e) {
    System.out.println("FileNotFoundException in getQuery: " +
                        e.getMessage() );
}
catch (IOException e) {
    System.out.println( "IOException in getQuery: " +
                        e.getMessage() );
}
finally {
    return retVal;
}
}
```

The GeneralDAO Class: The setAggregateVO Methods

The `setAggregateVO` method is used to set the internal `ResultSet` (`resultSet`) to the values of the internal aggregate value object (`gvo`). Since the strategy in this implementation of the data access object is to use the aggregate value object as a data cache, at various points during processing we would expect to have updates applied to the aggregate value object that must be applied to the internal `ResultSet` so that the two objects are synchronized. (Ultimately the `ResultSet` will be used to update the database, so we want the updates that have been applied to the aggregate value object to be applied to the `ResultSet` before we perform our database update using the `ResultSet`.)

The method begins with a `for` loop that iterates through all of the rows in the internal aggregate value object. For each row, it performs a series of checks to determine whether or not updates are needed, first for the row and then for the column in the row. Whether or not the aggregate value object has been updated can be determined using various flags within the general aggregate value object (`gvo`).

Before checking the update flags, the general aggregate value object is positioned with a call to its `absolute` method. This method behaves as does the `absolute` method within the `ResultSet` class–it moves to the requested absolute position, the position from the first record in the contents of the aggregate value object. (Note that unlike the `ResultSet` class that uses one-based positioning, the aggregate value object shown here uses zero-based positioning.)

The `getUpdateStatus` method is called to determine the update status of the currently positioned row. If this method returns `true`, then there are updates in the current row in the aggregate value object, and the corresponding row in the internal `ResultSet` must be updated. The internal `ResultSet` is positioned to the current row, and then a loop is executed to loop through all of the columns in the current row. Within this loop, the `ResultSet` `updateObject` method is called for the current column as controlled by the loop. The `updateObject` method is called with parameters for the column and an object reference to use to update the column. In this case, the object reference must come from the internal aggregate value object, the source of our update value. The `GeneralAggregateVO` method `getObject` is then called and is passed an integer value for the column value to retrieve. This method will retrieve an object reference, which will be passed to the `ResultSet` `updateObject` method to update the designated object. The code for this method follows:

The GeneralDAO Class: The setAggregateVO Method

```
public void setAggregateVO( ) throws SQLException {
//
// Sets the internal ResultSet (resultSet) to the values of the
// the internal aggregate value object (gvo).
// Effectively synchronizes the two objects.
//

    for ( int n = 0; n < gvo.getRowCount(); n++ ) {

        //
        // move to the row in our aggregate value object
```

```
   //
   gvo.absolute( n );

  // if true, there are updates in this row
  if ( gvo.getUpdateStatus( n ) ) {
                          //
          // move to the row
          //
          resultSet.absolute( n + 1 );

     //
     // set all columns for the row to values stored
     // in the value object
     //

     for ( int z = 0; z < gvo.getColumnCount(); z++ ) {

          //
          // update the object in the resultset
          //
          resultSet.updateObject( (z + 1),
                                     gvo.getObject( z ) );

     }

  }

}
```

The GeneralDAO Class: The loadAggregateVO and deleteRow Methods

The `loadAggregateVO` method is used to set the current `GeneralDAO` to the value of the `GeneralAggregateVO` object being passed into the method. This method effectively synchronizes the data access object to the value of the aggregate value object passed as a parameter.

The method is passed a parameter for the `GeneralAggregateVO` object to use for the synchronization. It sets the internal aggregate value object (`gvo`) to the object reference passed into the method. The `setAggregateVO` method is then called to synchronize the internal `ResultSet` to the values of the internal aggregate value object.

The `deleteRow` method deletes a specified row from the internal `ResultSet`. It first positions to the row to delete (and assumes the parameter being passed in is zero-based) and then calls `ResultSet deleteRow` to delete the row from the `ResultSet`. The code for these methods is shown next.

The GeneralDAO Class: The loadAggregateVO and deleteRow Methods

```
public void loadAggregateVO( GeneralAggregateVO  gvo )
                    throws SQLException {

    this.gvo = gvo;
    setAggregateVO();    // set our resultset to look like the gvo

}

public void deleteRow( int row ) throws SQLException {

    // delete our current row
    resultSet.absolute( row + 1 );
    resultSet.deleteRow();

}
```

The GeneralDAO Class: The applyUpdates Method

The `applyUpdates` method takes the cached updates in the internal aggregate value object and applies them to the database, using the `updateable ResultSet` features of the internal `ResultSet`.

The method will loop through all of the rows in the internal aggregate value object (`gvo`) and will check the update flags of the aggregate value object. If updates need to be performed, the `ResultSet` will be updated and then, through the `ResultSet`, the updates will be applied to the database.

The loop, which will move through the aggregate value object, is started. For each iteration of the loop, the internal aggregate value object is moved to the current row, and the internal `ResultSet` is moved to the same position so that both structures are now synchronized.

Since `insert` operations are treated differently than `update` operations: The current aggregate value object row is tested to determine if an `insert` update operation must be done on this row. The `GeneralAggregateVO` `getInsertStatus` method is called and passed the row number of the current row. If this method returns a `true`, then the current aggregate value object row must be inserted into the database, and the `ResultSet moveToInsertRow` method is called.

The `GeneralAggregateVO getUpdateStatus` method is called to determine whether or not the current aggregate value object row must be updated. Note that the update in this case can be either a SQL `update` of an existing row or a SQL `insert` of a new row—both are considered to be updates and will lead to the update flag being set. If this test for updates tests `true`, then a loop is started that is used to determine specifically which columns need to be updated. The `GeneralAggregateVO getUpdateStatus` method is called with an additional parameter (it is an overloaded version of the method used) to test the update status for a row and column combination. If this method tests `true`, then the current column (as controlled by the loop) is updated using the `ResultSet updateObject` method. This method is passed the column to update and the object reference to update the column with. The object reference to use for the update is the object reference returned by the call to the `GeneralAggregateVO getObject` method.

At the conclusion of the loop, which iterates for each of the columns in the row, the `ResultSet` is ready to be applied to the database. The internal `ResultSet` has either an update or an insert to apply. The code then tests to determine if the row contains an inset row. If this tests `true`, then the `ResultSet insertRow` method is called to insert the row. If the call tests `false`, then the row must be updated, which is done with a call to the `ResultSet updateRow` method.

The GeneralDAO Class: The applyUpdates Method

```
public void applyUpdates() throws SQLException {
//
// apply updates from the generalAggregateVO
// asserts that setAggregateVO() has been called previously
//

    for ( int n = 0; n < gvo.getRowCount(); n++ ) {

        // move to the row
        gvo.absolute( n );              // our aggregate VO data
        resultSet.absolute( n + 1 ); // the underlying resultset

        //
        // if this is an insert update then
        // we need to move to an 'insert' row
        //

        // is this an insert row ?
        if ( gvo.getInsertStatus( n ) ) {
         resultSet.moveToInsertRow();
        }

    if ( gvo.getUpdateStatus( n ) ) { // any update in this row ?
        //
        // update only those columns that need updating
        //
        for ( int z = 0; z < gvo.getColumnCount(); z++ ) {
            //
            // get update status for the row & column
            // combination
            //
          if ( gvo.getUpdateStatus( n, z ) ) {
             resultSet.updateObject( (z + 1),
                                     gvo.getObject( z ));
```

```
            }
        }

    if ( gvo.getInsertStatus( n ) ) {     // this an insert row
        resultSet.insertRow();            // insert the row
    }
     else {                                    // this is an update
        resultSet.updateRow();            // update the row
    }
  }
}

}
```

The GeneralDAO Class: The loadResults Method

The `loadResults` method is used to load results from the internal `ResultSet` into the internal general aggregate value object (`GeneralAggregateVO`), where it will most likely be delivered to a client program to use. The method is over-loaded to allow the use of a no-argument version, which calls the version with a single `ResultSet` argument.

The `loadResults` method that actually does the work starts with a call to the internal aggregate value object to clear its contents. This call will not only clear some of the internal collections in the aggregated value object of values, but will clear the various flags in the value object that are used to track updates to the value object.

The method begins by gathering the column labels of the columns in the `ResultSet`. A loop is started which uses the internal `ResultSetMetaData` object (`resultMD`) to return the column count used in the `for` loop and to return the column label. For each column in the `ResultSet`, the column label and the corresponding column number are stored in the aggregate value object using the `GeneralAggregateVO` method `setColKey`. (This method stores the information needed to associate a column name with a column number in the value object.)

Next, a loop is started for each of the rows in the `ResultSet`. (This asserts that the internal `ResultSet` is positioned before the first row.) For each row in the `ResultSet`, a loop is conducted over each of the columns in the `ResultSet`. For each of the columns, the type of the column is mapped to a Java String type with a call to the `JDBCTypeMapper getColumnDataString` method. The `getColumnDataString` method will perform some type-mapping operations and apply data formatting.

The output of the `JDBCTypeMapper getColumnDataString` method will be passed to the `addObject` method of the aggregate value object. This will add the object to the current row in the aggregate value object. When all columns have been iterated over, the `GeneralAggregateVO addRow` method is called to add the current row to the aggregate value object and prepare the value object for the next row to add. The listing for this method is shown next.

The GeneralDAO Class: The loadResults Method

```java
public void loadResults() throws SQLException {

        // by default we use the internal resultset
        loadResults( resultSet );
}



//
// load results from the resultset into the GeneralAggregateVO
//
public void loadResults( ResultSet rs ) throws SQLException {
        //
        // clear GeneralAggregateVO
        //
        gvo.clear();

        //
        // set the columns in the gvo
        //
        for ( int c = 1; c <= resultMD.getColumnCount(); c++) {

            gvo.setColKey( resultMD.getColumnLabel( c ), (c-1) );
        }

        //
        // for each row
        //
        while ( rs.next() ) {

          for ( int n = 1; n <= resultMD.getColumnCount(); n++ )  {

              //
              // apply some general conversion
              //
              gvo.addObject( JDBCTypeMapper.getColumnDataString(
                            n,
                            rs ) );
          }

            //
            // add the row to our aggregate object
            //
            gvo.addRow();

        }

}
```

The GeneralDAO Class: The clearUpdates and getGeneralAggregateVO Methods

The `clearUpdates` and `getGeneralAggregateVO` methods perform simple operations on the instance members of the `GeneralDAO` class. The `clearUpdates` method simply maps to the internal aggregate value object to call the `clearUpdates` method on that object; this will clear the update flags in the general aggregate value object but will *not* do anything to the database, nor does it reload the general aggregate value with data from before the update.

The `getGeneralAggregateVO` method returns the internal reference to the aggregate value object of the `GeneralDAO` instance. This allows client applications to use the value object to examine the data and potentially update the data without requiring interaction with the `GeneralDAO` object. The code listing for these methods is shown next.

The GeneralDAO Class: The clearUpdates and getGeneralAggregateVO Methods

```
public void clearUpdates() {

    // reset update flags
    // does NOT reload data to pre-updates state
    gvo.clearUpdates();
}

public GeneralAggregateVO getGeneralAggregateVO() {

        return gvo;
}

}
```

THE GENERALAGGREGATEVO CLASS

The `GeneralAggregateVO` class demonstrates one possible implementation of the aggregate value object pattern. As discussed previously, this design pattern encapsulates fine-grained access to the data in an aggregated form. While the value object pattern is sometimes referred to as *immutable* and unchanging, this pattern is specifically designed for updates, since one of the main goals of the object is to cache update operations at the client level (see figure 35-2).

The `GeneralAggregateVO` class makes heavy use of object-oriented "has a" type of object associations. A great deal of the code in this class is devoted to the process of keeping these various objects synchronized .

The Java Development Kit provides a number of very useful collections for the aggregation of objects. These collections are heavily used by this class. Since

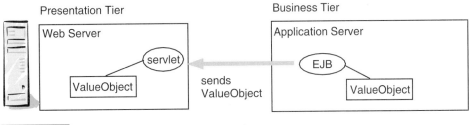

Presentation Tier

Web Server

servlet

ValueObject

sends
ValueObject

Business Tier

Application Server

EJB

ValueObject

Figure 35–2   *The Value Object as a Data Cache*

the aggregate value object represents the results of a query operation, results that can often be ordered; the Vector is the Java collection of choice for this operation since it is an ordered collection.

The following sections present the GeneralAggregateVO class. The discussion is divided into sections on each code block, starting with the class declaration.

The GeneralAggregateVO Class: Instance Members

A number of instance members are declared for the GeneralAggregateVO class. These instance members contain either data or flags that indicate the update status of the data. A combination of java.util.Vector and java.util.Hashtable are used.

A Vector object is declared for the rows. This Vector will contain a set of objects; each of the objects will represent a row, which itself will be a Vector object for each of the columns in the row.

A Vector object is declared for the current row. During an insert operation, the various objects that represent the data for the current row will be added to the current row Vector, then the current row Vector will be added to the rowsVector and a new current row Vector will be created.

Adding and viewing the data stored in the aggregate value object is fairly straightforward. The process of updating the value object is more difficult. Various flags must be set for each row that has been updated and for each column. Since we do not assume that each and every row in the aggregate value object will be updated, we do not need to create some type of array to track the updates on each row. Instead, it makes more sense to just store the rows and columns that have been changed and use a mechanism that allows it to be easily searched for updated rows and columns. For this reason, a Hashtable is used for the process of tracking updates.

The names of the columns must also be stored and a mechanism provided to allow them to be retrieved easily. Two Hashtable instance members are created for this purpose. One stores the column number as a key and maps to the column name. The other stores the column name as a key and maps to the column number. The code listing for these declarations follows:

```
General Aggregate VO

rows:                          Vector
current_Record:                Vector
update_Flags                   Vector
update_Cols:                   Hashtable
col Keys:                      Hashtable
col Nums:                      Hashtable
rowCount:                      int
col Count:                     int
```

Figure 35–3   *The GeneralAggregateVO Class*

The GeneralAggregateVO Class: Declaration and Instance Members

```java
import java.util.Hashtable;
import java.util.Vector;
import java.io.*;

public class GeneralAggregateVO implements GenericVO, Serializable {

// internal vectors

//
// stores and array of currentRecord vectors - one for each row
//
private Vector     rows       = new Vector();

//
 // an update flag for each row - indicates update status
//
private Vector     updateFlags  = new Vector();

//
// the column values (object references) for the current record
//
private Vector     currentRecord = new Vector();

//
// stores a HashSet for each row containing the columns
// updated in that row
//
private Hashtable updateCols    = new Hashtable();

//
// for column name mapping
```

```
//
private Hashtable colKeys        = new Hashtable();
private Hashtable colNums        = new Hashtable();

//
// current position
//
private int        currentRow    = 0;

//
// maintain counts
//
private int        rowCount      = 0;
private int        columnCount   = 0;
```

The GeneralAggregateVO Class: The set Methods

Various methods are used to set values of the aggregate value object. The setColKey method is used to update the column name and column number Hashtable objects with the column name and number. The colKeys Hashtable stores the column name and maps it to the column number. The colNums Hashtable stores the reverse—the column number mapped to the column name. The Hashtable put method stores these values in the appropriate Hashtable.

The setObject method takes two arguments: the integer column for the object to set and the object reference for the column value. The Vector set method is then called on the current record Vector to set the object reference at the designated position to the value of the object reference passed into the method.

An alternative version of the setObject method. This overloaded version of the method is passed the String name of the column to set and the object reference value. The method performs a lookup in the column name Hashtable (colKeys) and retrieves the object reference. The object reference in the colKeys Hashtable is an Integer class reference, the wrapper class for Java integers. The object reference returned by the Vector get method is cast as an Integer, and then the intValue method is used to retrieve the value of the entry as an integer. This position value is then used to set the value of the reference at the designated position (as retrieved from the colKeys Hashtable). The code for these methods is shown next.

The GeneralAggregateVO Class: The setXXXX Methods

```
//
// set keys for colname to positional mapping
//
public void setColKey( String name, int pos ) {
```

```
    // map column name to position
    colKeys.put( name, new Integer( pos ) );

    // reverse map. for lookup position and match to name
    colNums.put( new Integer( pos ), name );

    columnCount++;

}

public void setObject( int col, Object obj ) {
    currentRecord.set( col, obj );
}

public void setObject( String keyName, Object obj ) {
        int pos  = ((Integer) colKeys.get( keyName )).intValue();
        setObject( pos, obj );
}
```

The GeneralAggregateVO Class: The addObject and addRow Methods

The `GeneralAggregateVO addObject` method adds an object to the value object, and the `addRow` method adds the completed row to the internal list of rows.

This method takes a single object reference argument. It then makes a quick check to see if adding the current column will not exceed the number of columns in the current record (as set by the `setColKey` method, which we assert has been called before this method is called).

If the object being added does not exceed the column count limit, then the object reference is added to the internal current record `Vector` using the `add` method. If the current record does exceed the number of columns, an error message is displayed.

The `addRow` method is used to add the current row `Vector` to our internal `Vector` used to store all of the rows in the table. The `add` method is called on the rows `Vector` and then the `updateFlags Vector` gets a new row, a blank string indicating nothing has been updated yet.

Next, a new `Vector` object is created and assigned to the current record `Vector` reference.

The `currentRow` counter and the `rowCount` integer variables are incremented to track the size of the current row and the number of rows.

The GeneralAggregateVO Class: The addObject and addRow Methods

```
public void addObject( Object obj ) {

    // will fail if we attempt to go beyond columnCount
```

```
    if ( currentRecord.size() <= columnCount ) {

        // add the object
        currentRecord.add( obj );
    }
    else
        System.out.println(
            "Attempt to get beyond number of columns in VO.");
}

// add the current VO to our rows
public void addRow() {
    rows.add( (Object) currentRecord );
    //
    // create a new row
    updateFlags.add( new String( "" ) );      // null for 'no updates'
    currentRecord = new Vector();
    currentRow++;
    rowCount++;

}
```

The GeneralAggregateVO Class: Row Action Methods

The `GeneralAggregateVO` object allows rows to be cleared, deleted, and appended. The `clearCurrentRow` method simply clears the contents of the current row by calling the `removeAllElements` method of the `Vector` class (which is the data type of the `currentRecord` object).

The `deleteRow` method calls the `remove` method of the `Vector` class on the current row. It then decrements the current row pointer (`currentRow`) and decrements the internal row count (`rowCount`).

The `appendRow` method adds a row onto the end of the current row list. This requires that the various flags that track updates also be appended with new objects. Then a new `Vector` object is created for the new row to be appended.

A loop is then started to create a set of objects for the new row by calling the `addObject` method for each column. This allows `updateObject` to be called successfully to update the contents of the new row. If this were not done, then the `updateObject` calls would fail.

The record for the new row is then added onto the end of the internal list of rows. The row count (`rowCount`) is then incremented, and the current row pointer (`currentRow`) is set to point to the newly added row (which is the total count of rows less one). The code for these methods follows:

The GeneralAggregateVO Class: The deleteRow, clearCurrentRow, and appendRow Methods

```
// clear our current row
public void clearCurrentRow() {
```

```java
        currentRecord.removeAllElements();

}


// delete our current row
public void deleteRow() {

    rows.remove( currentRow );
    currentRow--;
    rowCount--;

}


//
// append a row onto the end of our data set
//
public void appendRow() {

// This is considered an 'insert' row.
// It will need to be placed into the underlying database
// with an 'insert' operation.
// Will append a blank row onto the current set. The new row
// becomes the current record

    //
    // this is an insert row
    //
    updateFlags.add( new String( "" ) );
    currentRecord = new Vector();

    //
    // create empty object references. Assert they will be updated
    // by updateObject calls.
    //
    for ( int n = 0; n < getColumnCount(); n++ ) {
        addObject( "" );
    }

    rows.add( (Object) currentRecord );
    rowCount++;
    currentRow = rowCount - 1;        // we are at the last row

    //
    // set the update flag for this row. This is an
    // 'insert' row.
    //
    updateFlags.set( getRowPos(), new String( "I" )  );

}
```

The GeneralAggregateVO Class:
The updateObject Method

The `updateObject` method is used to update a column member of the current row of the aggregate value object to the value of the object reference supplied. It is passed two parameters: the column to update in the current row and the object reference to use for the update. The process of updating or setting an internal object reference to a reference passed in is a straightforward matter. It is the process of maintaining the update flags correctly that involves some additional effort.

A `Hashset` reference is created and a variable which stores the current row position as an `Integer` object is also created. These variables will be used to maintain the update flags of the aggregate value object.

An update is either a SQL `update` operation or a SQL `insert` operation. If a row has been inserted into the aggregate value object, both the update and insert flags will be set.

Next the insert status of the row is checked with a call to the `getInsertStatus` method and passes in a parameter for the current row position. Note that this call, which returns a boolean `true` if the insert status flag has been set, is negated so that the body of the conditional statement will be executed only if the method returns `false`, that is, only if the insert flag has *not* been set will the call be made.

The update flag is set for the row with a call to the `set` method of the `updateFlags Vector`. (For purposes of this class, and this is behavior that is reflected in the `updatable ResultSet`, the SQL `insert` operation is treated differently than a SQL `update` operation, which is why we make an effort here to indicate with the update flag whether this is a SQL `insert` or an `update`.)

Update flags are maintained not only for the row but for each of the columns in the row. But column update flags are stored only if they are needed because a column has been updated in a row, so not every row will have a set of column update flags. We must therefore check for the incidence of column flags for this row. A call is made to determine if a set of column update flags exists for this row. The update flags for the columns are stored in a `Hashset` for each row; only columns that have been updated are added to the `Hashset`. The `updateCols containsKey` call will return `true` if there is an entry in the `updateCols Hashtable` for the current row position (`rowPos`). If this call returns `true`, then the `Hashset` for the column list of updated columns is retrieved from the `updateCols Hashtable` and the integer value of the column being updated is added to the `Hashset` (as an `Integer` object). (Since we are working with a reference to the `colSet` object, we have updated the `Hashset` that is stored in the `updateCols Hashtable`.)

Next we deal with the contingency that there is currently no column update flags `Hashset` stored in the `updateCols Hashtable` for the current row. If that is the case, then a new `Hashset` will be created. An entry is then added to the

Hashset for the column being updated, and the Hashset is added to the updateCols Hashtable.

At this point, we have finished setting the appropriate update flags. We finally call the setObject method to set the value of the designated column to the designated value. The code for this method is shown next.

The GeneralAggregateVO Class: The udpateObject Method

```
//
// update an Object - set flags to indicate update status
//
public void updateObject( int col, Object value ) {
HashSet colSet = null;
Integer rowPos = new Integer( getRowPos() ); // current row position

    // set the update flags
    // only set this if the 'insert' flag has NOT been set
    //
    if   ( !( getInsertStatus( getRowPos() )) )    {
        //
        // set the update flag for this row
        //
        updateFlags.set( getRowPos(), new String( "U" ) );

    }

    if ( updateCols.containsKey( rowPos ) ) {
        //
        // get the cols hashtable for this row
        //
        colSet = (HashSet) updateCols.get( rowPos );
        //
        // add this column to the list of updated cols
        //
        colSet.add( new Integer( col ));
    }
    else {
        // create the cols hashtable for this row

        colSet = new HashSet();
         //
        // add this column to the list of updated cols
        //
        colSet.add( new Integer( col ));

        //
        // add to the updateCols Hashtable
        //
        updateCols.put( rowPos, colSet );
    }
```

```
//
// set the object with designated value (update the object)
//
setObject( col, value );


}
```

The GeneralAggregateVO Class: Get Status Information

A number of methods are used to return status information for the aggregate value object. This is information on the insert and update status of certain rows and row and column combinations, information needed when it comes time to synchronize the aggregate value object with a database.

The `getInsertStatus` method returns the insert status for the specified row. This method retrieves the object in the `updateFlags Vector` at the designated row position, casts the `Object` as a `String`, and calls the `equals` method for the `String` to determine whether or not the flag is set to a value of "I". This setting indicates an insert; any other value would indicate another type of update. The method returns a boolean `true` if the flag is an insert value; otherwise, it returns a value of boolean `false`.

The `getupdateStatus` method tests for an update status at a specified row and column position. The method first tests to see if the update flag is set to an value of "I" for inserts, and if it is, it sets the return value for the method to a boolean `true`, since for inserts we want all columns in the internal aggregate value object row to be updated in the database.

If the row is an update row, then the test will return `true`. This code indicates the update status flag for the row is "U", indicating that updates have been performed on the row. If this is an update row, then the `Hashset` for the update column flags is retrieved and the `Hashset` (`colSet`) is tested to see if it contains an entry for the column that is being tested. The `Hashset contains` method is called to perform a lookup based on a key value passed as a parameter. This method will return a boolean `true` if the `Hashset` contains an entry for the column; otherwise, it will return a boolean `false`. The return value (`retVal`) is set to the value returned by the `contains` method. Finaly the return value (`retVal`) is returned by the method.

Next we see an overloaded version of the `getUpdateStatus` method is declared to take no arguments. This method assumes that the update status of the current row is required and simply tests the `udpateFlags Hashtable` to determine if there is an entry for the current row (as returned by the `getCurrentRow` method).

Finally the `getUpdateStatus` method is overloaded again to accept a single integer argument, which is considered to be the row to test for update flags. The method makes a call to the `updateFlags Hashtable` to determine the update status. As with the previous method, if the `Hashtable` contains an entry for the row, the method assumes (correctly) that the update flag has been set and returns a boolean `true`; otherwise, it returns a boolean `false`. The code for these methods follows:

The GeneralAggregateVO Class: The Get Status Information Methods

```
public boolean getInsertStatus( int row ) {
        if ( ( (String) updateFlags.get( row ) ).equals( "I" ) )
            return true;
        else
            return false;
}



// get the update status for a specific row and column
public boolean getUpdateStatus( int row, int col ) {
boolean retVal = false;

    // is this an 'insert' column ?
    If    ((
            (String) updateFlags.get( row )).toString().equals("I") ) {
        retVal = true;    // all columns need 'updating' for inserts
    }

    //
    // is this an 'update' column ?
    // if so, then check the column for updates
    //
    if ( ((String) updateFlags.get( row )).toString().equals("U") ) {

        // get the Hashset for this row
        HashSet colSet = (HashSet)
                            updateCols.get( new Integer( row ));

        // is this column in the HashSet ?
        retVal = colSet.contains( new Integer( col ) );
    }

  return retVal;
}

// get the update status for the current row
public boolean getUpdateStatus() {

    //
    // if non-null, then the 'update' flag has been set
    //
    if ( ((String) updateFlags.get( getRowPos() )) != null ) {
        return true;
    }
```

```
    else {
        return false;
    }
}


public boolean getUpdateStatus(int row ) {
//
// get the update status for a specific row
//

    //
    // if not null,then the some 'update' flag has been set
    //
    if ( ((String) updateFlags.get( row )) != null ) {
        return true;
    }
    else {
        return false;
    }

}
```

The GeneralAggregateVO Class: Get Internal Counts and getObject Methods

A number of methods are provided to return the values from internal flags. The getRowCount method returns the value of the internal row count variable (rowCount). The getColumnName method is passed an integer value and returns a column name string for the column in the aggregate value object. The getRowPos method returns an integer value of the current row position (currentRow).

The overloaded getObject method returns an object reference for the object at the integer column value passed into the method. The first version of this method takes an integer argument and retrieves the object from the internal Vector for the current row (currentRow) using the Vector get method.

The second version of the getObject method takes a string argument that is assumed to be the name of the column to retrieve. The colKeys Hashtable contains key/value pairs of column names and corresponding integer values for the column position. This Hashtable is searched for the column name value using the get method, which returns an object reference that is cast as a java.lang.Integer value, and then the intValue method is called to return the integer value. This returns the integer position of the column being requested, and this position is then passed to the getObject method (the first version of the method) to retrieve the object at that column position. The code for these methods is shown next.

The GeneralAggregateVO Class: The Get Internal Counts and getObject Methods

```
public int getRowCount() {
    return rowCount;
}
public int getColumnCount() {
    return columnCount;
}
public String getColumnName( int col ) {
    //
    // column name must be String
    //
    return (String) colNums.get( new Integer( col ) );
}

public int getRowPos() {
    return currentRow;
}

// get the String value at the column offset
public Object getObject( int col )  {
    return currentRecord.get( col );
}


 // get the String value at the column name position
public Object getObject( String colName ) {

    int pos = ((Integer) colKeys.get( colName )).intValue();
    return getObject( pos ) ;

}
```

The GeneralAggregateVO Class: Positioning Methods

A number of methods are used to provide positioning for the internal pointers in the aggregate value object. The `absolute` method is used to position the aggregate value object to the *absolute* position of the row that has been designated by the parameter. This is the absolute position from the start of the internal set of rows. Within the rows `Vector` there is a `Vector` that corresponds to the column values of the designated row. This `Vector` is retrieved and is used to set the value of the `currentRecord Vector`.

The relative method takes an integer parameter for the relative position to move, relative to the current row. The internal `currentRow` pointer is incremented based on the position parameter, and then the `Vector` for the specified row is retrieved from the rows `Vector` and used to set the value of the `currentRecord Vector`. The code for these methods follows:

The GeneralAggregateVO Class: The Positioning Methods

```
// move to the absolute position
public void absolute( int pos ) {

    currentRow = pos;
    currentRecord = (Vector) rows.get( currentRow );

}

// move to the relative position
public void relative( int pos ) {

    currentRow += pos;
    currentRecord = (Vector) rows.get( currentRow );

}
```

Positioning Methods and Negative Values

Note that the current version of the GeneralAggregateVO class does not support negative positioning values and does not test for out of bounds positions. This could obviously be added to these methods, but for the sake of clarity and brevity, it has been eliminated from this presentation.

The GeneralAggregateVO Class: Clear Contents

Two methods are available to clear the update flags and values of the aggregate value object: the clearUpdates method and the clear method. The clearUpdates method clears the update flags for the current set of updates; it does *not* set the value of the aggregate value object to the values that existed before the updates were made. (If the database had not been updated by the controlling program, then this could be done by simply executing a *refresh* operation from the database and then reloading the aggregate value object.)

The clear method clears all internal objects and pointers and allows the aggregate value object to be reused. This method clears the rows Vector, the updateFlags Vector, and the currentRecord Vector by calling the removeAllElements method. New Hashtables are then created for the objects that store column names (colKeys and colNums) and the columns that have been updated (updateCols). The internal pointers for the current row (currentRow), the number of rows stored (rowCount), and the number of columns in each row (`columnCount`) are set to zero. At this point the aggregate value object is ready to receive the contents of a new query. The code for these methods is shown next.

The GeneralAggregateVO Class: The clearUpdates and clear Methods

```
//
// clears update flags ... does NOT reset data to
// pre-update state
//
public void clearUpdates() {

for ( int n = 0; n < getRowCount(); n++ )
    //
    // set the update flag for this row
    //
    updateFlags.set( n, new String( "" ) );

}


//
// clear internal counters and vectors and
// allow this object to be reused
//
public void clear() {

//
// clear the vectors
//
rows.removeAllElements();
updateFlags.removeAllElements();
currentRecord.removeAllElements();

//
// need a new object reference for the Hashtables
//
colKeys     = new Hashtable();
colNums     = new Hashtable();
updateCols  = new Hashtable();

//
// clear the counters
//
currentRow    = 0;
rowCount      = 0;
columnCount   = 0;


}


}
```

SUMMARY

In this chapter we examined the process of integrating EJBs into our movie store application. EJBs are not a requirement for every application, and EJBs could be used partially in an application. In fact, this chapter demonstrated a partial implementation; the demonstration code shown in this chapter used EJBs only for the shopping cart portion of the movie store.

We refactored the shopping cart bean in this chapter to use an EJB to perform the processing of the shopping cart. A presentation tier component, a JavaBean, is used as a proxy to communicate with the EJB. The shopping cart EJB simply extended the shopping cart JavaBean developed in the previous chapter and exposed the methods needed by the presentation tier proxy.

We also looked at some of the helper classes used in the previous chapter. We examined the BlobView servlet which retrieves a Blob, a graphic image, from a database table and outputs to the servlet response stream.

The DAO and value object design patterns have been used extensively throughout this text. In this chapter we looked in detail at general implementations of these design patterns.

CHAPTER 36

JSP in Development: A Discussion Group System

INTRODUCTION

The previous chapters examined the development of a movie store shopping cart application. In this chapter we will take a look at a different application, a discussion group application.

The system developed in this chapter is a discussion group system designed to maintain a database of messages stored by topic. The system tracks message threads, and users of the system can start a message thread or add to existing message threads. The code behind this system is used to demonstrate login security, the creation of dynamic HTML tables, storing data in session variables, passing request parameters, and other important concepts.

A basic design strategy of separating presentation logic from business logic is used. To maintain this separation of business logic from presentation logic, the use of Java scriptlets on the JSP page are kept to a minimum and Java *design patterns* introduced are applied whenever possible.

These design patterns are also heavily used in the development of the classes for data access and workflow control. Data access objects (DAOs) are used to model and encapsulate database operations, and value objects are used to encapsulate and model the logical data records used throughout the application. *Facade patterns* are used to manage the workflow control and marshal the resources of the DAOs to facilitate the creation of the dynamic Web pages.

Discussion Group System: Application Description

The application shown here is designed to allow users to enter messages. These messages can be part of a thread so that a user can enter an initial message, and then users can add to that message, either providing additional information relative to the message or providing a reply to the message. These additional messages added to the initial message are referred to as *message threads*. This type of application is often referred to as a *threaded message list* or a *knowledge base* where knowledge or information is stored.

The Message

The focus of the discussion group system is the manipulation of messages posted to various discussion groups. These messages are tracked in the system using information about the user that entered the message, the date the message was entered, and the type and category of the message. This information about the message is used to store, manipulate, and sort the message when it is output on the message review pages.

Each message has a message type and message category. The valid message types and categories can be defined for a particular installation of the message system so that different installations of the message system can be used to track different types of messages. (This adds flexibility to the system but for us, the developers, implies additional work, since these dynamic values for the message types and message categories must be managed by the message system application.)

The use of the message system to create a common problem-tracking system demonstrates the flexibility of dynamic message types and message categories. This system would store information on problems as messages, and potential solutions to those problems could be posted as responses to the initial problem message. The initial problem message would be created with a message type of `problem`, and the message response, a message that is posted as a threaded message to the initial message, would be created with a message type of `resolution`.

Another use of the message system would be as a system to store online discussions. A message could be created with a message type of `post` for initial posted messages. Responses to the initial message, added as threaded messages, would be created with a message type of `reply` for replies to those messages.

Message Threads

A message that has been entered into the message system is either an initial message posting (or *base message* of a message thread) or a response type posting to an initial thread, also referred to as a *threaded message*.

Using the example of a problem-tracking system, a user may enter an initial message, perhaps identifying and explaining a particular problem identified. Another user of the message system may then read that initial message and further identify the problem by adding to that message. At this point, two messages would be considered part of that message thread: the initial message or the *base* message entered by the user that identified the problem and the message that was added by the second user, a *threaded* message. Both of these messages could be entered with a message type of `problem`, indicating that they identified a problem, as shown in Figure 36–1.

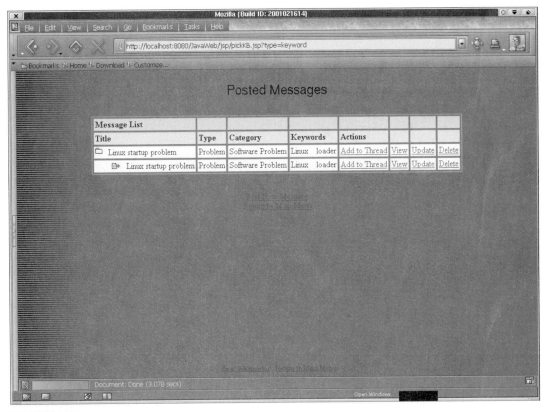

Figure 36–1   *Message listing page.*

Finally, a message system user may read both messages and provide a resolution to the problem identified. This message would also be added as a thread of the initial message, but would be added with a message type of `resolution`, indicating it provided a resolution to the problem identified by the other users. See Figure 36–2.

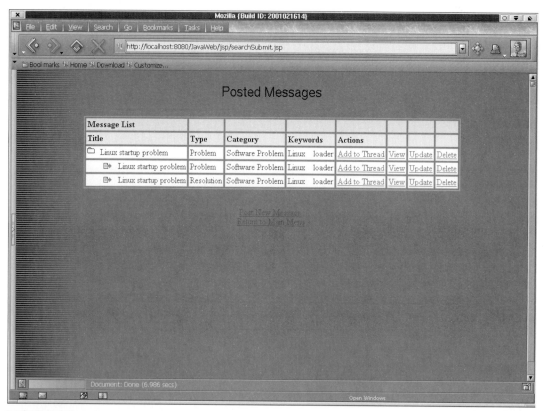

Figure 36–2   *Message listing with problem resolution.*

Message Categories

Each message is associated with a message *category*. This association is maintained in the database through a field in the message header that contains the category for that message. For a problem-tracking system, these categories could be `hardware` for hardware problems and `software` for software problems. Messages could be posted to either category, and dynamic JSP pages that searched or listed the message database could use these categories to restrict listings to either hardware or software problems.

Alternatively, the message system could be used for a discussion group, and these categories could be used as topics for discussions. Users could be allowed to add categories for different discussion topics. Other users could read these user postings and add additional postings. In essence, the message system application could provide a communication forum for a user community.

Database Structure

The message system uses a relational database to store configuration information for the system (message types, message categories), user login IDs and related security information, and messages and related information.

Each message entered in the message system has a primary key, known as a document key (`doc_key`). This primary key is automatically maintained by the database as a unique integer number. Maintaining the list of messages involves tracking the *base* key for the initial message in each of the threaded messages for that initial message.

Also stored with the message is the date the message was entered and the last date the message was modified. When the message list is displayed, it is sorted by the base document key and the date the message was entered, so that the initial message is at the top of the sorted list followed by the messages that have been posted to the initial message. The posted messages are displayed in the order in which they were entered, based on the date they were entered and the last date they were modified.

APPLICATION FLOW FOR THE MESSAGE SYSTEM

Any Web application is constructed using a certain procedural flow, which assumes the user of the application is going to move through the application in a certain fashion. With larger Web sites, a great deal of consideration is applied to this process, creating large wireframe diagrams that detail the flow of the system.

The message system, though not as complex as some Web sites, does contain a number of pages that you would expect on a Web site: a login page, a main menu, a search page, a message listing page, a message view page, and a message input/update page. Taken together, these pages comprise the message system Web site.

But our Web site is not just static HTML pages; it includes JavaBeans code that supports these pages and a database and corresponding database schema. The JavaBeans code for this application is comprised of business objects, control objects, and database access objects.

Keeping the flow of the application in mind, our discussion of the message system begins with a discussion of the pages of the message system in the order in which those pages would most likely be accessed. Following this discussion, the database schema for the message system is discussed. This discussion provides the framework for a discussion of the code behind the message system in Chapter 37, "J2EE Applied: Coding the Discussion Group System."

Login Page

A login page on a Web site is used to perform several different functions. First, it should authenticate the user and verify his or her identity. This usually involves checking a user ID and password entered by the user against a user ID and password stored on the system.

Next, a login page (or the processing behind the page) retrieves some information about the user and retains this information for the user session. For many sites, this information includes the user name and user preference information. The message system performs these operations, though it does not collect the copious user preference and history information that many commercial sites may collect. The login page initially asks the user to enter a user ID and password (see Figure 36–3).

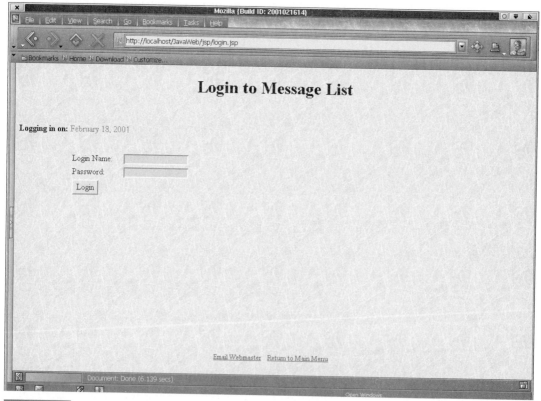

Figure 36–3　　*The user login page.*

Once the user has entered his or her user ID and password on the login page (`login.jsp`), the form is posted to another page, which processes the information (`loginSubmit.jsp`). If the user login is successful (the user is known to the system and the password is valid), then the successful login page is shown (see Figure 36–4).

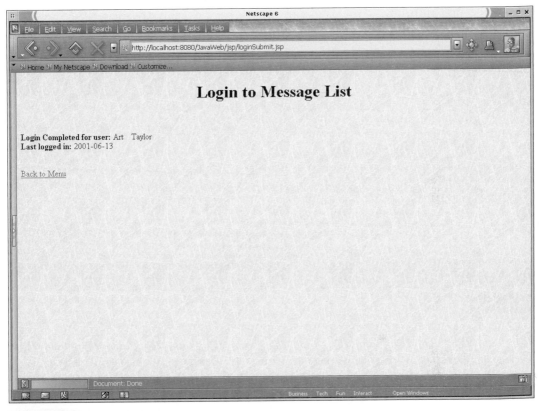

Figure 36–4   *Successful login page.*

If the user login is not successful, then a Java exception is thrown; the error page (`ErrorPage.jsp`) is shown in Figure 36–5.

The message system does not require every user to log into the system. A user who is not logged in is allowed to review the messages on the message board, but is not allowed to post a message unless he or she has completed the login process.

The login page retrieves user information (user name, location, last login date) from a database table and ultimately stores this information in a `session`

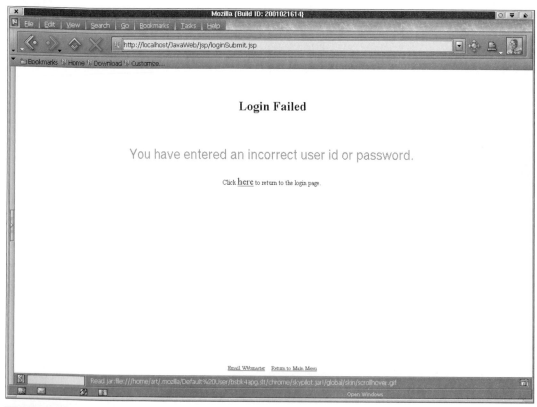

Figure 36–5 Login failure page.

object, an object available to all the pages in the user session (defined as pages called as part of a list of pages starting with the first page accessed). Other pages in the session use the user information in the `session` object. Some pages use the information to determine whether or not the user has logged in and whether or not he or she is a valid user. The message input/update page uses the user information to populate part of the input form for the user, information that will become part of the message record to be inserted or updated into the database.

The Main Menu

The main menu for the application is a simple static HTML page. This page is accessed by the user through the Apache Web server, using server-side includes to display information on the current date and to retrieve the header and elements to be used throughout the application (see Figure 36–6). Since the page is static HTML, it can be served by the Apache server, which has the benefit of reducing some of the workload for the Tomcat server.

Figure 36–6   *Main menu.*

The options to search the message base, to list all messages, and to later view the contents of the message base do not require a valid login. The option to post a new message does, however, require a valid login. These options and their associated pages are explained in more detail in the following sections.

Post New Message

The post new message process allows the user to create a new message in the message database. This option executes the `inputKB.jsp` page, which requires the user to have valid login entries in the JSP `session` object. If the user does not have a valid login, then he or she is redirected (using a JSP forward) to an error page indicating that he or she must log in before posting a message. See Figure 36–7.

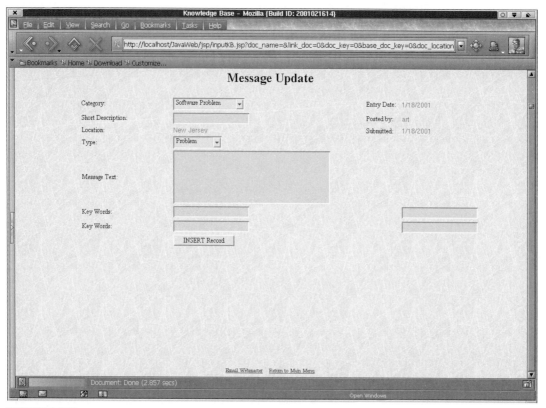

Figure 36–7   *Input new message.*

Note that some fields are displayed but cannot be changed by the user; these fields are either generated programmatically or obtained from the `session` object as part of the login record.

Search Existing Messages

The message search page allows messages to be searched using the keywords assigned to the messages. The page provides fields to input up to four keywords to be used to perform the search. See Figure 36–8.

Once the keywords have been entered, the submit query button on the page is pressed by the user. This sends a request to the message listing page (`pickKB.jsp`), passing parameters that indicate that the user has requested a filtered list. The filter operation selects not only the messages that match the search criteria, but also the messages that are part of the message thread for those messages.

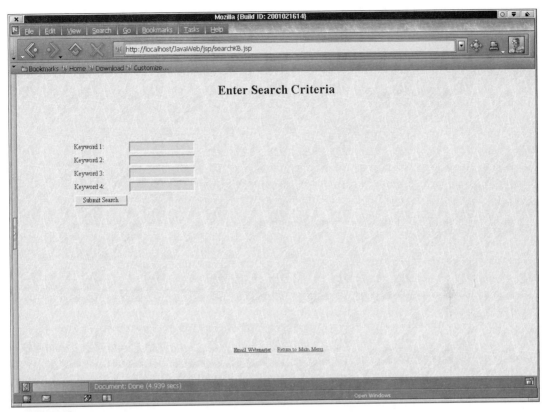

Figure 36–8   *Enter search criteria.*

Message List: All Messages

The message list page provides a listing of all messages currently in the message database. (The current implementation of this feature displays all messages in the database. A more refined production version should limit the number of rows returned for efficiency purposes.) See Figure 36–9.

Message List: Filtered

The message listing for a filtered set of rows uses the same display as the listing for all rows but applies the filter before producing the page output. See Figure 36–10.

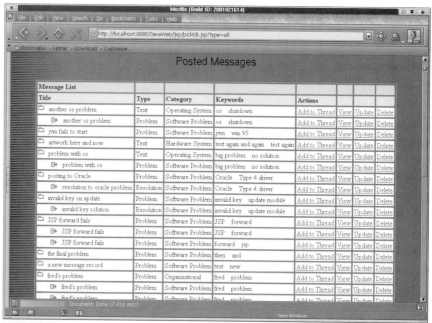

Figure 36–9   List all messages.

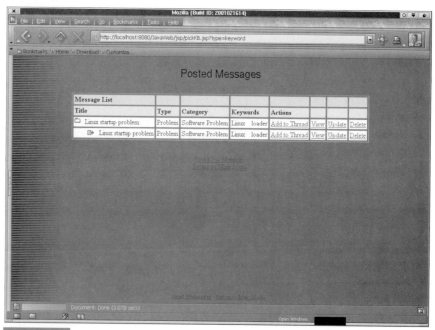

Figure 36–10   Filtered message list.

Update Message

The update message page is called with parameters that indicate the message document that should be displayed. The message document is then retrieved, and its contents are displayed in a form that allows the user to modify components of the record. Note that some fields are displayed but cannot be changed by the user; these fields are either generated programmatically or obtained from the `session` object as part of the login information. See Figure 36–11.

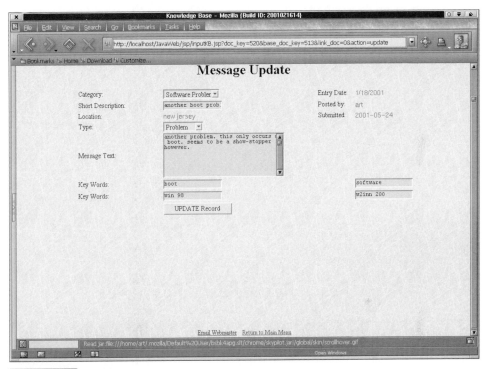

Figure 36–11 *Update existing message.*

Delete Message

The delete message operation allows the user to delete a message but checks to determine that the user attempting to delete the message is actually the user that entered the message or is a user with permissions to delete the messages entered by another user (for example, a system administration user or a message group moderator). Messages are deleted using a link on the message listing page to the message view page. This process allows the user to view the message before it is deleted.

If the message delete operation is successful, a page is displayed indicating that the delete operation was successful. If the delete operation fails, an exception is thrown, which displays the error page with a message about the failed delete operation. If the update is successful, then the page shown in Figure 36–12 is displayed.

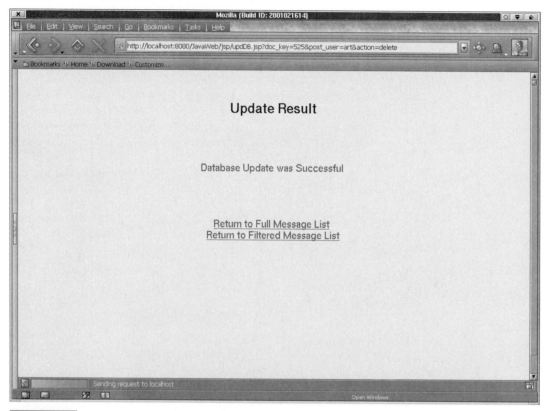

Figure 36–12   *Update successful message page.*

THE MESSAGE SYSTEM: TECHNICAL DESCRIPTION

The message application uses a number of *facade* classes on the business tier. The purpose of these facade classes is to manage the dynamic output of the pages. Their job is to marshal resources of the DAOs, send the value objects back and forth to the DAOs, and provide wrapper methods for the value objects. They are essentially the interface between one or more of the JSP pages and the database resources they access. They encapsulate the business logic of the application and control the flow of work being performed. (While this use of these facade classes allows the DAOs and value objects to remain focused on their tasks, it creates what was ultimately a very large and complex facade class for a number of the pages. A design revision would most likely include the use of multiple business objects by the facade classes to reduce the exposure of the facade class.)

These business tier objects are used by the JSP page to build the pages and perform the processing required of the pages. They are effectively helper classes for the JSP pages. To simplify the operations performed on the JSP page, a single session facade object, an instance of the KnowledgeBaseFacade class, is used by the various JSP pages in the application.

Two integration tier patterns are applied to the database operations. DAOs are used to provide access to the database, and value objects are use to encapsulate database objects in a form that can be conveniently passed from method to method in the application (these value objects are also used on the business tier). The use of these design patterns allows database operations to be isolated, tested, validated, and then easily shared by other objects. This allows the database resource to be protected and controlled in the application and provides a means of reducing the amount of work required to access the database. Code for database access is shared among the multiple business objects that access the database and, should the database vendor change (an all too common occurrence), the code change is isolated to a small set of classes.

The database operations are further abstracted in this application. A database utility class (dbUtil) is used to provide the low-level access to the database. This database utility class is accessed by the DAOs and contains virtually all JDBC database calls (with the exception of some ResultSet manipulation that appears elsewhere). This abstraction of database operations from the business classes of the application is used to encapsulate the low-level database operations and provide some flexibility in how they are managed. For instance, while the code used in this sample application does not use database connection pooling, it could easily be inserted into the database utility class in a manner that would be transparent to the rest of the application.

MESSAGE SYSTEM DATABASE DESIGN

The message system uses a number of relational tables to store pertinent information for the system, including information about the system users, information concerning the messages that have been posted, the text of the messages, any keywords applied to the messages, security information for the system, and message categories and message types. The design of the database is a relatively normalized relational structure with tables and descriptions, as detailed in Table 36–1.

These tables and their contents are explained in more detail in the following sections.

Table 36–1	*Message System Database Tables*

Table	Description
message_user	Contains information on the users of the system, including the user name and their password.
base_keys	Contains the keywords associated with the messages in the system. Currently, messages can have up to for four entries in this table. Optionally, the message can have 0 nozero entries in this table (which is true for many threaded responses to existing message entries).
categories	Contains the categories of messages that exist on the system.
knowledge_base	Contains the header information for messages entered into the system.
knowledge_messages	Contains the message text for the message. This is a child table of the knowledge_base table, meaning that every record in this table must have a corresponding entry in this table.
message_types	Contains the types of messages that can be entered in the message system.
message_security	Security information for users of the message system, including the security role of the user.

The knowledge_base Table

The knowledge_base table stores the base information for the message, the message header, or parent in the parent–child relationship for the message database. This table uses a document key (doc_key) column as the primary key for the table—the column that uniquely identifies the row in the table. This column is an integer value that is automatically incremented and maintained by the database. (For the PostgreSQL database, this is managed using a sequence in the database; the Oracle database uses a similar approach, while the Informix database uses a serial column, and SQL Server and MySQL use an AutoNumber column.)

The date the message was first entered is stored in the date_submitted field. This field indicates the date the message was submitted to the system. Like the entry_date field, this field is stored in the database as a date data type, but is managed by the JSP pages and Java code as a string.

The knowledge_base table stores the category of the message, the date the message was submitted, and the last date the message was updated (entry_date). The date columns are stored as date data types in the database, though for convenience and a certain amount of portability, they are treated as strings by the JSP/Java code, which uses the database to perform the conversion on inserts and updates.

The `knowledge_base` table also stores the location (`doc_location`) where the message document was entered and the user name of the user (`post_user`) that entered the message. This information appears in the `knowledge_base` record, but is not entered by the user. Instead, it is retrieved from the `session` object, where it has been populated based on the entries in the `message_user` table for the current user.

A short description of the document is contained in the `doc_name` field. This provides a description or *name* for the message. The `level` field is intended to store the level of the message within the message threads for the initial posting. This field is currently not used. (Messages are displayed in the date order based on the date the message was first submitted or entered in the system.)

The `post_user` field is used to store the name of the user who first entered the message. This field is automatically inserted based on the user login information stored in the `session` object (which is stored in the `message_user` table). The user entering the message is not allowed to change this information.

The `link_doc` field is used to store the document to which this document is linked. (This field is not currently used.) The `base_doc_key` field is used to store the base document key (`doc_key`) for the message thread to which this document belongs. This key is used to select and display message documents for a particular thread. The complete schema for this table is shown in Table 36–2.

Table 36–2   *Schema for the knowledge_base Table*

Column Name	Data Type	Description
doc_key	integer	Primary key for the messagessage document.
doc_name	varchar(50)	Short name/short description for the message.
doc_location	varchar(50)	Location where the document was entered.
level	integer	Level of the message in the message thread list.
category	varchar(50)	Category for the message.
post_user	varchar(50)	User name for the user who posted the message.
date_submitted	date	The date the message was submitted (or last changed).
link_doc	integer	The link document for this message; the message for which this document represents a response.
base_doc_key	integer	The document key for the base document in this message thread.
entry_date	date	The date this message document was entered.

The knowledge_messages Table

The `knowledge_messages` table stores the actual message text for the message. The message is stored using the `doc_key` as the primary key and foreign key for the corresponding header record in the `knowledge_base` table.

This message system stores the message as a variable-length character data type with a limit of 500 characters—a `varchar(500)`. (The database, not the application, enforces the limit on the size of the message, so the size of the column could be increased at the database and the application would support the larger size.)

The `message_type` field is used to capture additional information about the message being stored. While the message category groups the message based on a category name, the message type indicates the general nature of the message. For example, the message type could be a `post` message or a `response` message for a message system that was providing a forum for discussion groups. Or, the message type could be used to store a `problem` message to identify and describe a problem and a `resolution` message to describe a possible resolution for a problem. These message types are configurable and are contained in the `message_types` table in the database. The contents of this table are used to produce a list box for the message input page. The schema for this table is shown in Table 36–3.

Table 36–3   *Schema for the knowledge_messages Table*

Column Name	Data Type	Description
doc_key	integer	The primary key for this message document.
message_txt	varchar(500)	The text of the message.
message_type	varchar(10)	The type of the message.

The message_user Table

The `message_user` table is used to store information on the users for the message system. This table stores the user first name and last name, the location of the user, and the user password. Information is also stored on the location of the user, the date the user login record was submitted, and the date of the last login for the user. The complete schema for this table is shown in Table 36–4.

The base_keys Table

The `base_keys` table is used to store the lookup keywords for the messages stored in the database. Currently, the system allows four keywords to be stored for each message (though there is nothing in the schema for this table that enforces a

Table 36–4   *Schema for the message_user Table*

Column Name	Data Type	Description
login	varchar(20)	Login name for the user.
first_name	varchar(30)	First name (given name)for the user (given name).
last_name	varchar(30)	Last name (surname)for the user (surname).
location	varchar(50)	Location of the user.
date_submitted	date	Date login record was submitted by the user.
last_login	date	Last login date for the user.
pwd	varchar(15)	Password for the user.

limit). The keywords are referenced using the doc_key column and there can be zero, one, or many entries in this table for a given message document key.

If a user enters no keywords for a message (this is common with threaded responses to an initial posting), then no entries would be stored in this table. The schema for this table is shown in Table 36–5.

Table 36–5   *Schema for the base_keys Table*

Column Name	Data Type	Description
doc_key	integer	The primary key for the message document.
keyword	varchar(50)	The keyword to be associated with the message document.

The categories Table

The categories table stores the various categories of messages that can be stored in the system. This provides some flexibility for the system, allowing categories to be customized for the particular installation. For instance, for a problem-tracking system, categories could be stored for hardware problems, software problems, installation issues, and so on. For a group discussion system, categories could be entered for politics, gardening, dogs, cats, and so on. This table contains a column for the category name and a column for a description of the category. The schema for this table is shown in Table 36–6.

Table 36–6   *Schema for the categories Table*

Column Name	Data Type	Description
category	varchar(20)	Category name.
description	varchar(30)	Description of the category.

The message_types Table

The `message_types` table stores additional information on the type of message being stored in the system. For instance, for a problem-tracking system, the message type could be a `problem` message for a message that identifies a problem and a `resolution` for a message in the same thread that provides a resolution to the problem identified in the thread. The complete schema for this table is shown in Table 36–7.

Table 36–7   *Schema for the message_types Table*

Column Name	Data Type	Description
message_type	varchar(20)	Message type.
description	varchar(50)	Description of message type.

Additional Database Components

The logical concept of a message document has no natural primary key, a field that uniquely identifies rows in the table. For this reason, a generated primary key was needed. This required a counter within the database that could be used to generate unique integer ID numbers. The PostgreSQL database (and other databases) provide this feature in the form of a `sequence`.

The `sequence` is created in the database and then accessed using certain database functions. The statement to create a sequence named `doc_key` with a starting number of 500 is as follows:

```
create sequence doc_key start 500;
```

To access the next value of a sequence, the `nextval('<sequence_name>')` function can be used. In the message system, the `insert` statement used to insert the message into the database uses this function. The value generated by the `nextval('doc_key')` function call is used as the primary key for the record being inserted.

Since the other records related to the message header must use the `doc_key` generated by the database `insert` operation, the insert function for the message header record (`knowledge_base`) must return the `doc_key` generated during the `insert` operation. This `doc_key` is then passed to other methods to perform the insert operation.

SUMMARY

This chapter described various technical aspects of the discussion group system. As we saw in this chapter, this application demonstrates the use of JSPs with Java design patterns. We examined the overall architecture of the application, the flow of the application and the database tables the application uses. In the next chapter, we will examine the actual code of the application: the JSPs, JavaBeans and helper classes.

J2EE Applied: Coding the Discussion Group System

INTRODUCTION

In Chapter 36, we introduced our discussion group sample application and provided details on the design of the system and the database tables used by the application. In this chapter, we will examine the application in detail, examining the packages, the code and the JSP pages used. We will start by taking a look at the organization of the discussion group system.

THE ORGANIZATION OF THE DISCUSSION GROUP SYSTEM

The code for the message system is divided into three distinct Java packages based on the functional responsibility of the code in those packages. These three packages are listed in Table 37–1.

| Table 37–1 | *Message System Packages* |

Package Name	Description
JSPCal	General-purpose calendar classes.
db	Database utility access routines. This class is used to wrap the JDBC calls to the database.
knowledgebase	Classes used to manage the access to the message system, including the value object classes, the database access object classes, and the session facade classes.

Within the application, there is quite a bit of interaction between the classes in the db package and the knowledgebase package. The classes in the JSPCal package are used as needed throughout the system. The following sections explain these packages and their classes in more detail.

The JSPCal Package

The JSPCal class contains a number of utility methods to provide access to the current date and to display a calendar in HTML format. The two classes contained in this package are Cal and TagCal.

The db Utility Package

The db utility package is used to abstract the details of low-level database access from the data access object (DAO) classes. While the DAOs are still used to manage the database access operations and return results in the form of value objects, the db utility class methods are used to load the database driver, open and close connections to the database, create prepared statements, and execute queries against the database.

These methods are fairly flexible in dealing with database connections; if a connection has not currently been made to the database, a connection is made. Likewise, if the database driver has not been loaded, the driver is loaded before an attempt is made to create a connection. This removes the responsibility of managing these low-level database details from the DAOs. All methods share the same active connection for the instance, thus avoiding the overhead of creating additional connections for each query. (Use of connection pooling reduces this overhead.)

The knowledgebase Package

The `knowledgebase` package contains the bulk of the code used by the message application. This package contains the facade classes, the value objects, and the DAOs used by the application.

The value objects in this package contain internal data members that mirror the attributes or columns of the database tables that they represent and 'get' and 'set' methods that are the accessor and mutator methods respectively for each of these class members. Each value object will not be covered in detail since the description of each method in these classes would quickly become redundant.

The methods listed in Table 37–2 are common to the DAOs used in this example.

Table 37–2   *Common Methods for DAOs*

Name	Description
`public int insertDAO( ) throws SQLException, Exception`	Inserts the current contents of the DAO into the database.
`public void updateDAO( ) throws SQLException`	Updates the current contents of the DAO into the database.
`public void deleteDAO( ) throws SQLException`	Deletes the current DAO from the database.
`public void loadDAO( int doc_key ) throws Exception`	Loads the DAO from the database using the key passed as a parameter.
`public void loadDAO( Knowledge_baseVO knowledge_base )`	Loads the values of the DAO from the value object passed as a parameter.
`public void setVO( Knowledge_baseVO vo ) throws Exception`	Sets the value object to the current contents of the DAO.
`public void createPreparedStatements( ) throws Exception`	Creates the prepared statements used by the DAO to perform database access.

A DAO may also contain `getXX` and `setXX` methods for retrieving and setting local members, though these are generally not used. The preferable method for setting or retrieving the values of the DAO is to pass a value object to set the values of the DAO and retrieve a value object reference from the DAO to get the values of the DAO. This is done using the `loadVO` and `setVO` methods.

The KnowledgeBaseFacade Class

The KnowledgeBaseFacade class provides an *interface* between the JSP pages used to provide the visual access to the message system and the logic and work-flow required of the application. The division of responsibilities is that the JSP pages manage the display, the facade class manages business logic and workflow, and the DAOs and value objects manage access to the resources of the system. The KnowledgeBaseFacade class includes the methods listed in Table 37–3.

Table 37–3   *KnowledgeBaseFacade Class Methods*

Method	Description
public void setRowsUpdated(int rows)	Sets an internal member to the number of rows updated.
public void setAction(String action) throws Exception	This method is used to define the action (add, update, insert) for the inputKB.jsp page.
public void setSubmitTitle(String submitTitle)	This is used to set the title for the submit button on the inputKB.jsp page.
public void setNextKBVO(boolean val) throws Exception	This method is used to move to the next Value Object in the list of value objects retrieved to popu-late the pickKB.jsp page.
public Iterator getCategoryList()	This method is used to retrieve a list of categories used to populate an HTML select list on the inputKB.jsp page.
public Iterator getMessageTypesList()	This method is used to retrieve a list of message types and is used to populate an HTML select list on the inputKB.jsp page.
public String makeCategoryString(Object obj)	This method is used to convert an Object parameter into a character string representing a category. (It essentially wraps a Java cast operation and avoids having to place this code into a JSP page.)
public String makeMessageTypesString(Object obj)	This method is used to convert an Object parameter into a character string representing a message type. (It essentially wraps a Java cast operation and avoids having to place this code into a JSP page.)
public boolean isDefaultCategory(String category)	Returns a boolean value indicating whether a cate-gory passed in is the default category.
public boolean kbRecsHasMore()	Returns a boolean value indicating whether or not there are more knowledge_base records to be retrieved.

Table 37–3   *KnowledgeBaseFacade Class Methods (cont.)*

Method	Description

`public void setFilterKBRecs(`
`ServletRequest request, HttpSession`
`session )`
	Used by the `filterKB.jsp` page to pass the filter criteria for the JSP page.

`public void setFilterSelection(`
`ServletRequest request, HttpSession`
`session )`
	Used to set the filter selection for the `pickKB.jsp` page. This method reads the `'type'` parameter of the request and processes two selections: `'all'` for viewing all records, or `'keyword'` for a keyword filter.

`public void setAllKBRecs( boolean val` `) throws Exception`	This method retrieves all message system records from the database. (The boolean parameter is currently not used.)

`public void insertKBRecs(`
`ServletRequest request, HttpSession`
`session )`
	Used to insert message system records into the database. Data for the operation is contained in both the `request` object and `session` objects, which are passed as parameters.

`public void deleteKBRecs(`
`ServletRequest request, HttpSession`
`session )`
	Used to delete message system records from the database. Data for the operation is contained in both the `request` object and the `session` objects.

`public void processParameters(`
`ServletRequest request, HttpSession`
`session ) throws Exception`
	Used to process parameters for the operation.

`public void updateKBRecs(`
`ServletRequest request, HttpSession`
`session )`
	Used to update message system records. Data for the operation is contained in both the `request` and `session` objects.

`public void doUpdate( ServletRequest` `request, HttpSession session )`	This method is called by the `updDB.jsp` page to perform database update operations.
`public void loadKnowledgeBase( int` `doc_key ) throws Exception`	Loads a message system (`knowledge_base`) record for the `doc_key` passed.

Message System Application Flow

It is difficult, if not impossible, to understand the operation of a Web application without understanding the process flow of the system. With Web applications, this flow is indicated by the pages that are loaded as the user progresses through the application. Therefore, to understand the message system application, the following sections detail the page flow through this system. For starters, Table 37–4 lists the pages used in the system.

Table 37–4 *JSP Pages in the Message System*

Page	Description
pickKB.jsp	Lists the existing messages in the system. Provides menu options for viewing, updating, and deleting any of the messages listed. Must choose a type of listing as either 'all' to list all messages within the system, or 'keyword' to filter on a set of keywords (as contained in a Ccollection in the session object).
viewKB.jsp	Views all elements of a single message, including the message header (knowledge_base), message text (knowledge_messages), and keywords (base_keys). Provides menu options to delete the message (if allowed) and to return to the main menu.
inputKB.jsp	Provides data entry form for a new message, or to update a current message.
menu.html	The main menu for the message system.
login.jsp	Provides a form for to execute the login for the message system.
loginSubmit.jsp	Posted to by login.jsp. This page is used to process the login information and forward to an error page if the login failed.
ErrorPage.jsp	The error page for the message system.
updDB.jsp	Updates the database and forwards to the error page if there is an error during the update.
searchKB.jsp	Provides a search page using a form that allows searching the message system database based on four keywords. This page links to the pickKB.jsp page with the submission of the search criteria form.

The flow into the system begins with a user login. If the user successfully logs into the system, then the user can proceed to the main menu, which provides a number of choices:

- Login
- Search Messages
- List All Messages
- Post New Message

The most common course of action is to proceed to the search page (searchKB.jsp). This page allows the user to enter search criteria to narrow the search to a set of keywords. This page displays an input form, which posts to the pickKB.jsp page when the submit button is pressed. See Figure 37–1.

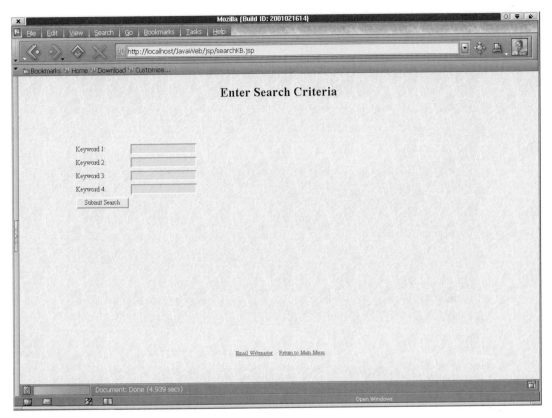

Figure 37–1 *Message system input form.*

After the user enters search criteria, the message list page (`pickKB.jsp`) with a filtered list of messages is displayed. The `pickKB.jsp` page provides menu options with each message listed. These menu options allow the user to optionally display the contents of the message (`viewKB.jsp`) or to update or delete the message (`updDB.jsp`). See Figure 37–2.

If the user chooses to display the contents of the message, the message view page is displayed (`viewKB.jsp`). This page allows the user to view the complete contents of the message, including the message header, the text of the message, the message type, the message category, and the keywords for the message. See Figure 37–3.

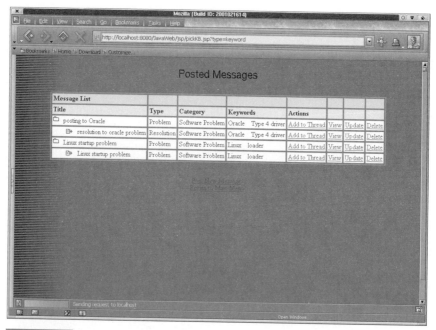

Figure 37–2   *Message listing page with options.*

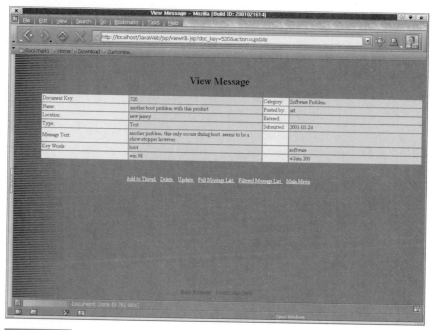

Figure 37–3   *Message view page.*

The menu options on this page allow the user to add a message to the message thread, delete the message, update the message, return to the message list, or return to the main menu. If the user chooses to update the message, then the message update page is displayed. See Figure 37–4.

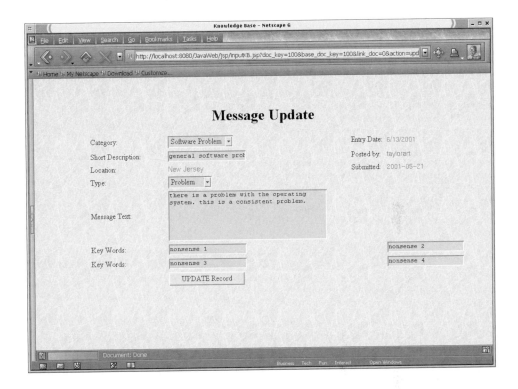

Figure 37–4 *Message input page.*

The message update page displays an input form that allows the user to make changes to certain fields and then submit the form. The form provides a drop-down list box for the message category and message type. The user is allowed to change any field on the page. Once submitted, this form will post to the update page (updDB.jsp), which will perform the work necessary to update the changes to the database. If there is no error, then the updDB.jsp page will display a rows updated message indicating that the change was updated to the database. See Figure 37–5.

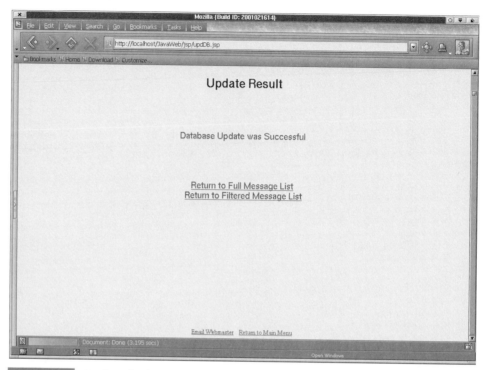

Figure 37–5   *Update database page.*

If the user chooses to input a new message, then the message input (`inputKB.jsp`) page is displayed with a blank form. (This is the same page used for the message update operation.) Once the user completes input for this form and chooses to submit, it is posted to the database update page (`updDB.jsp`) to send the changes to the database.

If the user chooses to delete an existing message, then the view message page is displayed, forcing the user to first view the contents of the page. At this point, the user must select the message delete link to delete the message from the database. The delete link on this page submits a request to the `updDB.jsp` page to delete the message. If the message deletion is successful, then the message update page outputs the number of rows updated message.

If an exception is thrown in any of these pages, the `ErrorPage.jsp` is invoked with the exception that has been thrown. This page outputs the exception that was thrown and provides a menu option to allow the user to return to the main menu page. This page displays the contents of the exception that triggered the message and provides links to allow the user to move back to the main menu. See Figure 37–6.

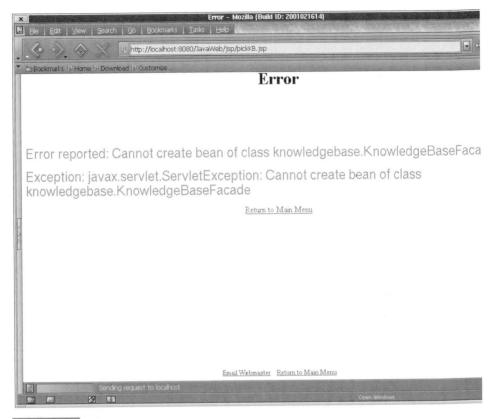

Figure 37–6 *The Error page.*

The preceding section explained the page execution that the user would use to move through the message system. This explanation provides a good basis for understanding how this system was developed. But now we need to examine these JSP pages in detail as well as examine the code behind the JSP page, the code that is executed when the JSP page is accessed.

Since we have kept close to the separation of roles concept in developing this application, the majority of the processing for a JSP page is performed by JavaBeans classes that are accessed by making a small number of method calls in the scriptlets on the JSP page. The following section shows both the JSP page and the Java code behind the page, and provide a detailed explanation of both.

The Rest of the Story: JSP Pages and JavaBeans Code Explained

The page flow gives us half the story. At this point, we need to see the contents of the JSP page and understand the interaction of the page with the Java code behind the page, the JavaBeans. To understand the actions performed by the page and to understand the process for programming a JSP application, the code behind each of the pages is explained *in-line* with the JSP page. This means that if a JSP calls a method, which in turn calls another method (as many of the facade class methods will do), then all of those methods are examined at that point in the text. This means that some of the more complex JSP pages is examined in fragments, while the code behind them is examined in detail. This leads to a better understanding of the procedural flow of the application and of the reasoning behind the approach to coding the application.

Managing the Login Process: The login.jsp and loginSubmit.jsp Pages

The login page provides a simple input form for the user to enter his or her login name and the corresponding password. The bulk of this form is HTML, with the exception of the output of the current date on the top of the form. See Figure 37–7.

This date is output with the use of the `loginFacade` class, using the `currentDate` property, as shown in the following code. This is used to output the current date in a string format. The date is output using green text to indicate that the user does not need to enter this information.

The login.jsp Page

```
<html>
<!-- <body bgcolor="#FFFFFF" background="/JavaWeb/img/bggradient.gif">  -->
<body bgcolor="#FFFFFF" background="/JavaWeb/img/bg2_grey.jpg">

<jsp:useBean id="loginFacade" class="knowledgebase.loginFacade" scope="page" />
<center>
<h1>Login to Message List</h1>
</center>

<br>
<br>
<b>Logging in on:</b> <font color="green"><jsp:getProperty name="loginFacade" prop-
erty="currentDate" /></font>
<br>
<br>
<br>
```

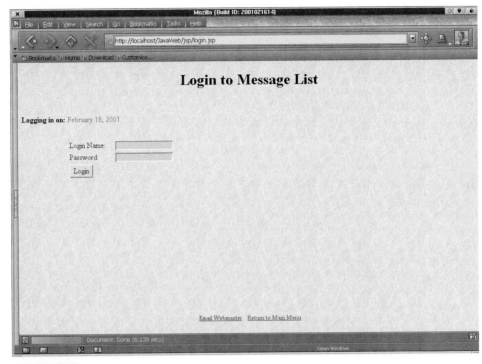

Figure 37–7 *The login page.*

```
<center>
<table border=0 width=100% >
<form method="post" action="loginSubmit.jsp">

<tr>
<td width=10%>   </td>
<td width=10%>Login Name: </td><td><input name="login" type="text" value=""></td>
</tr>

<tr>
<td width=10%>   </td>
<td width=10%>Password: </td><td><input name="pwd" type="password" value=""></td>
</tr>

<tr>
<td width=10%>   </td>
<td width=10%> <input name="submit" type="submit" value="Login" > </td>
</tr>

</form>
```

```
</table>
</center>
</body>
</html>
```

This page submits its contents to the `loginSubmit.jsp` page, which is responsible for processing the login information passed to it. If the login is successful, then a message is displayed indicating that the login succeeded.

If an error occurs, then the page forwards processing to an error page, which indicates that the login failed and allows the user to return to the main menu, where he or she can choose the login option and try the login again. (Alternatively, the user can press the browser's Back button and move directly to the login page.)

The loginSubmit.jsp Page

The login page (`login.jsp`) posts the input from the form to the `loginSubmit.jsp` page, which uses the `loginFacade` class to process the information input on that page. The `handleSubmit` method is passed both the `request` object and `session` object as parameters. The information entered in the input form is available as request parameters, and the `session` object is used to store session parameters to be used elsewhere in the application. If the `handleSubmit` determines that there is a problem with the login—for example, the login name is not found in the database or the password entered is incorrect—then it throws an exception and forwards processing to the error page for the `loginSubmit.jsp` page, the `errorPage.jsp` page. The JSP code for this page follows.

The loginSubmit.jsp Page

```
<html>
<body bgcolor="#FFFFFF" background="/JavaWeb/img/bg2_grey.jpg">

<%@ page errorPage="ErrorPage.jsp" %>

<jsp:useBean id="loginFacade" class="knowledgebase.loginFacade" scope="page" />
<center>
<h1>Login to Message List</h1>
</center>


<% loginFacade.handleSubmit( request, session ); %>

<br>
<br>
<b>Login Completed for user: </b> <jsp:getProperty name="loginFacade"
property="first_name" />    <jsp:getProperty name="loginFacade" proper-
ty="last_name" />
```

```
<br>
<b>Last logged in: </b> <jsp:getProperty name="loginFacade"
property="session_last_login" />
<br>
<br>
<br>
<a href="menu.html">Back to Menu</a>

</body>
</html>
```

The `handleSubmit` method performs the bulk of the processing for the login process. This method is part of the `loginFacade` class, which acts as a facade for the login process. This class creates a `message_user` value object named `message_userVO` and a `message_user` DAO named `message_userDAO`; both of these relate to the `message_user` table in the database. The calendar utility class `JSPCal` is imported, and a local `HttpSession` object reference is added as a local member of the class.

The loginFacade.handleSubmit Method

```
package knowledgebase;

import javax.servlet.*;
import javax.servlet.http.*;
import java.util.*;
import java.sql.*;

import db.*;
import JSPCal.*;

public class loginFacade {

Message_userVO      message_userVO;
Message_userDAO     message_userDAO;
Cal cal;
HttpSession localSession;
...
```

The `handleSubmit` method receives `ServletRequest` and `HttpSession` arguments. The local `HttpSession` reference is assigned to that of the `HttpSession` parameter. The login name has been passed as a parameter to the request, so this parameter is retrieved and then passed to the `message_userDAO.loadDAO` method as a parameter. This method uses the login passed (which is the primary key for the `message_user` table) and loads the DAO with the `message_user` table values for that login. The code for this section follows:

The loginFacade.handleSubmit Method

```
. . .
public void handleSubmit( ServletRequest request, HttpSession session) throws
Exception {

try {

localSession = session;

// load the user information
message_userDAO.loadDAO( request.getParameter( "login" ) );
message_userVO = message_userDAO.getVO();

// load the role for this user
// current implementation allows a single role
message_securityDAO.loadDAO( request.getParameter( "login" ) );
message_securityVO = message_securityDAO.getVO();
. . .
```

Once the login record has been retrieved, the password is checked to determine whether the password entered matches the password in the message_user table. If the password does not match, then an error message is written to the log file and the page is forwarded to an error page.

```
. . .
//
if (!(message_userVO.getPwd().trim()).equals(request.getParameter( "pwd" ).trim()))
{ // an invalid login

    System.out.println("Login error: " + message_userVO.getFirst_name() + " - " +
message_userVO.getLast_name() );
    throw new Exception( "Login error." );

}
. . .
```

As shown in the previous code example, if the login authentication is successful, then a series of message_user table attributes is stored in the session object, including the user name, location, login name, and date of the last login. Once the session attributes have been set, the database is immediately updated with the *new* user's last login date (which would be the current date). Errors are caught in the try/catch block, where they are logged and then thrown to the calling method.

```
. . .
else {   // a valid login
```

```
    // store session information about the user
    session.setAttribute( "first_name", message_userVO.getFirst_name() );
    session.setAttribute( "last_name", message_userVO.getLast_name() );
    session.setAttribute( "last_login", message_userVO.getLast_login() );
    session.setAttribute( "location", message_userVO.getLocation() );
    session.setAttribute( "login", message_userVO.getLogin() );
    session.setAttribute( "role", message_securityVO.getRole() );

    // immediately update the database with the new last login date
    message_userVO.setLast_login ( getCurrentDate( "mm/dd/yy" ) );      // the new
last_login date
    message_userDAO.setVO( message_userVO );                               // update
the database
    message_userDAO.updateDAO();
}
...
```

This current implementation of the login page does not forward the user to a menu, which could easily be done using the JSP forward tag. Instead, it merely displays a message confirming that the login was successful, displays the last login date for the user, and provides a link that allows the user to proceed to the main menu.

```
...
<br>
<br>
<b>Login Completed for user: </b> <jsp:getProperty name="loginFacade"
property="first_name" />    <jsp:getProperty name="loginFacade" proper-
ty="last_name" />
<br>
<b>Last logged in: </b> <jsp:getProperty name="loginFacade"
property="session_last_login" />
<br>
<br>
<br>
<a href="menu.shtml">Back to Menu</a>
...
```

Storing Information in the session Object

Following the login operation, the message system now has a `session` object populated with separate attributes for the user first name, last name, location, login name, and security role. These `session.setAttribute` calls are a good example of how to add objects to the session object. The syntax for the `HttpSession.setAttribute` method is as follows:

```
setAttribute( String name, Object obj);
```

In this example, the `name` parameter is a string name, which is associated with the object to be stored; this name is used to retrieve the attribute. The `obj` parameter is an `Object` reference that contains the *value* to store for the attribute. Since an `Object` reference is being stored, and any Java object can upcast to an `Object` reference, this allows any Java object to be stored in the `session` object. Once this information is stored in the `session` object, it becomes global (visible) to the entire user session.

Note that while it would be easy to store a large amount of information in the `session` object, this should be avoided. It is a more modular and flexible solution to pass information via the `request` object as parameters than to use the `session` object.

Using Static HTML and Server-side Includes for the Main Menu

Once the user has completed the login process, he or she must choose a link to the main menu. The main menu is an HTML page that displays the various menu options available to the user, as in the following example.

The menu.shtml Page

```
1.<html>
2.<body bgcolor="#FFFFFF" background="/JavaWeb/img/bg2_grey.jpg">
3.<!--#config timefmt="%A %B %d" -->
4.<br>
5.<br>
6.<center>
7.<h1>Welcome to the Message System</h1>
8.</center>
9.<br>
10.<h3>Date: <font color="blue"> <!--#echo var="DATE_LOCAL" --> </font>
11.<br>
12.<center>
13.<table width=100% border=0>
14.
15.<tr>
16.<td width=20%>
17.</td>
18.<br>
19.<br>
20.<td width=30%>
21.<font size=+2>
22.<br><a href="login.jsp">Login</a>
23.<br><a href="searchKB.jsp">Search Messages</a>
24.<br><a href="pickKB.jsp?type=all">List All Messages</a>
25.<br><a href="inputKB.jsp?doc_name=&link_doc=0&doc_key=0&base_doc_key=0&doc_loca-
tion=&action=insert">Post New Message</a>
26.
```

```
27.</font>
28.</td>
29.</table>
30.</center>
31.<br>
32.<br>
33.<br>
34.<br>
35.<!--#include file="footer.txt" -->
36.</html>
37.</body>
38.
```

The `menu.shtml` page uses *server-side includes* (SSI) to retrieve the current date for display on the main menu and to retrieve the footer for the page. (The `footer.txt` file is the same file included by the JSP pages for the footer.)

The highlighted tag on line 3 is an SSI directive used to set the format for the time to be displayed, using the `DATE_LOCAL` variable. This is the format used in the highlighted statement on line 10 to display the date. (This will be the date the page was served by the Apache server to the client browser, not the date on the browser's computer.)

On lines 21 through 24 in the listing, various menu options are displayed as links on the Web page. On line 33, an SSI directive is used to include the footer for the site into the page.

The discussion group menu provides the option of displaying a list of messages in the message database. The user can optionally list all messages or filter the message list for a listing of messages that contain a specific keyword. See Figure 37–8.

The user can optionally select one of the options from the menu page. The most common path would be to search the discussion group database based on search criteria. These search options provide a listing that is displayed, and then, based on what the user views in the listing, the user can choose to add to a thread or post a new message.

The following discussion proceeds with the assumption that a user has chosen to search the discussion group database for a particular set of topics and then review the listing that the search returns.

Collecting and Passing Search Criteria: The searchKB.jsp Page

If the user has selected the search option from the main menu, he or she will be allowed to search the message system database based on keyword entries. The `searchKB.jsp` page displays an HTML input form that allows the user to enter up to four search criteria. See Figure 37–1.

Figure 37–8 *Main menu page.*

The page itself is a standard HTML input form with the exception of the one JSP directive, the JSP `include` directive highlighted at the bottom of the page, as the following code demonstrates. (This page could easily have been implemented in HTML by changing the JSP `include` directive at the bottom of the page to an SSI include directive and renaming the page with a `.shtml` extension.)

The searchKB.jsp Page

```
<html>
<body bgcolor="#FFFFFF" background="/JavaWeb/img/bg2_grey.jpg">

<center>
<h1>Enter Search Criteria</h1>
</center>

<br>
<br>
<br>
<br>
```

```
<table border=0 width=100% >
<form method="post" action="searchSubmit.jsp">

<tr>
<td width=10%>   </td>
<td width=10%>Keyword 1: </td><td><input name="keyword1" type="text" value=""></td>
</tr>

<tr>
<td width=10%>   </td>
<td width=10%>Keyword 2: </td><td><input name="keyword2" type="text" value=""></td>
</tr>

<tr>
<td width=10%>   </td>
<td width=10%>Keyword 3: </td><td><input name="keyword3" type="text" value=""></td>
</tr>

<tr>
<td width=10%>   </td>
<td width=10%>Keyword 4: </td><td><input name="keyword4" type="text" value=""></td>
</tr>

<tr>
<td width=10%>   </td>
<td width=10%>            <input name="submit" type="submit" submit value="Submit
Search" > </td>
</tr>

</form>
</table>

<br>
<br>
<br>
<br>
<br>

<%@ include file="footer.txt" %>
</body>
</html>
```

Loading Request Parameters into a Collection

The search criteria that have been entered on the `searchKB.jsp` page are needed to execute the database query, so these parameters must have a way of making
it to the DAOs that will ultimately interact with the database. While the parameters could have been forwarded as a request and then retrieved by the DAOs, we

would prefer to completely shield the database access code (on the integration tier) from the details of the presentation, which certainly include the request object (an instance of `ServletRequest`). For this reason, we place the contents of our filter criteria into a `Collection` object, which is added to the `session` object. Since we would like to be able to allow the user to move back to the filtered selection page and redisplay it using the same filter criteria (as when a user adds to an existing message thread and then wishes to continue examining the same filtered list for additional messages to read or respond to), we store this filter criteria in the `session` object. With the criteria stored in the `session` object, when the user is linked to the posted messages page and the `type` parameter is set to `keyword`, the `session` object is examined to determine if there is a `Collection` of keywords; if there is, we execute the query again with those keywords. If the query criteria were not stored in the `session` object, then it would be difficult to implement this functionality.

Aggregating and Forwarding Request Parameters

The `searchSubmit.jsp` page is responsible for aggregating or collecting the search criteria entered on the `searchKB.jsp` page and then forwarding processing to another page. This page demonstrates both the use of the `session` object for storing session-specific information and the use of the JSP forward directive to forward request processing to another page.

The request parameters from the `searchKB.jsp` page are loaded into a `Collection` object and processing is forwarded to the `pickKB.jsp` page to execute and display the results of the query. The code for this page is shown next.

This page uses the `searchFacade` class as a JavaBean; this is loaded using the `jsp:usebean` tag on line 6. Only one method in this class is called on line 12, and on line 16 processing is forwarded using the `jsp:forward` tag. If an error occurs in the `searchFacade handleSubmit` method, then an exception is thrown and the error page declared for the page (`ErrorPage.jsp` declared at line 5) is invoked. If no exception is thrown, then the `jsp:forward` statement at line 16 is called. This is passed a single request parameter, the type of which is set to the `keyword`, indicating that a keyword search should be conducted based on search parameters that have been stored.

The searchSubmit.jsp Page

```
1.<html>
2.<!-- <body bgcolor="#FFFFFF" background="/JavaWeb/img/bggradient.gif">  -->
3.<body bgcolor="#FFFFFF" background="/JavaWeb/img/bg2_grey.jpg">
4.
5.<%@ page errorPage="ErrorPage.jsp" %>
```

```
6.<jsp:useBean id="searchFacade" class="knowledgebase.searchFacade" scope="page" />
7.<center>
8.
9.<h1>Login to Message List</h1>
10.
11.</center>
12.
13.<!-- load the search criteria into a collection which is stored in the session
object -->
14.<% searchFacade.handleSubmit( request, session ); %>
15.
16.<!-- forward to pickKB.jsp which will execute the query and display the results
-->
17.
18.<jsp:forward page="/jsp/pickKB.jsp?type=keyword"/>
19.
20.<br>
21.<br>
22.<br>
23.
24.</body>
25.</html>
39.
```

Storing Search Parameters: The searchFacade.handleSubmit Class

The searchFacade class is used by the searchSubmit.jsp page to manage the details of storing the search criteria collected on the searchKB.jsp page. This class contains a single method, the handleSubmit method, that is called on the searchSubmit.jsp page shown in the previous example.

This method is called with two parameters: the request parameter and the session parameter. The method merely creates a new Vector (which implements the Collection interface) and then adds the values of the four keyword parameters to the Vector.

We then want to add the Vector object into the session object for our session. This can be accomplished using the setAttribute method of the HttpSession class. This method takes two parameters: a String name and a corresponding Object reference. Once an object has been added using this method, calls to the HttpSession.getAttribute method can be used to retrieve the attribute value, using the corresponding name that was used when it was added. In this example, the Vector object that has been loaded with the filter criteria is added to the session object and assigned the name filter_criteria. At this point, the session object has been populated with the filter criteria for our session and we are ready to execute the JSP page, which will ultimately execute the database query using these parameters and display the results.

The searchFacade Class

```
package knowledgebase;

import java.util.*;
import javax.servlet.*;
import javax.servlet.http.*;


public class searchFacade {

public void handleSubmit( ServletRequest request, HttpSession session ) {

Vector v = new Vector();

v.add( request.getParameter("keyword1"));
v.add( request.getParameter("keyword2"));
v.add( request.getParameter("keyword3"));
v.add( request.getParameter("keyword4"));

session.setAttribute( "filter_criteria", v );

}

}
```

Building Dynamic HTML Tables with JSP: The Posted Messages Page

Because of the nature of page formatting with HTML, tables are often used to format and present content. So, it is not uncommon when dealing with dynamic content to need to create an HTML page based on some combination of request parameters and the results of a database query. The creation of the posted message list is an example of just such a page. To understand this page, portions of the JSP code are examined, and then the portions of the JavaBeans code that support the page are shown, effectively tracing the program execution from the JSP page to the JavaBeans code and then back to the JSP page.

The posted message page (`pickKB.jsp`) provides a listing of a set of message from the discussion group database. As explained previously, this listing can be either a listing of all messages in the database or a filtered listing based on filter criteria that has been made available to this page.

This listing is an HTML table that is dynamically created with columns for the topic of the message, the keywords entered for the message, and links to pages that allow the user to view the message in full, to update the message, or to delete the message. This page shows links for update and delete even though the user may not have permission to perform these operations on the message (see Figure 37–2). Permissions are checked before the operation is attempted, and if the user does not have the appropriate permissions, he or she is not permitted to perform the operation.

This page provides a good example of techniques for building dynamic table output using JSP. The listing is sorted based on the primary key of the message document, the date the message was submitted, and the last date the message was changed. The message listing includes not only the messages selected, but threaded messages that were posted to the message selected—that is, posted to a *base message* or a *threaded message*. Any messages that are part of the message thread are indented from the left margin so that the base message appears flush with the left margin, and all messages posted to the base message appear below the base message and are indented from the left margin. A different .gif image is also placed on each line of output, depending on whether the line being output is a base message or a threaded message.

Though this approach to creating the table with indented entries improves the readability of the table content, the code required to perform this indentation adds to the complexity of the control loop used to produce this table. The JSP code for this page (pickKB.jsp) is shown next.

The pickKB.jsp page performs its work using the Knowledge BaseFacade class. The KnowledgeBaseFacade class is a JavaBean and is identified on the page (and assigned a reference ID) using the JSP:useBean tag on line 4. Through this tag, the KBFacade name is associated with the knowledge-base.KnowledgeBaseFacade class and is given the ID of KBFacade. Other HTML content is used to display the header and set the suggested font for some of the text on the page. On line 16, the controlling method for the page is called: setFilterSelection. This method is passed the reference for the request object for the page and the reference for the session object.

The pickKB.jsp Page

```
1.<HTML>
2.<body bgcolor="#FFFFFF" background="/JavaWeb/img/bg0020.gif">
3.<%@ page errorPage="ErrorPage.jsp" %>
4.<jsp:useBean id="KBFacade" class="knowledgebase.KnowledgeBaseFacade" scope="page"
/>
5.<br>
6.<font face="Helvetica, Sans-serif" size=+2 >
7.<center>
8.Messages
9.</center>
10.</font>
11.<br>
12.<br>
13.<center>
```

```
14.<font face="Helvetica, Sans-serif" size=+2 color="blue">
15.
16.<% KBFacade.setFilterSelection( request, session ); %>
17....
```

The setFilterSelection Method

The `setFilterSelection` method, shown next, is called from the `pickKB.jsp` page. This method is part of a facade class (`KnowledgeBaseFacade`) and as such is designed to reduce the coupling (the calls) between the JSP page and the business classes and DAOs that retrieve the data for the page. This method performs a simple test of the requests passed into the `pickKB.jsp` page and determines what type of filter is to be used.

This method acts as a traffic cop of sorts, examining one of the request parameters passed to it and determining which action to perform (which method to call). If the `type` parameter is set to the value `all`, then all entries in the discussion group database are listed. This is achieved by calling the `setAllKBRecs` method with a boolean value of `true`.

If the request parameter is set to `keyword`, then a keyword filter is applied to the database lookup operation using the `setFilterKBRecs` method and passing both the `request` and `session`. Since exceptions may be thrown up the call stack to this method, a `catch` block is used to trap and report messages. (The `setAllKBRecs` and `setFilterKBRecs` methods will in turn call methods in the `Knowledge_baseDAO` class to perform the low-level database operations required to retrieve the data; the code for these methods is shown later in this chapter.)

The setFilterSelection Method

```
...
public void setFilterSelection( ServletRequest request, HttpSession session ) {

try {
    if ( request.getParameter("type").equals("all") )
        setAllKBRecs( true );

    if ( request.getParameter("type").equals("keyword") )
        setFilterKBRecs( request, session );
    }
    catch ( Exception e) {
        System.out.println("Exception in KnowledgeBaseFacade.setFilterSelection() : "
+ e );
    }
}
...
```

The setAllKBRecs and setFilterKBRecs Methods

The `setAllKBRecs` method takes a boolean argument and simply wraps a DAO method to retrieve the records necessary for the message listing of all message records. The method calls the `knowledge_baseDAO.getAll` method to retrieve all message records currently in the discussion group database and returns an `Iterator` object reference named `iterateKBList`, which is an instance member of the `KnowledgeBaseFacade` class.

The setAllKBRecs Method

```
...
public void setAllKBRecs( boolean val ) throws Exception {

//
// get a collection of Value Objects for
// all knowledge_base records
//
iterateKBList = knowledge_baseDAO.getAll();


}
...
```

The `setFilterKBRecs` method shown next is used to obtain a filtered list of messages based on the filter criteria contained in the `session` object (in code explained previously, the filter criteria is assembled as part of the processing for the `searchKB.jsp` and `searchSubmit.jsp` pages). This method wraps the `Knowledge_baseDAO.getFilteredList` method, which returns an `Iterator` reference that is assigned to the `iterateKBList` reference, which is part of the `KnowledgeBaseFacade` class.

Before the `getFilteredList` method is called, the `Collection` object stored in the `session` object must be retrieved, since this object stores filter criteria for the database query. This is accomplished with a call to the `HttpSession` `getAttribute` method.

As explained in the previous section, the session attribute `filter_criteria` stores an object of type `Collection` that contains the filter criteria for the page to use (see the description earlier in this chapter of the `searchSubmit.jsp` page processing that populates this collection). The `session getAttribute` method is used to retrieve the filter criteria. This method returns an `Object` reference, which is cast to a `Collection` reference and stored in an object named `filterCriteria`.

This object is passed to the `getFilteredList` method of the `Knowledge_baseDAO` class. This method accesses the database, retrieves the records that match the filter criteria, and places those records (in the form of value objects) into a Java `Collection` (a `Vector`). The `Vector` object is then converted to an `Iterator`, and the reference to the `Iterator` object is returned and stored in the `iterateKBList` reference of the `KnowledgeBaseFacade` class.

The setFilterKBRecs Method

```
...
// use a filter to retrieve the list of knowledge base records
public void setFilterKBRecs( ServletRequest request, HttpSession session ) {

try {
    // filter criteria passed as a Collection in the session object
    Collection filterCriteria
      = (Collection) session.getAttribute( "filter_criteria" );

    iterateKBList  = knowledge_baseDAO.getFilteredList(
            filterCriteria );
}
catch (Exception e)
  System.out.println("Exception in
KnowledgeBaseFacade.setFilterKBRecs(): " + e );


}


}
...
```

Once the DAO `getFilteredList` method has returned the list of records (value objects) from the database, the `KnowledgeBaseFacade` object will see to it that the `Iterator` that has been returned (from the DAO) is kept internally. This `Iterator` is later used by the JSP page to loop through the value object records stored in the `Collection` and to create the dynamic table output for the posted messages table.

Back to the pickKB.jsp Page

At this point, we have established the filter criteria for the page and have populated the `Iterator iterateKBList`, an instance variable of the `KnowledgeBaseFacade` class, with the results of the query operation. We now need to use the results in the `Iterator` to create the results to be used in the `pickKB.jsp` page.

The approach shown in this example minimizes the use of scriptlet code and maximizes the use of JSP tags and directives. Since the `jsp:getProperty` tag can be used to retrieve values from a JavaBean using an HTML-like tag, we use an approach that uses an instance member of the `KnowledgeBaseFacade` class to maintain a collection of records that have been returned from the database for display on the page. The `get` and `set` methods called by the `jsp:getProperty` tags return values or references to instance members of the `KnowledgeBaseFacade` class; we must set these instance members with the correct values from our collection of rows returned by the query. Since this collection is stored in an `Iterator`, we use a loop increment method to move through the `Iterator`, and for each new row, we set the instance members of the `KnowledgeBaseFacade` class to the same values as those in the `Iterator` row. The following code sample uses the `setNextKBVO` method to perform this operation.

As shown below the `hasNext` method is called to determine if there are more elements to the `Iterator`. If there are, then the `next` method is called to retrieve the value object from the `Iterator` and assign it to the instance member, `knowledge_baseVO`.

A call to the `NextKBVO` method of the `KnowledgeBaseFacade` class moves to the next element of the `Iterator` and sets the internal reference for the value object representing the current message (`knowledge_baseVO`) to the next value object within the list stored in the `iterateKBList Iterator`, as shown in the code below. A `catch` block is used to catch any exceptions that may be thrown by any of the methods called in this block.

The NextKBVO Method

```
...
/ increment the iterator and make the next knowledge_baseVO our current VO
public void setNextKBVO( boolean val ) throws Exception {


try {

if ( iterateKBList.hasNext() ) {
    knowledge_baseVO = (Knowledge_baseVO) iterateKBList.next();
    loadKnowledgeBase( knowledge_baseVO.getDoc_key() );
  }
}
catch (Exception e) {
      System.out.println("Exception in
knowledgeBaseFacade.setNextKBVO(): " + e );
    throw new Exception("Exception in
 knowledgeBaseFacade.setNextKBVO(): " + e );
 }
}
...
```

Building the Dynamic Table

The next task in creating the output for this listing is to create the HTML table to hold the listing. This table is created on line 3 in the JSP page fragment shown next. On line 5 in this listing, a row is created to hold a header describing the table, and on lines 8 through 15, empty cells are added to the table to provide a consistent, spreadsheet-like appearance to the table. On lines 18 through 29, another header row is created to output the columns headers for the table.

The pickKB.jsp Page (Continued)

```
1....
2.<!-- build table for output of selected messages -->
3.<table border=2 cellpadding=2 bgcolor="white">
4.
5.<tr>
6.<td bgcolor="#C0D9D9"><b>Message List<b></td>
7.
8.<td bgcolor="#C0D9D9" >     </td>
9.<td bgcolor="#C0D9D9" >     </td>
10.<td bgcolor="#C0D9D9" >     </td>
11.<td bgcolor="#C0D9D9" >     </td>
12.<td bgcolor="#C0D9D9" >     </td>
13.<td bgcolor="#C0D9D9" >     </td>
14.<td bgcolor="#C0D9D9" >     </td>
15.</tr>
16.
17.<!-- header row -->
18.<tr>
19.<td bgcolor="#E0E0E0" > <b>Title      </b> </td>
20.
21.
22.<td bgcolor="#E0E0E0" > <b>Type       </b> </td>
23.<td bgcolor="#E0E0E0" > <b>Category </b> </td>
24.<td bgcolor="#E0E0E0" > <b>Keywords </b> </td>
25.<td bgcolor="#E0E0E0" > <b>Actions   </b> </td>
26.<td bgcolor="#E0E0E0" > <b>    </b> </td>
27.<td bgcolor="#E0E0E0" > <b>    </b> </td>
28.<td bgcolor="#E0E0E0" > <b>    </b> </td>
29.</tr>
30....
```

Creating the Table Rows

The table is now ready to be constructed. Since there are multiple records to use, it makes sense to perform this operation within a loop. At the start of the loop on lines 4 and 5 in the listing, two control variables are set. These variables are used later in the loop to make decisions about whether or not to indent records based on their settings.

Within this loop, a `jsp:setProperty` tag is used to make a call to the `nextKBVO` method. This `jsp:setProperty` tag ultimately executes the `nextKBVO` method and moves to the next record in the internal list (`iterateKBList`). This process of moving the pointer in the list sets the internal `knowledge_base` value object to the next value object in the internal list of value objects so that once this call has been made, all calls to the `get` methods of the

KnowledgeBaseFacade class will return the values of the current knowl-edge_base value object.

The contents of each <td> tag within the message listing table represents a column on that row. The contents of the columns for this table are now stored in instance members of the class and will be retrieved using jsp:getProperty tags (which will in turn call the get methods of the KnowledgeBaseFacade class). These tags are used on lines 22 through 28 and are used to retrieve the short description of the message document (doc_name), the message type of the message (message_type), and two of the keywords associated with the document (keyword1 and keyword2).

The output of the columns is fairly straightforward, but the code on lines 13 through 21 requires more explanation. The purpose of this code is to provide the indentation of the output lines. This indentation is based on whether or not the line is a base message or a threaded message. If the message is a base message, then the short message description will not be indented and an image of a closed folder will be output on that line. If the message is a threaded message, then the short message description will be indented and a different image will be output on that line.

The determination of whether or not a message is a threaded message requires examination of the base document key (base_doc_key). A variable is used to track the current base document key and is set equal to the base document key of the current record at the end of each loop iteration. At the beginning of each loop iteration, the value of this current base document key is checked against the base document key of the record currently being output. If the base document key of the current record is the same as the current base document key, then this record is assumed to be a *threaded* message (since some previous record must have been used to set the current base document key to its value).

The first pass through the loop represents an exception to this rule. Since the value of the current base document key is not set until the end of the loop, on the first iteration of the loop, this value will not have been set. For our purposes, we assert that the first message in the loop is a base message and we ignore the setting of the current base document key.

```
1.<!-- columns -->
2.<!-- use program logic to indent threaded messages -->
3.<%
4.
5.   // start of loop
6.   int currBase_doc_key = 0;
7.   boolean firstLoop = true;
8.
9.while ( KBFacade.kbRecsHasMore() )  {
10.
11.%>
12.
```

```
13.
14.<jsp:setProperty name="KBFacade" property="nextKBVO" value="true" />
15.<tr>
16.<td> <% if ( !firstLoop && (currBase_doc_key == KBFacade.getBase_doc_key()) ) {
%>
17.
18.    <!-- indent if this is a thread off the base message -->
19.
20.                 
21.<img src="/JavaWeb/img/quote.gif">  
22.
23.    <% } else { %>  <!-- not a thread - the base message - display a closed
folder -->
24.              <img src="/JavaWeb/img/folder_closed.gif" name="Base Folder"
align=left >  
25.
26.    <% } %>
27.
28.
29.    <jsp:getProperty name="KBFacade" property="doc_name" /> </td>
30.<td> <jsp:getProperty name="KBFacade" property="message_type" />
31.</td>
32.<td> <jsp:getProperty name="KBFacade" property="category" /> </td>
33.
34.<td> <jsp:getProperty name="KBFacade" property="keyword1" />
35.             <jsp:getProperty name="KBFacade" property="keyword2" />
36.    <jsp:getProperty name="KBFacade" property="keyword3" />
37.</td>
40.
```

Next to the output of the message header are table cells that contain the actions that can be executed for the message document in the row. The JSP code that produces these actions is shown next.

The cells in this output contain anchor references that reference other JSP pages in the application. Parameter values for these references are set according to the current message document key. These settings are made by using jsp:getProperty tags, which retrieves the appropriate values for the current message document being processed.

Note that the jsp:getProperty tag can appear within the double quotes of the anchor href attribute, as follows:

```
 <a href="viewKB.jsp?doc_key=<jsp:getProperty name="KBFacade" property="doc_key"
/>&action=update" >View</a>
```

The final section of this listing contains the termination of the loop that produces this table. The firstLoop flag is set to false, and a conditional statement is used to determine how to set the base document key. If the base document key is nonzero, then the base document key for the current record is used to set to the value of the current base document key variable. Alternatively, if the base document key is 0, then we assert that the document is in fact the base document and sets the base document key to the value of the document key for the current document (which is the base document for this thread). Two URLs at the bottom of the page are provided to allow the user to return to the main menu or to post a new message.

```
...
<!-- actions -->
<td> <a href="inputKB.jsp?doc_key=0&action=insert&base_doc_key=<jsp:getProperty
name="KBFacade" property="base_doc_key" />&link_doc=<jsp:getProperty name="KBFacade"
property="doc_key"/>">Add to Thread</a> </td>
<td> <a href="viewKB.jsp?doc_key=<jsp:getProperty name="KBFacade" property="doc_key"
/>&action=update" >View</a> </td>
<td> <a href="inputKB.jsp?doc_key=<jsp:getProperty name="KBFacade"
property="doc_key"/>&link_doc=0&base_doc_key=<jsp:getProperty name="KBFacade" proper-
ty="base_doc_key" />&action=update">Update</a> </td>
<td> <a href="viewKB.jsp?doc_key=<jsp:getProperty name="KBFacade"
property="doc_key"/>&base_doc_key=0&link_doc=0&action=delete">Delete</a> </td>
</tr>


<%
 firstLoop = false;
 if ( KBFacade.getBase_doc_key() > 0 )
    currBase_doc_key = KBFacade.getBase_doc_key();
else
    currBase_doc_key = KBFacade.getDoc_key(); // this IS the base
} %>
</table>


<br>
<br><a href="inputKB.jsp?doc_key=0&link_doc=0&base_doc_key=0&action=insert">Post New
Message</a>
<br><a href="menu.html">Main Menu</a>

</font>
</center>
</BODY>
</HTML>
```

The user of this page will have options to view the current document, add to the message thread, update the current document, or delete the document. The code for these pages is shown in the following sections.

Creating Read-Only Output: The View Message Page

If the user chooses to view an existing message, then the `viewKB.jsp` page will be displayed. Each message is composed of messages from a number of different tables. This page retrieves all related message records for a single message and displays them in a table. The page does not allow the user to update any of the information on the page. Menu options, however, are provided to allow the user to add to the message thread, update the message, delete the message, or return to the main menu.

The coding of this page is fairly straightforward. The page merely needs to load the document key passed as the request parameters for the page and then use the `jsp:getProperty` tag on a JavaBean that contains all of the appropriate values. Fortunately, the `KnowledgeBaseFacade` class contains all of the necessary `get` and `set` properties to create the view page. Since only one message will be displayed, it isn't necessary to create a loop and iterate through multiple records as with the posted messages page (`pickKB.jsp`).

This page begins by using JSP directives to set the error page for this JSP page and to load the `KnowledgeBaseFacade` class and assign the class to a JavaBean named `KBFacade`. The document key for the message document to view is passed as part of the `request` parameter.

The contents of this page require data from a number of different tables in the message database. For this reason, the method that retrieves the data for this page must load not only the appropriate DAOs and value objects from the `knowledge_base` table, but also the `knowledge_messages` for the `message text` and `base_keys` for the message keywords tables.

The viewKB.jsp Page

```
<title>Message</title>

<center>

<%@ page import="java.util.*" %>
<%@ page errorPage="ErrorPage.jsp" %>

<jsp:useBean id="KBFacade" class="knowledgebase.KnowledgeBaseFacade" scope="page" />

<!-- set the doc_key first, before setting 'action' -->
<% KBFacade.setDoc_key( Integer.parseInt( request.getParameter("doc_key").trim() ));
%>
<% KBFacade.setAction( request.getParameter("action")); %>

<br>
<br>
<H1>Message Display</H1>

</center>
```

Once the current message document has been loaded, it is just a matter of describing the output of an HTML table, where the <td> tags will contain bodies that use jsp:getProperty tags to retrieve the appropriate values for the document being viewed.

A table definition is made and a blank cell is created. The document key for the document is retrieved using a jsp:getProperty tag for the output. (A space is added after every output on the page because some browsers will not render the cell color correctly if it does not interpret output for the table cell.) Table rows and cells are created and output is generated using jsp:getProperty calls.

```
...
<table border=0 cellpadding=2 >

<tr>
<td width=5%><br></td>
<td width=5% bgcolor="#E0E0E0"> Document Key: </td> <td width=30%
bgcolor="#C0C0C0"> <jsp:getProperty name="KBFacade" property="doc_key" />  
</td>

<td width=5% bgcolor="#E0E0E0"> Category:      </td> <td width=30% bgcolor="#C0C0C0"
> <jsp:getProperty name="KBFacade" property="category" />   </td>
</tr>

<tr>
<td width=5%><br></td>
<td width=5% bgcolor="#E0E0E0"> Name:           </td> <td width=30% bgcolor="#C0C0C0"
> <jsp:getProperty name="KBFacade" property="doc_name" />   </td>
<td width=5% bgcolor="#E0E0E0"> Posted by:    </td> <td width=30% bgcolor="#C0C0C0" >
<jsp:getProperty name="KBFacade" property="post_user" />    </td>


</tr>
...
```

The remainder of the table uses additional jsp:getProperty calls to retrieve data for the creation of the table. At the end of the table, a menu is created to allow the user to perform certain actions on the current message. The user can add to the current thread, delete the current record, update the current record, see a full listing of messages, or return to the main menu page.

Note that these options are output for this page regardless of whether or not the user has the appropriate permissions to perform these operations. The user permissions are checked but not until the user attempts to load the page to perform that operation; at that time permissions are checked, and if the user does not have permission to perform that operation, an exception is thrown and the page is not loaded.

```
<font color="white" family="times roman">
<p><a href="inputKB.jsp?doc_key=0&action=insert&base_doc_key=<jsp:getProperty
name="KBFacade" property="base_doc_key" />&link_doc=<jsp:getProperty name="KBFacade"
property="doc_key"/>">Add to Thread</a>   
<a href="updDB.jsp?doc_key=<jsp:getProperty name="KBFacade" property="doc_key"
/>&action=delete">Delete</a>   
<a href="inputKB.jsp?doc_key=<jsp:getProperty name="KBFacade" property="doc_key"
/>&base_doc_key=<jsp:getProperty name="KBFacade" property="base_doc_key"
/>&link_doc=0&action=update">Update</a>   
<a href="pickKB.jsp?type=all">Message List</a>   
<a href="menu.html">Main Menu</a> </p>
</font>
</center>
```

Performing Input with JSP: The Message Update Page

From the posted message list, the user who has requested the message list has various options available. If the requesting user is the user who entered the message, he or she will be allowed to change the text of the message, change the category or type of the message, or delete the message. Or, the user may choose to add to the message thread—that is, to add a new message under a specific base message. The inputKB.jsp page is used for all message updates, either to modify an existing message or to enter a new message as either a base message or an addition to a message thread.

The inputKB.jsp page uses an input form to insert a new message or update an existing message. The page uses the same HTML input form for insert or update, the difference being in how the existing field values are populated. If the page is being used for update, then the document that is being updated is loaded into the internal value objects. See Figure 37–4.

If a new message document is being input, then default values are loaded into certain fields and the remaining fields are initialized to default Java values for the data types (this is done by nature of the fact that the JavaBean carrying these value objects is of page scope and is therefore created anew each time the page is loaded).

If an existing message document is being input, then the document key for the message document is passed into the page. The KnowledgeBaseFacade JavaBean then loads the corresponding document for the document key. If the page is a threaded message, then the message description defaults to that of the base for the message thread, but the user is optionally allowed to override this text.

As shown next, the inputKB.jsp JSP page begins by importing the java.util package (which contains collections used in scriptlets for the page) and identifying ErrorPage.jsp as the error page to be used if an exception is caught. A jsp:useBean tag loads the KnowledgeBaseFacade JavaBean class and associates it with the `KBFacade` name for the page. The `Knowledge BaseFacade.processParameters` method is then called to perform the work necessary for the page to be output with the HTML form. This method is passed the `request` and `session` objects for the page.

The inputKB.jsp JSP Page

```
<html>

<body bgcolor="#FFFFFF" background="/JavaWeb/img/bg2_grey.jpg">

<%@ page import="java.util.*" %>
<%@ page errorPage="ErrorPage.jsp" %>

<jsp:useBean id="KBFacade" class="knowledgebase.KnowledgeBaseFacade" scope="page" />

<!-- the 'action' parameter indicates whether or not this is an insert,update or
delete operation -->
<% KBFacade.processParameters( request, session );   %>

...
```

Prepare Input Form: KnowledgeBaseFacade.processParameters Method

The `processParameters` method of the `KnowledgeBaseFacade` is shown next. This method performs the work necessary to prepare the `inputKB.jsp` page for processing. For that reason, it is useful to look at the code for this method to understand what is required to get this page (or any input page) ready for user input.

This page is called at the start of the `inputKB.jsp` page and is passed the `HttpRequest` object for the page (`request`) and the `HttpSession` object (`session`) for the page (and for the session). The method begins by creating a new `Calendar` object using the `Cal` convenience class described in Chapter. The parameters, specifically the parameter `doc_key`, which should always be passed into the method, are checked through a series of conditional statements.

The document key (`doc_key`) value is an integer but is sent in the `request` parameter as a `String` data type. It must therefore be converted using a call to the `Integer parseInt` method.The results of this conversion are immediately passed to the `setDoc_key` method of the `KnowledgeBaseFacade` class. This sets the document key for the local value object to the converted value of the request parameter.

The same test is performed for the `request` parameter for the `link_doc` (the document key for the document to which this document is linked). This converted value is passed to the `setLink_doc` method of the `KnowledgeBaseFacade` class. (Though this is stored in the value object and stored in the `knowledge_base` database table, the value of this column is currently not used.)

A number of the values are stored in the `session` object to be passed to the `updDB` page, which performs the database update for the values entered on this page. The document key (`doc_key`), the link document key (`link_doc`), and the base document key (`base_doc_key`) are stored as `Integer` object values in the `session` object.

The next block of code is used to set the default date for the `entry_date` field on the form (and ultimately in the database record). The definition of the entry date field is the date when the record was last updated, so logically this field should be set to the current date. A conditional statement then evaluates the `action` parameter to determine if an `insert` or `update` is being performed. These are currently the only two valid actions for the page, but this conditional testing allows different actions to be added at a later time.

If the conditional statement tests true, then an `entry_date` attribute is set using the current date as returned by the `Cal` class `getCurrentDate` method. The `setEntry_date` method for the internal knowledge base value object is also called to set this date to the current date. The remainder of the method is used to set default values for the form fields, depending on the action being performed.

KnowledgeBaseFacade.processParameters

```
...
// called by inputKB.jsp at the start of the input page

public void processParameters( ServletRequest request, HttpSession session ) throws
Exception {

Cal cal = new Cal();
int doc_key = 0;

 // assert these parameters are always passed to inputKB.jsp which will call this
method
   if ( request.getParameter("doc_key") != null )
       setDoc_key( Integer.parseInt( request.getParameter("doc_key").trim() ));

// set action will load the DAOs and the value objects for the knowledge_base (in
loadKnowledgebase() )
   if ( request.getParameter("action") != null )
       setAction( request.getParameter("action"));

  if ( request.getParameter( "link_doc" ) != null )
      setLink_doc( Integer.parseInt( request.getParameter("link_doc").trim() ));


  // add some of these to our session object, since they may not be passed via the
input form
   session.setAttribute( "doc_key", new Integer( request.getParameter("doc_key")));
   session.setAttribute( "link_doc", new Integer( request.getParameter("link_doc"))
);
```

```
    session.setAttribute( "base_doc_key",
                        new Integer(request.getParameter("base_doc_key")));

// store the dates as String ... let the database perform conversion
    if ( request.getParameter("action").equals("insert") ||
        request.getParameter("action").equals("update")  )  {
      session.setAttribute( "entry_date", cal.getCurrentDate( "mm/dd/yy" )); // date
last changed
      knowledge_baseVO.setEntry_date( cal.getCurrentDate( "mm/dd/yy" ));
    }


...
```

The next block of code is executed only for an `insert` operation—`action.equals('insert')`—and is used to set a number of default values for the `insert` operation. A number of these fields are set in the internal value object and in the `session` object to be sent to the `updDB.jsp` page for the database update operation.

The user name (login) and the user location (location) are retrieved from the session object where they were placed by the login process. They are placed in the appropriate fields in the current `knowledge_base` value object (`post_user` and `doc_location` respectively).

The next block of code deals with the contingency that the message being inserted is a threaded message. Since this is a threaded message, the short description of the message will most likely be the same as the short description for the base message for the thread. In this application, then, the default short description for a threaded message should be the short description for the base message, but this is not a requirement. This block of code will get the short description from the base message and then use that description for the current message. (This description will be placed in the input field, and the user will have the option of optionally changing the description.)

The contents of the document key for the base message for the thread (`base_doc_key`) are then examined. If this is currently set to 0, then the value of the link document is used and is retrieved. Otherwise, the value of the base message document key (`base_doc_key`) is retrieved. Then a local `Knowledge_baseDAO` object is created and uses the document key (`doc_key`) populated on the previous lines to load the DAO with the database values for that document key, which will be the base document for this message thread. The short name for the local message document is then set to the short name from the base message `knowledge_base` DAO.

We then perform a series of security checks are then performed to determine whether or not the user has permission to perform the operation he or she has requested. This block of code checks to determine if the user is performing an update operation (`action='update'`), and if so, whether he or she is the user who created the document or the system administrator (which is currently *hard-*

coded as a user role of `admin`). If the user does not have correct permissions, then they are not allowed to continue and an exception is thrown.

KnowledgeBaseFacade.processParameters (Continued)

```
...

  if ( request.getParameter("action").equals("insert") ) {

      // date first entered (submitted)
    session.setAttribute( "date_submitted", cal.getCurrentDate( "mm/dd/yy" ));
    knowledge_baseVO.setDate_submitted( cal.getCurrentDate( "mm/dd/yy" ));

 // get the user name and location from the login information stored in the session
object
    knowledge_baseVO.setPost_user( (String) session.getAttribute( "login") );
    knowledge_baseVO.setDoc_location( (String) session.getAttribute( "location" ) );

// if this is a threaded message, get the doc_name from the base_doc_key record
// since this is an insert, knowledge_baseVO has not been loaded, so need to create
a DAO to
      // get the base_doc_key

      // no base_doc_key value passed
    if ( Integer.parseInt(request.getParameter("base_doc_key").trim()) == 0  )
        // then use the link_doc
      doc_key = Integer.parseInt( request.getParameter("link_doc"));
    else
        doc_key = Integer.parseInt( request.getParameter("base_doc_key"));

    Knowledge_baseDAO baseDAO = new Knowledge_baseDAO( );
    baseDAO.loadDAO( doc_key );
    knowledge_baseVO.setDoc_name( baseDAO.getDoc_name() );

  }


  // if this is an update or delete,
  // does the user have permission to do this ??
if ( request.getParameter("action").equals("update") ) {

 // if this isn't the user that posted the message
if ( (!((String) session.getAttribute("login")).equals(
        knowledge_baseVO.getPost_user() )) ||
  (!((String) session.getAttribute("role")).equals( "admin" ) ) ) {  // this is
the sysadmin

      throw new Exception("You do not have permission to perform this func-
tion.");
```

```
    }
   }
}
```

The inputKB.jsp Page *(Continued)*

The next section of the `inputKB.jsp` page as shown below outputs a header and then starts the HTML table that will house the input form. The table is created and a form tag that directs the output of the form as a `post` operation to the `updDB.jsp` page.

We then create hidden fields to store the action and the link document as `request` parameters. (Though still included on a number of these pages, the `link_doc` field is not currently used by the discussion group application.)

```
<title>Knowledge Base</title>
<center>
<br>
<br>
<H1>Message Update</H1>
</center>
<table border=0 width=100% >
<tr>
   <td width=10%><br></td>
<form method="post" action="updDB.jsp">
<input name="action"   type="hidden" value="<jsp:getProperty name="KBFacade" proper-
ty="action"/>" >
<input name="link_doc" type="hidden" value="<jsp:getProperty name="KBFacade" proper-
ty="link_doc"/>" >

<td width=10%> Category: </td> <td width=20%>
...
```

The next section of the page displays a list box of categories, which must be dynamically created. In order to format the form fields, including the list box, the list box is placed in table cell using the `<td>` tag.

To dynamically create the list box based on the current contents of the database table containing the categories, the `getCategoryList` method retrieves the contents of the `message_categories` table (by calling a method in the `message_categoriesDAO`) and returns the results as an `Iterator` on line 9.

The `while` loop is started and loops through this `Iterator` and converts the members to a `String` data type. A conditional test is then performed to determine if the category is the default category. If this conditional test is `true`, then the category will be displayed as the selected list box item (an `option`), as shown in the output produced.

The inputKB.jsp Page (Continued)

```
...
<td width=10%> Category: </td> <td width=20%>
<!-- create category list box -->
<select name="category"
<%
String category = null;

// iterate through category list to create a listbox of categories

Iterator i = KBFacade.getCategoryList();
while ( i.hasNext() )  {
 category = KBFacade.makeCategoryString( i.next() );
 if ( KBFacade.isDefaultCategory( category ) ) { %>
   <option selected> <%= category %>
<% } else { %>
    <option> <%= category %>
<%
   }
  }
 %>
</select>
</td>
...
```

Following the creation of the category list box, a series of input fields are produced by the JSP. As shown below, in order to provide some spatial formatting for
the fields on the form, each field is enclosed in a table cell. Since the `entry_date`
field being output is not an input field, it is output in a different color than the
fields that allow input. A `jsp:getProperty` tag is used to retrieve the contents
of the `entry_date` field in the current `knowledge_base` value object in the
`KnowledgeBaseFacade JavaBean`.

Additional input fields are also defined using a `jsp:getProperty` tag to
provide a value for the field. The value of the `doc_name` field is used to provide
a value for the short description field. Using this JSP tag, the contents of the
`doc_name` field in the current `knowledge_base` value object are output as part
of the value attribute for this field. The contents of the `doc_location` field are
also retrieved using the same manner.

The `date_submitted` field does not allow user input (it is retrieved from
the database), so the contents of this field are output as simple text, without an
input field. To clarify that this field is not like the other fields on the form and does
not allow input, the contents of this field (as returned by the `jsp:getProperty`
tag) are output in a different font color. The code fragment for this processing is
shown below.

The inputKB.jsp Page (Continued)

```
...
<td width=5%> Entry Date: </td> <td width=20%><font face="helvetica, sans-serif"
color="green">
<jsp:getProperty name="KBFacade" property="entry_date" />
</font></td>
</tr>

<tr>
<td width=10%><br></td>
<td width=15%> Short Description: </td> <td width=20%>
<input name="doc_name" type="text" value="<jsp:getProperty name="KBFacade" proper-
ty="doc_name" />"> </td>
<td width=5%> Posted by:    </td> <td width=20%> <input name="post_user" type="text"
value="<jsp:getProperty name="KBFacade" property="post_user" />"> </td>
</tr>

<tr>
<td width=10%><br></td>
<td width=15%> Location:      </td>
<td width=20%> <input name="doc_location" type="text" value="<jsp:getProperty
name="KBFacade" property="doc_location" />"> </td>

<td width=5%> Submitted: </td> <td width=20%> <font face="helvetica, sans-serif"
color="green"> <jsp:getProperty name="KBFacade" property="date_submitted" />
</font>
</td>
</tr>
...
```

The message_type field also requires the user to choose from multiple selections. This is accomplished using the list box created in the JSP scriptlet code shown below. A call is made to the getMessageTypesList method to retrieve the values needed to populate the list box. This call returns an Iterator that is used to iterate through the contents of the message_types table.

The while loop is used to iterate through the contents of the iterator. The page output should have a list box that has selected the current message type of the message being displayed. To make sure the page is formatted so that this is accomplished, a conditional statement is used to select the message type of the current record in the select list. This is done by comparing the contents of the message type value object contained in the KnowledgeBaseFacade class with the contents of the message_types list being used. If the message type of the current record is found, then it is output as the selected item. If the message type of the current record is not the message being iterated in the list, then alternative output is provided.

```
...
<td>
<select name="message_type">

<%
// iterate through message types list to create a listbox of message types
String message_type=null;
i = KBFacade.getMessageTypesList();
while ( i.hasNext() )   {
      message_type = KBFacade.makeMessageTypesString(
                              i.next());
if ( (KBFacade.getMessage_type() != null ) && (
   KBFacade.getMessage_type().equals(message_type) ) ) {
%>
   <option selected><%= message_type %>
 <% }  else {   %>
   <option><%= message_type %>
 <% }
   }
%>
</select>
...
```

The remainder of the `inputKB.jsp` page contains a series of form fields for the input or update of the message. The form fields are wrapped in table cells and contain values retrieved using `jsp:getProperty` tags, as shown in the listing below. A submit button is created for the page, and since the page is used for both inserts and updates, the button title is generated based on the action for which the page is being used. This is accomplished by retrieving the value of the `submitTitle` property.

The inputKB.jsp Page (Continued)

```
<tr>
<td width=10%><br></td>
<td width=15%> Message Text: </td> <td width=20%> <textarea name="message_txt"
cols=40 rows=5 wrap><jsp:getProperty name="KBFacade" property="message_txt"
/></textarea> </td>
</tr>

<tr>

<td width=5%> <br>
<td width=2%> Key Words: </td> <td width=2%> <input name="keyword1" type="text"
value="<jsp:getProperty name="KBFacade" property="keyword1" />"> </td>
<td width=5% align="left"> </td> <td width=5%> <input name="keyword2" type="text"
value="<jsp:getProperty name="KBFacade" property="keyword2" />"> </td>
</tr>
```

```
<tr>
<td width=5%> <br>
<td width=2%> Key Words: </td> <td width=2%> <input name="keyword3" type="text"
value="<jsp:getProperty name="KBFacade" property="keyword3" />"> </td>
<td width=5% align="left"> </td> <td width=5%> <input name="keyword4" type="text"
value="<jsp:getProperty name="KBFacade" property="keyword4" />"> </td>
</tr>

<tr>
<td width=10%><br></td>
<td width=10%><br></td>

<td width=5%> <input name="submit" type="submit" value="<jsp:getProperty
name="KBFacade" property="submitTitle" />" >
</td>
</tr>

</form>
</table>

</body>
</html>
</tr>

</form>
</table>

</body>
</html>
```

Performing Database Updates

This page is posted to by the inputKB.jsp page and is responsible for performing the database update operations required by any input done on that page. The page contains very little presentation output, and the bulk of the work is performed by the KnowledgeBaseFacade.doUpdate method. If the update succeeds, then the page produces output indicating the number of rows updated. If some part of the update operation throws an exception, then the error page is displayed with information about the error. If the update fails to update any rows (which usually indicates a problem, since at least one row should have been updated), the current implementation of this page simply indicates that 0 rows have been updated.

The errorPage directive is used to indicate that the error page will be ErrorPage.jsp. The jsp:useBean tag is used to indicate that the bean to be used for this page will be the knowledgebase.KnowledgeBaseFacade class and will be identified on the page using the KBFacade.

A header is output and then the doUpdate method of the KnowledgeBaseFacade class is called to perform the database update operations required for this method. This method is the workhorse of this page, performing the relatively complex processing required to update the message database with form input it has received. (The processing performed by this method is detailed in the next section.)

Following the call to the doUpdate method, a value is placed in the rowsUpdated member of the KnowledgeBaseFacade bean. This value indicates how many rows have been updated by the page. The current implementation merely reports this number using a jsp:getProperty tag, without comment. (An alternative implementation would be to interpret a "no rows updated" condition as an error condition and forward control to an error page.) We provide URLs to allow navigation back to the main menu page or to return to a full listing of all messages.

The full processing of this page is performed off the page, in the doUpdate method. You can't really understand the processing being performed without examining the code behind this method which we will examine next.

The updDB.jsp Page

```
<html>
<body bgcolor="#FFFFFF" background="/JavaWeb/img/bkg.gif">
<%@ page errorPage="ErrorPage.jsp" %>
<jsp:useBean id="KBFacade" class="knowledgebase.KnowledgeBaseFacade" scope="page" />
<br>
<font face="Helvetica, Sans-serif" size=+2 >
<center>
<h1>Update Completed</h1>
</center>
</font>
<br>
<br>
<% KBFacade.doUpdate( request, session ); %>
<center>
<font face="Helvetica, Sans-serif" size=+2 color="blue">

<br>Updated <jsp:getProperty name="KBFacade" property="rowsUpdated" /> Rows.
<br>
<br>
<br><a href="pickKB.jsp?type=all">Return to Message List</a>
<br><a href="menu.html">Return to Main Menu</a>
</font>
</center>
</body>
</html>
```

Updating the Database: The KnowledgeBaseFacade.doUpdate Method

The `doUpdate` method is responsible for updating the database with the input from the HTML form generated by the `inputKB.jsp` page in the following code listing. This method receives two parameters: the `request` object (`HttpRequest`) and the `session` object (`HttpSession`).

This method is responsible for marshaling the resources of other methods within the `KnowledgeBaseFacade` class to execute the update and for enforcing security. A great deal of code within the method is spent validating that the user has permission to perform the update operation he or she is requesting.

The document key is first examined to determine whether or not it has been set correctly. Since the document key is the primary key for any messages, we must have a document key to be able to perform any update operations. If the `doc_key` is found, it is converted into an integer and stored in a local variable, where it can be used later without having to perform an integer conversion.

We then check to see if the `doc_key` is 0 and the action is an update. If this condition is true, then an exception is thrown, since we cannot perform an update without a `doc_key`.

We also check to see if an `insert` operation is being performed. If an insert is being performed, then the user must be logged into the system. If the user is not logged in and is not attempting an insert, an exception is thrown.

We use the method again to determine whether or not the user is logged in and to determine whether or not the logged in user is allowed to perform the operation he or she has requested. If the user is neither a system administration user or the user who entered the message, then he or she is not allowed to perform the operation, and an exception is thrown.

If we survive all the various tests and validations then the user is allowed to perform the update operation. The `request getParameter` method is used to retrieve the `action` parameter. The content of this parameter indicates which update action the user wishes to use. If the user has permissions to perform the operation, then the `insertKBRecs` method is called and is passed both the `request` and `session` objects. The method returns immediately once the `insert` operations have been performed.

The update option involves assigning a session attribute for the `doc_key` and calling the `updateKBRecs` method passing it both the `request` and `session` objects. The delete option is managed by setting a session attribute for the `doc_key`, and calling the `deleteKBRecs` method passing both the `request object` and the `session` objects.

If we fail all previous conditional tests, then we have not received appropriate parameters. We log an error and then throw an exception, thus returning control to the calling method.

KnowledgeBaseFacade.doUpdate Method

```java
public void doUpdate( ServletRequest request, HttpSession session ) throws Exception
{
int doc_key=0;

try {

// let's make sure we have a doc_key
if ( request.getParameter("doc_key") != null )
    doc_key = Integer.parseInt( request.getParameter("doc_key").trim() );
else
  if ( session.getAttribute("doc_key") != null )
      doc_key = ((Integer) session.getAttribute("doc_key")).intValue();

// if our doc_key is still 0 and this isn't an insert, throw an exception
if (( doc_key == 0 ) && ( request.getParameter("action").equals("update")) )
    throw new Exception ("Invalid document key.");

// update can be an insert,update or delete operation
// check security before allowing an update
// user must be logged in to perform an insert
if ( request.getParameter("action").equals("insert") ) {
   if ( session.getAttribute("login") == null ) // the user has not logged in
      throw new Exception("User must log in to add a message.");
}
// if user is performing an update or delete, then
// this must be the user that posted the message
if ( session.getAttribute("login") == null ) // user has not logged in
    throw new Exception(
                    "User must login to perform this operation." );

if ( request.getParameter("action").equals("update") ||
     request.getParameter("action").equals("delete") ) {
   if ( (!((String) session.getAttribute("login")).equals(
request.getParameter("post_user") )) ||
        (!((String) session.getAttribute("role")).equals( "admin" ) ) ) {  // this
is the sysadmin
      throw new Exception("User does not have permission to perform this func-
tion.");
   }
}

// security is ok, so perform the update
if ( request.getParameter("action").equals("insert") ) {
    insertKBRecs( request, session );
    return;
}

if ( request.getParameter("action").equals("update") ) {
    session.setAttribute("doc_key", new Integer( doc_key ) );
    updateKBRecs( request, session );
```

```
    return;
}

if ( request.getParameter("action").equals("delete") ) {
    session.setAttribute("doc_key", new Integer( doc_key ) );
    deleteKBRecs( request, session );
    return;
}

// if at this point, then we have not been passed a valid action
// log an error and throw an exception
System.out.println("knowledge_baseFacade.doUpdate() called with invalid action: " +
                    request.getParameter("action"));
throw new Exception( "KnowledgeBaseFacade.doUpdate called with an invalid action " +
                    request.getParameter("action"));

}
catch (Exception e) {
   System.out.println("Exception in KnowledgeBase.doUpdate(): " + e );
   throw new Exception ("Exception in KnowledgeBase.doUpdate(): " + e );
}


}
...
```

All of the update methods in the message system facade class use the DAOs for the various tables involved in the update operation. These objects encapsulate the insert, update, and delete operations for the database tables they represent. (Note that DAOs do not need to wrap a single relation but can in fact map to multiple relations, though that is not done in this example.)

Since the doUpdate method can optionally call either the insertKBRecs, updateKBRecs, or deleteKBRecs methods, this is a good point to discuss the code behind these methods. Each of these methods uses one or more DAOs to manipulate the database. So that we can focus on the business logic of the facade class, the detailed operation of these DAOs is not covered in this chapter. The following sections discuss each of the insertKBRecs, updateKBRecs, and deleteKBRecs methods in turn.

Inserting Records: The insertKBRecs Method

The insertKBRecs method in the KnowledgeBaseFacade class is used to insert records into the database. Since discussion group messages are stored in multiple tables, this method is responsible for managing these multiple inserts into several tables, using DAOs for each of the tables.

The `insertKBRecs` method shown below is passed the `request` (`HttpRequest`) object and the `session` (`HttpSession`) object from the JSP page. The first order of business is to set the DAO members with the values from the input form. This is done using data values retrieved from the request object.

We begin by retrieving values from the `session` object, data values that are not entered in the input form that provides the data for this method. We provide some conditional logic to set the base document key (the base message document for a threaded message) if it has not yet been set. The result of this logic is that if the base document key is not set and the link document key is set, then the link document key is used as the base document key for this message. We also retrieve the date submitted and the entry date for the message from the `session` object.

Note that up to this point the document key (`doc_key`) for the message document has not been set, because the document key for the discussion group database is a database-generated unique key. Its value is set by the DAO (ultimately by the database) as part of the insert operation into the `knowledge_base` table. But since there are a number of related tables that must be updated as part of the message insert operation, this unique key generated by the database must be returned to this method to be used in `insert` operations for the related tables. This is done at the point where the `Knowledge_baseDAO.insertDAO` method is called. This method returns an integer corresponding to the document key (`doc_key`) of the `knowledge_base` record just inserted.

The remainder of the method is devoted to updating the multiple tables related to the `knowledge_base` table. The `knowledge_messages` table is updated and the document key (`doc_key`) from the `knowledge_base update` operation is used to set the document key for the `knowledge_messages` table. The data for the `knowledge_messages` fields is retrieved from request parameters, and the `insertDAO` method of the `Knowledge_messagesDAO` class is called to perform the database insert.

The insertKBRecs Method

```
public void insertKBRecs( ServletRequest request, HttpSession session ) {

int doc_key;

try {

// use the request to get the values for our DAO members
knowledge_baseDAO.setDoc_location( request.getParameter( "doc_location" ) );
knowledge_baseDAO.setDoc_name( request.getParameter( "doc_name" ) );
knowledge_baseDAO.setCategory( request.getParameter( "category" ) );

knowledge_baseDAO.setPost_user( request.getParameter( "post_user" ) );


// these parameters aren't in the form, they're stored in the session object
```

```
knowledge_baseDAO.setLink_doc( ((Integer) session.getAttribute( "link_doc"
)).intValue() );
knowledge_baseDAO.setBase_doc_key( ((Integer) session.getAttribute( "base_doc_key"
)).intValue() );


if ( knowledge_baseDAO.getBase_doc_key() == 0 )
    if ( knowledge_baseDAO.getLink_doc() > 0  )
        knowledge_baseDAO.setBase_doc_key( knowledge_baseDAO.getLink_doc() ) ;

knowledge_baseDAO.setDate_submitted( (String) session.getAttribute( "date_submit-
ted") );   // only set on initial insert
knowledge_baseDAO.setEntry_date( (String) session.getAttribute( "entry_date" ) );

doc_key = knowledge_baseDAO.insertDAO();

// should throw an execption if we get a 0 back from knowledge_baseDAO.insertDAO

// knowledge_messages
knowledge_messagesDAO.setDoc_key( doc_key );
knowledge_messagesDAO.setMessage_txt( request.getParameter( "message_txt" ) );
knowledge_messagesDAO.setMessage_type( request.getParameter( "message_type" ) );
knowledge_messagesDAO.insertDAO();
...
```

The next set of statements performs the `insert` operation for the `base_keys` table. In the current implementation, four keywords are stored in this table. These keywords are each inserted into the table in separate insert operations. The document key from the `knowledge_base` insert operation is used for the document key for these records and is set in the DAO. Each `insert` operation inserts a separate row into the database, using the values from the keyword parameter values.

No specific success or failure flags are returned by this method; if any part of the database `update` operation fails, an exception is thrown by the `insertKBRecs` method, which would be caught and then thrown to `doUpdate` method, which will in turn throw an exception to the JSP page that called it. (Note that the current implementation does not use a transaction for these multiple updates, so it could leave the database in an inconsistent state.)

```
...
// base_keys - the keywords for our message
base_keysDAO.setDoc_key( doc_key );
base_keysDAO.setKeyword( request.getParameter( "keyword1" ) );
base_keysDAO.insertDAO();

base_keysDAO.setDoc_key( doc_key );
base_keysDAO.setKeyword( request.getParameter( "keyword2" ) );
base_keysDAO.insertDAO();
```

```
base_keysDAO.setDoc_key( doc_key );
base_keysDAO.setKeyword( request.getParameter( "keyword3" ) );
base_keysDAO.insertDAO();

base_keysDAO.setDoc_key( doc_key );
base_keysDAO.setKeyword( request.getParameter( "keyword4" ) );
base_keysDAO.insertDAO();
}
catch (SQLException e) {
    System.out.println( "SQLException caught in KnowledgeBaseFacade.insertKBRecs():
" + e.getMessage() );

}
catch (Exception e) {
    System.out.println( "Exception in KnowledgeBaseFacade.insertKBRecs(): " +
e.getMessage() );
}


}
```

The updateKBRecs Method

The `updateKBRecs` method is responsible for updating the records updated on the `inputKB.jsp` page. This method, like the other update methods, receives the `request` object and the `session` object as parameters.

For updates, the document key (`doc_key`) must be known. The value of the current document key is stored in the `doc_key` attribute of the session object as an `Integer` object reference. This object reference is retrieved and converted into its integer value and stored in a local integer variable.

N ext, the values of the `knowledge_base` DAO are set to the corresponding parameter values from the input form. The `entry_date` for the `knowledge_base` record is set to the current date, as stored in the `session` object attribute `entry_date`.

The `knowledge_messages` table is prepared for the `update` operation. In creating the processing for the table that stores the keywords for the messages (`base_keys`) we must deal with the fact there there is no primary key for this table. We manage this by simplifying the update logic. The table is *updated* by deleting all existing rows for the document key and inserting the values that have been returned by the input form into the table. The deletion is accomplished by first setting the value of the DAO then calling the `deleteDAO` method.

The updateKBRecs Method

```
public void updateKBRecs( ServletRequest request, HttpSession session ) {
int doc_key = 0;
```

```java
try {

doc_key = ((Integer) session.getAttribute("doc_key")).intValue();

// use the request to get the values for update
knowledge_baseDAO.setDoc_key( doc_key );
knowledge_baseDAO.setDoc_name( request.getParameter( "doc_name" ) );
knowledge_baseDAO.setPost_user( request.getParameter( "post_user") );
knowledge_baseDAO.setDoc_location( request.getParameter( "doc_location") );
knowledge_baseDAO.setLink_doc( Integer.parseInt( request.getParameter( "link_doc" ))
);
knowledge_baseDAO.setCategory( request.getParameter( "category" ) );

knowledge_baseDAO.setEntry_date((String) session.getAttribute( "entry_date")); //
date last changed

// knowledge_messages
knowledge_messagesDAO.setDoc_key( doc_key );
knowledge_messagesDAO.setMessage_txt( request.getParameter( "message_txt" ) );
knowledge_messagesDAO.setMessage_type( request.getParameter( "message_type" ) );
knowledge_messagesDAO.updateDAO();

// base_keys - the keywords for our message
// no true primary key in this table - it's just a list
// so delete all existing recs and then insert them again
base_keysDAO.setDoc_key( doc_key );
base_keysDAO.deleteDAO();

base_keysDAO.setDoc_key( doc_key );
base_keysDAO.setKeyword( request.getParameter( "keyword1" ) );
base_keysDAO.insertDAO();

base_keysDAO.setDoc_key( doc_key );
base_keysDAO.setKeyword( request.getParameter( "keyword2" ) );
base_keysDAO.insertDAO();

base_keysDAO.setDoc_key( doc_key );
base_keysDAO.setKeyword( request.getParameter( "keyword3" ) );
base_keysDAO.insertDAO();

base_keysDAO.setDoc_key( doc_key );
base_keysDAO.setKeyword( request.getParameter( "keyword4" ) );
base_keysDAO.insertDAO();

}
catch (SQLException e) {
    System.out.println( "SQLException caught in KnowledgeBaseFacade.updateKBRecs():
" + e + " - " + e );
    throw new Exception( "Database exception in updateKBRecs." + e.getMessage() );

}
```

```
catch (Exception e) {
    System.out.println( "Exception in KnowledgeBaseFacade.updateKBRecs(): " + e );
    throw new Exception( "Database exception in updateKBRecs." + e.getMessage() );

  }

}
```

The deleteKBRecs Method

The `deleteKBRecs` method is responsible for deleting all references to a specified message in the discussion group database. The method only needs the document key to the message to accomplish this, but for consistency it receives both the `request` and `session` objects as parameters.

The first step is to extract the document key for the message to delete from the `session` object. The `Object` reference returned by the `session` object is cast as an `Integer` reference (its *real* type), and then the reference resulting from that cast is used to call the `intValue` method to return a primitive integer value. This integer value is stored in a local variable and is then used throughout the method to reference the message being deleted.

The `loadDAO` method of the `Knowledge_baseDAO` class is used to load the message header for the document key passed to the method. Once the DAO has been set to this document key, the `deleteDAO` method is called to delete the referenced message document from the `knowledge_base` table.

The `knowledge_messages` table, which is used to store the text of the discussion group message, is then processed. The `setDoc_key` method of the `knowledge_messages` DAO is called to set the document key to the value of the document key that is passed. The `knowledge_messages` records for that document key are deleted using the `deleteDAO` method.

The `base_keys` table, used to store the keywords for a discussion group message, is then processed. The `Base_keysDAO.setDoc_key` method is called to set the document key to that of the message to be deleted. Once this has been set, the `deleteDAO` method of the DAO can be called to delete all references to the message in the `base_keys` table.

The deleteKBRecs Method

```
// delete this knowledge_base record and all of the related records
//
public void deleteKBRecs( ServletRequest request, HttpSession session ) {
int doc_key;

try {
```

```
doc_key = ((Integer) session.getAttribute( "doc_key" )).intValue();

// knowledge_base
knowledge_baseDAO.loadDAO( doc_key );
knowledge_baseDAO.deleteDAO( );

// knowledge_messages
knowledge_messagesDAO.setDoc_key( doc_key );
knowledge_messagesDAO.deleteDAO();

// base_keys - the keywords for our message
base_keysDAO.setDoc_key( doc_key );
base_keysDAO.deleteDAO();

}
catch (SQLException e) {
    System.out.println(
        "SQLException caught in KnowledgeBaseFacade.deleteKBRecs(): " +
        e.getMessage() );
    throw new Exception( "Database exception in deleteKBRecs." +
                        e.getMessage() );
}
catch (Exception e) {
    System.out.println( "Exception in KnowledgeBaseFacade.deleteKBRecs(): "
                        + e.getMessage() );
    throw new Exception( "Database exception in deleteKBRecs." +
                        e.getMessage() );
}

}
```

The Error Page: ErrorPage.jsp

The `ErrorPage.jsp` page is, as the name implies, used to handle exceptions that are thrown on various JSP pages in the application. This page displays a message concerning the error and provides links through the page footer that allow the user to return to the main page. (See Figure 37–6.)

As shown in the following listing this page does little more than display the error message as contained in the `exception` object and then displays output for the `exception` object by printing the object (which will eventually call the `toString` method on the object). A link in the middle of the page allows the user to return to the menu page. A JSP `include` page directive is used to include the `footer.txt` file (which contains a page footer used throughout the discussion group application) into the page.

ErrorPage.jsp

```
<%@ page isErrorPage="true" %>
<html>
```

```
<body bgcolor="#FFFFFF">
<head>
<title>Error</title>
</head>
</body>

<br>
<br>
<center>
<H1>Error</H1>
</center>
<br>
<br>
<br>
<br>
<font face="helvetica,sans-serif" size=+3 color="red">
<p>Error reported: <%= exception.getMessage() %>
<p>
<p>Exception: <%= exception %>
</font>
<center>
<a href="menu.html">Return to Main Menu</a>
</center>

<br>
<br>
<br>

<%@ include file="footer.txt" %>

</html>
```

Using the JSP include Directive: Inserting a Page Footer

It is not uncommon to include a footer on an HTML page. This footer would most likely include links to other sites that may be of interest to the user of your site. The insertion of the `footer.txt` file for the JSP `include` provides an example of just such an approach.

The file `footer.txt` is inserted at the bottom of most of the pages in the discussion group application, as shown in the following code. Using this file provides a consistent look for the application and, though it appears trivial in this example, on larger projects with more complex pages, this could save a significant amount of work by allowing some portion of the site to be duplicated code to be shared among developers.

The text in this file contains HTML and provides a link to the menu page as well as a link to send email to a specified email address (this is done using the URL `mailto` as the reference for the link).

The footer.txt File

```
<center>
<br>
<br>
<br>
<br>
<font size=-1>
<a href="mailto:webmaster@nowhere.com">Email Webmaster</a>    <a
href="menu.shtml">Return to Main Menu</a>
</font>
<center>
```

Summary

In this chapter we examined the code behind the discussion group system introduced in the previous chapter. This provided a working example of how to use JSP and Java classes to create a working Web application. We implemented various Java design patterns in the development of this application, including the session facade design pattern, DAO and value object design patterns.

Since we did not implement a strict controller component for the entire Web application, this was essentially an implementation of the Model 1 Architecture for JSP applications. But by implementing the facade design pattern we did effectively use a control object for a large portion of the application logic and thus did gain some of the benefit of that approach. For an application of this size, this is an acceptable approach. But for large, more complex applications, the Model 2 Architecture and the requisite use of a control component is recommended.

INDEX